The Commonsense of Gardening

Read not to contradict and confute, nor to believe and take for granted, nor to find talk and discourse, but to weigh and consider.

Francis Bacon 1561–1626

The knack of finding lies in knowing where to look.

Jean-Jacques Rousseau 1712–1778

The
Commonsense
of Gardening

BILL SWAIN

MICHAEL JOSEPH · LONDON

First published in Great Britain by
MICHAEL JOSEPH LTD
52 Bedford Square, London, W.C.1
1976

ISBN 0 7181 1382 9

Filmset and printed in Great Britain by
BAS Printers Limited, Wallop, Hampshire
and bound by Dorstel Press, Harlow, Essex

Contents

Section IV : Vegetables

Section V : Herbaceous and Bedding Plants

Section VI : Bulbs and Corms

Section VII : House and Indoor Plants

Section VIII : Greenhouse Practice and Principles

Section IX : Seeds and Sowing

Section X : Lawns

Section XI : Soils, Compost and Fertilisers

Section XII : Pests and Fungus

Section XIII : Paths, Patios and Rockeries

Section XIV: Eradication and Removal

Section XV : Aquatics

Section XVI : Poisonous Plants

Section XVII : Miscellaneous

List of Illustrations

(illustrations by Chris Evans)

Introduction

One of the effects of modern affluent society has been to provide many people who would otherwise have remained mere spectators with the means and the opportunity to become active participants in a wide range of arts, crafts and leisure activities.

Once largely the preserve of the more well to do, golf is now a sport for the masses, you no longer have to be rich to own a boat, and more families have cars it seems than those who don't. Squash courts proliferate and one can learn to emulate the masters of art and sculpture at evening classes. This is the age of active participation and do-it-yourself—and, as is to be expected, this is reflected in what is broadly referred to as the media, the communications industry.

Never before in history has so much information been so readily available on such a wide variety of subjects. Napoleon called the British 'a nation of shop-keepers'. More astute minds have more correctly observed us as 'a nation of gardeners'—an opinion never more vindicated perhaps than by the vast number of spades that 'dug for victory' during the last war.

And indeed, Britain still remains very largely a nation of gardeners and gardening retains an indisputable claim to the title of number one leisure activity. Examine the shelves in the bookshop and public library and you will find more books on gardening than any other subject: books on how to grow this, how to grow that, what to do and when to do it. Yet despite the absolute plethora and wealth of information, still people ask questions. Producing answers to specific questions is an integral part and an important service provided by the gardening journals and radio programmes . . . but still the questions flow.

It is difficult to avoid the conclusion that a lot of the gardening information available is not getting through to the majority. There may be explanations as to why this should be so. Researching information is a technique that doesn't come easily to many people. Many people don't know where and how to look for their information; others can't be bothered to wade through chapters in the hope that the answer will be found.

The book shelves may be full of what to do, how to do it, and when—but search those shelves again and you will find very little that explains—WHY. I believe that if people ask questions, the answers should try to convey enough of why, so that what, how and when are not only self-evident, but enable the questioner to vary his actions to suit the circumstances.

Section I

Roses

1 Greenfly—controlling their breeding rate

This year my roses have been inundated with greenfly. I have used every spray I can find; most of them seem to kill the insects because shortly after spraying they have gone, but in a day or two they are back again as bad as ever. I have read that aphids multiply fast but surely not as fast as this? Where do they come from and what can I do?

Every gardener knows that roses are particularly prone to attack by greenfly, but I fear not enough recognition is given to the damage they cause or enough measures taken in time to control them. Admittedly, the sight of the first one or two in spring and early summer does not equate with and evoke a sensation of serious plant destruction. It is only when the one or two have suddenly become thousands or even millions, usually within a few days, when shoots and buds disappear under a seething mass, that it occurs to us that we must remember to get something 'next time we go to the shops'.

The cumulative effect of so many insects, each sucking the life sap out of a plant, is enormous—stunting and damaging growth, weakening the plant so that it is more prone to mildew and other fungal attack, and quite often directly introducing virus. To realise fully the size and nature of the problem in dealing with greenfly, you have to appreciate their peculiar breeding methods.

In early spring, eggs that have overwintered on host plants in the garden, hatch into female greenfly—there are no males at all—many of which are winged and blown to other plants. These soon begin to give repeated birth to living young wingless females, which in turn within a short time each begin to produce living young females, which in turn within a short time . . . and so it goes on, multiplication upon multiplication, generation upon generation. Millions of offspring in a very short time and not a male involved! The ultimate in Women's Lib!

This process, called parthenogenesis, explains how a plague can arrive almost overnight. It continues through the summer months, encouraged by mild weather and suitable host plants like your roses. Overcrowding is one condition—there are others—that triggers the production of more winged forms that become airborne and set off to start colonies elsewhere. In due course, the onset of shorter colder days in late autumn also triggers another development—the same live birth, but of a generation of male greenfly. Mating follows—this is the only time it does—and results not in living young, but in eggs being laid to overwinter. The parents later die in the cold weather—unless they find a convenient warm greenhouse and a careless gardener who doesn't spray often enough.

Eggs overwinter on some plants better than on others, but a very cold winter will kill off many of them. However, enough survive with living forms on host plants and in greenhouses to ensure that the population explosion occurs again in the spring.

Being soft-bodied, greenfly are easily killed by a contact poison—there are several on the market—but if I had to take just one specifically for greenfly, it would be one containing the ingredient Lindane. Frequently in their search for soft plant tissue, greenfly congregate more to the undersides of leaves and crawl into the innermost crevices of buds and shoots—who hasn't found them right inside a lettuce? Contact sprays do not then reach them so we have to resort to other methods.

Where it is practicable we can introduce into the sap stream of the plant, merely by spraying the leaves, a chemical that renders the entire sap system poisonous to greenfly and other sucking insects. The plant remains toxic and pest free for varying periods, usually two or three weeks, sometimes a little longer, after which you will need to spray again.

It is safe enough for you to eat crops that have had systemic insecticide applied to them providing, of course, that you have left a safe intervening period: always follow the maker's instructions carefully, which will be printed on the bottle.

You will now see why achieving a 90–95% kill is so quickly followed by a new heavy infestation—the remaining 5–10% can replace their lost sisters in a matter of hours.

Heavy infestation is always predictable following a mild winter because so many eggs, and adults, successfully escape from dying in the cold. The lesson in this case is don't wait for the plague to occur: be prepared, act early and regularly, and you will keep your roses liberated.

2 Improving clay soil for roses—and understanding why

For the past two seasons I have planted roses in my garden, the soil of which is heavy clay. During the winter, the roses appear healthy but in the spring the stems yellow off and brown patches appear, causing a fair amount of die-back. New growth starts healthy, but after a while the leaf growth dries up and drops off. I have followed lots of advice to little avail and I am despairing of ever growing good roses. What do you suggest?

The first thing I suggest you do is to stop despairing, and the next to stop following advice until you understand why you are going to carry out a particular job. Good cultivation of roses, as with any other plant, has very little to do with knowing what to do, or how to do it, or when, but *why*! Understand why—and every other question of what, how, where and when answers itself.

Roses prefer a dense soil to a light sandy soil with no body in it, but they will not thrive in a heavy, sticky, badly drained, airless soil—which probably describes your clay exactly.

You may have heard of the use of 'Nottingham marl' in the preparation of cricket pitches. Marl is a heavy dense clay which does not settle into a sticky mess like ordinary clay. Many of the finest rose growers in the world are based in the Nottingham area and you would be right in concluding that there is a connection between the two.

You have the best raw material for healthy roses—heavy clay. What you have to do is to turn your garden soil into a little Nottingham by converting your clay into marl.

Here, I suggest you pause and read *No. 475* about cultivating a lawn on heavy clay. The one big advantage your roses will have over a lawn is that you can disturb the soil and help the assimilation of gypsum by hoeing.

I suggest you set about the job as follows. You can begin at any time of the year—in fact, whenever you read this. Spread agricultural gypsum on the soil surface at the rate of 2 ozs. per sq. yd. Scratch this in with a claw hoe, being careful not to snag roots which can easily lead to suckers. Now spread a very liberal mulch cover of peat, well-rotted garden compost or spent mushroom compost. Don't use stable or any form of farmyard manure if they are at all fresh—stack and rot down with frequent turning for at least a year.

This mulch layer should be at least 1½–2 ins. thick. It helps to conserve moisture, leaches nutrients slowly into the soil underneath, and gradually will become absorbed into the soil and thus increase the humus content. For this reason you will need to replenish the mulch cover from time to time.

Onto this mulch, spread more gypsum at about 2 ozs. per sq. yd. This makes a total of 4 ozs. per sq. yd. and is quite heavy enough for the time being. Repeat the 2 oz. dressing at three-monthly intervals indefinitely, but not more frequently—this is the fastest rate at which soil can assimilate the gypsum.

Gradually your clay will change, the physical structure will improve and the locked up fertility will become available to plant life.

At the same time as improving the soil structure with the steady incorporation of humus into the soil, you will need to ensure an adequate and continuing supply of plant nutrient—and this should be applied in the steady feeding of 'natural' organic-based manures, instead of quick-acting, but short-lived chemicals.

Fertility, as you will often read elsewhere in this book, depends, among other things, on a maximum presence of bacteria. These are responsible for the decomposition of once living—organic—animal and vegetable matter with complex chemical composition into the simple compounds that can once again be absorbed by living forms.

Each organic substance will have its own 'bacterial chain'—i.e. strains of bacteria that step by step carry out the many stages of decomposition, and at any point in time the numbers of the respective strains of bacteria to be found in a soil sample will clearly reflect the kinds of organic matter that have been reaching the soil.

If you haven't been putting down compost containing oak leaf mould, you will not find many bacteria associated with the breakdown of oak leaves, but if your compost was made from grass, leaves and kitchen waste for example, you would find plenty of bacteria that are concerned with the decomposition of grass and kitchen waste.

This is why, when first applying organic manures, the initial response to be seen in plants is not so great as with later applications. You have had to wait for the numbers of the particular bacterial chain to proliferate in response to the sudden availability of their particular—and probably artificial—food source.

The second application finds greater numbers of the right kinds of bacteria waiting for it and breakdown begins more quickly. This also explains why it is foolish to use different manures and fertilisers to find out what best suits your garden. All this does is to build up bacteria populations which, before they can work for you and be of real benefit, are redundant when you try something else. The moral is clear—choose one material and stick with it. But what is the right material?

It is clear that this must be something which supplies all three basic plant foods—nitrogen, phosphorus and potash (N, P and K respectively) in balanced proportions. The breakdown of the constituent compounds that provide N, P and K takes varying lengths of time, and therefore it is not only balance in quantity that is needed but balance also in availability. It is no good giving a hungry man a so-called balanced diet of meat, potatoes and greens for three months, if that turns out to be all meat for a month, all potatoes for a month and nothing but greens for the third month. One minute he is not getting enough to eat, and then you give him dietary chaos. It is the same with roses.

When you buy a bag of fertiliser or manure, you should find an analysis printed on the bag. This analysis will indicate, in percentage, the proportions of N, P and K. The P content is often indicated as soluble phosphoric and insoluble phosphoric—if so, add these together to give a phosphate total. A balanced plant food diet would then be indicated by the three percentages N, P and K being equal, or nearly so. In my view, it is much safer for the amateur gardener to deal with balanced diets than to risk the difficulties that can arise when an unbalanced diet is given to the plants—and this you can avoid by checking the analysis before you buy.

In Humber Eclipse Garden (be careful: there is also a Humber Lawn dressing with a high nitrogen content and a weedkiller) N, P and K are equal at 6% and I suggest that you spread this excellent manure at the rate of $1-1\frac{1}{2}$ ozs. per sq. yd. beginning in late March and repeating every five to six weeks or so until mid–late July, then no more. The dry materials of which fertilisers and manures are comprised cannot be absorbed at once by plants while they are in that form, they have to dissolve—or undergo bacterial decomposition into simple compounds that will dissolve—in water, i.e. the moisture in the soil. In the case of Humber Eclipse Compound, this breakdown process takes approximately eighty days before a peak of soluble plant food availability is reached, which means that from mid July, it will be about the end of September when the plant food supply begins to decline—this is a long sustained feeding action.

There is no reason why you should not be able to grow first rate roses, and if you follow the above there is no doubt that you will be much more successful than you have been. Bear in mind however, it is no good slavishly following this—or any other—advice, without understanding it, which is why I have gone to so much detail.

A good gardener never does anything without understanding what he is doing. If he doesn't understand—he doesn't do it, he finds out.

3   Not so super 'Super Stars'

I have a bed of fifty 'Super Star' roses which I planted three years ago. Why are they covered with mildew each year when other neighbouring varieties are unaffected? I feed them well with various rose fertilisers so it can't be that.

On the contrary, it could have something to do with the fertilisers. Another cause could be capsid bug, but if that were the case, other varieties would also be affected. In my opinion, grown hard and vigorous from good and properly ripe budding material implanted on good stock, 'Super Star' is one of the most marvellous roses ever produced. It is not in the least surprising that from the moment of its introduction and first showing, it should have achieved immense international popularity as quickly—if not more so—than any other rose in history.

And that at once has been the cause of a lot of the trouble that so many have experienced with 'Super Star'. Indeed, at one time it was being widely called Super Flop, as the blooms fell and flopped over on weak necks.

Too eager to cash in on the popularity whilst the early price was high, many growers were cutting buds from any material they could get their hands on, without worrying unduly about ripeness and condition. I've seen a lot of 'Super Stars' offered to an unknowing gardening public that would have been better labelled Super Rubbish.

Now, whilst it is a fact that the reds and pinks are a little more prone to mildew than the other colours, and certain varieties earn reputations for this under certain localised conditions, for other varieties to remain unaffected makes me suspicious of the origins of your plants and your subsequent cultivation. I cannot question the vigour of your plants at this stage other than to point out again the wisdom of only and always obtaining roses from first-class growers with reputations to uphold. Read *Nos. 2* and *4*—there is a lot there that you could apply here, especially the point about using different fertilisers.

I would also take a look at your soil structure and if heavy, consider whether gypsum could help to open it up. Constant replenishment of a mulch helps—use Humber Eclipse, supplemented three weeks after each Eclipse dressing by a 1 oz. per sq. yd. dressing of sulphate of potash. The potash hardens and matures the growth and texture of the foliage and new shoots to make them more resistant to mildew.

Since lack of air movement between the plants helps mildew to settle and spread, consider whether you have planted them too close. Karathane and Benlate fungicides will give good control but you should realise that growing shoots grow out of the protective sheath of fungicide and therefore need to be protected by frequent subsequent spraying.

Here is another idea that you may like to consider. With the multiplicity of hose fittings available today, it is a simple matter to rig up a permanent irrigation system. You will need standards about four feet tall and six to seven feet apart with, connected to their tops, the type of mist spray head used to produce the very fine mist that is used inside greenhouses for automatic irrigation and mist propagation. Bury the main water supply line as deeply as you can between the roses without causing any more disturbance than you can manage. The depth is important because you will want the water to remain as cool as possible especially when the air temperature becomes hot during summer. If you leave the hose connecting-point well clear of the rose bed, you will be able to connect to the water supply very quickly by using Snap Lock fittings.

Rose enthusiasts who have installed permanent watering systems of this kind can often be heard enthusing over the discovery that their watering 'washes off' all the black spot and mildew. This may well be true but if you use as much water as that, you will spoil a great many blooms as well. In fact a different principle entirely is being used, which is well-known in laboratory practice.

What stops the fungi is the slight but sudden drop in temperature at the leaf surface: not enough to shock the plant—the volume of water used is not enough to lower the temperature more than a very few degrees—but it is enough to inhibit the fungus spores from developing. You should use the special fine mist spray head instead of a normal sprinkler spray so the water volume is reduced to the minimum. The supply pipe is buried deeply in order to keep the water cool. Several times a day, give a 30-second mist spray, by a turn of the tap—and you'll not see much mildew or black spot.

Using Hoselock special plastic hose and fittings, setting up a spray system of this kind is quite easy and inexpensive.

4 Rose buds which will not open

A rose bush I bought cheaply two years ago from a local garden centre to replace a dead bush bloomed quite well the first year, but I noticed this year that some buds on this bush seem solid and fail to open. Could you tell me the reason for this? I have over eighty other rose bushes in my garden and none of them have had this trouble.

Presumably this trouble hasn't happened with your other roses and for it to have occurred with a new two-year-old planting suggests that it is not pest or disease, but an example of 'balling'—a physiological problem that is inherent in some varieties. It also occurs when the material used for the original bud graft has not been of the best quality—as I am sure is the case here. Flower buds do not develop properly, the petals fail to expand and then turn brown as they collapse and rot. These are all indications of a very severe growth check, possibly caused by a cold spell made worse perhaps by excessively wet weather, and it may be that this new variety is more intolerant than all the others in your garden of cold winds and an excess of wet.

Short of moving it into a more protected position or screening it, there is little you can do about the weather to which it is subjected. So you should do everything you can to improve the growing conditions (see *No. 2*) so at least you will know that it is not your cultivation that is at fault. If the trouble persists, you should remove the plant to a position where it can be left to its own devices. If the plant were mine, I should scrap it; rotting buds can soon pick up

botrytis fungus and spread it to the other roses. Then replace it with a proven good variety obtained from a reputable and known nursery.

Never, never be tempted to buy roses 'on the cheap'. A first-class grower will have put a lot of experience, knowledge and effort into producing a rose that he is prepared to put his name to. Pay him for it—you cannot get good roses if you don't start right.

5 Suckers

One of my 'Super Star' roses last year made foliage of a different colour from the rest of the bush and also had a bloom like a 'Queen Alexandra' rose day flag. I should like to know if this is what is called a 'sport' because several more of my roses are doing the same thing this year.

No, it is not a sport. The abnormal growth of your roses is undoubtedly due to sucker growth and is quite common with these plants and many others where budding and grafting techniques are used. Put at its simplest, budding is where a growth bud is implanted in the bark of another plant, and grafting is where a twig or piece of young wood is similarly joined on.

This is done for several reasons, but mainly because many choice varieties of roses—and fruit trees—do not develop a vigorous enough root system of their own. Therefore, their performance—be it colour, bloom or fruit production—can be improved by pushing into them the extra vigour of the 'natural' or 'wild' rose used for the root stock. Almost all bush roses are propagated by budding and standard roses by implanting the bud high up on a briar stem. As soon as the nurseryman can see that his bud has 'taken', he cuts off the original 'wild' stock foliage and growth above the bud so that growth is now concentrated in the choice variety bud.

It sometimes happens that the root or 'stock' wants to push up more vigour than the bud or 'scion' can take, and it therefore tries to find an outlet for its excess energy. This it will do by sending up growth of its own—i.e. the suckers —which can usually be distinguished by their different colour, wild habit and often by many more thorns on the stem.

When this happens to roses, fruit trees or anything else, never cut off these suckers. A clean cut with secateurs or a knife creates healing tissue called callus and from which new shoots called adventitious growth will assuredly form. This explains why you should always be very careful when hoeing or working the soil near roses. A 'cut' wound on the root caused by a hoe can easily throw up a sucker from the healing scar. Suckers must not be left because they will soon take all the energy and swamp the choice variety which, if by-passed in this way, will sooner or later wither and die.

Where suckers arise from the root, trace them underground, pull them away completely, apply a fungicide like Benlate to the wound and cover up again.

The stem of standard roses and fruits will often throw off sucker shoots. These should be removed while they are still young enough to be rubbed off with the fingers, thus causing the minimum of shock to the plant. If you neglect and thus allow sucker growth to become so established that there is risk that pulling will snap the choice variety or the standard stem from which it arises, cut the sucker away but roughen up the wound with a rasp so that the callus tissue does not form so easily and encourage yet more sucker shoots. Then treat the wound with a protective compound, like grafting wax, to stop fungus disease spores from getting in.

6 Rose culture in acid soil

I give my three rose beds a dressing of Top Rose every month in the growing season, and a spray of Murphy FF each week. I mulch with well-rotted manure, but many of the leaves are small and misshapen. On testing the soil, I find it is very acid; the soil is well-drained and not heavy.

Roses prefer the soil to be a little on the alkaline side of neutral, so you have some correcting to do. There is an old saying about taking a horse to water and not being able to make it drink. Perhaps it ought to go on, 'and if you do force it to drink, you will only make it

feel sick!' For this is what you are doing. Plants should not go short of food, but it does not follow that you can grow better plants by forcing a super-abundance of food down their throats, and you are overdoing it with this rate of fertiliser and foliar feeding.

You should cut out all feeding for at least one whole season, and give the over-abundance a chance to weather and disperse. You will have to get the acidity reversed, but you cannot do it quickly because a heavy application of lime will cause an even heavier release of plant nutrients and lush growth which would be prone to attack by diseases. Spread around a light dressing of hydrated lime at no more than 1 oz. per sq. yd. You already have the soil mulched with a well-rotted manure—that is good.

Keep it well-rotted and when you replenish the mulch cover, don't use fresh manure—'short' as it is called—because the high nitrogen content from the fresh urine encourages soft, sappy growth which is no good for blooms and attracts all sorts of pests and diseases. Scratch the lime into the mulch—a five-pronged claw hoe or a long handled border fork is good for this, because it is very easy to snag a root with a blade of a dutch or drag hoe and that is the forerunner of briar suckers.

Keeping the soil/mulch surface scratched open is important so that air can more easily enter the soil and encourage bacterial activity. Repeat the lime a month after the first, and again a month after that. However, *before* putting down the fourth dressing and any subsequent monthly applications, carry out a soil test for acidity, see *No. 472*. Make the test before a lime dressing is applied because you cannot expect a true reading of soil acidity/alkalinity just after fresh lime has been put down.

When the soil test shows a slight alkaline reaction you can stop the monthly dressing, and then carry out a soil test every three months —only lime dressing if you find the acidity coming back.

About the end of October—after the roses have fed for a full year at least on the residues of the earlier fertiliser dressings—scratch into the mulch cover Humber Eclipse, Growmore or other balanced plant food at no more than 1 oz. per sq. yd. The purpose of this very light dressing is not to produce a significant nutrient supply for the plants, but to encourage the proliferation of the particular bacteria strains that are concerned with the decomposition of this plant food source—see *No. 2*. There will, therefore, be much greater numbers of the right kinds of bacteria ready to go to work when, in spring, you put down 2 ozs. per sq. yd., or about a small tablespoonful around single plants of the same plant food. Beginning in late March, scratch the fertiliser into the mulch cover and repeat at six- to seven-week intervals until, but not later than, the first week in August. This means about four dressings in all. The long-lasting feeding action—especially in Eclipse—means that any dressing put down after early August would encourage too much growth too late in the year when they should be slowing down and going into their winter sleep. With the return to slight alkalinity plus a slow release organic feed, your roses will soon regain good health.

7 Black Spot disease

My floribunda roses have become badly infected with Black Spot. I have been told the only thing to do is to dig them all up and burn them, and on no account to plant new roses in their place. Please let me have your advice on this matter.

Read *Nos. 2, 3* and *4*—much of which is also relevant to Black Spot. Healthy, vigorous bushes are better able to resist and recover from attack.

There is no need to destroy roses attacked by Black Spot fungus—indeed it would be quite pointless to do so unless you modify your cultivation methods which have allowed the plants to become badly affected. Planting them elsewhere in the garden would not stop it either: fungus doesn't recognise frontiers like fences or hedges, and in the same garden your new plantings would be at risk at once.

Prevention is better than cure, but as you may be in an area that is prone to Black Spot and perhaps surrounded by other gardens

from which it may spread, anti-Black Spot precautions must become a basic and regular part of your cultivation technique. Strangely, an increase in Black Spot has resulted from our clean air policies—the polluted sulphur-laden air of years ago was an effective deterrent.

Spray at seven- to ten-day intervals with either a Captan-based or Benlate fungicide to which you have added a few drops of liquid washing-up detergent so that the spray spreads on the foliage and achieves a good cover. Incidentally, spray on dull days or in the cool of evening to prevent the sun scorching the leaves when they are wet with spray. Repeat this spraying as part of your routine from May. This is when the disease puts in its first appearance as spots, but by which time is already into and affecting the plant tissues.

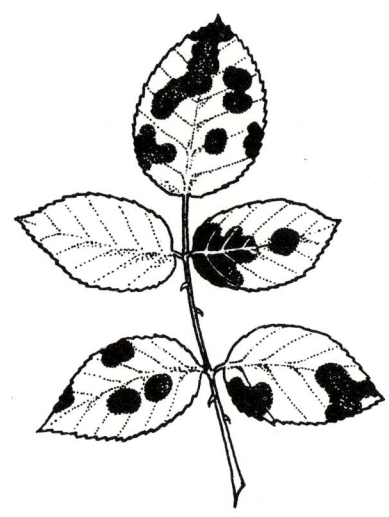

No. 7 *The unmistakable disfigurement of Black Spot disease which affects rose leaves.*

Like the precautions for Botrytis and other fungus diseases, cleanliness is vitally important. Pick up all fallen leaves at once—better still, pick off all affected leaves before they have the chance to fall—and of course burn them. After leaf fall, drench the bushes and surrounding soil with Ovamort Special to destroy overwintering spores. Resistance by the plant is important and as this depends upon good growing conditions, pay attention to correct feeding and soil structure as outlined in *No. 2* and *No. 11*.

Black Spot is a particularly destructive and weakening disease to which your roses are exposed throughout the growing season. You cannot prevent that but you can prevent it gaining a hold, by cleanliness, timely counter measures, and good cultivation techniques. It is a persistent disease so if you relax your routine of precautionary spraying all your previous work will have been wasted.

8 Only roses get Black Spot

I want to plant sweet peas on ground that was a rose bed. Would any Black Spot spores that may be on the ground have any effect on my sweet peas?

No effect at all. The spores of Black Spot fungus are specific and only have one host—the rose. It cannot attack sweet peas or any other plant.

Because you have had roses growing here, you will not have had opportunity to do anything about the soil structure deep down—and sweet peas like to send their roots down deep into plenty of moisture-retaining organic matter.

Prepare by trenching two spits deep, with plenty of well-rotted compost in the bottom, and you'll grow good sweet peas with no trouble from rose Black Spot.

9 Cutting blooms does no harm

Could you tell me whether it is harmful to rose bushes to cut their blooms for the house.

You won't do any harm provided that you don't overdo it; indeed, it might be regarded as a form of pruning that will encourage further bloom on new growth produced from lower down.

The important point to bear in mind though is that you should pay more attention to the still growing bush than the bloom you cut off. Like all pruning, what you cut off doesn't matter; it is the condition of what is left that does matter.

Cut the flower stems just above a leaf joint so that a growth bud can grow out quickly, but cut, not with scissors since they will only crush the tissue. Use secateurs that are sharp and in good condition, so that you leave a clean fast healing wound on the still living bush.

10 Why old flower heads should be removed

The pride of my garden is the lovely shrub rose 'Ballerina'. Should I cut off the dead flower heads or leave them on?

Unless you have purposefully cross-fertilised varieties and want to save the seed, you should cut off old flowers as they fade in order to concentrate the plant's energy into subsequent blooms and growth. As soon as a plant, any plant, begins the process of producing seed, it also begins to lose the need to put up more bloom because it has achieved its primary purpose in ensuring the next generation and the perpetuation of its own species. By taking off fading blooms and the developing seed which will be in the swelling pod or seed capsule adjacent to the fading flower, the plant has to go through the process again of trying to produce seed by first producing more flowers. The principle applies not only to the rose 'Ballerina' but in greater or lesser degree to most other roses, and for that matter to most other plants.

It is not always the case—some roses, like the well-known climber 'Albertine', produce one flush of bloom, and even if every fading flower is removed, they are very reluctant to produce secondary blooms. However, most bush roses are 'perpetual flowering', i.e. they produce bloom continually over a long period, and will be encouraged to do so by removing flowers as they fade.

11 Peat for roses and limited usefulness of bonemeal

I have about four cwt. of ordinary peat which I intend using on my rose beds—about three hundred plants. The peat is in a good condition, i.e. it is well separated, but rather dry. How should I use the peat to its best advantage and when should I use it? I also have about one cwt. of bonemeal, bought direct from a factory which manufactures the material. How and when should I use this?

I am not sure what you mean by a factory that manufactures bonemeal. The product that is intended for horticultural use has to be quite clear of anthrax—a dreadful disease—and you should be quite certain that this bonemeal has been prepared explicitly for garden use and is certified safe to handle.

In any case, bonemeal will only provide phosphate and is in no sense a balanced plant food, so I would suggest you can spend your money in a better way. Four cwts. of peat for three hundred roses is not very generous, but I would use it in the following manner. On a hard surface—garage floor, driveway, or even a polythene sheet on the lawn—spread out the peat, crumble any lumps and mix into it, not bonemeal, but 28 lbs. of Humber Eclipse garden manure; 7 lbs. into each cwt. of peat. If ever you have to buy it by the bale (in which case it will be measured not by weight because it is compressed and variable in moisture content and therefore variable also in weight), mix in 7 lbs. of Eclipse to a 'polybale' of peat. It is easiest to mix the peat while it is dry, but you should make sure that the mixture is well wetted before use on or in the soil. The best way to use the peat would be as a mulch—a thin covering to the soil, although to be effective you would need a layer an inch or two thick. Your three hundred roses would take more than your four cwts.

Lightly scratch open the soil surface with a dutch hoe and spread down the peat/manure mix as a light surface mulch. If you put it down dry and rain does not soon follow, put the sprinkler on to make sure the peat is well wetted. The best time to put down this feed mulch is in the spring, so that the plant food promotes good healthy growth at the right time. Addition of a plant food plus organic dressings like this makes for a dramatic increase in beneficial soil bacteria. Best advantage of this is gained by using exactly the same

plant food for subsequent dressings so that the right kinds of bacteria are already present in the soil and ready to go to work on your fresh dressings. It is not prudent to increase bacteria populations in this way, and then change to fertiliser or plant food because this will entail different kinds of bacteria, and you will have to wait whilst they in turn increase their numbers in response to the new food source. Read also *Nos. 2* and *6*.

12 Methods of propagating shrub roses by cuttings

Can I take cuttings from a lovely old-fashioned rose with scented flowers that must be at least fifty years old? If so, what is the likelihood of success, and when should the cuttings be taken?

Cuttings of roses, especially the species and old-fashioned types which, because they haven't been hybridised and crossed, and recrossed, have retained much of their natural vigour, can be rooted without much difficulty.

Follow the procedure for climbing rose cuttings described in *No. 13* but make the cuttings a little shorter—about 6 inches maximum. These can be prepared from July onwards, provided the wood is no longer sappy. The important point is to pare the cutting heel absolutely smooth and clean, so that a layer of healing callus cells forms quickly. These callus cells are the ones that lead to the formation of 'adventitious' root cells and thus roots.

Cuttings can be set until as late as October, by which time the wood will be well ripened and of course you can try both methods—cuttings set in a sand-lined slit trench, and the water rooting method. See *No. 13*.

13 Propagating climbers by cuttings

Could you tell me how to take a cutting from a climbing rose? I have never taken cuttings before, and a friend would like a cutting from my yellow climber 'Casino'.

It is quite simple to propagate most climbing roses by cuttings, but peculiarly, and unfortunately, not so well with yellow varieties, and you may well have to prepare a fair number of cuttings for each one that will root satisfactorily. There are two methods to try, both using the same cuttings.

Sand-lined slit trench method : During October—or later in November if the season is late—select shoots of the current year's growth, pull them away with a heel from the main stem, and cut off the top just above a leaf joint so that you are left with a cutting about 9–10 inches long. Remove any leaves except the top two and with a very sharp knife, trim the heel end very lightly so that the cut surface is smooth.

While the sap is still moist, dip half of your cuttings at once into Seradix or Murphy rooting hormone powder; put the other half of the cuttings aside.

With your spade, chop a slit trench about 6–7 inches deep, turn the spade over, chop down vertically and, leaving one side firm and undisturbed, pull the soil towards you to leave a V-shaped slit. Put an inch or so of sand along the bottom, and set the cuttings down firmly on this sand 3 inches apart, holding each upright against the firm trench side with a handful of sand.

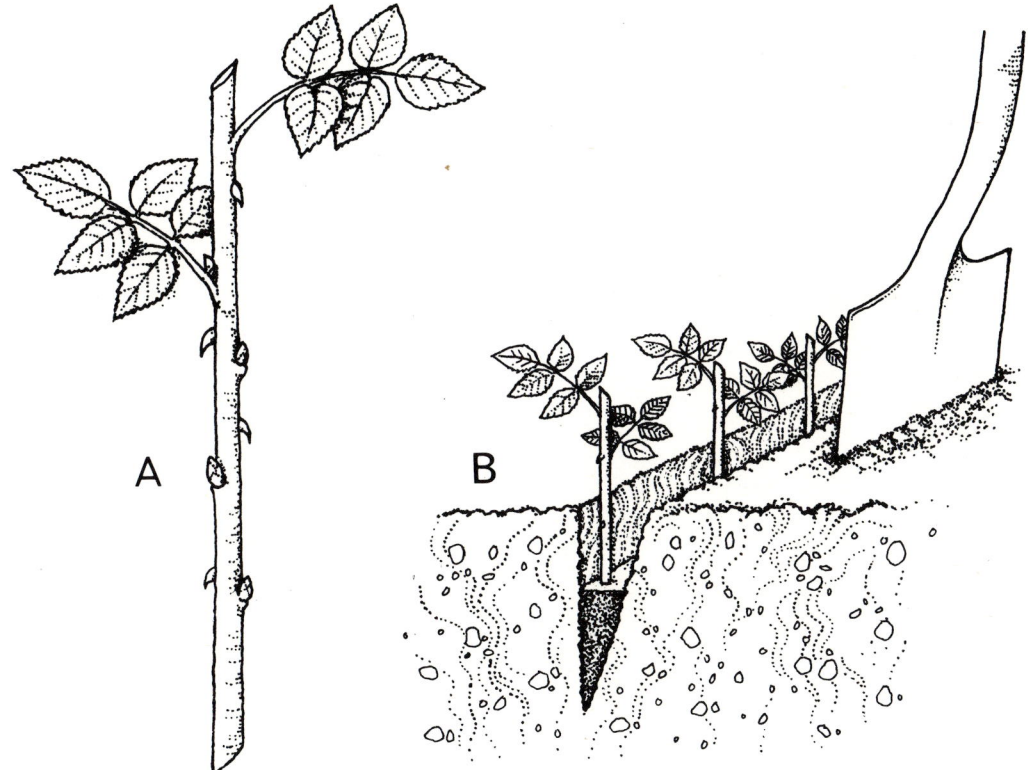

Nos. 12 & 13   *Propagation of roses by cuttings.*
A.   *Cutting made with heel pared clean, two leaves left with buds in leaf to grow out. Other leaves trimmed.*
B.   *Inserted in slit trench, cuttings set 5–6 ins. apart. Spade used to lever soil hard against cuttings.*

Insert the spade again a couple of inches away and lever the soil over to fill the original slit so that the cuttings are rammed hard against the firm vertical side. Leave this second slit open alongside. If dry weather sets in, simply run the water can or hose along the slit and fill it with water. As frosty weather sets in, mulch down both sides of the row of cuttings, filling in the slit.

The leaves left on the cuttings will of course fall during winter, but in spring, with good fortune, shoots growing out will show you which ones have rooted. Leave them here until next autumn when you can take them up and plant them into a permanent position.

Water rooting method: The other half of your cuttings are worth trying by the water rooting method; you won't need hormone powder. Simply stand the cuttings in a jar of rainwater 5–6 inches deep. It must be rainwater; tap water very much reduces the chances of rooting.

The water may become green with algae; if it does, clean it out and replace with clean fresh rainwater. After a few weeks, you should observe roots forming.

Many plants can be rooted in this way, but gardeners often experience difficulty in making the transition from having rooted in water to growing in soil. The reason why this difficulty occurs is that the roots that form in rainwater are water roots. They are different from soil roots and are not able to make a sudden transition to doing the work of normal soil roots. You will have to make the change gradually from water to soil. Here is a method I have used successfully.

When the water roots are an inch or two long, take a flower pot—about 3–4 inches in diameter in this case—and stand this inside another vessel, like a decorative pot holder that fits the pot, but it must hold water. You don't need space between the two pots. Fill the flower pot with rainwater and put the water-rooted cuttings into this. Each day tip in a dessert-spoonful of soil—John Innes No. 1 will do well. Gradually, day by day, the water will become paste, then mud, then wet soil, and finally moist soil. The inner pot can then be lifted out of the pot holder, with the cutting now nicely rooted in soil—the gradual transition from water having taken two or three weeks.

In spring, the soil-rooted cutting can be planted in a permanent position. Knock it out of the pot, complete with its root ball of soil; this will avoid root disturbance and the plant therefore becomes established quite quickly.

14 Causes and control of rose mildew disease

Last year I bought three climbers. I found they were affected with mildew which has now spread to 80% of my roses. I have dug out and burned the climbers. Could you please help me to get rid of this mildew?

Some varieties of rose are much more susceptible than others to mildew, and of course it is quite arguable that to include one or more such varieties in your collection must increase the chances of spreading it to others that might well have escaped attack.

Without knowing what varieties of climber you introduced, it is impossible to say whether the 80% infection was due to their introduction, or whether a particularly bad mildew season was responsible when you would have had that rate of infection anyway.

The lesson to be learned, from your experience, is that you should be very very careful about the varieties you buy. It is not only you and your fancies that have to be considered; the collection you already have in your garden has something to say about it too, and you should always consider to what risks you may be exposing them by bringing in a newcomer.

Furthermore, are you quite sure they were clean when you bought them, that they were not already infected from a dirty nursery or garden centre? Once again, I must emphasise the wisdom of only and always buying from a first-class reputable source.

Whatever the cause of the trouble, I think that you over-reacted by destroying them—before positively resolving what happened and at least giving them a fair chance for another season, with the benefit of a reasonable anti-mildew routine spraying.

There is no complete answer to mildew, the spores are everywhere in the air, and your roses are liable to be attacked every day of their life. Like ourselves, and every other form of life, plants are liable to constant attack by other forms of life—microbes, insects, bacteria, fungi, etc. There is little you can do to avoid the attack—that is life, and life lives upon life. As with ourselves, what you can do is to help your roses resist the constant attack upon them, and not only by protective measures. In this case protect against fungus by spraying with Karathane or Benlate; but also by ensuring good healthy growth by good cultivation.

Read all the adjacent questions and answers on rose culture especially *No. 2*, and bear in mind that as in life, first predatory attack is always against the weakest. So with your roses, mildew gains access into the leaf tissue that is soft and limp—the correct word is 'flaccid'—and this is more likely to occur after prolonged periods of dry weather when dryness at the roots is liable to occur. This is a real problem with new plantings that have not had enough time to develop sufficient root growth to support foliage, and bloom—and indeed could well have been the cause with your three new plantings.

15 Precautions to be taken when moving old-established plants

I want to turn my front garden into a lawn, but it is at present overgrown with sadly neglected large bushes of 'Peace' rose. They must be at least twenty years old. Is it possible to move these roses and replant them in another part of the garden and, if so, what is the best way to go about the job? They are still amazingly attractive and very healthy.

You must accept a big risk in moving any shrub or tree in an advanced state of maturity and, whilst it is always possible, the probability is that you will have a high degree of failure.

Tackle the job in late autumn when all leaves have fallen, and very much in the same way as for an evergreen—see *No. 65*. Begin by preparing the new position, taking out a large

hole and digging plenty of compost into the bottom.

It is not absolutely essential to lift these roses with a ball of soil attached, but your chances are much greater if you carry out the half and half 'sheet under' technique, described in *No. 65*. Before lifting, cut all top growth by half: some people advise hard pruning, but as it is going to have its root system mauled, it's rather like kicking a rose when its down. So don't slaughter the top growth more than is necessary to keep the thorns out of your eyes and from tearing your shirt whilst you man-handle the bushes.

Plant firmly, to the same depth as before lifting, and water in. Unless you are in a very exposed position and get very high winds, mature plants with a sizeable root ball ought not to be as liable to wind rock as would young plants.

This is another reason why a lot of the top growth is removed—too much up top can act as a sail to catch the wind causing the plant to sway. What can and often does happen especially in heavy soils during periods of wet weather, is that the wind rock creates a funnel shape of compacted soil around the neck of the stem as it emerges from the soil, and the repeated swaying and rock causes this soil funnel to glaze—clay soils are particularly prone to this. Water cannot easily drain through this glazed soil surface with the result that the 'funnel hole' fills with rain, which doesn't drain away and your rose spends many winter days standing up to its neck in water. It's not likely to happen in your case because the shrubs are so large, but watch out.

With old neglected roses, it is problematical whether and to what extent new growth will break from old, long dormant buds in what have become woody barky stems.

New growth shoots develop much more readily from younger growth and this is why old shrubs, particularly shrub roses, are so often seen tall and overgrown with all fresh growth two, three and even four feet high, with no fresh growth at all emanating from the old woody stems below. These old woody stems will contain growth buds, however, that have been long dormant and hard pruning will certainly encourage them into life. However, drastic hard pruning into old, barky, woody stems can easily cause the rootstock to blow a safety valve too; with the woody stem reluctant to send out new shoots, and taking the sap thrust from below, the rootstock finds its own way out for its energy—by sending up suckers.

With more gentle cutting back, you will have at least some buds breaking in early spring, indicating that root activity is established and the bush is still alive. Before these are an inch long—and certainly before individual leaves are discernible—prune back to the lowest two or three shoots per stem, so that new growth arises from low down near ground level—not up in the air!

'Peace' is a vigorous top grower and for the first year or two after transplanting will be at risk through making more than enough top growth for its renewing root system to sustain. The shrubs will therefore be susceptible to dryness at the roots and limp flaccid foliage is wide open to fungus and pest attack.

Therefore keep the soil surface well mulched with a thick compost layer to conserve moisture and, if a dry spell sets in, make sure the mulch has something to conserve by giving it a good soak. The plants will need a little bit extra by way of feed, but keep this down to a minimum, because once a vigorous rose like 'Peace' gets going it will react with a lot of growth.

16 When a climber doesn't flower

A filipes 'Kiftsgate' climbing rose was planted to ramble over an old 6 ft high tree trunk. This it has done with great vigour, but has not yet flowered apart from two sprays last year. What treatment does it require?

I'm afraid this is yet another example of planting something without first finding out exactly what it will become.

R. filipes 'Kiftsgate' is an extremely vigorous rose, and would be more at home against a field fence where it could run twenty or more feet. You cannot really expect it to stop at six feet and any form of pruning is only going to

make matters worse because it will react with even more vigorous growth.

If you don't want to uproot it and plant something more suitable, the only way to control it and make it throw bloom is to do something similar to what the fruit growers do to make logans and blackberries throw a lot of fruit. Restrict the sap flow by bending the young supple shoots, causing the plant to fight against the restriction. This it does by producing much more bloom, and subsequent fruit. The principle can be applied to many other plants, and is particularly suitable to

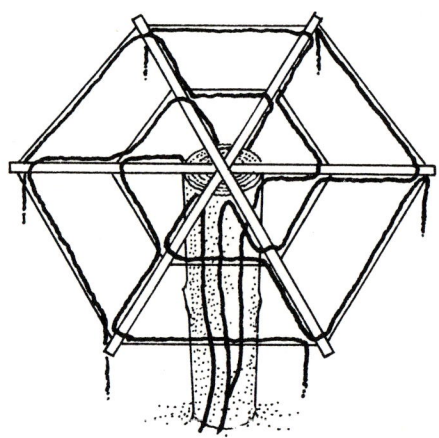

No. 16 *View of an umbrella canopy showing how a climbing or rambling rose can be planted against an old tree trunk. This method can also be used for other climbing and rambling plants— clematis, honeysuckle, jasmine and the blackberry 'Himalaya Giant'.*

many of the 'old fashioned' and 'species' roses which, whilst very vigorous, do not produce such an abundance of bloom as do the more modern varieties.

If you have the space to do it, here is a way to solve the problem to advantage, and provide yourself with an attractive feature.

Obtain three lengths of 2½ in. sq. timber—
or redundant piping or something similar—
about 6, 7 or 8 ft. long and fasten these to the
top of the tree trunk, like spokes of a flat
Japanese parasol. Fasten a length of stout wire
from end to end of these spokes to keep them
evenly apart like the rim of a wheel, and again
half way between trunk and spoke ends. As
the long vigorous stems rise up beyond the
trunk top, bend them over rather sharply
whilst still soft and pliable, and tie down along
a spoke. As the growing tip reaches half way,
bend it again and tie it in along the middle wire
to the next spoke; then bend it again so that it
is pointing to the edge of the wheel or parasol.
When the tip gets there, turn it again and run
it round the outer wire rim. This repeated
bending restricts the sap flow at each turn and
diverts the energy into flower production, and
thus you will have a lovely rose arbour, an
attractive solution to your problem.

17   Training a weeping rose

*In the spring I planted a weeping standard in the
centre of a bed of 'Papa Meilland' hybrid tea.
The tea roses flowered, the weeping standard
didn't. What did I do wrong and how do I train
a weeping standard?*

This may be a blessing in disguise. You should
not expect a weeping standard to bloom well—
if at all—in the first season after planting,
because it is usual for them to take the transplanting shock considerably harder than a
bush type and also harder than a conventional
climber or rambler. This is because of the
distance between the growth points at the top
of the standard, and the root system some 5 or
6 ft. below.

When the weeping head is in full foliage and
bloom the plant will have a considerable
evaporation area, and the evaporating moisture
has to travel a long way through the long narrow
bottleneck of the standard stem. The inherent
danger is dryness at the root, because it can
take a long time for the salvaging moisture—
when restored—to get to where it is wanted.

Normally a weeping standard is pruned after
flowering, cutting out old flowered growths
and training in new arching shoots to hang and
curtain down as replacements.

With a new planting however I would not
prune it very much in the first year. Let it
become fully established with plenty of new
root action before asking it to support the
invigorated growth response that will come
from hard cutting. Put down a good mulch,
feed it well with a balanced plant nutrient.

Weeping roses best display their beauty
when the long weeping stems are arranged
over, and allowed to fall from, a wire 'umbrella'
frame fastened firmly to the top of the supporting stake. These long weeping stems will often
curtain down to ground level and growing
among shrub roses in a bed could well produce
something of a tangled mess as they intermingle
with the smaller shrub roses.

In my opinion, a weeping rose should be
grown as a solitary specimen—not in a bed—
but on a lawn where it can be seen and admired
unobstructed by other plants.

18   Safe weed-killers for rose beds

*Is there a weed-killer I can use around my roses
to keep them free from weeds for a long period?*

If you were maintaining a good mulch cover on
your rose beds you would not be suffering
from weeds, at least to the extent that a stab
with a dutch hoe could not control them.

The roses would also benefit from the steady
addition of humus and better retention of
moisture and nutrients, and in addition to
making weed control easier, is a move towards
better cultivation.

However, if you want to practise chemical
control of weeds, first clean off all the top
growth of weed, scratch the soil surface lightly
and use one of the many flower bed weedkillers that are becoming available: Ramrod,
Casoron G., Rose Bed Weedkiller, and Herbazin Selective.

Always bear in mind when using weedkillers among plants you don't wish to harm,
that the selectivity between what is killed and
what is not depends upon the strength of the
rate of application; follow the manufacturer's
instructions to the letter.

19 Use of seaweed on roses

I am preparing a small garden for roses. It has been suggested that I should use a mulch of sedge peat with fish manure, or chopped-up seaweed for a spring fertiliser. Living near the sea, I can obtain the latter without cost, but do roses really like seaweed?

You are particularly fortunate in being able to collect seaweed. It is rich in potash and most trace elements, and rots down fairly quickly. The type known as bladderwrack is the best. It is naturally organic, has a very high degree of moisture absorption and is particularly beneficial in putting 'body' into light sandy soils.

You may find the salt a problem, unless you are using it fresh and as a mulch in conjunction with crops like onions and asparagus which quite like a little salt. This is how I would suggest that you use it.

Spread it out on the garden path or any other hard surface and either wash the salt off with the hose or let the rain do the job. You will not be able to use it in large lumps so, as you are going to save money by collecting the stuff, invest in a Rotochop, a most useful tool, quite inexpensive and rather like a large coarse mincer. Use this to chop up the seaweed into smaller pieces to produce an ideal mulching material.

The nitrogen and phosphorus content is so low as to be negligible; therefore, don't dig it in fresh or alone. It is far better to put it through the compost heap so that it can become admixed with other materials and so balance up the deficiency.

Mulching is not so critical in this respect, provided you rely upon other material for the balance in the nutrient supply. The moderate extra potash to be derived from a seaweed mulch will then be beneficial to roses both by encouraging mature wood and by putting extra colour in the blooms. It is also valuable used for all plants that bear large blooms—Dahlias, Chrysanthemums etc.

Potash is vital at ripening time, so you can also use seaweed to advantage in the vegetable and soft fruit plots.

20 Buttercups are persistent weeds among roses

My rose border is smothered with buttercups that get worse every year. How can I control them?

There are several forms of buttercup, and for a rose bed to be smothered and getting worse can only mean creeping buttercup or bulbous-rooted buttercup—or both. Control is difficult because of the risk of chemical weed-killers to other plants in the bed. If there are only a few weeds, you should touch each weed with a Touchweeder. This is a small stick of hormone-impregnated wax, which does not wash off.

But it would be a tedious job dabbing all the weeds in a smothered bed, and painting would probably be much quicker. Begin by applying a brushwood killer sold under the name SBK, but you will have to be very, very careful not to let the liquid touch the roses. Make up a water solution at half the directed strength—plus a few drops of washing-up liquid—and paint the solution onto the foliage. At half-strength, the hormone will be carried into the bulbil root before the foliage dies and then the hormone stops moving within the weed. A second half-strength dose ten to fourteen days later should then kill the entire plant. If the weed has not died by that time, give a third dose fourteen days later.

As soon as the rose border is clear, put down a heavy mulch of garden or mushroom compost. If the buttercups appear again, physical removal will be very easy in the friable mulch. As this mulch is gradually absorbed into the soil, replace it with more—you *must* keep up the cover.

If you are not confident that you can put down SBK without risk to the roses—perhaps they are congested and the job awkward for you—try the modern 'emergent' weed-killers that take out soft growth like seedlings and new shoots, but leave more established plant tissue unharmed. This process takes longer than SBK, but with persistence you can wear down the weed. Use Gesal Weed Preventer, Murphy Ramrod, Herbazin Selective, or Casoron G, and adhere strictly to the manufacturers' instructions. Don't expect miracles overnight; buttercup is a persistent and resistant weed.

21 Special treatment for Mare's Tail weed

My rose bed is full of Mare's Tail weed during the summer. I hoe and hand-weed it but I just seem to be wasting my time. Is there any selective weed-killer which will destroy this but not kill the roses?

Hoeing and hand-weeding only makes matters worse because you are stimulating the plant to produce underground side shoots. Hormone weed-killers will kill it, but the problem is how to get the hormone inside the plant.

The leaf shape is perfectly designed to shed every drop of weed spray, and the waxy texture of the leaf surfaces ensures that it does so. Add to this the proximity of your roses, and there is the sum of your problem. Fortunately it is not so difficult, if you use a little guile.

You will need a long rubber glove that will come well up your forearm—these are sold for use as household cleaning gloves. Over this pull on a woollen or old leather glove. Make up a solution $1\frac{1}{2}$ fluid ozs. of SBK brushwood killer in half a gallon of paraffin. Mix this in a plastic bucket, and as you move it around on the job for heaven's sake be careful not to kick it over.

Put your gloved hand in the solution—the rubber under-glove will stop your hand becoming oily—and 'wipe' the main shoot by gently grasping the lower part of the main stem and pulling so that it slips through your hand.

Where there is a chance of the wetted Mare's Tail blowing against and touching the roses, wipe only the lower parts. Gradually the weed will wither and die. Any young fresh emerging growth can be dealt with the same way—it will succumb much more quickly than older mature growth.

This is the easiest, safest and most effective way of dealing with this weed in cultivated ground—but you will have to be persistent.

Another chemical you could use is Amcide which is a total weed-killer that becomes ineffective after eight weeks, leaving the soil safe for planting. But it is risky to use it among other plants that you dare not harm.

Section II

Trees and Shrubs

22   Ailanthus growing too tall

Can you tell me how and when I can stop my Tree of Heaven from growing. It was just 18 ins. when I bought it and now, after only three years, it has already reached 8 ft. tall and I hope it won't grow much taller.

Your Tree of Heaven, previously called *Ailanthus glandulosa* is nowadays correctly named *A. alticima*. It has ornamental leaves shaped very much like those of the ash but much longer, sometimes 3 ft. or more. It is extremely active and frequently presents problems when it insists on growing taller than its owners originally had in mind. When it has reached the desired height, cut out the growing point. This will encourage the tree to spread by putting out side growths which, in turn, will eventually need cutting out in the same way.

23   Almond in decline

I have had a flowering almond for about four years. It has trebled in height but the flowers are getting fewer and fewer. This year there was only one flower. I thinned it out a bit last year and I have never fed it. Could you give me any suggestions of how to get it to bloom?

If your tree has trebled in height in four years, it can hardly be a standard tree—so it must be a bush type shrub which could have been grafted or budded onto a more vigorous stock to make it bloom younger and more profusely than it would on its own roots. Trebled in height? I wonder if the bottom part of the vigorous rootstock has put up growth of its own and increasingly ignored the choice flowering top part—the scion—so that it has been by-passed and is in decline.

Compare the foliage very carefully—shape, colour and size. If you can detect two different kinds, then it is almost certain that your flowering almond is nothing of the sort—but a sucker. To be quite sure, follow the stems from which the differing leaves arose, back to the base and you should be able to see where the root stock was cut just above the point where the intended choice variety emerges from an implanted bud or a graft. If this was

propagated at a good nursery the cut-off wound in the rootstock would have been painted with protective paint and after only four years it is quite likely that you will still be able to detect traces of this.

Now, if you can find a stem or stems from below the graft carrying different leaves from the intentional stem, there can be little doubt that the rootstock has broken out. You can try cutting this 'broken out' or 'unintentional' growth of the rootstock back to base. I should use a saw—don't use secateurs—so that you leave a rough surface. A smooth clean cut will merely produce healing callus tissue which will encourage several shoots to come where you had one before. The rough surface discourages this but you *must* paint the wound with protective grafting wax or paint to prevent the entry of fungus spores.

The above operation could be rather risky because it sounds in this case as though the rootstock growth has got a good hold—but there is nothing else to be done.

On the other hand, the problem may be nothing to do with rootstocks. Almonds, indeed all stone fruits, prefer an alkaline soil and your description of trebled growth could mean that your almond bush is putting on leaf and stem instead of flowering. It is probably being encouraged to do so by a very fertile soil which contains plenty of humus and a good nitrogen supply. You say the tree has never been fed, so the trouble isn't artificial fertilisers out of balance. Therefore, if you can be sure it isn't rootstock trouble, you can try increasing the alkalinity by putting down hydrated lime at a rate of 4 oz. spread over 2–3 square yards around the tree every three months. This must not be hoed or dug in as you may damage the roots and cause suckering. Midway between the lime dressings, spread 3 ozs. super phosphate and 1 oz. sulphate of potash over the same area. This will help to build up the phosphate and potash in the soil and tend to depress any nitrogen excess, so that the wood then hardens and matures, encouraging it to bear blooms.

If this treatment fails you will have to get positive identification of the foliage, so you can be sure that you are not still making a mistake—and if it really is almond, the only thing left to do is shock treatment by wounding—root pruning or stem bark ringing—as practised to bring reluctant fruit trees to bear fruit.

24 Amelanchier, the Snowy Mespilus

Last year I was given an Amelanchier cana-densis, *but I know nothing about this plant. As I am now re-arranging my garden, I would be grateful if you could tell me something of the habits of this plant.*

A member of the rose family, although quite unlike a rose, this is a small genus of about a dozen species of hardy shrubs or small trees deriving mainly from the North American continent. All are attractive in spring with racemes of white, sometimes slightly bluish flowers, five petalled. These are followed by berry-like fruits coloured from scarlet to black. They prefer a soil that is a little acid and thrive in positions of full summer sun which they must have to enable them to develop the sugars and starches that provide the most beautiful colours and tints in autumn.

There has become apparent, however, some confusion about the best-known species, *A. canadensis* which has for a long time been commonly called Snowy Mespilus or June Berry. Strictly this is a medium to large sized shrub, although it is often run up as a standard, and which has a tendency to put up suckers. The leaves are quite oblong shaped and the bloom held more erect than the two species with which it has been confused. First, *A. laevis* which is a strikingly beautiful small tree in May when a profusion of fragrant white bloom mingles with the young foliage which is pink, and which again in autumn is richly coloured.

Secondly, *A. lamarckii*, similar in stature to *A. laevis* but a little more spreading. The young foliage is a deeper copper and also quite downy—the bloom is much more lax and is produced more profusely along the branches. The tree in full bloom is a wonderful sight, and although it has been naturalised for very many years in Europe, it is only recently that it has been distinguished from *A. laevis* and *A. canadensis* and given a separate name. It is more than likely that confusion will remain for some time with nurserymen continuing in their conservative way to hang on to old names, therefore don't be surprised if your *A. canadensis* is in fact *A. lamarckii*.

You may be able at this early stage of your plant's life to identify it from the above brief descriptions, but whatever it is, you have a very beautiful plant which according to the way it has been grown on could either become a large shrub, some 10–12 ft. high, or a small tree up to perhaps 18–20 ft. In each case it will require space to develop. If you transplant it, get plenty of organic material underneath it while you have the chance.

25 Andromeda, Lily of the Valley tree

I have been given a small plant called Andro-meda paniculata *which has small white flowers. Should it be thrown away after flowering or can I keep it from year to year? Does it like sun or shade? I can't find any information about it.*

If you have been given an *Andromeda pani-culata*, then you have a positive gem, and it certainly shouldn't be discarded. The reason why you cannot find out anything about it is because nowadays it is more correctly called *Lionia ligustrina*. It is very closely related to the well-known Lily of the Valley bush, Pieris, and requires the same moist, peaty, lime-free soil. It is a medium-sized shrub getting up to a small tree dimensions in mild districts or even more in very well-sheltered areas. In July and August it is a marvellous sight with its millions of lily of the valley-like blooms. Although they look as though they would be evergreen the leaves are in fact deciduous. It seems to appreciate some shelter from the worst excesses of our climate. If you can provide sheltered conditions, I should get it planted out without delay. Plenty of peat in the soil and as a mulch empty the (cold) teapot occasionally around it so that it receives the iron and tannin from the tea.

Pruning is the same as for Rhododendrons, Pieris and Kalmia, don't—unless you have to to stop it growing too big.

26 *Araucaria, the Monkey's puzzle*

Whilst visiting a garden centre I could not resist buying a monkey puzzle tree and would be grateful for advice on the correct cultivation for this and any other useful information, e.g. how on earth does it have such a peculiar name? At present, it is in a container and is about 1 ft. tall.

It is one of the joys of gardening to grow plants that 'take your fancy' but you really must be careful that your joy doesn't give way to disappointment. Buying on impulse is all very well but you should always consider factors like how big will this plant eventually become? And the long spidery-branched monkey puzzle is a case in point.

These trees can quite often be seen in small front gardens, lower half quite bare of branches. These have either withered and fallen in the cramped conditions, or have been cut because they have become too big and have taken all the light from the 'downstairs front room'.

Of course, the curious scaly branches are the main attraction but to be seen to advantage the tree needs to stand alone with plenty of space around it so that it can grow and develop at will; definitely *not* a tree for a small garden.

Many gardening books refer to it as *Araucaria imbricata* and many nurseries still list it under that name, but it is now correctly called *Araucaria araucana*. It is a conifer and one of the very few trees from South America that are hardy in Britain. It originates from the high Andes Mountains area of Chile and Argentine called Patagonia, and here is the clue as to how the peculiar scaly 'leafless' habit has evolved. Patagonia and Cape Horn have very high winds and it is first to reduce wind resistance and prevent the tree being blown over that all the leaves and stems and twigs are 'drawn in' close together and are tightly packed close to the branches. Secondly, to resist drying out too readily and to conserve moisture, the leaves have become thick, leathery, overlapping and spine-tipped. These are so sharp that climbing the tree presents a considerable problem—indeed it is reputed to be the one tree that a monkey cannot climb and,

true or not, that's how it has come to have its common name!

It grows best in a moist loamy soil and despite the frequency with which it is seen in towns—due no doubt to the Victorian craze for anything bizarre, and they planted it in hundreds—it does not like smokey town air. This is another reason why the older lower branches eventually succumb and fall off. Being evergreen, this plant must have as little root disturbance as possible which is why it came in a pot. Before planting prepare the site with plenty of moisture-retaining peat or compost worked in first. Stake it for the first few years and never, never, let it dry out.

If you don't have the space for a tree that will eventually reach 80 ft. or more and at least half that across, you will have to content yourself with enjoying it while you can, until one day, you will have to face the unhappy necessity of cutting it down.

27 *Aucuba, a much underrated shrub*

Will you please identify and give me any useful information about a shrub in my garden which looks like a large laurel but has leaves spotted with yellow? It does not seem to flower.

This is most commonly called Japanese Laurel and known botanically as Aucuba. An evergreen, it was extensively planted in Victorian times and the early part of this century, but has since suffered a decline in popularity. Perhaps with the growing appreciation of colour and form in the planning and design of gardens, it will enjoy a revival.

The type most commonly seen in town gardens, public squares and parks—and very likely the one you have—is the wild type, *A. japonica*. Aucubas grow in almost any soil and condition; they will tolerate shady situations that never see the sun, but as with all the variegated plants, we have to understand that the basic and strongest influence affecting variegation in leaf colouring is 'intensity of light'.

Plants develop sugars and starches and then further develop these into cellulose and the material of their own structure—leaves, stems, roots, flowers etc.—by using light as the source of energy. This is done in the presence of special cells containing chlorophyll which gives plant tissue the characteristic green colouring. If the light intensity is diminished, then the plant will have to make more chlorophyll or green matter to keep up the elaboration of sugars. That means extra green and if the leaf has areas which normally do not contain chlorophyll—i.e. yellow, white or colourless areas like the spots and areas on your Aucuba foliage—then those patches will be utilised and greened over, the whole leaf perhaps becoming green.

Let the plant have access to full light so that there is no need for the extra greening and the pale variegated areas will remain ungreened and therefore prominent in their contrast.

In its former heyday, the Victorians raised many varieties with different leaf markings— striped, mottled, golds, and yellows, some indeed with scarcely any green in the leaves at all. Some dozen or more named varieties are still obtainable. The most striking is *A. crotonifolia*, which received an Award of Garden Merit in 1969—so that is recommendation enough.

Aucubas do flower, although quite insignificantly and the female plants carry bright scarlet berries.

28 *Azalea : causes of leaf drop*

Last spring I was given a three-year-old indoor Azalea in a 5-inch pot, at which time it was in full bloom. When flowering was finished, I repotted it using the same size pot and using John Innes compost No. 3. I sunk the pot in the garden as I had been advised and everything went well for about two months. But it has now started to drop all its leaves, even the new ones, although I keep it moist but not wet. What have I done wrong, if anything, and how can I save the plant?

The presence of lime is the most important factor here, aided and abetted by irregular watering causing periodic dryness at root, the entire situation sparked off by your entirely incorrect 're-potting', if not indeed begun even before then. Many shrubs that are brought

indoors to bloom dislike the wide variation in temperature that can occur between day time and night, and even when this is evened out by a controlled temperature system, the air resulting from most central heating systems is likely to be too dry. Periods of dryness at the roots, or in the air, can cause arrested development of next year's buds which are already forming in embryo as this year's blooms fade and fall.

Re-potting into the same size pot means that to have used fresh compost, you probably dislodged much of the old soil, thereby causing root disturbance. When re-potting Azaleas, you should always try to cause as little root disturbance as possible and, furthermore, don't use J.I. No. 3 compost because it is much too rich and also contains lime. Use the next size pot—just big enough for a thin layer of new compost to be carefully packed around the outside of the root ball with no root disturbance at all—and of course you must use lime-free compost. You can buy this from your garden centre under the name 'ericaceous compost'; or alternatively use pure peat. Use only the next size pot, because too much increase and freedom for root expansion can result in lots of leaf growth at the expense of the bloom.

If by 'plunging in the garden' you mean plunging in the garden soil, this could be another reason for failure—the danger of lime creeping in from the soil. Plunging outdoors is good practice during the summer months to enable the plant to receive maximum light, but only plunge into peat. You must make sure that the peat is very wet to begin with because the peat is meant to give moisture, not take it, and dry peat will absorb a great deal of moisture, possibly robbing the plants of what they need.

Also you must realise that a plunge pot can easily be worse off because water from your can may be diverted outside the rim of the pot instead of inside as it soaks down, so that the roots do not get as much as you think. Always insert the pot so that its rim is very near the surface.

Lime-hating plants should always be plunged into lime-free peat, because of the danger of lime creeping in from surrounding soil. Arrange some retaining boards to confine a good depth of peat so that you have a neat and tidy plunge box, and insulate this from the soil underneath by setting it up on a sheet of plastic. Pay careful and regular attention to watering and during dry spells, spray the foliage frequently with clear rainwater to try to keep the air moist and prevent the leaves losing too much moisture by evaporation. *Always* use rainwater, not tapwater because of the likelihood of it containing lime.

This is what you *should* have done, and if you leave your ailing plant, it will have a speedy demise, so you must quickly undo all the damage that has been caused. As you have little to lose, you will have to take chances. Take it out of the pot at once and try to shake off most of the J.I. compost—you will have to risk the root disturbance. Re-pot into peat and keep well-watered with rainwater. If you are fortunate enough to save the plant and new leaf begins to appear, you can help it further by putting a layer of used tea bags around the stem of the plant so that the roots receive a weak solution of tea. Tea is acid and they will like that. Secondly, spray the new foliage daily, and into the clear rainwater in your sprayer, add a few drops of Murphy FF foliar feed. This will help the plant quickly to get back on its feet.

29   Azalea : dry root ball

I have several Azaleas bought from a well-known nursery. I have fed and looked after them, but the leaves are all going brown. Could you let me know what has gone wrong?

Azaleas and Rhododendrons have very fibrous root systems which hold the soil and develop a dense clump called a root ball. These roots do not like disturbance, which is why they are wrapped with hessian and plastic, or the plant is grown in a pot. In this way the root ball is preserved intact at planting time. It is so permeated with fine roots that if this root ball is allowed to dry out, water tends to shed off it like water off a duck's back and very drastic measures will have to be taken to get it moist again. You'll never get it moist right through

with a watering can and won't fare much better with a hosepipe; so you can see it is quite possible for an Azalea or a Rhododendron or other root ball plant to be dying of thirst, even while you are watering it!

If your plants have been hanging around in a nursery with the root ball exposed, albeit wrapped, waiting for you to come along and buy, it is quite likely that drying out will have begun. Therefore before planting, *always* thoroughly soak the root ball—not in tap water because of the possible lime content, but in rainwater. Surround the root ball in the ground with very wet peat to guard against the loss of moisture into the adjoining soil and of course, until it is well-established—three or four years at least—keep it well-watered, especially during dry weather. Overhead spraying will also help to reduce some of the moisture being lost by transpiration and only being replaced with increasing difficulty via the roots. It will also help to replace the moisture in the leaves.

Members of the Ericaceae family, to which Azaleas and Rhododendrons belong, need more iron and magnesium than most other plants. You can ensure adequate magnesium by dissolving Epsom Salts in the overhead spraying—very weak—no more than $\frac{1}{2}$ oz. per gallon, unless you are in a chalky area where you will have to use an entirely different method of cultivation (See *No. 117*). The iron supply can be taken care of by a very diluted solution of iron sulphate, no more than $\frac{1}{4}$ teaspoonful in a couple of gallons of water, and of course it is a good idea to empty the teapot (cold) round all lime-hating plants like these so that they can get the iron from the tannin in the tea leaves. See also *Nos. 28, 30, and 31.*

30   Azalea gall and deformed foliage

What treatment can I give to a Japanese Azalea on which some of the leaves have become enlarged and blown-up? In the later stages these swellings turn hard and dark brown in colour. None of my other Azaleas in the same border is affected. I have kept the plant well-watered and have top-dressed the soil, which is yellow clay, with chicken manure on a peat base. I do not like killing insects and do not use any insecticide or artificial manures in my garden; cow manure in plenty is all that is used in the rest of the garden.

This is not an uncommon problem—all the indications are that the disease is Azalea Gall which is a fungus called *Exobasidium vaccinii*. The life cycle is not fully understood, but the white 'bloom' that follows the reddish swellings on the foliage is the spore or fruiting stage of the fungus and it is thought that these spores are carried to other plants by insects. The best method of control is to pick off infected leaves, being careful not to drop and lose one or 'shake' any spores into the air; burn all infected leaves. Do this as soon as you spot the white bloom and before the spore stage develops. At least this will check the spread of the disease.

Spraying with Bordeaux Mixture used to be the standard procedure and gave some protection against infection but a more modern method is to use one of the new systemic fungicides which enter the plant's sap stream system and gives the plant a degree of immunity or increased resistance. Fungicides such as Zineb and Maneb are also effective, so if you know that you have been affected before and the disease is likely to occur again, begin your anti-fungus precautions at the beginning of the fungus 'season' in early spring and again in autumn. Repeat at intervals of about sixteen to eighteen days, but if the leaves still show signs of disfigurement, off with them at once. Insects are not likely to be harmed by these fungicides.

An unbalanced diet—and reliance upon poultry and cow manure which are high in nitrogen is an unbalanced diet—encourages leaf texture that is lush, soft and more prone to fungal attack. Use Humber Eclipse or Growmore, both of which have equal ratios of nitrogen, phosphorous and potash.

Read *No. 2* which, although primarily concerns roses, will help you to understand the need for balanced feeding.

31 *Azalea : reasons for poor flowering*

In spite of treating a seven-year-old indoor Azalea well—I liquid feed it, give it the occasional steam bath, and foliar feed and re-pot it regularly—it persists in flowering poorly. Why?

Why should it bother? It's doing so well as it is—too well in fact—and you will have to use a little plant psychology. The reason a plant blooms is because this is part of the natural process of reproduction. Your plant is obviously doing so well and is so confident of being around next year that it doesn't feel any particular need or reason to ensure perpetuation of its species by trying to produce seed which must be preceded by bloom. So give it a bit of a shock. Let it get a bit worried about the future. Neglect it, make it do some work for a change.

Don't do anything silly, of course, like letting it dry up completely, but cut the over-kindness and, for a start, omit the re-potting part of your programme. The liquid feeding could well be reduced if not cut out for a while. I should think it has enough food resources to satisfy a horse so make it live on them for a bit. Foliar feeding is a supplementary boost only and is no substitute for a correctly-developed and hard-working root system.

Cut out the foliar feed and rely upon a balanced nutrient source like Growmore or better still, the slower acting semi-organic Humber Eclipse. Just a pinch or two scratched into the soil surface before watering. As soon as you discern the flower buds expanding before they burst into bloom, a little potash will help to accentuate the colour. Use sulphate of potash not nitrate of potash because that would add nitrogen which will encourage leaf. Again, just a tiny pinch scratched into the soil surface before watering.

32 *Bacterial canker*

I'm bothered about the lumpy appearance of my Forsythia stems, and which I am told is called fasciation. What do you advise?

Fasciation is a problem that affects Forsythias probably more than any other shrub, but it usually takes the form of hideous flattened stems (see *No. 67*) not lumps or swellings, and it is more likely that these are bacterial cankers.

Certain bacteria invade the tissue of shrubs and trees and such swellings result. Fruit trees are very prone to similar attack. Once in the plant, the spread of the bacteria is internal and your main problem is to find out how far it has gone. If it is practicable, you could try cutting back the affected stems to ground level. Paint the wound with a sealing paint or wax like Arbrex to prevent possible ingress of fresh trouble and wait for new growth to generate. This should be normal and unaffected but if the trouble appears again, do not hesitate—grub out the shrub, burn it, and replace with a new healthy specimen. And whilst you're about it, try one of the modern, much improved hybrids like 'Arnold Giant' or 'Beatrix Farrand'.

33 Bay trees—potted and poorly

My 2 ft.-high potted bay tree is looking yellow and sickly. Can you describe what I should do to restore it to health.

A bay tree is evergreen, which means that during winter, although it undoubtedly slows down, it doesn't have a dormant stage like deciduous plants, but still continues to 'tick over', constantly drawing moisture and nutrients from the limited soil within the pot. The nutrients are not everlasting, and even if you have been applying liquid feeds and fertilisers, the growing root system increasingly competes with the soil for space in which to exist. The pot is not elastic, so as roots develop and take up more space they compress the soil so that the soil ball gets compacted and it becomes increasingly difficult for water to penetrate. Absorption by roots becomes more and more concentrated upon the thin layer between the root ball and the inner surface of the pot, so that the plant becomes thoroughly 'pot bound'. This condition is the most likely cause of your bay looking yellow and sickly.

First, make sure you have a larger pot available—about 3 ins. wider across the rim and a little deeper than the pot it is now growing in.

Carefully turn out the bay from its pot—do this by turning it upside down and, with the fingers of one hand placed two each side of the main stem, gently tap the pot on a table or bench so that it loosens and comes out cleanly.

Depending upon how much root is massed round the soil ball—be careful not to damage the root any more than you can possibly help—tease out some of the old soil and carefully replant into its new bigger home. Put a wad of peat underneath to serve as a moisture bank and top up with John Innes No. 2 or No. 3 compost—or failing that, a mixture three parts loam and one part peat with an ounce of Humber Eclipse or other long-lasting, slow-acting balanced manure. Water the plant well and stand in a position away from full sun, and away from draughts.

The ideal time to do this is in late autumn but, with a bay as sick as this one sounds, it would be better not to wait provided the newly potted plant will not be exposed to frost.

During mild spells, a daily light spraying with clear water will help to keep the leaves plump and fresh. After the turn of the year as spring approaches, spray more frequently with a few drops of Murphy FF foliar feed added. In late March or early April trim back straggly shoots and work the plant to a nice even shape. This will encourage new growth. Always keep the pot well-moistened especially in dry weather. If, at any time it dries out, don't waste time with a watering can, plunge the pot under water and leave it for an hour. This is the only way to get a dried-out pot thoroughly soaked through. Keep away from full unprotected sunlight, frosts and strong winds and you will have a bay tree of which you can be very proud. See also *No. 34.*

34 Bay trees in winter

I have two bay trees four or five feet tall which have recently been given to me in large pots. Could you please tell me if I can have them in the open in the winter, or should I take them inside?

Bay trees, *Laurus nobilis*, will have taken several years to reach this height and will be worth several pounds each. It is therefore worthwhile going to considerable trouble to keep them in good condition. The basic fact to bear in mind is that evergreens, unlike deciduous plants that lose their leaves during the winter, are always transpiring—giving off moisture from the leaves. This moisture has to be replaced by moisture uptake from the roots and in the case of pot-grown plants, the difficulty is the limited moisture in the soil within the pot, and the speed with which the soil itself can dry out. The larger a tree becomes in its pot, and the longer it has had to rely upon the soil resources since its last re-potting, the more the basic problem becomes aggravated. All plants are prone to suffer from cold winds in winter, but the danger is intensified if the moisture loss is not replaced, causing collapse of leaf structure, usually around the edges of the leaves. This is the familiar 'scorch', where the collapsed part has withered, died and turned an unusual brown.

If you can move them into the protection of a conservatory or a sheltered position during the winter so much the better. Otherwise enclose them in a wrapping of hessian or straw during bad spells, but they should be uncovered to the air and light during milder spells or the leaves will spoil. Feed with slow-acting fertiliser like Humber Eclipse during summer, since it is then living faster than in winter when it is slowed down and resting. It can build up its resources, ready to face the rigours of winter. Lightly tease the fertiliser into the surface of the soil and never allow it to dry out. If this does happen—if for instance, you go away on holiday—there is only one way to get the root ball moist again. You won't manage with a can or a hose, so immerse the entire pot in a tub of rainwater and leave for at least an hour after the last air bubbles have risen. See also No. 33.

35   Bladder Senna pods

I picked up some pods that fell off a senna bush in the garden and dried them in my greenhouse. The seeds inside these pods are still green. Will they ripen and germinate if I sow them?

A member of the same family as peas and beans, the Bladder Senna—*Colutea arborescens*—is a large shrub or a small tree which is interesting for a number of reasons: attractive foliage, the very long period in summer over which the racemes of yellow-red flowers are borne, the curious large inflated bladder-like pods that dry out to a paper-whitish colour in autumn, its ability to grow on poor soils and chalky soils and also for its extreme hardiness and tolerance of salt sea winds.

Its area of origin is the Mediterranean and this is the important clue as to the viability of the seed that you have saved.

To compare with the intensity and number of hours' sunlight it would normally get in the hot south, we should need a particularly bright summer to get a really ripe seed. If the seeds were still soft when you shelled them from the pods—which seems likely as they were still green—they were not ripe and were not worth sowing. If they were hard, however, you may be lucky and get germination. They should be brown, hard and plump—not shrivelled—so you should wait for the last of the remaining pods in the hope that they will ripen. Normally, nurserymen do not bother with the uncertain seed because it propagates fairly readily from half-ripe cuttings inserted in the autumn.

Pruning is not needed other than to keep the shrub to size and shape, but if it has to be done it is best done in early spring by cutting back the flowered wood, or the offending parts, as near to the base of the shrub as is practicable.

36   Brooms : moving and pruning

We have a broom plant in an inconvenient place. I know brooms don't take kindly to being moved, but it has to be moved. Could you tell me the best time to do this?

October would be the best time to move a broom, while the soil is still warm enough to permit root development and the plant to become reasonably established before winter sets in. You are quite right: brooms dislike root disturbance, but if you prepare the ground and lift with as much soil attached as you can, you should be quite safe.

Read *No. 65* and the procedures relating to passing a sheet under the soil ball, and to spraying with S600 transplanting spray.

Brooms are often allowed to become tall and leggy, because they have not been pruned correctly. If this has happened, use a supporting stake if necessary (you should always get the stake firmly implanted before planting a shrub up to it), and trim back the top growth by a third. You will have to do this to avoid wind rock (see *No. 15*) which brooms will not stand at any price. The cutting back should encourage new shoots to form, and it is these that should be encouraged for they will carry the best bloom.

Prune in the normal way immediately after flowering to promote long flower-bearing shoots—unless it is a late flowering type, when it should be pruned in early spring. Remember, however, that you should not prune brooms over-hard into old hard wood since this can cause die-back which invariably results in the death of the plant. This is why it is so important to prune out those stems that have flowered to their base point of origin. Failure to do this—or only partly cutting them back—gradually allows the old mature wood to 'creep out' and the plant then becomes long and leggy.

37   Camellias : general care

As I want to try to grow Camellias outdoors, should they have full sun or semi-shade? I understand they really like a warmer climate, therefore is it necessary to put them flat against a south-facing wall, or build removable polythene covers? I have tried growing them in a pot in a mixture of loam peat and leaf mould but the buds refused to open.

The Camellia family come from tropical and sub-tropical Asia and although they have proved reasonably hardy in the U.K.—some varieties more so than others, of course—the big danger is frost damage to the flower buds, which are particularly susceptible. This is why Camellias are best planted against a south-facing wall so that the buds are not chilled by freezing north winds; alternatively, they can be planted in a woodland setting like a glade where they can get plenty of light, and also the protection of other trees around them. Cam-

ellias make very fine pot plants and you can move them outside during the summer and bring them under cover during cold weather. However, pot culture has an inbuilt problem because the flower buds that open in spring are being formed during the previous late summer and any dryness at the roots whilst the buds are being formed is almost certain to cause the bud development to be arrested. Pots are far more liable to dry out than outdoor soil, and copious watering is therefore necessary throughout this period; not just a splash from the can which is more than likely to run straight off a dried-out root ball, but a thorough soaking.

However, copious watering then introduces two more dangers. The first is that plant nutrients can very quickly be washed out of the soil and will have to be restored by regular feeding. Secondly, copious watering in many gardens and homes means relying upon tap water. In many parts of the country, mains water all too often contains lime, and as the Camellia is a confirmed lime-hater, each can of tap water is like a douche of poison. You will *have* to try to collect rainfall in water butts and tanks as it comes off the roofs. If this is impracticable, you can at least go a long way towards counteracting the lime in the tap water by watering your Camellias with the cold remains from the tea-pot. Camellias need iron and acid conditions, and both are derived from the tannin in the tea leaves. This is understandable when you realise that tea is derived from a related species of Camellia, so in putting down tea leaves you are putting back into the soil around the Camellia its own humus so to speak.

Planting time is your one and only opportunity to affect the soil under your Camellia, so incorporate peat into the soil and mulch liberally each autumn so that a high density of peat is built up which will act as an enormous sponge to soak up moisture and resist drying-out in warm weather.

Concerning polythene covers: there is very little protection in a flimsy film of the stuff. Indeed, trying to keep down the cost by buying the thinnest gauge can do more harm than good because it can rip and tear so easily in the wind and lose any protection it may have had, and might well tear and break the shrub as it flaps around. If experience indicates that protection is necessary, don't waste your money on half measures. Provide the best protection you can, either by planting in a good sheltered position or by erecting substantial screens during the worst of the weather. See also *No. 38*.

38   Camellias : causes of yellowing

A Camellia in a pot did extremely well in my porch for about four years, flowering well each spring. However, after flowering last spring, all the leaves looked very pale and almost yellow. Eventually many of them turned brown and dropped off. Could you tell me what happened?

After four years in the same pot, you can expect a steady decline in your Camellia as the soil becomes tired and clearly your plant is telling you that it wants a change of soil.

Camellias tend to react quite definitely to conditions that they don't like. Usually it is the buds that suffer first (see *No. 37*) and in addition the buds are prone to frost damage. Dryness at the roots and the other extreme, overwatering, each cause reaction. Nutrient starvation is serious enough for any plant, but with plants like Camellias, Azaleas, Magnolias, Pieris, Rhododendrons etc., there is the added problem of iron shortage induced by the presence of lime.

Now, all these problems can beset the Camellia in the open ground, and even more so in a pot with limited soil—washing out the nutrients, the presence of lime in mains water and the roots freezing through the pot sides in winter.

An evergreen like a Camellia is never completely dormant and, although it can be done at almost any other time, repotting should avoid the period when flower buds are being carried and especially in the run-up to flowering. This is because the shock can easily cause the buds to abort.

Just after flowering would, therefore, be the best time to re-pot, but it is not always possible or wise to wait too long for the right time to come around again. Particularly when that remedy is re-potting, you may have to get on with it and take the risk of disturbing the buds.

Carefully knock out the plant, and gently tease away some of the old soil from between the roots. Re-pot into a larger size pot so that the plant can have more soil than before and a little more room to move. Use a lime-free compost—two parts lime-free loam or soil collected perhaps from an area where rhododendrons thrive in the wild, and one part peat. Don't use John Innes composts because they contain lime—unless it is the special lime free 'ericaceous compost'.

Water very carefully, never allowing the pot to dry out and likewise never over-water to a wet soggy mess. Always use rainwater if you can collect it, but if you have to resort to mains water, always make sure that it has been through the tea pot—by watering your plant with the dregs and left overs.

During summer, stand the pot outdoors in a position where it can receive dappled sunlight; bring it into a well-ventilated greenhouse or conservatory during September or October. Be careful at this time to avoid yet another pitfall. Even in an unheated greenhouse, sun heat can rapidly raise the temperature and create a dry atmosphere—which camellias positively dislike. Professional gardeners 'damp down' by frequently watering the greenhouse floor; you can create humidity more tidily by suspending a piece of old blanket material so that the end lies in a bowl of water like a giant wick. Modern capillary benches can be a great boon. Absorbent mats soak up water from a reservoir and not only supply moisture to plants stood on it, but also evaporate it from the entire area, so creating humidity.

39   Camellias : seedlings that are slow to flower

I have a bush Camellia 3 ft. tall which I raised from seed sown eight years ago. During this time, the bush has shown no sign of flowering and the leaves are yellow-green, not the same dark myrtle green as the other bushes I have. What can I do to encourage this Camellia to flower?

Read *Nos. 37, 38* and *40* which should give you a better understanding of the Camellia. In the normal course, one would have expected an eight-year-old seedling to have flowered by now, but the yellow-green leaf indicates that the plant is not making enough chlorophyll—the green colouring matter with which plants make hydrocarbons, sugars, starches etc. in the presence of light. These make up the structure of the plant, i.e. leaves, stems, flowers etc. Leaves it must have because that is where the work goes on but it will only develop flower buds if enough carbohydrate is left over from healthy leaf production to provide the energy for flower bearing. As your other plants are apparently healthy, possibly this one is in a position where it is being affected by lime either in the soil or your mains water.

To make chlorophyll, plants need—in addition to light—the presence of iron; a Camellia makes a lot of chlorophyll and so needs plenty of iron. A pale-coloured leaf indicates that it is not getting it. This condition is called chlorosis—iron shortage. Either the soil in which the Camellia is growing is deficient in iron, or there is sufficient but it is locked up in chemical combination with lime in a form that the plants cannot absorb.

This is why it is fatal to have lime in the soil where you are growing Camellias and other lime-hating plants. You will therefore have to do all you can to overcome the effect of lime—don't water with mains water because of the likelihood of it containing lime—use only rainwater, and also put down extra rations of iron for the roots to pick up. You can do this by watering with weak iron sulphate solution and also by emptying the teapot around the plants, so that they can make use of the iron in the tannin in the tea. If there is lime in the soil, it will of course immediately begin to lock up this iron, but frequent emptying of the teapot has been shown to be an effective way of keeping pace with this locking up process.

Alternatively, you can put down iron in a chemical form called a 'chelated compound' that the lime cannot lock up. You can buy this chelated iron in the garden shop under the trade name 'Sequestrine'. A solution of this is simply watered into the soil around the plant but in order to keep a steady iron supply you will have to repeat the Sequestrine treatment every six months. Overcome the chlorosis, keep the soil area round about well mulched with compost or bark fibre to conserve moisture and prevent bud abortion, and I think you should see your long-awaited bloom.

40   Camellias : growing from seed

Four seed pods were produced on my Camellias last year. After they ripened and dropped off, I saved them and would now like to know how to grow them.

Camellia seeds should be sown in early spring in a mild compost like John Innes Seed, but with extra peat added. They will need a temperature of about 65°F–75°F which is easy enough if you have a propagating frame, and in seven to twelve weeks—they are very erratic—you may get about half the seeds germinating.

Then comes the task of weaning the seedlings away from the inside of the propagating frame to the bench outside. Try to make the change gradually so that the seedlings do not get a sudden shock. Take the heat off for a few days and then place in a shaded position away from draughts. After this they should be placed in dappled, i.e. partially shaded, sunlight: never in full, unobstructed sunlight. In the propagating frame the seedlings were in an enclosed 'mini-atmosphere' and which, isolated from the outside air, remained nicely humid. Now in the outside air, watering becomes very important because away from the humid mini-atmosphere of the frame, conditions become drier and the young plant is made to rely very heavily upon using young underdeveloped roots. Keep well-watered but remember that you should never use water from the tap—use rainwater and occasionally dregs from the teapot. As the young seedlings grow and progress, you will be able to apply the cultural methods outlined in *Nos. 37, 38,* and *39.* When it comes to planting outside, prepare the site well with plenty of peat and lime-free compost worked into the soil. How long you will have to wait for bloom, nobody can say and when it does you should not be at all dismayed if the bloom is unlike the parents. Most Camellias are hybrids and do not come true from seed.

If, at any time the young leaves begin to look yellow, particularly near the edge, suspect iron shortage to which camellias are particularly susceptible and either treat with Sequestrine or water with the teapot exclusively. See *No. 39.*

41   Ceanothus : care and cultivation

I have been given a pot-grown Ceanothus floribundus. *The only information the label gives is that it grows 8–10 ft. high. I cannot find it in any of my gardening books : can you please give me any more information, and how should I look after it?*

You have probably been thrown off the scent by the sometimes annoying habit of garden centres and nurseries in abbreviating long names by leaving out words—partly for their own convenience and partly the kind of disregard for the gardening public that assumes that they will not know any better.

The word *floribundus* is derived from *flori* (flower) and *bundus* (abundance), and it could be applied to almost anything that has an abundance of flowers. The Ceanothus family is very large including both evergreens and deciduous species of widely varying growth and habit. A considerable amount of both natural and man-instigated hybridising has produced many named varieties. Strictly, *floribundus* should be applied to the evergreen species *C. dentatus* which is smothered in a rich blue bloom in May but which needs ideal conditions to get it to grow much over six feet, let alone the ten feet indicated by the nursery. It would be worth your while to try and get a more positive identification by sending a sprig to the Botanist at the R.H.S. gardens at Wisley, Surrey.

Most of the Ceanothus family come from the far south-western side of North America hence the common name Californian Lilac. None of the evergreen species is particularly hardy, and in cooler districts they frequently drop their leaves which makes them look more deciduous than evergreen. They are all best planted in a sheltered position facing from west to south where they can receive full sun. A little surprisingly perhaps they are fairly tolerant of sea air and they therefore form a staple planting in many seaside parks and gardens. They are not lime haters in the same way as Azaleas and Rhododendrons, but will not do at all well in shallow chalky conditions.

They prefer a deep fertile soil, that is well-drained and the best planting preparation is outlined in *No. 71.* Pruning should be kept to the minimum, merely to tidy up any long outgrowths; and, if it is necessary, prune immediately after flowering. These are magnificent shrubs, one of the very best of blue flowering kinds that we have, and an absolute must in any collection of ornamentals. This is reflected in the large number of Awards of Garden Merit and First Class Certificate awards that have been given to the numerous varieties.

42   Ceanothus : pruning 'Gloire de Versailles'

How and when should I prune a Ceanothus 'Gloire de Versailles'?

The pruning treatment for 'Gloire de Versailles' is typical of that required for all the Ceanothus family. You should prune in early spring before new growth begins in earnest. Cut back the previous year's shoots to within 3–3½ ins. of the older wood forming the framework of the shrub. This stimulates new growth and a lot of bloom. If stems should become straggly, shorten them back to a point where they are well clothed with foliage, and of course cut out any that are weak, misshapen or broken.

However, in order to be able to prune hard enough to stimulate plenty of young growth, growing conditions must be right. So often pruning is talked about as though it were a subject on its own with nothing to do with other factors. This is quite wrong; clearly you cannot prune properly unless a shrub is growing properly. All Ceanothus prefer an acid soil and there tends to be some variation between the species in the degree of toleration of alkalinity.

Intolerance shows by yellowing—usually around the edges of leaves and by diminished and impaired foliage. If these symptoms appear, don't suspect disease as is frequently advised, but carry out a soil test instead. It is quite likely you will find the soil is alkaline. Put down a good mulch of peat—bracken peat if you can get it—or cut green bracken from the countryside and chop it up small. You must not allow the shrub to become overdry, but do not use tap water which is likely to contain lime. Collect and use rainwater, and if you haven't any, use the dregs from the teapot. The liquor is acid and the tannin contains iron which Ceanothus need.

43 Ceratostigma : care and cultivation

As I have just been given a container-grown Ceratostigma willmottianum *and as I have not grown this before, could you tell me if it needs a shady or sunny position and what kind of soil it prefers? When it has grown, does it need pruning?*

Awarded an R.H.S. Award of Garden Merit in 1928, *Ceratostigma willmottianum* from western China is often referred to as Hardy Plumbago and is particularly valuable for the shrub and herbaceous border because the intense blue flowers are borne from late July through the autumn—a period when there is not a lot of blue about. It forms a low shrub about 3–4 ft. high.

When planted in a sheltered position against a wall, pruning is merely a question of keeping it tidy and trimming back overlong shoots. In open ground, it is very likely to be cut back severely by winter frosts with new shoots appearing in spring rather like the hardy fuchsias. Indeed, in open ground it is generally best to treat it more as a herbaceous perennial than a shrub, cutting away all remaining growth to ground level in late March to early April so that fresh shoots are thrown up. These will carry plenty of bloom the same summer. In a position where it can receive plenty of direct sun, the build-up of anthocyanin in the leaves will often ensure a pleasant red tint in the autumn. It will tolerate a chalky soil but it thrives best in a light, well-drained soil containing plenty of moisture-holding organic matter.

The best time to set out a container-grown specimen is in autumn while there is still some warmth in the soil. Incorporate plenty of peat or compost, and spread a thick mulch, of garden or mushroom compost.

44 Choisya and Arbutus slow to bloom

Two years ago I planted a Choisya ternata *and an* Arbutus unedo, *obtained from a reliable nurseryman. Neither shrub has flowered yet, although they have grown very well. How can I get them to bloom?*

The important clue is, 'although they have grown very well'. Both shrubs are getting on with their most important task which is getting firmly established, putting on growth and reaching for maturity. Choisya has the common name of Mexican Orange Blossom, which is not at all surprising as it has the most fragrant flowers like orange blossom, and it originated from Mexico. *Arbutus unedo*, the Strawberry Tree, comes from southern Europe and although it may seem surprising at first, but not on reflection, it is also indigenous in the mild south-west of Ireland. The factor that is common in both places of origin, and in both plants, is intensity of light. The clean air in south-west Ireland enables Arbutus to thrive, as indeed the same clear air coupled with the warming effect of the Gulf Stream enables many plants to thrive in the north-west of Scotland, many hundreds of miles north of where one might have expected them to have reached their limit.

As your plants are growing well, there is nothing you need worry about with your soil, and providing you have them positioned where they can get full sun there is nothing much you can or need to do but exercise patience. The Choisya will probably be the first to produce bloom, and in another year or two will make the most of the growth it has been putting on. The Arbutus will probably take another four years or more. Do not prune either, apart from keeping them to size and shape.

45 *Choisya : propagation*

I have a Mexican Orange Blossom in my garden and would like to transplant a cutting or two from it to another position. How and when can these cuttings be taken?

This magnificent evergreen with the aromatic foliage and sweetly-scented white flowers in late spring and summer can be propagated by cuttings taken in September or October, but by far the easier and more certain method for most amateurs would be to layer it.

Anytime during spring, choose a suitably positioned stem and select an optimum spot along the stem where you will be able to place a peg to hold it down comfortably in the soil. With a sharp knife, cut a slit an inch or so long into the stem through a leaf joint, remove the adjacent leaves, dust the bare surfaces with rooting powder and slip a small twist of peat into the slit to hold it open.

Scoop out a shallow hollow in the soil with the trowel, lay the prepared part of the stem in this hollow, hold it down firmly with a couple of pegs or stirrups—which you make quite simply by bending a piece of wire in two like a hairpin. Cover the stem with an inch or two of soil, press this firm and place a stone the size of an orange on top to prevent disturbance, and by next spring you should have a well-rooted young plant ready to sever from the parent and plant elsewhere.

46 *Clematis : soil preparation before planting*

Please advise me on the soil preparation needed for Clematis. I so admire a porch wreathed in bloom and think it is a lovely welcome to a visitor. I have tried and tried but I just cannot get Clematis to grow, and have come to the conclusion that there is something wrong with my soil.

Growing a lovely Clematis round the front porch is something that many try—and fail with miserably. It is quite surprising how many people will persist in buying a new plant every year, in the forlorn hope that it will grow where all the others have failed. All that is required is understanding.

There are several classes or groups of Clematis, and although it is essential to know to which group a particular variety belongs in order to prune to produce maximum bloom and not cut it away, they are all similar in their demand for an open sunny position that is well-drained—with the emphasis on the 'well-drained'.

Species Clematis and *montana* types are not so demanding as a rule, but if you want to be really successful with the spectacular hybrids and large-flowered types, you will have to go to some trouble to get the right conditions. Indeed, if you are not willing to prepare the site properly before planting Clematis, don't bother to waste time and effort.

There may be paths or lawn or flower beds around the front porch or other area where you wish to plant the Clematis but, as best you can, dig a hole 2 ft. square and 2 ft. deep; if you are prepared to dig deeper, so much the better, but 2 ft. is the minimum. Keep the top spit and get rid of the subsoil remaining. If you are in a clay or heavy soil area, you will have to do something about the clay or it will be like planting the Clematis in a bath. Spread 1 lb. of gypsum over the bottom of the hole and fill to within a foot of the top with a mixture—of equal proportions by bulk—of plaster rubble and spent mushroom compost—or, if you cannot get the latter, moist peat. Mix it well, and tread it firmly in the hole. Thoroughly mix a couple of pounds of gypsum with the top soil you have set aside and refill the hole.

You now have a planting chamber that is not only immediately well-drained, but which also contains moisture-retentive organic material, in which plaster figures prominently. The gypsum, as it washes down, is going to take care of the porosity of the bottom of the pit, and the lime in the plaster will lead to the alkalinity that Clematis prefer.

Now you can plant: autumn or spring are the best times, but as you should never think of buying a Clematis that is not pot-grown, you could, if needs be, plant at almost any time providing it isn't frosty and blowing a blizzard.

Dig a hole just large enough to take the pot.

If the plant has been in the pot some time, as likely as not the root will be coming through the bottom. Don't try getting it out since you will inevitably damage the root. If the pot is plastic, cut it away; if the pot is a clay one, smash it. Spoil the pot and spare the root. It is a good idea to plant two or three shrubs around the Clematis to give shade to the soil of the planting area—*Senecio greyi*, *Olearia haastii*, or some similar flowering evergreen. Clematis must have their roots kept cool and this is the best way to shade the soil.

As soon as growth indicates that root action is taking place and the plant is becoming established, you will be able to think about pruning in accordance with whatever system it requires—see *No. 47*. With that amount of organic material underneath it, your Clematis will not need feeding for some time, but you will need to maintain the porosity of the area and you can do this by simply sprinkling an ounce or two of gypsum over the 'pit' area every three months or so. The gypsum will have no effect at all on the other plants.

47 Clematis: pruning rules are important

A Clematis planted last February formed plenty of leaves but there wasn't a flower. Is this usual? Can you please tell me how it should be pruned?

If it is growing in fertile soil and doing very well for itself, pushing up plenty of leaf growth, it is not unusual that it sees no reason why it should go through the motions of perpetuating its own species by producing bloom.

Refer to *No. 46* and you will realise that the preparation of a Clematis pit involves creating very rapid drainage and not much plant nutrient. If you want lots of Clematis bloom, don't feed it, make it work and treat it hard. a soft lush growth is easy prey to diseases.

Pruning has a great effect on the bloom, not only by enhancing flowering when done correctly but by spoiling everything when it is done wrong. To prune properly you must know the name of the variety or at least the group to which it belongs. Therefore, you should never buy an unnamed Clematis unless you want to take chances. Clematis pruning is a subject that is often made to look unnecessarily complicated and confusing.

Species Clematis generally do not need pruning beyond the removal of dead and useless wood, and shortening back long growths which have gone farther than intended. The exceptions to this rule are the later flowering species like *C. tangutica* which are cut back fairly hard in spring to promote strong flowering growth from the base.

The large-flowered varieties can be divided into two main groups. The first group includes *C. florida*, *C. lanuginosa*, and *C. patens* which flower on the previous year's wood in May and June.

Clearly any spring pruning with these would cut away bloom. Therefore, pruning consists of cutting back old flowered growth immediately after flowering. If a plant has been allowed to become overgrown and dense, really hard pruning should be delayed. It should be thinned after flowering but really hard pruning of very old and thick stems should be delayed until dormancy in February, although for one season this will mean the loss of bloom arising from the wood you are cutting away. The job has to be done, however, and bloom will be all the better for it the following year.

The second group includes *C. jackmanii*, *C. texensis* and *C. viticella* which flower on the current season's growth. These flower in late summer and autumn and should be pruned hard to within a foot of ground level in late February. Old unpruned plants carry bloom aloft (and not a lot of it) and become quite bare at the base. You must take your courage in your hands—spare the secateurs and you will spoil the plant. More Clematis are spoiled by timidity with the secateurs and lack of understanding than any other cause.

48 Clematis: propagation by cuttings

Can you tell me how to take a Clematis cutting? We have a four-year-old plant and would like to take a cutting for another part of the garden. I have tried taking shoots of both soft wood and hard stems without success.

Every rule has to have an exception to prove it, and Clematis cuttings are the exception to the usual practice of cutting just below a leaf joint, called a node. Clematis cuttings are different—they are inter-nodal; i.e. the cut being made midway between the leaf joints.

Having taken your semi-ripe cutting material from the parent plant—it can be a two or three-foot long stem—you will leave the plant cut just above a leaf joint so that no stem is left to die back to the next leaf joint which could possibly become diseased. Now, from the cut piece, you can prepare several cuttings. Starting at the lower end of the semi-ripe wood, cut into pieces 2 ins. below each leaf joint until you reach soft younger wood which can be discarded. You will now have several semi-hard cuttings with leaves emanating from the middle of each and they are now ready for trimming. With a sharp knife, cut off the top part of the stem to $\frac{1}{2}$ in. above the leaf joint, and 2 ins. below. At one time, cuttings were simply made by chopping the long stem midway between the leaf joints, leaving at least 2 ins. of stem wood above and below the joint, but the top part doesn't make much difference and is nowadays trimmed very much shorter to $\frac{1}{2}$ in.

Cuttings are inserted usually during the May–June period in a moist sand/peat mixture at a temperature of 75°F—you won't do much good at a lower temperature than this, so a propagating case or hot bed in an outdoor frame is necessary. The most satisfactory way for the amateur to do this is to install a soil heating cable. When the cuttings have rooted, usually in a few weeks, and shoots are growing out from the leaf joints, the cuttings can be carefully lifted and transplanted.

However, most amateur gardeners are likely to be more certain of success by propagating Clematis on their own roots; not by cuttings but by layering. Take a young shoot, make a small cut with a sharp knife from below a node (leaf-joint) up and through it and wedge into the cut a small piece of wet sphagnum moss dipped in hormone rooting powder. Scoop a little soil away, throw in a handful of sand/peat compost and peg down the prepared shoot.

Cover with more compost and then hold down with a piece of tile or flat stone. If you do this in the spring, the shoot should have begun rooting by autumn, and early in the following spring it can be severed from the parent and moved with as large a ball of soil as practicable —Clematis don't like their roots disturbed. (See *No. 46* concerning soil preparation for Clematis.)

49 Clerodendron, turquoise-coloured berries

In early autumn I spotted a small shrub clustered with turquoise berries set in maroon 'cups'. Can you name it for me and tell me something about it?

This sounds very much like one of the Clerodendrons, natives of China and the Far East that richly deserve their common name of Glory Tree or Glory Bower. They do best in sheltered gardens away from cold east winds and spring frosts. They are not terribly demanding as to soil, provided that it contains plenty of humus: annual peat dressings are therefore beneficial. The plant you saw is probably *Clerodendron trichotomum* which can grow up to 15 ft., bears white, very fragrant flowers, set in deep red/maroon calyces or 'cups' followed soon after by bright turquoise-blue berries still set in their cups. The harder variety *C. fargesii* differs little but is not quite so large—up to about 10 ft.—but is generally preferred because it usually fruits more freely.

50 Conifers slow to grow

I have some Cupressus lawsoniana *and* Thuja lobbii *which have been planted for two years. They are 18–24 ins. high and do not seem to be growing as well or as fast as they should. Could you give me suggestions for treatment? How often are fertilisers applied and would they do for my other conifers. Living not far from the coast, salt winds are my main problem.*

All conifers, especially evergreens, need careful treatment at planting time and for a few years after until they are thoroughly well-established. There are three main steps that you should take: guard against drying out; feed well, and protect from the wind. If you put down a really heavy mulch of organic matter—peat, compost, hops, pulverised bark, rotted straw or manure—you will keep the roots moist and cool by preventing the wind carrying away moisture by contact with the soil and so you will avert the biggest danger facing all evergreen plants—drying out. A four-inch thick mulch would not be too thick to begin with, although you should keep it away from the main stem of each plant so as to leave the shrub growing out of a little cup-shaped hollow.

Secondly, put down a balanced and complete plant food like Growmore or the semi-organic Humber Eclipse at the rate of about 1–2 ozs. around each plant, starting in early spring and repeating at about 4–5 week intervals until early July, and then stop. Especially with Humber, the slow-acting long release of plant nutrients will ensure that the plants get all they want for the rest of the growing season. It will also help to foliar feed, but add just a couple of drips of washing-up detergent, so that the leaves become thoroughly wetted and the spray doesn't run off them. Use a very fine spray so that the droplets stick; bigger droplets from a coarse spray bounce off and the material is wasted. Thirdly, Netlon make a fine plastic mesh net especially for wind protection. This allows the wind to filter through having taken the brute force out of it. Either put up a fence-like screen above 3 ft. high on the windward side or, if the plants are too far apart for this or the wind too strong, make individual V-shaped screens pointing into the wind, leaving the young tree nestling cosily in the angle behind.

51 Conifers and other plants for a Silver Anniversary

My parents are nearing their silver wedding and I should like to give them a silver-leaved tree. Can you please suggest a few names of suitable trees, and a park or famous garden open to the public where they might be seen. We live just south of London on high ground where there are a lot of conifer trees in nearby woodland so it seems that the soil around here is particularly suited to them.

It depends upon how tall and wide you are prepared for the tree to become eventually. When planting trees you should always bear in mind the final full-grown dimensions and consider if there is a risk that one day the tree could become too big—although you would have many years of enjoyment whilst it is smaller and growing to full proportions. I feel it is always best to spare yourself the heartache of having to chop down a tree when in its growing prime because it has become too big for your garden.

Starting from the top and working down so to speak: if space isn't a problem the Blue Cedar, *Cedrus atlantica* 'Glauca', makes a most imposing silver-blue tree. It will one day reach 80 ft. or more and probably more than 30 ft. wide so it really is a big one. Although not so silver-grey, the Deodar Tree, *Cedrus deodara* has much lighter coloured growing tips that droop and hang to give an overall silver appearance which gives it another common name, the Fountain Tree.

Then there are several pines in the species Pinus and Picea—notably *Picea glauca* and several varieties of *P. pungens*. Reducing in size, there are several varieties of Chamaecyparis, notably 'Pembury Blue'—perhaps the best of the species—and 'Grayswood Pillar', a rather narrow, grey-green pillar-like tree. The many steel-grey growing tips of *Chamaecyparis* 'Boulevard' seen against the grey-green older foliage makes this a very attractive small tree. Finally, among the conifers which are not much more than tall shrubs is perhaps the most silvery-white of all, *Chamaecyparis* 'Chilworth Silver'.

All of the above are readily available from the best nurseries who should be able to offer various sizes, but remember the bigger and older the tree, the less likely will be your chances of a successful planting and the more the precautions you will have to take to prevent drying out whilst the tree becomes established. You should be able to see examples of one or more of those mentioned in one of the gardens open for charity from time to time. Probably the best place in the south of England to see nearly all the conifers that can be grown in the

U.K. is the National Pinetum at Bedgebury in Kent, just off the main A21 Hastings road.

Among the non-coniferous silver trees are Eucalyptus, which is more hardy than is often supposed. These have unusual leaf shapes and forms that make them doubly attractive. One or two of the willows like *Salix alba* 'Sericea', a striking small tree, and *S. exigua* the Coyote Willow a small tree from Mexico, and finally a tree that is worth a place in any garden, the willow-leaved pear, *Pyrus salicifolia* 'Pendula', a graceful, medium-sized weeping tree with narrow leaves made all the more attractive by an abundance of white bloom in spring.

52 Conifers : precautions to take when transplanting

When is the best time to transplant a Leyland's cypress that is 4 ft. high and growing in the wrong place?

The best time to transplant an evergreen conifer like this would be in November when the tree has slowed down its rate of growth. Read *No. 65*, and use the 'sheet under' method as indicated for Mahonia and other evergreens. If it is growing in the wrong place you will of course wish to move it, but I think you would be very well-advised to take some insurance steps.

I believe most professional gardeners would agree that with all their skill and expertise, the chances of successfully transplanting a growing *leylandii* fall away rapidly after it has reached 2 ft. tall, and the larger and older it becomes, the less chance it has of surviving. It is therefore only reasonable to expect the odds to be even more heavily against most amateurs getting away with moving one already 4 ft. tall.

Cupressocyparis leylandii has been in great demand in recent years for its speed in producing an evergreen screen. You can obtain a 3–4 ft. tall specimen that is container-grown and which can easily be set into a planting hole with no root disturbance or check at all. In the north of England, Rex Greenfield Farms at Louth, Lincolnshire, always have a stock of this size, and in the south of the country try Keydell Nurseries, Horndean, Hampshire, who are specialists in large trees.

As soon as planted with plenty of moisture-retaining peat or compost around its roots, spray these large size conifers with S600 transplanting spray which you can obtain quite easily from the garden centre. This helps to reduce moisture and evaporation from the leaves. Keep the planting area well watered, don't let them dry out at the roots—that is fatal. In the spring as new shoot growth develops, spray the foliage with clear water at evening time during dry spells. For the first year, until the new root system has developed sufficiently to pull moisture up fast enough to replace loss from the foliage in harsh cold dry winds, keep your tree wrapped around with sacking or plastic during wintery weather. You will not want it spoiled and harmed by wind scorch and cold drying winds can play havoc with new plantings.

53 Conifers : how to straighten bent trees

I have two conifer trees, which are now nearly 8 ft. tall. Being in an exposed and very windy position they are both leaning at an angle, and I wish to move them back into an upright position. Can you please advise on the best way to do this. We had such a job getting them established and we don't want to risk losing them. Should the branches close to the ground be removed to leave just the main stem?

Obviously, you will have to disturb the root system and this will involve some risk but it can be minimised by not disturbing it any more than you are forced to. With eight-year-olds it's worth a try. It would be impossible to straighten them if they were much older.

During October–November, spray the trees thoroughly with S600 transplanting spray and repeat the spraying two days later. This will reduce transpiration loss and help the trees over the shock of what will be virtually a replanting. After another forty-eight hours, take up a position on the windward side—that is to say, with the tree leaning away from you—

and start taking out a semi-circular trench about 2½–3 ft. away from the main trunk. If you find that you are cutting through a lot of the tree's fibrous roots, you will have to move out further. Take a second spit, from the bottom of the trench, then a third, working your way under the tree. Always be careful not to chop out any more fibrous roots than you can help.

You may have to widen the trench a little towards the outside to give yourself room to work under the tree, but with the third spit removed, or at least loosened, you can try heaving the tree gently so that the 'root ball' rolls into the hole that you have made. You may need to remove a little more soil and you can judge this by the way the tree responds to your heave.

As soon as you have heaved it upright, arrange a prop to keep it that way whilst you work back some of the finer soil into the hole that remains. Put back a little at a time, washing it in with water from a can so that the soil is carried down and under: this will ensure that the severed roots get a thorough soak. A water can is better than a hose in a job like this, because it is all too easy to splash water around where you will need to carry on working and get the ground muddy underfoot. Firm down the soil as best you can and keep watering daily for a couple of weeks, each time trying to wash down the soil and, of course, topping-up with more soil as it settles. Keep the prop in position until the tree has established itself again. This way, at least half the root system remains in position with the minimum of disturbance and the tree has a fair chance of growing on without too much trouble.

The lower branches may look a little askew for a while and give the tree a lop-sided appearance. They will adjust to their new position, but don't do anything drastic like severely pruning them back until the tree is clearly well-established and growing away again.

This method can be used to straighten any tree or shrub that is leaning from the base, but the older the plants are, the greater the shock and the greater you must expect the risk to be of the shock proving fatal.

54 Cornus : a case of mistaken identity

I planted a Cornus alba *'Siberica' three years ago and although it seems to be healthy enough, it hasn't bloomed yet. Does it take a long time, or do you think that there is something wrong?*

Perhaps you have planted this shrub under a misapprehension because it is normally grown for the colour effect of its variegated foliage and the bright red leafless stems in winter and not for the bloom, which is yellowish-white, borne in small clusters and quite insignificant.

If you want a flowering dogwood, you should have planted one of the six or seven named varieties of the North American Flowering Dogwood C. *florida* which have very conspicuous flowers, and whilst they do not give the vivid coloured stems of 'Siberica' they more than make up for this with the rich colouring of the autumn foliage. With flower arrangement becoming more popular, however, the brilliant red winter stems of C. *alba* should be useful to you and the best way to encourage 'arrangers' stems' is to cut back all growth in April to within 2–3 ins. of the soil level. This will encourage new long stems to be thrown up from low down and it is these that give the best coloured foliage followed by the brightest winter colour.

55 Crataegus : the Christmas-flowering hawthorn

Somewhere I have read that there is a winter-flowering hawthorn which grows in the West Country and often blooms at Christmas time. If this is true, could you please tell me its name and something about it?

There is a variety of the common hawthorn or May tree, *Crataegus monogyna*, which is presumably a natural sport that carries its main flush of bloom noticeably earlier than the type. Often this is preceded by a very early, premature and partial flush in mid-winter. This double flowering gives it the name used by some botanists—C. *monogyna* 'Biflora', whilst others add the word 'Praecox' which simply means early. Whether C. *m.* 'Biflora' or C. *m.* 'Praecox', neither sounds as romantic or evocative as the common name it has acquired —the Glastonbury Thorn, after the particularly good specimen which stands in Glastonbury churchyard in Somerset.

As you might expect, any bloom in midwinter is at the mercy of winds, snow and Jack Frost. Therefore, if this tree's freakish ability to herald the New Year is what attracts you, try to give it a protected and sheltered position so that it is encouraged and the early bloom not spoiled.

Propagation is vegetative, i.e. it is grafted and young trees are generally available as half or full standards from the better-class nurseries.

56 Daphne, a difficult shrub needing protection

I have difficulty with a Daphne odora *'Aureo-marginata' growing in a slightly exposed position. The soil is clay with lime and flints and a high water table. What conditions does the plant prefer?*

As the *odora* part of its name suggests, *Daphne odora* bears fragrant bloom and coming very early in spring or even late winter (in fact, it is one of the earliest shrubs to bloom) needs some protection from winds. Generally *D. odora* is hardy enough to withstand even severe frost but a bitter cold wind is something else besides, and your Daphne is out in it all the time. You can put up a temporary wind shield made up of the special Netlon wind break mesh, plastic netting, rot-proofed hessian attached to simple frames, or surround the Daphne by other shrubs.

D. o. 'Aureo-marginata' has yellow edges to the leaves and it could well be that, as very often happens with variegated leaves, a nutrient deficiency which would normally show up as a variation in leaf colour is masked by the variation.

Whilst not as intolerant of lime as are Azaleas and Rhododendrons and other 'lime-haters', Daphnes definitely dislike lime and positively will not tolerate waterlogging. Therefore, with clay that is slow to drain at the best of times, a high water level and alkalinity as

well, your best chance of growing Daphne is to build up above the natural soil with a raised peat bank as described in *No. 117*.

57 Davidia, The Pocket Handkerchief Tree

Can you tell me anything about a tree I saw in Cornwall in June which had hundreds of papery-white flowers fluttering from its branches? Where can I obtain one? My local garden centre cannot identify it from my description. Would it grow in south London?

Unmistakably, this is *Davidia involucrata*, commonly called Dove Tree, the Ghost Tree, or the Pocket Handerchief Tree. It is medium-sized, ultimately reaching about 25 to 30 ft., and originated in China where it was discovered only as recently as 1869 by a French missionary M. David whose name it bears. Exactly one hundred years later, our own Royal Horticultural Society recognised its beauty and worth by awarding it an Award of Garden Merit. It is quite hardy in the U.K. and will grow in a wide variety of soils. You should have no difficulty in south London—indeed, you will find a nice specimen in Dulwich Park about 250 yards from the Dulwich Village gates opposite the entrance to the yard. The actual blooms are very small, and during late May or early June are borne grouped into small heads about an inch in diameter. Each head, however, has a pair of large white bracts which are curiously unequal and flutter in a breeze just like a lot of pocket handkerchiefs—hence the common name. A mature tree will bear a large number of these 'handkerchiefs' and is an attractive sight.

Davidia is still quite rare and it is doubtful if you will find many garden centres in the U.K. offering it because most of this kind of trade caters for, and depends upon, a relatively quick turnover of more common and widely-known subjects. However, you should have no difficulty in obtaining a nice specimen from a quality nursery like Hilliers of Winchester or Treseders of Truro, but you should be warned that it will take several years for the tree to mature and the 'hankies' to appear.

58 Eccremocarpus, a pretty social climber

Last year I grew from seed the climber Eccremo-carpus scaber *against a south wall, and it went up to 5 ft. 6 in. and flowered well. Can you advise me how to attend to it during the winter, and does the old growth have to be pruned back in the spring?*

The Chilean Vine is only half hardy—in a cold winter most of the above ground stems will be killed back but new growth will arise from surviving stems, and from the root stock. This root stock needs protection from frost by the provision every November of a really heavy mulch. The best planting position, in fact, is against a south or protecting wall of a house against which it can be trained and with its roots behind and below other shrubs, preferably evergreen, which will keep the soil cool in summer and help to keep off the frost in winter. However, don't rely solely on the protection of other shrubs—mulch as well. You will be able to tell how well it has come through winter in April when live stems will be showing green shoot buds. This is the time to go over the entire plant, cutting away every piece of die-back you can find, no matter how far back to base it goes; to leave any dead wood is to contribute to further tangle. No other pruning is really desirable or necessary. Nature will decree when you should be drastic; after a bad winter you may well cut away so much die-back that very little live wood is left. However, provided you have protected the rootstock, new growths will soon replace the loss.

59 Elaeagnus : why so droopy?

When the leaves of my lovely variegated Elaeagnus pungens *started to hang down and its new growth began to curl, I gave it three gallons of water, but it is not improving. Can you suggest a treatment?*

There are four or five different varieties of *E. pungens*—'Maculata' is the most commonly grown and popular—and all make very attractive shrubs, their variegated foliage giving colour contrast to others around them. The leaves have that leathery texture that is usually a hallmark of a shrub that is resistant to drought; therefore, you can be certain that when a drought-resistant shrub shows signs of distress like this, the soil has become very dry indeed and three gallons of water is far too little to do any good at all.

Recovery with this, as with other evergreens in a similar condition, may take several weeks, but the following procedure is the most likely way to achieve it. Lay the hosepipe close to the shrub and allow it to trickle slowly for several hours every day, moving it around about every hour so that the entire root system gets a soaking. Each evening flick water from the hose over the foliage so that it remains wet during the night. If you cannot spare the time to do this each evening, at least spray the entire shrub thoroughly with S600 transplanting spray to try to reduce the loss of moisture by evaporation from the leaves. It is best, however, not to do this unless you are forced to because you will need to foliar feed through the leaves later and this may prove an obstruction. Cover the area around the shrub with a heavy mulch compost to obstruct daytime drying-out.

In a couple of weeks or so, the foliage should be responding, looking more plump and fresh, and less limp and lifeless. Now with the leaves living and working again—but not until then— you should try to get nutrient into the plant's sap stream by foliar feeding. Use Murphy FF, but put a few drops of liquid washing-up detergent into the spray so that it spreads on the slightly glossy surface of the leaves.

When the shrub is clearly responding, put down a feed, 2 oz. per sq. yard, of Growmore (this acts more quickly than the organic-based Humber); hoe it into the mulch layer and water it in. The hose watering can now be reduced to one good soak once a week, unless heavy rain falls when it can be dispensed with. Repeat the feeding after a month and maintain the mulch cover as it is gradually taken into the soil by earthworms.

In good health, this is a most attractive and colourful shrub; treat it kindly and it will repay you well.

60   Elaeagnus growing in limy soils

Could you please let me have any information on the shrub Elaeagnus pungens *'Maculata'. I have had one or two unsuccessful attempts at growing it and before I buy any more plants I should like a few hints. My subsoil is limestone, and it is quite near the surface in places, but other shrubs do not give the same trouble.*

The leaves of *E. pungens* 'Maculata' have a central area of golden yellow which gives a bright effect to what otherwise might be a dull-looking shrub. It is perhaps most useful in shrubberies where its dense evergreen foliage deflects winds and so gives protection to more delicate plants in its lee. It is also used for hedging and would no doubt enjoy greater popularity for this purpose if it were not for its relatively high initial cost compared with most other hedging subjects. It is to be seen growing and thriving in many different parks within the London area and in such places as urban railway stations, a distribution from which several conclusions may be drawn. It is tolerant of widely differing soils, of a degree of atmospheric pollution, and of exposure to cold.

I think that it is fairly certain that the reason for your repeated failure is that you are offering the one condition that this very accommodating plant doesn't like—a shallow alkaline soil. Because your soil cover is so thin, rather than to dig out a planting hole and back fill with the limestone soil, you would stand a better chance by back filling with peat, compost and non-alkaline ericaceous soil which you may have to buy. This will enable it to grow in a less limy soil pocket. You would stand the best chance of all, if you would be prepared to raise the shrub away from the limestone with the raised bank method indicated in *No. 117.*

A consequence of growing on limestone and severely alkaline soils can be the locking-up of essential elements in chemical combinations so that they are denied to the plants. One of the elements most likely to be affected in this way is magnesium, and it would be worth trying several foliar feeds of epsom salts—magnesium sulphate—at the rate of about 1 oz. to a gallon of water applied a month apart during spring and summer with a watering can so that the leaves are well wetted and the run-off to the soil can then be picked up by the roots.

Try to maintain a two- to three-inch mulch layer of compost or peat over the soil in the vicinity of the shrub. This not only helps to prevent drying out of the soil and the roots, but will also absorb the magnesium and any other nutrient chemicals that are put down, releasing them slowly into the soil underneath so that a steady nutrient supply is maintained.

61   Elm disease: is protection practicable

In my garden I have a young Cornish elm tree. This is the slender, spire-shaped species with small leaves. Can you tell me if the Dutch elm disease attacks the Cornish elm as well as the common kind and, if so, is there anything I can do to protect it?

There has been a lot of research into this dreadful disease but a great deal more remains to be done and there is a lot that is simply not known. All elms are susceptible to Dutch elm disease but there does seem to be a variation in the degree of susceptibility which may, or may not be a reflection only of the preference of the carrier beetle for one elm to another. The Cornish elm, *Ulmus stricta*, does appear to be one of the most resistant types.

Cleanliness undoubtedly helps to check the spread so make sure that any elmwood lying around, which could be harbouring the beetle, is cleared up and burned. Any dead twigs or branches should be removed from the growing tree: use secateurs or, if the branches are too thick and you have to use a saw, pare it clean and smooth with a knife, cutting back to clean, healthy wood which shows no signs of brown staining anywhere in the tissue under the bark, and seal the wounds with a fungicidal paint, such as Arbrex. At the first sign of dieback in the foliage—it might show first on a single branch—cut immediately into the infected wood to see if you can discover the tell-tale staining and cut back, again and again as necessary until healthy wood is reached. You may have to do this several times, and virtually slaughter the tree in the attempt to check the advance of an attack.

Immunisation by injection has been practised but it is by no means infallible. A fungicide called Lignasan is injected into healthy, disease-free trees every year in May-June, but protective treatment is only really worthwhile at the earliest signs of the disease in the small twigs at the periphery of the tree. Beyond that stage, you will most likely be too late.

Compare the cost of annual protective treatment with the cost, time and labour involved in felling, cutting and burning a diseased tree—to say nothing of the loss of a fine tree—and if you think it is a worthwhile insurance, contact the Forestry Commission at 25 Savile Row, London W1 who can put you in touch with your local forestry officer and probably also the nearest approved tree surgeons capable of carrying out this work.

To put the problem into perspective, it would be well to bear in mind that during 1975, official policy recognised that the spread and intensity of the disease had become so overwhelming that it was being left to run its own course. See also *No. 62*.

62 Elm : be careful when using infected wood

I have been offered the trunk of an elm tree affected by Dutch elm disease as firewood. If I accept, would the trunk endanger the many other trees, none of which is an elm, in my garden?

Dutch elm disease is caused by a fungus called *Graphium ulmi*, which is peculiar to elms, and does not infect other trees. It is spread from tree to tree by bark beetles, and the risk you may be running—if you store it in the open before burning it—is not in introducing elm disease as such but in bringing other beetles and grubs into your garden which, given half a chance, may very well play havoc with your other trees. Elm wood does not burn well in any case and is best used in conjunction with other hotter-burning solid fuels or in a furnace where a draught aids combustion.

However, if you decide to take the trunk, I would suggest that you take the precaution of flaking off the bark first, and burning it on site before transporting the de-barked timber to your place.

63 Eucalyptus getting too tall

From a pot plant eight years ago, I planted a Eucalyptus urnigera *in the thin soil of my comparatively small garden. It is now nearly 30 ft. high; how tall will it grow?*

There are some two dozen Eucalyptus species grown in the U.K. of which *E. urnigera* from Tasmania is one of the least common. If yours really is *urnigera*—two clues are dark green rather than grey leaves, and peeling bark that is grey—you have to face the prospect of it becoming about twice as tall as its present height and ultimately quite wide. Once they get their toes in, most eucalyptus make vigorous growth when young and with 30 ft. in eight years, yours has done this. The rate will slow down now, but in the next eight years you can expect it to reach at least 40 ft. and then start filling out and becoming wider.

It is possible to keep the height down by judicious cutting, but you will need a very long and very efficient long-arm pruner to head it back. Even so the shape would be spoiled and would encourage laterals and side growth.

To keep it under control and try to preserve a balanced overall shape, you can do this cutting very early in spring before the sap starts rising fast when there is a risk of bleeding; also from July onwards when the sap rise has slowed down. Do this pruning carefully; cut just above suitable lateral shoots so that filling-out is encouraged and you will soon be able to take a sizeable crop of foliage from your tree which your local florist should be very willing to receive.

If, on the other hand, you decide that it must be grubbed out, do it soon before it becomes a too big job for you to manage—but sell the foliage first! Then you can replace the *E. urnigera* with a much slower growing kind; try *E. niphophila*, the Snow Gum, a very hardy species that is only a small tree in its natural habitat, with a beautifully marked main stem.

64 Eucalyptus: hardy or not?

I'd like to plant a Eucalyptus tree but am told that they are not hardy against frost. Is this true? Which is the hardiest kind, and what soil does it need?

Eucalyptus are a very large genus of evergreen trees valuable for their ornamental foliage and for their form and colour contrast. They come from Australasia, some parts of which are positively tropical so that it is not surprising that of the seventy or so species that have been grown in Britain, only a handful have stood up to our most severe winters. This has led to a widespread but mistaken regard that all eucalypts are not frost-hardy, which is a pity because more might otherwise be planted.

Fortunately this 'handful' of hardy species covers a range of size from large to small so that whatever size your garden, there is a hardy eucalyptus to suit it. Starting with the largest size, *E. gunnii* is usually regarded as the hardiest and certainly the most commonly grown and offered. It can grow up to seventy feet or more so it needs plenty of room. Perhaps, surprisingly, it stands cutting provided it is not allowed to bleed when early spring sap is rising. Lasting well in water, the foliage is in great demand for flower arranging, selling well to florists. *E. coccifera* is another 'large' tree species, coming from Tasmania, the mature tree bearing very glaucous leaves. *E. parvifolia* comes next in size and is one of the hardiest of all. It is a medium-sized tree that is particularly notable for its tolerance of chalk soils, and has leaves which are narrow and blue-green.

Then comes *E. niphophila*, the Snow Gum, which is decidedly smaller and slower-growing with large grey-green leaves and a very attractively mottled trunk with patches of greens, greys and creamy white. Smaller still comes the Cabbage Gum, *E. pauciflora*, a very striking tree with large leaves some 8 to 9 inches long and a very white trunk.

Eucalypts will grow in a variety of soil conditions and will tolerate a degree of wetness but not waterlogging. Only one variety however, *parvifolia*, has proven to be indefinitely tolerant of severe chalk. There is one very

important but unusual precaution to take especially with the larger-growing species. When young and as soon as they get their toes in, they tend to grow at a tremendous rate and seem for a time at least to outstrip the anchorage of the root system, rendering the young tree very susceptible to being blown over by strong winds. Therefore, if you plant in an exposed position, take the precaution in winter and early spring months of fitting guy ropes to hold the tree steady.

65 Evergreens: all need special care when transplanting

What is the best time to move a 3 ft. tall Mahonia japonica *which is growing too big for its present position? Also, when is the best time to take cuttings?*

A lot of confusion reigns over the difference between *Mahonia bealei* and *M. japonica*. Both have very similar striking foliage, and the sprays of yellow bloom are similar but in *japonica* they are longer and more pendulous than *bealei* and they are deliciously fragrant.

If your shrub really is *M. japonica*, then you have one of the most beautiful of all shrubs and it is worth going to considerable effort to make sure that the transplanting does not cause distress. To be fair, you should realise your mistake in planting this valuable shrub in a position where subsequent growth would necessitate later removal; always check on the ultimate size of plants before planting so that this risky situation does not arise. The best time for an enforced move is March–April, just after flowering so that next year's bloom has the maximum length of time to develop and so that re-establishment is secured before the crucial late autumn run-up time to flowering. The following procedure can be used for all evergreens and other shrubs that dislike root disturbance although, of course, it won't always be in spring.

First, prepare the new planting position; you do not lift a shrub and *then* think about where it is to be replanted. For a 3 ft. Mahonia, you are going to need a planting hole at least 2 feet in diameter and 18 inches deep. Take the first spit and lay it to one side; then take out the crumb and the second spit, spading it straight into a wheelbarrow, where you leave it. Fork in plenty of compost, plus a couple of handfuls of a balanced nutrient source—Growmore or Humber Eclipse. Do this a week before the move, and at the same time give the shrub itself a really good soaking.

The day before the move, spray the plant thoroughly with S600 transplanting spray, making sure that all leaf surfaces, especially the undersides, are well wetted. As this material dries, a very thin plastic sheath is formed which effectively prevents moisture evaporation from the leaf surfaces and helps the plant over the period when its root system will be hard pressed to absorb moisture from the soil.

You will need a heavy gauge plastic sheet about 5–6 ft. square; roll it up to half way.

Begin extraction of the plant by digging a trench in a semi-circle on one side only of the shrub and no nearer than 2 ft. from the main stem. If roots are damaged, it cannot be helped; sever them cleanly with secateurs as they emerge into the trench. Work this trench down deeply under the shrub so that when you have half the root ball free, you can work the sheet under the shrub with the rolled-up half under the shrub. Replace as much of the soil as you can by packing it *under* the sheet. When the soil has been packed into the trench to support the shrub, do the same from the other side; dig round, down and under so that you can reach the rolled-up sheet and pull it out the other side. Wrap the sheet around the soil ball; the shrub is now free and you can lift it clear— another pair of hands will help at this stage— and move it to the new site. Don't drag it, that could snag a thin sheet; if it is too heavy to lift into a wheelbarrow, at least get it on to a tray, a board or an old sack, in order to move it carefully without harming the roots, and preserving the root ball intact and as firm as you can.

Line it up at the side of the hole, facing the way you want. Estimate the hole size to soil ball and adjust as required so that it can be lifted in complete with sheet; you should have a few inches to spare all round. Ease the weight and drag out the sheet, fill in the gap with the original top spit soil that has been lying at the side all this time, plus a little compost, and tread the soil firm as you go. Now you can wheel away the barrow load of second spit

A   B

No. 65   *Moving evergreen and established shrubs.*
A.   Rolled half-sheet packed into bottom of trench dug halfway under shrub.
B.   First half-trench refilled to support shrub and soil ball whilst second half of trench is dug until it reaches roll of sheet which is then withdrawn as indicated. After the edges of the sheet are wrapped and bound to the trunk, the entire shrub can be lifted and removed to new position.

to fill the hole from where the shrub was lifted.

Give a new planting a good watering, and if you have done the job with care, it will hardly know it has been moved and your bloom next year will be as good as ever.

66 Evergreens: judging the right time to make a move

What is the correct time for moving shrubs? We want to alter their positions.

It is important to bear in mind that evergreens do not have a dormant period like deciduous plants which shed their leaves, but retain them and through which they go on transpiring moisture. They therefore need a little more attention. Always spray evergreens with S600 transplanting spray which, as it dries, leaves the foliage encased in a plastic sheath that very effectively reduces evaporation and drying-out whilst the plant is struggling to replace the fine absorbing roots that inevitably will have been damaged or lost during the move.

Prepare new positions by digging in plenty of compost—remember, this is your last chance to do anything about the soil underneath where the shrubs will grow. As a general rule—there will be exceptions as in *No. 65*—move evergreens in October or November during a mild spell. Three or four days before lifting, give the evergreens a really good soaking; then forty-eight hours before the job, spray with S600, and again twenty-four hours later. Then up and out with a good ball of soil into the prepared positions.

After the evergreens, shift the others. If you can move them at the same time, all well and good, but if your time is limited, move evergreens first since they need extra care; then the deciduous types can follow on as soon as you have the time.

If you are moving anything large and valuable read *No. 65* and carefully follow the method suggested there for pulling a sheet under the shrub to retain the soil ball.

For at least twelve months, be very careful to avoid dryness at the root; maintain a good mulch cover, and in dry spells help the foliage

of all transplanted shrubs to remain fresh and turgid by spraying each evening with cool water from the hose. Limp, flaccid foliage predisposes a plant to attack by fungus disease and pest attack.

67 Forsythia: familiar monstrous growth

What has caused my Forsythia to develop abnormally wide, flattened stems?

When side shoots fail to grow normally and do not 'separate' at the growing tip of a shoot—usually a main stem—and remain joined together, the growing stem builds-up into a monstrous-looking and, in the case of Forsythia, flattened growth. It can happen in similar form with almost any plant, and is not uncommon with Forsythias. Indeed, the phenomenon can have a commercial value as in the plant Celosia, commonly called Cockscomb, which you can often see offered by garden shops and nurseries each summer for bedding or as a pot plant. Being annuals, these are grown fresh from seed each year and the characteristic is even inherited through the seed. Exactly what causes fasciation is not certain, and there are many opinions about it.

What seems clear however, is that there is a disturbance of the genes controlling cell division and growth and there is some evidence that it occurs, or can be induced, in shrubs that are continuously used for propagation, being cut and cut repeatedly for cuttings to the point it seems of overworking, and this abnormal growth is a reaction. Possibly the shrub is asked to produce so much healing tissue so relentlessly—rather like repeated severe pruning—that the growth-controlling hormones get a little punch drunk. This observation is borne out (a) by the fact that it can be seen occurring in Forsythia more frequently when the plant is misused and repeatedly clipped to a hedge than when it is allowed to grow normally and unclipped as a specimen shrub and (b) other genetic breakdowns which have occurred in all manner of plants which have been vegetatively propagated over-intensively. Perhaps the two most notable examples of this are the strawberry Auchin-cruive Climax (see *No. 247*) and the very popular Dahlias, 'Baby Royal' and 'Glorie van Hemsteede'.

There could well be a correlation therefore between plants grown from cuttings taken from a parent stock tree that is being over-worked—the abnormal tendency showing up in the cuttings. For this reason, it is not altogether certain that cutting out a fasciated growth from your Forsythia will cure the trouble. The increased rate of cell division resulting from this 'pruning' could trigger the breakdown in a worse form than before. However, if this is the first time that it has happened to this bush, it is worth taking a chance. Cut out the fasciated growth—it is not very nice to look at anyway—but watch out very carefully for it happening again with all further growth. If it occurs again, you will have to start thinking about replacing the shrub, and if you decide on this course, go for one of the new hybrids like the triploid 'Arnold Giant', or the tetraploid 'Beatrix Farrand'. These new Forsythia types are even better than the old varieties.

68 Forsythia : *wrong treatment can wreck the bloom*

A Forsythia in my garden is cut back every autumn, but in the spring it only bears about four yellow flowers. How can I encourage it to produce more flowers on its branches?

The short answer to this is to leave it alone. All rules have exceptions, but the golden rule for pruning spring-flowering shrubs is to prune *after* flowering, not in the autumn. This is to allow the maximum period between flowering and the onset of winter for the production of new growth and for that growth to ripen and set flower buds. Therefore in pruning your spring-flowering Forsythia in autumn, you have been cutting away all the flower buds that have been developed during the summer months, and which would have lain dormant during winter to burst out their colour in the spring. See *No. 70* concerning the pruning of Forsythia.

Your experience is another example of the other golden rule of pruning and which I think is one of the most important rules in gardening. When you have secateurs in your hands and are about to cut—stop! Think: why am I going to do this? Do I understand *exactly* what I am going to do? What will happen as a result?

If you don't understand *why*, don't do it— go and find out, and be sure that what you find out makes sense to you.

69 Forsythia : *to prune or not to prune*

I planted a new Forsythia called 'Beatrix Farrand' in October and the following spring, although only a young plant just over 2 ft. high, it was smothered in bloom; then it grew four enormously long shoots over 5 ft. high and two shorter ones. But this year, there has hardly been a flower on the whole plant. Should I have pruned it in the autumn?

No, leave it for a year or two, other than to develop a nice open shuttlecock framework, then follow the principles outlined in *No. 68* and *70*. You are very fortunate in having this Forsythia—actually, it is a peculiar hybrid called a tetraploid and also in getting it to grow away so quickly. Obviously it likes the conditions where it is planted but you will have to be a little patient. Spring-flowering shrubs often bloom profusely in the first season after planting, then disappoint in this way. The long stems are a characteristic of this Forsythia and you will most likely find that these will branch out in the second season, and then the shrub will quickly fill in with branches and probably with more stems. The fast development of these long stems before the plant could have been expected to have made much root growth, indicates just how vigorous the variety is, but even so, it has put on this growth at the expense of developing bloom buds. Don't feed this shrub, it is doing well enough as it is. It will soon settle down and give a glorious display.

70 Forsythia : *early formative shaping is important*

Would you tell me the best way to prune a Forsythia bush?

The wonderful show of yellow bloom is borne in the spring on growth made during the previous year. The basic principle, therefore, will be to promote strong shoots that will bear bloom in the following spring. This is achieved by pruning away flowered stems as the flowers fade, and before too much energy has been used up in putting out the foliage that follows after blooming. Cut back such stems to strong healthy buds close to the base of the stem, or in the case of a young plant that you want to grow larger, merely shorten back the stem to healthy buds. Keep an eye on the shape and direction of the basic framework that you are building, try to form an open shuttlecock-like construction, and avoid crossing stems.

A particularly attractive feature for the garden can be produced with the true 'weeping' form of Forsythia, *F. suspensa*. Unhappily, very few nurserymen take the trouble to spend the few years of training and growing required to produce a standard 'weeper'—but there is no reason why you should not try.

Run-up a young plant—a cutting perhaps—as a single stem, rubbing off all side shoots and reducing any divisions of the lead shoot to one. Tie on to a straight cane or support until 6–7 ft. tall, then encourage side shooting at the top by nipping off the soft lead tip, and then the tips of the resulting side shoots which will then produce even more side shoots which can be allowed to grow out. The long shoots will curtain towards the ground like an umbrella screen covered with masses of yellow bloom in spring; the effect is very impressive and very much worth the effort.

The quality of bloom can be spoiled and its duration shortened by allowing stems and shoots produced during the summer, after the heavy pruning, to grow with abandon. Don't allow overcrowding to occur; as the new shoots form, cut out any weaklings so that the stronger ones can have plenty of space in which to develop. Energy thus directed into a few strong vigorous shoots will give better bloom and growth than allowing it to be shared amongst too many overcrowded, competing and therefore not so well-developed stems.

Finally, do realise that the heavy performance of blooming, then pruning and new stem production, means a heavy demand on nutrient resources in the soil. Every time you prune, you are taking away an awful lot of organic matter. Put it back by maintaining a substantial mulch cover of garden or mushroom compost and each spring scratch into this 3–4 ozs. per plant of Growmore or Humber Eclipse.

71 Garrya : planting preparation

I wish to plant a Garrya elliptica *this autumn. Could you supply information about the extent and depth of soil preparation required, and whether good drainage and deep manuring would be an advantage?*

The cardinal rule to realise with all plantings of trees and shrubs is that this is the last opportunity you will have to do anything about the soil underneath, where the roots are expected to go to work. Garryas like a deep, well-drained soil and as you are presumably going to grow it for the long, greyish green catkins that festoon the shrub in early spring, which make the shrub a glorious sight at a time when there is not much in the garden worth looking at, it's worth doing the preparation properly.

Take out a hole about two feet square and two spits deep, keeping the top one and removing the second. Break up the bottom of the hole with a fork, sprinkle in a handful of balanced fertiliser and incorporate compost, leaf mould, or moist peat so that you have a roughly 50/50 mix of soil/organic matter. This will raise the level so that on replacing the top spit with a little more organic matter added, the original soil level will have been reached. If it is a little low never mind.

Try to do this about the end of September or early October, which will be about a month to six weeks before you should plant. This will give the hole and its new soil and compost time to warm up from the surrounding soil, and for the bacteria to start working on the organic matter and the fertiliser.

When the new shrub arrives, take out a hole just large enough to accomodate the root system comfortably; it will not be as large as the first hole. Firm the new shrub in with the heel of your foot, dragging in enough of the surrounding soil as required so the shrub is planted firmly at the centre of a saucer-shaped rain-catching depression an inch or two deep. The phosphates from the fertiliser which are going to encourage root action will take a few months to decompose before they become useful to the plant, but in the spring, when the plant is beginning to establish and grow, working hard to make new roots, the needed encouragement will become available just at the right time.

Whenever possible, this procedure is an ideal one to follow with all tree and shrub planting. The top fertile spit is retained, the less fertile second spit is removed and its bulk replaced with an equal bulk of organic, spongy, moisture-retaining, humus-making matter.

Garrya eliptica is unisexual, the male plant bearing the long catkins, so make sure you obtain the right sex and don't let yourself in for disappointment later on. If you can locate it, the variety 'James Roof' is a vigorous male form with extra long catkins. Tolerant of both seaside conditions and town atmospheric pollution, the Garryas are normally hardy enough to withstand a cold winter but in the north it needs some protection against the fierce drying Northerlies to avoid wind scorch.

72 Garrya: when the leaves turn brown

Are the leaves on my evergreen Garrya elliptica *suffering from a disease? A few of them started turning brown and this trouble has gradually spread all over the shrub, which is now about 9 ft. tall and 8 ft. wide. I have read about wind scorch but I do not see how it can be this, as my garden is in such a well-protected position that even the strongest winds blow over and scarcely ripple the leaves.*

In a position as well protected as this, it is unlikely that the browning could be due to wind scorch and, furthermore, it would not

start with a few leaves and gradually spread to the whole tree; the windward side would be be blistered at one blow. This gradual spread and the protection from air movement suggest that the Garrya is being attacked by fungus—the most likely being the Leaf Spot disease, which has been known to affect mature trees. If this is so, you have a problem on your hands that will need patience and perseverance, because if the conditions have been conducive to the onset of fungal attack, presumably they will also be conducive to its continuance. You will either have to change the conditions by encouraging more wind/air ventilation, or try to control the fungus under conditions that are favourable to it, and adverse to you.

If the foliage and younger growth is badly damaged, you should cut this away and burn it—but don't cut more than a quarter of the whole. Then the entire remainder will need drenching with a fungicide—drenching meaning in this sense not using so much liquid that it runs off and is wasted but ensuring that every surface area is wetted and thus covered by the fungicide.

Thiram or Zineb are likely to be the two most effective fungicides. Make up the spray solution exactly as the maker's instructions, and add about 6–10 drips of liquid washing-up detergent so that the spray spreads over the waxy leaves instead of running into large globules and dropping off.

You will need to spray fairly frequently—probably every 2–3 weeks for several months to really get on top of it, and then you will have to spray whenever the trouble occurs again, as it assuredly will do. You must do this job properly; it is a complete waste of time and money to only half do it.

The type of sprayer you use is most important, of course; you can't work well with inadequate equipment and the nature of the job almost determines what you will need. Spraying enough liquid to wet thoroughly, up to 9 ft. high, means that a single-handed puff-puff is not enough. You'll need a fine spray on an extension lance to reach up under and around the top. You will need a reservoir of at least a couple of gallons so that you don't have to keep stopping to mix up and refill. A double-action Solo sprayer—which sucks liquid from a bucket —is ideal for the job.

73   Gorse likes poor conditions

I would like to plant some ordinary yellow flowering gorse. I grow flowers and vegetables very well and I am wondering if the soil would be too rich for gorse?

Gorse is one of those unusual shrubs, like many of the heathers, that grow best in sandy, dry, acid soils that have a low degree of fertility. There are a great many areas like this throughout the country, generally on heaths, commons and downs that are too infertile to support intensive agriculture and therefore remain wild and more or less natural. *Ulex europaeus*, the common gorse, is found in such situations and is well-known both for its vicious spiny growth and the wealth of the yellow bloom during spring and summer.

When grown in more fertile soil, such as it will undoubtedly find in your garden, there is not the need for it to fight so hard for its perpetuation and invariably it does not bloom nearly so freely. If you want to grow gorse for its spiny protection, it would be a wise policy before planting a whole hedge to try one or two first to see how they make out in your soil. They are not at all easy to establish and are usually grown in pots to give them a better chance of transplanting. It is usually propagated from seed, so instead of buying-in plants, collect well-ripened seed from plants growing wild in the countryside. Sow them in early spring, either in boxes for later pricking-off into pots and then into their final positions, or sown directly into a drill in situ, thinning-out or transplanting into gaps as required.

If however, it is a yellow bloom that you are after, and not the spines, you would probably do very much better by growing Spanish Gorse, *Genista hispanica*, which will grow to 2–2½ ft. high and never fails to give a mass of yellow bloom during May and June and received an Award of Garden Merit in 1969; or its dwarfer-growing companion *G. lydia* which received a similar award in 1946.

74   Grassing down a shrubbery

I would like to increase the number of shrubs in my small shrubbery. It is grassed all over : is this a good idea, or should I dig in all the grass? I am curious because when I was young and living in Kent, all the orchards were ploughed every year, but now they are grassed over because, I am told, it is better for the trees and fruit.

Apart from saving time and labour, the reason for the modern practice of grassing over orchards and the adoption of the system in some gardens is because many of the nutrient and trace element deficiencies that beset a lot of fruit growers a couple of generations ago were proved by East Malling Research Station— set up in Kent to tackle this very problem—to be due to the practice of ploughing the orchard floor. By ploughing and exposing the soil to the air, more rapid decomposition of the organic matter in the soil was accomplished, producing a surge in nutrient availability and an increase in fertility—to begin with.

The trouble, however, is that this rapid decomposition doesn't stop and the nutrients are quickly washed out of the soil. The humus content quickly becomes exhausted in the aerated soil. When none or very little organic matter is put back, the soil structure deteriorates and fertility is lost.

Grassing down, apart from mowing being easier than ploughing, works on this principle. Grasses which have comparatively shallow roots do not compete directly with the trees for available plant nutrients. Even when fertilisers are put down for the trees, the small proportion absorbed by the grasses is returned to the soil via the cuttings every time the grass is mown. This constant return of cuttings builds-up humus and so the result is retention and increased fertility compared with the leaching and 'washing out' resulting from repeated ploughing.

Now to the practicalities of your particular shrubbery. If the shrubs are spaced as specimen plants, grassing-down has a number of advantages to commend it and, indeed, it is a wide-spread and growing practice; but if the shrubbery is of the conventional close-planted type, it would be very difficult to get at the grass to cut it and think of the laborious job of clipping out the long stuff that the mower cannot reach. Hoeing and/or mulching is much more practicable maintenance.

Digging grass into an already established shrubbery is highly dangerous because you could not possibly turn the grasses in deep enough to prevent their regrowth without damaging the roots of the shrubs. It is much better to cut the grass out with a spade, with a layer of about 2 in. of soil, so that most of the grass root disappears and the possibility of re-emergence is minimised. Spread a liberal layer of compost or peat mulch each autumn to compensate for the lost grass.

75 Hawthorn : how long does it take a seedling to bloom?

After waiting two years, I have managed to germinate some seeds from a very pretty May tree that grows near by. Its flowers are white with a pink edge. How long shall I have to wait for my seedlings to flower?

After your patience has been rewarded with germination of the seeds of your May tree, it is sad to warn you of possible disappointment if you are relying upon these seeds to produce a May tree the same as the parent. It will very likely be seven or eight years, perhaps longer, before the seedlings—young trees by this time —are mature enough to bear bloom and although you may be lucky enough to get a bloom like the parent, the chances are very slim.

The only way to be absolutely sure of getting the bloom you want is to reproduce the tree vegetatively—by grafting a shoot of it on to the common 'hedgerow' species, *Crataegus monogyna*, young plants of which you can get in the autumn from a nursery offering them as hedging material or perhaps from a hedgerow in the countryside.

Grafting not only ensures that you get exactly the bloom you want, but also that you get that bloom three or four years earlier.

76 Heathers : propagation by cuttings

I grow both winter- and summer-flowering heathers and I wish to increase my stock. What is the best time of the year to take cuttings, and what size shoots should be used? Does it help to use a rooting powder?

Heather cuttings can be taken in August, September or October. Use short shoot ends of the current season's growth, no more than $1\frac{1}{4}$ inches long. Dip into rooting hormone powder and dibble into pots containing a mixture of four parts silver sand to one part fine sieved soil taken from immediately below and around the parent plant.

Place the pot in an outdoor frame, buried to the rim, shaded from the sun, and keep just moist. Rooting usually occurs during late winter, and by early spring, the rooted cuttings should be ready for potting-up.

Handling cuttings an inch long is a fiddly job though and there is a much easier method. For most amateur gardener's requirements, by far the most satisfactory method of propagating heathers is by layering.

Prepare for this by rubbing peat through a $\frac{1}{2}$-inch sieve and carefully work this under, through and around the heather so that you have a good layer $1\frac{1}{2}$–2 inches thick. Now thoroughly moisten the peat and at the same time give a good soaking by putting on the sprinkler for an hour or two. If you have to resort to rainwater because of the limy content in the tap water give several waterings with the can and a fine rose.

You now need a good supply of stones about the size of a tangerine. Simply press semi-soft stems of the heather into the moist peat, put a wodge of peat on top and hold each in position with a stone. Done in spring, this should produce sufficient rooting to enable most of the shoots to be severed and moved to new permanent positions during autumn. See *No. 77*.

The most important points to watch with this very simple method are firstly, keep the propagation area well moist; don't let the peat mulch dry out or the newly-forming roots will be ruined. And secondly, if you lift a stone and test a stem for rooting, always replace the wodge of peat between the stem and the stone. During the heat of summer, in the sun, that stone can become so hot that you wouldn't want to hold it for long, and it would harm the heather stem if it were in direct contact.

77 Heathers : propagation by division, and soil fungus

Can I divide my heathers as one does with perennial plants? I could lift them with plenty of soil attached to the roots and ensure they have plenty of water afterwards.

It is not at all clear from your question why you want to divide these heathers; there is no point in dividing them just for the sake of it. They are far better left alone undisturbed to merge together. If you are intending to increase your stock by this division, you would do far better to follow the method described in *No. 76.*

Repeated top dressing with peat, in fact, often leads to plants becoming a colony of side stems that have self-rooted into the peat and, provided that rooted sections are lifted carefully with as much peat and soil adhering as possible, such colony plants can be divided.

If you plant up a fresh site, always take a little extra soil from where the plants originated. This is because heathers live in association with certain special soil fungi that in turn rely upon the heather, a partnership in which both depend upon each other. Transferring to a new site means there may not be any of these special fungi in the soil and your new planting will have to depend entirely upon the fungi it brings with it in the soil adhering to its roots. The old site will abound in these fungi and that's why you should bring some of it to help the new planting on its way.

With few exceptions, heathers are lime haters, and it goes without saying, therefore, that as you will need to keep the new plantings well moist to get them growing well, not *one* drip of water should come from the tap. Use rainwater only, and if the storage butt runs dry and you are forced to use tap water, make sure that it has had its lime content counter-acted by the tannic acid of tea. Empty the tea pot into a bucket and when cool use the liquor, with tea leaves or bags keeping the soil moist in addition to the peat mulch.

78 Heathers for Christmas, and after

A friend gave me a lovely pot of heather at Christmas with very large, white-tipped, pink bells. Unfortunately, now that I have had it in the house for three weeks some of its needles are beginning to drop off and the plant doesn't look so healthy. Please tell me how to treat it.

In all probability, your plant is one of the tender South African Cape Heath hybrids, known as *Erica hyemalis.* These are not easy to keep by any means for most amateur gardeners, and the way they are so often grown doesn't make it any easier.

The plants are produced specifically for the Christmas trade, a time of year when little other bloom is available. They are usually crammed into pots which are much too small, meaning that their root systems are cramped with insufficient space and are dependent upon a soil volume so small that drying out easily occurs. They are grown under glass in a controlled environment so that they bloom at the right time for market, and as space under glass is at a premium and has to produce as much as possible, these heaths are sometimes grown close together in greenhouse beds, and moved into pots with inevitable root damage just before being sent to market.

Deprived of its proper root system, it is only with extreme care, and the most favourable conditions, that you will be able to nurse these through this sort of shock; the dropping 'needles' are an indication of just how bad this has been.

Try to keep the plant in as equable a temperature as possible: cool but frost free and the atmosphere humid—the dry air of modern home central heating is certain death. Mist spray daily with tepid rainwater to which has been added a few drops of Murphy FF foliar feed; this will help to compensate for the loss of assimilation through the missing roots. To help this foliar feed thoroughly wet and penetrate into the foliage (hence foliar) add just one or two drips, no more, of liquid washing-up detergent.

Keep the plant in partial shade away from full light. If you are able to arrest the decline (or avoid it perhaps on a future occasion) and notice signs of new growth—indicating that it is making new roots and fighting hard to live— then encourage the plant with a little liquid feed. If you are able to keep the plant going, you will get a show of bloom but don't expect the overall quality that you had the first time. That was the result of controlled and specialised growing techniques and you can hardly reproduce these. All this seems a lot of bother to go to, which is why potted Christmas heathers are usually regarded as expendable. If they were grown in such a manner that they were easy to grow on for the next year, like Christmas trees, the demand would be reduced. Like modern motor cars, and many other things, many plants are sold with a built-in short life expectancy, but in the same way that a lot of care can keep a car going for longer than it was designed for, so a lot of care is often needed to keep a pot plant on the road.

79 Heathers growing in limy soil

I have a slightly limy soil but would like to grow some heathers. Shall I have to plant them in specially prepared soil?

Since your soil is slightly limy, you will inevitably experience disappointment and many losses if you try to grow any heathers other than the winter-flowering varieties: *Erica carnea, E. mediterranea, E. terminalis* and *E. × darleyensis.* Varieties other than these are intolerant of any trace of lime. You will need to avoid using tap water and any fertilisers containing lime.

If, by your reference to specially prepared soil, you plan to plant into pockets of special lime-free soil, forget it. Young plants may last a year or two, but they are doomed to decline and failure as the lime inexorably seeps in from the surrounding soil.

The only way to grow lime-hating plants in a lime soil area is to put down an insulating plastic sheet and construct a raised bed—see *No. 117*—and to avoid lime in every shape and form. You will need to build this raised bed with lime-free soil, of course. One further tip when planting heathers, is to try to collect some soil from commons or the countryside under natural-growing heather. This is to make sure that there will be present plenty of the soil fungi that live in association with heather and without which they will not thrive. See *No. 77.*

80 Hedges: cutting back overgrown Escallonia

I have a short hedge of Escallonia which is very overgrown. When can I cut back the hedge and take cuttings? I have a few gaps in the hedge; can these cuttings be put in place before they have rooted?

Ideally, the best time to cut back an overgrown Escallonia hedge is late March or early April, depending upon your north/south location, the weather beforehand and during the time that you do the job, because the plant will have a lot of open wounds which would be damaged by frost. Some people advise autumn pruning, but I have seen too many early autumn frosts do untold damage.

Don't bother with cuttings to fill the gaps; whilst waiting for the right pruning time to arrive, bend round and peg down into the soil of the gap some of the lower stems or branches from nearby plants. These will layer quite quickly and by also pulling around and 'lacing in' some of the higher growth, you can quickly fill in the spaces.

If you want to see Escallonia at its best, you should aim to have the hedge respond to hard pruning by sending out long arching stems which cascade down like a curtain and these will bear the best blooms. Escallonia should not be repeatedly clipped back into a formal shape like a privet. Pruning is done once a year and once only, and then don't be afraid to prune back hard.

81 Hedges: cutting back overgrown privet

Despite frequent cutting, my privet hedge has gradually grown to 4 ft. wide. I would like to cut it back to 1½–2 ft. How and when should I do this?

A privet hedge, or any other clipped hedge for that matter, is not green all the way through but only near the outside edges where light can reach. The dark interior is leafless, and you must therefore accept that cutting back to this extent inevitably means that, for a while at least, the hedge is going to look awful, bare and lifeless. Therefore, the best time to do the job is in early spring so that the new growth season can be expected to produce at least some green fairly soon afterwards. If you prune in the autumn, you will have to wait a lot longer for new growth to hide the mess.

You will need secateurs and pruning saw for the most part; hedging shears will not be used much unless they have a special lopping notch and even then you will be wiser to use secateurs or the saw.

I am assuming that the hedge consists of a single row and is not a staggered planting, making an 18 inch width impracticable. The first thing I do with a job like this, is to get the height down to where it is wanted, and as most people want a straight line and not a switch back, you will need, with a hedge already 4 ft. wide, some 5 ft. canes. Push one right through the hedge at each end at a couple of inches below the new hedge height you eventually want, so that they protrude each side. Now push others through at something less than 5 ft. intervals adjusting them as required so that the protrusions both sides are dead straight, by eye, with the end ones. When you are satisfied that they are all straight, level and in line, lay on the protruding cane ends some of the left-over canes and use these to sight a straight edge guide to cut in about a foot each side. There is no need to cut right across at this stage—4 ft. wide is too wide and awkward.

You now have a wide ledge each side, with a narrow overgrown ridge in the centre. Now you have to get a straight line indicator for the sides and this can be done either by pushing canes down vertically through at each end and tying string between them or by laying canes on the ledge to sight a straight line in a similar way as before. Again make the cutting line an inch or two in from the final dimensions you want the ledge to be. This is so that new green growth can grow out an inch or two to where the final face will be. All later clipping can then take place without the danger and annoyance of repeatedly catching on old wood or producing unsightly 'black holes' by cutting right through the new growth to the bare interior.

Start at one end and make a cut down vertically to floor level, then use this 'face' as a guide as you work gradually to the other end; do the other side and then, with access now a lot easier, you can remove the centre ridge of old growth on top.

There is no need to be too precise at this severe cutting back stage—the remains of the hedge is going to look a shambles in any case. The time for finesse and pin-point straight faces and edges comes later when you are trimming the soft new green growth that emerges. Clear the clippings away, put down a slow-acting balanced nutriet like Growmore or Humber Eclipse and soak the soil thoroughly by laying the hose under the hedge and letting it dribble slowly. If the weather turns dry, spray the hedge overhead. With old woody growth reluctant to make new shoots, green leaves may come spasmodically and unevenly, but as soon as this new growth becomes long enough, begin clipping so that side shooting is encouraged and a new face quickly developed. Cut back resolutely to this face each time; if you are timid and let it creep out on you, it can only be a matter of time before you have to do this job all over again.

82 Hedges: a better and brighter replacement for privet

I want to replace a miserable dying privet hedge with something that's hardy, with perhaps flowers too. What do you suggest?

It rather depends upon whether you want a formal clipped hedge or whether you'd like to try something just a little more informal with a firm core sending out stems bearing flowers and/or berries. In this case you can try the evergreen Escallonia; this sends out stems wreathed in white and rosy-pink and crimson bloom in late summer and autumn. The variety 'Apple Blossom' tends to be a slow grower, and is therefore very suitable for hedging. 'Donard Beauty' is aptly named and has the added attraction of being aromatic when brushed, bruised or cut; and 'Donard Gem' has large sweetly-scented flowers. Or you could try Pyracantha, the Fire Thorn, or Cotoneaster, both of which are smothered in berries in autumn. The method of pruning in all these cases is the same as that described in *No. 80*.

The spectacular yellow-flowered Forsythia can also be used for hedging, but if you decide to try it, prune it as above; don't ruin a beautiful shrub as so many do by close clipping it like a privet.

If you want something with a closer growth habit, and without the long arching shoots, try the Daisy Bush from New Zealand *Olearia haastii*. Every so often one comes across an idea, a solution to a problem and the thought occurs, why wasn't that thought of before? Or why isn't that grown more often? Olearia is a case in point. It is evergreen with grey-green leaves, smothered with fragrant white flower heads in July and August. Very hardy, it has the added advantage of being remarkably tolerant of polluted air and town conditions. An Olearia hedge in full bloom is a glorious sight—and one of the most underrated and neglected of all shrubs, especially for hedging.

83 Heeling-in: what it means and advance preparation

I'm about to receive a consignment of shrubs but the ground won't be ready. How can I keep them fresh and healthy?

A lot depends upon how long you are going to be before you plant them. Most nurserymen pack well before despatch, and another few days spent in a cool garage or shed away from cold draughts won't harm them. However, the wise gardener always makes sure that he has a heeling-in trench ready before the plants arrive and this is how to prepare one.

Take out a short trench, two spits wide and one spit deep, throwing the soil on one side only of the trench to form a steeply-shaped ridge close to the edge. Shovel out the loose crumb and pile this on the other side. Then when the shrubs arrive, unwrap and examine the bare roots. If they look dry, soak them overnight by immersion in a bucket or bath. Lay the shrubs in the trench with their stems and twigs laying against, and supported by, the ridge of soil. Keep the plants as close together as possible and cover the roots loosely with the crumb soil from the other side of the trench. Use whatever remains from the packing—paper bags, sacking—to wrap lightly around the shrubs to protect them from wind, and cover the open trench with wood wool from the packing, straw, compost or peat, to prevent them drying out. Called 'heeling-in', this method will tide them over for a few weeks until you are ready to plant. As the plants are only lightly covered, it will be easy to lift them.

The cardinal rule, however, is to have the trench ready beforehand. If you don't, it is all too easy to leave the plants in their packing or

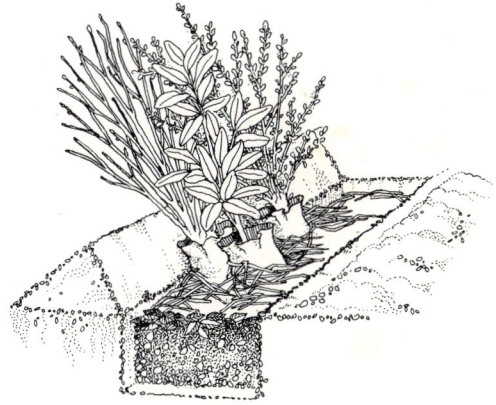

No. 83 *Heeling-in, the way to protect plants that cannot be planted as soon as they are delivered.*

half out of it for a few more days. Then it's no good trying to tell the nurseryman that 'they were wonderfully well looked after but they still died', and blaming him for sending you half dead shrubs!

If you pay good money for shrubs, it's only common sense to look after them when they arrive.

84   Hibiscus : always slow to flower

What is the reason why my Hibiscus will not flower? It is three years old and is in a sunny position. The soil is light. Should I prune it?

For heaven's sake, don't prune it! Hibiscus is notoriously slow to mature and come to bloom. Five, six or even seven years is not uncommon, so your three-year-old is still only a youngster. The species comes from Syria, so there is the first clue to the conditions that it likes and needs —full sunlight. Although it is known to have been grown in this country in the sixteenth century, it still hasn't got used to our climate and still hankers after its own.

It is too late now to do anything about preparation of the soil under the shrub but you can do one or two things to help and encourage it to 'grow up'. First, hoe in plenty of peat or humus-forming compost and mulch every spring to keep the roots cool and moist during the summer months. Put this mulch down over a 3–4 oz. spreading of a slow-acting organic-based balanced manure like Humber Eclipse so that the nutrients' gradual availability encourages steady growth all summer. Then, if there is no bloom at the fifth summer, you can encourage the maturing process by offering the shrub an extra helping of the element that all plants like if they are to mature and ripen—potash. This will ensure that any continuing shyness to bloom is not due to a shortage of that, so at monthly intervals, starting April until August, hoe in four or five dressings of about 2 oz. of sulphate of potash spread over an area of a square yard around the shrub. There is little else you can do; the Hibiscus will not flower till it is ready. But when it does, after all your encouragement, you should get some very fine blooms.

85   Holly : why no berries?

My large holly has never berried. Why?

If you mean that you've not had even one from time to time, then almost certainly your holly tree is a male. Hollies are unisexual; i.e. plants either bear male or female flowers and in order to get a good set of berries it is normally necessary to have plants of both sexes growing close to each other so that pollination can take place. Hollies are not very fast growers and even if you immediately buy a known female holly, you are not likely to get berries next year or for a few more after until it matures, so you have time to find out positively whether your tree is a male or female—it could be either— and know which mate your tree needs.

When it flowers, usually about late May, look carefully at the small white flowers. If they have four tiny little stalks in the centre these are stamens and your tree is male, but if it only has one club-headed stalk in the centre this is the pollen-receiving female pistil and your tree is therefore female. As soon as you are sure, order another appropriate tree from a good nursery stating clearly which sex you want.

86   Holly : disfigurement of foliage by leaf miner

Our holly tree has never shown any signs of disease until this year. Now almost every leaf is affected with whitish markings which zig-zag about haphazardly. Spraying with a general insecticide has made no difference.

Many plants are attacked by leaf miners—in this case the holly leaf miner *Phytomiza illicis*, minute caterpillar-like grubs that bore into a leaf and then live between the two surface skins, upper and lower, devouring the material in between and leaving tell-tale marks where they have tunnelled or 'mined'. These tunnels do not heal, the damaged part does not become green again and even if an insecticide reaches and kills the grub, the markings remain. Hollies are often troubled by the pest and so are softer tissued plants like Chrysanthemums. It is, of course, very damaging to the plant because it seriously reduces the manufacturing area of leaf and interferes with the ability to pass the elaborated sugars and hydrocarbons back to the main body of the plant and it seems that your plant has suffered a particularly severe attack.

The problem with leaf miners is always the same—to reach the grubs protected within the two skin layers. Where about half the leaves have been attacked, one could expect the tree to withstand the shock of having all affected leaves picked off. These should be burned. If it is impracticable to do this, you will have to hope that the remaining functioning portion of the foliage can at least keep the tree going whilst you try to prevent further attack by spraying. Use Malathion—with a few drops of washing-up fluid added to enable the spray to adhere to the glossy surfaces of the leaves. Repeat this fortnightly until winter, or until the cold weather or the pupae stage of the insect will stop the tunnelling. However, the pest is around and you must expect renewed attack next year. So from March-end onwards you must start Malathion spraying again, every ten to fourteen days, in an effort to kill the flies as they come in to lay their eggs.

You can try a systemic insecticide to poison the plant's sap stream and remember to add a few drops of liquid detergent to the spray to help the liquid get through the tough leathery skin of the leaves to the sap inside. This may not be very effective with holly because it is a slow living plant, and the slow movement of sap within the plant does not make for efficient distribution of the poison. You must therefore spray very thoroughly, wetting every leaf and repeating at three or four week intervals to keep up the toxicity level as the poison disintegrates.

Leaf miner is a very debilitating trouble and it weakens the plant and disfigures the oranmental leaves. If you don't get on top of it, the consequences could be very serious. Help the holly to fight and recover by putting down a balanced nutrient like Humber Eclipse or Growmore and mulch heavily.

87 Honeysuckle: when mildew is a problem

I have a Dutch honeysuckle against a south wall and last summer it was virtually defoliated by what seemed to be a sort of mildew. The young shoots are already showing signs of a similar white discolouration. Can you tell me what this disease is likely to be and the remedy?

Honeysuckle is a hedgerow plant and there are two basic environmental differences between its natural habit and growing against a wall. In a hedgerow, its root system—although obviously in competition with other plants—is nevertheless unrestricted and, receiving an annual mulch with each autumnal leaf fall, is not likely to suffer from nutrient deficiency. Against a wall, it is denied half of its potential root spread area.

The other difference is more important: the wind blows through a hedge giving good ventilation. Against a wall, air movement is usually very much reduced and this is likely to be the important factor in this problem case.

It is difficult to give a reasonable diagnosis without seeing the plant, but with a restricted root system the plant will not be as vigorous as it should be. With impaired ventilation, honeysuckles are prone to attack by aphis, a very debilitating pest, and when this happens the weak, ailing, flaccid foliage is wide open to a knockout blow. The spores of mildew are always in the air; every plant in your garden is constantly under attack from other forms of life—that is Nature. Whether the attacker gains a foothold or is thrown off depends primarily upon the resistance it meets; and your honeysuckle hasn't much resistance, so you must come to its aid.

Many people advise spring pruning, I prefer autumn. Clean out tangled growth—it cannot all bear bloom and only harbours pest and disease—let in the air, and let it have the equivalent of a natural leaf fall by putting down a heavy mulch—spent mushroom compost is perfect. In early spring—February to March—hoe in 4 oz. of balanced plant nutrient like Growmore to the two square yards of the root spread area, and repeat this once a month

—at the end of March and again in April. You can expect early growth to be invigorated, but don't let it fall easy prey to aphis. Spray regularly with a fine mist spray containing a two-pronged attack—Lindane or Malathion for a knock-down contact kill, and a systemic insecticide which in this soft new foliage will be quickly assimilated into the sap stream to build-up internal toxicity to the pest.

Your plant will now present an entirely different proposition to the inevitable onset of mildew when it comes, and should therefore not become nearly so devastating. However, at the first signs, move quickly to prevent its development, by spraying with Karathane or Dinocap. Follow this procedure each year, and you will get plenty of deliciously perfumed honeysuckle.

88   Honeysuckle : the variety with the gold tracery

I have a young honeysuckle with gold pencil-like markings on its leaves which I rooted from a cutting. It is now in a 5 in. pot on a window sill and is growing at a terrific rate. Can it be planted outside?

This is *Lonicera japonica* 'Aureo-reticulata', and it is perfectly hardy, so plant it outdoors where it can scramble over a fence or pergola like the natural habitat its near relations in the hedgerow. As you have found, it roots quite easily from cuttings and this is particularly useful because the 'gold net' patterned leaves make particularly fine pot plants for the cool greenhouse or patio, climbing over a fan-shaped trellis. It is made even more attractive by highly-scented creamy yellow flowers.

The leaf colouring is better when it is grown in rather poor soil. If you treat it generously, the foliage becomes rather too lush and the veining will tend to disappear.

89   Honeysuckle : sweet scent and golden-white flowers

I have a climber called Hulliana japonica. *I cannot find it in any gardening book or catalogue. It is evergreen with lovely perfumed yellow and white flowers and I have it climbing up the side of the garage. Can I prune it and if so, when? Is it a form of honeysuckle?*

You haven't found this honeysuckle because you have been looking for it under the wrong name; in fact, it is called *Lonicera japonica* 'Halliana'. It is not quite a true evergreen, semi-evergreen is more correct and, as you describe, the creamy-white bloom has a wonderful perfume and turns yellow with age. It doesn't need pruning to a set formula, but it will form a tangled mass of trailers and stems if neglected. It cannot all reach the sunlight and bear bloom, so clear out the congested growth and let the air blow through it. Otherwise, don't prune unless you have to restrain its size. Let it clamber and climb at will.

Normally it is more resistant to mildew than other honeysuckles but aphis can be a nuisance and is another reason for not providing the pest with overwintering quarters by leaving congested growth. Clear it out in November. See also *Nos. 86* and *87.*

90   Hydrangea : how to influence blue or pink flowers

Some years ago I purchased three Hydrangea plants, each with red blooms. These were planted in three different places in the garden. Now they are large bushes; one is blue, one blue and mauve and one is mauve. What is the reason for the change of colour and can I do anything to bring them back to their original shade of red? Do you think that feeding them with Growmore fertiliser could have caused the change in colour?

Hydrangeas are often likened to litmus paper which turns pink or blue depending on whether it is dipped into an acid or alkaline solution, except that with Hydrangeas it works the other way; an acid soil tends to turn the Hydrangea blue and an alkaline soil turns it pink and red. The various degrees of blue, mauve, pink or red depends upon the degree of acidity or alkalinity working with or against the degree of colour vigour in the particular plant. The indications therefore are that your soil is acid and your difficulty is a similar one to the problem that another gardener would have on a limy soil trying to prevent blue Hydrangeas from turning pink or red.

To keep the red colour of your Hydrangeas you will have to isolate them from your acid soil and you can do this by replanting them during the dormant season in pots or tubs in a compost containing lime. If this is impracticable and they have to stay 'in ground', you could try applying hydrated lime to the soil around the plants—a cupful per plant three or four times a month apart during early spring and summer.

Bear in mind, however, that if you have other plants growing nearby and they are lime-haters (something you may suspect if they are growing well in your acid soil) they will definitely not appreciate the limy habits of their neighbours. In this case, it is better to keep your Hydrangeas in a special part of the garden where they can be limed without risk to other plants. I doubt if Growmore is likely to affect the colour of Hydrangeas. The colour should not change unless you repeatedly use straight chemical fertilisers that have a marked acid or alkaline reaction. Growmore is fairly neutral. You can buy special Hydrangea colourant at garden shops, or you can make your own by mixing sulphate of iron with aluminium sulphate.

Dissolve $\frac{1}{4}$ oz. of each chemical into four gallons of water and with the rose on the can spout, sprinkle the solution over the shrub so that the leaves are well wetted and the liquid drips off into the soil. Use this quantity of solution during the course of each fortnight for each plant from early spring until the flowers begin to open and you should get better blues in the first year and really good blues in the second year. Repeat the treatment each year.

91 Hydrangea : dividing an overgrown plant

Some of my Hydrangeas have grown very large and 'woody'. I would like to prune them but I do not know the correct time for doing it, how much I should remove and whether old blooms should be removed. Should I give them any fertiliser?

The best time to split or divide a Hydrangea is late winter, just as the milder weather begins, but before the new growth buds begin to swell and turn green. If you do it later when the new green shoots are appearing, you will give the plant an enormous shock. Having lifted the plant, try to split the root clump by carefully inserting two garden forks back to back and bringing the handles together to lever the clump apart. Do this gradually, try to tease it carefully, encouraging it to fall apart, rather than ripping it apart regardless. When you have finished pulling them about, trim down the stems and top growth to about one foot. This will encourage new strong shoots to grow from the base. Before replanting you will have your last chance to get moisture-retaining organic matter and plant food underneath them. Fork some peat or compost into the bottom of the planting holes enriched with a handful of slow-acting balanced plant food like Growmore or Humber Eclipse. Or you can use an enriched organic manure like Maskells Hop Manure. If replanting in pots or tubs, take the opportunity to replace the soil and compost similarly.

Plant firmly and keep watered in the early stages until they are well-established. You shouldn't normally expect the plants to throw bloom in the first season after replanting but if they do quickly get well-established they might try to put on a show later in the summer —but *don't* let them. The most important thing they have to do is to build up strength after their amputation and not overspend their energy in carrying premature bloom. Cut out any bloom that appears; indeed, if the new stems look like becoming long and spindly, head them back so that a single stem breaks into several side shoots and a better, thicker bush is produced to carry the maximum amount of big blooms next year.

Give your plants a light mulch of peat or compost with a little Growmore or Humber Eclipse added, or Maskells Hop Manure. Mulch again in spring, a little heavier this time and you should have fine plants and magnificent bloom.

It sometimes happens that Hydrangeas become too unruly and have to be reduced. Of course, try to prevent this happening in the first place, but if it does happen, don't make a drastic reduction all at once. Remove half of the oldest and thickest timbers by cutting as low as you can. This will encourage some fresh shoots from the base during the growing season whilst the remaining old wood sustains the plant. Then next year, with the new growth growing in stature and able to take over, the remaining old wood can come away. Do it in two stages—more drastic treatment will mean an equally drastic reaction in the plant, even its loss. In future take the old wood out bit by bit each year so that new growth is encouraged as a continuous process. Clearing old wood regularly each year will avoid the need for desperate and drastic remedy.

Spent blooms are usually left on Hydrangeas to give protection during winter to new emerging growth buds just beneath. When you remove the dead flower heads in early spring, cut back to the firm pair of buds which will all grow on to flower.

92 Hydrangea growing in a tub— and no flowers

A Hydrangea I have growing outdoors in a tub did not flower last summer. Do I leave it as it is or cut it down?

First, read and think about the answers to questions Nos. 89 and 90. Hydrangeas respond to good feeding and your plant is growing in a tub. Therefore it is likely that the soil in the tub is exhausted and your shrub is starved.

Follow the advice given for dividing and replanting. As it has had a bad time during the summer, mollycoddle the plant for a year or two, move the tub into a sheltered position during winter and give an extra feed every other week or so with a quickly assimilable liquid manure. Sangral, Bio or Maxicrop would do, but as these are available in various forms use the one that has balanced proportions of N, P and K—the figures will be printed on the side of the bottle; don't buy a product if the figures are not provided. When the plant is responding you can help further with foliar feeding but do remember that foliar feeding is only an added help to a plant that is working and thriving and in no way replaces the natural method of nutrient intake via the roots. In early spring, merely trim back any winter withered shoots to healthy swelling buds.

Finally, never forget that your plant is in a tub and can dry out much more quickly than the natural ground. Keep it watered regularly.

93 Hydrangea: flowers that don't colour properly

I own two Hydrangeas which are in pots. They were pink but have both turned to green. Can you help?

This is not unusual. What you probably regard as flower petals in the Hydrangea are not petals at all. Botanically, they are modified leaves and therefore it is not so surprising that when they have finished their splendid colour period, they should revert to their basic function whilst they still have life in them. They make chlorophyll and turn green before finally withering to the familiar winter straw colour. Some varieties do this more noticeably than others. Soil conditions also have an effect and of course weather plays a big part as well— a mild late summer encourages the condition.

There is nothing basically wrong but growing in a pot could mean that the soil is getting played out. I should consider re-potting with fresh compost, plenty of peat and a good mixing-in of a balanced nutrient compound, such as Humber Eclipse. Or if you decide to carry on for a little while without re-potting, scratch some Eclipse or Growmore into the soil surface two or three times whilst the season's growth is forming. This will ensure that it doesn't go short of food, and allow its 'bloom' to go prematurely green because it is hungry. As soon as the buds begin to form, stop the Humber feed, which will go on acting for another three to four months; instead, scratch in a teaspoonful of sulphate of potash, water it in lightly and repeat again in a fortnight. This will put extra colour into its cheeks and encourage the flowers to hold it and not go prematurely green. See also Nos. 89, 90 and 91.

94 Hydrangea : growing the climbing kind

*How should I care for a climbing Hydrangea (*Hydrangea petiolaris*) planted against a north-facing wall?*

Although there are many plants that sprawl, ramble and clamber over supports like fences, sheds and tree stumps, there are very, very few that actually climb unaided. One that does, perhaps surprisingly, is a member of the same family as the familiar potted Hydrangea.

H. petiolaris doesn't like dryness at its roots and this is what it can suffer if you plant it close in to the foot of the wall. Don't be put off by thinking that the soil is moist enough because the surface looks moist after rain; it's what it's like three or more feet down that matters.

If you have any doubt, move it farther away before it becomes too established and take the opportunity—your last—to get plenty of moisture-retaining humus underneath it. Or you can sink in two or three 9 in. pots nearby and make a point of filling them from the hose pipe once a fortnight in the growing season. Do this regularly and don't go by dry spells.

Don't expect it to make a lot of top growth in the first year after planting when it will be preoccupied with making root and becoming established. After this, it will climb unaided by means of ivy-like suckers that arise on the stems whenever they rub against a wall or other support.

The white 'hydrangea' bloom heads are at their best in June and this is one of the best subjects for covering an old stump or climbing through the branches of a host tree. Pruning is not necessary unless it becomes invasive through windows and other openings.

95 Ivy : does it kill trees?

We let an ivy grow up into our oak tree. Now the tree looks unwell. It lost its leaves in September and the branch tips are dying. Is this the ivy's fault?

A lot of controversy rages around the question as to whether ivy kills a tree when it is allowed to climb up into it. Scientific investigation will have it that the ivy does no harm and that when the tree does have ivy on it, it is dying anyway. Ivy, they say, is not a parasite and the masses of sucker-like roots that attach it to the host tree are merely anchoring the ivy and, as such, do not take anything from the tree.

That may or may not be true, say the other school, and it certainly seems a remarkable coincidence that the ivy only selects those trees that are destined to die shortly, despite outward healthy appearances. The indisputable fact is that one does not often see a healthy tree smothered in ivy and that all too often we do see that the trees that are so smothered are dead—or nearly so. Parasite or not, smothering light or not (and I have never heard of an oak tree being deprived of light which is blacked out by ivy, but I have seen far too many dead trees festooned with ivy except near the branch ends where the leaves are) it is always wisest to play safe.

Cut through all the ivy stems near the ground and pull away as much as you can, as high as you can get with safety to yourself. Always be careful when climbing ladders! Never let ivy get a stranglehold and if the ivy is so thick on the ground as to constitute a danger of recurring attack, put a check on it by spraying around with paraquat weedkiller.

Whether ivy has been the cause of your tree's trouble is not quite certain. Is it an old tree, showing signs of a final decline, or a younger one growing in conditions that are not ideal and not conducive to longevity? Does it show signs of nutrient shortage? Is your soil sandy and too well-drained, indicating dryness at roots? These are all possible causes of an ailing tree that should be looked for and put right. If the tree is young enough to suggest that it would respond, and is worth the experiment, try spreading a balanced long-lasting manure such as Humber Eclipse or the quicker-acting Growmore, 2 ozs. per square yard over the entire area covered by the tree; do this three times, a month apart, each spring commencing early March. Place the hose close to the roots and let it dribble slowly, moving it around every couple of hours or so.

96 Japonica : should it be pruned?

I have moved to a house with a small garden and it has a japonica. I would like to train it round the door, but I have never had one so I don't know what to do. Has it to be clipped or pruned?

The word 'japonica' applies to a great many plants and merely means 'originating from Japan' in the same way that 'sinensis' or 'chinensis' means originating from China. In common parlance, however, the name Japonica has come to be associated with the popular spring-flowering Quince. This has undergone a lot of name changes in recent years; it used to be called Cydonia and several nurseries still offer it under that name. However, the correct name is *Chaenomeles* and your plant will most likely be a named variety of the species *speciosa* or the hybrid × *superba*.

The quinces are particularly suitable for training against walls. However, they are not climbers in the sense that they adhere to the wall like ivy or twist and twine like a runner bean. In time the shrub will become woody and stand of its own volition but it is always best to train young growth to wires and this is all you will need to train it around your door. Pruning should be kept to a convenient minimum, merely shaping and confining to size where necessary immediately after flowering. All quinces are hardy and grow well in practically any soil, but thrive best in full sun.
See *No. 230.*

97 Jasmine and loss of bloom

Why do you think my summer Jasmine (Jasminum officinale) makes plenty of leaves but few flowers? I tend it well with artificial fertilisers and each November I cut it back drastically.

This beautiful climber which is a very, very old favourite in cottage gardens and surprisingly hails from Tibet, throws its fragrant white flowers best where it can clamber about on a support in a sunny position. By 'feeding well' and 'pruning drastically' you are doing your best to ensure that it doesn't bloom. Pruning is best confined merely to thinning-out weak or overcrowded shoots, leave alone the long stems which remain. Drastic cutting will only produce a lot of leafy shoots as the plant tries to reassert its natural habit and, of course, the fertilisers don't exactly help as they also encourage a lot of leafy growth. You must give the plant a chance to live its own natural life: no more fertilisers since it has had enough to last it for years. No more drastic pruning: make it work for its living and you should get masses of bloom.

98 Laburnum: when it becomes too dry at root level

Two Laburnum × vossii trees about fourteen years old have always produced masses of bloom about Whitsun-tide. For the last two years, however, neither tree produced any blossom. They appear to be healthy, except at the points where the blossoms would normally appear. Here the leaves are somewhat shrivelled. I was recommended to feed with sulphate of ammonia, but it has made no difference. Can you explain what has happened?

This really is a good example to prove the point which you should always follow in gardening, viz, before you do anything—stop, think and ask yourself why are you going to do this? What are you trying to do? What actually is going to result from your action? If you cannot give yourself correct and sensible answers, don't do it! If you don't really understand what you are doing; leave it alone, and find out! Don't follow other people's recommendations unless they make sense to you.

What was the sulphate of ammonia supposed to do? It supplies nitrogen and because it is quick-acting, the effect is more like a short-acting tonic than a long-lasting feed. In a case like this where the plant is ailing from another cause, it can do more harm than good by prompting a burst of energy that the plant has not the resources to sustain. Furthermore, the absurdity of the advice given to you will be seen when you consider that Laburnums belong to the botanical order called Leguminosae (others in the order are peas, beans, sweet peas, vetch and clover) which has a peculiar ability to use nitrogen that has been 'fixed' from the atmosphere in the soil by special bacteria that are within the root-systems. In other words, they have their own independent nitrogen supply, so what is the point of putting down more?

I don't think there is much doubt that your Laburnums are very thirsty. Consider: they are fourteen years old, they have been growing all this time and have reached the stage where their increasing demands on the moisture supply around them have proved too much. It sometimes happens that this explanation is given when the recent weather has been wet and one risks being thought a bit strange, but the fact is that the flower buds of Laburnums, as well as many other subjects, form on the previous year's growth and a period of severe or sustained dryness at the roots will affect the development of the buds. The bloom fails because of adverse conditions months before.

The problem can be accentuated by planting near a wall or building so that they are shaded from rain. *L.* × *vossii* is a very much better form than the common type and is well worth taking some trouble with to get the glorious golden-yellow bloom—so spare your trees a thought during dry weather. It takes little trouble to lay the hose near them and let it dribble for a few hours—slowly, so that the soil gets a good soaking but does not become a muddy mess.

Finally, do remember—especially where children are about who could pick up seeds— Laburnum is poisonous. See *No. 553*.

99   Lavender: some plants will never bloom

I planted a lavender bush four years ago as part of a scented garden. It has made a lot of growth in that time, but has never flowered. Is there anything I can do and if I plant another, what is the best variety for scent and flowers?

Try by all means to get this shy bloomer to do its stuff, but I wouldn't waste much more time before grubbing it out. It sounds as if it could be growing too well, making all leaf and stem.

It could be that the soil is nitrogen-high, but unless you are putting down fertilisers it is most unlikely that a soil would remain nitrogen-high for four years.

However, to combat this possibility, try several dressings of sulphate of potash from early spring to mid to late summer—about 1 oz. every two to three weeks sprinkled around the plant and lightly scratched in. Potash is a ripener and hardener of plant tissues and would be an encouragement for the plant to start to bloom. You can also try shock treatment by giving it a good clipping all over, removing about a third of the old wood, but no more than that. If this heavy treatment doesn't bring bloom, I doubt that it ever will, so out with it and plant anew.

I have never seen a blind lavender, but I have heard of it several times and it is quite possible that yours is one of these unfortunates.

Most of the lavenders give some scent and among the best is Old English Lavender, *Lavandula spica*, once grown extensively in southern England, especially on the outskirts of towns where it was in demand as a welcome change to the unpleasant odours of mediaeval life. This species has been developed into many varieties of height and colour, probably the most highly scented being 'Grappenhall' a vigorous form that can get up to $3\frac{1}{2}$–4 ft. tall. Another form 'Vera' is usually referred to in the trade as Dutch Lavender and is not quite so vigorous as 'Grappenhall', and has broader leaves.

The strongest smell without doubt comes from *L. stoechas*—the French Lavender and the one mostly used in the French perfume industry. You may not find it quite so suitable for your scented garden because it is a dwarf that can hardly be called a shrub. The flowers are purple and form a dense head. Native to the Mediterranean area, it needs a warm, dry growing season, so if you do plant it, give it the sunniest position you can find. It may be difficult to find a nurseryman who can supply the genuine thing, but it's worth finding. A few leaves and flowers chopped up in a little sachet and placed in a cupboard soon pervades the room with a delightful aroma.

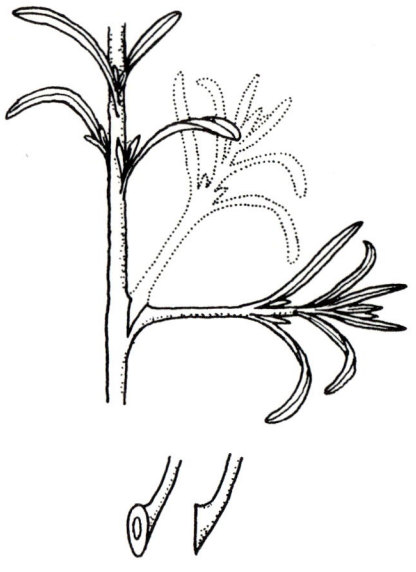

No. 100 *Cuttings propagated by taking a 'heel'. Bend down a young side shoot as shown until it snaps away, taking a 'heel' of the main stem with it. With a sharp knife or razor, trim the face of the heel smooth, dip into hormone rooting powder and the cutting is ready for striking into pots or nursery rows.*

100 Lavender hedges and pruning

I need advice on the culture and pruning of a lavender hedge which has been neglected over the past three or four years.

Lavender is extraordinarily reluctant to make new growth from old wood, and hard cutting back in an effort to repair neglect often—no, invariably—kills the plant. Therefore, it should never be neglected and allowed to become overgrown, old and unruly because this can only shorten the time before the plant becomes worn out and has to be replaced. On the other hand, you can prolong the useful life of the plant by sensible pruning.

Don't use hedging shears; a good cropping all over which is so often advocated is crude and downright lazy. If you want good lavender, you will have to prune properly. During late August and using secateurs, deliberately and selectively snip out all flowered shoots to just above their point of origin. It is inevitable that the plants will gradually grow out, and with no new shoots being produced from the old wood they must eventually become bare and 'leggy'.

Fortunately they root easily in September from short cuttings of firm non-flowered shoots taken with a heel, trimmed smooth with a razor blade, dipped in hormone rooting powder and dibbered firmly either into a cold frame or into open ground where they can be covered by a cloche during harsh winter weather. When these have been planted out and made up into nice young plants, you can strip out the old hedge and replace with one of your own propagation.

However, if you don't want to wait whilst you produce your own replacements, and would prefer to buy in young plants, contact a good lavender specialist.

101 Lawson's conifer: does it harbour pests?

I have been asked by a new neighbour to remove some Lawson's conifers from between our bungalows 'because they harbour pests and diseases harmful to woodwork in the house'. Is there any truth in this?

It is most unlikely that your neighbour's fears are justified. Most conifers are remarkably free from pests and diseases because the resin in their foliage, stems and trunks repels most insects. Wood-boring beetles—and this is what they are evidently afraid of—usually spread out from dead or dying trees or branches and so there is just a glimmer of justification.

Lawson's cypress—*Chamaecyparis lawsoniana*—has an unfortunate habit, especially when growing in association with others in a hedge or screen, of the foliage dying from the bottom up. At one time, it was planted extensively as an alternative to the common privet and the sight of hedges and informal screens, with their lower regions severely and horribly browned and dead, is all too common. The hybrid Leyland's cypress, × *Cupressocyparis leylandii*, does not have this fault, and in addition, being much quicker growing, is much more in demand than Lawson's.

If your trees are affected by this die back of the lower older growth, there could be some insect or beetle attack, but I would have thought that the trees would have had to be so close to your neighbour's building to present risk from insects, as to give them better reason to complain by loss of light. If there are any that are dying, you should consider cutting them down—at least it would help to appease your neighbours a little—but if the trees are healthy, your neighbours have nothing to fear.

102   Leyland's conifer: popular for hedging

Last year I planted a screen of × Cupressocy-paris leylandii *evergreen conifers. The planting positions were prepared beforehand, precautions at planting time and aftercare have been careful. The trees seemed to get away well right from the beginning and have grown remarkably well. However, I am now getting worried by what appear to be little growths near the tips of many of the leaves and, when I brush past them, there seems to be a little cloud of dust. Could this be some fungus disease that is attacking my trees?*

The probable explanation is that your conifers are in flower. If you look very carefully, perhaps with a magnifying glass, you will be able to discern that the little growths are, in fact, minute catkin-like flowers that emit a small cloud of pollen as you brush them. Both male and female flowers appear at about the same time, and later in summer you may see little cones form. No action is necessary; indeed, the appearance of bloom in this way so soon after planting is evidence of the way that they are thriving and testimony that proper preparation beforehand and good aftercare are very worthwhile. See *Nos. 65* and *66.*

An object lesson, I might add, to the many people who, despite all the advice available, simply dump their plants in holes, and when they fail to grow, complain bitterly.

103   Lilac suckers: no use growing them for blooms

Last autumn I planted six lilac tree suckers taken from a deep purple-flowered variety. I've now been told they won't bloom. What do you think?

Well, they will bloom one day but it could be very much later than sooner and then you'll quite likely be so disappointed with the bloom that you'll wish you hadn't bothered to wait. It all depends upon how the parent plant was propagated. If it was layered from its own parent, then it is on its own roots and your young suckers are 'vegetative' parts of their parent and will be exactly the same. How long they will take to bloom will depend upon how long they take to mature enough to carry the bloom. It could be three years or as much as five or six.

On the other hand, if the parent tree was grafted, then your suckers are vegetative parts, not of the dark purple top 'scion' which you probably expect, but of the lower root or 'stock' part which as likely as not would be the common lilac, *Syringa vulgaris.*

If you do not know which way the parent tree was propagated, look at the base of the stem just above soil level. If it was grafted, you should be able to see a swollen scar or definite join mark where the graft union was made. If this is not clear, then it is probably a layer on its own roots and began life in the same way as the suckers you have taken. If you cannot identify either way, all you can do is to wait and see what happens to your suckers.

However, I think it would be wisest to scrap these suckers and plant properly propagated plants obtained from a good nurseryman. You can then be sure that you will receive good quality stock, but why stick to all deep purple? You can make your collection much more interesting by growing other colours as well.

104   Lilac: patches on the bloom

I have a double white lilac tree, the flowers of which tend to brown even before they have fully turned from pale green to pure white. Is there anything I can do to prevent this?

Browning is a problem that is more noticeable with white bloom than with the colours because of the contrast of brown scorch against white, but it is prevalent with all cultivated lilacs. The reason why, takes little deduction. The lilac is usually very floriferous, and with a lot of bloom giving off a lot of fragrance at a time when the tree is in full leaf, adds up to a very large surface area that is transpiring a lot of moisture which, of course, has to be replaced within the plant. When in full bloom, or coming up to it, the lilac is pulling hard on the moisture in the soil and it is therefore very prone to dryness at the roots. When this happens, and the tree is perhaps put under stress by strong drying wind, the bloom is the first to suffer and shows it by browning. In quick-draining soils the problem will be very common.

This shows how important it is to prepare the site properly before planting, by digging in an abundance of peat, compost or other moisture-retaining organic material. You can't dig it under the roots once it is planted; all you can do then is to mulch very heavily so that a blanket of organic matter delays drying out and itself is gradually carried down into the soil by earthworms. Don't try digging it in around a lilac because you are bound to damage the shallow roots and the wounds will encourage a lot of suckers. As soon as you can discern the embryo bloom buds developing at the shoot tips in early spring, lay the hose-pipe to the base of the tree and let it dribble slowly without it creating a puddle. Do this for a couple of hours twice a week until blooming is over and unless your lilacs are growing in a very exposed position which, at this stage, it will be something you can't do much about, you should have no further trouble from the browning of the bloom.

105   Lilac : overgrown and straggly

We have a badly neglected and unpruned lilac, about ten years old. It has so many stems we cannot find the main one and it produces very few flowers. What can be done with it?

You have a difficult task on your hands or, at best, a hard decision to make. Choice varieties of lilac are propagated either by grafting shoots of them on to the more vigorous rootstock of the common lilac *Syringa vulgaris*, or by cutting or layering in which case they grow on their own roots.

As often happens with budding and grafting —and you can see this for example in roses, fruit trees, and many ornamental trees and shrubs—the vigour of the rootstock is greater than the grafted-on scion. The top part of the graft cannot take all the upthrust energy, and the bottom half bursts out by sending up its own growths, called 'suckers'. These often make roots of their own and, of course, suckering is a natural method by which many plants spread and multiply.

When it happens to a grafted plant, you must rip off the sucker and confine the rootstock's vigour in its own strait-jacket, because if the rootstock can by-pass the restriction of the graft by putting up enough of its own stem and foliage, it will increasingly neglect the scion top graft which, increasingly deprived, gradually declines and withers.

You must not cut suckers—that is merely a form of pruning and many shoots will form from the healing tissue at each clean cut. This is why you must also be very careful not to cut or snag lilac roots with a spade when digging nearby; a sucker shoot is almost bound to spring from such a wound. Suckers must be ripped away from the root, and the rough wound then painted with an antiseptic, anti-fungal paint like Arbrex. What you have to find out next is whether the original top graft of your tree is still alive, if indeed there was one at all, and whether ten years of neglect has ruined it. The way to do this is to try to send up a massive injection of vigour by removing as many of the useless suckers as you can. The smaller, weaker ones you can pull away but after ten years some wood will, of course, be too thick and will have to be sawn off. Do this during the winter and watch out carefully for signs of variation in any bloom that is carried in the spring.

Tie a label on all shoots carrying bloom so that you will know, the following winter, whether it is different and stays, or the old common colour and comes out. Any new growth that occurs from ground level must be pulled and you may have to keep this up for a couple more years to give a graft fair chance to show whether or not it is still alive. This may sound a great deal of trouble to go to, and then comes your difficult decision—is it all worth it, or is it better to take the bull by the horns—that is, to heave out the lot, with mattock and spade, clear the site and make a completely fresh start.

You can then choose the colour bloom you want and have it the first year after planting. Read *Nos. 103* and *104* which are also relevant.

106 Liquidambar, aptly named for its autumn foliage.

Is Liquidambar a shrub or a tree? And what kind of soil, cultivation and pruning does it require? Does it need full sun or can it tolerate shade?

Liquidambar is a small genus of three species and as many again varieties of small medium-size trees, so handsome in their brilliant autumn colouring as to be a literal translation of their name, liquid amber. They will grow in a variety of soils but not chalk or severely alkaline. *L. styraciflua* from the eastern part of North America, where it is called Sweet Gum, is by far the most commonly grown and in nursery catalogues virtually exclusively so. It is therefore most likely to be the species that you have.

Given a sheltered position in the soil type it prefers—mildly acid, high moisture-retaining capacity, but well-drained, i.e. a mature woodland glade on a hillside—it can get up to 50 ft. or more. *L. styraciflua* usually takes about eight to ten years to reach a stage of maturity to give really good autumn colouring, but before then it will have begun to produce curious horny bark that forms on twigs and branches in long ridges.

Pruning is not necessary but if you have to correct the shape of the tree as it grows, wait till all the leaves have dropped and the tree is dormant, usually by mid-November or a little later if the weather has been mild. Certainly don't prune in spring when the sap is rising, because although Liquidambars are not maples, although often confused with them, they are alike in the respect that cutting when the sap is rising can cause 'bleeding' as the sap exudes and forms a gummy mess. This is very seriously debilitating especially to a young growing tree and I have seen it happen many times after March winds have blustered and hacked at the nursery rows.

The brilliant autumn gold and amber colouring derives from the breakdown of sugars and starches built up in the leaves during summer and as these can only be built up in sunlight, it follows that the best colours come when the tree is planted where it can receive full sunlight. This is a lovely subject for giving form and colour contrast to neighbouring trees and shrubs, and also makes a fine lone-standing specimen on a lawn.

107 Magnolia unhappy in chalky soils

The Magnolia × soulangeana *I planted on my chalky soil last year died within six months. What went wrong? I am told that* M. stellata *would do better; what do you think?*

There are a great number of species of Magnolia and even more hybrids and crosses. Most of them dislike lime but not all by any means; indeed, one or two positively thrive on the stuff. However, most people when planting Magnolias will choose *soulangeana*, almost as though it were the only Magnolia to grow. In full bloom, it is a spectacular sight but although moderately lime-tolerant it would rather be without it to give off its best. Your chalky soil however is much too much for *soulangeana*, so don't try to grow it again.

Furthermore, Magnolias tend to have soft, fleshy roots which do not like disturbance and which die-back if damaged. This could be an additional cause of the quick death of your tree; so next time, handle your Magnolia very carefully and plant in lots of soft peat.

There are two Magnolias that you could try that are not all that unlike *soulangeana* as regards size and stature, and which are sufficiently lime-tolerant to be worth a try. *M. kobus* is a very hardy species from Japan, whose flowers are white and slightly fragrant but which, although borne with extraordinary freedom when it does start blooming, will take twelve years or even longer to mature and bloom for the first time. The second is a hybrid grown with conspicuous success in, and named after, a world-famous garden, Highdown, in Sussex, constructed and planted by its owner the late Sir Frederick Stern, which proves that a beautiful garden can be grown on chalk. *Magnolia × highdownensis* bears large, pendant, fragrant, white flowers. It received an Award of Garden Merit in 1936 and is without doubt your best bet. *Magnolia stellata* is considered by many to be better on lime soils than *soulangeana* but bearing in mind the rapidity with which your tree died, I should think that your conditions are too severe for it.

Read *Nos. 65, 66* and *109*—there is much in them which applies to your problem.

108 *Magnolia: lichen does little harm*

Last year I bought a young Magnolia soulangeana *sapling and I have just noticed what seems to be a dark and pale green fungus on the stem and branches. Could you advise me of the treatment required for this?*

'Dark and pale green'—this is virtually certain to be not a fungus, but lichen and it is unlikely to have any detrimental effect on your Magnolia. Lichen is usually a sign of damp, humid conditions, but can also be encouraged, as can moss, to grow prolifically on walls and roofs as well as trees by local conditions. Perhaps the most frequently encountered local condition is an incinerator in which large quantities of paper are burnt; when surfaces are wet from rain, smoke and ash 'stick' produces exactly the right kind of fertility for mosses and lichens to thrive. Maybe that is a clue for you to watch out for.

I don't object to lichen and feel that it adds to the 'naturalness' but it is all a matter of personal taste—if you regard it as unsightly and want to remove it, you can get rid of it quite easily by brushing with a solution of ferrous sulphate made by dissolving 2 oz. to the gallon, or by brushing with a weak, half-

strength tar oil wash. In either case, the job should be done during early winter and full dormancy. Treat only the woody stems; don't let these washes get on to green shoots or foliage because it will cause brown scorch and do unsightly damage. A good practical tip when doing this job is to reach into the shrub to paint the centre and main stem first, working out gradually towards the outside. This way you'll keep your sleeves dry; getting even weak tar oil on soft, white forearms isn't at all comfortable.

109 *Magnolia: precautions to take when moving*

When can I move a young Magnolia to another part of the garden?

Magnolias have fleshy roots that tear and damage easily and they react badly to growth check. The usual planting time for trees and shrubs is late autumn and therefore has to be modified in the case of Magnolia. Depending upon the weather and early spring temperature, sometime in March or April when the soil is warming up is normally regarded as the optimum planting time. Or you can plant earlier than usual in the autumn whilst the soil is still warm, but not in winter when it is cold.

Read *Nos. 65* and *66* to appreciate the importance of preparation beforehand. There will not be a lot of foliage yet, unless it has been exceptionally mild and wet, so there won't be so much need for transplanting spray. Everything else will have to be done thoroughly; the new planting position prepared and the sheet underneath etc. Immediately before lowering into the planting hole, peel back the sheet, so that you can examine the soil ball for broken root ends. Trim any broken or ragged roots with secateurs, and then lower the root ball into a good thick bed of moist peat. Backfill little by little, making quite firm as you go.

After-care is important; planted in spring, foliage will shortly be developing fast and you have only an impaired root system to sustain it. Mulch heavily to conserve soil moisture and hoe in three 2 oz. dressings of Humber Eclipse four weeks apart, beginning a couple of weeks after planting. Don't let the shrub dry under any circumstances, and if a dry spell sets in during the first twelve months, give the foliage a thorough wetting in late evening so that it remains wet during the cool of the night. This helps to reduce transpiration loss and keep the foliage firm and turgid.

110 Maples do not like draught and wind

An Acer palmatum '*Atropurpureum*' *growing in an open position in my garden had half its young leaves badly cut by frost in the late spring, and died. This was replaced the following year and the plant appeared to be well-established. But in July, all the leaves shrivelled up and dropped, and the plant seems almost dead. Can you advise me please?*

Japanese maples are tender, but so beautiful that they are worth considerable effort to try to provide the rather exacting conditions that they need to grow well. They detest high winds, especially cold winters; they need light but not full sun, and they need plenty of moisture but not water-logging.

This can be interpreted as a soil containing organic moisture-retaining material, and shelter from other trees which are large enough to give partial shade. A woodland setting, whilst being the best culturally, is also the best in which to appreciate them. A canopy of trees overhead permits shafts of sunlight to high-light the lovely colours of their foliage. Whilst a woodland setting would be ideal, it is not very practicable in a small garden and this is where the fascination of gardening comes in. You have to contrive to get as near to the ideal as you can.

A. palmatum 'Atropurpureum' is a small, almost dwarf-growing subject, so that even in a small garden it should be possible to find a space between some protective neighbours. This is preferable to the advice, sometimes seen and heard, to wrap them in hessian or plastic sheeting during winter because you merely convert the shrub into a sail to catch the full force of the wind and do worse damage than before.

It seems to be the most likely explanation that exposure to winds has caused your losses, and before risking another, you will have to consider whether the steps that you can take towards providing ideal conditions are worth another try. If you do, take the opportunity to put plenty of peat or compost into the soil beforehand, but also pay very particular attention to getting the planting depth exactly the same as in the nursery. Maples are sensitive to being planted too deeply. If the new plant has a wrapped root ball, you'll be able to see a soil mark on the main stem. If pot-grown, both pot and ground levels will be the same. Never, never, never let the root ball dry out at any time—it is absolutely fatal.

The dead wood of maples seems to be readily attacked by the coral spot fungus; you can often see it as small coral pink spots or clusters growing on decayed timber. Any damaged or dead shoots or stems should therefore be cut back at once to healthy and living wood. To leave them is to risk a spread of coral spot into existing healthy wood.

111 Metasequoia, the Fossil Tree

Could you please advise me about a specimen conifer that is supposed to be very rare. I only know it as Dawn Redwood. It appears to be growing well, and is over 8 ft. high but the top 12 inches or so are bending over and I wonder if it will ever straighten up. Would it help to stake it?

There are several conifers whose leading shoot does tend to flop over; indeed, in some cases, all the growing tips flop and hang with beautiful effect. There are some notable examples among the larches and the very beautiful Fountain Tree *Cedrus deodara*, and the blue-grey *Chamaecyparis* 'Boulevard' are well known.

Dawn Redwood has an upright habit and although it sometimes has this floppy leading shoot, it is by no means common. It is possibly due to the speed of the growth, and because the soft new tissue is not strong enough to hold an upward-pointing position, it flops over. Generally, as the growth hardens and becomes thicker, the shoot straightens out but the extreme tip may still bend over. One can sometimes see a kink in the otherwise quite straight main stem, although this is usually absorbed by the growing trunk and disappears as the years go by.

It would certainly help to keep the leading tip straight if you lightly looped it to a 4–5 ft. bamboo cane. The young trees will not be strong enough to place a ladder against so always use a step ladder to do this job. You should gradually move the cane up to keep pace with the growing tip, keeping it straight as it grows.

Dawn Redwood is the modern common name that does justice to a most beautiful tree and is easier to pronounce than its tongue-twisting botanical name *Metasequoia glyptostroboides*. Deciduous, the new foliage is pink in spring, light green in summer and turns to pink-gold in autumn. It was common throughout the world several millions of years ago and is thought to be responsible for most of the world's coal deposits. The tree was considered quite extinct, like the fossil fish Coelacanth, until a few trees were discovered in the remote regions of Hupeh province in China in 1941. Assuming that you can somehow get up to the 30 ft. maximum height you desire, I don't think you will have much problem in limiting its height but you will have to head it back two or three times a year. It may react by growing wider, and you will then have to trim all round to preserve its natural shape since it will clearly show that it has had its head taken off.

112 Mini-shrub border for a small garden

In my garden I have a border measuring 3 ft. by 5 ft. facing south, which I have previously planted with annuals. But now I would prefer to plant it permanently with small shrubs. Could you suggest some suitable kinds for this purpose, preferably which will provide interest from spring to autumn.

If your soil is acid, you can do no better with a small area like this than plant a few of the dwarfer kinds of heather, chosen for variation in bloom, foliage and season, or a small collection of dwarf Azaleas.

If your soil is alkaline, you could grow the dwarf *Berberis thunbergii* 'Atropurpurea Nana' with *Arundinaria pygmaea*, a dwarf bamboo, to give form and colour contrast. *Caryopteris clandonensis* will give you a further contrast of grey-green foliage and intense blue bloom in late summer, but plant it in the centre of the bed as it can get up to 2 ft. *Genista* 'Peter Pan' has bronzy-red flowers and gets up to 1½ ft. and the *Fuchsia* 'Tom Thumb'—not usually thought of as a subject for shrub planting—is suitable nevertheless because it is both dwarf and hardy. *Lavandula* 'Munstead Dwarf' has intense violet-blue bloom and is never much more than 18 ins. high or even shorter. If you can find a supplier, try the white dwarf variety 'Nana Alba' which is not to be confused with 'Hidcote' sometimes called 'Nana Atropurpurea'.

Remember that the period over which you can have something in bloom can be considerably extended in a bed of this small size, by underplanting with summer and autumn-flowering bulbs, as well as those that bloom in springtime.

113 Paeonies, tree : care and treatment

My Japanese tree peony is five years old but it hasn't bloomed yet. It is planted against a west-facing fence, and during winter I have been covering it at night with a polythene sheet, but wonder if this is sufficient protection. Also, does it need any special feeding?

There are several species of 'tree peonies', but the term is more commonly applied to *Paeonia suffruticosa*—sometimes called the Moutan tree—and its varieties, the blooms of which are amongst the most gorgeously coloured of all shrubs. Whilst quite hardy through even severe winters, the early growth and emerging buds are susceptible to frost, which so often occurs well into the spring. Unless it is a thick gauge, I doubt whether polythene film is protection enough—it needs something more substantial. Each evening that frost threatens, drape a screen of hessian or sacking in addition to the plastic. On a free standing plant, a screen may be erected in wigwam fashion on a tripod of bamboo canes. Remove the covering each morning when the frost has lifted, and as soon as growth has hardened and the night frosts passed, the screens may be put away till next year.

It may seem to be a lot of trouble but, like the Camellia which has the same frost-prone problem with its flower-buds, the glorious show of bloom is worth any trouble. Given full sun and a site reasonably sheltered from cold winds, they thrive best in a light, well-drained soil that has had plenty of organic matter applied. Put this down as a mulch, each early spring after a light dressing of a balanced fertiliser such as Growmore or Humber Eclipse.

Tree peonies usually take at least three or four years from planting to come into bloom so there is nothing very unusual in a five-year wait. Pruning should be avoided as far as possible, being confined basically to the removal of weak or dead shoots, or those that are badly positioned. Do this as soon as flowering finishes so that the maximum summer time is left for fresh growth to mature.

114 Pampas grass and disappointing plumes

How can I encourage more luxuriant growth in the pampas grass plant in my garden? It doesn't do nearly as well as it used to.

It sounds as though you have had your pampas for some time, in which case the soil is probably exhausted or the plant needs dividing. Cortaderia hails, as its common name suggests, from the pampas, the high plains of South America, and does best in a rich deep soil with plenty of humus that never dries out. As its place of origin indicates, it likes the sun and warmth. This has to be borne in mind when you select a planting position because this is the last opportunity you will get to put plenty of humus underneath it.

If your plant is large, it will probably have a centre of old leaves and the remains of dead shoots. Lift it in late autumn, split it by implanting two garden forks back to back and levering the two handles together, teasing and easing the clump into two or three pieces. Take the opportunity to dig very deeply, take out a hole at least two spits deep, breaking up the bottom and incorporating plenty of manure, compost or moist peat (never use dry peat because it absorbs the moisture from the soil and robs the plant). Work in about 4 ozs. of a slow-acting balanced manure like Humber Eclipse and if you want really good strong plumes, hoe in about 2 oz. of Eclipse about three or four times—a month apart—during early spring and summer.

You may not get good plumes in the first year after planting; in fact, it would pay you not to let them develop but to conserve and build-up energy. Then you can expect really good plumes in the second and succeeding years.

115 Passion flower—why no flowers?

A passion flower planted three years ago has made lots of twining shoots but there's never a flower. Where am I going wrong?

This plant sounds as though it is living it up too well with its roots unrestricted in too rich a soil. It doesn't feel the need to go to all the trouble of trying to perpetuate its own species by setting seed—i.e. throwing bloom and nourishing a fruit. If you want lots of blooms, you should have planted it in a root restricting pit like a fig (see *No. 189*) but as it is too late to do this with your established shrub, you will have to try to simulate the effect.

Try to obtain some old asbestos sheets from a builders' dump or even the municipal tip; you will need enough to make a box 3 ft. × 4 ft. and about 2½ ft. deep. Whether you will be able to manoeuvre under the plant will depend on how much room you have. You can probably dig a vertical narrow trench and throw the soil to one side without a lot of trouble, but you will not be able to work under the plant from the bottom of the trench without making the trench much wider to give you room to work. However, this is about the size box you will need *in situ*. Dig the sheets into position one side at a time, chopping through any roots that you encounter. Do this after autumn leaf fall, and in February shorten back all main shoots to about half their length, to an outwards facing bud. That should give it the fright of its life and prompt a bit of passion into it. Don't feed it after this—make it work hard for its living.

116 *Peat bank: how to grow lime-haters on chalk and lime soils*

It has always been my ambition to have a lovely show of Azaleas and Rhododendrons, but I will soon be retiring to an area where the soil is chalky and I know that this is supposed to make it impossible to grow these plants. Is there really nothing I can do to grow them?

Azaleas and Rhododendrons put on a spectacular show every spring and the desire to grow them is high on every gardener's list of ambitions, but there is this problem of their not liking lime or chalk in the soil. Of course, they are not alone in that—many other beautiful plants are also lime-haters. However, it doesn't mean that they cannot be grown at all—we have to use a little ingenuity. It is fairly evident that a hole or pocket of peaty acid soil has to be provided, but then often the lime will creep in from the surrounding soil and gradually the plants will languish and succumb. Lining the hole with plastic is a barrier but is not infallible by any means.

The safest solution is to get away from the chalk and lime by building above it—the chalk will not so readily creep upwards. Lay down a sheet of heavy gauge plastic—this should be unbroken and not for instance several plastic bags, which would allow roots to find their way through into the chalk. Build on this an 18–24 in. bank or wall of materials of suitable appearance and to the desired shape and size. Peat blocks are sometimes used but will very gradually weather and crumble. Hypertufa, which you can make yourself (see *No. 524*) is inexpensive and very durable. Fill up the enclosure behind the retaining wall with acid peat soil which will rest on the polythene sheet and as lime cannot creep upwards through this barrier your shrubs are permanently safe from alkaline soil.

You should bear in mind two precautions: firstly, a raised bed is more exposed and plants near the edges will be liable to dry out more quickly than in the ground proper. Secondly, never under any circumstances, use tap water because if the natural soil of the district is too limy for Rhododendrons, it is more than likely that your local water supply will also reflect this. Try, by means of collecting in water butts etc., to conserve rainwater. A good tip is to collect all the drainings from the teapot and use the liquor to water in new plantings. An old wives' tale, but true nevertheless, and by this method in my own garden, I manage to keep a nice collection of Azaleas and other lime-haters in thriving condition where the tap water is not infrequently clouded with lime content.

By the raised bed method, many gardeners have been able to grow and enjoy rich displays of these beautiful plants and others like Camellias, Kalmias, Pieris and Crinodendrons.

117 *Pernettya without berries*

Why does my Pernettya never have berries?

You indicate that you only have one Pernettya and this is the clue to your trouble. Some of the genus are hermaphrodite, but many are unisexual—i.e. plants are either male or female, and it is clear that your plant wants a mate. You will need a lime-free soil if you want it to do at all well, and also a group of about four plants which will include a male form to ensure fertilisation and berries.

The variety *P. mucronata* 'Bell's Seedling' is generally regarded as a hermaphrodite form and is therefore most commonly offered as one that can be relied upon for berries, but as it is predominantly dark red, the planting of this alone will miss out on all the pinks, whites, lilacs and purples for a more varied collection. Much rarer and more difficult to find is a comparatively recent variety listed as 'Davis's hybrids'. The berries are larger and the colour variations very wide. Pernettyas are among the most showy of the dwarf evergreens, very hardy and form a dense thicket of growth about 1½–2 ft. tall which is ideal for ground cover.

118 Philadelphus: the common confusion

My Syringa mock orange is the one with large double white flowers and strong scent. It was fine as a young shrub, but each year as it has grown bigger, the amount of bloom has become less. Why is this?

First, you are a little muddled with your naming. Syringa is the botanical name for *lilac* and not mock orange, the correct name for which is Philadelphus. The confusion is very common, and how it comes about is strange because the two plants are not at all alike.

The double flowers and strong scent, in this case, suggests that the variety is very likely *Philadelphus* 'Virginal' a strong growing very scented variety that received an A.G.M. as long ago as 1926 and despite several later introductions is still the best double-flowered variety.

The gradual deterioration is quite natural in a shrub allowed unrestricted growth; the best bloom and scent is borne by young wood, and to keep a steady supply of new long arching stems you will have to remove wood before it becomes 'old'.

What is 'old'? A good rule of thumb method of determining this, not only with Philadelphus but also with other flowering shrubs such as Buddleia, Deutzia, Forsythia, etc., is to compare the latest growth with an older stem. Whereas the young stem is generally light in colour, and even green as with a rose, the older wood—apart from being thicker—is generally harder and more 'woody' but always darker and either developing, or has already developed, a definite 'bark'.

This is the sign that it is of no further use, and instead of having lots of weak poorly-bearing new growth developing from high up, encourage fewer but stronger and more prolific bearing stems to arise from the base of the plant by taking out the old wood to ground level. Use a saw, don't strain your secateurs.

With a grossly overgrown shrub, there is likely to be too much to come out in one go—pruning does not mean slaughtering. Take a third out immediately after flowering, then next year another third, and the following year the final remains of the old wood, by which time some of this year's 'new growth' will be distinctly woody, and showing signs of being ready for the chop. Try to keep to a regular replacement cycle and in addition to the old, always take out weak or misshapen stems so that by concentrating the plant's energy into constant replacement of strong growth from the base, you will see this lovely shrub at its best.

119 Plumbago needs correct treatment before blooming

Each summer I have stood my Plumbago plants out of doors in their pots, but this year I took them out of the pots and planted them in the ground, thinking this might improve them. However, they have not flowered and there is no sign of any flowers coming. Is this the result of the dull wet summer or would it be better to keep them in their pots in future?

If a Plumbago has been grown in a pot for a few years, maybe with the soil unchanged, it will be in a state of decline due to the gradual exhaustion of the soil. It is therefore a natural reaction to feel that planting into the ground instead of another summer spent in pots would encourage them to make better growth and bloom. As it happens, Plumbago—and many other plants and bulbs—are encouraged into prolific bloom and, in some cases, even to bloom at all, by a different factor altogether.

This is one way of illustrating the principle that plants are alive in much the same way as we are and react to the same stimuli. For example, they do not like conditions that are too hot or cold, too wet or too dry, and plants do not like being overfed or underfed any more than you do. Another similarity is the threat to the life of the individual, the natural reaction being an attempt to ensure perpetuation of the species. This is the 'psychology' that is used when severely wounding a non-fruiting fruit tree to make it throw flowers and seed—i.e. fruit—to ensure another generation before it meets its anticipated death. Severe overcrowding acts in the same way; the plant tries to throw flower and set seed that will then carry on elsewhere and stand a better chance in more congenial conditions. The overcrowding effect is stimulated by the cramped conditions of a pot which is large enough to contain enough soil to sustain the plant but too small to permit a free and unrestricted root run.

The Plumbago bloom is carried on young shoots of the current year's growth and flower bud development can very easily be hampered by cold and strong winds. This is why, when they are used in open beds, they are usually trailed up canes to achieve height and then positioned as contrast 'dot' plants—i.e. dotted or spaced out in a bed. They are not planted out until they are well into bloom and the strong winds of spring have gone. This planting-out is done 'in pot' and not knocked out, so that the root restriction is retained whilst in the beds, and this is where you went wrong. Your plants decided to have a welcome rest from flowering.

You should lift them carefully before the frosts come, remove most of the soil from the roots including much of the original root ball, choose a pot into which the roots can be reasonably closely packed and pot up with a rich compost like J.I. No. 3 with a thick wad of peat at the bottom. In future, when planting potted plants into the open ground, always ensure that the top rim of the pot is an inch or two below soil level in a saucer-shaped depression and never allow the bed to dry out.

A plant in a buried pot like this relies upon moisture that sinks in from above, *not* that soaks in from the sides—which of course it cannot do through a pot. With the plant roots extracting moisture, the pot of soil can soon dry out and if it does, permeated with so much root, it will so literally shed water that if you rely upon a hose pipe to get it wet again, the plants will probably die of thirst whilst you stand hosing them!

If the plants show signs of flagging and wilting, there is only one safe way to save your plants and it is drastic. Lift the pots from the soil and soak in water until the plants firm up again; then replant in a depression and follow the golden rule which is to water regularly every day.

120 Polygonum, the beautiful steam-roller

Can you give me some advice on how and when to prune a Russian Vine?

Once *Polygonum baldschuanicum* becomes established the problem can very easily become one of how to prevent it from taking over the whole garden! It is extremely vigorous and can grow an extraordinary distance in one season. The best time to prune it is towards the end of March, and it can be cut back as hard as you like, but you should bear in mind that the harder you hit it, the more vigorously will it react. It is often planted to cover a fence or provide a screen around an eyesore, and is left to its own devices for years on end. Whilst it undoubtedly performs such functions very well, it usually means that a whole thick mat of withered and decaying growth accumulates. This is not only a haven for birds in which to build their nests, but can also be a haven for overwintering pests and insects. It is a dusty dirty job cleaning away such long accumulated growth, so the obvious answer is not to let it become neglected so that the rubbish accumulates.

Every year, regularly, take out the old wood from the base so that the replacement growth of young bloom bearing stems is constant. Having severed the old stem near the base, follow it into the top growth, pulling out as much as you can and, of course, as much old rubbish as possible.

Pruned hard and regularly, the plant finds an outlet for its vigour in masses and masses of white bloom that completely smothers and hides the foliage. Because of the neglect it so often receives, this plant is seldom seen to its full potential advantage.

121 Pomegranates need an Indian summer to ripen

We have six pomegranate seeds germinating in a 4-inch pot in seed compost. These have been germinated in a propagator, and placed on top of the kitchen water heater to give them warmth. Are these likely to be annuals or not, and are they trees or bushes? Could they be planted out of doors, or should they be kept in pots indoors. Are they likely to bloom, or to fruit?

The pomegranate, *Punica granatum*, is a native of Persia and Asia Minor. It is a deciduous shrub, certainly not an annual, and will grow in this country but requires the encouragement of a south or south-west facing wall. When well-established, the shrub will produce scarlet-orange flowers with crimped petals during later summer, which means it needs to have a long, hot and very late 'Indian summer' to have a chance of ripening any fruit that may form. They would undoubtedly stand a better chance in a greenhouse but there are many more productive plants to occupy such valuable space.

You have done very well indeed to raise seedlings and these should be potted-off singly into 3-inch pots, using a mild compost like J.I. No. 1 at this stage. Then when there is a nice layer of root around the inside of the pot, move it on to a 5-inch pot with a little added nutrient like Humber Eclipse or Growmore. It will then be ready for planting out against a wall in April or May, taking care at all times not to let it dry out.

122 Poplar: the kind with balsam-scented leaves

Would you please identify a tree which has been in my garden for several years? When coming into leaf in spring, it has a lovely smell similar to that of Azaleas, and as the summer progresses it exudes an aromatic sap from the leaf joints. The leaves are rather like those of a lime, but the tree is much more slender. It gets taller each year.

There is not much doubt that this is a Balsam Poplar. Most people think of Poplars as the tall, narrow, very upright trees which are commonly grown as screens and windbreaks—but that isn't the only variety by any means. There are several dozen species of various shapes and sizes, including several that have the characteristic of exuding a balsam-like odour.

Your description seems to whittle the identity of your tree to one probable and one other possibility. First, the probable: *Populus balsamifera* is listed by some as *P. tacamahaca*. It is a large erect-branched tree with large sticky buds that burst into leaves which are whitish on the undersides. The other possible, *P. candicans*—the Ontario poplar—is not so large or upright, and is a broad-headed tree with downy twigs. The leaves of both are strongly aromatic but the differences described should pinpoint the identity of your tree. Both also have the notorious Poplar tendency for invasive roots, see *No. 122*.

123 Poplars: are they dangerous to buildings?

Five years ago we planted seven robusta *poplar trees thirteen yards from our bungalow. Could you tell me if the roots will eventually harm the foundations of the bungalow? Can you advise me how high they could grow?*

Populus robusta is a hybrid and as its name indicates, is a vigorous and fast-growing tree. Apart from sheer speed of growth, poplars also have very extensive root systems that persist in seeking out things like drains and house foundations. A drain run is a potential moisture and nutrient source and, given half a chance, the roots will become positively invasive and damaging—hence the general advice not to plant poplars anywhere near buildings or drain runs.

Certain factors may increase the importance of adhering to this advice. Clay, for instance, shrinks as it dries, and a poplar can drain-off an amazing amount of water from the soil, causing foundations to move, walls to crack and expensive bills to be paid. A vigorous type of poplar will explore considerably further away than its own height in all directions from its own main stem. *P. robusta* can easily reach 50 ft. high. Therefore, you are running a considerable risk with the trees only thirteen yards away and there is little doubt that you must have the trees out before any damage is done. They are still young, and will be relatively easy for you to move and can be replaced by other subjects that will not present the same risks; flowering trees or tall-growing shrubs would do admirably.

124 Pyracantha : why no berries ?

A Pyracantha planted about two years ago has grown well, but has not, so far, had any flowers. Is there any way to encourage it to bloom and set berries next year ?

You are in a little too much of a hurry. Your firethorn is concentrating on getting established before flowering and setting berries. Pyracanthas flower best on about two-year-old spurs. If there are any long sappy shoots, these can be shortened to about a third of their original length. Sprinkle two light dressings, each a month apart, of about $\frac{1}{2}$ oz. of sulphate of potash around the plant in later summer which will help to harden up the wood and encourage the shrub to get on with flowering.

125 Pyracantha : why the berries fall off

My Pyracantha sheds most of its berries before they ripen. Can you suggest what I can do to remedy this ?

When a Pyracantha, and many other plants for that matter, sheds most of its berries—but not all—before they ripen and change colour, the most likely cause is that they are being aborted. That is to say that the pollination was poor at blossom time but the shrub carries on with the natural process of developing its fruit. When it realises that they have not been fertilised and are useless, it has no further need of them—and so it drops them!

The first things to look for then are reasons for bad pollination. If it happens once, or occasionally, you can probably look back to bad weather at blossom time with very few

insects on the wing. If it happens regularly, you will have to think in terms of repeated exposure to bad insect conditions, like a cold windy position since insects don't like being blown about in draughts.

It is probably too late to move the Pyracantha, so you will have to do what you can in helping the insects; the berries you want are the result of their handiwork and nothing else will do the job. A quick-growing conifer or two planted nearby would give some protection which would be helpful.

Another cause of berry dropping is fungus attack—examine the fruits that remain and if they show signs of brown or black spots, you will have to suspect scab. This can cause premature berry drop about July–August when the fungus begins to reach the fructifying stage, and another very close and careful inspection, using a simple magnifying glass, should confirm whether or not the berries are infected.

The best precaution is to spray with Orthocide garden fungicide as soon as the bloom clears and the minute berry pinheads can be seen, and repeat at about ten to fourteen day intervals until the berries are nearly full size. Try to control overwintering of the disease by spraying a winter wash over the plant and the surrounding soil where the berries will have dropped. If it is practicable, clear up and burn all prematurely dropped berries, to try to prevent, or at least interrupt, the overwintering stage.

126 Rhododendron : why no flowers ?

My Rhododendrons were in bloom when I bought them, but have not flowered for the last three years. Growth seems healthy ; what is the trouble ?

This sort of thing is not at all uncommon in the first spring or two after planting and results from the upheaval of transplanting. Bear in mind that the plant is relying upon the ball of soil and root system that it brought with it, and after that flush of bloom that it bore when you first had it, will have been torn between wanting to make fresh root into the surrounding soil, getting established, and beginning the construction of next season's flower and growth buds. It's not surprising, therefore, if the plant has decided to give the bloom a miss and concentrate on growth and getting established during the following year or two.

When the bloom fails for the second time, and even as in the case here, for three years, we have to suspect another but still related cause. The bloom borne in spring comes from the buds that are built-up during the previous summer and autumn—indeed, the embryonic buds are already forming whilst the previous bloom is still there.

A severe check like a dry spell in summer or autumn during the bud development can cause these to abort and, in addition, the as yet under-developed root system is still unable to pull in an adequate moisture supply from deep down. So don't neglect your plants; they flower in spring but need looking after all through the year. Then if they fail to bloom again, you'll have to resort to the shock treatment of wounding in the same way as fruit trees some-times have to be wounded to induce them to bloom and fruit.

127 Rhododendron: why the leaves fall off

My Rhododendron 'Ascot Brilliance' is looking very sorry for itself; its leaves develop small black spots, after which the whole leaf seems to gradually brown off and die. Some have fallen off completely. The plant is growing in a tub in a mixture of soil and peat and I'm sure I'm watering it correctly. Can you suggest what is wrong?

There are many pests and diseases that are not particularly choosy and which will attack plants of different kinds. Plants are also attacked by the 'specialist' pests and diseases which pertain to that one plant, type or species. It sounds as though your Rhododendron is being attacked by one of the latter—a leaf spot fungus called *Glocosporium rhododendri*. The treatment is not unlike that for Azalea gall (see *No. 30*).

Pick off and burn all affected leaves and apply fungicidal sprays. Rhododendrons, some

of the evergreen Azaleas, and indeed many other plants have a thick leathery-textured, glossy leaf, off which water runs very easily. It is difficult therefore to achieve a good 'cover' with a protective spray. This is due mainly to what is called a 'waxy cuticle', that is a waxy skin covering and you can see the same effect when sprinkling water on a cabbage leaf. Add a little washing-up detergent to the spray and you will get a better wetting cover. Also make sure you spray a fine mist since small droplets stick while big droplets bounce off, run together, drip and are simply wasted on the ground.

Leaf spot has a serious weakening effect so try to make it up to your plant with a little extra care and attention to feeding, especially with regard to iron and magnesium.

128 Rhododendron: preparation for planting

I would like to grow Rhododendrons and Azaleas. The acidity of the soil is pH6, and there are docks and other similar weeds. What should be done before planting; if you recommend peat, can you tell me how much to buy?

With a degree of acidity of pH6, you won't need to use peat in order to create acidity but only in regard to soil structure and moisture retention. Adequate moisture after planting is absolutely vital, so if your soil is sandy and well-drained you will need to incorporate plenty of peat—special Rhododendron peat if you can get it or baled moss peat will have to do. Put this into the holes at planting time and also as a thick moisture retaining mulch over the soil surface. Planting and mulching an area of this size could take anything from 80 to 100 bushels, even more would not be wasted.

To prepare the site, all perennial weeds have to be removed; paraquat weedkiller will clear the green tops off. But any with big root systems, like docks, will only grow again and will have to come out anyway, so it is better to leave the tops intact so that you have something to pull on as you dig them out. Most of the smaller weeds will be blanketed out and controlled by the peat mulch layer.

Provided that you can be absolutely sure that no lime-containing materials have been used to 'case' the beds, spent mushroom compost which you can have delivered loose in 6 cubic yard loads or more, is a less expensive substitute for peat but, in either case, money spent in providing depth of mulch that will mask out weeds is money well spent, because apart from the fertility you will be creating, overcoming weeds after the Rhododendrons and Azaleas have been planted and are growing will not be easy.

If the soil is heavy, you will have to make sure that waterlogging does not occur. Should this be likely, you may have to dig trenches across the site and backfill with rubble. Pipes are not likely to be effective because in heavy clay soils, if the water cannot percolate through to the drain pipes, they may as well not be there and trenches are better.

Drying-out within the first two or three years of planting is the biggest danger, so another very important preparation is to ensure either that your mains water is lime-free, or make arrangements with water butts and tanks to collect every drop of rainwater from the roofs; literally, it could be a matter of life and death if you get a prolonged dry spell. In the first few years after planting, rainwater will be worth its weight in gold to you.

129   Rhododendron: rootstock takes over

My 'Lady Clementine Mitford' Rhododendron is being swamped by a thicket of non-flowering shoots which sprout from the base. Is this typical?

For several reasons, many plants like roses, fruit trees and ornamental cherries, are grafted, which, to describe it crudely, means cutting off a vigorous plant's head and putting in its place something that will look better, smell better, taste better or whatever. It is not uncommon to find the bottom 'stock' or root part of this shotgun marriage to be rather dissatisfied with the ability of the top half—the scion—to take all the vigour and energy it wants to give. This is why it quite naturally breaks out of its constraint by sending up its own growth.

This is what is happening with your Rhododendron. If you allow the suckers to remain, the stock will increasingly ignore the choice variety which will become deprived and possibly die.

Therefore, get to the point where this sucker growth emerges from the rootstock. You may have to scrape below soil level to pull the suckers away. Don't cut them since this is merely a form of pruning and they will grow again, worse than ever. Pull them away and treat the open wound with a grafting compound like Arbrex to prevent fungus entry. This should be done early whilst they are young and the stems then pull away easily. If you have left them there too long and you cannot easily pull them off, saw them away leaving the surface rough. This is less conducive to the formation of new shoots, as will certainly happen if you make a smooth clean cut. Protect with Arbrex as above, then replace the soil.

130   Romneya: care of a summer beauty

I've been given a potted Californian tree poppy. Where do you suggest I plant it, and how should I treat it?

Romneya coulteri is a shrubby perennial with leaves deeply cut into segments and solitarily borne large, white, fragrant poppy-like flowers, occasionally as much as six inches across, with a most conspicuous central mass of golden yellow stamens. Like many plants with thick, fleshy, rhizomotous root systems, they are sometimes difficult to get established but once settled in, can spread—sometimes too quickly—by the underground stems (rhizomes).

Our climate can be too severe, especially in the north; therefore select its planting position with care. As its common name suggests, it hails from the western part of North America which is the surest indication about the conditions it requires, i.e. a warm spot out of doors where it can get full sun. Cold winter winds can kill Romneya, so protect it by planting near the south-facing side of a sheltering wall or by surrounding it on all sides by other shrubs, preferably evergreens or those with sufficiently heavy growth to deflect the winter blast.

The ideal planting time is in the autumn, whilst the soil is still warm from the summer; however; container-grown plants can invariably be planted at any time without trouble provided that the weather is not too cold. As its roots like a free run, aim to get it out of its restricting pot as early as you can. If your soil is heavy and at all inclined to be wet, set the roots on a small bed of sand to encourage drainage away from direct contact with the roots. In autumn whilst the soil is still warm from summer, spread a thick mulch layer of peat or compost to blanket in the warmth. The ranging root system usually is able to search out adequate plant nutrients, but if you feel that the plant needs extra feeding, always use a balanced manure, applied sparingly in early spring so that the nutrients become available to the plant some weeks later when it is making growth and throwing its bloom.

131   Santolina : easy to propagate

Could you please identify and tell me something about two plants in my garden? They have furry greyish-white growth, and leaves like no other plant. These have a very curious scent when brushed with the hands. They have small yellow flowers in summer. I should like to know what it is called because I want to get a lot more so I can plant them alongside my drive.

This sounds very much like what was called *Santolina incana*, but it is now called *Santolina chamaecyparissus* and, indeed, its foliage is shaped remarkably like the conifers that bear that name.

Commonly called Cotton Lavender, it is a low-growing, evergreen sub-shrub up to about 1½–2 ft. tall. It is a native of the hot dry areas bordering the Mediterranean and as with all grey and white foliaged plants, the grey and white is the visual effect, either of myriads of hairs or waxy cuticle—see *No. 132*.

You can buy this plant quite cheaply and in quantity to form a low ornamental hedge on a similar scale and manner to normal lavender or, if you wish to propagate your own, young semi-hard shoots pulled away with a heel in late summer and inserted in sandy compost will root very easily. During the winter, put the cuttings in a cold frame or cold greenhouse and plant out in spring.

When the hedge is big enough, an annual light clipping over in spring will help to keep its shape and also encourage side shooting and more yellow button blooms. As these blooms are borne well above the foliage on long stems, it is quite a simple matter to quickly run along the hedge with the trimmer to remove the dead heads after blooming.

132   Santolina : lack of flowers

My twelve bushes of Santolina incana *are now three years old, have a definite greenish colour and haven't had a single bloom on them. Yet the advertisement claimed they would be literally covered with blooms. My soil is well cultivated clay, but it is not well-drained. Would this account for the failure?*

Santolina incana is an out-dated name; the correct name is *Santolina chamaecyparissus*.

Invariably, the silver or grey appearance in plants is due either to minute hairs all over the leaves which makes them feel soft like velvet, or it may be due to what is called 'waxy cuticle', something like a waxy or glaucous skin—hence the words *glauca* and *glaucophyllum* which are sometimes seen in botanical names. This may exist like a thick bloom on the leaf and stem surfaces making them appear grey or even silver. Hairs or wax are just two of the ways in which nature tries to reduce evaporation of moisture from within the plant by creating a barrier to prevent air and wind from coming into direct or close contact with the sap in the plant cells. It is important to understand this because when we see grey or silver leaves, we may fairly deduce that the plant is specially adapted to growing in open, probably very sunny but certainly dry conditions where it has to conserve its moisture.

So there is the first clue to what is wrong with your plants. When greys and silvers get too much water and there is not so much need to conserve moisture, equally there is not so much need to develop hairs or wax. The silver and grey then diminishes and the plant begins to look much more green than it otherwise would. It could well be that your conditions are so wet that your plant's flowering is also being upset. Therefore, using the knowledge that you now have about grey-leaved plants, make them suffer a bit, move them into a hot, dry position which is very well-drained so that they have to work hard to conserve their moisture. The silver-grey colour should then improve and because the plant will become a bit more concerned about its own future, it will do what plants and many animals do when faced with the possibility of death—try to ensure perpetuation of their own species. In the case of the plant, this means putting up flowers as the prerequisite to setting seed. Thus, you can expect to get the masses of yellow button blooms that the advertisement promised you.

133 Senecio : wrong growth habit

I am having a problem with my Senecio greyi—*it was planted for its grey foliage and yellow bloom and, whilst we liked this very much, it is becoming too much of a good thing and spreading all over the place and swamping other plants nearby. Would it be safe to cut it back? It is now nearly 8 ft. wide.*

It is fairly certain that your plant is not *Senecio greyi*—but you can check by the leaves. If they are rounded, then it *is* probably *greyi*, although it is most unusual for it to be behaving like this. However, if they are narrow and pointed, then the species is more likely to be *S. laxifolius*. The one big fault with this species, and one that makes it quite unsuitable for a small garden, is the way it will keep extending its lower branches along the ground, sprawling over everything else. Of course, it makes ideal ground cover and, like all greys, the silver colour is best on poor soils so it is particularly useful for covering sandy banks where hardly anything else stands a chance.

In your case, it sounds as if the plant is sufficiently well-established to take a hard

knock. Have a look at some of the older stems to determine just how far they can be cut back without leaving an irreparable hole, and cut these out as far as you can. Do this just as spring growth is commencing so that any holes or blanks are soon filled in. In future, prune back the branches to a convenient length—this will have the effect of encouraging more laterals and flowering side shoots. To prevent the whole thing becoming a thick overcrowded mess, remove the oldest wood as required. Do not feed or mulch this shrub; it needs to work hard to give of its best.

134 Skimmia : why it does badly when it is lonely

Recently I moved a bush of the evergreen Skimmia 'Foremanii', but it is too large for its present site. It is growing well and we would like to know how much can be safely cut away. Although this variety is supposed to be a hermaphrodite, the bush has only ever carried two berries and it has a decidedly pinkish tinge to the leaves. Apart from planting another Skimmia to encourage cross pollination, is there anything we can do to get more berries?

Most of the Skimmias prefer a rich, well-drained soil that is rather alkaline, and they will generally grow quite well in partial shade. Lack of berries invariably means faulty fertilisation, and factors like cold or draughty positions which do not encourage pollinating insects are therefore suspect. However, as the berry shortage is long-standing and the plant in another position too, we shall have to look deeper.

Hermaphrodite is the word used to describe the many plants that bear both male and female flowers on the same plant. However, there can be marked variations in the proportions of male and female flowers so that some varieties may have a male tendency whilst others are more female. Furthermore, whilst many hermaphrodite plants are self-fertile, much better fertilisation occurs when there is cross-pollination between two separate plants.

The description of your Skimmia being large and having a decidedly pink tinge would indicate that it is not 'Foremanii' but the variety *S. japonica* 'Rubella', and if it carries red buds through the winter that open in early spring into white, yellow anthered flowers, you may be fairly certain that that is what your plant is. *S.j.* 'Rubella' is a predominantly male clone, and this is why you have had so few berries. The solution therefore is to plant, close by, another Skimmia that has a female tendency, and for this you cannot do much better than the true *S. japonica* which will give you plenty of brilliant red fruits. Contact a really good nursery, tell them your problem and exactly what you want.

Concerning cutting your plant back—remember that pruning does not reduce growth but encourages more vigorous shoots to be produced and therefore you must never plant a shrub in a position where it will out-grow the available space. There is, also, the risk that cutting back will remove a lot of your flowering buds.

135 Sorbus, a Mountain Ash

About four years ago, I planted a mountain ash which was then two or three years old. This tree, of weeping form, is growing very slowly and is very limited in foliage. Can you suggest any method of improving it? The tree is in grass and if root pruning can be avoided, this would save damage to the lawn.

The name Mountain Ash is often loosely—and misleadingly—applied to many of the Sorbus genus, a very large family of wide diversity in size from shrubs to trees. Mountain Ash itself, also called Rowan, is correctly *Sorbus aucuparia* but there are a great many varieties of it and at least ten are separately named, and commercially available. Although they do not grow much above small to medium size trees, they are not normally slow-growing.

There are two exceptions however: one is a very upright growing form called *S. aucuparia* 'Fastigiata' (sometimes *S. scopulina*)—a re-markable tree both for its columnar shape and many large branches of bright red berries. The other slow grower is a weeping form *S. a.* 'Pendula' and as this tallies with your

description, this is the most likely identity of your tree.

Apart from its natural habit, soil conditions will also have considerable influence. The Mountain Ash is very tolerant of acid soils but on shallow soils, especially if they are chalky, they are not at all happy or long lived. If this latter description in any way fits your soil, you should try to help your tree by covering the soil beneath its branch spread with a three-inch layer of peat or compost and replenishing it as it is gradually absorbed into the soil by earthworm activity.

Avoid the nearby use of any fertilisers with an alkaline reaction and, of course, don't let lime get anywhere near it. I don't think that you would be justified in root pruning, bark ringing or otherwise wounding a tree so young in order to obtain more foliage. Making plants react and grow faster by any form of pruning is all very well provided that there are sufficient resources to support the extra and faster growth. On the other hand, retardation could be caused by nutrient deficiency and to pro-voke extra effort in this case is to ask for weakening of the plant, and even exhaustion.

It would be far better, therefore, to ensure adequacy of plant nutrient by putting down a balanced compound fertiliser like Growmore or Humber Eclipse over about three months, beginning a month before the main growing season begins so that nutrients become avail-able just when the plant needs them most. Starting about mid-February spread 2 ozs. per sq. yard around the tree, and repeat twice more at monthly intervals.

Of course, it would mean less competition for a young tree to cut out a circle of grass around the base to bare the soil and cover this with the compost mulch, but if you don't want to do this, at least leave the box off the mower when mowing in the vicinity of the tree so that the cuttings and resulting humus are returned to the soil.

136 Special beauties for milder climates

I have a sheltered garden in Cornwall and would like to plant some really colourful, but out of the ordinary, shrubs. What do you suggest?

Tucked away in the warm south-west, you should be able to grow several subjects denied to gardeners in other parts of the country, especially if you can offer a lime-free soil. One of the most exciting to grow must be Mimosa—*Acacia dealbata*—because it has everything to offer: attractive foliage, masses of little puff balls of yellow bloom ideal for cutting. No wonder it's a florists' favourite. Camellias, often spoilt by frost damage to the buds, grow wonderfully at Torpoint and should be quite at home with you.

Everyone knows the Butterfly Bush, Buddleia, in the several varieties of *B. davidii*; the scented willow-like *B. alternifolia* and the orange ball *B. globosa*. Your climate should suit a rare Buddleia often considered to be rather tender—*B. colvilei* has large tubular deep rose flowers in June and can be relied upon to tease most people to identify it. *Crinodendron hookeranum*—which the modern craze for renaming is trying to call *Tricuspidaria lanceolata*—is one of the gems of the garden. Aptly called the Chilean lantern tree, it is a superb evergreen, and in May and early June smothered with long-stalked rose-pink coloured flowers, for all the world like little lanterns.

Although hardy in most parts of the U.K., *Desfontainea spinosa* thrives particularly where the warm Gulf Stream keeps the climate mild. An evergreen with holly-like leaves, the flowers always evoke admiration. They are crimson-scarlet tubular-shaped with a yellow mouth, hanging in hundreds throughout late summer.

The spectacular Chilean Fire Bush, *Embothrium coccineum*, is ideally suited to south-west districts, and another shrub-like small tree that is hardy elsewhere but which seems to grow better than ever in Devon and Cornwall is *Corylopsis willmottiae* which is smothered in yellow bloom in spring.

Finally, a couple of climbers that you will find interesting are *Eccremocarpus scaber*, a vigorous, fast-growing climber with the admirable habit of producing its scarlet-orange flowers continuously throughout summer and autumn, and *Actinidia kolomikta*, remarkable for the tri-coloured variation of its foliage and fragrant flowers.

All the subjects mentioned are obtainable from good quality nurserymen and, indeed, enquiry to Treseders in Truro should also bring further advice on subjects suitable to your particular part of Cornwall.

137 Spindle Tree: where have all the berries gone?

Why does my spindle tree fail to bear any berries? I have had it for three years and it is covered with greenish flowers every spring; it had plenty of berries when I bought it to give me material for autumn and winter flower arrangements. Is it necessary to have both male and female shrubs?

The spindle tree Euonymus is not unisexual like holly, and you have to have two trees, male and female growing in close proximity to ensure pollination and the production of berries. However, in the case of the spindle tree, it is nearly always necessary to have them growing in groups of at least three or four to get berries. This is because the flowers are often imperfect and not fertile enough and the tree needs pollen from another spindle. The fact that your plant bore berries when you first bought it, bears out this contention—they were fertilised by other trees in the nursery—and, furthermore, you will see proof of this where they grow in the wild.

The common spindle, *Euonymus europaeus*, is found in hedgerows and thickets where its curious winged or lobed rose-scarlet seed capsules or berries are very conspicuous in the autumn, but you will seldom, if ever, find one growing alone. There, then, is another clue to the conditions it likes, hedgerows and thickets. It likes other shrubs and trees about it to give a little shade, so that it is never fully exposed. Ideally, it is best grown in a thicket-type shrubbery and in addition to others of its kind, you could plant other subjects that are useful for flower arrangements such as the Golden Elder, *Sambucus racemosa* 'Plumosa Aurea', which will give you lovely blooms of brilliant red berries and deeply cut, fern-like golden foliage. Also try the Snowberry, *Symphoricarpus albus*, and its related species.

The spindle tree is noted for its ability to

thrive on chalk and, indeed, it is to be found growing luxuriantly in places where the soil cover over the chalk is scarcely an inch or two thick; but you'll always find it in groups, never alone.

138 Spraying with care

I have four well-established apple trees in my garden. Three of them have clematis growing up through them, and the fourth is underplanted with hardy cyclamen. I want to spray the apples with winter tar oil wash. Will it harm the clematis or cyclamen?

Tar oil is used to destroy overwintering pests and fungal disease on plants that are protected by their own lignified tissue, i.e. plants that are woody like roses and other shrubs, or covered with bark like trees. Any parts that are showing green—leaves, shoots, buds—will be scorched and most likely destroyed.

Whilst you may be able to protect the cyclamen by covering them with a plastic ground sheet, covering clematis is impracticable because it is the bark of the tree behind them where your quarry lies. Even dormant in the winter, clematis carries well-developed buds especially in the axils of last season's woody side shoots, and unless these clematis are varieties that have to be pruned back hard to the ground level each year, it would be very risky to spray with tar oil and you should use an alternative non-oil, non-corrosive, winter wash.

139 Sycamores are a risk near buildings

My front garden contains three fairly large sycamore trees that were small saplings when the house was built in 1939. I am now wondering whether they are a danger to the foundations of the house which is about 20 ft. away from them.

There is no doubt about this; sycamores are like poplars in having an extensive root system, and it is generally reckoned to be unwise to plant them within 50 ft. of buildings or drains. It is clear therefore that with three large trees

only 20 ft. away, you are running a considerable risk. They should be removed as soon as possible.

Grubbing them out by the roots, whilst the safest and wisest method, will also be quite expensive if contracted professionally. If you take on the job yourself, drop each tree in pieces that are not too big for you to handle safely. Felling a whole tree in the direction you want it to go is not as easy as it looks, and it could be dangerous with the buildings only 20 ft. away. If you feel capable of digging out the main root bole, leave the main trunk 6–8 ft. high so that you have a long 'lever' to push and pull. If you cut a trunk to ground level you will have to dead lift the bole, and unless you know what you are doing this can be dangerous to your limbs, so 'lever' it out.

On the other hand, if digging out the roots is beyond you, cut the trunk down as low as you can. Then fit a carpenter's swingbrace with a $\frac{3}{4}$ in. woodbit (an Irwin bit is best—it is shaped like an Archimedean screw and enables you to drill deeply pushing up the drillings so that you don't block the hole) and drill out holes 3 inches apart and 5–6 inches deep all over each stump.

The first job is to kill the root bole and you can now do this by filling the holes with sodium chlorate solution, made by dissolving the weedkiller in water until the liquid will not dissolve any more; this is called a 'saturated solution'. As the liquid slowly diffuses into the wood over the next few days, refill the holes but, this time, not with sodium chlorate but with a saturated solution of saltpetre, potassium nitrate, made in the same way. Keep topping up the holes with saltpetre solution for a couple of months, by which time the boles should be thoroughly impregnated. Cover them in wet weather, leave them to dry out, and then sprinkle a few drops of paraffin into each hole and ignite. Any flames will quickly subside and each stump will then smoulder away like a big cigarette without causing smoke annoyance. Don't be in too much of a hurry, the effectiveness of the burning out depends entirely on the thoroughness of your impregnating preparations. If at any time you see signs of suckering growth arising from the remnants of the root system, simply paint these with a little SBK weedkiller.

140   Sycamore with pimples

I have a diseased sycamore tree in my garden standing on a lawn and would be pleased if you could identify the disease. The tree is very late coming into leaf and then the leaves develop red patches which turn into red pimples on the upper surface. Finally, the leaves fall prematurely. Is there any remedy and is the disease likely to spread to other trees? My soil is sandy.

The symptoms you describe don't sound like a disease, but the results of an attack by a mite—called the Acer Gall Mite—that causes these little pimples or galls.

It will affect the whole Acer family—maples, sycamores and acers.

The method of controlling the pest depends largely upon the practicality of the situation. If it is possible for instance to reach all the affected leaves of a small tree, and there are not so many as to denude the tree, the best control is to pick off the affected leaves and burn them. But failing that, you will have to spray: use a 5% lime sulphur solution made up strictly according to the instructions on the can, and at the end of February, drench every tree of the Acer family in your garden and get your neighbours to do the same. Spraying lime sulphur can be a really messy job, so choose a windless day.

Fortunately, unless the incidence builds up, the effect of this pest is not seriously damaging and control measures need not be undertaken unless the tree becomes unsightly. Like a rash on a pale under-nourished skin, blemishes of this sort always look more prominent on foliage that is pale and below par. You can reduce the visual effect and help the tree to live with the pest by ensuring that there is no deficiency of plant nutrients.

Put down a slow-acting, long-lasting balanced compound manure like Humber Eclipse at the rate of 2 oz. per sq. yard over the entire area under the tree spread. Do this three times each a month apart starting in March. When the tree is standing in broken ground, hoe it in and cover the soil with a mulch of well-rotted compost, peat, or spent mushroom compost. However, since your tree is in grass you can either put the fertiliser down on the turf—it will not harm it—or you can lift a divot here and there and drop in half a handful until you reach the equivalent total quantity. Either way, don't collect the cuttings when you mow the lawn near the tree; fly them with the box off and return the humus to the soil.

141   Veronica: care and cultivation

How should I treat a veronica after the blooms have finished? It doesn't bloom as well as it used to; what should I do?

The correct name for veronica is Hebe. There are a great many species which all originate from New Zealand. You don't say which one yours is but this advice can be followed for them all.

Whilst it is growing and getting bigger each year, merely remove the old flower heads by cutting them back to just above where new young shoots can be seen beginning to form, and which will bear flowers next year. If the shrub is growing a little more one side than the other, you can take out a stem more severely; the aim should be to avoid having a straggling lop-sided shrub.

Provided that the soil is reasonably well-drained, Hebes will grow in almost any type but naturally will benefit from being fed with a balanced compound manure. In fact, exhaustion of available plant nutrients is the most likely cause of the deterioration of your shrub. Trim it off as described to promote the development of new flower-bearing shoots, mulch and feed well and there is no reason why the Hebe should not prosper.

You do not say either whether yours is a pot plant, but as many of the Hebes like 'Midsummer Beauty', 'Mrs. Winder', 'Autumn Glory' and *H. salicifolia* are often used for pot work, it is useful to remember that, in pots, the plants have even more limited soil resources. Plant nutrients can, and do, soon wash out. Foliar feeding and top dressing both have their uses but these are 'extras'. There is absolutely no substitute to a plant living as nearly naturally as possible, i.e. through a healthy root system.

Therefore, with a pot plant, try to adopt the following procedure. Don't overwater, but make sure that the plant never dries out, and during the growing and blooming season, add a little liquid feed. In autumn, lift off as much soil as possible, from the top of the pot without pulling up the roots, and replace with fresh soil compost—J.I. No. 3, or one containing plenty of humus and a balanced compound manure. Every third or fourth year, re-pot by knocking out the plant, teasing and shaking out as much soil as you can without too much root damage. Replant—using the next size of pot if necessary—with J.I. No. 3 and a good wodge of moisture-retentive compost or peat in the pot bottom.

142 Viburnum : one of the finest of all shrubs

Last autumn I planted a Viburnum bodnantense *'Dawn' but it failed to flower around Christmas, as promised by the nursery.*

You really are being optimistic in planting a Viburnum in the autumn and expecting it to flower after a couple of months. Of course, it can and often does happen that way but it is not something that you can rely on and the nursery should have known better than to 'promise'. It will take a year or two to settle down and become fully established and as the bloom comes in late winter or early spring, it derives from and depends upon good growing conditions during the previous spring, summer and autumn.

You can help it to grow strongly by hoeing in a balanced organic-based manure and when the young plant is clearly responding and doing well, but not before, encourage it more by spraying lightly at two to three week intervals during the summer with Murphy FF foliar feed. Bud development must not suffer because of moisture shortage at the roots; this is nearly always a likely cause of disappointment with newly planted spring flowering shrubs, so keep

it well-watered and the soil above covered by a liberal mulching to prevent drying out. The bloom that you will enjoy is a reflection of the conditions and effort that you put in, and few shrubs can repay you like viburnums. An ideal preparation is outlined in *No. 71.*

Viburnum × *bodnantense* is a hybrid between *V. farreri* from China and *V. grandiflorum* from the Himalayan regions of India and Nepal and in the 1930s was raised, as its name indicates at Bodnant in North Wales, the home and gardens of Lord Aberconway, Chairman of the Royal Horticultural Society. It produces clusters of slightly rose-tinted very sweet-scented flowers over a very long period, sometimes as early as November until as late as January or early February. Remarkably, these flowers are very frost resistant and are a surprising sight on a cold winter's day. Equally remarkable is the length of time the cut flowers last in a vase of water. The variety 'Dawn' received an Award of Garden Merit in 1960 and is one of the top dozen flowering shrubs.

143 Viburnum, reluctant to bloom

My Viburnum tinus *planted two years ago seems perfectly healthy but hasn't produced a single bloom yet. Why?*

Your two-year-old shrub is most probably concentrating on getting established, making root and top growth before turning its attention to bloom. Until a lot of new root growth is made so that the plant's ability to absorb moisture has been developed, it will be very susceptible to lack of moisture in the soil. This one factor is the cause of a lot of the problems and difficulties we get with spoiled bloom in all young plants especially evergreens. Any plant that is seriously short of water cannot make the extra bulk of buds, blooms, new leaves and shoots, or, for that matter, roots. Or, what it has started to make has to be abandoned. If you are in a sandy, gravelly or other quick-draining soil, even long-established plants have to be helped. When a new planting grows away well, this doesn't necessarily signify that it is not suffering from dryness—it could be and if this happens at a time when buds would normally be forming, they simply abort and fail to develop. The disappointed plant may well try to make up for it by putting on yet more shoot and leaf growth as soon as the rains come. Water at the wrong time is almost as bad as no water at all.

Perhaps you did not work in enough moisture-retaining organic matter at the time of planting. It's too late to dig it in now; disturbing the shrub will only damage the fine root hairs and set them right back, so you'll have to content the plants by heavy mulching each autumn and again in spring with compost, peat, spent hops or mushroom compost, and get out the hosepipe more often.

Although dryness is the most likely cause of your trouble, you will always find *Viburnum tinus* doing best where it can receive plenty of sunlight, so if the two-year-old is in a shady position, you'll have to combine the risk of further root disturbance that moving it entails, with the opportunity to plant it properly and get more organic matter underneath it.

Physical damage from insects is unlikely to be involved in this case, but take the precaution of looking very carefully at the buds and new shoots frequently during the summer months to see if there is any sign of minute red creatures indicating attack by red spider needing control by an insecticide containing Mesrethrin. Alternatively, blemishes, spots, stunting or even nibbling could be 'thrips'. A monthly spraying will take care of them and put your mind at rest.

144   Weepers : a selection of the best

About seven years ago I bought a weeping willow. This has since overgrown the part of the garden where it was planted. I have decided to remove it and replace it with another variety, this time dwarf-growing. Please recommend a suitable variety to suit an average sized garden. Could you also recommend a smallish slow-growing type of weeping cherry tree?

Clearly you fell into the trap of planting something without first checking out the ultimate size it could grow to. Furthermore, to buy a tree and plant it merely as a 'weeping willow' is asking for trouble because there are well over a hundred willows, many of which could be described as weeping and some of them are monsters. However, only two are what can fairly be called dwarf-growing: *Salix caprea* 'Pendula', the Kilmarnock willow, and *S. purpurea* 'Pendula'. The ultimate height of each depends upon the stem height at which they are grafted. They are rare, and only a top-class nursery is likely to be able to offer you a specimen.

But why stay with a willow? The weeping effect can be obtained with other subjects. For instance, Young's weeping birch, *Betula pendula* 'Youngii', is easier to train, makes a flat dome or mushroom-headed small tree with long stems reaching to the ground. It received an A.G.M. in 1969, so there is proof that it is good. The most popular weeping cherry, often wrongly called Cheal's Weeping is the beautiful dwarf Japanese cherry, *Prunus* 'Kiku Shidare Zakura', a name awkward to look at but easy enough once you get your tongue round it. This variety is propagated and offered as though there were no other weeping cherries; a pity, because there are several others to choose from. Hilling's Weeping has a curtain of long vertical stems which in April are smothered in pure white flowers. *P. mume* 'Pendula'—an apricot—is charming, with pale pink flowers in February and March.

Two peaches are weeping: *P. persica* 'Crimson Cascade' and *P. p.* 'Windle Weeping', rather more pink and winner of an A.G.M. in 1949. Finally, two more cherries; *Prunus subhirtella* 'Pendula Rosea', and the darker coloured *P. s.* 'Pendula Rubra'.

Many shrubs make wonderful small weeping trees when run up as standards and then topped out so that the branches fall and weep, or they may be worked as grafts or buds onto 6–8 ft. stems. This sort of work was more commonly practised in the old days in private gardens and nurseries, then for some reason, probably labour costs, it went out of fashion. There are signs of a very welcome revival and although still rare, standard worked shrubs are worth searching for. Perhaps your enquiries will help to prompt an enterprising nursery to get cracking. Suitable subjects include the fragrant lilac-coloured *Buddleia alternifolia*, the shrub form is good and well known, but a standard weeper shows it to advantage. *Cotoneaster* 'Hybridus Pendulus' is an evergreen with the added attraction of brilliant red berries during the autumn; try *Forsythia suspensa*, a weeping form of the well-known yellow spring-flowering shrub; and finally try the so-called Chinese Beauty Bush called *Kolkwitzia amabilis*. To see a weeping standard of this in May and June, draped in masses of pink and yellow bell-shaped flowers, is to make one lost for words.

Finally, how dwarf is dwarf? It depends upon your garden. The best way to avoid a repetition of the problem you now have, is to decide the maximum height and width you can allow and then visit and ask questions in parks, private gardens open to the public for charity, National Trust gardens, horticultural shows etc. This way you can get to see and know mature specimens so that you know exactly what the subject is going to look like before you plant it.

145 *Woodland shrubs suitable for shaded positions*

I have a peaty woodland garden and need a few really outstanding shrubs to give it interest after my late Rhododendrons have flowered. What do you recommend?

How fortunate you are! It sounds as if you have ideal conditions, shelter from the elements and plenty of humus in the soil for growing some of the most beautiful of all shrubs and trees. Here is a short list that can be relied upon to give a succession of charm and delight.

Flowering in May at the same time as many of the Rhododendrons, but to be included because of the unsurpassed beauty of autumn foliage is the yellow-flowered *Enkianthus campanulatus* from Japan and its related species, *E. cernuus* 'Rubens' which has red-fringed flowers, and the remarkable *E. chinensis* with large flowers of yellow and red.

The aptly-named Silver Bell or Snowdrop tree *Halesia carolina* is a beautiful large shrub or small tree from America, and similar in size is *Crinodendron hookeranum* Chilean Lantern tree from South America, covered in May and June with beautiful rosy-pink lantern-like blooms. Search out the Calico Bush *Kalmia latifolia* with its masses of beautiful corrugated, pleated, little pink lantern flowers, one of the gems of the woodland garden.

A beautiful small tree that will be a delight, if you give it a sunny position in an open glade, is *Koelreuteria paniculata*; it goes under the common names of Golden Rain Tree and Pride of India, and deserves both.

Beautiful examples of a lovely family are the two lacecaps: *Hydrangea sargentiana*, a noble shrub whose stems and shoots have curious hairy covering, large velvety leaves and large blue white florets and the graceful *H. villosa* one of the loveliest of all late-flowering summer shrubs. Both of these Hydrangeas are seen to their best in the dappled sun-shade of a woodland setting.

The Sweet Pepper, *Clethra alnifolia*, positively hums in August with the insects attracted by its sweet-scented white bloom, the fragrance carries some distance in a slow moving woodland air. If it's interest you want, you will get it unfailingly each August with a beautiful shrub from the Andes mountains, *Desfontainea spinosa*. The evergreen leaves are very much like holly and the masses of large orange-scarlet flowers never fail to win admiration.

Finally, to end this short list, if you can grow Rhododendrons you can grow one of the most vividly coloured of all plants, the Sorrel tree, *Oxydendrum arboreum*. The white flowers are produced in clusters from the tips of shoots in August and alone make the shrub worth its place, but the vivid crimson and yellow foliage that follows put this at the forefront of all woodland plants.

146 *Wisteria: its care and cultivation*

Two years ago, we planted a three-year-old wisteria on a south-west facing wall, which it now covers. So far there has been no sign of flowers. What can we do to encourage it?

Wisteria can take three or four years from planting before they produce their first flowers, so you may have to wait a year or two yet. This plant has evidently made plenty of growth and is well-established, so I think you can begin the pruning procedure that will speed up flowering and lay the foundation for prolific bloom in future. Stage 1 comes in late summer when all laterals or side shoots that have formed to date can be cut back to 12–15 inches from the main stem—unless you want one of them to grow on to cover a particular area of wall, in which case you then treat it as main stem and spur the side shoots off that. This cutting back encourages development of 'basal buds' at the foot of each shoot.

Then in February, Stage 2 consists of cutting back further the same side shoots to three or four buds only from the old wood main stem. This creates the spur from which the best bloom is borne. Train the main shoots to go where you want and spur new side shoots each late summer as they form.

As the plant has put on a lot of growth, it is likely that the soil is already rich in plant foods, but a light scattering of sulphate of potash would encourage wood ripening and the development of those flower-producing basal buds.

147 Xmas tree: can it be kept after Christmas is over?

I've managed to get a shapely Christmas tree with plenty of roots, and would like to keep it growing after Christmas. How should I care for it so that it recovers quickly when I plant it outdoors in the New Year?

The odds are stacked heavily against you, and it is most probable that you will fail to establish the tree. Christmas trees are lifted and intended for use as Christmas decoration—not for growing on as specimen trees—and not much attention or care is therefore taken with the roots. With a mutilated root system, the tree then has to spend a spell in the warmth and dry air of your home. By the time you remove the lights and the fairy off the top, it will be in an advanced state of dehydration and

the first step will be to correct this. Trim any broken and ragged roots with secateurs and soak as much of the tree as you can in water for at least forty-eight hours. The roots can go in a bucket but if you have a water butt, you might be able to get a lot more immersed; and if the tree is small enough to go in the bath, so much the better.

Plant the tree with plenty of well-soaked peat or compost around its roots, firm it well, and thoroughly spray the tree with S600 transplanting spray from head to foot—repeating the spray twenty-four hours later.

This spray reduces transpiration of moisture from the foliage; it will not be going in through the impaired roots, so you cannot afford to let too much go out through the leaves. It would have helped to have begun this transplanting spray process before Christmas, and in fact S600 is sold in an aerosol can to prevent the tree dropping its needle leaves. At this stage, you will have done all that you reasonably and economically can and if it doesn't manage to survive despite these efforts, it would be most expedient to cut your losses and obtain a pot-grown specimen for planting and growing on.

Finally, a word of caution: do consider carefully where you plant the tree since you will need plenty of room for its growth. Your charming little Christmas tree can grow up into a hulking great Norway Spruce!

148 Yucca: why it is slow to flower

Could you please tell me if it is true that Yuccas only flower once in every seven years? Mine flowered eight years ago, had two blooms at once, and hasn't bloomed since!

Provided we are not faced with some peculiarity, like plants of the wrong sex, completely unsuitable soil, or persistent annual frost pockets, the first thing to suspect when plants do not flower—when they apparently should—is light intensity. Our temperate climate allows us to grow and enjoy many plants from warmer climates. However, the one thing that our climate cannot make up for is the lower light intensity. Even a brilliant summer's day is dull compared with the intense light in some parts of the world where certain of our plants come from. See *No. 149*. Such plants need this bright sunlight to enable them to build up the reserves for flowering, and a dull summer or even a partially shaded position can put them off altogether.

However, there is no truth whatever in the idea that Yuccas only bloom every seven years. A succession of hot dry summers will bring a succession of flowers, the number of spikes depending upon how many mature growths develop within the rosette of leaves. This is why they grow better and are more frequently seen in the clean bright air of seaside towns than in the polluted hazy air of industrial towns inland.

If your Yucca is in any way shaded and is not too large, move it into a sunny position in about October when the soil is still warm and can make root growth before winter. That apart, there is little you can do about the sunshine. All Yuccas benefit from heavy mulching with peat or compost enriched with a balanced plant food like Growmore or Humber Eclipse. If you do this every autumn, the question of blooms is then up to sunshine.

149 *Yucca: care and cultivation*

Could you give me some advice on the cultivation of a Yucca? I have had one for two years and, although not dead, it seems a bit reluctant to extend itself skywards. New leaf growth is there, but there is no sign of any stalk. The bottom leaves are all brown and look untidy. The soil is quite clay-laden and I have added some sand to counteract this.

Although members of the lily family, Yuccas are really shrubs or small trees native to Mexico, Arizona and other parts of Southern U.S.A. A family of about fifteen different species, several are hardy in the mild climate of the British Isles, where they create a sub-tropical effect in the garden. They are almost unique in form and habit and have rosettes of narrow rigid leaves from which rise tall stems bearing panicles of drooping bell-shaped lily-like flowers with a colour range from mostly green-

white to cream. Yuccas will grow in most soils provided that it is well-drained and, as might be expected from their place of origin, they need plenty of sun.

Our climate which, even at its best, is less sunny than its native land, is one of the contributing factors why Yuccas are so notoriously slow to reach flowering maturity and are reluctant to bloom every year unless conditions and sunlight are to their liking.

The lower leaves of the Yucca, as they become old and eventually die, should be removed and not allowed to collect. This removal can be done in late spring or early summer. In April, side shoots can be removed —taking care not to harm any roots that may be attached—and planted out into prepared positions, similar to that of the parent. A little bonemeal will encourage root action and help to get the plant established, and a light dusting around with a balanced plant nutrient, each spring, like Growmore or Humber Eclipse, will be beneficial. Its position is the important factor—a hot well-drained position in full sun.

Where a Yucca is going to be planted or already is planted in clay, something must be done to improve the drainage. Spreading sand will do no harm, but will not do much good either. Read the questions and answers on clay flocculation *Nos. 2* and *456* so that you understand the action of gypsum. Hoe this into the soil around the Yucca; 2 oz. per sq. yard every three months indefinitely.

150 *Yucca: an easy propagation method*

Can you tell me how to propagate the underground buds known as 'toes' on a Yucca?

Yuccas have thick rhizomatous roots, and these are the easiest means by which the plant can be propagated. During early March, carefully uncover and sever two or three of these roots, about the thickness of a pencil, and then cut them into pieces—'toes'—about 3 or 4 inches long. Prepare 3–4-inch deep seedboxes with a compost of equal parts peat and sand and set the pieces $\frac{1}{4}$–$\frac{1}{2}$ inch deep.

Wat er well, and place the boxes either in a

propagator case or on soil-warming cables, so that the root cuttings can be influenced by gentle heat rising from below. A temperature of 55°–60°F is usually sufficient. This 'bottom heat', as it is called, is one of the strongest factors influencing rooting. Keep the compost nicely moist, watering as required with tepid water, and by mid-summer you should have several nicely rooted cuttings, each putting up a shoot. These can be carefully lifted with as much compost adhering and with as little root disturbance as possible. They must not be damaged in any way at this stage.

Pot them into 5–6-inch pots using the same compost plus a handful of the soil from around the parent plant; this is to introduce plenty of soil bacteria which you now set to work producing plant nutrients, by mixing a level teaspoonful of Humber Eclipse or Growmore. Scratch in another teaspoonful three weeks later, and as they grow larger, pot into bigger pots. Keep in an unheated greenhouse or in a frame during winter and by the following spring they should be ready for planting into a permanent position in the garden.

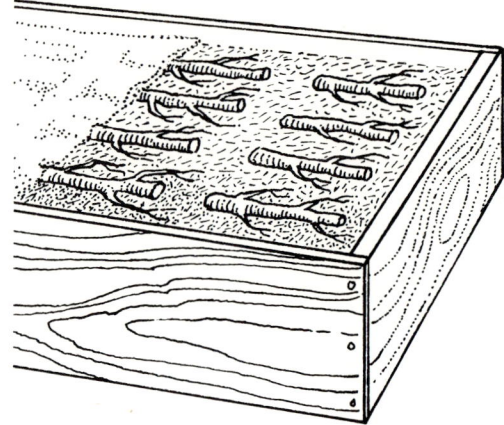

No. 150 *Propagation of Yucca by root cuttings which are laid flat on compost, lightly covered and placed in gentle heat.*

Section III

Fruit

151 Apples: cordon growing on clay soil

I understand that cordon apple trees planted upright do not crop so well as when set at an angle of 45°. Is it correct that they have lengths of bare stem from which they are unable to produce side shoots? Also, is Bramley's Seedling unsuitable for training as cordons and espaliers? My soil is very heavy clay and although I would like to grow a Cox's Orange Pippin, I understand that Laxton's Superb is more suitable for this soil.

Although most amateurs think and work in terms of a single stem, trained at an initial angle of about 45°, there are various growing systems: U cordons, double-U cordons, and single stems in both upright and oblique directions.

The objectives of the cordon system are twofold. Firstly, to divert vigour from growth into spurring and thus into fruit production and, secondly to get as many bushes in and as much fruit as possible from a given area. See *No. 152*.

On the face of it, a cordon grown vertically is a mistake and pointless because the growth has the greatest incentive to remain upright and does not present any restriction and diversion of vigour. The distance between spurs must be expected to be greater and the opportunities to bear fruit per foot run, so to speak, are less than the more closely distanced spurs of the oblique cordon.

If a cooking apple has to be grown this forcibly shaped way, Early Victoria or Lane's Prince Albert would probably be better than

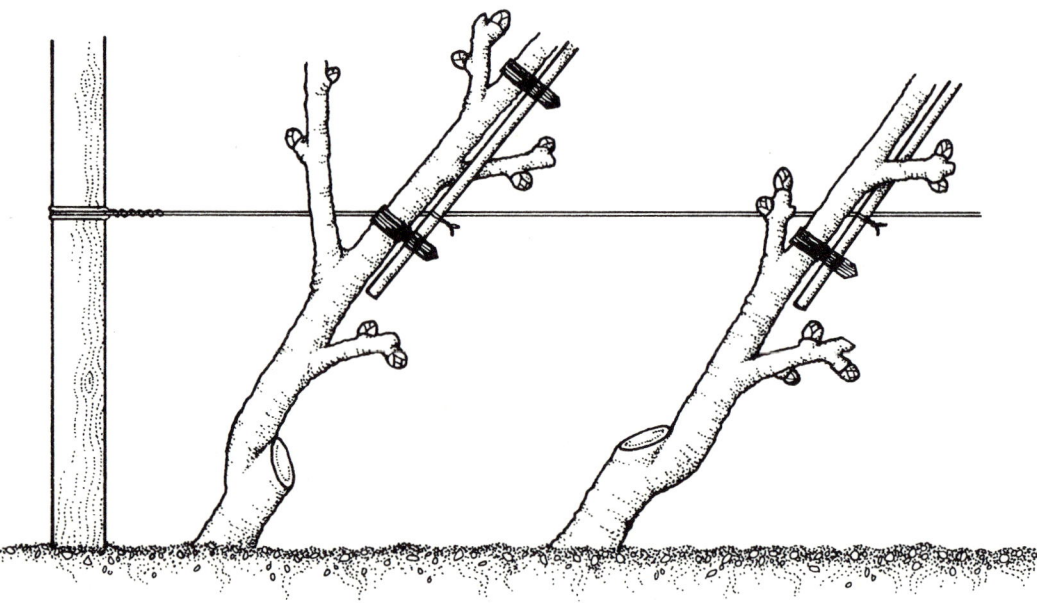

No. 151 *Oblique apples cordon, the right and wrong methods. The one on the right will always be in danger of cracking open at the union with the rootstock. It would be even worse if planted upright and then pulled into the oblique position. Any fracture or splitting immediately exposes the tree to invasion and attack by fungus spores.*

The left-hand tree is planted correctly. The first growth bud should be allowed to grow on and break again in order to fill the otherwise vacant corner, see illustration to No. 152. Note also how the bending over of the rootstock causes a sap flow restriction which helps to keep early growth shorter and encourages fruit bud production.

Bramley, but either is suitable provided that they have been grafted on to a Malling IX stock.

There are very many different stocks upon which choice apple varieties and other fruits are grafted. These stocks impart specific characteristics to the resultant trees, such as stature, vigour, time taken to reach fruit-bearing maturity etc. They are produced vegetatively so that the same characteristics are imparted uniformly. This is very important in an orchard, for example, where the farmer wants all the trees to be of similar size and the fruit to be borne about the same time when the labour is available.

Apple stocks are classified by Roman numerals plus the name of the research station where this work was begun—East Malling in Kent. A stock called Jaune de Metz had been used on the continent for a long time where early cropping and a pronounced dwarfing effect was wanted. After testing a selection of the very best strains, this became Malling IX stock. Today, this is the most popular stock for bush cordon and dwarf pyramid apples, and is certainly the best for the amateur gardener.

There wouldn't be a lot to choose between the performance of Cox and Laxton's Superb on your heavy soil, but if you can—it might be hard going—dig in plenty of very well-rotted organic matter under the bushes before planting; it will be the last opportunity you will have. After planting, keep the rows mulched heavily so that organic matter is always being carried into the soil by worms. The porosity and drainage of the soil will be greatly improved by dressing the area with 2 ozs. per sq. yard of gypsum, every three months. Read *Nos. 2* and *456* about the improvement of clay soil.

152 Apples : training of cordons must be right

I have ordered three cordon apple trees for my new garden. Please advise me as to the best way to support these trees?

Cordons need horizontal wiring and to support this, posts are required. These need to be strong and rigid to take the strain of several tight wires, plus the extra weight of fruit. Posts must be examined and tested by deliberately trying to break or push them over every early spring. There is nothing worse than having a post collapse under a full crop. The posts should stand 6 ft. out of the ground and wires strung every 9 ins. or so, starting 18 ins. from the soil level.

The best way of supporting your cordons is to wire bamboo canes at an angle of 45° and tie in the cordon stem to this cane. The tip will always try to turn and grow upright, so whilst still soft, it must be bent down to the cane and tied in. This bending back is an integral part of the cordon growing system, since each bending back is a restriction to the sap which helps to divert plant energy into producing fruit buds rather than making leaf and stem growth. This illustrates the misconception concerning vertical cordons, see *No. 151*.

Most gardeners only grow half the number of cordons they could, failing to realise that a second row can be grown on the other side of the 'fence', with canes lying in the opposite direction, criss-crossing with the others. However, planting a second row to an already established cordon row is risking root disturbance and damage to those already there. Since you can only plant to this plan at the outset, bear it in mind when making your plans.

How long your cordon 'fence' can be, will largely determine to what extent you will be able to practise a refinement of cordon training that can increase yield very noticeably. When the growing tip reaches the top wire most gardeners imagine that this is the limit and cut out the top to restrict further growth. This is not at all necessary and, indeed, is more likely to promote an outburst of growth from lower down.

A better practice is to bend down the tip and take it along the top wire, parallel to the ground; the bending causes further restriction and yet more inducement to produce fruit spurs.

If your rows are long enough, the ultimate refinement in cordon growing is to set off each

No. 152   *Oblique trained apple cordons showing how the angle is gradually increased at each support wire so that the main stem is horizontal to the ground by the time it reaches the top wire. The second row on the reverse side, and growing in the opposite direction, is shown by dotted lines.*

year's new tip growth at a flatter angle so that by the time it reaches the top wire, it may be 20 ft. or more long. Each successive bend, becoming increasingly level with the ground, turns vigour into fruit bud production and the cropping is tremendous. The resulting shape of the stem is then not a straight stem at an angle of 45° to the ground but, instead, the shape is more that of a gentle curve beginning at 45°, then arching over to the horizontal level at the top bar.

Bear in mind, however, that what comes out, must go back, and if you take heavy crops by the cordon method, you must expect to repay your soil by heavy mulching and correct feeding. See *No. 153*.

153   Apples need regular feeding for good fruiting

My two eating apple trees, which are Cox's Orange Pippin and a Laxton variety, bear plenty of fruit, but appear to be bearing smaller and smaller apples. What is the cause of this?

Apples are no different to any other plant in that they need an adequate supply of the three basic plant nutrients—nitrogen, potash and phosphorus. The primary purpose of the apple tree, as far as you are concerned, is to make plenty of ripe fruit, and this means that nitrogen and potash are very important and should never be under-supplied.

Provided that soil texture, drainage and the health of the tree are in order, there is no reason why an apple tree shouldn't fruit and fruit well. From the early part of summer when the fruits are swelling rapidly, the trees are relying very heavily upon nutrients—sugars and carbohydrate supplies—that not only have been and are going to be elaborated by the leaves, but also on the reserve that has been built up within the tree at periods when fruit bearing wasn't making heavy demands.

It should be clear, therefore, that although nitrogen, which is involved in leaf growth, and potash, which is involved in the ripening processes, are important, feeding is really a matter of constant steady availability and not one of the quick-acting remedies to meet or cure specific short-term requirements.

Feeding, in short, means two things. First, the regular provision of nutrient material containing balanced proportions of nitrogen, phosphorus and potash, which is released gradually rather than in a mad rush; and secondly, steps taken constantly to improve the soil structure, so that the assimilation of these nutrients by the root system is assisted.

As important as putting down nutrients, are steps that you take to retain them instead of their being washed-out of the soil—leaching. In this sense, moisture retention also means nutrient retention and this will mean regularly mulching the soil beneath the tree. Alternatively, you can grow a permanent ley like grass or, better still, nitrogen-fixing plants like clover. Then, when mown, the cut material can be left as a mulch ultimately to be carried down by earth worms into the soil as it decomposes.

This is where the benefit of a slow-release nutrient source like Humber Eclipse can be used to real advantage. Hoe in three dressings, each of 2 ozs. per sq. yd. over the whole area covered by branch spread, a month apart commencing in February. This could be augmented by a nitrogen boost to get leaf growth strongly established; give 2 ozs. per sq. yd. of nitro chalk in early April.

The basis of good fertility—indeed all fertility—is that there must be air in the soil. Because the supply of nutrients depends upon the decomposition of organic materials which is performed by bacteria, which in turn depend upon air, a waterlogged airless soil must be avoided. A heavy solid wet clay, therefore, cannot be expected to grow good apples and curing it can take a long time to accomplish.

However, if you are on clay, *accomplish it you must*, and you can do this by spreading down, at three-monthly intervals, 2 ozs. per sq. yd. of agricultural gypsum, allowing the weather to take it into the soil. Keep this up indefinitely, even after several years. You can only go on improving the clay soil and the cost is negligible.

154 Apples : curing the curse of biennial cropping

In my garden there is a Charles Ross apple tree, planted in 1937. Since I took over in 1951, the tree has been allowed to grow naturally except for some overcrowded branches which have been cut out. Since I've owned it, it has carried a heavy crop of apples every other year; in the alternate years it bears only ten or twenty fruit. Is this usual and what can be the reason for it?

Refer first to *No. 153* to appreciate the necessity of adequate feeding and reserve build-up within the tree.

It not infrequently happens, more so with young trees perhaps that have not built up much reserve, that a tree will carry a crop of fruit that is somewhat heavier than its maturity or stature can really stand. There are several reasons why this should happen. There could be bad frost damage to bloom causing a poor crop; this causes a reserve build-up which enables the tree to react the following year by throwing a heavier crop to make up the previous year's loss. Inclement conditions such as excessive dryness and cold winds, for instance, can cause a reduced crop which then rebounds the following year with a heavier crop. If this rebound coincides with favourable conditions, like plenty of pollinating insects, you can then get a heavy overcrop. This might make you happy, but does the tree no good at all because it can start a dangerous 'pendulum' situation.

A heavy, overdemanding crop can mean that the tree has to cut its bud production, then the tree has a rest and throws a much reduced crop the following year; this is followed by a heavy crop again, a rest, a small crop, and the tree is into a stop-go rhythm that is called biennial cropping.

Some varieties tend to be especially prone: Charles Ross is one such and other notable examples are Ellison's Orange, Laxton's Superb and Newton Wonder. Your experience shows that even an established tree can get into the habit, and for it to have been settled in this stop-go pattern for more than twenty years it will probably take a lot of coaxing to make it behave itself.

You will have to be satisfied with an average crop instead of a heavy one. To begin with, thin out a quarter of the fruits before they begin to swell and so create a demand on the tree. Try to select apples evenly spaced and not touching, and remove the others as soon as they are big enough to handle. Because there is no certainty at this stage that the apples remaining will not be affected later by June drop—this is when a tree will abort fruits that are growing from flowers that were not pollinated—wait for the

June drop to occur and sometime towards late July take out a third of those remaining on the tree. You should now be down to below half the original embryo crop on the tree immediately after blossoming.

This should throw the tree out of its stop-go stride but, as it has been set in its ways a long time now, you may have to persevere several times before getting it to behave normally. Since the tree is nearly forty years old, it may well be sizeable and it is a fault with many large fruit trees not under commercial or professional supervision, that when pruning time arrives with all the fuss, bother and time involved of climbing up a ladder, pruning tends to get done rather haphazardly or not at all.

This may be another direction in which management could be tightened up: if it persists in 'stop-go', go over the tree in the August of a cropping year, and prune back leaders and the current year's growth shoots to one bud. This should get the tree's mind off growth and concentrate on producing fruit buds during the remaining summer months that will then develop in what would otherwise have been a lean following year.

155 Apples: pruning espaliers

My problem relates to espalier apple trees. I have three trees which are growing against a six-foot wooden fence; how should these be pruned and when?

The purpose to be borne in mind when pruning an espalier is to preserve the basic form and to divert the tree's energy into producing fruit buds on short spurs.

During the first half of August, cut back all side shoots that have formed along the branches to two or three leaves only. This lets in light and sunshine to finish colouring and ripening any fruits, and helps firm up any exposed buds into blossom buds which, under conditions of lessened light and dispersed energy, would probably have remained weak leaf buds only.

In November when leaves begin to fall, cut back these side shoots further still, to one bud only. Cut out hard any secondary growth that

may have formed since the August pruning; it will be soft and immature anyway and useless for fruit bearing. At the same time, all leads of the current year's growth can be cut back by a half to a *downward* facing bud.

This downward facing may seem strange; it is 'unnatural' and meant to be so. It is a further restriction to sap flow, to add to what you will have been doing all year. As they grow, shoot ends will turn to grow upright. Every three or four inches and while still soft, bend these down and tie them in; this bending down is deliberately intended to cause restriction to sap flow, reduce growth and so encourage fruit bud formation. There is considerable similarity in this bending to cordon growing, see *No. 152.*

156 Apples and Pears suitable for cordon growing

I wish to plant nine cordons of well-flavoured dessert apples and four cordons of dessert pears. Which varieties and rootstock do you recommend? The soil is sandy. I am using 2 in. diameter galvanised pipes as stakes at the ends of the row of cordons. Is it possible to hide these with pillar roses and clematis?

Make sure that you obtain young cordons from a top-class nurseryman and that they are grafted onto the dwarfing Malling IX stock. See *No. 151.*

Good varieties for cordon training are, in order of ripening: James Grieve, Fortune, Cox's Orange Pippin, Tydeman's Late Orange, Ribston Pippin and, if you want a russet, try Egremont which is ready for eating in November and December.

Pears respond very well to summer pruning and, as this is an important part of cordon training, pears do very well grown by this method. The popular varieties Doyenne du Comice and Conference make very satisfactory cordons; Louise Bonne would make a good third, and no collection of four would be complete without the grand old variety Williams' Bon Chrétien. This variety is all the better for cooking, and when put in a tin is the variety you know and buy as 'Bartlett'.

There is no intrinsic reason why clematis or

roses should not be used to hide the posts—but both would probably be much too vigorous for the purpose, and get in the way—but why waste valuable fruit-bearing space? Allow a side shoot or two to be trained into the 'vacant space' by the posts.

157 Apples: what is a 'beef apple'?

An apple tree near us produces large bright red fruits which hang on the branches until the following spring. They have a sour taste and are known locally as 'beef apples'. How did they get this name?

This is a classic example of how a name can be handed down through the vernacular, get altered a little and lose its original meaning. The term 'beef apple' is a common name that has derived from 'Norfolk Beefing'—a cooking apple that is very sour to begin with, that keeps exceptionally well and remains firm from autumn right through winter into early spring, and doesn't ripen until March or even April when it changes colour and takes on a very pleasant flavour.

After all that waiting, a beautiful ending—and that is the clue to how it got its name. It hails from France where it was called 'Beaufin' which, translated means 'good end'. The corruption of 'Beaufin' into 'beefing' is understandable, both by pronunciation and the appearance of the written word.

158 Apples: the maximum yield for a small garden

What is the best way to grow a range of apple varieties in a small garden? Would the family tree be suitable?

In a small garden, there is only one way to grow a range of apple varieties. Cordons can be planted as little as two feet apart and if grown away from boundary fencing—i.e. on their own supporting fence—the number of trees can be doubled by planting both sides (see *No. 152*).

The 'family tree', which is a name tagged on to the idea of grafting three or four varieties onto one stock, is very popular. Cross-pollinating varieties ensure a good crop and a succession of ripening fruit, but the total weight of the crop and the number of varieties cannot compete with a collection of cordons.

159 Apples: the curse of Brown Rot disease

Can you tell me what has gone wrong with my Laxton's Superb apples? Last December, the tree was sprayed with DNOC winter wash and later with lime sulphur. Despite this, many of the fruit are spoilt by brown patches of rotten flesh, and they do not keep.

Spraying cannot do much good here, because neglect and bad management must be the most important causes. This is a particularly persistent fungus disease, which first enters a fruit through wounds to the skin, and then develops rapidly to show the familiar brown rotten areas. These are very soon followed by dusty pustules, which can then spread fungus rapidly by contact. It is this disease, in fact, that gives rise to the old proverb about 'not taking long for one rotten apple to spoil all in the barrel'. Near ripening time, the fungus is very virulent and the air is full of spores. Bird-pecked and damaged apples are wide open to attack and soon develop the fungus.

Keep a sharp look out for affected fruit; try to pick them off before they fall. Some varieties, however, react more quickly than others by shedding the affected fruit which the tree knows can never ripen properly and produce viable seed. If affected fruit is found lying on the ground, try to discover exactly where they have come from. The risk is that, before the fruit falls, the fungus may have crept up the stalk involving the spur from which it was hanging and perhaps even extended into the branch. Rotten apples lying against branches can also very quickly infect that branch, and many a tree has been ruined by a rotting apple falling into the crotch of the tree, and not being removed.

Thinning out young fruit in June is clearly important in order to ensure that fruits swell and develop without touching, so that any fruit that succumbs doesn't pass on its malaise by contact. Absolute cleanliness is the most important remedy, at all times.

Apart from watching the fruit on the tree, never leave fallen fruit on the ground because this will certainly ensure that you get the disease again. The tonnage that does fall and rot every year in average gardens is enormous. Search frequently for fallen fruit in long grass. Of course, you can use any good flesh that you can find, and consign any rotting fruit to the incinerator at once. Not a slow smoky smouldering pyre that spreads unkilled spores all over the district, but a fierce blaze.

The same hygiene also applies to fruit in store. Examine them frequently and remove any at the first sign of trouble.

160   Apples : spotted fruit

When the apples are picked from our Bramley's Seedling apple trees, they are plentiful and look in perfect condition. They are stored in the proper manner, but when taken out and cut open they have small brown spots in the flesh. This has happened for the past three seasons; could you please explain and tell me what to do?

This is an almost classic description of Bitter Pit. The dark brown spots in the flesh of the apple suggest that the trouble is a disease, but in fact it is physiological disorder. The reputed causes are legion and not known for certain, and quite possibly the trouble is due to an accumulation of two or more contributory factors. It seems to be worse following dry summers, and more prevalent in conditions that encourage vigorous leaf growth. Lack of calcium also seems to be involved and this appears to be confirmed when a spraying of the tree three or four times with a solution of calcium nitrate, half a pound in ten gallons of water, reduces the incidence. Other opinions are that it is due to a deficiency of one of the trace elements. Boron is one element indicated, because a handful of Borax spread around and hoed in often seems to have cured the trouble. Some varieties seem more prone than others, Newton Wonder being particularly prone and excessively extra heavy wet and dry seasons also have been blamed.

The truth of the matter is that we just do not know the real cause. The one thing that is recognised and certain is that there is no 100 per cent certain or quick solution. Putting together all of the available information about causes, it seems a likely explanation that affected trees have been expected to do too much, and where over-heavy cropping has been boosted by nitrogen feeding and heavy pruning. Read *No. 153* concerning apple feeding and try to achieve a better balance between N, P and K. This, plus plenty of organic material resulting from annual heavy mulches, should make sure that a trace element deficiency is avoided.

Thin out the crop as though you are trying to break biennial cropping, see *No. 154*; that will reduce the cropping load. It will take a year or two to affect the tree's system but then, if the trouble continues, at least it will not be due to overcropping or nutrient deficiency.

161   Apples : James Grieve needs a marriage partner

I have a solitary poor cropping James Grieve apple. I understand it needs a partner. Which do you recommend?

Although James Grieve is popular with many amateur gardeners, it is most frequently commercially grown, not for its fruit but as a pollinator for the very important commercial Cox's Orange Pippin. So what better apple is there than that for you to grow?

Some apples set no fruit at all when they have only their own pollen, others self-pollinate fairly well, but even those varieties which set fruit well with their own pollen, will set more fruits and more regularly when pollinated by another variety. This is why it is always advisable to plant at least two or more varieties, of course ensuring that they are compatible. Other varieties that would pollinate James Grieve are the well-known Charles Ross; Sunset, which is a very prettily coloured apple similar to Cox in flavour; Merton Worcester and, for a dual-purpose, sharp dessert-cooker try Allington Pippin.

162 Apples: little prospects from growing pips

I planted some Cox's apple pips and the seedlings are now about a foot high. Would you let me know if they will ever be of use and, if so, would you advise me how to grow them on?

Whilst it is very satisfying indeed to germinate pips from a fruit you've eaten, don't expect them to be another Cox. You cannot know for certain what the pollinating variety was and you will have to wait anything up to ten years to find out if the progeny are any good. If you can wait that long and have space enough to plant them out, go ahead, but if you really want to put the space to its best possible food-producing use, don't bother! It just isn't worth it! On the other hand, if you just want to grow a Cox's apple, you will only do this by purchasing a properly grafted tree from a good nursery.

Furthermore, you should appreciate that grafting 'choice' varieties onto stocks, is done basically because the variety fruits more prolifically, better, heavier, or earlier than it would do on its own roots and the eventual size of the tree is also influenced. See *No. 151*. Many a pip from a small tree has grown into a poor cropping monster, and although it may by very satisfying to germinate your own pips, in a properly-run efficient fruit garden such a tree has no place.

163 Apples: woolly aphis, the American Blight

My apple tree has white fluffy patches growing all over it. Can you suggest what it is, whether it is harmful and how to deal with it?

This is almost certain to be Woolly Aphis or, as it is commonly called, American Blight. It is often argued that American Blight looks far worse than it really is, which is difficult to believe for anyone who has seen a really bad attack, and the mere fact that even a mature tree's fruit bearing can be disrupted shows just how debilitating the pest can be if it is allowed to get out of control.

The aphis is quite unlike any other aphis

which lay eggs to overwinter. This one persists right through winter which is not the hardship that it might at first seem, because coming from the eastern U.S.A. where winter temperatures can be very much lower than those we experience, our conditions, by comparison, are a holiday in the sun.

The same remarkable reproduction procedure of parthenogenesis is followed as with greenfly (see *No. 1*), which means that an attack can develop into plague proportions in a very quick time. The main problem in controlling the pest is making physical contact. During winter, they cluster several layers thick in the crevices of the bark so that even if a toxic spray penetrates the fluffy waxy covering of the top layer or two, it doesn't reach the innermost pests and enough of them escape to replace the loss in no time at all.

Advice is often given to dab the white patches with methylated spirit and petrol which is supposed to penetrate the wax. This is impracticable when you have a whole tree to deal with and the only way to get on top of the pest is to spray the tree during winter with a tar-oil-based wash. After that, if white patches are seen in spring, spray these at once with Malathion plus a little detergent. This treatment will clean your tree, but you will have to maintain a close watch if the pest is about in the neighbourhood. Re-infection is all too easy with this pest.

164 Apples: maggots in the core

Most of my apples had maggots in the core this year. Can you say what the pest is and how to prevent the trouble next season?

When you bite a ripe apple and find a grub inside it, you can be fairly certain that it is a caterpillar of the Codlin Moth, an absolute beast of a pest. An attack begins with disc-shaped eggs laid singly late in the evening by the night-flying adult moths on a leaf or fruit. These are very small indeed, a mere speck which you are most unlikely to see unless it happens to glint in the sunlight.

The first readily visible sign comes about July when marks appear on the fruits that look like a sting wound. Usually these are very small and have a dry centre spot with a surrounding pinkish ring. This forms because of the premature oxidation of the sugars and pigment substances which are forming just under the skin of the fruit ready to change colour during natural ripening. In this small area, therefore, you have a situation that is analogous to a localised area of premature ripening.

At this stage the grub is very small indeed, but it is inside the apple, out of reach of anything you spray at him. However he is feeding on the pulp of the fruit and very soon the minute sting hole conceals a sizeable

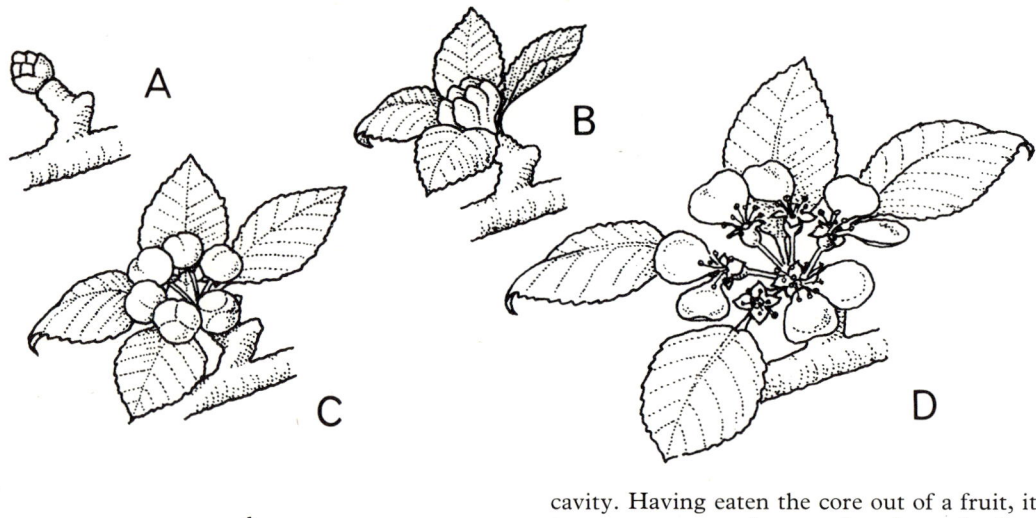

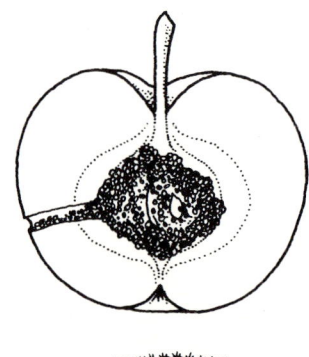

No. 164   *Typical damage done inside an apple and the exit hole made by the larva of the Codlin moth.*

To combat the Codlin moth, spraying should be carried out at the following stages of leaf and bud development : A. dormant   B. green cluster C. pink bud   D. petal fall.

cavity. Having eaten the core out of a fruit, it is not uncommon for a grub to leave the first course and start on the second, boring straight into the side of a nearby fresh apple, leaving a very much larger hole. Fruit damaged in this way will eventually fall and the grubs crawl out and move towards the trunk which they climb, looking for bark crevices in which to hibernate until next spring when adult moths emerge to lay eggs on the small fruitlets, and so begin another life cycle.

It is necessary to look at this life story in detail, not only to appreciate the serious damage that the pest can do, but also to realise the difficulty of the problem of stopping it. So much of the time when Codlin is doing the damage, you can't get at him; the egg stage is so resistant as to be regarded as invulnerable and almost as soon as the egg is hatched the grub bores through the skin and is holed up inside, where he can't be reached.

Commercial growers often use lead arsenate, but this material is extremely poisonous and much too dangerous for amateur use. Many hibernating grubs will be killed by routine winter tar-oil washes but some, of course, will escape and others will arrive from other trees along the road. This is when the one and only short period occurs when control is practicable. From the beginning of petal fall, spray thoroughly with liquid Derris and repeat every week or more often if possible throughout the fruit setting stage and well on into July, in order to blanket the egg laying period and to try to catch the grubs as they hatch and bore straight in. By the end of July, it is too late to do any more, they are out of reach.

When thinning your apple crop, watch out carefully for Codlin signs and, of course, take off all affected fruits first. If they are too unripe to use, throw them to the chickens or burn them. It is unwise to put them on the compost heap because you cannot guarantee that the maggot is going to be killed by generated heat and won't somehow find its way up the tree again.

As soon as apples are seen to drop, or when you know that your tree is affected, put grease bands on the trunks (see *No. 204*) low down to catch the grubs as they climb the trunk. Inspect these grease bands and renew them frequently because trapped and dead grubs very soon become a bridge for the latecomers to cross in safety.

165   Apricots from a stone

I have a nice apricot tree, nearly six years old, which I grew from a stone. It is in a tub and looks delightful, but hasn't produced any blossom. Is it too young, or does it need more root room?

If your expectations extend to anything more than an odd fruit or two, your seedling apricot will certainly need more root space than is provided in a tub. Apricots do come reasonably true from seed but unless you can be quite certain as to its parentage, your seedling is bound to be something of an unknown quantity; an imported apricot could be unsuitable for conditions in this country. How long you will have to wait to find out is also problematical if you leave it in the tub. If you

plant it in the garden, you should not have to wait much longer.

Apricots budded or grafted onto plum stocks generally come into fruit earlier than those on their own roots but the latter live longer. By all means, carry on growing your own apricot and at the very least you will be able to regard the fruit with more pride than anything you buy at the shops.

However, it would have been far better to have taken this as a one-year-old seedling and trimmed back its roots in order to provoke more fibrous root which increases the plant's nutrient absorption ability. Since this was not done then, I suggest that you do it during next autumn after leaf fall. Choose a site near to a wall that will give it shelter from cold northerly winds, and where it won't be shaded from sunlight.

Take out a hole, somewhat larger and deeper than the tub, and then take out a further spit from the bottom. Remove this subsoil and replace it with broken brick and rubble rammed down hard. This is to discourage tap root formation and, by creating an obstruction, encourage the formation of a branched root system which can absorb more nutrient and thus support better crops of fruit.

Lay the tub on its side near the hole. Roll it to and fro to loosen the ball and slide it out. Try to sort out the main root stem which will have been deflected by the bottom of the tub, and is now probably concentrated around the outside and bottom of the root ball. Any of this root stem that is not carrying thin fibrous root, can be cut away with secateurs; if you do this carefully you should be able to retain intact most of the soil ball and a good proportion of the root with it. Position the plant in the hole, and back-fill with plenty of rotted compost well mixed into the soil; back-fill a little at a time, and firm the soil well before adding more. Put down a good mulch of compost around the tree, and as it is absorbed into the soil, keep it replenished.

Read the adjacent items concerning peaches and other stone fruits and follow the general advice concerning feeding and proper training, etc.

166   Avocado pear from a stone

Can I plant an avocado pear raised from a stone eighteen months ago, outdoors for the winter?

The avocado pear, *Persea gratissima*, sometimes called *P. americana*, originates from the warm south-east of U.S.A. and it is only in our extreme south-west areas—Devon, Cornwall, Scilly and Pembrokeshire—that an avocado stands a chance of overwintering outdoors. Even these areas get bad frosts from time to time so planting out is a very risky business.

It will eventually make a large tree and as it has to be overwintered in a well-lit position—a greenhouse or conservatory with a minimum temperature of 50°F—it is only suitable for pot culture, until it becomes too large and has to be disposed of. However, until you have to part company, avocados are worth growing for the satisfaction and reward of germinating seeds that eventually give large handsome evergreen foliage.

167   Bacterial canker attacks the cherry

The branches of our sweet cherry are dying back and some are wet and sticky. Is the tree diseased?

Yes, it is diseased and from the sound of the stickiness, most likely with one of the most serious diseases the cherry can be attacked by—bacterial canker. The disease also attacks plums, and there are several other types of canker which affect other fruits. Infection can be via the leaf in mid-summer, but is more likely to occur in late summer and autumn through open wounds, and can be spread not only by free airborne spores in the case of fungal canker but also by insects and birds carrying both fungal and bacterial infection. This emphasises how important it is to be careful when removing shoots or suckers to protect every wound at once with a fungicidal paint like Arbrex.

There is no satisfactory remedy for the disease. Once the bacteria gain a foothold under the bark, they spread to more and more tissue until the stem or trunk is girdled. Sometimes severe winter comes before this encirclement

is complete, the disease is arrested or dies out, and the tree sets up an isolating healing tissue. However, the chance isn't worth taking. Grub out the tree and burn it before it spreads more infection. See also *No. 179*.

168   Bark-splitting: cause and precautions

Although my eight-year-old Victoria plum tree appears healthy, its bark is splitting. First, small marks appeared, then these spread into long vertical slits; it looks as though the bark was too tight for the tree. It is worst at the base of the trunk, but continues to the top. Could this be a canker?

No, this is not canker although, of course, being an open wound, infection is possible, not only by canker but by several other diseases as well, and it is obviously necessary to prevent organisms gaining entry.

Although it is not entirely unknown in other trees, it is fairly common with plums and greengages in the first half of their lives whilst they are growing to full stature and the main trunk is growing thicker. Plums and gage fruits contain a lot of liquid and there is a period, therefore, when the main trunk is called upon to rapidly pass a considerable volume of sap to the swelling fruit. Indeed, like a tomato splitting when watering follows a dry spell, the onrush of sap can cause enough pressure to cause the bark to split.

Some commercial growers avoid restriction to the sap flow by deliberately slitting the bark, so that bark tension is released and a full flow of sap can rise. They usually do this in April and the wound is healed before too many fungus spores are about.

Don't forget that any wound in the garden, at any time, especially on such fungus-prone trees as plums and gages, should be painted with Arbrex protective. Keep a careful watch, not only for bark splitting to occur in the first place, but also where it has already occurred and been painted. The painted wound can split open further and re-expose living tissue again through the paint layer.

Pay attention to your soil condition, and try

to avoid variation in moisture levels leading to erratic sap flow. Heavy mulching is of vital importance and you can hardly put down too much compost on the soil.

169 Blackberries: how to grow them and avoid the thorns

I have seen the Oregon thornless blackberry described as lusciously sweet, of good quality and on the sharp side. Can you give me your views as I am looking for a variety which crops fairly late, is sweet and thornless? I am now growing Himalaya Giant which I find crops too early, and the thorns are vicious.

The flavour of the Oregon thornless blackberry is largely dependent upon the weather prior to fruiting and it needs an adequate rainfall and intensive sunshine for enough of the natural sugars to form to effectively sweeten the taste. The cropping season is not materially different to Himalaya Giant which, in my

connected criss cross by stout wires like the poles in a hop field. A 'Giant' blackberry planted against each pole is trained up it and the canes fanned out along the wires, to look something like a gigantic pergola. You should be able to adapt this method. If you only have space for one plant, try the umbrella method described in *No. 16*.

There is a tremendously heavy set of fruit this way and most of it hangs down clear of leaves and stems and thorns. Picking is therefore greatly simplified. Heavy cropping also very materially extends the fruiting season because the plant cannot ripen all the fruit at once and in waiting to take its turn much of the fruit is delayed, and a good picking in November is by no means unusual.

Sweetness can be enhanced by encouraging the fullest ripening process. Try putting down sulphate of potash at the rate of 4–5 ozs. spread evenly within a 4 ft. radius all round each plant during May and June.

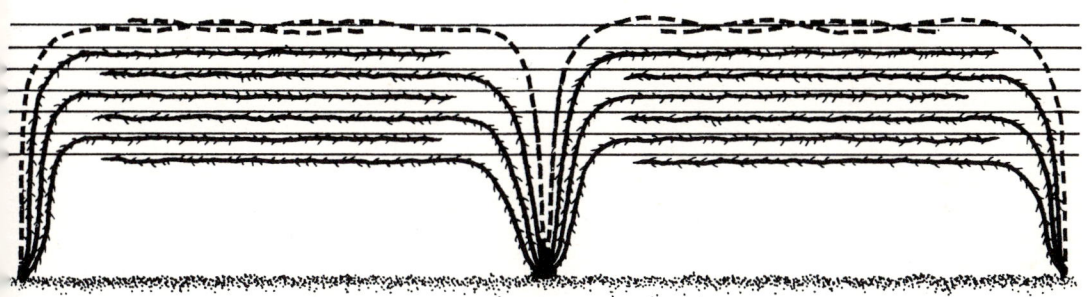

No. 169   *An interesting variation for training blackberries. The dotted lines represent the two strongest new canes destined to replace the top fruiting canes which will be cut out at the end of their third crop. Extra wires are needed to accommodate the canes as they slot together.*

experience, is a much heavier cropper.

Thorns are a problem with the 'Giant', so why not consider growing it in a different way —like the commercial growers do. They grow a great many plants and their method is to erect 5–6 in. diameter poles about 6–7 ft. high and about 8–9 ft. apart to allow the tractor to pass through the rows. The pole tops are

170 Blackberries: a thornless variety growing thorns

I have had an Oregon thornless parsley-leaved blackberry for several years. This year it threw up from the centre a shoot with the same shaped leaf, but with thorns. Is this to be expected, and what should I do about it?

The thornless blackberry is a chimera—this is, one plant growing inside the skin tissue of another. The skin tissue in this case is a thornless form and thus you have a thornless blackberry. The heartwood, however, is of a normal thorned type and sometimes this breaks through and is mistakenly called a 'sport'. It should be pruned at once from the point of emergence.

Thorned growths that arise from the base are much more frequent. Close inspection will reveal these to be suckers arising from the roots. The chimera only extends over the above-ground part, and does not include the root section. Suckers arising from the root are therefore from the heartwood and bear thorns. They are best pulled away if possible, not cut, as this will merely encourage several side shoot growths to arise where only one stood before.

Pruning away old fruited wood should follow normal blackberry practice. Fruiting side shoots will form and can be allowed to grow for two or three years and then taken out as the wood becomes old and tough. When you cut down this variety, it is best to cut not right to ground level but to leave 4–5 ins. to show a couple of embryo buds which can break from above ground level and so preserve the chimera. If you cut too hard and low, you reduce the chances of a chimera bud being left to break and so increase the risk of a thorned root sucker bursting up from below.

There is nothing physically wrong with your blackberry—and thorned growths like this are just one of the expected hazards to be dealt with.

171 Blackberries: fruit mouldy and misshapen

Every year my cultivated blackberry ripens with badly-shaped, mouldy fruits. Why should this be?

The most likely cause is an attack of grey mould following an attack by the raspberry beetle. This pest often begins by damaging a few fruits, which can easily go unnoticed and then, if not detected and dealt with, can in a few years build up to such an infestation that the entire crop can be lost. This is one of those cases where control consists not of attacking the obvious target, but of controlling something entirely different that causes it. Often, but not always, the beetle and mould go together. The larvae of the beetle, which attacks all the Rubus family, damages the berry and the fungus strikes immediately after.

Raspberry beetle is the little wriggling grub that is sometimes met when picking blackberries, and is nearly always in the scum when boiling fruit. As soon as your blackberry flowers have opened, look very carefully in the cup of the petals; if you see a tiny brown beetle about $\frac{1}{8}-\frac{3}{16}$ in. long, you can be sure that it is raspberry beetle. Dust all the blooms with Derris dust and follow this up a little later with a Derris wet spray on the small embryo fruit.

Fruits damaged by the emerging beetle larvae, are open to attack by grey mould and once it starts it can quickly spread to adjacent good fruit. Lime sulphur spraying is the best way to control it. Beginning in early spring, just as the fruit buds are breaking into growth, spray with lime sulphur or Captan just before the blooms open and again just after petal fall. Of course, the blackberry carries its bloom for a long period and you will often find buds opening and petals falling all at the same time— several sprays will therefore be needed.

Cure is all very well, but prevention is better, and it may be worthwhile looking to see if you can improve conditions which may be conducive to fungus. By far the best precaution is to ensure adequate ventilation; fungus is encouraged by stale, stagnant, humid air, so be methodical and ruthless about cutting out and burning old fruited canes so that there is no unnecessary wood causing obstruction to airflow. Try also to keep new canes that you are going to retain, separate from the fruiting canes that will be cut away later; this avoids contact transmission of the disease.

172 Blackcurrants: importance of correct formation

What do I look for when I buy a blackcurrant bush? When is the best time to plant and the best way to feed them?

Don't just buy any nondescript blackcurrants; contact a top-line nurseryman—there are not many of them—pay the price for good clean unreverted stock (see *No. 173*) and make a sound beginning. This is the best advice I can give to anybody about growing blackcurrants.

Choice of variety depends upon how much trouble you are going to take. Wellington XXX is grown a lot commercially for its reliability and is therefore popular with many amateurs. The variety Seabrook's Black produces a heavy crop of fruit which if not so large as some varieties is tip-top for flavour. If you can find room for two varieties, you can spread the season by adding an early variety such as Boskoop Giant or Mendip Cross; to either of the two previously named varieties and if you have room for a third, the variety Baldwin bears very late fruit.

Strong young bushes will have three to five main stems about 2 ft. long or a little longer, of the current season's growth, all light brown in colour and have a root system that is already making a lot of fine fibrous roots. A spindly, uneven double shooter, or even a third uneven one with a thick main tap root and a minimum of fibrous root, may be half the price, but is not worth a tenth.

There is no need to worry about pollination since all varieties are self-fertile and all that is needed for lots of excellent fruit is the absence of late frosts to affect the blossom, cold winds resulting in the loss of bees and insects to do the pollinating, and freedom from the worst pest of all—greenfly.

You must therefore thoroughly spray dormant bushes during each winter with a tar oil winter wash to kill overwintering aphis eggs and, as the buds are breaking green, spray regularly every seven to ten days with an insecticide containing Lindane which is a specific aphis contact killer. Then as foliage and flower buds expand and toughen up, and the pests move off to the succulent soft growth tips, keep after them with a single handed puff-puff spray.

Prepare the planting site by working in plenty of organic material which must be very well rotted. If you can still discern the leaf, stem or other constituents of the compost, it will be too 'short' and must not be dug in. Compost can cause nitrogen starvation if dug in before being thoroughly rotted down, and because blackcurrants must never go short of nitrogen, short compost is better utilised for mulching.

Planting time is November to March, the earlier the better. Fork in a small handful of Growmore or Humber Eclipse under the bush, and position the crown—the breaking point of side shoots—2–3 ins. *below* soil level (as distinct from red currants). Cover the planting area with a two to three inch thick mulch layer. The common practice at this stage is to cut the stems back to about 3 ins. above soil level.

This is all right if you can easily identify an outwards pointing bud above which to cut. If in doubt, shorten back the stems to one third their length and then in early spring, as the buds begin to swell and show, cut back again to about 3 ins. This should be completed well before any green colour shows in the shoots.

Of course, this means that no fruit is borne in the first season, but you will get strong new stems thrown up which will be ready to bear heavily next year. Roots and establishment are always more important than any haste for fruit. See *No. 175*.

Blackcurrants need lots of nitrogen and can take it on a scale that would make other plants sick. If you have poultry, rabbit, pig, cow, or horse manure available, this can be put down fresh as a spring and summer mulch when the fresh urine is rich in nitrogen. This is the very finest way you can feed blackcurrants, but if fresh manure is unobtainable, use dried blood or hoof and horn at an ounce per sq. yd. or an inorganic fertiliser like sulphate of ammonia at the rate of $\frac{1}{2}$ oz. per sq. yd. every two weeks from mid April till end of June early July. Mix the appropriate quantity of fertilisers with peat or grass cuttings and put down as a mulch.

Do not dig around blackcurrants because of the risk of root damage; surface hoeing with a dutch hoe is all that is required to control weeds—but if a thick mulch is maintained, they should never pose any problems or difficulties.

173 Blackcurrants: how to recognise and prevent 'big bud'

My blackcurrant bushes are badly infested with 'big bud'. Should I plant new bushes within 4–5 yards of them?

To the unsuspecting and uninitiated gardener, the promising-looking big fat blackcurrant buds suggest that a big flower truss is coming which therefore promises a healthy crop. But education is cruel when the only crop that emerges is a distorted unyielding fruit truss. These 'big buds' contain many thousands of mites so small that you cannot see them—and you are left wondering what has caused the trouble.

The 'big bud' Gall Mite is microscopically small—several thousands in one single bud; it is so small that it spreads merely by drifting in the wind from garden to garden and bush to bush. After feeding on the leaves of the currant unlucky enough to catch it, females enter the newly forming buds to lay their eggs. Hatching mites feeding within the buds cause abnormal

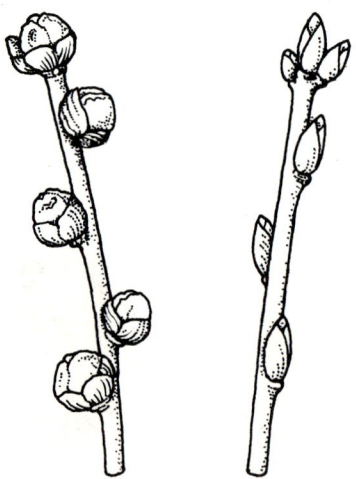

No. 173 *Detecting an attack of Big Bud mite on blackcurrants by the shape of the buds. The infected shoot is on the left, and the healthy shoot on the right.*

development and distorted growth, which is seen as a big, fat, promising-looking bud.

Where the attack by 'big bud' mite is new and only a few buds are affected, pick them off and burn them, and follow with a lime sulphur wash as described later. Where the attack involves over half of the buds the bushes should come out at once and be burned. This is because 'big bud' mite is the carrier of the disease called reversion—see *No. 174*—for which there is no known cure and, as any serious or long-standing infestation will have also led almost inevitably to infection by the reversion virus, there is only one remedy—burning.

'Big bud' mite does not infest soil, and consequently there is no risk in planting into ground once occupied by infected bushes—apart from the fact that it would be better husbandry to change the demand on the soil by planting in a different spot. As the mite travels on the air, new plantings placed near infected stock are virtually doomed from the outset.

In addition to tar-oil spraying which is an absolutely essential part of the blackcurrant programme to keep them clear of greenfly, spraying with lime sulphur must be undertaken against 'big bud'. The time to do this is when the leaf is no larger than a five-penny piece. When you know that the pest has been present, you should use the very strong rate of 1 gallon lime sulphur to 11 gallons of water. This strength of solution is drastic and some foliage scorching must result. The bushes will survive however, and fruiting won't be much affected.

Even when there has been no sign of the pest, annual spraying is essential at the same time of year, but with the strength reduced to 1 part to 50. Some scorching to young leaf will result, but this is acceptable in face of the necessity of keeping 'big bud' under control.

174 Blackcurrants: reversion and how to recognise it

My blackcurrants have not borne fruit for years and when I compared them with the new plants that I put in last year, the leaves were quite different. Could you please tell me why this is so?

No. 174   *Detecting reversion of blackcurrants by the leaf shape. The healthy leaf on the left is even in shape with a definite serrated edge. On the right is a badly reverted leaf which is much more simplified with fewer veins and only a little serration.*

By itself, this is the most serious of all the troubles which affect blackcurrants and within three or sometimes even two years, cropping ability is quite destroyed. As it is also associated with the 'big bud' Gall Mite, definitely proven to be a carrier of the reversion virus, and aphides, which have been under suspicion for doing so, the combined onslaught makes one wonder that we get any fruit at all.

Particularly if you have had occasion to pick off the swollen buds affected by 'big bud', you must regularly and closely examine the leaves —you are looking for leaves that are different. On a reverted bush, the foliage is often darker than normal and each leaf—normally even in shape with a serrated edge—is much simplified, with no serrations, and the lobe ends of each leaf are no longer pointed, but rounded. The bloom, also, of the reverted bush is a different colour—ginger red instead of a pale lavender purple. Instead of currants developing in trusses, those on reverted bushes strip off with perhaps only a single specimen here and there.

There is no remedy: the one and only control of reversion is grubbing out and burning. The removal of a whole branch can sometimes leap ahead of a spreading virus, but the risk isn't worth it. If you read *No. 173*, you will realise how easy it is for the 'big bud' mite carrying the virus to spread, not only from bush to bush, but from garden to garden. If you have detected an infected plant, it is odds on that the others will be affected also, even though they may not yet be showing symptoms.

Blackcurrant bushes are relatively inexpensive and the safest course is to grub out everything, burn them and start again with fresh clean stock and spray regularly to keep the carrier 'big bud' mite and aphides under control.

175   *Blackcurrants : special pruning*

How should I prune blackcurrants I planted last winter? I cut them hard back then.

The basic purpose of pruning blackcurrants is to encourage plenty of growth, and for this reason preparation before planting with plenty of compost dug into the site, and subsequent heavy mulching, must be seen as an integral part of pruning. This will maintain the moisture and nutrient availability that will be required to meet the heavy demands of constant regeneration of growth.

Therefore, at planting time, scatter down into the mulch a small handful of a balanced fertiliser like Growmore, or better still, a slow-release balanced nutrient like Humber Eclipse.

After planting, a one-year-old should be pruned very hard to just above soil level; timidity is the first mistake made by most amateur gardeners. Cut to an outward-facing bud, as close as possible to soil level. This should promote new shoots to grow out from the basal buds; 'should' is the operative word, because it can do this only if it draws on adequate nutrient sources. Pruning hard means feeding well.

During the first summer, strong young shoots should develop. There should be no suggestion of fruit at this stage and, by autumn, the plant will be looking more like a 'bush'. A couple of weeks after the last leaves have fallen from it, indicating that all growth and development has finished for the season, you must prune again. If the plantings were small one-year-olds, you will now have two, three or perhaps four stems.

During autumn, replenish the mulch, and each spring spread the same plant nutrient as before.

It is now a two-year-old and at this stage you can pick up the procedure as if the bushes you planted were two-year-olds. Prune the bushes down again, except for one strong stem which can be left to carry a little fruit next season. Then at the third year you will have

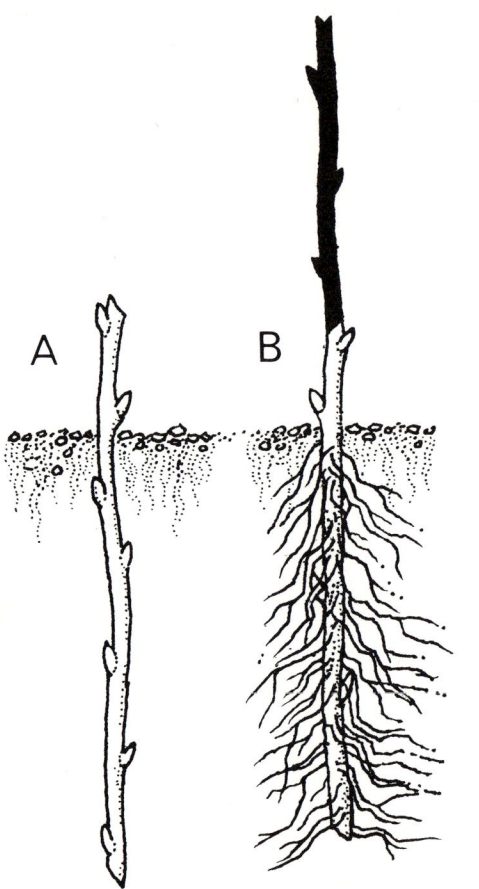

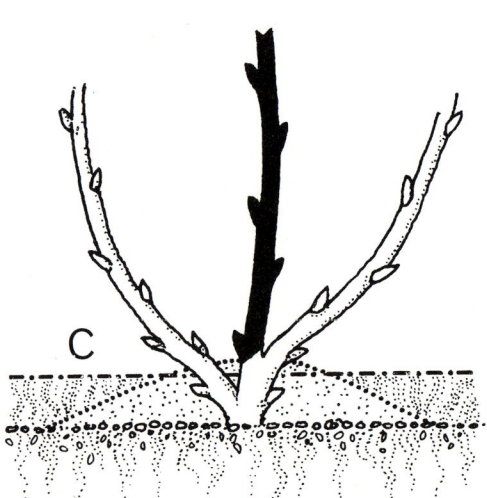

No. 175   *Stages in the propagation of a blackcurrant bush.*
A.   An autumn planted cutting, set with only two buds showing above ground.
B.   The same cutting a year later. One of the two buds has grown to make a single shoot, with growth buds closely set at its base. This shoot is cut back hard to within an inch or two of soil level.
C.   Another year later and last year's basal buds have grown out to three or four strong shoots. One (if three) or two (if four) can be left to carry the first crop. The other shoots should be cut back hard to their basal buds. When the bush is planted into its permanent position, it should be planted to a deeper position or, alternatively, the original depth can be raised by heaping the soil into a mound—called a clone— indicated by the dotted line.

No. 175   *The same blackcurrant plant at four years old. The two-year-old wood is shaded and the wood which needs removing is shown in black. Note two new stems arising from below ground level. These should be cut back hard in order to encourage the basal buds to develop into stems which will replace the two-year-old wood when it is removed next year. This will be a continuing pattern and each two to three years old wood must be ruthlessly removed to leave room for new growth to develop fully.*

many more stems; cut back half of these to basal buds at soil level, leaving the outer half to carry a crop next summer.

From these cropping stems, some growths will develop which will bear fruit the following season. The close cutting back will have produced new shoots, arising from, at or below the soil surface. Subsequent pruning after each leaf fall should then consist of cutting back hard one stem at least, or perhaps two of the two-year-old stems which have fruited if the bush is growing strong and vigorously. This is where your planting preparation and subsequent mulching and feeding will begin to tell.

This hard cutting back of the older wood is done in order to encourage the strong growth stems to form from just below soil surface. Therefore, the bush is composed of a constantly regenerating regularly-spaced cluster of strong young growths, each mainly supported by its own roots and not dependent upon the roots of the old original base stem. This is important because if your pruning is not hard enough to produce stems from below the soil surface with their own roots, you will inevitably produce a bush 'on a leg'. You cannot expect much top growth or fruit if the bush has to depend upon such a limited root system. A blackcurrant is a gross feeder. It must have as much root system as you can encourage it to develop, and this is why it must be mulched and fed regularly as an integral counterpart to pruning.

176 Blackcurrants : blistered leaves

What is causing the red raised bumps on my blackcurrant leaves and what is the cure? Will this trouble affect the fruit?

These small discoloured distortions of growth cells, that look like blisters, are caused by the currant blister aphis. This pest is normally much more common on redcurrants than on black. Although it is often considered that only a very severe attack and much leaf distortion will significantly affect the fruit crop—and, for that reason, does not evoke such swift and drastic counter measures as do many other pests—the real danger of the pest is not so much in what it does, as what it indicates.

Greenfly aphides occur in many forms and if the currant blister kind are around, it is certain that the others are too. The greenfly, in sucking sap from the plant tissues, has the disgusting habit of regurgitating saliva and sap back down its sucking tube into the plant's sap stream. Plants often react to this 'injection' of regurgitated liquid by distortion, curling, blistering etc. which can, and often does, prevent the leaf from fully performing its proper function, so that fruiting and growth are impaired.

There is also danger arising from a side effect. As you are probably aware, aphis secrete a sugary liquid called honeydew and sometimes in such quantities that it drops to the ground— as many owners of cars parked under lime trees know to their cost! This sugary residue is the perfect material for the culture of moulds and other fungi. In a damp muggy season, fruit can often be lost through going mouldy and there is no need to encourage it by letting aphides practise their filthy habits. Sooty mould can also develop, living on the honeydew; see *No. 212.*

Serious as all this is, it is minor compared to the risk of virus infection, and aphides often take an important and primary role in spreading virus. It has been found that many viruses cannot be transmitted, even by grafting infected plants onto healthy ones, and in order to become capable of infection have to pass through an incubation stage within the body

of the aphis. All very alarming you may think— and it is a measure of the risk you are running in not keeping the aphides under control.

Spray your bushes with tar oil wash during the dormant winter period to kill any over-wintering eggs and as soon as the foliage emerges in spring, keep a sharp look out on shoot tips and other areas of soft growth where immigrant aphides make for first. Spraying with a contact killer containing Lindane or Malathion will quickly destroy them.

177 Blueberry : its soil requirements

I want to grow some blueberries. What conditions do they like?

Blueberries are definite about their dislike of lime so the first thing you must do is to establish whether your soil is acid or alkaline by testing with a soil-testing kit which you can buy quite cheaply from Boots or a good garden shop.

An acid reaction is ideal, but if your soil is alkaline you will find that the most satisfactory —if not the only—way to grow blueberries is to plant them in raised beds on a plastic sheet to insulate the acid bed from the alkalinity underneath. See *No. 116.* Use acid soil, or the proprietary preparation 'Arthur Bower's Eric-aceous Compost' to 'fill in' the raised bed. Plant young bushes in late autumn and do not prune for three years. Older stems will now be becoming woody; cut these back hard to new shoots arising from the base. Pruning, from then on, consists of steadily removing old wood in order to promote the constant upthrow of vigorous growth.

In March and April, delicately scented white flowers are borne which are noted for their ability for withstanding late frosts. Berries start to ripen towards the end of July and swell to the size of marbles. The flavour is unusual, rather like the quince. The best modern blueberries are hybrids and you should plant at least two bushes so that flowers cross-pollinate and produce a heavy crop.

Being shallow rooted, they benefit from mulches of peat or garden compost provided you can be quite sure that lime is not being introduced from the soil adhering to plants put on the compost heap. For the same reason, it is preferable to avoid farmyard manure or mushroom compost.

Keep up the plant nutrient availability by dressing with a slow, organic-based manure that is N.P.K. balanced—i.e. Humber Eclipse —at the rate of 1 oz. per square yard. Put down two dressings a month apart, March and April.

178   Capsid bug and understanding it

Last year my apples were disfigured with smoothish brownish lumps. What caused them?

This sounds like capsid bug, a pest that attacks all manner of plants besides apples, upon which it is probably best known. The control of it is the most convincing argument for equipping yourself with a highly efficient sprayer, one that is capable of projecting quantity with penetrating force. In my opinion, a pump-up sprayer using compressed air to propel the liquid is not strong enough, and a one-handed puff-puff is plainly ridiculous. The best type for the amateur is the double-action hand-held stirrup pump type—such as models 27 and 28 made by Solo—that sucks from a bucket, or from a tank on your back if you prefer to struggle with the straps instead of moving the bucket around. You'll need an extension lance to reach up into the taller trees.

If you see the bug before it sees you and gets round the back of a leaf out of sight, or drops to the ground, you'll notice that the full-grown capsid is built like a streamlined aphis, but with wings and the ability to run very quickly indeed. Control by contact killing is not very satisfactory because of the short period available in which to get at the pest.

Egg laying is done in June to July and the eggs are inserted deep into the crevices of bark, twigs, branches, fruit spurs, etc. These eggs do not hatch until the following year in April and May and the active young bugs begin feeding at once, making minute punctures which soon develop a reddish margin and which may be detected on the leaves and shoot tips. But under the suede-like down that covers the apple fruitlets, they are virtually impossible to see.

Distortion is going on under the skin, however, and as the fruitlet grows, the punctures become scars and blotches as the flesh erupts and swells into the familiar lumps, and when several of these merge together, the fruit becomes shapeless and deformed.

Fortunately, the egg is easily killed, but the problem is a physical one of getting the killing agent deep into the crevices where the eggs have been laid—hence the special sprayer needed. An effective control is either Ovamort, Thiol, or DNC winter wash, applied with penetrating force to the bark and all woody parts—branches, twigs and stems. Merely spraying and wetting is no good: the tree must be forcibly drenched.

179   Cherry: fruit on an ornamental tree

For the past nine years we have watched our flowering cherry growing wider and taller and it is now huge! This year, the only branch that flowered with the double pink blossom was the centre one—all the other branches were covered with a single white blossom. Now we have lots of cherries ripening. Is it possible for a flowering cherry to revert to a normal cherry? The fruit looks perfectly normal but tastes very bitter.

This is not a case of reversion but of 'growing out' by the stock. The double flowered cherry was originally budded or grafted onto another more vigorous-growing variety—either a wild cherry or a stock called Mazzard, often used for this purpose. The stock, finding that its new head could not take all the energy it wanted to give, simply burst out with new growth shoots of its own. This sort of behaviour can frequently be detected in many grafted and budded plants by the different appearance of foliage and/or flowers. You will very often see it in a rose bed, for instance, with a many-thorned and light-coloured briar arising among the other darker foliage of the choice rose varieties.

This is what happened, unrecognised, several years ago with your cherry and the growth shoots of the stock, bursting out and not having been removed, have grown on to become branches at the expense of the choice flowered variety.

You now have to decide which you want: fruit, such as it is—and it doesn't sound very appetising—or to embark on a drastic and possibly risky operation of removing the firmly established wild branches so that the solitary ailing double cherry receives a shot in the arm.

If you decide on the second and lengthy course, obtain a good supply of fungicidal protective paint such as Arbrex and make sure you protect all cuts as soon as you make them. With a root stock nine years established, you cannot remove all the wild branches at once and expect the one double flowering shoot to take the full flood of sap; you will have to do it gradually. Sometime during the winter, start with the two largest wild branches: take these out as close to the main trunk as you can in order to try and preserve a nice shape, and protect the wounds at once. In the spring, the choice flowering part will be galvanised into activity. If this takes the form of a forest of shoots, make sure they are of the double flowered variety above the graft and thin them out as they occur. These shoots should be developed into an open frame-work, rather like a shuttlecock. On the other hand, the removal of two branches may provoke an outburst of shoots from the remaining wild wood. Rub these out as soon as they appear.

If you do get a quick reaction of new shoots from either choice or wild wood, it is a sign that you can tighten the screw a little more. Don't do this by taking off another branch in full growth with the sap flowing; this would be too great a shock for the entire tree. Instead, cut back all the wild main stems and leading shoots by up to a quarter of their length—and, of course, protect all cuts. Next year, you can take another branch, or even two, and so on according to how the choice double variety grows and is able to take over the entire thrust coming from the stock below.

The entire transformation may take several years—you will have to be patient but, with care and understanding, the job can be done. The big danger, at all times is Silver Leaf and

bacterial canker getting in. You have a lot of cutting to do and the tree will be open to infection through every wound for a long time. Don't take a single chance. Paint every wound as it is made.

180   Cherry and its die-back

I should appreciate advice regarding my Cheal's weeping cherry tree. This was bought two years ago and last year bloomed quite well. This year, one arm seems to have died off and the others, although coming into bloom, seem to have lengthened considerably. Can you tell me whether the tree should be pruned? There are a number of smaller arms starting to grow from the top. I have removed the old shoots I found on the trunk. What happens when the arms reach almost to the ground?

This sounds like die back caused by fungal attack. Unfortunately, all members of the Prunus family are liable to be attacked by several fungus diseases. Silver Leaf is the most well-known, but there are several others, and it is impossible to be precise on just this evidence. They have a similar effect in causing shoots and stems to die back from the point where the fungus spores gained entry, i.e. a wound, whether deliberate or accident, that was not covered and protected at once. (See *No. 167.*) Although not necessarily inevitable, the result, more often than not, will be death of the tree unless you do something about it as soon as suspected.

These fungi spread along the cambium layer—that is, the very thin green-coloured layer just below the bark—or woody skin that covers shoots and stems before they are old enough to have 'bark'. Within the cambium, runs the very life stream of the tree. The fungus stops this and as it proceeds, so foliage and side shoots wither—and the die back evolves.

Infected cambium turns brown, which you can see by pulling back a very thin pinpoint sliver of skin with the blade of a knife. Therefore, at the very first signs of anything untoward in the foliage, you should lift a tiny sliver of bark to see if the tell-tale brown staining is present. If you do detect it, snip through the stem or twig with secateurs and you will see the stain has caused a brown ring at the cut instead of a green one. Then snip more and more, inch by inch until you have overtaken the fungus in its travels and are into clean healthy wood. Continue to the next bud or lateral shoot, paint over the wound with Arbrex and finally, most important of all, clean up *all* the clippings meticulously and burn them. Any clipping of diseased wood, however small, left lying on the ground is a possible source of further infection.

As they near the ground, the long pendulous branches of weeping cherries should be stopped an inch or two short, and the cut end painted. Odd shoots on the trunk are best removed whilst they are still small enough to be rubbed off or, at most, pulled out by finger and thumb. Never wait until they have to be cut by knife or secateurs. The clean cut is tantamount to pruning and to allow even a small leaf to form is to allow a food build-up at the base of the shoot to provide the reserve for another shoot to be developed.

Don't forget to paint every single cut you make.

181 Cherry: its complicated pollination rules

I have just bought a Black Heart cherry tree. Will it pollinate itself, or do I have to buy another one?

Pollination of cherries is a very complicated business, and it is quite useless planting only one tree by itself and expecting to get a crop. No cultivated variety of sweet cherry will set fruits with its own pollen; the flowers can only be fertilised by a different variety. Furthermore, cherry varieties form into groups within which pollination between varieties is useless, so fertilisation has to be not only from another variety, but also from another group. There are twelve of these groups, so you can see the advisability when buying cherries of not only buying no less than two but of ensuring their compatibility. A really serious and good class nurseryman will be able to advise you all about this. Don't take for granted that the two

varieties he is anxious to sell you are compatible. Ask to see his copy of the fertility tables and if he cannot or will not, go elsewhere.

For your Black Heart, you will need another that flowers at about the same time. Suitable varieties would be Early Rivers, a black cherry that is ready for picking in June; or Knight's Early Black; or Elton Heart, a yellow and red cherry, very large, which flowers a little later than Black Heart, but usually with sufficient overlap to ensure adequate pollination.

182 Cherry: pruning method for a Morello

We have had a fan-trained Morello cherry for four years, so it is probably six years old. It bears some fruit, but the vigour of its shoots is worrying us since we wish to keep it to a frame 7 ft. high and 14 ft. wide. We intend to thin the laterals drastically, but the question is, should we carry out root pruning as well?

The pruning of the 'sour' or Morello cherry is a bit of a puzzle to some professionals, as well as to the amateur. A lot of people prune it as though it were an apple, trying to produce fruit spurs. This is quite wrong, as almost all the fruit is borne on wood that has developed during the year prior to fruiting. This means that if you look at a tree in fruit you will find extending growth shoots growing on from a section of fruiting wood, and further back behind the fruiting section bare branch wood with, here and there, an occasional spur that may hold a cherry or two.

This means that the tree will naturally grow long slender branches and take up a lot of space. The only way to avoid this is to cut back one or two of the older branches each year and to replace them by selecting young basal growths which break from the centre of the tree, and then allowing these to grow out and in due course bear fruit. The object should be to take out just enough each year to keep a succession of stems growing out from the centre, and your tree appears to be at just about the right stage to commence this procedure.

Most gardeners, not knowing about this process, watch their Morellos getting bigger

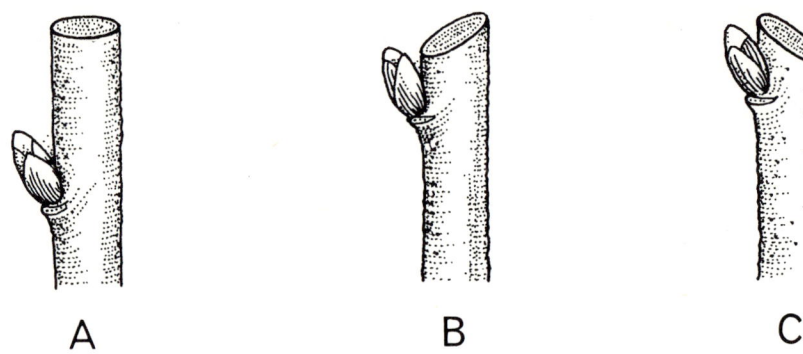

No. 182   *Common pruning faults.*
A.   This is totally wrong; square cut and too far above the growth bud.
B.   Still incorrect. The cut is better but slopes in the wrong direction; the cut should always slope away from the bud. Both A and B are liable to die back.
C.   The correct method.

and bigger until, in desperation, something drastic has to happen. The main cutting back should be done in October to head back the young growths at the centre to single pointed growth buds; double buds are fruiting buds. For the time being, we want no fruit on these shoots, but more growth.

It is most important that you realise with all this pruning and heading back that there is always the very severe risk of infection with Silver Leaf fungus and all cuts should be immediately painted with a fungicidal protective such as Arbrex. See *Nos. 167* and *180.*

183   *Cobnuts : involved pruning method*

I have a seedling cobnut bush that is five years old, but so far it hasn't produced any nuts. Can you tell me how old it must be before it begins cropping?

Even from a seed taken from a named variety, seedling cobs are very much like wild hedgerow trees, in that nut bearing is very erratic. You can expect the first nuts in about six or seven years' time, but you will only get very small nuts and a small crop unless you carry out a rather elaborate pruning programme.

With cobs, pruning is everything. It starts when a sucker or seedling is first cut down to about 18 in. from soil level so that the topmost buds grow out to form shoots. These are then reduced to three, spaced evenly apart which, by heading back the following year and taking the two foremost and strongest shoots on each, are induced to become six evenly-spaced shoots. By repeating the process next year, you will have twelve. The object is to produce an open centred form like a shuttlecock, and achieve this by selecting the buds at each stage best placed to grow in the desired direction.

This pruning is best done at the earliest stage of a bud's growth into a shoot, by nicking off the unwanted buds with the thumb nail. When the twelve leaders reach the required height, a light tipping back each year to a bud suitably placed to grow on, encourages the side shoots—which should be spurred back—to produce the twiggy growths upon which the nuts will be borne. Cutting back like this is repeated on a lessening scale each leaf fall, always to an outward-facing bud and thus a strong shuttlecock frame is built-up, clothed with these twiggy nut bearing shoots.

Male catkins will eventually form to shed

pollen that will be received by the small female flower tufts which will form the nuts. As soon as no more pollen falls when the catkins are shaken, indicating that the pollination stage is finished, spring pruning can begin. Shorten back the catkin-bearing side shoots to three or four buds. This will have the effect of producing vigorous side shoots from basal buds. In July or August, snap these between finger and thumb, but leave them hanging. This restricts growth and induces the production of both catkin buds and the small red coloured female flowers. Then, at the next leaf fall, at the same time as the main stem heading back is done these broken shoots should be cut out just above the second or third—whichever is upward-facing—bud from base.

At this time, also thin out old wood which has borne nuts in the current year, so that a constant replacement of new twiggy wood is produced. Any strong growths that arise from the centre, additional to the main leader system, should be cut out; better still, rubbed out whilst still very young. Suckers may spring from near to the main stem, prompted by the severe topping and restriction going on above. Watch for them and pull them out, but do not cut.

This rather involved pruning system may be altogether too much for many gardeners. Cultivation then can be a compromise between diligent attention and neglect, but you will not get such big nuts or such heavy and regular cropping. Simply let the tree follow its own inclination, subject to keeping it to required size. Keep the centre open and remove any sucker growths that arise. See *No. 184*.

184 Cobnuts and how to deal with cob suckers

What should I do about suckers on a cobnut tree; cut or not?

First see *No. 183* concerning cob pruning. Under no circumstances should you cut these suckers; this is only a form of pruning and inevitably will produce side growths and your problem will be worse than before.

Clear the soil around the base of the suckers if necessary in order to trace them back to the point of origin at the main roots. Then twist and tear them out so that the basal buds are removed. If you cut, you will almost certainly leave basal buds that will then spring into growth. Tear the sucker away and paint the wood at once with Arbrex protective paint, and cover up again.

185 Crab apple : why no fruit?

I planted a half-standard Pyrus eleyi *two seasons ago, so that I could have a supply of crab apples. It is about 10 ft. high but it has never flowered. Do these crabs have to reach a certain age before flowering? Also, can I give it the same treatment as apple trees?*

This crab apple is correctly *Malus eleyi*, not Pyrus which is now used specifically for pears. It is rather unusual for *eleyi* to be so reluctant to bloom even if only just one or two flowers—but not unknown.

It is possible that it could be concentrating upon making growth and becoming thoroughly established at the expense of flower, in which case it will soon settle down and behave normally. Conversely, it could be struggling in conditions that it does not like or suffering from dryness at the roots.

If you read the other notes on the planting of shrubs and trees, you will realise that one of the most important aids to flowering and fruiting comes before planting. This is the incorporation of plenty of compost into and around the planting hole so that moisture is held, and with it plant nutrients in solution.

If you didn't prepare properly before planting, it is too late now, so mulch heavily and put down three dressings of a balanced fertiliser, Growmore or Humber Eclipse—2 oz. per sq. yard hoed in; the first in March, the others following a month apart. Repeat each spring for the next three years by which time the tree will have been growing for five years, and not until then will it be really firmly established. Do not hesitate to get the hose out in dry weather and let water dribble slowly for a few hours.

At least now, any refusal to flower will not

be because of dryness at the roots or nutrient shortage. If the tree still has not flowered in a couple of years, you will have to be brutal with it; root pruning or bark ringing will shock the tree into thinking it is about to suffer death. The natural reaction to this is to try to ensure the continuance of its own species, which the plant does by trying to produce seed which, in turn, has to be preceded by flowers.

If you haven't already got it and have space for another tree, plant the variety 'John Downie'; this is the best fruiting crab apple of all.

186   Damsons and the dreaded Silver Leaf disease

This year some pale mauve fungi have grown from the bark of an old damson tree in our garden. Some branches appear to be dead and I think the tree is dying. What do you suggest?

There is not much doubt here. The parasitic fungus *Stereum purpureum* is usually associated with plums, and stoned fruits—but it will also attack other trees, including apples (see *No. 180*). The symptoms of attack are well decribed by the common name Silver Leaf but the fully-developed fungus eventually appears on dead wood as a purple or lavender-coloured crust, usually with a whitish rim later fading to a dirty brown. Crusts may appear in layers and at this stage the disease is extremely infectious. There is no remedy for this disease and any silvering of leaves must be met by cutting back all wood until clean wood is reached and then sealing the wound with fungicidal paint. Infected, but still living wood, will show patches or traces of brown staining in the green cambium layer just below the bark. Clear green cambium will be reached beyond where the fungus has spread.

Clearly this old damson tree must be removed at once and your clearing up afterwards must be immaculate. The very smallest piece left lying around merely harbours the disease. Don't store the timber for logs. All infected wood must be burned at once in a fierce blaze—not a slow smouldering heap which can spread spores for miles around. If you cannot burn

the wood properly yourself, contact the local Council to have it removed to the public incinerator. The Silver Leaf Order of 1923 makes it an offence not to remove an affected branch or to allow a killed tree to remain standing. Little notice seems to be taken of it these days which is crazy, because Silver Leaf is a very dangerous disease.

187   Damsons: cross-pollinator   for plums

I already have Victoria and Coe's Golden Drop plums and an Early Transparent gage, and I would like to add a damson this autumn. Could you give me the name of a dessert damson that would cross-pollinate the best?

This is a good idea for a reason other than your desire to crop damsons. The damson suckers freely and in several parts of the country where plums and greengages are grown commercially, growers often set damsons in the hedgerows, where they not only provide a marketable crop, but perform a useful function as a pollinator.

As often happens, even with trees that are self-fertile like your Victoria plum, fertilisation and fruit setting are better with the aid of a cross-pollinator. The variety Merryweather, which has large black fruits almost plum size, is best for your purpose, as it is compatible with your two gages which will also benefit.

188   'Family' trees and the problems of varied pruning

Will you tell me how to prune a 'family' apple tree planted last year and fruiting this autumn? The tree is grafted with the varieties James Grieve, Merton Worcester and Sunset. Some of the branches have grown very long, particularly on James Grieve which has produced only one apple.

'Family' trees are available in certain fruits other than apples and with two, three or even four varieties grafted on a stock, have attained some popularity and admittedly enable a 'variety of varieties' to be grown where space is limited. However, before planting, you would be wise to think very carefully about the disadvantages. This 'variety of varieties' factor has at once to be considered when pruning because some varieties are stronger growing than others and will both take and require heavier pruning—and likewise can respond with stronger and variable growth. This is not by any means unusual and you will have to be careful to avoid one variety becoming dominant and trying to overpower the others. In my opinion, sloping cordons are a very much better proposition especially if you practise sap flow restriction by bending—see *No. 152.*

For the first two or three years, 'family' trees need a little time spent in trying to develop a good framework structure. Don't be in a hurry for fruit; get a nice evenly-spaced open-centred frame, from which later fruit-bearing wood can develop.

During winter dormancy, cut back the best and strongest branches to downward-pointing buds. It is quite impossible to be precise about this because, as noted above, the vigour varies, both of stock and the union made by each graft etc.

In general terms, the branches of Merton Worcester and Sunset can be shortened back by six to nine inches, depending upon where the downwards-facing bud is positioned; those of the more vigorous Grieve can go back by about twice as much, some twelve to fifteen inches. Apart from this, all that should be needed is thinning out of weak or congested growth as required; and always cut back and/or remove shoots that cross, touch or rub. This is a most important factor with this kind of tree because, by its very nature, you are trying to pack a lot into a small space and it is quite easy to allow rubbing damage to occur which provides a wide open door to fungal attack.

Finally, when pruning, *always* touch over the pruned exposed cuts with a protective paint like Arbrex.

You will now see why you should not be conditioned by any thoughts of getting a balance in the amount or length of growth or symmetry in the final pruned shape. You will realise also why it is imperative that each variety must be separately labelled.

189   Figs : care and cultivation

I am a relative newcomer to gardening and would like to grow figs. Could you advise me on the best way to grow them, and something about the different varieties.

Figs come from the eastern Mediterranean region, and to properly ripen their fruits—if indeed to grow at all without suffering—need more light and warmth than our summers usually bring. They have, however, been grown in England since the twelfth century and it is an old maxim that figs should be grown within sight of the sea. This observation should not be taken literally; it arises because it is only in the south of the country—Sussex, Hampshire, the Isle of Wight, Cornwall, Dorset, Devon, and where the Gulf Stream reaches the west coast, i.e. Pembrokeshire, Lleyn Peninsular and Anglesey—that the fig can be grown with any real confidence of getting a worthwhile crop.

Since they dislike draughts, it is no good growing them against a fence through which the wind can whistle. You will need a south-facing wall in full sun to which it can be trained fan-wise. A rich fertile soil is fatal because it results in rank growth and no fruit. If you want figs the tree has to be kept in a prison, with little room to move.

According to the space you have available, take out a hole about 5 ft. long by 3–3½ ft. wide by 2 ft. deep, at the base of the south-facing wall. Keep the two top spits of soil and cart the rest of the subsoil away. Line the pit walls with bricks—you can use old ones for this purpose, making sure that they fit together tightly with no gaps—or erect shutter boards and make a pit lining of concrete. Now fill in the bottom 9 inches with paving stones, brick or hard core; pack it carefully and ram it tight. This is going to allow drainage of water, but as it is going to discourage formation of a single main root, other vigorous roots will form to seek out any weaknesses the pit walls and floor may have, so they must therefore be made impenetrable.

When set hard, refill with the two top soil spits and, if you can get it, half a dozen buckets of plaster rubble—or failing this, gravelly grit—

and sprinkle 14 lbs. of gypsum on the surface to allow it to weather-in during the winter. No manure or fertilising is necessary yet. You can carry out this construction work as convenient during autumn and winter ready for planting in the early spring. Buy a young tree that is pot-grown. Brown Turkey variety is best; it is the hardiest and crops well in late summer with large, brown richly sweet fruits. Set it so that it can be trained against the wall. Hoe in 3–4 oz. of Humber Eclipse balanced manure and mulch over with rotted compost or mushroom compost. The top of the pit wall should be clear of top soil or mulch because if you allow it to become covered and submerged, the restricted roots will try to grow over the top into the soil outside and immediately give the tree an outlet for its energy by throwing up suckers.

Allow long shoots to form and train these so that they grow like the spokes of a cartwheel about a foot apart. The fig's method of fruiting is unusual, with the fruit being borne at the shoot ends. Therefore, pruning must be designed to ensure a succession of new growth arising from the base to grow out like a spoke to the edge of the wheel. You may have side shoots arising from the main spokes—these will help to fill in the spaces and will also bear fruit. Eventually, the fruit-bearing shoot growths, ever extending outwards, will reach the limit of available space. Try to plan therefore to take out not more than one such main leader or 'spoke' in any one year, and train into its place a new shoot to grow on and produce fruit. Next year another may come away, then another, so that by the time you have replaced all the spokes the first replacement has reached its limit and with the wheel having turned full circle, you can begin the cycle again.

During the winter, the embryo figs will need protecting from frost. You can wrap the shoots individually in straw, like great big finger stalls, or cover the entire tree with straw hurdles or straw mattresses, made by tucking straw into draped netting or branches of evergreen material.

Some authorities recommend lifting the fig every fourth year—the idea being that the root

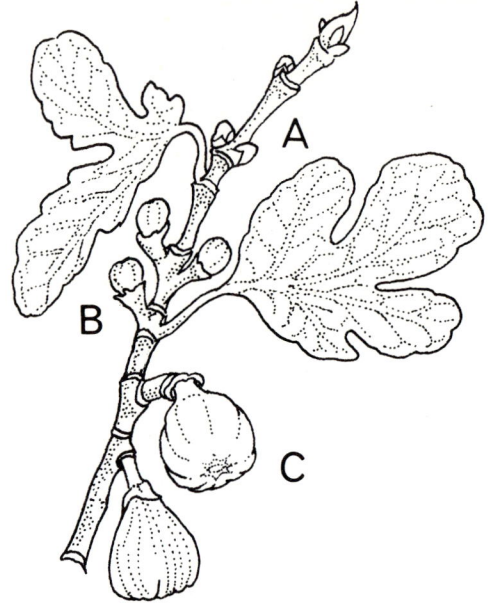

No. 189 *Fruiting of the fig.*
A. Embryo figs which develop next year. These will need protection during the winter.
B. The early figs produced during the current year and which will not ripen so they should be removed so the plant's energies are directed into the fruits it can ripen.
C. Last year's embryos and this year's crop.

system will inevitably be damaged and thus pruned. To deliberately prune with secateurs is a tremendous job as the tree becomes bigger; it should not be necessary if the pit has been built securely with a hard-packed floor. But if you want to go to a little extra trouble, here is a method I have seen practised with the variety Brunswick—the largest outdoor variety growing in Britain, and which regularly gives a most prolific crop of green figs each August. The fruit is green and although the flavour is good, it is not so sweet and sugary as Brown Turkey. Make the pit 18 ins. longer and 10 ins. wider than the dimensions above and, every fourth year, dig a trench inside the pit wall just a spade width and two spits deep, down to the hard core floor chopping with the spade any roots that are met.

Always pick the figs off the tree as soon as they are ripe—if the birds don't get them first. Never drop a damaged fig on the ground or leave a ripe one lying about. This only encourages birds, so much so that they turn their attention to other fruits. This is one of the risks you take in growing figs.

In addition to the varieties mentioned, Black Ischia gives medium-sized deep purple figs with a good flavour, a little earlier than the others. White Marseilles, on the other hand, fruits later into September bearing pale yellow very sweet figs.

190   Figs : growing in a tub

Please advise me how to grow a fig in a tub, against a north wall with a southerly aspect.

First read *No. 189*. To translate this to tub-growing, the first point to realise is the risk during winter of exposing the roots to frost through the sides of the pot. It must, therefore, be moved into a greenhouse or conservatory or some frost-free place during winter. Next, fan training in the tub would produce an unmanageable size; therefore, a tub-grown fig should be grown as a bush, and is placed in the garden where it is sheltered and gets full sun.

Follow the same pattern of rubble and soil except that because the tub is so much smaller than a pit and the soil contents are therefore so much less, make it one-quarter rubble to three-quarters soil. A tub is more liable to dry out than even the fiercely draining pit; therefore it will have to be kept watered during the summer and because this will wash out nutrients, you will need to replace them. I would suggest 1 oz. of Humber Eclipse which is slow to break down into plant nutrient and therefore resists the rapid leaching. This should be scratched into the soil surface each month from February to August.

Other than to keep the bush shaped and nicely balanced, pruning will not be necessary until it comes into fruit—again, see *No. 189*.

After you have taken fruit, remove the longer of the fruited shoots during winter; this will mean sacrificing some embryo figs, but it cannot be helped and, in any case, they will be replaced by other younger shoots arising from lower down. The object is to maintain a nice balance between taking out over-long stems and replacing them with new shoots coming forward. This way the tree doesn't become too big and you can keep up maximum cropping.

191   Figs : growing from seed

Can I grow a fig tree from the seed of the fruit? If so, do I sow the seed just as it is, or should it be washed?

The seed of figs grown in Britain will not germinate, however ripe the fruit becomes. This is because pollination is effected, astonishingly, by the larvae of an insect called Blastophagus and as it will not live in our climate the seeds grown here are infertile and it is no good sowing them.

You may be able to germinate seed from uncooked figs imported around Christmas time. There is no need to wash them; you can separate them rather like those of a tomato by laying them out to dry and sowing the seed into John Innes seed compost. They will need a minimum temperature of 50° F and germination may be erratic and take some time.

It is, however, very questionable whether you will ever get a sufficient crop of figs—indeed, if any—to warrant the trouble. A seed from a tree growing abroad is hardly likely to be of any use in our conditions and whilst you will, of course, derive satisfaction from successfully germinating fig seeds in this way, you would be much better advised to grow a variety more suitable to our climate if you want to grow and pick your own figs. See *Nos. 189* and *190*.

192   Figs : and a curious method of fruiting

I have a Turkey fig tree growing against a south-west facing wall. It is loaded with fruit about the size of walnuts but as they formed late in the summer, there seems no chance of them ripening. Can I ever expect to get ripe fruit?

First read *No. 189.* You will then see that the figs that ripen on trees grown outdoors in Britain (always and only providing that we get a long sunny summer) are the embryo figs that formed near the tips of the previous seasons growth.

These infantile fruits are naturally soft and very susceptible to frost and overwintering damage, so unless you are living in one of the very few parts of the country that never sees a frost and are prepared to take the risk, these embryo-bearing shoots will have to be protected by wrapping or covering with straw or, as the trees are growing against the wall, by shielding them with straw hurdles or mattresses.

Next season, these young figs will swell, and hopefully ripen by autumn. This will be helped by the removal of the secondary figs that form on the new growth in spring—the very ones that you are waiting in vain to ripen, but never will. Beyond these, in summer and autumn, the small embryos will appear that twelve months later should be the next crop of ripe figs. See the accompanying illustration.

193 *Fruit cages and how to select them*

I want to erect a fruit cage to keep out birds which are a real problem in my garden. Can you give me some good advice?

There are several points to bear in mind about a fruit cage. First, it must be high enough to enable you to stand up reasonably erect inside; working for any length of time with a stoop will surely produce aches and pains. Secondly, if you intend taking it down for the winter, it must be light enough to handle and easy to put up; or if you leave it in position it must be completely impervious to the weather. It must be easy for you to get in and out, but impossible for the birds.

The two basic types are either a permanent frame with wire netting which by its very nature is not easily moved; or a simple, easy-to-erect sectional frame over which is draped a lightweight netting made of solid extruded plastic, or woven from a synthetic fibre yarn.

Permanent wire netting cages can be obtained from Gassons of Rye, Sussex, and Garden Relax of Rainham, Essex; and lightweight netting on sectional frames by Sutton Nets, Bridport, Dorset, and Henry Cowles, Porthleven, Cornwall.

194 *Gooseberries : their cultivation*

Last October, I was given twenty three-year-old gooseberry bushes, most of which have survived the move. However, although the crop is quite good in quantity, the fruit is only very small, mainly about the size of peas. Is this normal, or am I being too impatient? The ground is heavy clay and tends to get waterlogged in wet weather.

Two things that the gooseberry is absolutely insistent about are that the soil must not be waterlogged and there must be plenty of potash available.

On top of that, it is expecting the impossible for any fruit tree or bush to give what you regard as a crop in the first season after a move. See *No. 195.*

Always assuming that you have prepared the site beforehand with plenty of organic compost in the soil, the primary task following the move must always be to replace the inevitably damaged root system with new roots; i.e. the plant has to get established again. Therefore, in the first year after transplanting, remove all the fruit and concentrate on getting good growth.

Over a period of a week to ten days, remove all the fruit as it forms; a few fruits each day, in order to spread and minimise the shock.

Pruning and training can then be commenced by removing all basal growth so that the bush stands on a pedestal-like leg; see *No. 195.* Thin out any overcrowding or overcrossing inner branches, then shorten all leaders by up to a third and lateral side shoots by two thirds, to encourage vigorous spur buds to develop.

As you are on heavy waterlogged clay, something has to be done about that too. Twenty bushes represents a sizeable planting and I would suggest that a quick and beneficial first step would be to form a surface drain by taking out a trench one spit deep through the plot leading to the lowest spot, with side trenches coming in. Take the soil off site and fill the trenches with hard core, clinker, stones, bricks—or, if you cannot get any of these simply leave the trench open.

The badly-draining nature of clay can be improved by putting down 2 ozs. of gypsum about 18 in. away from the stem of each plant; do this four times a year, three months apart, and keep this up indefinitely. The clay has to be cracked and gypsum is the best way to do it. As the surface water open trench falls in or, crock-filled, gradually soils up and becomes inoperative, the gypsum will be taking over the role by making the clay more permeable. Maintain a mulch of compost—mushroom compost or leaf mould—and as it gradually breaks down and is absorbed into the soil, renew it. Gooseberries need plenty of potash to harden the wood and ripen new fruit. Use slow-acting organic-based compound manures whenever possible, and start off in early spring with a 2 oz. per sq. yd. dressing of Humber Eclipse, plus an ounce of sulphate of potash, spread over the growing area. Follow this up a month later with an exact repeat of the above dressing.

Provided the bushes given to you were of a good variety, there is no reason why you shouldn't soon be harvesting a heavy crop. But don't be in too much of a hurry; the plants have to be given time to get over their shock and this might take a couple of years.

195   Gooseberries : pruning method

Having bought a number of gooseberry bushes, can you explain how I prune them and when this will become necessary?

First, no fruit must be allowed to form in the first year; that is absolutely definite. Every effort must be made towards establishment and growth training.

The first pruning will come in mid-summer, when all side shoots coming off the main stem should be shortened back to no more than five leaves. This heading back will encourage formation of fruit buds, and is a procedure to be followed every summer.

During the winter, when bushes are dormant, cut away any damaged shoots, weak shoots, shoots that cross others and old wood. Imagine plunging an arm into a congested bush to pick fruit, look at the thorns; you must give your hands and fingers room to twist and turn without being scratched and torn. Bear that in mind and aim for an open-centred bush with the main branches radiating up and out from the base like a shuttlecock, head them back if they grow too long or out of proportion with the remainder.

This pruning not only helps injury-free picking, but facilitates air movement through the bush which helps to avoid mildew to which gooseberries are prone.

Another important anti-mildew precaution is the provision of adequate potash, see *No. 194*, to harden the shoots and foliage. Vigorous growth resulting from pruning, but which may be soft and flabby due to insufficient potash, is wide open to mildew and aphis attack.

196   Gooseberries : and the sawfly caterpillar

The fleshy parts of the leaves of my gooseberries have been eaten away and only the veins of the leaves are left. This happened very quickly— within two or three days—and although I have found a few caterpillars, I don't see how these could have caused so much damage in such a short time. Can you suggest what else it could be and what I should do?

This is the most common gooseberry pest, the Sawfly, and fortunately it is easy to control— when you know how to detect that it is around.

You have followed the usual pattern in only becoming aware of the trouble when the damage has been done—apparently overnight. The caterpillars you found are the culprits, but the fact that you only found a few, illustrates one of the defence mechanisms that insects develop to avoid danger to themselves. The blue-green black spotted caterpillars hatch from eggs laid in the leaves around the time when the bushes are in bloom. Of course, minute at first, they can hardly be noticed but, as they grow, they develop a very nervous streak. At the slightest movement or vibration —a bird looking for a meal perhaps, or you poking around looking for the likes of themselves—they drop to the ground and feign death until danger has passed, when they climb back up into the bush again and get on with the job.

Having suffered from this pest, you should now expect to be attacked every year, but it only takes a minute or two to detect its presence. At least once a week from about a fortnight after flowering, take a large sheet of paper; plain is best as you will see them more easily, but failing that, newspaper will have to do. Lay this as carefully as you can under the bush, with a stone on each corner to hold it quite still and then, an hour or so later put their nervousness to the test, by giving the bush a few sharp taps. If there are any sawfly caterpillars on your bush, they will soon drop off and you will know that it is time to give them a change of diet.

Out with your sprayer, mix up Derris wash, at full strength as directed on the can and add a few drops of washing-up detergent to make sure the liquid spreads and wets thoroughly. Then drench the bushes completely, paying particular attention to the undersides of the leaves and, contrary to the usual advice about avoiding waste when spraying, spray the ground as well so that any caterpillars that have dropped to the ground do not escape. That will finish that brood, but sawfly produce three generations each year—roughly April, June and August— so you will have to repeat the sheet of paper ritual regularly and, in addition to what you may have cleared up, you cannot be sure about your neighbours sending their visitors over to you. Derris will settle the pest, if applied in time, and is non-poisonous to humans and animals.

197 Gooseberries: and American gooseberry mildew

How can I stop my gooseberries becoming infected with a white, mouldy fungus that ruined the fruit last year?

Undoubtedly, this is American gooseberry mildew, a very widespread and serious disease which, as you have found, can completely wipe out any ideas you may have about picking gooseberries.

Prevention is better than cure, so, control of this pest begins not by spraying to kill it, but by preventing the attack in the first place.

Examine your bushes in winter, looking to see if you can find any shoot tips that are browned over; this is the overwintering stage of the fungus and every tip so affected should be removed and, of course, burned.

In early summer, the disease may be seen on the leaves and on the berries as a white felt-like patch, getting worse as time goes on, affecting all the berries without exception. The white turns brown, and long before the berry is half-grown, it is ruined.

Some varieties are more susceptible than others and conditions can also encourage passing airborne disease spores to stay and take up abode with you. Soft growth resulting from unbalanced feeding—i.e. too much nitrogen and too little potash—predisposes all trees and shrubs to disease attack. As most gardeners use fruit cages, this is the biggest and most common single factor encouraging the disease. Not that there is anything wrong with cages; they are vitally necessary. The trouble is, that having a specific enclosed area to deal with, most amateurs try to cram as much into it as they can, as though the only way to make sure that they are making best use of the cage, is to pack it so tight as to be almost impossible to turn round in. Grown too close together, free air movement is virtually non-existent and fungi like mildew couldn't have it better than that.

Springtime spraying with lime sulphur is the old time recommendation for mildew and is still often advised. However, certain varieties, particularly the yellows like the favourites Leveller and Golden Drop, cannot take the spray without a great deal of scorching and crop loss. The modern procedure, and this should apply whether mildew is about or not, is to spray with Benlate fungicide just before the flowers open and repeat the spray ten to fourteen days later. If an attack does appear, it will be very weak and spraying with Dinocap will finish it off.

198 Gooseberries are hopeless in sandy soil

No matter how well I feed gooseberries in our poor sandy soil, they simply refuse to grow. What's the answer?

Gooseberries will not be happy in a heavy badly draining soil, nor will they like the other extreme which drains too fast. There are two courses open to you. Improve your soil or grow something else.

Your light sandy soil must have some 'body' put into it to make it more dense. You can do this by spreading around any clay that you can lay your hands on. A layer of clay 2–3 ins. thick when worked in, will stiffen up the sand to a depth of anything up to 6–9 ins. If you can't get any from friends who are often very glad to get rid of the stuff, you will have to buy it as marl. This is the material that is used to prepare cricket pitches and is a dry powdery form of a very dense clay. Improving sand in this manner is a long term procedure; you can't do the job properly in one season and digging it in near the bushes is dangerous to their roots, so it is better to spread the marl on the surface or let clay lumps dry out so that they can be broken up. Scratch it in where you can and leave the weather to do the rest.

Time and weather are in fact the best way to get marl and clay to work into the soil. Marl, being ready powdered will work itself into the soil the most quickly. Put down a dressing of either every three months, or repeat the dressing when you observe that the dressing has almost gone.

You may have to keep up this practice for several years, and maintain a good mulch cover in order to get humus into the soil but, with patience, you will be able to grow good gooseberries.

If you haven't the patience, try growing the Worcesterberry instead. Some people say that this is a cross between a blackcurrant and a gooseberry; others say that it is a true Ribes variety. Whatever the truth, it is a heavy cropper and, being a strong grower, will hold its own better until you can improve your soil. Plants will take up a good deal more room than the gooseberry so allow at least 6 ft. between plantings.

199 Grapes : causes of fruit shrivelling

This year the main rod on my grape vine has grown very well and produced about twenty embryo bunches of fruit. Can you tell me why all the berries shrivelled up and died when they were about the size of rice grains?

This sounds very much like the failure of pollination. Some growers have a useful technique for this and, with only relatively few flower trusses to deal with, you should be able to do it quite easily.

Knock the vine stem—called the 'rod'—smartly so that the flower trusses shake, then, holding up a truss with the palm of one hand, gently stroke it with the fingers of the other, working from stalk to tip. This has the effect of dispersing pollen over the female parts of the flowers. Try to do this every day or as often as you can manage during the flowering season. To fertilise properly, flowers should be quite dry, and to ensure that they stay dry, you can enclose each truss in a polythene bag during the flowering period. Close the bag with a wire twist so that it will let in the air but keep out the rain. All that is then needed is to give the truss in its bag a sharp shake each day.

With a Riesling vine I know being treated in this way, there is always a fine crop of grapes each year, so there's no doubt that it works.

200 Grapes : causes of fruit splitting

I have a five-year-old vine growing in my cool greenhouse and last year I allowed it to carry a full crop of grapes for the first time. Unfortunately, the skins of many of the berries split just before they were ripe. How can I avoid this happening again?

There are two basic reasons why this happens. The first is unequal watering; maybe the vine hasn't had all the moisture it would have liked whilst it was swelling its fruit so that it begins to harden the skins a little early, then when the soil gets a really good soaking, there is a belated rush of moisture to the fruits. But the skins are by now too tough to stretch and they split with the pressure.

The second cause is somewhat similar. If you want nice large grapes, you should have thinned out a lot of the little ones so that all the available sap and energy is concentrated into those that remain. Maybe you have overdone this a little, taking off too many at one time instead of a few every two or three days. In a wet summer especially, the grapes that are left cannot take all the moisture and with nowhere else to go, the sap bursts the fruits. See *No. 202*. This is why I think it is always a good idea to leave a safety valve by allowing a few laterals or side shoots to grow on a little instead of stopping them just beyond the bunches.

Finally—and this can make a lot of difference especially with vines growing in a greenhouse—always make sure that this internal sap pressure is not intensified by an inability to transpire. Always try to provide maximum ventilation.

201   Grapes grown under glass

Three years ago I planted a Black Hamburg grape vine in my unheated greenhouse. Last winter it was cut back to one centre stem, 10 ft. long, which is producing small bunches of grapes at almost every leaf joint. How many of these should I remove and how should I water and feed the vine?

Now that the central stem has been reduced to ten feet, you will have to choose between three or at the most four bunches of decent size grapes or more bunches of much smaller ones. These will have to be spaced equidistantly, about 2 ft. apart on the plant.

To get decent-sized grapes, on the bunches that you retain, two small but swelling fruits out of every three—or at least, every other one —should be snipped out as they swell. Don't take all in one go; take out a few every other day. See *No. 202*. Grapes do not like to be

waterlogged, but at no time should the soil be allowed to become drier than well moist.

Proprietary vine fertilisers are obtainable, but normally you will find a balanced organic manure quite adequate. The total fruit crop is going to swell to a sizeable volume, over a fairly long period and the high sugar content is derived from and depends upon a vigorous thriving foliage supported by an equally vigorous thriving root system, clearly all three main plant nutrients Nitrogen, Potash and Phosphorus must be in adequate supply over a long period. Quick-acting fertilisers are therefore not as beneficial as slow-acting organic manures. But only use very light dressings of artificial feed, grapes do not need a lot of feeding—no more than 1 oz. per sq. yard in spring and again in mid-summer.

More important is the maintenance of a thick compost layer over the root area to keep the soil moist and cool. You may have seen old vine houses which have the roots growing outside with the vine entering through a hole in a wall. Always remember, especially when growing grapes in the confined atmosphere of a greenhouse, it is most important to ensure adequate ventilation at all times. See also *Nos. 199, 200* and *202*.

202   Grapes : fruit to be thinned

My Black Hamburg vine is growing in a cold greenhouse and this year had a very good crop. A lot of the bunches are all black except for about nine grapes which seem to have difficulty getting darker than red, although they are quite sweet. I am wondering whether the cause is that I stopped watering about the third week of August? There is the odd bunch that is still all pink and sour; will these ripen, or wither?

Uneven ripening is usually an indication of insufficient thinning of the berries, and/or there is too much leaf growth. Thinning grapes is the most tedious, time-consuming job. It is bad enough where outdoor vines are concerned, but easy compared to the neck-aching pergatory of indoor thinning. The aim is to begin by clearing the grapes forming in the centre of the bunch—these will be covered by those forming at the outside and hidden from the sunlight. Then move on to the outer fruits, thinning where there is congestion and allowing each grape to swell without crushing its neighbour.

Beginning when the grapes are still small but are noticeably swelling, enthusiasts use special vine scissors with long thin blades to reach into the cluster and snip the fruit stems, but you should be able to manage with any scissors with pointed blades. Then as the bunch grows, snip out misplaced, undersized, blemished, and finally congested grapes, a few at a time so that you finish up with only a third of the small fruitlets originally formed after blooming.

Too many fruits left on to share the sugar supply means that most will not be able to ripen fully. Likewise, too much leaf growth causing obstruction to sunlight can also hinder ripening, so you may have to cut back to avoid overcrowding and congestion, but don't remove shoots that can be tied in without causing overcrowding and shading.

If you have been using artificial fertiliser, there could be a soil condition that is leaving you a little short of potash at the ripening end of summer. Overcome this by dusting lightly with sulphate of potash—1 oz. per sq. yard in June and again in July. On the other hand if you have not been feeding at all, put down a proprietary feed or a balanced manure like Humber Eclipse—1 oz. per sq. yard in April and May and again in August. It is most important to keep the root area around the vines well-mulched with compost, leaf mould, or mushroom compost in order to keep the soil moist and cool.

203 Grapes : propagation of

We have a sturdy vine (which produces small purple grapes in autumn) growing against the back of the house and along the garden wall. Would it be possible to take a cutting with us when we move to Wales in about a year's time? Could you tell me what would be the best way of going about this, when is the best time to take a cutting, and how do I do it?

There are several ways in which grape vines can be propagated, most of which are rather involved for the amateur and you haven't the time to spare on experiments that will take a long time and then may not come off. You don't have much time, furthermore, because when you move in twelve months' time, you will want to carry rooted plants with you. There are three methods that you should be able to rely upon to provide this: layering and two kinds of cuttings.

You can begin each method during October or November. For cuttings, first pull away side stems of this year's growth from the main stem so that a 'heel' of older wood also comes away. Cut the top part away just above the first bud which will be seen ready to grow out from the leaf joint; this will give you a piece of mature stem about 6–7 in. long. With a very sharp knife, carefully trim smooth the surface of the 'heel', dip it into rooting hormone powder and insert several cuttings at the fiercest draining position—round the edges—of a 6-inch pot containing peat and sand in equal proportions, as for Geraniums, see *No. 384.* This method can be tried as late as January, or even February, provided the growth buds have not begun to swell. Clearly the cutting must have roots before it can sustain the moisture evaporation of expanding foliage, so, stand the pots, shaded from sun and bright light, either in a propagating case or on soil cables where a little bottom heat can rise from under the cuttings— a strong encouragement to rooting.

The other cuttings method uses the material left over after making the 'heel' cuttings. You can use ripe light-brown coloured wood from this material to produce 'eyes'. Chop up the brown mature part of the stem into short pieces about ¾ in. either side of leaf joints and discard the soft green parts. Divide the chopped pieces into two equal numbers: you are going to try two variations, in order to improve your chances of success. One group can be set into seed trays of moist peat and sand, pressed firm. Examine each cutting to decide which is the right way up: the embryo leaf bud may be discernible above the leaf scar, or you will have to determine from this scar which way the leaf grew. Dip the 'bottom' end in rooting hormone powder and simply press it into the compost, making them firm with the embryo bud just showing.

The other group can be split end on; dip the split surface into rooting hormone, and press these down on the same compost. Whenever I use this method, I hold each eye down with two wire stirrups, bent like a hairpin, one each side of the bud—i.e. the eye. Sprinkle sand over the tray of eyes so that the embryo buds are just clear. Place these trays containing eyes alongside the pots of 6-inch cuttings where they can get bottom heat. From the one lot of material you will now have pots of 6-inch cuttings and a fair number of eye cuttings.

As a final insurance, the third method is to peg down some layers during early spring. Select a long side stem that will reach the soil and cut a tongue slit through a leaf joint where the growth is semi-hard. Dust with rooting hormone powder. Hold the tongue open by inserting a small sliver of peat and hold down firmly not into the soil because they are going to have to travel, but into pots buried to the rim. Later on, when well-rooted, you can then sever them from the parent plant and lift them with the root system intact inside the pot. Leave lifting to the very last moment before moving and plant as soon as you can in your new garden.

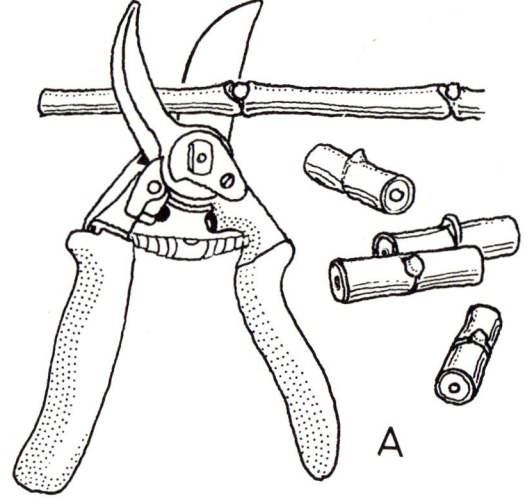

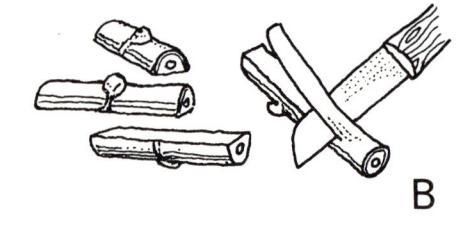

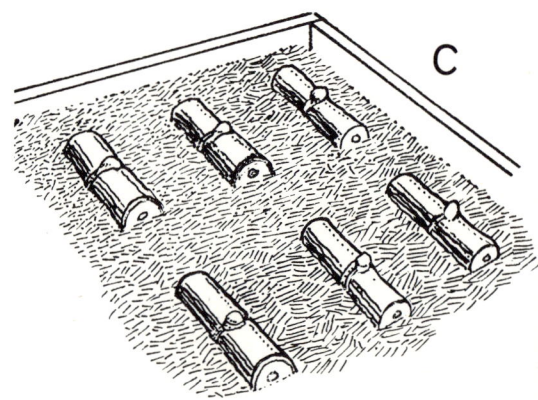

No. 203   *Propagation of vines by eye cuttings.*
A.   Ripe canes are cut into 1 in. long pieces containing a bud.
B.   With a sharp knife, pare a thin sliver from the side opposite to the bud to leave a 'flat'. This gives a long length of cambium to heal and form callus tissue. It is this tissue that throws the adventitious roots. The longer length of cambium, therefore, gives more of a chance of rooting.
C.   After touching the flat into rooting hormone powder, the cuttings are pressed into sandy compost, flat side down and bud uppermost.

204   Grease bands on fruit trees

Moving to a new house with an orchard, I found all the fruit trees had sticky bandages round their trunks. What are these for?

These are grease bands—i.e. bands of material smeared with a vegetable-based grease that remains sticky for a long time. They are put in place in September to trap those grubs and insects which, during their life cycle, climb the tree to feed or lay eggs among the buds and young shoots in the upper reaches.

However thorough your spraying with insecticides, there is always the chance that some will escape, or even visit you from along the road, and grease bands will help to trap them.

Two precautions which you must take are often overlooked in most gardens. A grease band is only effective if the insect or grub tries to cross on the sticky outside. Some of these varmints have more brains than you'd give them credit for and, if they get the chance, will pass on the inside like a lot of human motorists. Smear a thin band of grease onto the bark and pull the bottom of the band tight onto this in order to block off the inside lane.

The second precaution is to inspect the band regularly; don't just put it into place and, feeling that your tree is now immune, forget about it until the next time that you happen to pass by. So many grubs can be trapped that their remains become a bridge for those coming after to cross over safely.

Bear in mind, however, that greasebanding is not a substitute for a routine systematic programme of spraying and winter-washing appropriate to the type of tree. Spraying cannot kill every single overwintering egg; there is no such thing as 100% efficiency and greasebanding is merely intended to catch the odd ones that get away. If you do happen to snare a lot of bugs on the grease band, don't congratulate yourself too quickly; it is most likely that your spraying wasn't as effective as it should have been. See also *No. 164.*

205   Greengages : a long wait for fruit

I have a Dennison's greengage tree, about six or seven years old, on my lawn. Although growing well, it has carried neither blossom nor fruit and I would appreciate your advice on how to encourage it to crop.

As your tree is growing well, it should soon produce fruit. It is not at all unusual for gages to take several years to come to fruiting maturity and, even when your tree does, don't be too anxious and greedy. Thin them out carefully; imagine a hen's egg for eventual size and allow enough room for the fruits to swell and grow without touching.

It is, of course, possible that your tree has too much nitrogen, a gross disproportion of which, causes the effect of a deficiency of potash which is vital in the maturing and ripening processes. You could try, therefore, putting down sulphate of potash—1 oz. per sq. yd.—over the area of the branch spread, every three months until the tree blooms.

The only pruning that is necessary is the removal of weak or overcrowded shoots during the growing season but because of the danger of Silver Leaf fungus, always and at once, touch and cure a cut wound with fungicidal protective paint. If you do not have any Arbrex, don't simply remember to get some, and then continue on with the pruning. Read *No. 186* and see what can happen. Don't start cutting until you have secateurs in one hand and the Arbrex or protective paint in the other.

206   Greengages : causes of fruit splitting

I have a Transparent Gage that fruits well every year but just before the fruits ripen, the skins split open. I assume something is lacking in the soil. Can you please advise?

Unfortunately fruit splitting does sometimes occur in gages and plums and is due mainly to an unsatisfactory soil condition. Plums and gages contain a great deal of liquid, as much as 80%, and when the fruits are swelling fast, the trees will be pulling hard on soil moisture.

Dryness during this period can only mean undersized fruits and a hardened skin. Anything that then leads to an increase of moisture in the soil—a change of weather, even watering the lawn nearby—can lead to the resurgence of moisture and the fruits to swell. The hardened skin does not easily stretch and so it splits. Any unevenness in the moisture supply must put the thin-skinned varieties like Transparent Gage at particular risk.

Your short-term policy could be from the time that the fruits are the size of small cherries. Let the hose lie and trickle slowly for an hour at a time in several places once a week. For a long-term policy, I should start a regular annual programme aimed at improving the soil conditions. Heavy mulching with compost, leaf mould, or mushroom compost is essential —and the layer should be maintained at all times and not allowed to dissipate. Stone fruits need plenty of lime and ground chalk can be spread around so that it can work down into the soil. On the other hand, if you are on a clay soil you should spread gypsum at the rate of 2 ozs. to the sq. yard under the spread of the tree every three months, plus any old plaster rubble that you can lay your hands on.

Changing the soil structure, especially clay, is not a five-minute job and it may take several years before a significant improvement can be effected. It is well worth doing, however; the cost is negligible compared to the benefits.

In future, as the fruit is swelling up to the size where splitting has occurred in the past, you should keep a close watch on the tree and remove any fruit as soon as they are seen to be splitting. They are a little sour at this stage, of course, but can be made into a sharp-tasting jam rather like a marmalade. If you don't pick these fruits off and use them, the wasps will certainly make full use of them—and then turn their attentions to the sound fruit.

207   Hairs on leaves : eggs of the lace-wing fly

This summer, I noticed a leaf on my apple tree had about eighteen hairs around it on the underside, about an inch long. At the end of each hair was a little white blob. What are these hairs, and is the condition harmful?

The unusual hairs—which can occur on many other plants as well as the apple—are the egg stalks of lacewing flies, the white 'blob' at the end being the egg. These hatch into larvae which pray upon aphides and other pests and are the classic example to illustrate that all that crawls should not be killed regardless. Lacewing larvae are wholly beneficial and should never knowingly be destroyed.

The adult lacewing flies are in fact very beautiful, and their name aptly describes the four delicate, transparent lace-patterned wings.

208   Hollow trunks and how to deal with them

What should I do to the hollow trunks of two beautifully-shaped old apple trees? They bore fruit last year and were full of bloom in the spring.

When a tree trunk becomes hollow, it is because the woody centre has decayed. The problem can start where a branch has been broken or cut away, and the exposed wound not sealed with protective paint to exclude air, fungi and bacteria. This is another good reason why the advice to paint all tree wounds is repeated so often. However, when decay has set in and been allowed to progress to the advanced stage where the trunks have become hollow, something has to be done, and quickly.

First, the decay must be arrested and prevented from going any further. You will have to remove every vestige of rotten and decayed wood on the inside, which means chipping and scraping until every bit of decay is removed. You may have to reach down into the holes— an awkward job—but it will have to be done thoroughly. Professional tree surgeons have all sorts of tools for doing this work—long-handled gouges, rasps and scoops—and you may have to devise something of the sort yourself. When you have removed all the decayed wood and cleaned to healthy tissue, you should paint the entire exposed surfaces with fungicidal preservative paint, or Arbrex.

With the decay arrested, you will next have to decide whether the trees need in-filling to give them structural strength; holes are normally filled in with a concrete mix but in bad cases, where excavation of decayed wood leaves such a large hole that the strength of the trunk is suspect, steel rods may also have to be inserted as reinforcement. Smooth off the concrete filling flush with the trunk so that not even the smallest drop of water can remain in the lip of the hole which could start the decay going again. Paint over and seal the join between the concrete and the bark of the tree, and examine it frequently to ensure that cracks do not occur in this seal to let in rain.

209 Lemons: care needed in cultivation

My lemon tree is now two years old, about 2 ft. tall and looking very healthy. It was grown from a pip and is planted in a large lean-to greenhouse which is heated in winter. Will it bear any lemons and are the blossoms self-fertile?

Lemons require similar treatment to the other members of the citrus family—oranges, grapefruit etc. Seedling lemons will normally reach fruit-bearing maturity at about nine years old. The flowers are self-fertile and will cross pollinate; however, before then you have some work to do. Prune out the lead and side shoot tips, to build up a nice shape with plenty of twiggy fruit bearing growth. Read *No. 215* on the Calamondin Orange and you will realise why growing medium conditions—especially spraying and the mid-summer standing-out period—and minimum winter temperature are all very important.

Fruit bearing on 'schedule' will then depend upon the extent to which the necessary reserves are built-up by as ideal conditions as you can provide.

210 Loganberries: the correct way to train the canes

My loganberry is a jungle of long canes over a wire frame. Where do I start?

As the last fruits are picked, cut all ties and disentangle all the canes to expose the wire framework. Put this in good order, repairing and strengthening as required. Deliberately, try to break or push over the supporting posts; it is better to replace a weak post at this stage than see it break when loaded with a full crop of fruit. Cut all fruited canes to ground level and clear them away from the job.

From the canes remaining—new canes that have grown during the current season and which have not yet borne fruit—select six to eight of the very strongest of each plant and tie these up to the frame like a horizontal fan, tying the canes along the wires evenly, half each side, but leave the centre 'V' open. Next you should remove all remaining weak or branched canes and put down a heavy mulch of leaf mould or mushroom compost. You are now ready for fruiting next season—subject, of course, to routine spraying with a winter wash against overwintering aphides. Put down three well-balanced feed dressings, like Growmore or Humber Eclipse, 2 ozs. to the square yard in February, March and in April.

As new canes arise from the base, group these loosely into the centre 'V' of the fan and then as they reach the top of the supporting frame, select the eight strongest, bend them over and tie them three or four to each side along the top wire. Remove any other weak canes. After fruiting, remove the fruited canes as before, re-position the new canes to an open fan shape and the training cycle is ready for another turn round. Remember that it is very important to continue mulching and spraying. See *Nos. 169, 170* and *171*.

211 Loganberries lacking vigour

Normally, the ten loganberries I have trained along a south-facing wall for the past twelve years have produced good crops and ample quantities of new canes. However, this year, two of the plants are producing only masses of spindly, twiggy growth none of which is suitable for training to carry next year's crop. No selective weedkiller or fertilisers have been used near them, but they do look as though they have had something similar sprayed over them. What can the trouble be?

This sounds suspiciously like the onset of an attack by what is called rubus stunt virus; all the members of the rubus family to which loganberries, blackberries, raspberries and the various hybrids belong, can be affected. There was a time when the early loganberries were very prone to this trouble, but the vigour bred into modern varieties has virtually overcome it.

The virus is not soil borne, so there is no risk of infection through the soil. As with the transmission of virus in other plants, we have to look for something that transfers sap from one plant to another, and that points to a sucking or biting insect.

The first indication, therefore, is that you will have to be very stringent and painstaking about protecting the plants against insect attack, particularly against public enemy No. 1 —greenfly. Frankly, if you have had good crops for twelve years, they don't owe you anything and I would grub them out without further ado. But if you want to check out this diagnosis a little further, cut back hard all the affected canes to soil level and burn them. If new shoots or retained ones show any further signs of stunt or deformity, don't wait any longer. Further delay in clearing them away only increases the risk of other plants becoming infected. Indeed, this may already have happened and you should certainly expect it. Keep a very close watch and at the first signs of trouble, cut and burn.

Because of the risk of further infection, it would be unwise to plant new plants until you have had a season or two's growth from what is left to prove that you have stamped out the outbreak. By the same token, where did this outbreak come from? See if you have neighbours nearby who may be growing members of the Rubus family and who are wondering what has gone wrong with their plants. It is no good your being spotless if your neighbour has virus-ridden plants. When you are satisfied all is clear replant with the vigorous modern hybrid L.59. Don't spare the winter washes and spring-time spraying which will help to keep the greenfly at bay.

212 Medlar and its peculiar ripening method

I have a fine crop of medlars but they don't turn soft. How should I treat them?

Medlars are not native to Britain, although they have been grown here for nearly as long as the mulberry. They come from Asia Minor and the southernmost parts of Europe, and generally we have to adopt a special procedure to ripen them.

Leave them on the tree as long as possible. Try to gather them on a dry sunny day, if there is one, in November. Wipe clean with a cloth, and dip each fruit stalk fully into a strong salt solution and leave it to dry, so that the fruit stalk area has a fine coating of salt.

Place each fruit eye down in little pads of paper to hold them apart since they mustn't touch each other: tomato or apple trays are ideally suitable. They should stay in a cold, but frost-free place for two to three weeks. Gradually the green colour will turn to yellow and the flesh soften. The fruit is then fit to eat. The process is called 'bletting' in many country districts, and during the two to three weeks' ripening period, mould fungus can often be a problem. Ventilation and separation are the precautions, hence the little paper 'nests' for each fruit.

If it starts, the fungus generally begins around the stalk area—hence the stalk dipping. Therefore, examine the fruits regularly—daily if you can—and at the first signs of fungus, wipe clean, 'dunk' the *whole fruit* in salt solution and set it up again *away* from the main crop. You may accrue several of these suspect fruits, but it is worth trying to arrest the mould.

213 Mulberries : a long wait for fruit

Can you tell me anything about the mulberry? How long will it be before my newly-planted tree starts fruiting?

Originating from south-west Asia, but grown in Britain since as early as the sixteenth century, the mulberry grown for fruiting is almost exclusively *Morus nigra*.

The fruits have a unique, agreeably and slightly astringent taste and are only really sweet when they have become so ripe as to be almost too soft to handle without squashing, and at this time they have turned from red almost to black. For this reason, they are best left on the tree to fall as they become fully ripe. To avoid having to scrape up a splodgy mess, suspend netting—old lace curtains are ideal for this—under the trees from poles, like large hammocks, to catch the fruit relatively undamaged. You should collect the fruit two or three times a day otherwise the birds, especially pigeons, will beat you to it.

The mulberry isn't very widely grown, and the probable reasons for this are the difficult harvesting of the ripe crop (although the above solution greatly simplifies the problem), the ever-present risk of the brittle wood dropping a branch—large and very old branches have to be propped up to make them safe—and the serious risk of clothes being stained and ruined by falling fruit. This is a pity because the mulberry will grow almost anywhere that is sheltered and has remarkably few pests or diseases.

A young tree will take about ten years to reach fruit-bearing maturity, when it will pay handsomely for manuring and heavy mulching. See also *No. 214*.

214 Mulberries: the white fruited variety

I have been told there are both red and white mulberries. Could you tell me which would be the sweetest to eat and the best to grow? Also, could the mulberry be trained as an espalier on a west-facing wall?

First read *No. 213*. There is a white mulberry, *Morus alba*, in addition to the more common black mulberry *Morus nigra*. It is a much smaller tree, the fruits are whitish, but turn pink when ripe, and they are sweet to the taste.

Its importance, however, is not its fruits but its leaves which are heart-shaped and 6 ins. wide. It is upon the leaves of *Morus alba* that silkworms are fed. If it is fruit that you want—and mulberries are a most underrated fruit—grow the black mulberry *Morus nigra*. Both black and white forms are better grown as freestanding specimens, but if you cannot provide the space for a free-standing tree, plant it against the wall. However, don't bother with espalier training; it just isn't worth it. Simply train the growth to a broad fan shape to cover the wall space. No pruning will be required other than to keep to shape and avoid crossing and overlapping.

As most mulberries are grown with the expectancy that they will be required as standards, you may have some difficulty in obtaining a short-stem specimen suitable for fanning. If you are determined to go ahead you should try to obtain a young maiden which you can head back to provide the side shoots that you need for training. Furthermore, if you grow the black mulberry you will need a big expanse of wall because, naturally, it makes a large tree.

215 Oranges: care of a Calamondin ornamental

I have been given a dwarf orange tree (Calamondin) and would be grateful if you could give me full instructions as to the cultivation of this plant.

Citrus is the generic name given to all oranges, lemons, tangerines, grapefruits and limes, all of which can be grown in greenhouses. Most success is gained in the south, of course, and even in a few particularly well-favoured sheltered sunny spots in the open.

The best type for the amateur, both by virtue of size, neatness of habit, and usually prolific bearing, is the Calamondin orange. Like the other citruses, it has evergreen leaves, fragrant white flowers in springtime and small bright fruits similar to the familiar tangerine. It will need a large pot or small tub and although it may grow well in John Innes No. 2 alone, it is worth making the effort to make up the following special compost. Two parts by bulk of J.I. No. 2 and one part a mix of equal proportions of dried crumbled cowpat that has been passed through a $\frac{1}{2}$ in. sieve, charcoal, coarse bonemeal, and plaster rubble. The resulting compost is more open and porous than the J.I. compost alone. You should not disturb the root system more often than necessary, but if you are going to re-pot in order to get it into the ideal compost, do the job in February or March and whilst the plant is still young. Water freely from March till the autumn, and once a week from May introduce a balanced liquid manure into the watering.

Red Spider can be a problem so keep a very close watch for it. As summer approaches, mist spray the foliage daily (this will help to deter the pests) and in June the plants can be moved into positions outdoors where they can enjoy the sunshine and be sheltered from cooling breezes, but this is when you will have to watch your watering and spraying very carefully because drying out is the big danger. The spraying must be done regularly each day. Towards late summer, if the plant is ripening fruit, change the general balanced liquid feed to one with a potash bias—Tomorite would be suitable —to enhance the ripening process. At the appropriate time during autumn, i.e. as soon as the night temperatures show signs of dropping below 55°F., move the plants indoors.

When taking ripened fruit for the first time, don't be confused by the curious formation of fruit—i.e. that formed during one year does not ripen until the next. Discontinue the liquid feed as the fruit is picked and reduce the watering during October so that the soil is kept just moist. Maintain a minimum winter temperature of 45°F. and, in the second week of February, scratch into the soil surface a level teaspoonful of a long lasting organic-based manure like Humber Eclipse. Give a good watering with tepid rainwater, prune away any long straggly shoots to keep the plant in shape, and away you go again.

Repeat the feed dressings each March and April and with a good compost to begin with— bearing in mind also the need to avoid root disturbance as far as possible—you should only need to think about re-potting at four to five-year intervals.

216   Orange scale, a bad pest

The stems of my Calamondin orange are covered with sticky scale-like objects. What are these, as they seem to be affecting its health?

Scale insects are like minute limpets and barnacles in the tenacity with which they adhere and this is the pest that is attacking your plant. Feeding on the plant sap, they have a very debilitating effect on the plant and, like aphides, excrete the sticky, sugary fluid, called honeydew. This coats the leaves and surfaces and not only clogs the breathing pores but is the ideal food material to sustain sooty mould fungus—

and when that occurs your plant is in real trouble.

Most of the scales are females, and after several months feeding they lay hundreds of eggs which hatch into a crawler stage. These move about and so infection is carried from plant to plant.

Scale insects have a waxy protective covering, hence their name, and it is not at all a simple matter to get past this to kill the pest. The most effective control is a two-pronged attack: liquid Malathion contact killer sprayed on and, for those that this doesn't control, a systemic insecticide like Topguard, which makes the plant sap toxic to sucking insects. Bear in mind the ripening fruits, however, and don't use systemic poison within three to four weeks of picking fruits so that it has had time to dissipate and breakdown before you taste them! If you are not going to eat the fruit and are using them for ornamental uses only, so that there is no possible risk of giving yourself the collywobbles, persist with the systemic until all the scales have gone. Don't underestimate the ability of this pest to persist and come back at your plants, so keep the Malathion going for a month or two after the visual all clear. Your plant has been under stress, so be generous with feeding, and follow the advice in *No. 215*.

217   Passion Fruit: the Granadilla

Can you please give me the correct name of a purple fruit which I bought whilst on holiday in Spain where they called it a Granadilla. Some of the seed I saved has germinated and now I have plants 8 in. tall. I would appreciate advice on what to do next?

Granadilla is the common name for one of the passion fruits named botanically *Passiflora edulis*. Passiflora is a large genus of climbers that, originating from Brazil and neighbouring areas of South America, are almost all too tender for growing in the British Isles. For the most part, it is the passion flower, *Passiflora caerulea* that is grown here for its bluish flowers and, following a very sunny and warm summer, it is not uncommon for it to bear a fruit or two.

For a worthwhile crop, however, a better fruiting variety is required, and unless you are in the extreme south and south-west where a sunny, protected position can be given so that the plant will get full sun, a greenhouse or conservatory is advisable. If that is not possible and you have to grow it outdoors, you will need to protect the plant against frost by covering with straw hurdles, blankets or branches of evergreen cut for the purpose.

Very soon now, your seedlings will develop their method of climbing by twining tendrils. One single plant will become large enough for a medium-sized greenhouse or conservatory. Plant it in a tub using John Innes No. 2 or directly into the ground. As it grows, train it to trellis or wires fastened into the roof area of the greenhouse or over the wall surface if outside. Eventually, it will bear white and purple flowers followed by yellowish-purple plum-shaped fruits which turn deeper purple as they become ripe.

Any pruning which may be required to restrict its growth—it can become rampant if it likes the conditions—can be done in late autumn—October—or by clearing and trimming winter-affected stems in April.

218 Peach : how to hand-pollinate

My peach tree—which I grew from a stone—does not fruit very well, and I have read that this is because it has to be hand-pollinated. Can you please tell me how this is done?

Most flowers, especially those of fruit trees and bushes, are pollinated quite satisfactorily by visiting bees and insects. However, it sometimes happens that conditions, like a cold and draughty position, make life unpleasant for them and they go elsewhere.

Assuming that your consistently poor crop is due to bees and other fliers not pollinating the bloom, you will have to do the job yourself. The physical construction of flowers varies enormously so that with some it is quite easy whereas with others you would have to stand on your head—like a gooseberry for instance where the flowers hang like little bells. Indeed Nature sometimes go to some length to ensure that self-pollination cannot occur if the male and female parts of the flower reach maturity at different times, so that the female part of the flower has to rely on cross-fertilisation by pollen brought from a different tree. However, with most peaches, cross-fertilisation is not necessary and to be your own bee is a simple matter.

Acquire a rabbit's tail, or piece of fur equally soft, and use this to lightly dab into the open blossoms. This will transfer the pollen and put it where it will do its work. If you have blossom too high to reach, simply tie the tail to the end of a cane. This method will work with other fruits that have similarly constructed blossom—apples for instance—but before trying it, do be quite certain that the tree is self-fertile.

219 Peach tree pruning

My peach tree, which is trained to a wall, has a fine crop of fruit and is now making a lot of new growth which hides the fruit. How should I prune it?

It is quite usual for a considerable amount of pruning to be carried out on trained peaches during the growing season, but it is a little complicated. Bear in mind that the object is to allow for a fruit to develop whilst at the same time making provision for its successor—next year's fruit—to be encouraged.

First, take shoots that are already bearing fruits. Shorten these to 18 inches if they are longer than that; leave them if they are shorter. Any shoots adjacent to these and not bearing fruits should be cut back to two leaves. As the shorter fruit-bearing shoots reach 18 in. in length, take out the terminal growth bud and, at the base of the shoot, select the best of any basal shoots that may be growing out and remove the others. After harvesting fruits, prune out the fruited shoot to immediately above the selected replacement shoots growing from its base. Clear out all weak and secondary shoots; this will let in the daylight. Now tie in all the extension and replacement shoots, trying to keep them equidistant so that next year's crop of peaches can be spread out evenly.

220   Peaches : growing from a stone

I planted a peach stone last year. Having moved it to a larger pot, it is now 2 ft. tall. Should I re-pot again or transfer it to the garden?

Peaches do not take kindly to having their roots confined in pots or tubs. Read *No. 165* concerning an apricot grown from a stone. The same conditions apply in this case. So transfer your peach to the garden, and follow the same advice given for the apricot. If your stone came from an imported peach, it may need more warmth and sun than it is likely to find in this country. However, plant it in a sheltered sunny position, and provided it blooms in mild conditions, it could set fruit. If it does, be prepared to thin out drastically in the early days until you learn, by living with it, how many fruits your tree can ripen properly. Grown from a seed, it must be an unknown quantity and only experience will tell.

221   Peach leaf curl

I suspect that my peach tree is affected by peach leaf curl. Is there any protection against it?

Peach Curl is a fungus disease, *Taphrina deformans*, that can be recognised by the curled, bloated and coloured leaves, the normal healthy green being replaced by a reddish, sometimes purplish, hue. Sometimes the whole leaf is blistered, and sometimes only a few spots appear. When the leaf is seen to have a dusty surface, the fungus is in bloom and because it is giving off a lot of spores, it is then very highly infectious.

Whilst the disease is unlikely to kill the tree, it is serious because, if the leaves cannot work properly, the fruits will be under-nourished and the crop therefore suffers. Infected leaves die and fall, and often the tree has to produce secondary foliage which is debilitating.

Cleanliness is the very first step in prevention; all dropped and/or infected leaves should be collected with as little disturbance as possible and burned. Primary infection comes from spores which have overwintered in bud scales or on shoots. Therefore, as soon as leaves fall,

clear up and burn them and then spray the tree with a copper-based fungicide or with Captan. In February, the buds will be seen to begin swelling; spray again with Captan or with lime sulphur. If you want to be extra cautious, spray the merging buds again after February, using Captan only because lime sulphur can damage the maturing green leaf.

222   Pear : the curse of scab

I have a William pear tree growing on a chalky soil and the fruit is badly scabbed. Earlier in the year, I sprayed once with systematic spray and once with Captan. Can you suggest what I should do next year to prevent the trouble?

Pear Scab and Canker go hand in hand, and these two fungus diseases between them cause more dirty, cracked, rotten and useless pears than all the other pests and diseases put together. Pear Scab is similar to, but not the same as, Apple Scab and the treatment is the same.

It overwinters on fallen, decayed leaves and on young shoots that have become infected. In spring, these sources of infection pour millions of spores into the air, many of which must alight on opening buds and leaves, and soon after you will see the familiar sooty discoloration on the foliage. These infected leaves pour out more spores. It will not be long before the growing fruit receives its share, and where the spores attack the skin this becomes hard and unable to expand. Therefore, as the inside continues to swell, the fruit cracks open and now it is wide open to secondary infection, Brown rot—that is, if the wasps don't get in first.

In order to forestall the invasion, you must spray on a protective fungicide and maintain cover throughout the infectious period, which is late March to early July or, if the weather is mild and muggy, right through to picking. One single spray of Captan won't provide protection for that long. Instead, you will have to spray with lime sulphur made up as instructed on the can, at roughly fourteen-day intervals, which can be described approximately as the following stages of growth.

1. Bud burst, dormant buds just bursting green.

2. Green flower, buds showing green but *not* open.

3. White bud, buds about to open but do not spray open flowers.

4. Petal fall, 80 to 90 per cent petals will have fallen, pollination will be over and it will therefore be safe to spray over what is left of the flowers.

5. Three weeks after petal fall, embryo fruits.

6. Three weeks later, fruitlet stage.

7. Repeat at fourteen-day intervals if the weather is mild and muggy.

You will see from a programme like this that a persistent disease has to be met by persistent control. Systemic fungicides (incidentally the correct spelling is systemic, indicating that the chemical enters the system of the plant) may give a control but one application will not last long enough to give effective control throughout the whole period that the tree is at risk. Spraying would need to be repeated at intervals according to the instructions appropriate to the particular fungicide and repeated over the same period as the more conventional fungicides.

223   Pears, Williams : exception to the rule

My William pear fruits well, but every time I pick a ripe fruit, I find it is turning brown inside. Could this be due to a deficiency in the soil, or chemicals I use to spray against scab, or what?

It is always difficult to know just when to pick pears so that they will ripen to perfection. The time-honoured way to judge for fitness of the mid and late season varieties is to lift the fruit from its normal hanging position to just above the horizontal to see if it will part easily.

Early pears have a very short edible life and should be picked before they part readily from the spur and this is the case with Williams. This variety must be picked green if it is to ripen properly. If there is the slightest trace of yellow, this means that ripening has begun, and the chances are that you are too late. Get

these fruit off at once, and cook such flesh that is still usable: this pear is the Bartlett so beloved of the canners.

Store the unripe green pears in the dark and in a uniform temperature between 40°F and 50°F—a cool cellar is ideal. Stand the fruits apart in the normal hanging position—i.e. eye down, stalk up. In this way, a good proportion should ripen without beginning to rot inside. A few hours before eating, bring the fruit into a warm room, of at least 60°F. which will finish the ripening process very quickly. Without warmth the full pear flavour and aroma will not be present.

224   Pears : the cause of fruit drop

Every year, the pear tree in our garden is covered in blossom which forms a mass of tiny fruitlets. These later turn yellow and all drop off. What is the cause of this trouble?

This could be due to either of two causes; one possible, the other probable. It could possibly be a heavy infestation of pear midge which, not being controlled, is attacking your tree regularly. However it is surprising that all the fruits drop off and you don't get even one. You can check whether it is midge by cutting open several of the largest fruitlets before they fall to see if they are eaten away inside and contain a small cream maggot looking fat and contented. With the seed pip gone, the tree has no further use for the fruit and so aborts it, usually towards the end of June when the maggot crawls from the fallen fruit and enters the ground to cocoon and pupate.

If midge is revealed as the culprit, a good control, perhaps rather surprisingly, is Chlordane wormkiller. Apply this to the entire soil area and 4–5 yards beyond the spread of the tree. This will kill not only the earthworms, but all grubs that try to overwinter in the soil. A pity about the worms but the higher priority are the other grubs that do the damage. It will remain effective for at least twelve months and whilst it may give you a fair measure of control during that period, as you will see in a moment, you will have to repeat it for two or three years.

Adult midges that emerge from the soil, lay

eggs in the opening flower buds so that spraying at the crucial moment could well affect further pollination and is therefore rather dangerous. The best thing to do is to spray with Malathion at white bud stage, and again, if you can, as late as you dare just before the petals open. Finally, as the grub spends two years in the soil, however effective your spraying this year, there will be another generation to emerge next year. You will have to keep up the treatment for at least that time before you can expect to get on top of the pest. This is also the reason why you have to keep the soil toxic with Chlordane for more than just one year. Pear midge, however, is only a possibility.

The probable reason for no fruit, however, is that the pear is infertile to its own pollen and needs another variety to cross-pollinate it. This would explain why all the fruit falls without leaving even one or two. Very few pears will set fruit to their own pollen which is why it is always best to plant two or more and, furthermore, the varieties have to be compatible to cross-pollinate. There is no guarantee that a second tree will do the trick because without fruit you cannot identify the tree you have and a second tree may easily be the same variety or incompatible. Only if you know exactly what it is can you choose a suitable partner. Therefore two other different varieties which are themselves compatible or even a third variety may have to be planted to get worthwhile cropping of this tree.

225   Persimmon : conditions required for a Chinese fruit

Can you please give me any information about the Chinese persimmon tree. I have tasted the fruit abroad on holiday and would like to try to grow it here if it is hardy. I am told it is another name for passion fruit—is this so?

The Chinese persimmon, *Diospyros kaki*, makes a large shrub or small tree and is not passion fruit, which is Passiflora, a climber from a different part of the world, South America. However, originating in China and Japan, the persimon is now widely grown in the Middle East and the southernmost part of Europe,

where it has been selectively cultivated into several different varieties.

Male and female flowers are borne on separate plants and it is quite unusual in that the fruit-bearing female does not need to be pollinated to form fruits; this is why the fruit you buy seldom have seeds.

It can be grown in Britain, but requires warm sunny conditions in the south. In the north it will need to be under glass for the fruits to ripen freely. However, enough of the orange-yellow tomato-like fruits are borne in most summers to warrant growing it and, for added measure, the large leaves change colour to brilliant shades of orange and purple in the autumn.

226   Plums : a lot of work to do before fruiting

Last September I bought and planted two Victoria plum trees, three to four years old. Their branches were both long and thin. Should these be pruned this year and if so, how? When can I expect them to fruit?

There are two schools of thought about plums. One says 'leave it alone and never prune it' and you may get fruit a little earlier than if you follow the method which advocates that if you want a tree that will eventually bear really good crops, you must put fruiting out of your mind for a few years whilst you build a strong basic framework. If you go for the second method, shape the tree by cutting back the lead shoots just above opposed side buds to about 15 in. in early July. Paint the open wounds at once with fungicidal protective paint or with Arbrex. You should never prune a plum tree without sealing with protective; it is the only way to make sure that the fatal disease Silver Leaf doesn't attack your tree.

Next season repeat the process, cutting back new growth 15–20 in., aiming for suitably positioned opposed side buds. You should do this for up to five years in all to build up a frame work of branches spaced equidistant apart, like a shuttlecock, so carefully choose the buds each time and cut with an eye on the direction that the resulting growth will take.

If new growth is not strong and is inclined to

be thin and weak, cut back harder, take out unwanted, weak, misplaced, and crossed shoots
to concentrate all the tree's energy into building
the basic frame—always, repeat always painting
the wounds with protective. Remove any
blossom that appears in spring and after five
years' training there should be a good frame
work to carry good crops. From now on, prune
spur laterals or side branches but be quite sure
that you are cutting to a bud cluster *that contains a growth bud*. This is important because
the drag or suction of the leaf growth is necessary to pull the sap supply to the fruit. With
Victoria, many amateurs make the mistake of
spur cutting back to fat fruit buds. Invariably,
when this is done, fruits will develop but abort
and fall because there is no leaf area above them
to nourish them and to pull the sap up to and

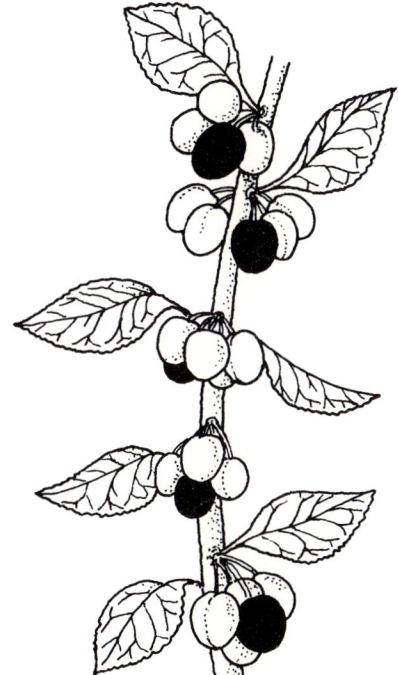

No. 227 *Overcropping of plums. Thin the small
fruits before they reach the size of small cherries
so that one fruit only remains on a 4–5 in. run of
stem.*

beyond the fruit bearing spur. So remember:
a cluster of fruit buds must *always* contain a
growth bud, otherwise the fruit will not develop properly.

Maintain a mulch cover of garden compost,
mushroom compost or leaf mould and follow
the same general procedure concerning feeding
with balanced manures and ground chalk as is
recommended for peaches and apricots. See
Nos. 165, 219 and *220*. If you have a heavy soil,
this can be improved by dressing with gypsum
(see *Nos. 2, 276* and *475*).

As the fruit ripens you will have to attend to
thinning. The cardinal rule to remember about
thinning, particularly with plums as with all
stone fruits, is that it is a multiplicity of pip or
stone production that debilitates a tree and
consumes its food reserves at an alarming rate.
Pulp production, the part of the fruit that you
are going to eat, causes little distress. It is the
production of stone that causes the strain. This
is why thinning out, so that fruits cannot touch
each other, can actually produce a heavier crop
than many more but unthinned fruits, and with
much less stress on the tree.

227 *Plums : keeping a Victoria clean*

*Is there anything that can be done to prevent the
annual occurrence of the black sooty secretion that
covers the leaves of our plum trees, mainly Vic-
torias, late in the season? The trees look healthy
and usually fruit well.*

You'll find another reference to sooty mould in
No. 240. This is a black furry fungus that
thrives on the sugary excretions of aphides, with
which your tree must have been infested, and
presumably still is. This black covering severely reduces the light intensity getting through to
the leaves. These are therefore prevented from
working properly and the fruit crop consequently suffers.

The fungus can be killed by spraying with a
contact fungicide like Dinocap, but the best
control is to stop the aphis infestation in the
first place from providing the food material of
the fungus. You should at once spray with
Malathion to clean the pest off the tree, paying
particular attention to the undersides of the

leaves where the pests will be concentrated. Fruit would be fit to eat after seven days, but it is safest to wash it first.

During winter, spray the trees thoroughly with a tar oil wash to kill all overwintering eggs to try to give the tree a clean start. Aphides can arrive on the wing, however, and you should either routine spray regularly from early spring with Malathion or Lindex or, at least keep a very close watch on their numbers, spraying as required. Basically, the best cure for sooty mould is to prevent it from occurring in the first place by controlling the aphides that provide the food for it.

228 Pomegranate : conditions required for ripening

I have two young plants of Punica granatum *'Nana', approximately 1 ft. high and growing in 7 in. pots. They have been standing outside all summer. Can they remain outside, or is the climate here in the north unsuitable? Alternatively, would they be suitable for house plants?*

The pomegranate is native to Persia and thereabouts so, as you may expect, it is not hardy enough to withstand our severest winters. The showy brilliant orange-scarlet blooms, however, make it worthwhile taking a fair amount of trouble with, and in the milder parts of the British Isles it can be grown in sheltered positions against a south-west facing wall, or planted in a greenhouse or conservatory.

The familiar multi-seeded fruits often form and may even grow to a size approaching those that we buy at the fruiterer's, but a very long sunny summer is necessary to ripen them here.

Punica granatum 'Nana' is a very dwarf form that is particularly amenable to pot culture and thus is often offered by nurserymen and florists as a spectacular blooming shrub. It can be grown for many years before it will need anything larger than its 7 in. pot—the normal practice is to re-pot every other year. Punica is an evergreen and thus it does not have a dormant period. It will, however, slow down considerably during winter, so early November would be a good time for re-potting or early spring just before it becomes more active.

Turn it out of its pot, tease some soil away without undue root damage and re-pot in the same pot, using John Innes No. 2 compost. During the intervening years, repotting is replaced by top dressing: scrape off as much soil as you can from the top of the pot until the roots begin to show. Then refill with the same John Innes compost.

Pomegranates have a peculiar liking for cow manure—it's a good idea therefore to make the soil level a little lower in order to leave space for mulch of crumbled cow pat on top of the soil. As it gets played out with successive waterings, this mulch can be renewed at frequent intervals, and it is worth taking a bucket in the car boot when going into the country to collect a cow pat or two.

In order to get maximum unhindered sunlight, the pots are usually stood outside in summer, but they should never be allowed to dry out. If it should happen, don't hesitate for an instant: plunge the pot into water with the rim submerged and leave for at least half an hour after the last bubbles have risen. To avoid drying out, pots are often submerged into the ground. This is risky as it is an encouragement to neglect; they still need watering as moisture does not move from the soil, sideways through the pot! Furthermore, roots have a nasty habit of finding their way through the drainage hole so that they then have to be cut off when the pot is lifted and that is a shock that is best avoided.

During winter, pomegranates must be given protection particularly in the north by bringing them into the greenhouse, conservatory or sunny window. In the latter case, turn the pot regularly to stop the plant growing lop-sided. For this reason they are not really suitable as a room plant as they need plenty of all round light.

229 Quince, the fruit of the flowering 'japonica'

Is it possible to use the fruits of what is commonly called japonica for jelly and jam?

A spring-flowering shrub once called *Cydonia japonica*—of which the *japonica* part has stuck and refuses to die—the correct name is now Chaenomeles. Your fruits are generally called quinces and although the best fruits derive from the cultivated fruiting quince, *Cydonia oblonga*, this closely related genus, Chaenomeles, will sometimes produce fruits which are usable if left on the shrub as long as possible, until ripe and come away easily when lifted.

The flowering Chaenomeles is unlikely to provide enough fruit to make into the very piquantly flavoured quince jam, but you can use them, one at a time, to add flavour to stewed apples and apple pie. See *Nos. 230* and *231*.

230 Quince : variety for growing in the north

What variety of fruiting quince would be suitable for Lancashire?

The fruiting quinces are generally hardy in Britain and of the several varieties that are available, Vranja would be a good choice because in addition to providing fruit in October, it is also attractive when in bloom in the spring.

In the south, it is grown as a free-standing bush, but in the north it would benefit from a sheltered position, perhaps against a wall, away from the wind where the spring blossom would not be harmed by spring frosts.

Prepare the soil by working in plenty of well-rotted compost before planting and mulch each spring with a dressing of compost either from the compost heap or mushroom compost; in each case bolster by mixing in a feed of Humber Eclipse or Growmore, equivalent to the rate of 3–4 ozs. per sq. yd. of the area over which the mulch is to be spread.

You will have to wait two or three years before fruiting maturity and then don't let your plant produce too many fruits for the first few years. Allow the fruits to remain on the bush as long as possible until they are ready to fall, or until the onset of frosts. Selected sound and damage-free quinces will keep for two or three months if wrapped in tissue paper and kept cool. An old trick is to place a wrapped fruit in a linen drawer or cupboard, scenting the air with a delightful pineapple scent.

231 Quince : a lot of growth but no fruit

Can you please advise me about fruit on my quince Vranja? The bushes were planted three years ago and flowered well in the first spring, but produced no fruit. Each succeeding year, they have produced less and less blossom, but make a great deal of spindly wood. They have been well manured and I have cut the weak growths when they are about 6–8 in. long and have then spurred them back in winter.

Quinces are often erratic in their early years after planting until they settle down—and three years is nothing to worry about. It is best not to try to induce fruiting by artificial means. The only pruning that is required is the removal of dead shoots and the thinning-out of congested shoots and cross shoots. Spurring back is quite unnecessary and may well delay fruiting by provoking alternative shoots which are likely to be weak and spindly—indeed, it sounds from your description that this is already happening.

It might also be that you have been over-doing the manure so that the shrub is responding by trying to put up too much leaf instead of flower and fruit. Maintain a mulch cover by all means but I should stop the manuring until fruiting is well established: leave the shrub alone and it will come into bearing in its own time.

However, give it a couple of light dressings of sulphate of potash during late spring and summer to harden the wood and hasten the formation of flower buds.

232 Raspberries : how to get two crops each year from Zeva

Can you tell me about a raspberry called Zeva that fruits continuously. Is its cultivation any different from other raspberries, and where can it be obtained?

Some confusion has grown up around the thornless raspberry Zeva. It has been called perpetual fruiting, autumn fruiting and even never fruiting by those who don't understand it or how to grow it properly. Some people get heavy crops of large sweet fruits while others get very little.

Zeva throws its heaviest crops and largest berries on the current year's growth. On commercial farms, these canes are not tied to support wires but are allowed to stand unsupported —I have seen them so overloaded with berries that they bend right over so that the fruit touches the soil and is spoiled. The berries are enormous, pleasantly sweet, but with just enough astringency to make it acceptable to all palates. Some varieties are a little too sharp for some people, but Zeva is just about right for everybody. Cropping is not continuous but can be extended over a period that is much longer than for any other variety—from June right through to November. In fact, the fruit keeps coming so late that it is almost inevitable that some will be lost to winter frosts.

Pruning depends upon whether you want a heavy autumn crop or whether you would be prepared to trade a little of this in order to have an early summer yield as well, i.e.—the long fruiting period. If it is to be an autumn crop only, shorten back all the fruited wood to about 18 inches to reduce wind rock during winter and then in spring, when new canes are appearing, remove the old canes completely as low as you can cut. On the other hand if you want an early crop as well, prune back as before except for three or four of the strongest canes and, with these, merely trim off the old fruiting head. In spring, side shoots will emerge from the leaf axils and these will bear fruit in early summer. As soon as these have been cropped, cut the canes right down to ground level. Following the early fruit, the second and main autumn crop will be carried on the new canes already emerging.

The canes of Zeva are generally not so long and floppy as normal varieties, they do not so easily tie onto wires, and as a rule, don't need this treatment. The best method is to fasten cross pieces 12–15 inches long to stakes at about 2 ft., 3 ft. and 4 ft. from the ground. Fasten wire strands, not to the stakes but to the ends of these cross pieces and as the canes develop and grow, tuck these between the wires so that they don't flop over with the weight of fruit they will bear. You will then have a loose thick hedge of raspberries, instead of the usual fan trained on wires.

One of the basic reasons for failure with Zeva is that gardeners are too kind and considerate to it. Light soils will grow raspberries best with plenty of organic material worked in first; don't try to work it in after planting or you'll harm the shallow roots. Heavier soils are better for the raspberry but under no circumstances must there be any form of wetness or waterlogging. If this occurs, as in a clay soil, dig out drainage trenches and put down gypsum at the rate of 2 ozs. per sq. yd. every three months. Slowly the clay will be broken and the wetness lessen. See *No. 194* concerning gooseberries.

Raspberry roots are fibrous, shallow, and do

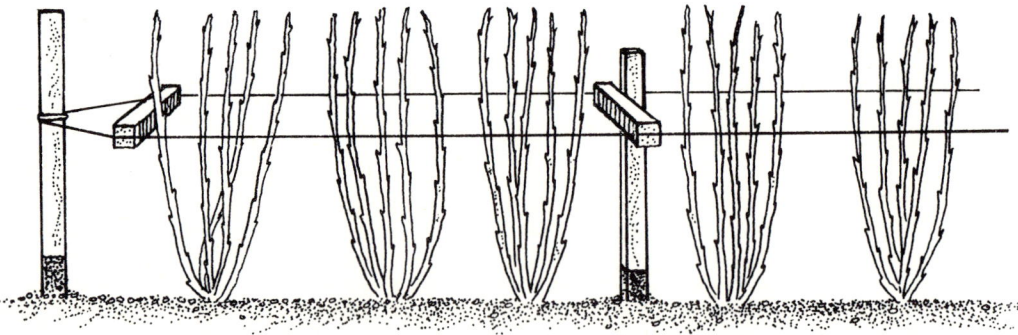

No. 232   *Support of a free-growing raspberry without the usual parallel wires and ties.*

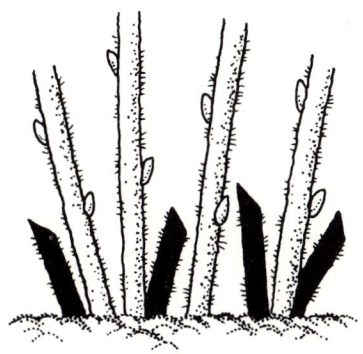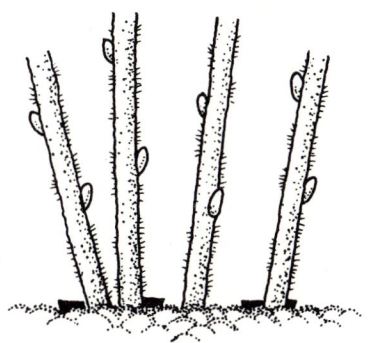

No. 232   *Pruning old fruited raspberry canes. The wrong way is shown on the left. The four strongest and most vigorous of the new shoots have been correctly retained to carry next season's crop, but the old canes have not been cut down hard enough. The correct method is shown on the right.*

not like disturbance; therefore, never dig near raspberries. Shallow hoeing for weed control or scratching in feeds is one thing, but never go near them with a spade or a fork. Plant firmly, water them in but not again unless the plant flags and is in obvious distress. More raspberries are ruined by watering than by any other cause—Zeva positively hates the stuff. If you have a sprinkler or other watering device, make quite certain it never reaches your raspberries.

Plants can be obtained from the raspberry specialist, W. H. Skinner, of Mount Pleasant Farm, Chart Sutton, Maidstone, Kent; and from Ken Muir, Honey Pot Fruit Farm, Weeley, Clacton, Essex.

233   Raspberries : no need to cut back tall canes

I am told that after tying in the best of my new raspberry canes, they should be cut back to about 6 ft. long. It appears that this is cutting off the best of the cane which bears most of the fruit. Is this so? Also can you tell me what fertiliser should be dug in for raspberries and when it should be applied?

Normal raspberry training is more closely akin to that for logans than the looser cage method used for the different growth habit Zeva variety. When growing really vigorously, some varieties of raspberry can easily reach 6 ft. or more. If this happens, two methods are open to you: (a) cut off the growing tip to try to encourage fruiting side shoots; or (b) bend over and loop the shoot, tying it to one of the topmost wires of your training fence. See *No. 210.*

In any case, you won't want them higher than a comfortable picking height—5 to 6 ft. at the most—unless you want to go in for the dangerous game of standing on step ladders.

The objective of the former alternative will be seen in February or early March when the soft tips of the canes that did not ripen before the onset of winter, will be seen to be for the most part, frost bitten and dead. So too will be the tips of the laterals which were prompted to form by the tip cutting method, but too late to ripen and become woody enough to withstand winter. Light cutting back in spring is then intended to form swelling, pushing buds which produce better fruit and a heavier yield. I personally prefer to bend the soft shoot ends to cause restriction to sap flow, and the production of fruit buds in much the same way as cordon apples. See *No. 152.*

It is not uncommon to see the soil adjacent to raspberries, and between rows, dug over with such abandon, as to indicate no regard for the rooting system of the plant. Raspberries make a mass of fibrous root, much of it near the surface. Competition from weeds and energy-sapping suckers must be controlled, and the best tool for this is a Dutch hoe. Use it frequently and maintain a mulch layer of compost, so that an open surface tilth is maintained and the soil not allowed to pan and cake hard.

If the soil is allowed to pan hard, rainwater—upon which you are going to rely—will run off without penetrating and therefore be wasted. Raspberries should not be watered artificially in any way unless prolonged drought causes distress. See *No. 232*. If the soil cakes too hard for the Dutch hoe—this is the type where you move backwards to leave an untrampled surface—turn to the drag hoe, with which you drag/chop with each blow, and move forward all the time into fresh ground. This means walking on the tilth you have created so, always finish by knocking out your footmarks with the Dutch hoe, putting down fresh or replacing the mulch cover as you go.

The constant production of new cane, its removal after fruiting, and new cane again, means that raspberries need something more than boosting tonics. The demand is over a long period and nutrient availability should be geared likewise. In addition to its moisture-retaining purposes, mulching forms an integral part of feeding, because as a material like mushroom compost, leaf mould or your own compost, decomposes and is slowly broken down, humus is gradually absorbed into the soil, and it is this organic sponge that is so important in soaking up and holding moisture so that it doesn't drain away, taking with it the soluble plant nutrients or fertilisers upon which you will have spent money to put down.

The demand of the raspberry is balanced—it will not be making all root like a turnip, or all leaf like a cabbage. But root and leaf are vitally necessary for good fruit to form—let alone ripen—so you will need a nutrient source that supplies the three basics, Nitrogen, Phosphorus and Potash, in a balanced ratio. Both Growmore and Humber Eclipse will do this but if I had to choose just one, I would go for the organic-based latter. You will also now realise why little and often over a long period to keep up a steady supply is better than up-ending a bucketful once a year.

The bacterial breakdown of Humber takes about eighty days, with Growmore usually considerably less. Therefore you have to try to gauge the correct time to put down a feed dressing before peak demand is reached. Accordingly with summer-fruiting raspberries, dressings put down in April will be providing a peak in July. So if you put down light dressings, $1-1\frac{1}{2}$ ozs. per sq. yd. hoed in a month apart from February until May, you will encourage good growth and good fruiting with enough residue to look after late cane production.

Autumn-fruiting varieties can take an extra couple of dressings, but don't put down any after mid-July to early August because the three month delay would be like encouraging your raspberries to continue growing vigorously until Christmas!

234 *Raspberries : no place for a yellow 'wildy'*

When picking some wild raspberries, I was surprised to find some of the canes had yellow berries on them. They were ripe and of a good size, but a little bitter compared to my garden raspberries. Would it be worth planting some of these canes in the garden?

Raspberries propagate very easily from seed and escape from garden culture into hedgerows and unkempt ground more readily than most other plants. Wild raspberries are to be found almost everywhere and it is likely that the wildies you picked were seedlings brought there by birds.

There are several varieties of yellow fruiting raspberries but whether this 'wild' form would be worth growing and whether you would be wise to try are both extremely doubtful propositions. Of course, it is possible that you have discovered a very acceptable yellow raspberry and may be on to a winner, but with an unknown and unplanned parenthood it is extremely unlikely that it will be worth your time and trouble. Also, plants which have developed qualities that enable them to withstand natural wild competition, will have probably lost out on yield and flavour. Furthermore because they have been growing wild and will not have been subject to the same care and attention as the plants already in your garden, it is quite possible that they will introduce some kind of pest or infection.

If you really want to grow unusual coloured fruit, buy clean healthy canes from a specialist nurseryman.

235 Raspberries, fly-ridden

This year my raspberries are covered with white fly, making the fruit practically unusable. How should I treat them? I shall shortly be cutting back the old canes, but this will leave the new canes still infected.

White fly is not usually regarded as a serious pest of raspberry or other outdoor grown crops but of course in favourable weather conditions, infestation does happen and is perhaps most likely to be met in a sheltered, windless garden that allows the pest to settle and build up.

If your fruit is so badly infected, it suggests that your normal early precautionary measures have been woefully inadequate. So determine now not to let it happen again, and resolve early next spring to spray regularly. This year's experience means that the pest will be around next year.

To get on top of white fly, or any pest for that matter, it is first of all necessary to study the beast a little. There are millions of this pest and they will be tucked away on the undersides of the leaves where it is difficult to get at them. Timid and alert, they fly off at any disturbance, looking like floating cigarette ash, to alight probably some distance away and then come back when you have gone. It is vital that control measures are very effective. One hundred per cent may be impossible, but try for 99·9%.

Liquid Malathion will kill white fly, but there are two problems to solve first: how to get it to stick to all surfaces of the plant so that it becomes wet all over, gets at the minute insects and penetrates into cracks and corners of leaves and fruit instead of 'running up' into globules and dripping off. You can solve this one by adding a few drops of washing-up detergent to the spray liquid when mixing.

Secondly, the spray will need to be projected from almost every conceivable angle so that you reach every nook and cranny where the fly can lurk and hide. Low down and upwards, high up and downwards—a sprayer with an angle bend is vital, and unless you want to stoop so low, an extension lance is also necessary in order to throw it up from ground level. The spray must be so fine that it sticks, and if there are several plants you will be using a lot of liquid. You see how a little thought about the nature of the job virtually determines the type of equipment you will need. A single-handed puff-puff is a waste of time, because it does not hold enough quantity or project it with sufficient force. I prefer and use the double action type hand-operated sprayer that sucks via a plastic hose from a bucket. The bucket is easily refilled and you don't have to struggle getting it on your back like a knapsack sprayer, nor risk spilling it down your trousers. A Solo Type 27 or 28 is an ideal sprayer for the job and try to choose a windless day. Malathion is lethal stuff so you won't want it blowing back in your face and, although it may be considered ultra cautious, tie a wet handkerchief over your nose and mouth.

You can begin picking fruit after thirty-six hours, but be sure to wash it before eating it.

236 Redcurrants: very brittle wood

My redcurrants crop poorly, and the stems and spurs seem to be so brittle that it is virtually impossible to pick fruit or prune the bushes without causing unintended snapping and breaking, and I often lose branches in a strong wind. I have sought advice but nobody can explain what is wrong— can you help?

Redcurrant shoots are brittle and break easily at the best of times, so much so that in the early years protection is advisable against wind in exposed positions. However, the brittleness can be made much worse by the activities of an insidious little beast called the Currant Clearwing Moth. It can often be seen as a white, black and yellow moth, on the wing during July and August and, being very partial to the shoot tips of red and white currants, this is where the eggs are laid. Caterpillars hatch and bore straight into the stems, tunnelling in the pithy centre, where of course you won't see it.

You can check out this diagnosis by examining a shoot either when pruning or when one has broken to see if it has a hollow, perhaps discoloured centre, and to explore it by cutting off half-inch sections with secateurs until the culprit is found.

Too much of this boring and, of course, the crop must suffer seriously, and in a bad infestation, the blackcurrant also can be affected.

Perhaps it is not so bad with the black because you are constantly regenerating new wood, and so the pest is cut away, but with the different pruning system of the redcurrant, this course is not open to you. Spraying the bushes with a contact killer, like Derris, should interfere with the egg laying activities during July and August, but this is a long period to deal with and it is easy to miss the early and late hatchings.

At one time, the only remedy for a bad attack was to grub out the bushes and burn them, but this did not necessarily stamp out the source of infection. Much better control is possible nowadays by commencing spraying immediately the crop is taken, with systemic insecticide and repeating at 15–20 day intervals right through the egg laying period into September. By this time the bush will be thoroughly permeated with poison so that any creature that bites or sucks is doomed.

237　Redcurrants: pruning methods

Could you please tell me how to prune my redcurrant bushes?

There is a fundamental difference between black and redcurrants, and the pruning procedure is naturally also quite different. Whereas black currants produce fruit on the previous season's wood, which is left unpruned save for the regular hard cutting back of old wood to produce young stems from below soil surface (see *No. 175*), the fruiting buds of the redcurrant are clustered closely at the bases of side shoots which grow out from the main stems. Fresh fruiting buds are formed at these points

every year and thus the fruiting wood of redcurrants can sometimes attain a considerable age.

Correct pruning depends upon correct training from the start and therefore begins with the planting of the new young plant. If the plants are established and have not been trained and pruned correctly you will have to adapt as best you can to bring your bushes into line. Beginning with a new planting then, examine the main stem and cut away any roots arising from bud scars on the stem leaving only the lower roots at the base. The reason for this is to leave a long clean main stem clear of root points from which sucker shoots may rise.

Plant into ground well-prepared with plenty of compost and a small handful of Growmore or Humber Eclipse lightly scratched into a mulch cover spread over the soil surface; then prune back side shoots to an outwards-facing bud, 3–4 ins. from the main stem.

Twelve months later, you will have—or if you have bought the plants as two-year-olds, they should have—eight or more shoots. These can be shortened back by about a third of their length, again to an outwards-facing bud so that the ensuing growth is away from a centre that will then remain open, rather than inward-facing buds the growths from which would tend to cross and congest each other.

Once established, redcurrants are apt to throw a forest of weak side shoots unless checked. This is where you may be able to make the best of old bushes by adapting them to the continuing procedure for young plants. During June begin to prune side shoots back to about 3–4 ins. from the main stems; this encourages fruit bearing buds to form around the bases of the spurs. You will have to be careful how you do this, as too much all at once whilst the plant is actively growing could easily produce shock. It is best, therefore, to spread this pruning over a period with only a few shoots being headed back at any one time with a few days' interval before you do any more.

When winter pruning will be done will really depend upon whether the bushes are protected by fruit nets. If the bushes are within a cage and beyond the reach of birds,

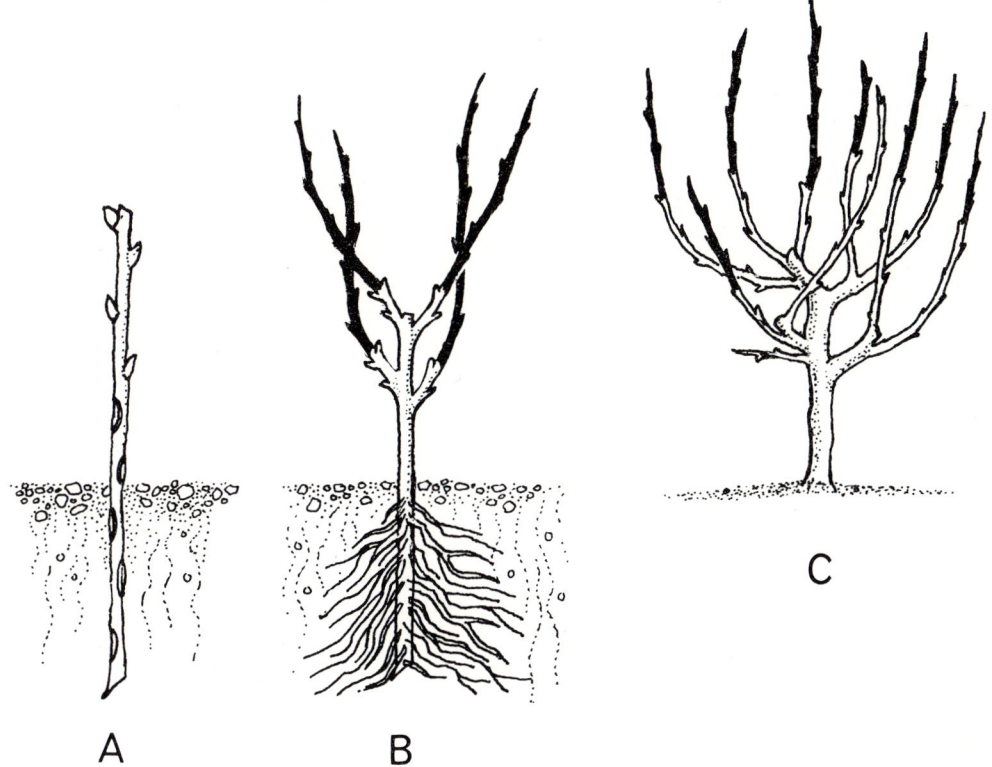

No. 237   *The propagation of redcurrants.*
A.   The autumn planted cutting has four growth buds well above ground level whilst all the lower buds have been nicked away with a sharp knife or razor blade.
B.   The same cutting a year later. The buds have grown out to become four shoots. These should be pruned back to two or three buds—indicated by the black marking.
C.   These will grow out to become the two-year-old plant whose shoots are again cut back, although not so hard.

the bushes can be pruned by shortening back the eight or so main stems by about half of the growth they have made during the previous season. As the bush becomes older and bigger, the heading back of the lead shoots will become progressively more severe so that eventually when you want them no longer they will be reduced each winter to half an inch or so. Now cut back the June pruned 3–4 inch spurs to about $\frac{1}{2}$ inch long, i.e. about the second bud from their bases.

On the other hand if the bushes are being grown in the open, birds may well peck out a lot of the buds and it is no good pruning to an outwards-facing bud until you know that it is still there and has not been taken by a hungry bird.

Pruning in the open will therefore have to be left until early spring when you can be sure which buds remain, and try to make the best of the directions in which they are pointing.

Because you need to counter the tendency to

push out a lot of weak side growths, do not use quick-acting fertilisers, especially nitrogenous ones. Redcurrants are the perfect example of the need for slow steady release of balanced nutrients.

238   Rhubarb easily acquires a tainted flavour

Last year I purchased four crowns of rhubarb advertised as a variety called Prince Albert. They are all growing strongly, but when cooked their sticks have an unpleasant strong earthy taste. I have followed recommended procedure—working in plenty of farmyard manure and mulching heavily, but something is wrong somewhere. Can you please suggest what it is—and a remedy? Or do I dig them up and plant another variety? If so, what do you suggest?

The rhubarb variety Prince Albert is very old, and not much grown now. It was regarded as an early variety and was grown mainly for forcing in the days when the first long bright pink stems brought high prices at market, until the canning industry effectively killed it. In other words, it is a commercial variety for forcing, and not the best for the garden.

Newly planted rhubarb should not be pulled for the first two seasons, to allow the plant to build up reserves and strength and you shouldn't have pulled yours so soon. Furthermore, pulling should not extend over a longer period than three months from the first pull.

The 'earthiness' could be something to do with the soil condition—perhaps enhanced by allowing the sticks to become mature and 'old' before pulling. A further clue is that, planted only last year, the rhubarb must have grown extremely fast for you to be able to describe it within twelve months as growing 'strongly' and for you to have pulled sticks at all. Quite apart from the mistake you have made in cropping much too early, this rapid growth is no doubt due to the farmyard manure and the probability that you have dug it in and used it as a mulch whilst still fresh. If this is so, you needn't look any further for the trouble. Rhubarb can pick up a taint from 'strong smelling' materials like cow, pig and fish

manures—although the latter is unfortunately now virtually unobtainable.

Replace with clean straw if you can get it. Time and weather, decomposition and/or leaching will gradually remove the trouble. Don't use any more farmyard manure, unless it has been stacked, turned and composted properly for at least a year; and if it contains cow or pig droppings I should make it two years at the very least.

Make a test pulling next year and if the taste is still there, clear them out. If you want to try a different variety, try Hawke's Champagne, a good variety for forcing; or The Sutton, a good maincrop type.

239   Rhubarb: preparation for planting

Some rhubarb roots I ordered, arrived whilst I was away and they are now very dried-up. Can they still be used, and are there any special preparations needed for this crop?

Unfortunately due to being delayed in transit or damage to the packing (no competent nurseryman sends out roots in bad condition) many plants with big fleshy root-stocks like rhubarb can dry out and look very shrivelled when you receive them. The first step is to reverse the dehydration by a long and thorough soaking, and it may take several days before they swell to become nicely plump and fleshy again.

Rhubarb is a gross feeder, and a deep rooter. Therefore, prepare for planting by working plenty of moist peat or very old compost at least two spits deep, three spits if you have the energy. Don't use farmyard manure or fresh mushroom compost unless it has been stacked and turned and composted, see *Nos. 476, 489* and *492*, for at least a year because of the danger of imparting taint to the rhubarb, see *No. 238.* Set the crowns three feet apart with the embryo leaf buds—or the base of young leaf shoots, if they are emerging—just an inch or two above soil level. Firm the soil, but be careful not to break or damage the root.

Spread a 2–3 inch layer of very well rotted compost—this is why the crowns were planted an inch or two above the soil—and scatter into this a balanced fertiliser that is clear of any 'smell' that rhubarb can absorb. Growmore would be quite satisfactory. Put this down at about 2 ozs. per sq. yd. and as leaf shoots are emerging, scatter down another 2 ozs. per sq. yd. If this second dressing is put down when the leaves are unfolding make sure that the fertiliser does not lodge in them since this can cause scorch.

Repeat this mulch and feed procedure each spring, and follow the general advice contained in the adjacent items about rhubarb.

240 Sooty mould on fruit : cause and control

Last summer the leaves and fruit on a peach tree in my garden were covered in a black substance which also dropped on to gooseberry bushes growing beneath the tree. It also spread to a plum tree growing nearby. No other part of the garden is affected with this trouble and we wonder whether an elderberry bush in the same area could be the cause?

The elderberry is only indirectly responsible and no real blame can be attached to it. The black deposit is a fungus, descriptively called sooty mould. This infects the wounds made by sap-sucking insects and proliferates at a fantastic rate in the sugary honeydew secretions of aphides. It is certain, therefore, that earlier in the year the peach tree was infested by greenfly, and the honeydew dripped on to the gooseberries—or, indeed the gooseberry itself could also have been infested with greenfly aphis.

Quite apart from the dripping honeydew carrying the mould with it on to the gooseberries below, the microscopic spores of the fungus are in the air by the million and, finding the perfect culture medium in the sugary film on the leaves, is in its element. Apart from anything else, the black suede-like fungus reduces the intensity of light reaching the chlorophyll in the leaves so that they cannot function, and later fruiting can therefore be seriously impaired. See *No. 228*.

The mould must be removed but, more important, it should not be allowed to happen in the first place. The first precaution is to clear all

overwintering organisms especially eggs of aphides from trees and bushes during the dormant winter season by spraying thoroughly with tar oil wash—and because the elderberry is a favourite host plant for overwintering greenfly—this is how it may be indirectly involved—spray that as well.

With the ending of winter hibernation, young leaves bursting from the buds are soft and luscious and are a magnet to the earliest hatchings of greenfly which, being winged, will look upon these landing strips as something from Heaven. This is the time to commence spraying with Lindane or Malathion, drenching the young foliage, especially the undersides. Then every few days, as emerging leaves and shoots grow out of the protective insecticide film, carry out supplementary spraying on all soft tips. You can do this quite easily with a hand-held puff-puff sprayer.

You should be able to clear the sooty mould attack with a fungicide spray like Captan and then if rain does not remove the dead mould in a week or so, clean the green leaf, by directing the spray from a hose pipe with just enough force to remove the soot but not to knock leaves and fruit about to cause bruising and damage.

241 Strawberries : growing alpine variety from seed

I have been given a packet of seeds of an alpine strawberry called Baron Solemacher. Will these be easy to grow and can you tell me something about the care of the seedlings and whether they can be grown in pots?

Many people like to grow alpine strawberries because of the alleged better taste over the more usual larger fruited kinds. These people can never have tasted the modern variety Domanil which, to many palates, mine included, is the finest flavoured strawberry yet produced.

Alpine strawberries can have erratic germination; sometimes it is poor and sometimes they come up like mustard and cress. The safest policy is always to sow plenty of seed; you will then get enough seedlings for your requirements if germination is poor, and if you have more of them than you need, you can always give them away.

To give them a month or more longer growing season, they are best sown in March in a cool or slightly heated greenhouse but, failing that, sow them outside in April or May covering them with a cloche. As soon as the seedlings are large enough to handle between the finger and thumb, prick them out singly into 2½ in. pots of John Innes potting compost —or into Jiffy 7 peat balls. Remember, the peat balls can dry out very quickly so only use these if you can be sure that you can give them regular daily attention.

As soon as the pots develop a root layer between soil and pot, or roots show through the mesh of the Jiffy 7, either pot into 4–5 inch pots with a John Innes No. 1 compost into which has been mixed an equal bulk of peat, or plant out in the garden in a position where plenty of peat or well-rotted compost has been worked in. Strawberries like plenty of moisture-holding humus in the soil, so that they are able to grow vigorously at all stages with no dryness checks.

In all probability, alpines will try to put up blooms in their first summer; pick these off so that the plants build up strong crowns and produce much more and better fruit next year. Each spring, February to early March, sprinkle a teaspoonful of balanced plant food around each plant. If you are growing the plants in pots, move them up into a 6 in. pot, working the same teaspoonful of nutrient into the extra soil.

Try to arrange that the pots spend a week or two during winter out in the open so that they can be chilled, or even very lightly frosted. This doesn't mean a fierce hard frost that will freeze them solid. The chilling (or to the technically minded 'vernalisation') is important as an inducement to flowering in spring and is probably the most important reason why amateur-grown greenhouse pot strawberries often give very disappointing results.

Alpine strawberries, although very tasty are usually somewhat small in size. The superiority of their flavour over the red bags of water that the fruit shops often sell (the primary ob-

jective of the growing industry is weight of crop and profit, not quality) is one reason for growing them. If you want to increase their size, thin the small embryo fruitlets to no more than eight to ten per plant and sprinkle half a teaspoonful of sulphate of potash around the plants as soon as the flower petals fall. This will enhance their taste and put a little extra colour in their cheeks.

242 Strawberries: growing out of season

I bought some strawberries last Easter and potted them on. Now they are in 9 in. pots and I have removed the flowers and runners so the plants are enormous. I feed them and I have a cool greenhouse, so would it be possible to have some fruit during the winter? I could fit a light if required. The strawberries in pots have so far been outside.

Getting strawberries to fruit out of season is a very difficult job; even the specialists who want them to show at exhibitions have a problem. You will not be able to grow strawberries in deep winter but by growing early varieties and using a little subterfuge and understanding, you should be able to get fruit considerably earlier than usual.

Strawberries need a period of chilling and light frosting to promote flowering (see *No. 241*). Potted plants can be brought in when they have been chilled. Now they will need all the light they can get and a steady temperature of 45°F. at night; if it is allowed to go much higher at this stage, you will only produce leaves. If you fix up a light, this really should be of a type like mercury vapour bulbs that can give high illumination for a relatively low current consumption—otherwise it can easily become uneconomic.

From now on your cultivation is directed to encourage the plants to think that spring is very early. Keep the lights on for half the night so that the length of daylight resembles early summer. As they respond with growth, hopefully about February, feed with Growmore or Humber Eclipse; a level teaspoonful to each plant scratched into the soil surface and then watered in.

As soon as flowers begin to show, gradually raise the temperature so that by the time the fruitlets have grown to the size of cherries, the greenhouse temperature is at 65°F. minimum. At petal fall scratch in half a teaspoonful of sulphate of potash to each plant to enhance flavour and colour. Generally speaking, the combination of this special application of sulphate of potash with slow-acting manures, working in association with a high humus content in the soil medium so that a vigorous healthy root system results, means that you should have no need for liquid feeding or foliar feeding. These, at best, are regarded as boosts and are no substitute for healthy vigorous root activity.

Natural growth, as it progresses, will increase transpiration and water uptake; you musn't allow a dryness check to occur but, by the same token, don't overdo it. Strawberries are not bog plants.

In the sheltered conditions of a greenhouse, greenfly could build up to plague proportions very quickly indeed, do keep a sharp lookout and at the very first signs of them, even on plants outside the greenhouse, spray thoroughly with Lindex, especially the undersides of the leaves where the first attack will show. Don't wait for the attack to set in. Protective spraying should start about the end of February and be repeated weekly throughout the growing season.

243 Strawberries : replanting a bed

I am going to replant my strawberry bed with fresh plants. This plot is always reserved for strawberries and I realise it now needs rejuvenating. Can you recommend suitable fertilisers to bring the soil into good condition?

Strawberries need plenty of humus-forming organic matter in the soil, and benefit during their three-year stint in the beds from copious

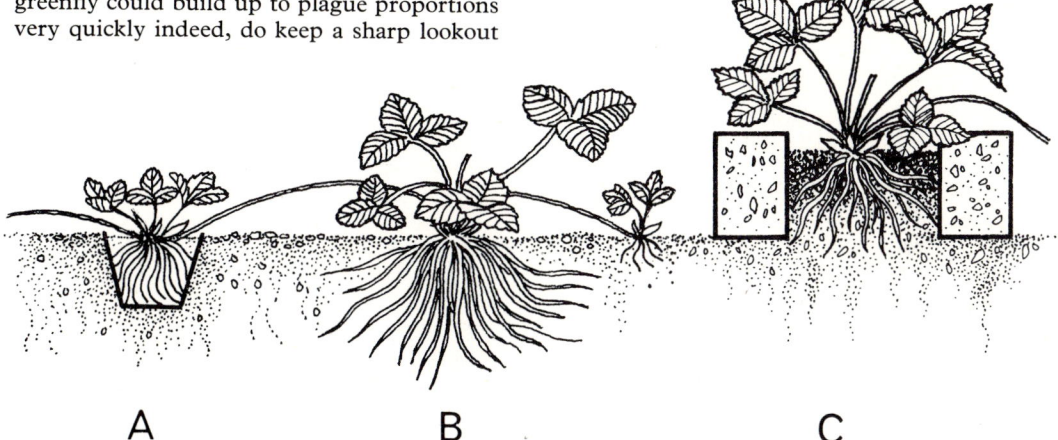

A   B   C

No. 243   *Three methods of rooting strawberries.*
A.   Wrong: it has been rooted into too small a pot. Insufficient root development and the fact that runners are allowed to develop into further plantlets will result in a poor specimen.
B.   Wrong: this is a self-rooted plantlet with a free root run which produces a better plant. But severe root damage is inevitable when it is lifted for transplanting.
C.   Correct: set two rows of house bricks 4–5 ins. apart and fill the channel with compost. The bricks will stop runners spreading. Being above soil level, the plants will have the added benefit of full light and full root spread beneath. If they are to be transplanted, pull the bricks apart and cut out the plants with square of root and compost intact.

mulching with well rotted compost, spent mushroom compost or peat. Advance preparation for a few years with heavy mulching will result in a substantial input of humus into the plot. You won't get really good strawberries unless the plant has a vigorous root growth, and adequacy of plant nutrients is best ensured not by quick-acting boost fertilisers, but by slower-acting long-lasting organic-based manures.

Instead of putting new maiden strawberries back into the same old strawberry bed, set them into fresh ground alongside and the next year plant maidens into fresh ground alongside that, and so on each year. See *No. 247*. Rotational cropping in the garden is proven good practice and should be carried out whenever possible, even in a small garden. By rotating the strawberries round the garden over the years, the organic input is taken over and utilised by succeeding crops. This way the strawberries benefit, the soil structure of the whole garden benefits, all other crops benefit.

244 *Strawberries grown under cloches*

Our strawberries are flowering well this year, but I have them covered with cloches. How will the plants be pollinated if insects can't get in? Do I have to do it with my hands, as with tomatoes, or are they self-pollinating?

Modern varieties of strawberries will crop quite satisfactorily under cloches without your being concerned about special pollination. The only extra precaution, compared to those strawberries growing entirely exposed, is to realise that growth and fruit-bearing are likely to be greater and therefore moisture and nutrient uptake will also be greater. Put down a little extra balanced plant manure and as soon as the first fruits reach cherry size, dust a little sulphate of potash along the rows to encourage ripening.

Ensure, also, that movement among the cloched plants—picking, manuring, spraying etc.—does not disturb the mulch cover and expose the soil. Cover your footmarks and maintain the mulch cover at all times. See *No. 242* and adjacent items on strawberry growing.

245 *Strawberries : greenhouse culture*

I have ordered ten Grandee strawberry plants and hope to grow them in a greenhouse. I would welcome advice about how to go about this.

For pot culture you need to take delivery of plants in autumn and to choose a variety that can withstand the strain of fruit-bearing in their first year. Grandee is one of these varieties and, of course, has achieved considerable fame for the large size of its berries.

Your strawberries may be delivered to you as young plants growing in 'Jiffy 7s', which are small balls of peat in a plastic mesh net, or perhaps growing in fibre pots or soil balls as knocked out of small pots before packing and despatch. In any case, before planting, make sure that the root ball is well moistened by soaking it for an hour or so. If they have become dried-out in transit, this is the only way to get the ball thoroughly moistened all through and it will take a lot of watering with a can to get them moist again. If the plants arrived with their root systems shaken out, free of soil and the plants feel dry and limp, immerse them completely in water for an hour or two so that they become plump again.

Strawberries like plenty of humus in the soil so, with well-moistened root balls or shaken-out but plump plants, plant into 6 inch pots using a compost containing plenty of moistened peat or well-rotted compost. If you have to buy potting compost, get John Innes No. 3 potting, and mix this in equal proportion with peat. The potted plants should now be plunged to their rims in an open exposed position in the garden.

This is because strawberries for indoor fruiting need to be chilled and vernalised during winter, see *241* and *242*, to encourage flower production. If the winter is mild, keep an eye open for slugs and be ready with baited traps, see *No. 511*. Leave the plants until late February or early March when they can be lifted, cleaned up, the dead leaves removed, and moved into the greenhouse or conservatory. If this is heated, keep them in the coolest part since they won't need much heat; in fact, the less heat the better. They don't want draught but ventilation is important; a stagnant atmosphere encourages Botrytis, a grey mould fungus that can play havoc. At the very first signs of attack, apply a fungicide to check it. Greenfly is a pest that must be controlled as it can introduce virus disease. Don't wait for it to appear, regard it as inevitable and spray regularly with Lindane every seven days as soon as you take the plants inside.

From early April when they will be growing away fast, feeding is important, so use a balanced feed like Growmore or Humber Eclipse or a liquid fertiliser.

Exposure to sun or full light is important from the time the flower buds appear and if you want to ensure a little extra something in the colour and flavour of the berries, add just a pinch of sulphate of potash each week in addition to normal feeding until fruiting is finished.

Grandee is capable of providing extremely large berries, even without thinning, but if you want to have really monster berries, thin each truss to leave only a couple or so to develop.

246 Strawberries : container-grown

I would like to make a strawberry barrel from a 40-gallon water butt. How do I set about it?

A popular idea, and very suitable for patios and balconies. Preparation is all important and you won't be successful unless you do the job properly. You must first realise that there is no particular quality advantage in growing strawberries in a barrel. The basic purpose of this growing method is simply that more plants can be grown in the area upon which the barrel stands than if the plants were in the ground. There is a limit to how much plants can be overcrowded, so there is only one direction to go—upwards.

Start by boring 1-inch diameter holes, 4–5 ins. apart in the base—these will be for drainage. You are going to have to look at the barrel whilst the plants are growing, so it's worthwhile taking a little trouble to make it look attractive. So instead of haphazardly boring holes in the sides, first mark the positions where they are to go with a piece of chalk, as

follows: on a line around the centre of the barrel mark out six positions equidistant—with a forty-gallon barrel, this will be about 10–12 ins. apart; with smaller barrels, reduce the number of holes to maintain this distance or in a larger barrel make more holes. A forty-gallon wooden barrel usually has three iron hoops at each end so, between the second and third hoops from each end, which will be about midway between the centre and the ends of the barrel (should the hoops be missing or your barrel different), mark six more holes opposite the spaces in the central row. This will allow fruit trusses of each plant to hang between, and not on top of, plants in the row underneath. You will now have eighteen marks on the barrel that are evenly spaced; you can get a clear idea of what it should look like by referring to the illustration. These, with six plants in the top of the barrel, will give you twenty-four plants. When you are satisfied that all the marks are evenly spaced, bore out 2–2½ in. holes in the eighteen places around the barrel, varnish it, paint the metal hoop bands and when dry, you are ready to fill your barrel.

No. 246 *The barrel method of growing strawberries which is ideal for patios and conservatories.*

When the barrel is filled with soil, it will of course be heavy and rather awkward to move, so put it into the final position where you want it before filling. Remember that this should be where the plants can be frosted (see *Nos. 241* and *242*) or you will have to move it afterwards. Stand the barrel on four bricks so that air passes under and water does not stagnate around the base. Put a three-inch layer of broken crock and stones in the bottom and cover these with some rough compost or peat. Roll a piece of wire netting or Netlon into a tube about 4–5 in. in diameter and set this upright in the centre so that the end comes level with the top of the barrel. Fill this tube with more crock and stones so that, when filled, the barrel will have a central drainage core. Fill the barrel with a compost of equal parts peat, John Innes No. 3 and sandy grit, but with a good layer of rough peat or compost over the bottom crock and around and against the central core. Set this filling in layers and tamp down firmly each time, otherwise too much settlement will occur later. Fill to within an inch of the rim. Each day, water lightly, allow the filling to settle for two or three weeks, making good the soil level if it should drop below 3 ins. from the rim. Aim to have reached this stage by August or September so that you are ready to set the plants.

Select July-taken runners that are strong and vigorous because, unlike open ground plants, you are going to want them to fruit in their first year as maidens.

Using a dibber, and plugging them firm with peat, set eighteen plants in the holes, and a further six plants around the rim.

Watering has to be done from the top and the success of this barrel method depends largely on your ability to prevent drying out at the top whilst ensuring that the bottom plants are not waterlogged, i.e. the moisture content should be uniform from top to bottom. The secret, therefore, is to water a little and often. If you fill the barrel as described, you should now have an interesting and very productive strawberry farm.

The Italian strawberry industry has for some time grown the crop in pots which are stacked up 6, 7, even 8 ft. high and, not surprisingly, they have earned the name 'Tower Pots'. The strawberries emerge, two plants to a pot, from protruding lips. The pots are each about 9 in. tall and in diameter, and set one upon another, a tower 6 ft. high or more is therefore not very stable. This problem is solved by passing a wire or a cane through the pots from top to bottom and attaching it to a top wire, so that the pile cannot fall over. These pots, made in white rigid plastic, are now available in Britain. Arranged as 5 ft. high units they are much more attractive to look at and are far lighter and easier to move than a barrel. Other plants will grow in them remarkably well and can look most attractive standing on a patio or balcony. Details can be obtained from Honeypot Fruit Farm, Weeley, Clacton, Essex.

Whichever method you try—barrel or tower—there is one precaution you must observe: grown in this manner the fruit trusses hang down and they can be buffeted around by wind. Air movement is very good to assist fertilisation of the bloom, but it can ruin the soft-fleshed strawberries if they bang together and bruise. Positioning your 'high rise strawberry flats' in a greenhouse, home extension or even a porch is fine, but if you try an open patio or balcony, make sure it doesn't catch the wind.

Another risk is that 'little and often' frequent watering can soon wash out plant nutrient from the soil at the top of the tower or barrel. It is beneficial therefore to always water with a weak solution of liquid feed—balanced N P & K—until the first minute fruits can be discerned. Then switch to a feed having a potash bias like Tomorite, in order to assist fruit ripening.

247 Strawberries : the yellows

For the last few years some of my strawberries have grown stunted yellow leaves and have had little berries that were hard and useless. Some seemed to grow out of this condition, but others stayed like it. This year it has happened worse than ever; spraying has made no difference. Can you suggest a cure?

'Sometimes they get over it, sometimes they

don't.' The symptoms are clear—this is a case of 'June Yellows'. With whatever you are spraying, you are wasting time and money because the trouble is due to neither pest, fungus nor virus, but due to a physiological breakdown in genetic make-up, and therefore arising way back in the variety's ancestry.

You do not say what variety of strawberry you are growing—the problem is known to affect several, and indeed hit the headlines several years ago when a magnificent new variety called Auchincruive Climax suffered a widespread and sudden collapse. The fruit growing industry in its enthusiastic acclaim had committed itself to this wonderful new variety to the exclusion of almost everything else and was badly hit when it suddenly collapsed with the 'yellows'.

Dig up and burn all disfigured plants. Better still, be resolute and burn the lot and start afresh with clean healthy stock from a reputable grower.

You can try the variety Grandee which has become well-known for its enormous sweet-flavoured berries. A new Belgian variety, Domanil, has given me good-sized berries, not overlarge but rich in colour and, for my palate, the finest flavour I've ever tasted; a remarkably strong pleasant aroma and quite the heaviest ever total crop per plant. There are also several other newer varieties like Tamella and Gento which have very greatly extended the fruiting season.

It would be a wise precaution to plant new stock in a fresh position. This is not because there is a danger of passing on 'yellows', but because after several years uninterrupted growing, there may well be mildew or other fungus spores left over from the old plants that could put your new ones under stress right from the beginning.

Good management of strawberries involves regular and systematic spraying against disease and pests—especially against greenfly which can transmit virus—and that can be just as lethal as 'yellows'. Constant renewal of your fruit-bearing plants is also essential—strawberry plants cannot be expected to fruit profitably after three or four years.

Peg down into pots the sturdiest of the plantlets that form on the runners—these will be next season's maidens. Pick off the bloom in their first full season to prevent them from fruiting. This will encourage heavy cropping in the second full year and a good crop again in the third year. Then scrap them, replacing with new maidens that you have previously produced for this purpose. Try to maintain constant renewal on this three-year cycle.

Put plenty of humus in the soil before planting, always maintain a good mulch layer of peat or compost, don't begrudge good-balanced feeding, using Growmore or Humber Eclipse —and you should stay clear of another attack of the 'yellows'.

248 Strawberries : underground attack by soil pests

I found several fat white grubs boring into my strawberry roots and the plants are wilting. Are the grubs causing this harm?

There are several grubs like weevils and chafers that feed underground and cause the collapse of strawberries, but the description 'fat and white' suggests that your trouble is one of the chafer beetles: if the grubs have shiny brown heads, you can be sure that is what it is.

Unchecked they could ruin not only your crop, but the plants as well. They can be controlled by working Bromophos or BHC Dust into the soil around the plants and I have seen Chlordane wormkiller, used to control wireworm, also wipe out a bad infestation of chafers. Chlordane can be watered down at any time; it is effective against soil creatures for twelve months. If you have used straw under the fruits, as soon as fruiting has finished, pick up all the straw carefully and quickly, so that any adult weevils lurking in it are gathered up before they can escape—burn the lot at once. Spray the plants and the soil around the plants with BHC spray and again every fourteen days until early September. This should prevent any egg-laying antics by late pests in the plant crowns.

As the Chlordane diffuses, the soil atmosphere is made toxic to grubs that breathe by diffusion and any grubs that do develop from late egg-laying will be quickly destroyed before they can do damage to your plants.

249 Tomatoes: causes of Botrytis in greenhouses

For the last two years my greenhouse tomatoes have gone milky white where the stalks joined the fruit, and dropped off. Then the plants became very sick and collapsed. Can you suggest what the trouble is and how to cure it?

Botrytis mould, as it is usually called, is a very common fungus disease in greenhouses, but not so much on plants grown in the open. The microscopic spores are carried in the air in countless millions and get everywhere. These spores are harboured in plant debris in the soil, on unclean pots and boxes and in spilled soil on the greenhouse floor. They are merely waiting for favourable conditions to grow away and then living plant tissue can be, and often is, attacked.

Dampness and stagnant air are encouraging conditions. Therefore, adequate ventilation, with sufficient movement of air and the avoidance of overwatering, are the two most important precautions to be taken.

Like most fungal diseases, Botrytis finds easiest entry into soft plant tissue, and when naturally soft tissued plants like tomatoes and strawberries are made even more soft by being fed too much nitrogen, they become very susceptible. So look to your feeding, and if the fertilisers you have been using are nitrogen high, replace them with a nutrient source where the NPK ratios are balanced. If anything is higher, let it be the K fraction—potash— and then only just a little. This will encourage maturity and resistance in the tissues instead of lush soft growth. Where Botrytis is attacking growing tomatoes in a greenhouse, you can tackle it in two ways. First, you can try to cure the disease by treating the plant. Benlate is a particularly useful material to ward off attack, but now that the Botrytis is active, you'll have to apply it frequently enough to suppress the fungus—every three weeks rather than the five to six weeks which is the preventive-

frequency before Botrytis puts in an appearance.

Secondly, you can utilise the captive atmosphere in the greenhouse and carry out fumigation with a fungicidal smoke. Use TCNB smoke cones or PBI smokes and fumigate strictly in accordance with the instructions. You'll be able to buy these at your local gardening shop.

At the end of the season, have a complete and thorough clean-out of the house: all soil droppings, old compost, rubbish, everything, and then fumigate again. Then bring in fresh soil, making sure that it has been sterilised. Next year, be certain to give the greenhouse plenty of ventilation and spray with Benlate every five to six weeks as soon as the first truss is set, and you should have no more trouble from Botrytis.

250 Tomatoes: where has all the taste gone?

I'm fed up with growing almost tasteless tomatoes. Is there a really sweet-flavoured variety?

This sort of thing often happens in all sorts of fruit and vegetables when they have been bred and selected for size and weight of crop, resistance to disease, and/or commercial factors like uniformity of size and period of ripening which help harvesting by machine. Other factors like taste and colour then often become diminished or even lost. I agree that the tomatoes that one buys in the shops are nothing but bags of tasteless water—they have been bred for weight of crop and profit. Until you pick and immediately taste a freshly picked tomato you haven't experienced the real thing.

Flavour is very much a personal matter: what one palate relishes, does not excite another, but you won't go far wrong with the old variety Ailsa Craig, or derivatives of it. A generation ago, Carter's Sunrise was regarded as something out on its own for flavour. Unhappily, Sunrise doesn't figure in many catalogues these days—probably because it wasn't a very prolific cropper. However, one of its parents is still there—Ailsa Craig. Some years this bears a good crop, other years it disappoints; that's where its progeny Sunrise was more consistent.

The wisest policy is to test out two or three varieties each year till you find one you particularly like. Then make this your mainstay. You will be able to rely on it each year whilst you experiment with other varieties. Make sure of consistent performance before you switch your maincrop.

Have you tried yellow and gold varieties? These are growing in popularity as more and more gardeners discover that these haven't been over-worked and 'improved' by the experts to the same extent as the red varieties and, in consequence, have retained much more of their flavour than the heavy cropping tasteless reds.

251   Tomatoes : dealing with leaf curl

The leaves of my greenhouse-grown tomato plants curl under, giving a claw-like appearance. The lower leaves are quite normal; the plants are vigorous; the fruit is setting well; there is no discoloration of the foliage nor any infestation by greenfly or whitefly. Some of the plants are in plastic pots, others are growing in the greenhouse border in new but well-rotted turf soil. They are given a proprietary tomato feed every fourth day. All show the same symptoms.

This is an almost classic description of what is usually called Tomato Leaf Curl. It is not a pest or disease but a physiological disorder. The cause is basically a conflict of growing conditions, i.e. vigorous plants feeding and growing but being held back by temperatures which are too low at night. Raise the night temperature and the curl should disappear.

As soon as you do this, however, the plants will very likely grow away quickly and make a lot of soft lush growth because they have been restricted. You must now keep a very careful watch for any signs of a whitish mould under the younger leaves and around the fruit stalks —Botrytis, see *No. 249*. Give as much ventilation as you can during the day. Also start spraying with Benlate a little more frequently —say every three to four weeks—than the routine precautionary anti-mould spraying

which is every five to six weeks. If you are unlucky and an attack develops you will have to fumigate—see *No. 249*.

252   Tomatoes : poor ventilation produces brown spots

Could you identify the disease which first attacks the lower leaves of my tomato plants and then steadily moves up the stems? So far, the tops of the plants seem to be unaffected. Brownish spots appear on the under-surface of the leaves and later become yellow, when they can be seen from the upper surface as well, giving the foliage a distinctive mottled appearance.

This is a fungus disease called Cladosporium and as with another fungus that attacks soft tissue subjects like tomatoes, Botrytis, is rarely encountered in plants that are grown in the open, but is common and quite often severe under glass. The symptoms are exactly as you describe them and the attack can come on quite suddenly, as early as April, but with increasing likelihood and severity as the summer progresses. As autumn approaches conditions often become ideal for the disease and it is not unknown for whole houses full of plants to be affected.

Like Botrytis, spores are everywhere and the conditions conducive to development of the fungus are a stagnant, dank, moist atmosphere, especially at night. Therefore, although ventilation is important at all times, it is imperative at night. This does not mean leaving open the top ventilator only, open the bottom ones too so that air circulates top to bottom and if your house doesn't have lower ventilators leave the door open and remove a pane of glass at the far end so that the air can sweep straight through. If you are afraid this may reduce the night temperature too much, and cause leaf curl, see *No. 251*, install an electric fan, or use a fan heater, to keep the air on the move.

Overcrowding of plants in order to achieve maximum possible total crops from a given area is a contributing factor. The leaves overlap as they grow and become congested, so that air movement is hindered. This is where the disease is usually first noticed and without waiting for yellowing or first signs of an attack, lower leaves or at least part of them could be removed in order to assist air movement—but first read *No. 257*. Plants that have been checked in growth or which are excessively lush and soft due to unbalanced nitrogen-biased feeding, are more likely to attack, and to be attacked badly, so check that your fertilisers are in the correct proportions, i.e. with N P & K in balance. In a case like this, don't let the plant suffer a dryness check—wilting will only make matters worse—but try to keep the plants a little on the dry side so that the plant's surface tissues harden a little and offer more resistance to invading fungal spores.

Even after careful management, plants can succumb when humid muggy weather encourages a determined attack. Such conditions should lead you to expect trouble and to exert greater than ever vigilance. At the first signs of the disease, some control can be attained by wetting all plant surfaces with a colloidal copper spray, or with Zineb. This is only partially effective though and if you feel like being extra cautious, you can respond to muggy weather with a precautionary half-strength spraying just in case.

Now that you have had Cladosporium, you will have to very thoroughly wash out the house using formalin or fumigate it with a fungicidal smoke, see *No. 249*.

253 Tomato: how to save your own seed

My tomato plants this year have given me by far the finest crop I have ever had, and I would like to save the seed to try again next year. How do I go about it?

Compared to the number of plants it will provide, the cost of a packet of seed really is very small and, of course, what you are buying is not only the seed but also the grower's knowledge and expertise involved in breeding various qualities into the particular variety. That is, growing the stock plants free from diseases and defects which may be carried over into the seed, harvesting, drying, cleaning and all the hundred

and one processes that go into placing a neat packet before you.

If it is the cost of the seed you are primarily concerned in saving—no matter whether it is tomatoes, runner beans, flowers or whatever—don't bother; it is false economy. Seed production is a skilled job, and it costs you very little to let the specialists use all their facilities to do the job properly.

However, there are other factors to be considered, not the least of which is the pride and satisfaction so dear to every gardener in saving and growing seed from a plant that you have grown yourself. So, if despite the above caution you really want to try with a tomato, here's how to go about it.

On a clean and healthy plant, select one or two nicely-shaped fruits and allow them to become fully ripe. It is best, if you can manage it with perhaps other fruits close alongside, to enclose the selected fruit in a paper or plastic bag and wait for it to fall naturally.

Pull the fruit apart and scoop out the seed into a fine sieve—like a flour sieve—and wash away the pulp under running cold water. Spread the seeds out on a piece of glass, formica or plastic sheet—some people advise cloth or absorbent paper because it helps to dry the seed more quickly. This is not such a good idea because the soft coating of the seed tends to adhere to the fibres of the cloth or paper and, when dry, they have to be forcibly scraped off, possibly damaging what has now become a delicate seed. They don't stick to a hard gloss surface.

Space the seeds so that they do not touch each other and place in a warm airy place to dry —the airing cupboard is ideal. When thoroughly dry, put them into a small plastic bag, add a small pinch of Murphy Combined Seed Dressing for protection, shake the bag so that it is mixed with the seed and fold or seal the bag airtight.

Store the seed in a cool but frost-free place during winter, and they should be in fine condition for sowing in the spring.

However, there is a cautionary warning to heed before you even start. Noticeable improvements in vegetables and flowers—such as you have remarked in this case—often come with the use of F1 Hybrid seed and, of course, especially when experienced for the first time, it is this improvement that you naturally wish to preserve by saving your own seed. If you try it with plants that were raised from F1 Hybrid seed you will be very disappointed, because F1 Hybrid means that the specialists have bred to a special genetic programme that only they or the seed firm know, and which produces the improved characteristics for only the one hybrid generation. The seed does not breed true; so don't make the mistake of saving it for another crop. This applies to all F1 Hybrids—not only tomatoes.

254 Tomatoes: the causes of fruit splitting

Why are my greenhouse tomatoes beginning to split? They were swelling fast and looked good, but now many have cracked open.

Tomatoes are very susceptible to variation, they don't like uneven temperatures or uneven moisture availability and if either or both of these two extremes occur, cracked fruits may result. A tomato fruit is nearly all water and sudden surges of sap create pressure inside a skin which cannot expand quickly enough, and so it splits.

Try to keep growing conditions as even as you can. Of course, you will have to use judgement whether or not to remove tomatoes damaged in this way. There is always the increased risk of infection until the exposed flesh in the split forms a healing callus tissue, but you should also remember that to remove damaged fruit is to reduce the available space for later surges of sap to expand into, and must therefore increase the risk of other fruit splitting.

255 Tomatoes which do not ripen properly

Every year that I've grown outdoor tomatoes I've ended up using them for chutney. How can I get them to finish ripening?

The most likely cause of non-ripening is insufficient potash at a time when the plant is needing it most. It is therefore prudent to make sure that non-ripening is not due to this deficiency by applying $\frac{1}{2}$ oz. sulphate of potash, spread and watered in around each plant just as the first truss is well set, and repeated twice more at fourteen-day intervals.

Are you sure that you are not trying to ripen too many trusses? Outdoor tomatoes should be restricted to no more than five trusses at the most, so that they can ripen before the late summer/autumn temperatures drop too low. Tomato fruits ripen by temperature and it is pointless to leave them on the plant until near frost time, or to place green fruits near the window where they can get plenty of light. To fully ripen five trusses on an outdoor tomato means that they have to be planted out very early in the season with the first truss of bloom already showing. If you do not do this, you are asking the plants to do too much in too short a time, and you will have to be satisfied with four trusses.

At the same time as improving your cultivation techniques to assist ripening, there is another idea you may like to try. An enormous amount of work has been going on in recent years to develop new improved strains of tomatoes, particularly with dwarf bush types that do not need the staking and supporting that the normal plants do. These dwarf types don't need so much attention either. For example, the side shoots are not pinched out as these form fruiting trusses and although individually not quite so large as those on the normal varieties, the fruits are far more numerous and form a month earlier, thus giving an extra month in which to build-up a considerable total crop. They are particularly applicable to those who have ripening difficulties, and needing no stakes or supports, these bush and dwarf varieties have another advantage in that they can be covered with cloches.

Try the varieties Sigmabush and French Cross; both are obtainable from Sutton's Seeds, Reading, Berkshire.

256 Tomatoes: removal of side shoots

Do I have to nip the shoots which are on the side of the main stem of my greenhouse tomatoes? I have been told, on the one hand, that only the main stem should remain, and on the other that one side shoot allowed to grow and become a second stem will increase the crop. Is this true and how is it done?

The usual method of growing tomatoes—other than dwarf and bush types, see *No. 255*—is on the single stem system which means that all side shoots are removed and growth concentrated into the main stem. The side shoots grow out of the leaf axils—i.e. the angle between the main stem and leaves—and should not be confused with fruit trusses which develop from the main stem between the leaf joints.

These side shoots can be taken out quite easily as soon as they are large enough to be fingered—about an inch long. At this stage they will snap out with a gentle sideways pressure between finger and thumb, but do be very careful that the shoot snaps clean and that a sliver of skin tissue does not remain attached to peal and tear leaving a long gaping wound to bleed.

However, if you are a smoker, do not under any circumstances take the shoots in this way; wear gloves and do it with a short thin-bladed knife. This is because tomatoes are susceptible to a virus that is rife in tobacco and which can and often has been transmitted by tobacco-stained fingers. I have seen tobacco mosaic virus in tomatoes at its worst and there are many gardeners like myself who won't allow smokers inside their greenhouses, let alone touch the plants.

Some growers prefer to grow on the twin stem system; this is done by taking out the growing tip of the young plant and allowing the first two side shoots to develop to form the fruiting stems. These are then allowed to develop as main stems and are side-shooted in the normal way. The idea is that, although the deviation takes time and puts the formation of the trusses behind the clock so that one less truss will be borne during the season, on each stem compared to the number on an un-hindered single main stem, there are however two fruiting stems and the total crop is much bigger. If you try it on outdoor tomatoes, remember that you are shortening the available time for ripening, and if you try it in the greenhouse, you will have to increase the spacing to avoid overcrowding of foliage and the hindrance to air movement and circulation.

Thus, whilst you may—and only may—be able to increase the yield per plant, it is very doubtful whether you will increase your crop in relation to the area occupied by the plants.

257 Tomatoes: the fallacy of leaf removal

At what stage in the growth of a tomato plant can the lower leaves be taken off, and would you advise half or one-third of a plant to be stripped in this way? Also, why is it advisable to strip tomato leaves?

There is more confusion on this matter than any other in tomato growing. Many gardeners seem to regard it as rule of thumb that leaves have to be removed. It is only necessary if the plants are so congested and overcrowded that they obstruct air circulating, and thus create conditions favourable to fungus diseases. This is only likely to happen in the greenhouse—seldom, if ever, in the open. See *Nos. 249* and *252*.

Healthily functioning leaves are the plant's factory in which are elaborated the carbohydrates and celluloses that help to make up the plant's structure and also the sugars and starches that are vital in the ripening process of fruit. If you remove healthy functioning leaves, you remove the factory and ripening is hindered rather than helped. Tomato fruits ripen by temperature not by sunlight on them, and the light is wanted on leaves. If the leaves become diseased, browned or scorched—the lower leaves sometimes become old and withered—that is another matter and the affected parts can be removed, otherwise leave the leaves well alone.

258 Tomatoes: modern growing methods

Because I thought it would be easier to renew straw bales than the soil in my greenhouse, I tried growing my tomatoes by the straw bale method, but was unable to make them heat up and decompose properly. Can you tell me about this method?

There are several difficulties involved in the use of straw bales for tomato growing, not the least of which nowadays is the cost of the stuff! First, the straw should be wheat straw from the most recent harvest. Secondly, it must have been baled dry and have remained dry: it should not, for example, have become wet whilst waiting in the field to be picked up and carted. This may have caused premature decomposition and a degree of heating-up, and almost certainly infection by fungus spores. The final difficulty is the part that defeats most amateurs, that of getting the bale to heat-up and decompose properly. This is usually due to a shortage of oxygen, nitrogen and bacteria. Read *No. 489* carefully, and bear in mind that a straw bale is organic matter at the very first stage of decomposition.

Of course, the tidiness and ease of complete removal of a bale from the greenhouse at the end of the season was a great advantage compared to replacing a lot of soil and that was an important attraction to many tomato growers, but the method has been completely replaced by 'growing bags', and the use of straw bales has fallen out of favour as quickly as the idea at first caught on.

Growing bags are simply plastic sacks containing peat-based compost, fortified with plant nutrients. The bags are laid in position, holes stabbed in for drainage, and slits cut through which the plants are inserted to grow. These bags usually take a couple of tomato plants and they have proved to be so successful that commercial growers have taken to them in a big way. With fresh, clean-growing compost coming in each year and removed simply by carrying sacks out again, the tedious, and very expensive annual process of sterilising the greenhouse soil is obviated. The same ad-

vantages also apply to the amateur—only more so—and in addition to being far less expensive, you will find this method much more easy to manage than straw bales. You can obtain very helpful instruction leaflets on growing bags, and their uses, from Alexpeat Ltd., Burnham-on-Sea, Somerset.

259 Walnuts grown from a nut are a waste of time

Please tell me about the cultural needs of a walnut because I have germinated one from a nut that I had at Christmas. At present, it is growing in a heated greenhouse.

In the southern milder parts of the British Isles, it is not uncommon in spring and early summer to find young walnut seedlings growing in beds or shrubberies near to a tree from which nuts have dropped and bounced, have become covered with leaves and debris, and then germinated. The seedling you have growing in a warm greenhouse will have to be moved outside. It cannot stay where it is. But you will have to make the move gradually, step by step, via a cooler part of the greenhouse, into a cold frame and then into a sheltered position before planting from the pot to its permanent position, so that the hardening process is spread over several weeks.

Of course, it is highly satisfying to germinate a walnut and you will be proud when your tree is growing away—but now comes the horrid truth. Seedling walnuts will not carry nuts until they are at least twenty years old, and then the quality and quantity is quite likely to be useless.

To be quite sure of good quality and a good yield of walnuts, a scion from a known and proven good tree has to be grafted onto a seedling and this is the only way to make sure that your plant has a worthwhile future; use it as a stock. You have been successful with germinating, so now you must try your skill with the more demanding and rewarding technique of grafting.

Walnuts originated in Persia and Asia Minor and still retain something of their ancestry in the vulnerability of young plants to frost damage, so seedlings or young grafts must be covered during periods of frost, especially when clear nights can produce radiation frosts. See also *Nos. 260, 261* and *262*.

260   Walnuts : harvesting and storing

What is the best way of harvesting and storing walnuts? Last year our tree carried a good crop and we left the nuts on the ground until October and then stored them in boxes of peat, but by the following month many of them were going mouldy.

The essential factor to observe in order to avoid walnuts going mouldy is to help them to dry out when harvested; and then to keep them dry. Walnuts for storage must reach full ripeness. Wait for the nuts to fall and make a daily search if you can—but at least collect them frequently. If you have a high squirrel population, you will have to resort to beating with a long pole to get them down before they are pinched to fill the squirrel's larder.

Break them out of the green shells and brush them with a really stiff brush—something like a scrubbing brush—to make sure that any of the husk fibre still adhering is removed. Husk fibre exposed to the air is the ideal material for the development of mould and so its complete removal is imperative. Spread out the nuts in an airy place so that plenty of fresh air can get at them to dry them. You will need a lot of space for this drying out; they should be laid separated, not two or three layers deep, so that mould, if it does start, does not spread to the next nut. Inspect regularly, removing any suspicious nuts and if you don't want any of them to disappear mysteriously, lay traps for mice.

When they are perfectly dry, hang them in string bags in an airy place. Greengrocers often have spare nets they can let you have.

Keep up the regular inspection to make sure that everything is in order. Nuts are like apples and the odd single bad one can soon spoil the rest. Keep them completely dry and you should be able to enjoy them until you start again on the next crop.

261   Walnuts : possible reasons for lack of crop

Last year, for the first time, my walnut tree, which is fifteen years old, produced eight nuts. This year, although it had a very good crop of embryo nuts, they all dropped off when the size of large peas. Is there any remedy for this?

The embryo nuts dropped because they were not fertile. Walnuts produce male and female flowers, but young choice grafted varieties often produce only female flowers for the first years. Pollination in this case depends upon wind-blown pollen from male flowers on other older trees, so unless you have such a tree nearby there is nothing you can do except to wait until the tree eventually produces male flowers. Until then, your tree will produce female flowers and embryo nuts, which not having been pollinated, will abort and fall.

262   Walnuts take a long time to fruit

Our walnut tree is about thirty years old and has never produced any nuts. Does it need pruning, or some special fertiliser?

First of all, read *Nos. 259* and *261*. Even trees from proven stock that bear male and female flowers set better crops when cross-pollinated with other trees, which is why walnut trees are generally grown in groups.

Most likely your thirty-year-old tree is a predominant male and will never bear a crop, so unless you like it for its ornamental value, it is only worth the value of the wood to a timber merchant.

Some grafted varieties can be expected to have come into bearing by their tenth year, others take longer. But to have waited thirty years for a nut means it must be a seedling and is now approaching the very limit when bearing should have started. The question is whether you are prepared to go on living with an ornamental, but non-bearing tree. If it were mine, it would come out at once and be replaced with something worth its space in the garden.

263 Feeding fruit trees: the basic principles

After reading an article on fruit trees, I have decided that my fruit trees all need feeding. In my third-of-an-acre grass orchard, there are apples, pears, plums and greengages, ranging between ten and twenty-five years old. Can you please tell me when to feed, what to feed, and how much to give per tree?

You do not indicate specific deficiencies so I am assuming that you wish to apply general feeding, which incidentally is sensible and a praiseworthy way to treat your trees. So many people expect them to crop year after year without any feeding at all!

You are following modern scientific and professional practice in growing fruit trees in a grass orchard, but you should realise fully that the primary purpose of grassing down is not convenience i.e. mowing is easier than tilling the soil and keeping it weed-free. The practice is aimed at improving soil structure and based quite deliberately on the regular return to the soil of humus—producing grass cuttings—so the box must be off the mower *at all times*. Never cut lower than $1\frac{1}{2}$ inches so that the long sward, and the cuttings, performs the same physical function as a mulch on open soil.

For ensuring the adequate supply of nutrients you cannot do better than to apply a properly based compound manure in which the relative proportions of the three main elements—nitrogen, phosphorous and potash—are balanced, preferably an organic-based one like Humber Eclipse so that nutrient release is slow and longer lasting, but Growmore will also do very well.

Achieving this balance is a highly skilled job and it is best to rely on such proprietary products, rather than to mix your own as it is so easy to get the proportions wrong, and this will do more harm than good. Apply the general feeds at the rate of 2 oz. per sq. yd. over an area equivalent to branch spread. Two applications every year, one in late February and one in March, will ensure that your trees won't suffer from nutrient starvation. Broadcast the fertiliser straight on to the grass which will grow like mad, but don't worry as it will all go back into the soil.

Stone fruits, plums, peaches, apricots, cherries and damsons etc., do best with some lime in the soil so, at about the same time as one of the nutrient feeds, spread a dressing of ground chalk at the same 2 oz. rate. Just the one application each year will be enough.

Section IV

Vegetables

264 Artichokes, globe: cultivation principles

Could you advise me how to grow globe artichokes?

It is the scales of the immature buds that are eaten. The taste is an acquired one and if you have not eaten globe artichokes before, you would be well advised to hesitate before you devote so much space, time and effort on a vegetable that may very well disappoint when it comes to the table. Its native habitat is the sandy sea-shore of North Africa and it is not surprising, therefore, that it requires a sandy well-drained soil.

Seed can be sown in the open ground in March and April, but much better plants can be obtained by sowing seed in heat in February, and the best seedlings planted out in April for cropping the following year. Although the plant is a perennial, it is seldom very much use after the third year, and sometimes even the second, which explains the practice of making a sowing each year in order to supply two plots—one of first year seedlings growing through, and the other of second year plants which are grubbed out after the buds have been cropped in mid-summer. Each plant needs a minimum of 2½–3 feet each way, and once planted and established, needs little attention other than copious watering.

The two-season wait for crops is one reason why growing from offsets is popular. These are suckers that arise in spring. As winter approaches, any remaining stem growth and leaves are cut down, and the crowns lightly earthed over and covered by a layer of straw, dry roughage or compost to keep out frost. In spring this is all carefully removed to reveal several suckers already shooting through. Any in excess of three can be taken and planted as offsets, and it is these that are offered by growers in spring and early summer. With plants grown from suckers, watering is very important: they are much more intolerant of dryness than are seedlings.

You will get better and bigger buds by incorporating plenty of compost into the soil prior to planting, and mulching heavily at all times in order to obtain really large buds, the smaller secondary side buds below the main terminal buds should be removed when they are about the size of an egg: it is these that are eaten raw or fried. The main bud then swells to maximum size, and is usually boiled. As soon as the main buds have been taken the stems should be cut down.

265 Asparagus: thin spindly stems

I bought asparagus roots through an advertisement. The first year, we had some poor thin stalks. The second year was no better and last year the crop was not worth picking. How long does an asparagus bed last? Should I scrap the bed or is there some knack in growing it?

You have been in too much of a hurry! Asparagus is a gross feeder and as the bed will

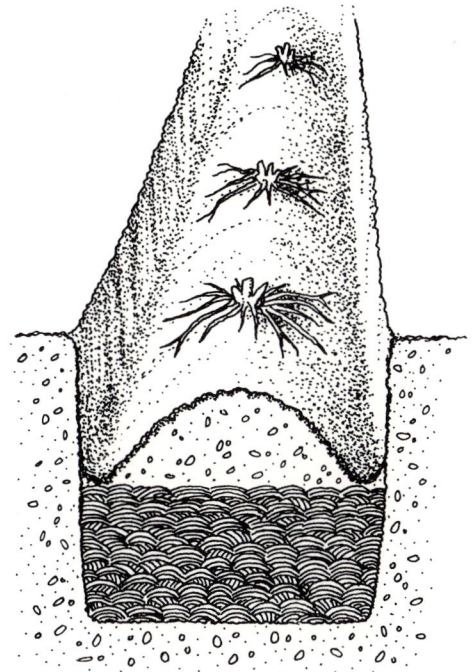

No. 265 *A single-row asparagus bed, where the young plants have their roots set astride a ridge of soil over a good spit's depth of compost.*

remain *in situ* for many years, it should be prepared well before planting by digging in plenty of well-rotted manure, spent mushroom compost, peat or humus-forming material, two spits deep. The bed should be no wider than 3 ft. so that you will be able to reach the shoots easily for cutting. The more compost you can dig in the better; this will raise the level of the bed and, indeed, it will get higher each year because you must apply a liberal mulch of this compost each late autumn. You will need to feed each early spring with an organic-based manure that will give a long sustained feed action. This is especially important for the first two–three years after planting because the plants need to build-up strength in order to be able to stand the strain of heavy cutting that will come later.

There should be no cutting at all during the first year. During the second year, if you cannot wait and must have a taster, just take an odd stalk here and there where a plant looks vigorous and well-established. Then, with good feeding, you should be able to cut a little heavier the third year—but don't overdo it—coming into good cropping in the fourth or fifth year. A well-prepared and annually manured bed should remain in good production for at least thirty years, so it is well worth waiting for two or three years and doing the job properly.

March to early April is a good time to plant the crowns, so newcomers to asparagus growing who would like to try this delicious vegetable can order during January, February and March for delivery later, whilst the bed is prepared. Two-year-old crowns are easier to establish than the three-year-olds that are often offered.

266 Balcony crops

We used to enjoy growing vegetables in the garden of our previous house, but now that we live in a flat all we have is a small area like a verandah over a garage. What could I grow in soil-filled boxes?

There must be a lot of people who live in flats, or who have patios or very small gardens.

Boxes can be used, of course, but these may not be all that easy to come by. A better idea is to use growing bags. Decorative plastic bags containing peat-based 'soil-less' composts with added plant nutrients can be bought at most garden centres or, better still, delivered direct to your home. You simply lay these bags in position and cut holes or slits for the plants or vegetables to grow through. There is no mess this way and, being clean and tidy, this growing bag technique reduces problems and failures. See *No. 258*. There aren't the pests and diseases that can be introduced with soil from perhaps unclean sources and there won't be stones or anything else to cut your fingers.

Many commercial growers of tomatoes and cucumbers are using these bags because they are able to clear out the old growing 'soil' so easily and bring in fresh more quickly and less expensively than having to sterilise the soil every year and if it pays the commercial growers, you can be sure it will benefit you too. Probably you will derive most benefit, therefore, by concentrating on tomatoes—and on other crops that are either expensive in the shops or are so much better for being ultra fresh.

Salad crops are favourite. Lettuce, radishes and small round beetroot grow at a tremendous pace giving several crops in one year. Almost anything can be grown in these bags although, as you only have a depth of about 7–8 inches when the bags settle, you will not be able to grow long-rooted parsnips, beets and carrots, but must keep to ball- or stump-rooted varieties. Peas do uncommonly well, but if you want to try beans, grow the non-climbing bush-type like Hammond's Scarlet or Dwarf French Climbers. Wonderful crops of the purple podded Blue Cocos have been grown this way.

Potato foliage can become rather big and awkward if space is limited, as on a balcony, but they are worth a try if you relish that extra something in the taste of absolutely new potatoes: two plants grown to each bag can give a yield that will astonish you.

Don't forget to put two or three small slits under the bag so that excess water can drain out, but don't make the slits over large or the bag may break up when you come to move it for replacement. Using powdered fertilisers through the small growing holes or slits is a little risky as there is the danger of 'burning' the plants, so it is best to use weak liquid manures after the bag has been in use six to eight weeks, and you are taking your second crops. Foliar feeding is particularly suitable for this kind of culture but if you do try it, use a fine mist sprayer; the big droplets from the watercan will bounce off and be largely wasted.

267 Beans: lumps and bumps on the roots

Would you tell me the cause of the disease on the roots of my broad beans, and sometimes on runner beans, which occurs every year, resulting in healthy plants but poor crops? The disease appears as little lumps on the roots. I manure the garden regularly and use fertilisers and foliar feed.

The little lumps on the roots of your beans are not a disease, quite the opposite. Instead of doing harm, the swellings,—which are a characteristic of leguminous plants such as peas, beans, clover, lupins, and many shrubs and trees like gorse, and laburnum—contain colonies of bacteria which have the peculiar ability to 'fix' atmospheric nitrogen, and in a form that the host plants can use. For this reason, peas and beans are very important in the rotation of your vegetables. As you clear peas and beans after cropping, always follow with brassicas— i.e. green leaf crops like cabbages, broccoli, kale, or with lettuce—so that the fullest use is made by the nitrogen left over from the legumes. It sounds from your description that you are being much too kind and over-feeding the beans. It doesn't follow that the more you feed a plant the better it will crop, especially when the crop you are going to take is the 'fruit', for that is what the bean is. Why should your plants be worried about ensuring the continuation of their species for next year? They are living a life of luxury. You are over-feeding and spoiling them so that they create a lot of leaf, and very little seed (bean).

Legumes have their own independent nitrogen supply, so you can cut that out for a start. If any part of your garden has not been manured and fertilised, or at any rate not so heavily for a year or two, plan to grow the legumes in this area next time. See *No. 268.* There should be enough residual nutrients to give you a good crop but if you feel that you really must use a fertiliser, choose one which is high in phosphate and potash, and lower in nitrogen so that a rough balance is struck with the plants' own nitrogen supply.

268 Bean pole 'fence': a substitute

I shall need new bean poles this year, but they seem to be quite unobtainable. The special gadgets one sees advertised are so expensive. Have you any ideas please?

Don't bother with bean sticks: they only last a couple of years or so before becoming brittle and are not worth the trouble. Instead, use six

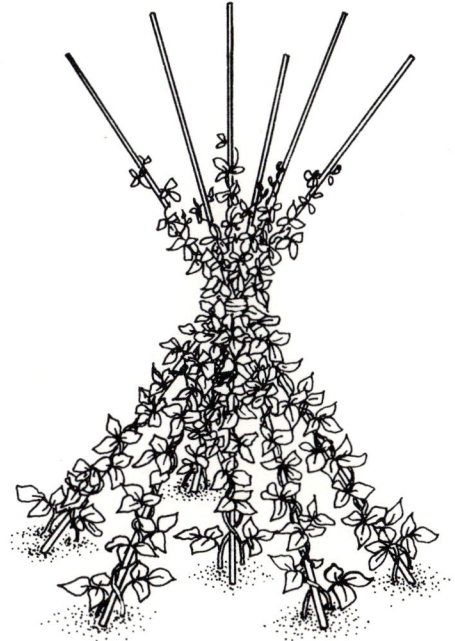

No. 268 *The wigwam method of training runner beans. The better air circulation helps pollination and produces heavier crops.*

heavy grade 7–8 ft. bamboo canes and place over a 3 ft. diameter patch into which you have dug a barrowload of compost. With one upright in the centre, arrange the others around it like a wig-wam about 2½–3 ft. wide. Push the ends into the ground firmly, and tie or wire them together just over half way up so that the structure fans out nearly as wide at the top as at the bottom. After soaking the beans for an hour, set two or three to grow up each pole. Not so much blossom gets buried in the foliage this way, and there is better air movement around the plants than with a 'fence' resulting in a better 'set' and bean formation. You can arrange these wig-wams in a line or—this is their great advantage—spread them about wherever you have the room for a single one, making full use of odd corners. You just cannot have a bean crop that is too heavy—they deep freeze very well.

Bamboo canes cost quite a bit more than bean poles but, as they last ten times as long, they are much cheaper in the end. The best way to buy them is to club together with a neighbour or two and get them by the hundred from the importers. It's a lot cheaper than buying them locally and they'll be delivered direct to you.

269 Brassicas: declining and failing seedlings

Would you please tell me how to prepare a seed bed for brassicas. Last year I sowed the seed in a bed inside a cold frame. They started off well, but after a while they stopped growing and after planting out, very poor cabbages and cauliflowers resulted.

All brassicas are going to need adequate nitrogen in order to produce leaf and for this reason are an ideal crop to follow peas and beans in the rotational plan, see *No. 267*.

The big problem with all brassicas is club root, a soil-borne fungus that gains entry and attacks the root system causing conspicuous swellings and stunted growth. If you know the disease has been present, rather than sowing in the normal way in the open, possibly infected ground, it would be safest to sow seed in a deep

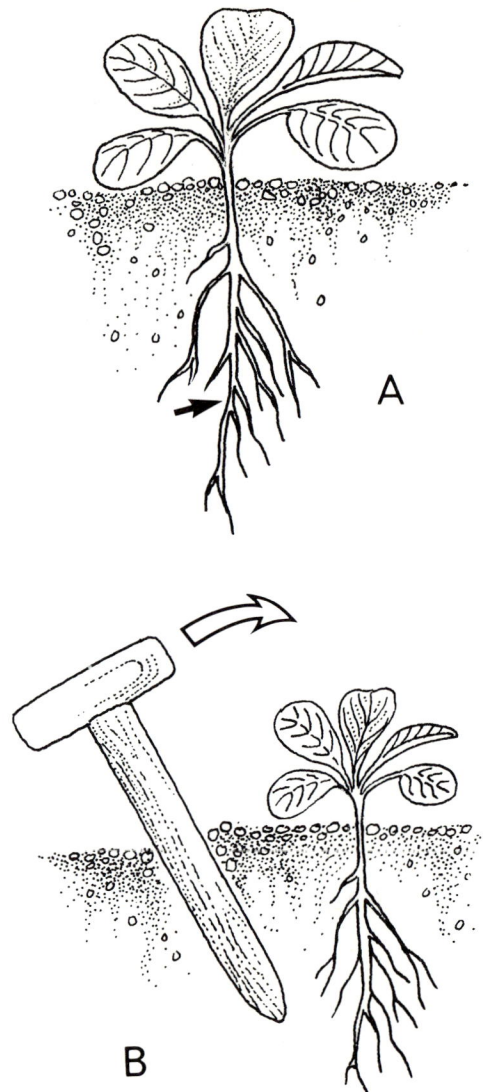

No. 269 *Preparing the seed bed for brassicas.*
A. *Seedlings should be set deeply, especially if they are leggy, and the tap root should be cut as indicated.*
B. *Force the dibber into the soil and lever hard against the root system, leaving the hole open as a water catchment.*

tray of sterilised soil to get them off to a clean start and then to puddle them in calomel/lime paste when planting out. On the other hand, if the soil has been clear of club root, a seed bed can be prepared in the open ground, covering with a cloche or two if the weather is likely to be cold. A 3 ft. row or two, a few inches apart, will supply more than enough young plants for most households.

Prepare the soil by dusting lime over the seed bed area at the rate of 1 oz. per sq. yd., plus, if you want to be really helpful, an ounce of superphosphate or an ounce of Humber Eclipse. Rake the soil to a level tilth, water well with a fine rosed can and again forty-eight hours later, then leave the bed for a week. Fresh lime can inhibit seed germination so by watering it in and letting it weather for a few days, you avoid the danger. This also gives soil bacteria time to get to work decomposing the Eclipse and releasing the nutrients for the seedlings to get off to a flying start.

When sowing, place a board on the soil as a straight edge, place your foot on the board to hold it steady and with the back of the rake pull in a shallow drill. Sprinkle seed very thinly along the drill and cover very lightly ¼ in. deep is quite ample. More seed is ruined by planting too deep than by any other factor. Water with a fine rose again and cover with a cloche.

An arch enemy of all brassicas is flea beetle. You will not see this pest—it is too small and nervous, hopping off as you approach, but what you will see is hundreds of small holes puncturing the leaves of your seedlings, doing them no good at all. Don't wait for the damage before going out to buy insecticide: have it on hand. Gamma BHC dust will control them: if you don't buy it in a special 'puffer', put some in an old stocking and shake this along the row. You shouldn't have any difficulty in obtaining BHC, but as an alternative, use 'whizzed' naphthalene from the chemist or crushed and powdered camphor balls. These act as deterrents rather than killers and will send most of the pests hopping off next door.

When planting in open ground, make up a bowl of puddle—equal parts lime, calomel dust and soil, clay if possible because it sticks better. Mix with enough water to form a thin sticky paste. Take each seedling separately, cut off the lower quarter—to a third of the main tap root—swish the root in the paste so that a good coating adheres all over and plant very firmly with a dibber. See *No. 272*.

Seedlings will probably flag for a day or two until new fibrous root, forming as a result of the root pruning, begins to bite into the soil and the leaves firm up again. As soon as they show that they are established and growing away, dust a teaspoonful of Growmore or Humber Eclipse around the plant, 3–4 in. away so that the roots have to work and go looking for it. Scratch lightly into the surface and repeat this feeding three weeks apart, twice more and you'll have the finest brassicas you've ever seen. Do remember however, Brussels sprouts need especially firm planting and the soil rammed hard, see *No. 271*.

270 Broccoli : how long to go on cutting

How long should I continue cutting purple sprouting broccoli? My plants keep on throwing out new shoots.

Just so long as the shoots are tender to eat, you can keep cutting. If you cannot use all of the shoots, don't let them blow and flower, pick all that you can in prime condition, clean, trim as though for cooking and put them in a new clean plastic bag, twist it tight, and put the bag in the ice box of your fridge where they will keep for a week or more—or better still, if you have one, put them in the deep freeze.

This is a most valuable crop, providing fresh greens throughout the difficult winter period. There are three main varieties: Early Purple, sown March–April, and fit for cutting the following January–February; Purple Sprouting, sown in April and ready the following March–April; and Late Purple sown in May and ready the following April–May.

The crop will be standing for some months and occupying the same plot. Therefore, guard against club root by always 'puddling' plants when planting out. See *No. 269*.

271 Brussels sprouts : why they 'blow'

I need advice about sprouts. Instead of staying closed as they grow, they have opened up into leaves with no hearts. Could you tell me if it is anything to do with the soil, or, if not, please suggest what else could be causing the trouble.

Unless they are grown well, Brussels are not worth growing—you'll do better with kale and broccoli. Brussels sprouts reflect the soil condition around their roots. If the soil is at all light and loose, that is how the sprouts will be. The cardinal rule for knobbly sprouts is a firm soil. Plant firm, tread them in hard, then as the plants are growing keep the soil between and around them, trodden and rammed firm. Brussels do best in a heavy soil and are ideal, for instance, for following peas and beans in order to utilise the nitrogen residue, see *No. 267*. Sow as early as you can: early March in a frame or under cloches, plant out into final positions in May or June.

Puddle the roots as you plant out young seedling plants, see *No. 269*, as a precaution against club root. Puddling will not positively stop club root if an attack sets in, but the plants will be able to put up greater resistance and make a better show. Finally, only sow the very best seed that you can get, you will certainly never grow good sprouts from second rate seed.

Try the variety Bedford Fillbasket for early sprouts, October–December; Bedford Winter Harvest for mid-season November–January; and Bedford Market Rearguard for a late crop, Christmas to March. All are obtainable from Sutton's, Reading.

272 Cabbages : why they do not heart properly

Why do you think the spring cabbages in my garden fail to heart up properly, although they made plenty of leaf growth and were planted in well-manured soil? Could it be anything to do with the distance apart that they were planted?

Many newcomers to gardening have this problem, and the mistake is quite a natural one to make. The clues are in your comments 'plenty of leaf growth' and 'well-manured soil'.

All brassicas—members of the cabbage family—do best in a firm soil, and it appears likely that the soil had been only recently dug over, and 'well-manured' prior to planting. The soil was therefore much too loose and, in addition, fresh manure could well have released too much nitrogen which encourages lush leafy open growth, and not firm hearts.

This is why it is best, wherever possible, to let brassicas follow peas and beans. See *No. 267*.

The requirement of firm soil also explains why professionals transplant brassica seedlings with a dibber—a pointed stick which you can easily make by rasping the shaft of an old spade or fork to a point. Cropping potatoes disturbs the soil a bit, and is not the best crop to follow, whereas peas and beans can be cleared with almost no soil disturbance. Pull off any weeds, of course, and merely pull the soil level with a rake, firm it by treading and with the dibber make the holes to receive the seedlings. Puddle the roots (see *No. 269*), hold the plant in the hole and plunge the dibber in again a couple of inches away and lever the soil over hard against the seedling. This serves the dual purpose of setting the soil firm against the roots and also, by leaving the dibber hole open, you have a little water catchment pit which you can quickly fill by running along with a can or hose. This ensures that every time you water, a holeful of water, at least, is trapped in close proximity to the roots. This plus the mud from puddling, enables the seedling to get away with the minimum of check.

273 Calabrese can be used as an asparagus substitute

I have been given some calabrese plants and have not been able to find out what the mature vegetable looks like. Can you tell me how to know when they are mature and how to cook them?

Calabrese is often called Green or Italian Sprouting Broccoli. Probably the best way to visualise it is to imagine a rather loose headed cauliflower with several small side cauliflower heads which are correctly called curds. These are cut whilst still immature, plus four to five inches of stalk, and can be cooked and served like asparagus for which they are an extremely good substitute. The cropping period extends from August to early October. This is a particularly easy green vegetable to grow, and an added advantage is that it is very suitable for deep freezing. Plant into firm soil, and grow as for other brassicas. See *Nos. 269, 270* and *272.*

274 Carrots: how to grow them long and straight

How can I grow straight carrots: mine are twisted every time? I thin them out, but they still twist.

This sort of thing often happens in stoney ground when the growing root tip is hindered and diverted by stones. You would doubtless do better with globe-shaped carrots like the wonderful new Parisian Rondo, or a stump-rooted kind like Amsterdam Forcing or Chantenay Red Cored.

However, you ask for long straight carrots, and this is how to grow them. With an iron crow-bar, bore a hole about 18–24 in. deep into the ground. Each time you drop the crow-bar into the hole lever a wider top to the hole. The idea is to produce a hole shaped like an inverted cone, pointed at the bottom with straight sloping sides to the opening about 4–5 in. in diameter. If you make the hole too deep too quickly and without levering each time you drop the crow-bar, you will get a wide bottom and top, and a narrow part in the middle, so the hole will be shaped like an hour glass—a shape that will be difficult to correct.

Having made your holes, fill them with John Innes No. 2 compost or fine sieved soil. Don't firm the soil, merely water it which will cause it to settle a little, top up with some more compost but leave a small depression into which you should sow about four seeds. Cover with cloches until germination is well-established. This will also help to keep the carrot fly at bay: this pest likes to lay its eggs around the neck of emerging young carrots

As the true leaves develop, thin the seedlings

to leave one seedling per hole and as the compost settles with more watering, top up with just enough compost to keep the forming roots covered, otherwise, exposed to light, they will become green. Feed occasionally with a little general fertiliser, and you will be well on your way to growing the longest straightest carrots you've ever seen. This method can also be used for growing long parsnips.

Incidentally, if you want to win a prize at the local show, the carrot must be absolutely undamaged and the only way to ensure this is to carefully dig them out, right to the very bottom of the root tip.

275 Carrots: storing them through winter

Could you tell me the correct method of storing carrots for winter use? Last year I tried keeping them in dry sand, but most of them went rotten.

Storing food is just as important as growing it. There is little point going to a lot of trouble to grow vegetables only to lose them through bad storage. Deep freezing works very well with carrots but there are far more useful and valuable vegetables and other foods to occupy the space in the freezer. Storing carrots in dry sand is the normal procedure and when rotting occurs, it is more than likely that one or two of the following prerequisites have not been met.

Carrots must be properly mature before they are stored, and they must not be damaged in any way. Apart from careful dislodging and rubbing off surplus soil, do not clean further and certainly do not wash them. This makes the skin wet, creating an ideal condition for fungal growth. Foliage should be cut off close —about $\frac{1}{2}$–$\frac{3}{4}$ in.—and the roots left in a cool airy place for the cut stalk ends to dry and callus over, and also for the soil remnants and the skin to become quite dry.

Using fresh, perfectly dry sand, pack them in boxes head to tail so that each carrot is completely enclosed and separated from its neighbours: they must not touch. Place the boxes in a dry, cool but frost-free shed, garage or cellar. Frosting (which is altogether different to deep freezing) will almost certainly start a collapse of tissue so that rotting begins—and it only needs one to start for the whole boxful to quickly become affected.

For this reason don't use large boxes, otherwise you may lose too many if a carrot starts rotting. Wooden tomato trays are useful for the job because they stack clear of each other on their corner legs with air passages between and should be not too difficult to get from the shops. Use fresh lime-free or washed builders' sand that has been spread out to become thoroughly dust dry, and do not use it a second time. Spread used storage sand on a compost heap so that it eventually finds its way to the garden soil.

276   Carrots : growing on heavy clay soil

What variety or varieties of carrots will grow in heavy clay soil? What should I add to the soil and when should I sow?

Potentially, clay is a very fertile soil and there is no reason whatsoever why you shouldn't be able to grow good carrots, but success will depend not so much upon varieties as upon the preparation of the ground. If sowing time is some months ahead, make use of the time. Give an immediate dressing of Gypsum, 2 oz. to the square yard over the area where you are going to grow the carrots, and repeat this dressing every three months. Gypsum will have no direct effect upon plant life, but can be put down over the entire plot to make the clay more friable and easier to work. If the clay is too sticky or hard to hoe in the Gypsum, leave it on the surface to weather in. There is no point in putting down Gypsum at a heavier rate than 2 ozs. per square yard every three months because this is the fastest rate at which the soil can properly assimilate it.

When the time comes for sowing, your carrot patch should have greatly improved, and because the entire plot is heavy clay it would be a good idea to plan another twelve months ahead, decide where the next crop of carrots are going and start improving that area too. The growing of carrots should come within a crop rotation plan. As much compost as you can make or buy, should be dug in before a potato crop so that this, with the action of Gypsum, gradually opens up the clay to become good carrot soil.

It will take several years to achieve much depth so until then, you will do best by growing globe or ball carrots (see *No. 274*) and as your clay improves you will be able to grow longer stump-rooted types very well. There are several new varieties available and these are a great improvement on the 'Intermediates' of a few years ago.

277   Cauliflowers running to seed

For several years I have attempted to grow cauliflowers. I say attempted because each time the heads begin to form, they suddenly go to seed. I have tried watering them often and growing them according to the textbook, but each time exactly the same thing happens. How can I stop this happening next year?

Cauliflowers are the most difficult of all brassicas to grow well. You should realise that the curd you are going to eat is really the immature flowering head and, as in many other vegetables, any check in their growth very soon makes them 'bolt'—i.e. run to flower and seed. In the case of the cauliflower, the flower bud is already there so it will not take much of a check to break up the nice tight curd you are looking for. Read *Nos. 270, 271* and *272*, much of which is directly applicable to cauliflowers, especially the references to the firm soil.

In addition, a sudden chilling east wind can upset them. Is your garden exposed? Try growing the crop in the lee of a sheltering hedge or wall. Bright sun on the curd can also upset them and you can avoid this by bending two or three leaves over the curd and either tying them down, or using a couple of clothes pegs to keep them in place.

Try the two new varieties Classic and Arcturus from Sutton's and, if by following the above basics, you are still unable to achieve a good cauliflower, you must accept that you just do not have the right conditions. Don't waste any more time and space with cauliflowers, grow broccoli instead.

278 Celeriac : how to grow it

What do I do with celeriac seedlings that are a few inches high in a seed box?

Celeriac, or turnip-rooted celery as some people call it, is in fact a true celery, but differs from the plant that everybody knows by building a basal food store which swells like a turnip instead of making elongated sheath-like leaf stalks. It is a lot easier to grow as well. Every part of the plant can be used: the root can be boiled and used like a beetroot, or sliced raw and eaten in salads, or used in soups and stews. The leaf stalks can be used like sea-kale.

Celeriac requires a long growth period and therefore seed should be sown in gentle heat in March and the seedlings will then be ready in May for planting out, 1 ft. apart and 1½ ft. between rows, into soil that contains the residue of a hefty manuring for the previous crop — following potatoes is ideal. Trenches are not needed as for true celery; just set in a shallow drill so that you can pass along quickly with the watering can and retain the water in the drill. The celery family are, by nature, bog plants and you will deduce from that, that they need copious watering.

It is often surprising to the uninitiated that instead of earthing up as with true celery, soil should be continually drawn away, preserving and increasing the depth of the drill as the roots swell so that they stand out of the soil and not in any part of it. As they form, all lateral shoots, suckers and fibrous roots arising from the swelling root ball should be removed so that it remains quite bald, and the leaf stems kept to a single stem-like cluster. The root ball will thus develop a rough surface caused by the leaf and root scars.

If you are going to feed at all, make quite sure that the NPK ratio is balanced. You cannot do better than Growmore or Humber Eclipse.

Celeriac is generally lifted in October but, if left any later, you will have to earth up as a protection against frost. If you are going to store them, remove all the leaf stems except for the tuft of unopened leaves in the centre. This is the mistake that most people make, because if you cut that off as well, the root will waste a lot of food and energy producing more leaves to replace the tuft. This has to be at the expense of the food stored within the root ball. Because the root is dormant and the food store cannot be replaced, the root becomes soft, withered and useless. Trim the roots, rub off any soil — do not wash — leave for three to four days to dry off completely and then store in dry sand, like carrots, see *No. 275*. Celeriac is a useful, easy-to-grow vegetable and, like Kohl Rabi, should be far more widely grown.

279 Chives : easy to grow

I would like to grow some chives. Should I buy seeds or plants, and when?

Chives are one of the easiest vegetables to grow, and one of the most useful for flavouring salads, soups and stews with a mild onion flavour, and yet it is one of the most neglected of all plants. Seed can be sown in March or April, or plants from divided clumps can be planted at almost any time of the year. Plant about 8–9 in. apart and, after about four years, lift the resulting clump, divide and start again. It is the grass-like leaves that are cut and used for flavouring, not the onion-like roots. Many people merely gather as many leaves as they require from the outside of each clump — this is wrong. It is far better to cut the whole clump back hard, because this prevents flowering and ensures a continuous growth of the young and tender 'grass' that is preferred in the kitchen.

280 Cucumbers : growing the ridge type

Can you tell me how to grow ridge cucumbers?

Also at one time called the prickly cucumber, the old varieties had pronounced short spines all over the skin. This feature has been largely bred out of modern varieties, and the length increased as well. The first step is to sow only the finest seed you can get. If this is the first time you have grown ridgers, try one of the F1 Hybrids like Burpless Tasty Green, because it has a vigorous hybrid resistance to several cucumber diseases, is relatively easy to grow and produces a very well-worthwhile crop.

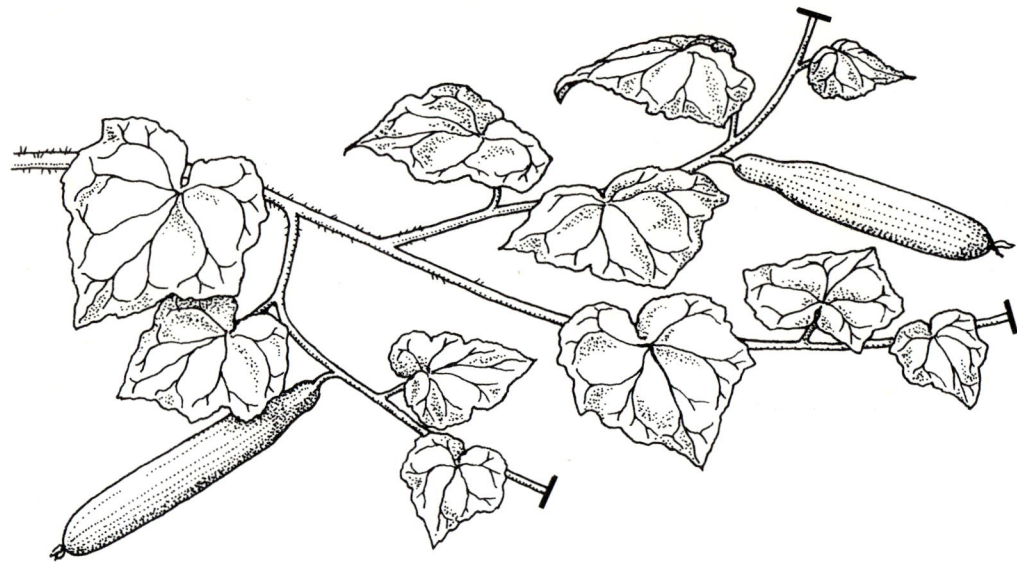

No. 280   *Cucumber stopping. Allow a couple of leaves to grow beyond the fruits, then stop as indicated.*

Although these modern varieties can be sown outdoors, you will get better plants and crops if you can start them off a few weeks earlier by sowing seed in a little heat in the first half of April. Otherwise, you will have to wait until mid-May when the soil begins to warm up. For outdoor sowing—or planting out young plants, as the case may be—take out holes 18 in. square, and a foot deep, 3 ft. apart. Half fill with fresh and hot fermenting compost from the heap or, if the compost is not heating up, half-fill instead with fresh grass cuttings (you will have started mowing by this time of the year) and cover with a 3 in. layer of rotted compost. Then replace enough loose soil to leave a rather pronounced hump. Don't firm the soil at all, otherwise you will exclude air and heating up will stop. The mounds will tend to subside as the cuttings and compost decompose. This process will appreciably warm the soil, and five to seven days later you will be able to sow seed or plant out.

If you sow direct into the ground, sow three seeds in each position and later thin out the two weakest seedlings. If you are growing more than half a dozen plants, make a continuous trench instead of separate holes and shorten the distance between plants to 2–2½ ft. with the soil forming a ridge. The cucumber is very susceptible as a seedling and a young plant to the main stem rotting just where it emerges from the soil, especially if the soil is wet. Clearly, this is a danger in heavy soils and this is the reason why these plants are grown on ridges so that water drains away quickly from the plant stem.

Ridge cucumbers do not need a lot of training. Take out the point of the leading shoot when it has made six–eight leaves—this will encourage branching. As soon as a shoot is bearing a cucumber that is safely forming, take out the growing point to make the shoot and its leaves concentrate on swelling the fruit instead of making a long travelling shoot. If a shoot goes on beyond a dozen leaves without producing a fruit, cut it back to six leaves. Water copiously especially if the weather is drying, and syringe or hose forcibly to make all leaf surfaces, upper and lower, well wet. Do this in the cool of evening so that they remain wet through the night.

Apart from keeping the leaves turgid and firm, frequent evening spraying is a most effective deterrent to red spider. However, if any leaves take on a dusty red colour or patch, you can suspect this pest. Look to the undersides of the leaves very carefully, and you may be able to confirm this by spotting the minute red creatures. Cut off the affected leaves, and syringe or spray more than ever because red spider does not like humid and damp conditions.

Feed with liquid manure only: do not use a dry general fertiliser unless you are absolutely sure that it does not contain phosphates, or the fruits will contain a lot of seeds. As most dry fertilisers contain some superphosphates, it is better to use a liquid fertiliser.

Baton Vert is an F1 Hybrid variety specially bred for outdoor cultivation and has long fruits of good flavour, and another F1 Hybrid, Marion, bears a prolific crop of cucumbers that are quite free of bitter taste. See *No. 281*.

281 Cucumbers: greenhouse cultivation

I have been given some seed of a cucumber called Kaga without any information about it. Can you tell me when to start the seeds in a cold greenhouse and something about the variety?

Kaga is one of the Japanese cucumbers that has quickly created demand by bearing out the claims made that it is a heavy cropper. Although it can be grown outdoors, it really needs an unheated greenhouse to do it justice. The seed is not all that plentiful, so you will have to forgo the normal luxury of sowing three seeds to a pot and then thinning out the two weakest. In an unheated greenhouse, sow seeds from early March—end down, not flat on their sides —about $\frac{3}{4}$ in. deep in 3 in. pots containing John Innes seed compost mixed with its own volume of peat. When the seedlings have two true leaves, plant into the greenhouse border or into prepared soil boxes on the benches or into peat compost filled bags. Set the seedlings

as deeply as is necessary for the seed leaves to be almost touching the soil.

An ideal method of training is to arrange for the plants to be positioned at the back of the bench or border near to the glass, and to place a piece of heavy gauge 6 in. mesh trellis (if it is plastic covered so much the better—then it will last for years) with one edge resting on the soil between plants and glass, and the opposite edge suspended so that the net or trellis leans forward over the plants, which will then be able to clamber up, through and over it. In favourable conditions, growing stems can reach the roof. They can then be trained across more trellis or canes suspended just below the roof glass. As the shoots grow and trail, you can then lead them through the mesh so that the leaves grow above the mesh to the light but the cucumbers hang free underneath.

Watering is important: at no time after planting must the plants be allowed to become in the slightest bit dry. Try to use rain water if you can, and at the same temperature as inside the greenhouse. This means always keeping a filled can in the house. Conditions should be like a Turkish bath and, in order to create the saturated atmosphere, it is a very good idea to suspend an old blanket in a bath of water to act as a giant water wick. Lightly mist spray the plants, foliage, glass and staging, twice a day— but with cold water from the tap or, better still, keep the sprayer in the fridge.

This sounds contradictory to the Turkish bath. The reason is that light spraying is not meant to project a large volume of cold water that will significantly chill the soil and the plant, but it will suddenly drop the surface temperature a couple of degrees or so for the moment and this is an effective deterrent to mildew, and combined with the overall humidity makes life distinctly distasteful to red spider.

Try not to let water splash and settle around the stem at ground level, because this can cause collar rot. If you can lay hands on some charcoal or a little plaster rubble to form a rapid draining protective ring around the main stem, this will help to avoid trouble.

Pinch out the growing point when the main stem has made four to five true rough leaves;

then also the points of the resulting side shoots when they have made four to five leaves. After this don't pinch out anything else until fruits are developing. By stopping the fruit-bearing laterals at one or two leaves beyond the cucumber, enough stem will be left above the mesh to support the weight of the cucumber, and a leaf or two beyond it will continue to pull up the sap to and beyond the fruit stalk.

Feed the plants with liquid manure; don't use dry fertilisers as most of them contain phosphate in some degree and this encourages the production of a lot of seeds. Some ventilation will be required because the air must not be entirely stagnant, so have the very lowest ventilators open, and the roof ventilator open just the smallest amount.

Kaga is generally considered to be able to take full bright unobstructed sun but if you are growing this variety in association with other varieties they will need shading. You can do this by erecting special plastic sheeting, blinds, or spraying a thin whitewash-like material over the glass to reduce the intense glare. Cucumbers are least inclined to be bitter when they are grown quickly and have straight and parallel sides, without the trace of a curve and whilst the dried out flower still remains at the tip. When grown more slowly, the fruits invariably develop a curve, especially at the blossom end; the flower remains drop off and they become bitter to the taste.

282   Fennel : growing from seed

Could you let me have cultural details for producing the fleshy base of fennel for use in raw salads?

There are two fennels: first *Foeniculum vulgare*, a perennial plant with feathery leaves that can get up to 4 ft. tall, or it can be treated as an annual with fresh sowings each April in shallow drills and the seedlings planted out later 18 ins. apart. The leaves and stems have an aniseed flavour and it is traditionally used with all fish dishes, to flavour other vegetables—potatoes especially—and in salads.

To get the fleshy stalks for salads, the plants need to be fed well (use a balanced fertiliser or one with a slight bias in favour of nitrogen to encourage leaf production) and keep it well-watered; never let the plants become dry or limp. Eventually the plants will make established clumps and these can be divided—much as you divide clumps in the herbaceous border as the first signs of growth appear in early spring. Offshoots may appear and provided that they are well-endowed with their own roots, these suckers can be severed and re-planted elsewhere in autumn, or during early spring.

The other fennel, sometimes called Florence, is *Foeniculum dulce*. This comes from Italy and is grown as an annual, shallow-sown in March–April in drills 18 ins. apart where they stay and grow. This one doesn't take kindly to transplanting, so you must sow thinly. Mix the seed with silver sand and this will help you to spread the seed. Thin the seedlings later to about 8 in. apart, using the leaves of the thinnings for flavouring like perennial fennel. Florence will get up to 2½ ft. in height (remove the flower heads unless you want the seed for flavouring) and later produce 'bulbs' which can be braised as a cooked vegetable or used raw in salads.

283   Leeks and rust disease

I have rust on my leeks. Please could you tell me the cause of it, and whether there is a cure?

Rust disease attacks several plants, and leeks appear to be especially prone to it. A number of factors contribute towards creating conditions favourable to an outbreak. Warm damp weather, an excess of nitrogen, and/or a deficiency of potash, poor soil structure, unclean seed and unclean management. Usually, as cold weather comes along, the rust is depressed, and later growth appears to be free of the disease.

With a standing crop carrying the rust, get the disease under control with fourteen-day repeat sprayings of a contact fungicide—Bordeaux and Burgundy mixtures, colloidal copper and colloidal sulphur have all been used in the past. The most widely used modern control is Dithane. As the crop is cleared—do not put leaves and refuse on the compost heap, burn everything—you must take every step to kill off all traces of the disease. Next year, get your seed from an impeccable source, and grow the leeks well away from this present position. In fact, don't grow leeks again in this spot for at least three years.

Do not grow leeks following legumes, because the nitrogen residue could lead to soft lush growth which means that your leeks would be wide open again to fresh attack in the next spell of warm wet weather.

If you use a fertiliser, make sure that the potash content is at least equal to that of the nitrogen and phosphate: in fact, it can even be a little higher so that the growth is hardened, and resistance increased.

Don't expect to have cleared rust off the site with these precautions; it will persist around on debris and other plants and you should expect further attack as inevitable. At the very first indications of another attack, get on to it at once with Dithane fungicide.

284 Marrows and how to grow monsters

I want to grow some monster marrows. Can you suggest a suitable variety and also give me some hints on how to achieve the largest possible marrow?

I've seen some really enormous monsters of the variety Long Green, a strong-growing trailing type obtainable from Sutton's of Reading, Dobies of Chester and Unwin's of Histon.

After soaking the seed in plain water for twenty minutes, sow it in slight heat during late March. Arrange them singly $\frac{1}{2}$ in. deep and on end in $3-3\frac{1}{2}$ in. pots. If you use peat pots, potting on can then be effected with no root disturbance. Then, when the first true leaf is nicely formed, pot on to a 5 in. peat or whale-hide pot using John Innes No. 2 or 3 compost and by mid to late May with three true leaves formed, the young plant is ready for planting out—preferably under a cloche—into a prepared position. Generally, cultivation involves digging in as much well-rotted compost as you can spare into an area 4 ft. square for a single plant or, if you are growing several plants, into a trench 3 ft. wide. Afterwards, draw the soil in low mounds up to the planting positions 3 ft. apart.

However, for a really special job take the soil out 18 in. deep and 3 ft. square. Put in a 9 in. depth of fresh lawn mowings, covered by 3 in. well-rotted compost followed by the original top spit of soil pulled to a mound or ridge. Incidentally, the heavy organic preparation of this crop is an excellent forerunner in your cropping rotation for your early potatoes. Remove the surplus sub-soil by spreading it around the plot: it will contain too much plant food residue to be thrown away. Don't tread or firm the compost or soil because this excludes air and you want the heating-up of the grass cuttings to continue as long as possible. This hot bed warms the soil, and not only helps to minimise any shock to the plants on being planted out, but gets them away fast. Seven to ten days after making the beds, plant out, water in and cover the entire area with a heavy mulch of compost, straw or spent mushroom compost. Put down a collar of slug bait around the plants or position a couple of slug traps per plant, see *No. 511*, and keep a cloche over each plant for a week. Trailers will soon begin to run; have a supply of stiff wire stirrups, like giant 6 in. hair pins, ready to peg down these trailing stems so that they can root into the soil.

To begin with, only male flowers are produced. These are obviously male, and have a central core covered with pollen. In a couple of weeks, females should be formed; if not, begin removing some of the male flowers. The females will have a small marrow beneath, and although insects should adequately pollinate, it is the established custom to make sure by hand-pollinating. There is considerable misunderstanding about this although it is quite simple. Take a fresh male flower in prime condition, pull back the petals and simply insert the core into the centre of the female flower, and leave it there. Cultivation is then similar to that of ridge cucumbers, see *No. 280*.

Marrows must be kept watered, never apply dry fertilisers, but for specials spray with Murphy FF foliar feed. You should lightly spray the foliage every day in any case to create the humidity that red spider doesn't like, so you merely add the foliar feed to the spray every five to seven days.

For that one special monster, select the best marrow when it is obviously well-set and beyond risk of aborting, remove and use the others, and let no more form. An old trick that the devotees swear by is to push a darning needle through the marrow stalk with some darning wool attached so that the strand comes out each side. Arrange a shallow dish underneath, containing sugar solution—3 tablespoonfuls in half pint of water—and let the wool dangle into this syrup. The idea is that the solution creeps up the woollen wick, and the extra sugar supply leads to a bloated flatulent marrow. It may well be true, the practice is certainly widespread but I have never had need to prove it really works, being more concerned with a total usable crop than producing corpulent freaks.

285 Marrow: special varieties for courgettes

I read that young marrows could be cropped as courgettes but when I tried it, the crop was very poor and not worth the space. Are there special varieties for courgettes and is their cultivation any different to ordinary marrows?

The preparation for and early stages of cultivation are very similar to that for ridge cucumbers, see *No. 280*. Sowing seed singly in Jiffy 7 peat balls or 3 in. pots under glass from late March for planting out in May—or if you haven't a frame or cool greenhouse to give the early protection, sowing during May direct into the prepared site where they are to grow.

The usual trailing type of marrow will not provide enough immature marrows for courgettes, and you will have to grow specially bred varieties.

These have a bush habit and, being much more compact, can be planted more closely than the sprawling trailing types, i.e. about 15 ins. apart. The Zucchini type obtainable from most seed firms is available in both green and golden skinned forms, and although they make up to small marrows some 12 ins. in length, they will be induced to produce more prolifically if these are picked, whether or not you want to use them at once, when they are 4–6 ins. long. Continuous picking in order to ensure continuity of production is even more important with varieties that are more specifically intended for courgette use such as the F1 Hybrid variety Green Bush Courgette from Sutton's or the two F1 Hybrids Aristocrat, a dark green, and Golden Courgette, from Thompson and Morgan, Ipswich, who also offer the true French courgette, which can be fried like sausages.

As with normal marrows, the cardinal rules in cultivation are the things to avoid. Plant in positions that will not expose them to draughts which may come through hedge gaps and between sheds etc. They must never be allowed to become dry at the root; but over-watering is just as bad. Never use dry fertilisers since this only encourages a run to seed and bitterness. Feed with liquid manure that is low in phosphate.

286 Melons growing in a garden frame

I would like to grow melons in a brick frame. The seed I have is Sutton's Sweetheart F1. What type of soil should I aim for? Also, how do I tell when it is ripe?

There is something peculiarly satisfying about growing melons well, and especially so with this variety for it has exotic grey-green skin, scarlet-orange flesh, and as it ripens, an equally exotic aroma. There is a similarity in the cultivation requirements of melons with those of cucumbers and marrows (see *Nos. 281 and 284*). After all, they are all members of the Cucurbit family, and you can safely translate and apply all that is practicable to a garden frame. No particular soil is required other than that it should be enriched with well-rotted compost. Plant them 2 ft. apart and don't use dry fertilisers because the phosphate content encourages the production of a lot of seed. Feed instead with liquid feed during July when the fruits are swelling, and do not allow more than four fruits per plant. With this variety, you will be able to tell when the melon is ripe by the change of skin colour to grey, the unmistakably wonderful aroma, and frequently by slight cracking in the fruit stalk. Growing in a frame, you won't be able to allow an unrestricted run and will have to take the lead growths out, and stop side shoots more than with marrows and cucumbers, but this is not a bad thing as you may need to do this anyway to encourage flowering.

At least to begin with, until you've gained some experience with melons, you will be well advised to restrict fruiting, to make sure that they ripen fully. If a fruit sets early and the plant is growing vigorously, you may be able to ripen two fruits in a good sunny summer; otherwise restrict each plant to one fruit only.

287 Onions: when to lift and how to store

Would you tell me how to know when to dig my onions up and how to dry them?

Whether onions can be stored successfully or not depends on proper ripening. You must not cut the leaves off until they have completely withered naturally. This may not always be possible in the unreliable British climate, but it is then one of the challenges that gardeners have to overcome. The solution is rather like the old epithet 'Early to bed, early to rise'.

Sow early ripening varieties in March into well-prepared soil so that they grow fast, and reach acceptable size in time for ripening to begin whilst there is still a fair chance of enough autumn sun and warmth being left to ripen the crop. Even in the south of the country, the very last day that onions should be left to grow is September 1st. You may before then have to begin encouraging the tops to dry off by bending them over, but come September 1st they must be lifted if they are going to be stored. Don't disturb the soil any more than you can help; put a border fork under them, prize them clear and lay them on their sides. If the weather is wet, cover them with cloches. Rub away the soil that will have adhered as it dries, and avoid banging the bulbs together unduly because bruised onions will not store. When the leaves

are crisp, dry and the bulbs covered by a dry skin, they can be taken indoors to complete drying out. Any with embryo flower stems, uneven shape or damage should be used first and then those selected for storage can either be laid on trays or roped. Leaves should be perfectly crisp before cutting—in fact, it is better to break off leaf growth by hand rather than cutting because the exposure of any leaf tissue not withered and perfectly dry is to risk fungal infection and rotting.

Alternatively, they can be tied together in bunches of six and hung up in a dry airy place. Roping, as practised by the French is a knack and you are not likely to be successful. Don't try it—an onion that falls to the ground is likely to be damaged or bruised, and will not then keep. It is therefore a lot safer for amateurs to imitate roping by tying them by the leaves, four at a time, to a length of sisal string.

288 Onions: growing sets from seeds

Will you please tell me how I can grow my own onion sets from seed and when should this be sown?

Onion sets are small marble-sized onions which are planted in March and April to grow and swell to be ready for harvesting in late summer. In this way, the gardener who does not have a cold frame or cloches and thus is unable to start his seed early, see *No.287*, hopes to catch up by planting small onions that are already well on their way. Another advantage is that these sets are not so liable as spring-sown seed to attack by mildew and the onion fly.

If you read *No. 289*, you will realise that the check of arrested development makes these sets much more liable to bolting. Special strains have therefore been developed for this method of onion growing but this seed is not generally available to the amateur. Frankly, you will do much better to buy your sets in from a seedsman, and thus be sure that they have been grown and harvested under ideal conditions. The strain Stuttgarter Reisen was for years regarded as the best variety and most resistant to bolting, but is now outdated and replaced by a much better variety called Sturon. You won't find the seed of either variety very easy to get. If you still want to try from seed, you must choose between spring-sowing varieties, sowing them two to three months late from April to June and stopping them over winter, or sowing autumn varieties much earlier than usual, stopping them, lifting and drying to store over winter—but again see *No. 289.*

Sow autumn varieties May to June in wide drills and by late July or August the bulbs should be marble-sized and ready for halting. Insert a small border fork under them and ease them up so that their roots are broken; a week later ease them up a little more and as the leaves yellow, cover with cloches to keep them dry. As the foliage withers and the bulbs form a brown skin, lift them clear and take them indoors to dry off quickly. The best way is to spread them out on a shelf or base of small mesh wire netting or Netlon so that air can pass through them and circulate freely.

They can be planted out 9 in. apart into prepared beds the following March or April. Set them so that the necks just protrude from the soil. Firm them by treading alongside: onions need firm soil but don't overdo it. Over-compaction causes stagnant soil moisture and this they simply will not stand. If you find them out on the surface, the culprits are birds pulling them out whilst looking for grubs underneath. Simply replace and firm them. Covering the sets for a week or two with cloches until they have become established and are making growth will overcome the difficulty.

289 Onions bolting : cause of

A year ago I sowed some onion seed to stand the winter. I put cloches over them in October and then transplanted them in the spring. They all bolted; where did I go wrong?

It sounds as though you have been growing an unsuitable variety. Although a lot of work has been done in recent years to improve the qualities of onions and the advantages and disadvantages of autumn vis-à-vis spring-sowing have tended to merge and disappear, I think you will be wise to regard autumn-sown onions as being for immediate use when harvested the following summer, and to rely on spring-sown for autumnal harvesting and storing.

It is best to visualise the difference between the two kinds as follows: the spring-sown onion grows as an annual— i.e. it germinates, grows and reaches maturity all in one season. The autumn-sown seed germinates and achieves partial growth before the onset of winter, and then naturally slows down virtually to a stop, starting up again as spring comes along—i.e. its growth pattern is that of a biennial.

As with many another plant that receives a check, its natural reaction, as soon as growth starts again is to ensure perpetuation of its own species, and this it tries to do quickly by putting up bloom in order to produce seed—in other words, it bolts.

You just cannot sow any variety in the autumn chosen at random and expect it not to bolt; you must sow one that has been bred specifically to resist running to seed. I suggest that you try again with the variety Solidity, or with one of the new Japanese varieties like Kaizuka or the F1 Hybrid Express Yellow— all of which you can get from Sutton's of Reading.

The second main source of your trouble is transplanting. If you will see this as another shock to the seedlings, you will also see that you are virtually forcing your onions to run to seed. In future, sow thinly and thin out further if necessary, and leave the seedlings *in situ.* If you have difficulty in handling the seed, use a pelleted seed. When thinning, don't select the larger seedlings to leave. These won't grow to make large bulbs—in fact, they are the ones more likely to bolt. Thin them out, and use them for salads. Cloches should only be put on if heavy snow or hard frost is expected. Apply no fertilisers at any time during growth— fertilising should be done before sowing, and make sure this is nitrogen-low. The only concession to fertilising during growth can be dusting down between rows with fresh dry wood ash towards harvesting time; the quickly soluble potash will encourage ripening.

290 Onions rotting at the base

After moving to a new house last winter, the vegetable garden was manured and limed and in the spring I planted some onion sets. Many of the onions now look very miserable and are rotting at the base. Can you suggest a cause?

Look carefully—but don't touch—at the base of the bulbs. If the rotting is accompanied by white fluffy mould, that will confirm onion white rot, a fungus disease that turns from the white mould to black 'seeds' which appear on the bulbs—or what is left of them. These 'seeds' are absolutely lethal because they are so easy to miss and dislodge that they fall to the ground. This is why you shouldn't touch the bulbs or foliage until you know exactly what you are up against and are going to do.

The disease infects the soil, making it quite impossible to grow onions there again for at least eight years—not only onions, but all members of that family which include leeks, chives, shallots, etc. Starvation by exclusion of host plants is the only way to eradicate the disease.

If you have been cultivating a plot for some time and know its history, and the disease appears for the first time, you still have a chance. But if you are new to a plot or garden, and don't know the history of what has happened by way of pests and disease, for safety's sake you must assume that the whole plot or garden is infected. So don't try to grow onions for a long time and then, when you do start again, do so well away from the position where the last attack occurred.

When it appears for the first time, and you spot the disease early, don't follow the usual advice to pull up the plants and burn them. This is not drastic enough. With a spade, carefully cut under the affected onions, and all others nearby, because if one is diseased you can bet that the neighbours are too. Cut a V-shaped sod under the affected bulbs and very carefully place it in a bucket and take it off the site, to a fire if possible. You must be very careful how you do this; not a crumb of soil must be dropped because you are trying to isolate and cut out a particularly infectious disease.

The procedure does not guarantee that you will be successful in avoiding its spread, or eradicating it, but at least you will have done everything possible and can carry on at least for a while treating your garden as 'suspect contaminated'.

Make the next sowing in a different part of the plot and dust the seed drills with Calomel dust at the rate of 1 lb. per 20–25 yds. Be on your guard in future and if the disease puts in another appearance, you will have to resort to the eight-year starvation routine.

291 Paraffin oil and pigeon manure : fallacy and precaution

Can you tell me if it is advisable to soak runner beans and peas in paraffin oil before planting them? And is pigeon manure suitable to dig into the ground for these crops?

This is widespread practice, not only with runner beans but with broad beans, french beans and peas as well. Dipping in paraffin was an old-time method of keeping mice away, and even then the seed was only dipped so that it picked up the smell and no more. This is not very effective; the defending smell soon goes, and furthermore, longer immersion by soaking could, and often did, mean that the testa or seed coat was penetrated by the oil, and the minute embryo laying between the two large food stores (cotyledons) was killed. Normally, runner beans are sown later than peas and broad beans which may well need protection, and this is best done by spreading a vermin deterrent or poison near the rows or sowing positions. If you want early vermin-proof beans and peas, soak them for 15–20 minutes in plain tepid water, and sow them three to four weeks earlier than usual, three to a 3½ in. pot of seed compost or one in a well-soaked Jiffy 7 peat ball. Raise them in a frame or cold greenhouse, and plant out when the first pair of leaves are well-developed, and the growing tip is appearing between them. When planting, cover with cloches for a week or so to guard against a late frost; and with runner beans try the wig-wam method, see *No. 268.*

Pigeon manure contains about four times,

or even more, as much plant nutrient, particularly nitrogen, as stable manure, and will make beans and peas very rank and overgrown with leaf at the expense of pods. The organic bulk is very small and the structural effect upon soil, especially heavy clay, is to make conditions sour and sticky, rather than opening it up. It is best spread in layers in the compost heap, in which it is an invaluable aid in the heating-up process—see *Nos. 476* and *489*—or it can be allowed to become powder-dry, put in a sack and by crushing it, reduced to a fine meal. Then, by mixing it with an equal volume of fine peat, and dusting very lightly along the rows; it can be used as a nitrogen boost to your brassica and lettuce seedlings, but wash off any dust from the leaves in case it scorches.

292 Potatoes : are seed potatoes different?

Are seed potatoes different from ordinary potatoes? They seem to cost so much more than those I can buy at the greengrocers, so why not just plant them instead?

There is no difference except that potatoes intended for sowing—and that is the only meaning of the word 'seed'—have been selected to a roughly uniform size that gives the best crop return per lb. of sown tubers. There is not much point in planting a bigger tuber than about 2 ins. diameter; better to cut up the big ones into the same size pieces—but why bother? you will do better with smaller ones. In fact, during the wartime 'Dig for Victory' campaign when 'seed' potatoes were scarce, it was a common dodge to buy up the greengrocer's 'chats' —the small potatoes that had gone through the sieve and were too small to sell. There is no reason why you shouldn't plant potatoes obtained from the greengrocers for one season— but don't save your own seed repeatedly.

The two dangers with this are firstly, you may easily pick up a variety that is not immune to wart disease, although with the concentration on immunisation to this disease, this risk is becoming increasingly unlikely. The two common varieties to avoid in this respect are Epicure and King Edward. Secondly, potatoes like many other plants, are troubled by aphides which are responsible for transmitting virus diseases. Repeated growing of potatoes in areas that are liable to aphis attack encourages a build-up of virus infection in your stock, and seriously affects yield. It is quite likely that potatoes or 'chats' you buy at the greengrocers will have been grown fairly locally, and will most likely have been exposed to the infecting aphides. By repeatedly saving your own seed, the great risk is that a build-up of virus results from repeated infection, and you not only suffer a crop failure, but become a high incidence source of infection to others around you.

Potatoes intended for seed are grown in the north where conditions are not conducive to aphides and the risk of virus infection is therefore much reduced or eliminated; hence, the almost total reliance on Scottish grown seed potatoes.

293 Potatoes : are green potatoes poisonous?

Why are my Desiree potatoes turning green in store? The skin looks all right, but when they are peeled the flesh is a light green.

If you read *No. 298*, you will see where you have been going wrong. Potatoes in store should be kept away from light. You may not be aware of the risk that you take if you eat greened potatoes; considering the extent to which the potato has become staple diet in many parts of the world, it may come as a surprise but the potato is a poisonous plant. All the green parts—stems, leaves and the greened tubers—contain solanine, an alkaloidal glycoside which causes prostration, gastritis and stupor. It is not soluble in water so that soaking does no good, and furthermore it withstands ordinary cooking or boiling and there have been many cases of fatality and severe illness in humans and animals.

Of course, you will probably not be affected by eating a potato that is partly greened, and no doubt have done so many times. It would take a meal of badly greened potatoes to give most people the collywobbles—two or three

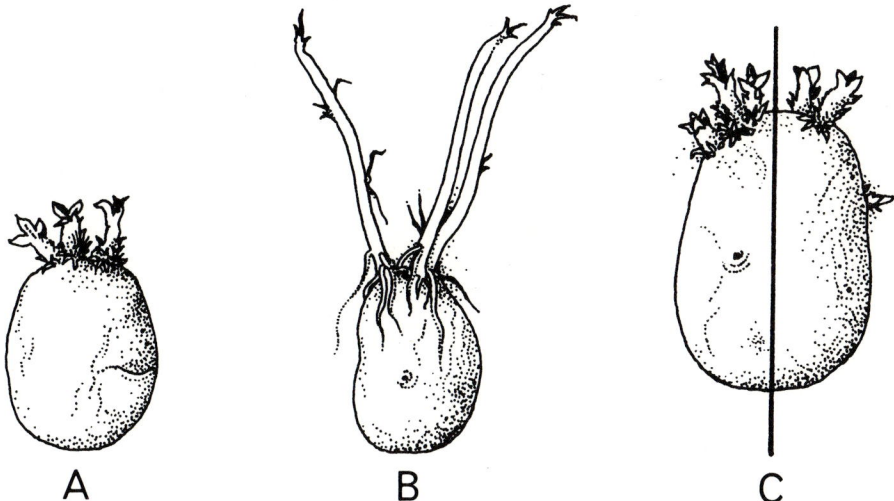

No. 293   *Potatoes for planting.*
A.   Well-sprouted seed potato ready for careful planting. Only two or three of the strongest sprouts are retained.
B.   A badly sprouted tuber with long weak and useless sprouts.
C.   A large tuber capable of producing several good sprouts can be divided into equal parts between the groups of sprouts.

meals almost certainly would. Some people seem to be more susceptible than others but it is far better, and a great deal more comfortable, not to find out if you are one of these.

When growing, earthing-up draws the soil into ridges. This is done not only to encourage the production of tubers, but also to exclude light from them. These are the reasons why earthing-up should be a regular continuous process. It is not at all unusual to find swelling tubers protruding from the soil of the ridge, and these have to be covered.

Greened potatoes need not be thrown away. Put them into complete darkness until the green colour has totally disappeared. This usually takes a couple of weeks and then they will be fit for eating.

294   Potatoes: why are they called a cleaning crop?

Can you tell me why potatoes are sometimes referred to as a 'cleaning' crop?

A better crop of potato tubers is obtained when you earth them up, and they are prevented from going green by excluding them from light. This is usually done progressively, by drag hoeing the soil up to the emerging shoots, a little to begin with, and then more and more to form ridges as the shoot reaches out of the soil until the ridges and valleys are so big that they meet and no more can be earthed up. These ridges have to be maintained with constant attention and finally the roots with tubers attached are dug out. The drag hoeing, cultivation and subsequent digging out cleans the soil of weeds and exposes pests to the birds so that after a crop of potatoes the soil is usually much cleaner than before.

Potatoes benefit from heavy manuring and this in turn has a beneficial effect upon soil structure as the residual organic matter becomes admixed with the soil—which then becomes in better condition to support other crops. This is why the beneficial effect of a potato crop, cleaning and improving soil structure, should always be part of a planned crop rotation so that the entire plot is regularly cleaned and improved in sequence.

295 Potatoes : early crop goes mushy

Last year my Sharpe's Express potatoes were caught by frost and without fail all disintegrated when boiled. The soil on which they were grown was cultivated for the first time, was rather acid and lacking in nourishment. How can I be sure of good potatoes this season?

I don't think that the disintegration of your potatoes was due to frosting; this is a hazard that potatoes undergo every year but still crop well. The more likely cause is growing in unsuitable soil conditions, a variety that is notoriously liable to go to pieces in the pot at the best of times. As this was soil freshly put to cultivation, it is likely that it was deficient in potash which is essential not only for a good crop but also for their condition—and Sharpe's Express needs soil in good condition.

Potatoes like a slightly acid soil, so don't put down lime for the time being. Read *No. 294* dealing with the use of potatoes as a cleaning crop, and the effect of heavy manuring upon soil structure. You must make or buy every ounce of compost you can—dig in as much well-rotted organic matter as you can.

The two main artificial potash fertilisers have marked but opposite effects upon the cooking qualities, so be careful. Sulphate of potash tends to increase the tendency for flouriness, whilst muriate makes them waxy. Therefore I think that you would be wise to use only slow-release organic-based manures that contain N, P & K in equal proportion. Next time you grow early potatoes try Sutton's Foremost—an extremely good cooker—or two recently introduced, but tested and proven very good 'earlies', Ulster Sceptre, probably the quickest to mature variety of all, and Pentland Javelin. The latter yields as heavy crop of early potatoes as any other variety. But don't be in too much hurry or you'll be disappointed because it has the peculiar characteristic of being slow to bulk whilst growing, and then quickly fills out at the end.

296 Potatoes : what to plant for 'french fried'

What's the tastiest and best-looking potato for frying?

The very best potato for frying—and, for that matter, boiling—is Pink Fir Apple, listed in some catalogues as the Salad Potato, since it is very popular for cold salads. The great merit is that the elusive 'new potato' flavour which all potatoes possess when freshly harvested, but which often fades when they are dried and stored, is retained throughout. Grow them in rich, well-manured soil, as for maincrop potatoes. This variety is not readily available, but you should be able to obtain it from Dobies of Chester or Sutton's of Reading, if you book your order very early. As a second choice try the variety Catriona on dense soils or Desiree where the soil is light.

297 Potatoes : a crop of tiny little ones

Will you tell me how I can grow larger potatoes instead of lots of little tiny ones? I use garden compost with a little manure in it, and some spent mushroom compost, but no chemicals.

Potatoes are amongst the most fickle things on earth. It is well-known that certain varieties will crop well in one place and not in another. What you can grow well, can be awful next door—I've known allotments where each end was as different as chalk from cheese in the varieties that could be grown.

The moral is to experiment, find the variety that suits you—and the rule then is to stick with it. By all means, try a row or two of something different, but don't rely on any one for your main crop until it is proven to be successful on your soil.

Although you have used garden and spent mushroom composts you will need to supply more by way of plant nutrients. Prepare for potatoes by trenching 18 in.–2 ft. wide, putting in a thick layer of compost, and feed with a slow-acting long-lasting manure like Humber Eclipse, at 2–3 ozs. per yard run.

Prepare the tubers by sprouting: three to

four weeks before planting—whilst you are digging out the trenches and laying in compost—stand the tubers in seed trays bulbous end uppermost just like an egg. Place them in a warm, light position—I like to sprinkle water over mine, every other day at this stage—and very soon growth shoots will begin spouting from the eyes. When these sprouts are about $\frac{1}{2}$ in. long, select the two or three strongest and remove the remainder by rubbing with the fingers. All the tuber's stored-up food reserve and energy will now be concentrated into producing the two or three strong vigorous stems that will develop large tubers, instead of dispersing energy into a lot of weak spindly shoots with equally weak tubers.

Carry on sprouting until the shoots are about an inch long, when the tubers are ready for planting. Rub off any other small shoots that may be trying to develop, and cover them very carefully with loose soil because the 1 inch shoots are extremely brittle at this stage. Earth up regularly, see *No. 293* and *295* and if the weather is dry, don't hesitate to put on the sprinkler—you won't get a big crop from dry soil.

298 Potatoes : storing through winter

Soon we shall be lifting our potatoes and would like to store them in boxes in our garage for use during the winter. What is the best method of doing this; should they be packed in peat or sand?

There are four basic rules for storing potatoes: no frost, no heat, no moisture, and no light. Potatoes that are intended for storing should be left until the foliage has died down—but don't leave them in the ground longer than you can help.

Start the hard job of lifting by cutting off the withered foliage—the haulm—and then clear it out of the way to the compost heap unless it is diseased. Choose a breezy, dry day and use a fork: if you have a wide-tined fork as distinct from the normal square-tined digging fork, so much the better. Don't drive it in too close or you will spear the spuds; get right under them, and turn them sideways onto the adjacent soil.

Break out the tubers by hand onto sacks or sheets laid on the surface and then move on to the next plant.

Do not leave potatoes lying exposed any longer than is necessary to dry the skins—if you pick the right day this will only be a couple of hours. If it rains, get them under cover. Continue the drying process for a day or two by spreading them on paper sacks or newspaper in the shed or garage. If this has to be in full light, put a sheet of newspaper over them, or they will begin to turn green. See *No. 293*.

The place for storing can be anywhere that conforms to the four rules above and the trouble you go to will obviously depend on the quantity you wish to store. You can build a 'clamp' by putting down a layer of straw or peat on the floor. Examine each tuber; it should be whole and undamaged. Watch particularly for any brown patches where the skin rubs off easily, exposing discoloured flesh. Spread a layer of perfect tubers, dust them very lightly with flowers of sulphur—preferably from a puffer—then a layer of fresh dry straw, another layer of potatoes, and so on in alternate layers. Finally, cover with a thick layer of straw or newspaper covered with peat. Don't make your clamps deeper than $2\frac{1}{2}$ feet. Fresh air but frost free is essential at all times: you must keep the storage room well-ventilated to prevent the build-up of dank stagnant air.

Smaller quantities can be set up in boxes or string bags, but do examine them frequently, and of course remove at once any that show signs of deterioration.

299 Shallots : cause of 'blueing'

Could you tell me the cause of my blueing Hative de Niort shallots? I have planted new seed in five different parts of the garden, but they are all discoloured.

Blueing can affect most of the onion tribe—some react more than others and shallots are particularly prone. There are two contributory reasons for blueing: soil structure and nutrient availability. The blueing is due to over-pigmentation, and this arises because of a starved and hastened growing life so that the bulb attains something like a 'premature maturity'. It is more prevalent in dry sandy soils after a dry sunny summer. This is the first clue—your soil probably needs humus. Your future preparation of the shallot bed must therefore include the incorporation of a very liberal amount of organic matter, compost or peat; this is why shallots are a good crop to follow on in that part of the plot previously used by heavily manured potatoes.

The second factor is allied to the first, in that a soil short of humus is also short of ability to retain moisture. Therefore plant nutrients, as soon as they become soluble, wash out very quickly. Shallots, like most other vegetables, benefit by being fed, and feeding means a steady balanced diet, not tonics and pep pills. Use an N. & P. K. balanced fertiliser as soon as the newly planted bulbs are established and showing an inch or two of green; dress lightly at 1 oz. per square yard. Water in, and cover with a light mulch of granulated peat. You can use garden compost, or mushroom compost that has passed through a half-inch sieve but you must be absolutely sure that, in the course of its making, it became well-heated. Otherwise there is the risk of introducing weed seed, and hoeing is a dangerous job with shallots because growing exposed on the surface you must be very very careful not to cut and damage them.

If hoeing has to be done, then it is best done with an onion hoe which is like a short-handled drag hoe. The control over the blade is that much better because you are that much closer to it, but it is a stooping tedious job and if it is difficult for you to get down to it, you will have to resort to a long-handled drag hoe. The stabbing 'push and chop' of the Dutch hoe is too risky.

A month after the first fertiliser dressing, put down another 1 oz. per square yard and hoe this into the mulch cover. If there are weeds present, this will probably be the last opportunity to hoe them out and clean the bed, because very shortly, the central bulb will start splitting into the clusters which, as they open out, can effectively close the space between the rows so that further hoeing becomes impossible.

The shallot bed should not be allowed to dry out during the growing period. Until the leaves begin to wither naturally after the spread cluster of bulbs have swollen to full size, don't hesitate to water if a dry spell ensues. This is the advantage of getting down that mulch of fine compost as early as possible, but don't overdo it: a sodden soil is the first step towards onion rot.

300 Spinach, a substitute for

Spinach always boils away to nothing when cooked; is there a similar vegetable which is more substantial?

There are a number of alternatives that can be tried as substitutes. 'New Zealand spinach' is preferred by many because it doesn't have the bitterness of true spinach. Once established and growing away, the plants will stand blazing sun—which true spinach will not. There are two disadvantages: the seedlings are tender and when sowing in March and for planting out in May need glass and a little heat; and secondly, the growth spreads and rambles, so much so that each plant will need 3 ft. or so from its nearest neighbour. Don't let it bloom: if buds appear at the shoot ends, take them off at once. Avoidance of bitterness depends to some extent upon the avoidance of dryness, so never let the plants dry out.

Another substitute is Perpetual Spinach, or Spinach Beet. The leaves are larger and more fleshy and, being more substantial, do not reduce as much as true spinach when cooking. Sow seed very thinly in shallow drills March to August, and thin to 8–9 inches apart. No special preparation is required and cultivation, other than keeping the crop weed free, consists of little more than picking leaves when ready. You should pick whether you need leaves or not, in order to promote a continuity of fresh growth. Leaves surplus to immediate needs can always go into the deep freeze, or will last for several days in the cold box of the normal household refrigerator.

Two leaf beets are worth trying: the first, sometimes called Swiss Chard, should not be confused with the blanched summer growth of

Globe Artichoke, called 'chards'. It doesn't produce edible root but the fleshy part of the leaf can be used as spinach and the stalks and leaf ribs can be used as Sea Kale. The second leaf beet, the Golden Beet, is a dual-purpose beet that deserves to be much more widely grown. In addition to using the leaf, the golden-yellow fleshed root can be cooked and served in the same way as red beetroot, or can be mashed and used as a second vegetable like swede.

Finally, there is the plant which has the curious name Good King Henry, widely grown a century or more ago, but hardly ever grown nowadays. The leaves can be used as spinach, and the health food addicts claim all manner of curative and dietary properties for it. The plant is very easily grown from seed sown in April, and should be earthed-up—in order to elongate and blanch the shoots. The young ones make a good substitute for asparagus. Seed for this vegetable can be obtained from Jack Boyce of Soham, Cambridgeshire, and the other spinach substitutes from Boyce, Sutton's of Reading and Dobies of Chester.

301 Sweet Corn: an improved growing method

I would like to grow some sweet corn. My soil is a light loam with good drainage. Please tell me the best way to prepare it and suggest a good variety.

Sweet corn is a form of maize, but it is not the same as the maize that is fed to poultry, pigs and cattle. Sweet corn contains more sugar and less starch compared with maize where the proportions are reversed. Probably emanating from the Americans and Canadians who came over during the last war, there has been a boom in its popularity ever since.

There are two schools of thought concerning the sowing time. The more common practice has been to sow in gentle heat at the end of March; the other school sow direct on site in mid-May and argue that the later sowing catches up. This is generally so, although the reason why is not always understood. Plants sown on site without root disturbance withstand dry conditions better than transplanted seedlings which need very extravagent watering.

In recent years a great deal of work has been done to improve the crop and as the vigorous new F1 hybrids grow and mature much more quickly, the old transplanting method is rapidly being dispensed with. Most gardeners grow sweet corn 15 ins. apart, in rows which are wide enough apart to walk between.

I prefer a different method that takes more account of the rather strange construction of the plant's pollinating methods. The plants have male and female portions: the male parts, which end in bunches of long flower spikes at the top of the plants, and the female parts lower down which consist of the embryo cobs which end in bunches of long flimsy tassels, commonly called 'silks' and whose purpose is to catch pollen as it falls from the male flowers above. It is clear, therefore, that there is a much better chance of catching this falling pollen if the plants are grown closer together in groups rather than strung out in single rows. I, therefore, plant sweet corn in groups of seven —one in the centre and six in a circle around it, 12–15 ins. apart with 2½–3 ft. between each group.

In an exposed position, difficulty is sometimes experienced in preventing the plants from being blown over; they can reach 5 ft. high, and earthing-up is sometimes recommended but this is not entirely successful. Grouping is better; the plants get mutual support, the wind can filter through the groups more easily, and if you are still seriously worried, put a firm stake in at planting time and loop the entire group of plants to it.

Some people like sweet corn very young and soft. Young cobs are ready about three weeks after the first appearance of the silks. An easy way to test for ripeness is to press a grain or two with the thumb nail. If the inside spurts— something like stiff cream, it is ready to cut and use. If you leave the cob too long, the inside becomes hard and mealy—but this is how some people like them. Do not cut more cobs than you need for immediate use, especially young soft ones because they don't keep very well.

The best varieties are all F1 hybrids. Earliking and Sutton's First Of All are early maturing varieties, and John Innes Hybrid, Kelvedon Glory and North Star Hybrid are later heavy-bearing main crop types.

302 Herbs : the best way to dry them

What is the best way to dry herbs from my garden?

Although there are other methods of preserving herbs other than drying them, this seems to be the most popular way. The essence of drying plant tissue is air and plenty of it.

Tie shoots and leafy stems in small bunches and hang these either side of a taut line erected in a shed or room where plenty of fresh air can circulate. As soon as they are brittle, rub them through a small mesh wire sieve and store in dry screw-cap airtight jars that have been thoroughly cleaned. Remember it is the lid that needs special attention to remove every trace of smell. If you do not completely clear other odours left by previous contents, like pickle or coffee, you can be quite certain that the very absorbent texture of this dried matter will pick it up and be spoiled.

303 Mint : how to pick it fresh throughout winter

How can I grow mint to give me pickings through late autumn and winter?

Dig up some root runners, cut them into 4-inch lengths and plant three or four pieces an inch deep in 6–7 inch pots containing a compost of equal parts peat and John Innes No. 1. Keep well-watered and as new shoots appear—which they will do very quickly—move them into a good light and keep free of frost. A few pots like this, provided you pick sparingly, will keep you supplied through the winter.

Section V

Herbaceous and Bedding Plants

304 Alstroemeria, the Peruvian Herb Lily

I am keen to grow some Alstroemeria Litgu Hybrids. I have bought some seeds and I would like your advice on how to sow them.

This most beautiful flower, magnificent for cutting, is easily propagated from seed provided the following points are borne in mind. Firstly, germination is sporadic and can sometimes take as long as a couple of months. Secondly, the plant develops a tuberous root system that detests disturbance. Sowing can be made direct into a sheltered, well-drained border in late spring when the soil is becoming warm but a better method is to sow seed singly during February into 2 in. peat fibre pots using John Innes seed compost, setting seed about ½ in. deep. Position in a frame or greenhouse where a minimum temperature of 55–60°F can be maintained. Water well once and thereinafter only very sparingly because a too wet growing medium can easily rot the seedlings.

In April or May, when all chance of frost has passed, planting out can begin into a soil bed already prepared. The site must be very well-drained, sunny and sheltered from cold wind—Alstroemeria is only half hardy. A light sand can be given body by digging in compost or peat; a heavy soil will need to be lightened if the plant is to have any chance and the best way to do this is to dig in and thoroughly mix with the soil 8 ozs per square yard of gypsum plus plenty of plaster and brick rubble if you can get it. Follow this every three months indefinitely with 1–1½ ozs per sq. yd. of gypsum sprinkled on the surface—you cannot work in later applications because of the roots just below the surface. Plant the peat pots—don't knock out the soil ball since the peat will rot away—and cover the planting area with a 2 in. thick mulch of teased-out rough compost, mushroom compost or straw. After planting out, the tops often die back but the rootstock soon sends up new shoots. It is best not to let these bloom in order to make the young, growing rootstock conserve and build-up its energy to give first quality blooms next year. As winter approaches, thicken up the mulch cover to at least 6 in. to keep frost away from the susceptible roots, carefully lifting off most of it in spring when frost has passed. Be very careful not to damage any emerging shoots.

305 Aster—Michaelmas Daisy: mildew is a prevalent disease

Each year my Michaelmas Daisies suffer from mildew. Can this be avoided?

All Michaelmas Daisies are particularly prone to a mildew fungus, seen as white powdery patches on the foliage, and soon spreading until the whole plant is affected. Although it can be controlled readily enough by spraying with Karathane plus a few drips of liquid washing-up detergent so that a good wetting cover is achieved, what the attack can indicate should not be ignored. This fungus is an illustration of the adage that predators always attack the weakest first and hardest.

Although it is likely that some of your plants will show signs of the disease at some stage of growth, it is always much more severe in plants that are dry at the roots and whose foliage is therefore limp and flaccid. This is one reason why it is so important when dividing the clumps and replanting to seize the opportunity to get a good thick moisture-holding wadge of compost or peat under each plant.

Other contributory factors are imbalance of nutrient availability, too much nitrogen causing soft lush foliage, and/or potash deficiency resulting in lack of vigour.

Each spring, use an N, P & K balanced organic-based manure—Humber Eclipse is ideal for this plant. Spread it down at 2 ozs per sq. yd., cover it at once with a mulch of compost or peat to keep moisture in, and in dry weather don't hesitate to water.

306 Aster: when healthy seedlings fail

I sow all my seeds in John Innes seed compost and water the seedlings with Cheshunt Compound. After planting out and growing on well, many of my Aster plants begin to wilt and die. Can you tell me what is the cause of this and what can I do to prevent it?

The most likely cause of the trouble is that your garden soil is infected with the soil-borne fungus disease, Aster Wilt. As soon as your young plants reach the garden soil they are attacked and succumb. You can grow modern wilt-resistant varieties and plant them into beds which you should previously soak for forty-eight hours with a strong solution of ¼ oz. per gallon permanganate of potash and again forty-eight hours after planting, this time at half strength. This usually checks the disease, but it will not eradicate it.

The only real effective way to do this is to starve out the disease. It has been shown that the fungus can live in the soil for up to seven years after the last Asters were grown and I'm afraid that is about how long you will have to wait to get your soil clean again. If the combination of resistant variety Asters and permanganate does not give you a worthwhile return next year, you will have to give up Asters for seven years. However, since the bed may still be slightly infected, it's wise to play safe and wait for ten years before planting Asters again.

307 Canna: how to care for over winter

Last spring I bought two Cannas and they have done very well. I would like to go in for them in a big way, and would like some information regarding their winter treatment.

Magnificent plants with blooms rather like a very exotic form of the more familiar gladiolus, but borne continuously over a much longer period, Cannas come from the warm climate of Central America and not surprisingly, therefore, the thick fleshy rhizomous roots must be protected from frost. The growing season outdoors must be confined to the period of late spring, summer and early autumn. Towards the end of September, lift the rhizome clumps, remove the loose soil, being very careful not to break or damage the roots, pack into boxes of moist peat to prevent drying out and store over winter in a place like a shed or cool greenhouse that will remain reliably frost free.

If you want to increase your stock, they can be moved during March. Keep them in their boxes of peat or, if you remove a clump from a box, repack it in moist peat into a greenhouse or conservatory with a temperature of 60–65°F. Water with liquid manure and with the encouragement of the heat, shoots will soon appear. When these are 3–4 inches long, pull the peat away very carefully so that the rhizome is exposed with any fibrous roots coming from it. Cut away a shoot with a good section of rhizome and root attached; pot this up into a 5 in. pot using a light compost—John Innes No. 2, peat and silver sand in equal proportion—and keep shaded until established and growing away.

Old clumps and new divisions can be planted out into pockets of peat/sand compost in beds and borders during late May, after all danger of frost is safely past. Never let them dry out, and remove the flowers as soon as they are past their best and fading, in order to keep up a succession of new blooms. You will be at the mercy of weather and rainfall, of course, but do try to reduce watering from the beginning of September so that they slow down and when lifted later in the month are not still in active growth. See also *No. 440*.

308 Carnations: cause and control of splitting

Why do the calyxes of my carnations split whilst flowering? Having just started growing these carnations, it is a disappointment to find nearly every bloom suffering from this complaint.

The calyx can be described as the green sheath that encloses the bud and which opens like a cup as the petals emerge to become the bloom. When the calyx splits, instead of being held tight and even, the petals flop through the split and the bloom becomes lop sided and bedraggled. Calyx splitting is more prevalent in some varieties than others but the cause is the same, and the prevalence or otherwise is due mainly to the ability of the variety to resist the cause, which is uneven environment.

Carnations must not be grown in too much heat, and must have plenty of ventilation. However the ventilators should not be left open at nights unless you can provide heating sufficient to maintain a minimum of 55°F, otherwise the buds become chilled. If this is allowed to happen, development of the bud is slowed. It only needs a burst of growth—brought on by moisture and warmth—to mean that the chilled calyx cannot expand and as the petal bases swell, it splits.

Special rings can be put round the buds near to opening time—some growers use rubber bands—but the basic remedy is to avoid sudden boosts, so do all you can to regularise conditions. An automatic ventilator control is very helpful and quite inexpensive.

309   Cowslips : growing unusual colour

Some years ago I sowed seed from a yellow cowslip and obtained a healthy batch of new plants, one of which produced russet-coloured flowers. Is this unusual and would it come true from seed, or would I have to divide it to get similar plants?

The cowslip, *Primula veris*, is normally yellow although some slight variation in the yellow may be seen in a batch of seedlings. Occasionally the variation goes a bit far and orange or even reddish flowered forms occur. Barnhaven Nurseries at Brigsteer in Cumbria have made a speciality of collecting the variations of primroses, cowslips and other Primulas and have a very varied range. They should be able to supply seed, seedlings, or plants.

By selective breeding, strains have been developed that throw a high proportion of colour variants and most of the bigger seed firms offer 'coloured' cowslip seed in a range from red/bronze through orange and yellow to cream and white.

There is no guarantee that seed sown from your russet will show the same degree of variation and the only way to be quite certain of increasing the stock of this colour would be to divide the roots as soon as the clump becomes big enough.

310   Cut flowers : a long cutting season

Can you suggest some hardy border flowers that I can grow to provide cut flowers for the house?

Suggesting flowers to grow is always a difficult business because tastes differ so widely, and what I enthuse about may leave you uninterested.

Therefore, the very best and fairest advice is to give a list of plants that are best suited to cutting—i.e. they will last a reasonable length of time in water, and not fade very quickly. And then I suggest that you send for illustrated catalogues, and identify the plants. Don't rush out and buy those listed below, just because I name them! Visit your parks and local shows if necessary to find out what they look like. It's what appeals to *you* that matters.

The following is a list of plants arranged according to the month when they are at their peak, although of course many will have more than one variety and carry on for longer than just one month. Bear in mind, also, the uses of summer as well as spring bulbs, and flowering material cut from ornamental shrubs.

April	Doronicum
May	Geum; Pyrethrum
June	Achillea, Aquilegia, Astilbe, Coreopsis, Erigeron, Gaillardia, Heuchera, Lupinus, Penstemon, Scabiosa, Thalictrum
July	Gypsophila, Helenium, Heliopsis, Monarda, Rudbeckia, Sidalcea
August	Aster, Eryngium, Phlox, Solidago, Verbascum
September–October	*Anemone japonica*, Chrysanthemums, Helianthus, Kniphofia, Physalis, Physostegia

311   Dahlia : taking cuttings from last year's stools

Can you tell me the correct way to take Dahlia cuttings from last year's stools? I have a heated greenhouse.

Although you have a heated greenhouse, for really good results you will need to provide an enclosed humid atmosphere and a steady temperature of 65–70°F. By far the best way to do this is to have a propagator that produces bottom heat through soil-heating cables, controlled by a thermostat that turns off the electricity when the required temperature is reached and automatically turns it on again when the temperature falls below a set minimum.

No. 311 *Dahlia cuttings are obtained by half-burying the tubers in moist peat in a warm greenhouse and as new growth shoots become 2–3 ins. long, they are cut away with a piece of tuber attached.*

In March, half-bury the Dahlia root tubers in a moist peat bed made up on the staging in the greenhouse. Watering and warmth will induce shoots to develop from the 'eyes' in the same way that sprouts form from potatoes. When about 2–2½ ins. long, cut the shoot away with a small heel of tuber attached, touch this cut surface into hormone rooting powder and dibble each cutting singly into a moist sand/peat mixture in 2–2½ in. pots or into Jiffy 7 peat balls. Place these in the propagator or, if you do not have one in the warmest part of the greenhouse, cover with polythene film to create a moist atmosphere underneath.

Cuttings should be shaded (a sheet of newspaper laid over will do nicely) because bright light can cause the young leaves to work and pull on a root system that doesn't yet exist. Cuttings should root quite quickly; examine them by inverting and tapping them out from

the pot—or if you are using Jiffy 7 peat balls, you will be able to watch the roots appear through the mesh covering. When roots appear, move the pots outside the propagator but near to it where they can still remain warm and cover with polythene film for a week. The move from the sauna bath of the propagator to the outside world should be done step by step —a too sudden and drastic change in their living conditions at this stage can easily be fatal.

Pot up into larger pots as required, aiming to plant out when all danger of frost is past.

312 Delphinium: overwintering and root division

I have had some lovely Delphiniums this year and they are now dying off. As I want to keep them for next year, is it advisable to dig them up and split the roots? Do they survive the winter?

Delphiniums are quite hardy enough to be left in the ground and can be treated the same as lupins—see *No. 319*—except that you are not likely to get a second show of main blooms by cutting right back early on. Don't let the main spike set seed capsules, however; the secondary side shoots bear blooms that are most acceptable for cut blooms.

Spring mulching and feeding are important. Slugs and snails are even more of a problem than with lupins. In addition to the slug traps described in *No. 511*, surround each plant in autumn with a 3–4 in. wide band of sharp grit; if they get across that, at least they'll have pretty sore feet! This is often enough to divert them into the traps.

When the clumps are large enough to break apart easily, they can be divided but you will get much better plants and much better blooms from 3 in. cuttings taken with a heel of root in March or April and rooted in sandy peat in a gentle bottom heat or in a cold frame from mid-April.

313 Geranium: overwintering without a greenhouse

As I haven't a greenhouse in which to overwinter my Geraniums, where else can I keep them?

Many gardeners lift their Geraniums, pot them up and contrive to keep them ticking over in a well-lit spare room, but I recommend that you treat these plants as stools, in the following manner.

Soft tissue is more susceptible to fungus disease than hardened ripened growth. Therefore, towards the end of the growing season, try to withhold water so that the growth becomes harder and the plants drier. Then, before the frosts arrive, lift them, shake off the soil from the roots and cut away to just above a leaf joint, up to about half to two thirds of top growth, to leave shortened stems around 6–9 inches in length. Pack these plants—stools—closely in boxes of moist peat, puff them with Captan fungicidal dust as a precaution against fungal attack and position them in good light—by the window of a spare room or frost-free shed. Watering from now on should be kept to a minimum—just enough to keep the stools alive.

The other two big dangers are lack of ventilation and dampness in the leaves and stems. Stagnant moisture is certain to bring on fungal attack; therefore, whenever outside temperature allows, open the windows. Examine shoots regularly and at the very first signs of disease, puff Captan dust. Pick off any faded leaves which may hinder air movement and invite attack.

In early spring when young shoots are forming, greenfly may put in an appearance. These must be snuffed out at once, and as wetting the foliage is an encouragement to fungus, if you spray liquid greenfly killer like Lindex, you should also begin regular precautionary spraying with a systemic fungicide like Benlate; otherwise, control greenfly by puffing Malathion dust.

New shoots forming on these stools in the spring can either be allowed to grow and bear bloom or can be taken as cuttings when they are 5–6 in. long and struck into sandy compost. Stooled plants, starting from shortened growth, bear more and better blooms and are much better for bedding than plants that are potted up, and which often become tall and spindly if they are not shortened back.

314 Gypsophila : difficult propagation

I have tried in vain for several years to propagate my 'Bristol Fairy' Gypsophila without success. Can you please tell me how it is done? I am very successful with Lupins and Delphiniums.

Gypsophila will not propagate from root cuttings and to be in any way successful you will have to adopt a rather involved technique. In mid-July, give the plant a good soaking and a week later carefully lift the plant with a good soil ball and the roots as intact as possible. Pot the plant, using for pot filling a quick-draining compost mix of equal parts John Innes No. 1, peat and crushed plaster rubble for preference—or failing this, sharp gritty sand.

Remove the plant to a frost-free greenhouse and grow on, allowing the foliage to eventually wither, but do not remove the stems. Keep the plant cool during the winter with the soil just nicely moist. Root activity will continue and with the protection of the house, growth will begin earlier than if it had remained outside. From January, water with liquid feed and manure water.

By the end of March—if not before—secondary shoots arising from the main stems should be 2–3 ins. long and ready to be taken with a heel of the older stem wood. Use a sharp penknife—experienced gardeners use an old many-times sharpened and therefore thin blade for this job. Until you have cut out a few heels to get the knack, make the cut from just above the shoot, into the stem down past the shoot and out again below the shoot. Most people will find it easier and more 'natural' to cut up from under the shoot but there is a risk, until you get used to it, of bringing the knife out a little suddenly and awkwardly and injuring the soft tissue of the shoot—or your thumb!

Whilst still sap-moist so that a coating adheres, dip the heel in a rooting hormone powder and set the cuttings six to a 5-in. pot, containing a mix of 2 parts silver sand, 1 part peat. First water the pot by immersion and allow the surplus to drain for an hour or two, and then insert the cuttings by making the holes with a small dibber around the edge rather like Geranium, see *No. 313*. Firm the cuttings so that they are tight against the inside of the pot with the heel facing inwards.

Place the pot in a propagator set at about 60°F. or in a polythene bag placed, if you have one, on a heating panel on soil warming cables. If all else fails, place it in the warmest part of the greenhouse—always provided that the cuttings are well-shaded from sunlight. Wipe away condensation at least once a day and with luck your cuttings will soon strike.

When they begin to grow away, indicating that they are drawing upon a root system, open up the polythene cover or lift the propagator cover a little to give them gradually increasing ventilation so that they are fully exposed in about two weeks or so, and then pot them up singly into 4-in. pots, planting them outside when the soil ball is enclosed and held in a nice layer of root.

Young Gypsophila is regarded as a gourmet meal by slugs and snails. When you plant outside, therefore, put down a slug trap baited as described in *No. 511*—you haven't gone to all this trouble simply to provide a free meal.

315 *Helleborus, the Christmas rose*

How can I get some new Christmas rose plants to form long flowering stems?

If you are to do well with *Helleborus niger*, the so-called Christmas rose, you have to start before you begin. That is to say, before planting, the soil needs plenty of compost or peat worked into it. The earlier this is done—a year or more is ideal—the better will the compost be assimilated. Hellebores do not like root disturbance and, as you won't be able to correct the soil under the plant after planting it is sensible to get it right at the start.

The best site is one that is well-sheltered and where the plants can get dappled light coming through overhead foliage. Planting can be in October or November well before blooming, or well after, in March. A mulch of well-rotted compost, leaf mould, or the lighter strawy parts of mushroom compost should be kept in

place at all times: not just a handful but a good layer 2–3 ins. thick.

In December, as the flower buds appear, put a barn cloche over the plants—or, if you don't have a cloche, at least support a pane of glass over them on upturned pots perhaps to protect the blooms from the weather. The thick mulch and overhead glass will have the effect of materially lengthening the flower stalks, but if you want to make certain they will be extra long, pack sphagnum moss lightly round the stems so that they are supported and not spoiled by flopping onto the soil.

After flowering, sprinkle down a little balanced manure like Growmore. Keep the mulch layer intact and in dry weather water with dilute manure water. Try to keep the foliage healthy and vigorous so that food reserves can be built-up to support a good bloom the following winter.

316 *Hosta needs to have the right conditions*

My front garden is on a high hill and it tends to have very dry soil and be very sunny. Would this be suitable for growing Hostas.

Having been widely advocated for ground cover, the charming Plantain Lilies—Hostas—like many other plants have often disappointed because of unsuitable conditions.

In order to do well, Hostas need a soil containing plenty of moisture-retaining humus. They like moisture and are at their best, perhaps, in a position near a pool where, although not boggy, the soil never dries out. They also need partial shade, dappled sunlight, provided by nearby and slightly overhanging shrubs. These are ideal conditions and whilst it is not possible always to provide the ideal, you will need to provide something like it if your Hostas are to show their blooms and remarkable foliage to anything like best advantage.

It would certainly appear from the description of your garden that you have a lot to do if you don't want to be disappointed. I am sorry if this sounds disheartening, but I will never advise anyone with false hopes, or difficult ones without pointing out the risks.

Always check whether any plants you intend to grow have special preferences. This will show you whether you already have or can adapt to provide them with the ideal conditions—acid, alkaline, well-drained, or boggy, sunny or shaded, etc.

317 Ipomoea, Morning Glory: difficult seedlings

I am having trouble with seedlings of the Morning Glory. Their leaves are very pale and tend to die off. Can you suggest what is wrong?

—A lot of gardeners have trouble with Ipomoea which is a pity because there is something about the clarity of that glorious morning blue that is not only very beautiful but is worth going to some trouble to achieve. Unhappily, the blooms only last one day and by late in the evening, the clarity has gone and the beauty past—however there are many more mornings and many more blooms to come. As with all plants, you can't do better than the way Nature made them, and if Man has the audacity to move plants half way round the world, he cannot expect the plants to be happy about it unless he contrives to provide conditions that are similar to where they came from.

Ipomoea comes from tropical Central America where there are several species; the one we grow here, commonly called Morning Glory, is an annual, *I. rubro-caerulea*.

The first requirement quite evidently is warmth, and like most plants from that area of the world, it needs steady temperatures with as little variation as possible. They do not like root disturbance and therefore the growing away of the seedling must be unhindered and preferably rapid. They are not overgross feeders but won't do well on starvation rations either. They prefer acidity as they need a fair amount of iron, and this gets locked up in a limy, chalky soil. Finally, the seed has a rather hard seed coat.

The first thing to do is to 'chip' the seed— i.e. cut through the seed coat so that water can

more easily get into the embryo to prompt the commencement of germination. Bare fingers and a sharp knife will probably result in your fingers being chipped too, so hold each seed in pliers or tweezers and with a nail-file rub through the seed coat. You will easily see when it is perforated by the change in colour. Do this in early March if you are going to grow them inside, late March if you are to grow them outside.

Next, soak the seeds for twenty-four hours preferably in rain water and in a warm place. Whilst you are doing this prepare the sowing medium. You must not disturb the roots by pricking out or turning out of pots, so each seed will have to be sown in a fibre pot that can later be planted intact and which will rot away in the soil. Use the 3-inch size and fill with a compost mix of equal parts John Innes No. 1, peat and sand.

Sow three prepared seeds per pot, just pushed below the soil surface, water with rainwater and place in a controlled temperature of 60–65°F. If you are going to grow them in the greenhouse in pots, whilst the seedlings are germinating (about 10–14 days), take as much of the above compost as will be required to fill the number of 7 or 8-inch pots you are going to use, and mix into the compost the same number of heaped teaspoonfuls of Humber Eclipse Garden Manure, i.e. one spoonful per pot. Place the compost aside so that whilst the seedlings are growing to 3 ins., bacteria can be working on the Humber Manure and the nutrient availability will be advanced when it comes to potting on. During these early stages, be very careful to keep conditions as stable as possible, particularly avoiding draughts.

At 3 ins. tall, plant the complete fibre pot into the prepared compost in the large growing pot, at the same time arranging the main frames that will support the trellis or whatever you want the plants to climb upon; to push canes in afterwards would inevitably damage or disturb the roots.

If you are planting outside into the garden, it would pay to take out a fair-sized hole and use the same prepared compost to backfill so that there is a nice food bank around the roots.

Water copiously at all times (they must not at any time suffer dryness) with rainwater. This should be simple enough if you have a greenhouse because you will naturally collect it off the roof in a butt, but if you have to rely on the tap, counter the probability of lime in the water by using the dregs from the tea pot.

318 Kniphofia : why never a sign of red hot pokers

Can you tell me why our red hot pokers do not flower? Should they be divided and what time is best for this? They have been in situ for about ten years.

Kniphofias do not like lime and this is known to affect their flowering. It could well be the cause of your problem. Natives of South Africa, they need all the available light and if your plants are in any form of shade, move them into the sun. Since they have been in the same place for ten years also suggests that the plants are congested and the soil exhausted. Between October and March, during a mild spell with no likelihood of frost, lift the clumps, divide if possible, choose a new position if necessary, dig in as much compost as you can spare (bear in mind that short of digging them up again, this is your last opportunity to do anything about the soil under the plants), work in a handful of balanced plant nutrient like Grow-more or Humber Eclipse and, after planting, cover the area with a mulch of rotted compost or peat. If your soil is chalky or limy, do not use plain tap water on this plant. Use the tea pot dregs to water Kniphofias, and any other lime haters, and add the tea leaves or bags to the mulch around the plants. The tannin from the tea is acid enough to overcome the lime in your tap water.

319 Lupins : how to get a second flush

Will you tell me what to do with Russell lupins when they have flowered? Do I cut them down or just take off the dead flowers?

It is not generally realised that lupins can be induced to give a second bloom. The longest spikes of bloom are borne on the main stems, and often the lower flowers begin to decline whilst there are still unopened buds at the top. Don't wait any longer: the entire flower spike should be removed before the lower flowers are replaced by seed pods—or at least remove these pods if there are a great many unopened buds still remaining. With the removal of the main bloom head, secondary blooms are encouraged to develop on shoots arising from the leaf axils lower down. These are never so long and large as the main bloom, but there are several of them.

However, if instead of merely removing the declining main bloom, the whole stem is cut back to just above the growth bud at the first leaf joint a few inches above ground level, this bud will quickly develop to form another 'main' stem bearing a long bloom. This treatment asks rather a lot of the plant and should not be attempted until the plant is well-established in its second or third year.

Lupins pay for generous treatment. Mulch each spring with well-rotted compost, and work into it a small handful of fertiliser with N, P & K in balanced proportions or even slightly nitrogen low. Never feed with purely nitrogenous fertilisers; lupins are like peas and beans and get most of the nitrogen they need from the colonies of nitrogen-fixing bacteria that live in the nodules on their roots.

Cut back the foliage when winter approaches and don't let foliage merely collapse and remain. This is a direct encouragement to slugs and snails to take shelter and hang around. These are arch enemies of lupins and can take chunks out of young leaves, and even ruin an active shoot. At the first signs of these pests, put down slug and snail traps as described in *No. 511*.

320 Lupins : replacement of washed-out plants

I would like to replace a border of washed-out lupins with better varieties. What do you suggest?

Lupins are not very long-lived and there is the tendency for them to decline, if not in colour, then certainly in vigour as they become older and exhaust the soil in which they are growing. Therefore, to keep a border of them in top condition—and there is not a much finer sight than a long border or lupins in full bloom—means constant replacement of older plants by young plants raised either by cuttings (like Dahlias, see *No. 311*) in which case they will be identical to the parent, or by seed.

Lupins are one of the relatively few flowers that include the three colours red, yellow and blue in their colour range of pure and bicolours. The Russell strain has the widest colour range of the strains available. For many gardens however, 3–4 ft. or more high is a little too tall and the plants are too vigorous for more than just a few gardens.

Therefore, a shorter-growing lupin of the Russell type called Minaret, and now available, will be attractive to many with limited space: the colour range is not quite so wide as the larger Russell strain, but there are many bicolours and by selecting and re-selecting the best colours and roguing out those that you don't find attractive, you can build a very colourful display.

A little smaller, but with a slightly different habit, is the Dwarf Lulu strain. These have a colour range similar to Minaret, not so wide as the Russells, but still including all the bicolours. The main difference, however, is that the plant is altogether sturdier, the main long bloom spike is not quite so pronounced and each plant, when fully grown, will carry a dozen or more closely set spikes of bloom.

Lupin seed has a cover that is hard and resistant to moisture; germination is better therefore for chipping the seed. See *No. 310*. Soak the seed in water for a little while before sowing. They are planted spaced out in boxes, or singly into Jiffy 7s in March, in a slight heat. Pot on into 4–5 inch pots and plant out in May or June into final positions previously prepared with plenty of compost dug in. After planting, cover the area with a good mulch cover—plus a slug trap alongside each seedling, see *No. 511*.

Many plants will try to bloom during their first year, but don't let them. It is too exhausting for an underdeveloped seedling's root system to support bloom. Make them concentrate on becoming established with a good root system. The second year bloom will then be much better.

321   *Lupins : older plants dying*

For several years my lupins have been fairly successful, but last year I lost some plants. The outside shoots shrivelled and died and the trouble then spread to the rest of the plants. I moved the survivors to a different part of the garden but it looks as if the trouble is starting again. No other plants in the border are affected and I cannot understand it. I apply fertilisers and lime each year so they are not short of being fed properly.

The lupin is not generally troubled by many of the pests, and diseases and troubles that beset so many other plants, but whilst not too particular about soil, it does prefer one that is slightly acid rather than one that is on chalk or limestone. You should not therefore, put down garden lime around lupins, so from now on and for a couple of years or so save all the dregs and leaves from the teapot and distribute these around the lupins so that the tannic acid in the tea neutralises and overcomes the alkalinity that you have built up over the years with your repeated liming.

This shrivelling of shoots suggest that the root system is impaired and a likely cause of this is unfavourable soil structure i.e. heavy, poorly-drained, an excessive wet stagnant condition causing the fine assimilative roots to rot away. With the ability to absorb moisture and nutrients gone, the growing points, the shoots, are the first to shrivel and collapse due to non supply of essentials. If this describes your soil to any degree, put down gypsum at the rate of 2 oz. per square yard every three months. It will take a long time but, as the gypsum works, gradually the sticky wetness will pass and the soil will be more porous so that root formation is encouraged instead of impaired.

Finally, Lupins are not long lived so it could be that these have lost all vigour and exhausted the soil. Read *Nos. 319* and *320* and then start again with new plants and a regular replacement scheme of new plants from seed and then cuttings taken from the best colours.

322   Peony : care needed when moving

I would like to split up an old clump of peonies but understand it's wrong to shift them. Why?

Unless conditions are markedly unfavourable to them peonies are very long lived and, like many plants that live to a ripe old age, they do not like their roots being disturbed, especially when young and thriving. However, this is not to say that they cannot be uplifted at all and indeed this may be advisable with an old clump that has exhausted the soil around it or that may be the better for dividing into pieces.

In late February–early March choose a mild drying day and lift the clump very carefully, dig around it well to begin with to loosen it and take every care not to break the large fleshy roots. If you do make a break, pare it clean with a sharp knife, keep the cut surface smooth and not jagged. Hopefully your Paeonia has never suffered from wilt, but just in case the soil-borne spores are about you should take the precaution of dusting the cut surfaces with Bordeaux powder as a further precaution against fungal infection and covering the cuts with cloth or paper in order to keep soil particles away from the surface before the healing callus tissue forms. It is almost inevitable that you will have to sever something somewhere to split the clump but having divided it and trimmed the cuts, leave the divisions for an hour or two for the cut to dry (this is why it is best to choose a mild dry day) whilst you get on with preparing the new growing positions.

The divisions usually react with energetic growth and this is the condition when the Paeonia is least tolerant of further root disturbance. Once replanted, the plant will have to remain undisturbed for several years and you should therefore take this one and only opportunity to incorporate plenty of rotted compost into the soil around and especially under where each piece will be planted. Sprinkle in a handful of Growmore or Humber Eclipse and cover the planted area with a mulch of compost or peat.

For the first year at least keep the plants well watered; Paeonia should never be allowed to become dry which is why you should have worked in the moisture-retentive compost.

During the first season after replanting, don't let the plants bloom. Their most important task now is to make root and become established—not dissipate their energies into putting up blooms that they haven't yet the root action to support. In the second season, the plants themselves may have realised this and be somewhat reluctant to bloom. Don't worry; by the third season, they should be well into their stride with much better blooms than you could have seen on your clump for a long time.

Paeonias are heavy feeders so replenish the mulch cover as it is worked into the soil, and scratch into this each early spring a handful of Growmore or Humber Eclipse, plus—as soon as the bloom buds are discernible—an ounce of sulphate of potash in order to harden the foliage and put extra colour into the bloom.

323   Peony buds fail and rot

Can you tell me why each year my peonies look healthy and have lots of buds, but many of them rot before they are fully open?

This is a very common problem with Paeonia; the blooms are sometimes damaged by frosts but this is hardly likely to be the cause of consistent non-development. The main cause of persistent failure like this is more likely to be unsatisfactory soil conditions—mainly excessive dryness at the roots. This is why they like a humus-rich, moisture-retentive soil. Peonies detest root disturbance, and will often fail to bloom for two or three years after transplanting —see *No. 322*—so unless you are prepared to risk even further delay by lifting and transplanting into lots of compost, you will have to do what you can with them where they are.

Put down a thick layer of well-rotted friable compost as a mulch, or use peat. It must be well rotted and friable so that earthworms are encouraged to work in it and accelerate the assimilation into the soil. As the mulch decomposes and is absorbed, restore the cover with more; this will also help to keep the soil moist.

It is a good idea to steep a sack of farmyard manure or mushroom compost in a spare water butt, pummel it around so that the liquor becomes heavily humus-laden—the colour of tea —and once a week from spring, when new growth and flower buds are being thrust up, give each plant half a bucketful of this liquid with three or four pin-head sized crystals of permanganate of potash dissolved in it. Renew the contents of the sack as the contents get worked out, using the old stuff as extra mulch, and with the increasing humus content and adequate potash to encourage maturity, flowers should not be long in forming.

324 Polyanthus: why are the second year plants so weak?

My Polyanthus were magnificent last year, but this spring my plants are small and weakly. Why?

Like its close relation the primrose which thrives in a semi-woodland floor, rich in leaf mould, and all members of the Primula family, Polyanthus do best in a soil containing plenty of organic matter. They are seldom quite so vigorous and spectacular as in their first year from seed, but they can certainly be encouraged to produce a more than worthwhile display in a second and subsequent years by providing the optimum conditions and not ignoring them as soon as flowering is over. They need part shade (dappled sunlight is ideal), overhead protection from frost and snow, a humus-rich soil that is moist but not wet, and a steady balanced nutrient supply over a long period.

If you remove flower heads as soon as they are past their best and stop them from wasting energy making seed, it is possible to extend the flowering season after the main spring flush. During May, dust in about a teaspoonful of Humber Eclipse or Growmore around each plant or, if they are in beds, spread a couple of ounces per sq. yd. between the plants, scratch it into the surface if practicable and cover with a thin mulch of spent mushroom compost or

peat. Repeat the fertiliser dressing twice more at six-week intervals and don't make the common mistake of allowing plants to dry out during dry summer weather. The more flourishing you can keep the foliage, the more energy the plant can store to make next spring's blooms.

Aphis can be a problem during spring and summer, so keep a regular careful watch on the leaf undersides and spray with Lindex at the first signs of the pest on the soft young leaves. This cultivation should produce nice sturdy dark green foliage, which will nourish and build-up plenty of reserves in large rootstocks. Keep an eye open for damage by slugs and if necessary bait with traps—see *No. 511*.

As the cold weather approaches, replenish the mulch, rather thicker this time, with coarse roughage and if bad frost or snow threatens, cover with cloches or, if in beds, cover overnight with polythene sheets which should be removed during the day. You should get good bloom again in the spring, when you should follow the routine again after flowering, but in the following September many of the rootstocks will be large enough to be split apart easily by hand; don't use a knife more than you have to, except to trim them.

Lightly fork in the old mulch, replant, water in and restore the mulch cover with new material. The plants should now become nicely established before winter arrives and in this way you will get yet another couple of years' worthwhile bloom. Don't expect them to go on for ever though; when they are past their prime, scrap them, and replace with fresh young plants raised from seed.

325 Primroses: old-fashioned sweet-scented doubles

In the village of Dean not twenty miles from here almost every cottage garden contains plants of a sweetly-scented pale lavender double primrose. I have never seen it anywhere else; could you tell me something about it?

Dean is in Westmorland, now called Cumbria; it is an area in which many variations of primroses are to be found growing both wild and cultivated in cottage gardens.

This sweet scented lavender double is the old 'double lilac', the origins of which go back to Tudor times when it was known by at least two names, Ladies' Delight and Quaker's Bonnet. It is a little more temperamental than the common primrose, which probably accounts for its not being much more widely grown, which is a pity because it can be grown well throughout the UK and, indeed, was so as late as the second half of the 1800s.

It needs a shady, dappled-light position, prefers a soil inclined to the heavy side, and likes a liberal mulching with well-rotted farmyard manure or spent mushroom compost, teased out and fluffed up. Give a very light dusting of Humber Eclipse or any other balanced plant nutrient once in early summer, again in early autumn and you should have no difficulty in growing this charmer. The clump develops very quickly and can then be divided fairly easily. Every two or three years, immediately after flowering or in autumn, are the best times to do this.

Several nurserymen list it: you may find it as *Primula lilacina plena*—its correct botanical name. If you have any difficulty in obtaining it, write off to Barnhaven, Brigsteer, Kendal, Cumbria.

326 Salvia: correct care and treatment

I have grown some Salvias from seed and although they were a dark green when pricked out, they are now tending to become light green, almost yellow, and the leaves are becoming brittle. Could you give me a remedy?

Few gardeners grow Salvias successfully: the secret is to look after the foliage and the flowers will look after themselves. Pale green leaves instead of nice dark green ones is a condition often seen in the plants offered for sale; such plants are hardly worth the trouble were they to be given you, so don't ever consider spending money on them. Plants looking like this have been chilled, grown too cold, so that root action is inhibited and nutrient uptake slowed or stopped.

To get the best results, sow seed early in January, in a shallow sowing in John Innes seed compost, temperature 68–72°F. Germination is quick, fourteen days only; don't let them dry and check at any time.

Prick out into boxes 1½ in. apart in John Innes Compost No. 1. Then, when they've produced four true leaves, instead of planting out which is what often happens at this stage, pot them into 3-in. pots, in a richer compost—J.I. No. 2. At six full leaves, take out the growing tip—if you let all the energy run into the lead flower, you won't get much of the prolific secondary bloom. When the 3 in. pot contains a good root layer pot on into 5-in. pots but don't be in a hurry to plant out; wait for the soil to warm in spring sunshine. They will only hang about in cold soil, and that is fatal for a good bloom.

Plant out in late May or June—the blooms should be just showing signs of red and, at this time, feed and keep well-watered for a few days.

I know of few flowers that repay better for a dressing of Humber Eclipse garden manure at this time and they relish the potash that becomes available late. Dust it down between the plants at up to 2 ozs. per sq. yd.—one dressing is enough. Grown well, Salvias provide a spectacular show but you can only achieve spectacular results, if the plants have dark green foliage and leaves that are working well and which have not been checked. The remedy for anaemic pale green foliage is to provide warmth, protection from cold draughts and feeding, plus a little extra nitrogen. In addition to the balanced feeding, a useful boost can be made by dissolving an ounce of nitro-chalk and half a teaspoonful of Epsom salts into 2 gallons of water. Put this down from a can with a spout so that you don't splash and mark the leaves, about 2 weeks after planting.

327 Scabious: propagation for 'Clive Greaves'

What is the correct cultivation for my 'Clive

Greaves' scabious? Whenever I try to divide the roots, like other plants, they always die and I have to buy new plants.

It is possible to divide scabious—but, as a general rule, autumn division of perennial scabious always proves fatal, so you will have to try another method.

Treat them as you would for the tuberous-rooted Dahlia, see *No. 311*. In spring, as shoots are emerging from the root clump, cut these away about 2–3 ins. long with a heel of root, dip in hormone rooting powder and dibber firmly into light sandy compost—six spaced round the edge of a 5-in. pot—and stand this in a frame or other sheltered spot and keep moist at all times.

Rooting is usually successful by this method and flowering shoots are produced in the first year. Although scabious grows wild in many parts of U.K., especially on chalky downland, the cultivated kinds are derived from types native to southern Europe where they revel in full sun. You should, therefore, always try to grow scabious where it will get plenty of light. Like most herbaceous plants, the withered foliage that is cleared away each autumn, represents a relatively large bulk of organic matter that has basically originated from the soil. It is no good clearing it away and not putting back the equivalent volume. Therefore, clearing away should be to the compost heap rather than to the bonfire, and where it can be turned into valuable compost to be returned to the soil as mulch. Maintaining a mulch cover of compost helps to keep up the supply of plant nutrients, but you can make sure of this by spreading and hoeing in a handful of general balanced fertiliser per plant every spring.

Finally in your efforts with 'Clive Greaves', don't become so preoccupied as to forget and disregard the superb range of colours available by growing scabious from seed sown in open ground in March under cloches to flower from June, or unprotected in April to flower from July onwards. Most of the major seed houses offer seed of different kinds, but there is a particularly fine strain of superb large flowered doubles available from Sutton's of Reading

that grows to 3 ft. tall, with blooms on long wiry stems which are ideal for cut bloom.

328 *Sweet Pea : saving seed*

I have collected the seeds from some mixed sweet peas and separated them according to colour. Will next year's flowers be true to the parent plant?

Although the flowers self-pollinate, insects will be responsible for some degree of cross-fertilisation and it is usual for the blooms of self saved seed to decline, both with regard to the intensity of colour and their number, and also for the vigour of the plants to suffer. More and more whites and weak colours appear each year, and the flower stems become shorter.

By growing plants on single canes, so that you can always be sure that you are taking seed from the best colours, it is possible to keep up the colour proportion of your seed for a few years, but I would not consider doing this for more than three or four years at most. However careful you are, the decline will be gradual and almost without realising you will be cultivating sweet peas much below par.

In any case the cost of the original seed will not owe you anything by this time, so it would be much better to get fresh first quality seed from a reliable seedsman and start afresh. If not every year, you should sow fresh seed at least every other year.

Incidentally, if you are thinking in terms of saving seed from F1 Hybrid plants, don't waste your time: such seed will not come true, either in colour or vigour.

Finally, you should realise that continued flowering and saving seed are incompatible. If you grow plants and allow the early flowers to set seed, which is what the seedsman does because it is the best, you will get no further flowers—or very little—because the plant has carried out its primary purpose in life, setting seed and ensuring the next generation. If you want the best flowers, concentrate on growing them well, and leave seed production to the specialists. Remove flowers as soon as they begin to fade, in order to encourage the production of more bloom.

329 Sweet Pea: treatment after flowering

I have successfully raised from seed an everlasting pea, Lathyrus latifolius. *It has grown to a tremendous size and has given a wonderful display of deep pink flowers. Now it has finished flowering, I am wondering if it should be cut down.*

Everlasting sweet pea can soon decline if it is not grown properly. At about the end of October, flowering will have finished and foliage will be at a stage when it will not be contributing much food reserves to the root system. Therefore, cut down all growth to within 6 inches of soil level, and put down a thick mulch of compost. This is very important because everlasting pea is a vigorous grower and quickly exhausts the nutrients in the soil. Put down an annual mulch every autumn, plus a good handful of a balanced plant food which has the N, P & K proportions equal—such as Growmore or Humber Eclipse—spread around and hoe in. Repeat in spring and replenish the mulch cover where it has been absorbed and become thin. This will ensure that you get a good show of bloom each year.

Extremely hardy, the everlasting sweet pea is one of the most underrated of plants, but too often is an object of neglect and a mere apology of what it can be.

Section VI

Bulbs and Corms

330 'Amaryllis': why no flowers the second year

Two years ago I bought a red Amaryllis Bella-donna Lily complete with a small pot and compost, and it made beautiful large trumpet flowers. I let it die down standing outside, and then repotted it in a larger pot. Last year I had a wonderful display of leaves, but no flowers. I left it in the garden until late summer, watering when required. This year the bulb has split and leaves are coming on each bulb, about 5 in. long, but still no flowers. Where have I gone wrong?

I wonder if you are falling into a trap due to a confusion over names. The bulbs sold in complete outfits as you describe are correctly named Hippeastrum. They are also called—incorrectly—Amaryllis, to which they are very closely related but are quite distinct. The modern Hippeastrums which are offered in the late autumn as specially prepared bulbs for blooming at Christmas are hybrids of species that originate from the tropics of Central America and therefore need warm greenhouse or 'store' treatment not 'standing outside'.

Unfortunately the specially prepared Hippeastrum often behaves in the way you have experienced, flowering well as a purchased bulb, and then in later years disappointingly producing all leaves and no blooms. The basic cause is that they do not like disturbance. After blooming, in fact almost whilst it is still blooming, the plant sets about creating an embryo bud deep within the bulb which will grow out and bloom next year. Your first successful bloom will have been in the bulb in embryo when bought and thus will have been produced virtually automatically. The shock of being sold and planted afresh will quite likely have upset a new bud being formed, and it may take a year or two to settle down.

Another cause is the size of pot into which you repotted. This plant blooms best as a reaction to being crowded and when it is made to compete hard with pressing neighbours. This is why, when a bulb is bought in a kit complete with pot and soil, the pot is only just large enough to take the bulb—it is not the nurseryman being stingy!

Inevitably, with such a small quantity of soil upon which to rely for nutrients, supplementary feeding is essential, with repotting into fresh soil only every four years. When in full leaf, they need plenty of light to enable the reserves to be built up to nourish the embryo bud within, but standing the plant outdoors is a very risky business not only because of chilling temperatures, but also the extreme rapidity with which the pot can dry out. If this happens, any embryo bud that was forming for next year will have checked and withered long before the foliage shows any sign of distress—and it takes a lot to make Hippeastrum wilt.

Therefore, leave the plant for one more season in its present pot; keep it in the greenhouse or conservatory in full light at all times and don't let it become dry. Liquid feed it using Sangral or Seaweed Maxicrop every seven to ten days. If you should see a bloom bud forming, switch at once to the special 'tomato' or 'flower' variations of these fertilisers. These have a higher potash content than the 'general' form and will enhance the bloom colour as well as keeping the plant growing well. It then has every chance to build up reserves and, hopefully, a bud for next year. Gradually reduce watering in September so that by October to November the pot is quite dry. Divide the bulbs—but only if they will part easily. Don't force them apart, causing damage; it would be better to wait for another four years or so until the next re-pot. Plant the splits or whole bulb as the case may be into 6–7 inch pots, no larger, using one part by bulk John Innes No. 2, a half part sand and to each 7-inch pot a heaped teaspoonful of bone meal and a level teaspoonful of Humber Eclipse or Growmore. Position the bulbs only two-thirds deep in this compost. At this point, you pick up the normal routine and continue as for bulbs that are not being repotted. Keep them quite dry and frost-free, of course, until the end of January when you should begin watering and weak-feeding, slowly at first and increasing as foliage grows.

You may be lucky and get a bloom in the first season after the repot; if not, carry on as directed for this year aiming for healthy hard working foliage, then during the autumn–winter rest, instead of another repot, simply scrape off the top inch of soil and replace it with J. I. No. 2 compost plus a level teaspoonful of Eclipse or Growmore.

If you don't get a bloom after this, you never will, and you can consider the bulb to be blind.

331 Bulb fibre

Can you tell me the formula for bulb fibre?

There is no specific formula for bulb fibre—proprietary and local nursery-made formulae vary a great deal. However, since 'bulb fibre' usually means fibre for spring-flowering bulbs like hyacinth, daffodils, crocus etc., here is a fibre you can make up yourself. I have used it, both privately and commercially with every success.

Rub new Moss Peat from a pack or bale through a $\frac{1}{2}$-inch sieve and moisten it. Do this by watering very lightly with a fine rose on the can, turning the peat, watering again, turning again and then leaving for fifteen minutes while the peat absorbs the moisture. Then repeat the whole procedure until the peat is uniformly moist, but not wet; moist so that when you squeeze it in the hand it still crumbles—and not so wet that it remains a congealed lump.

Most proprietary bulb fibres contain a little charcoal which is not always easy to obtain in the relatively small quantities amateur gardeners will need. You could make your own by burning wood but this is not convenient for many with limited facilities and you may, therefore, have to use an alternative. The primary use of the charcoal is to hold the compost open whilst being itself absorbent of moisture.

Ceiling tiles and a lot of commercial packaging is nowadays made of expanded polystyrene. This can be used as an alternative to charcoal—it is very friable and can be granulated quite easily by grating it against a $\frac{1}{2}$-inch sieve. You will need the equivalent of about seven to eight cupfuls of this crumbled polystyrene to each bushel of peat. Or you could cut up into very small pieces the soft kind of moulded polystyrene used for egg boxes.

The white flecks in proprietary bulb fibres are oyster shell, added so that the soluble lime keeps the fibre 'sweet'. Not everyone has a private supply of oysters so again an alternative is needed—and you can do this quite easily by crushing egg shell. You will need two cupfuls of shell per bushel and this will take a surprising number of eggs, so you will need to start collecting them well ahead. Allow the shells to dry—the remains of the egg white can smell if you don't—and then crush them very finely under a rolling pin. If you want to make more bulb fibre than you have egg shells for, use ground limestone instead—and if you can't get that, use half the quantity of ground chalk.

So into your bushel of peat, crumbled polystyrene granules and crushed egg shells mix 2 heaped dessertspoonfuls of Growmore or Humber Eclipse and a handful of garden soil to introduce the soil bacteria needed to decompose the plant nutrient, and you have an ideal bulb fibre.

332 Cyclamen : care and treatment

Can our pot-grown Cyclamen, which has just finished flowering, be preserved for another year?

Certainly it can; Cyclamen corns can be kept going for very many years. When the flowers have finished, put the plant in a cool greenhouse but away from full sun. If you don't have a greenhouse you will have to compromise, and do as best you can with a window ledge—and of course many people are very successful with no better facilities than this. Keep the soil moist and the foliage growing strongly until mid-April, when gradually reduce watering so that by May–June, the pot is almost dry and the foliage has died back. Then place the plant on a dark shelf or underneath the staging of the greenhouse, covered so that it remains dry. If you are using the greenhouse to grow crops that require heat and/or humidity it will not do for Cyclamen. Try to keep them cool, don't let the temperature get like an oven. Don't water for six weeks, until mid or end of July when the corm can be broken out from the old soil and repotted.

The corm should be on top of and only slightly pressed into a compost mix of two parts John Innes No. 2 compost, plus a half part each of peat and silver sand. Stand in a shady part of the greenhouse away from direct sun, and begin watering, slowly at first, gradually increasing as foliage develops. Take care to water only at the side of the corm, not letting the water reach the top and centre of it. This is especially important as the corm becomes old and increases in diameter; a wet corm can soon start to rot.

As soon as flower buds can be detected arising from the corm in between the leaves, scratch in a ½ teaspoonful of Growmore or Eclipse, plus a small pinch of sulphate of potash; repeat this every three to four weeks to enhance the colour of the bloom. During the winter keep Cyclamen at a steady 50°F, anything higher will only force them and shorten the flowering period.

333   Daffodil bulbs with a grub inside

I have just dug up some 'King Alfred' daffodil bulbs and every one was rotten with a grub inside it. What is this trouble and is there a cure?

The trouble—narcissus fly—is probably the worst pest affecting daffodils, narcissi, jonquils and other members of the narcissi family. As always, the best way to control a pest is to look at its life cycle, and work out the times and ways in which it is possible to attack it, and the times when it is safely holed up and a waste of time trying.

Adult flies appear in May and June and do not have to travel far to lay their eggs—back on the same bulb patch. This explains why once the pest announces its presence with a few bulbs going blind, widespread blinding invariably follows.

Eggs are laid low down in and on the neck of the foliage where it emerges from the soil, larvae hatch, enter the bulb and eat away the central core. This is where the embryo bud is poised waiting to burst into growth next spring, and once eaten away there can be no flower but only leaves from the outer scales of the bulb. In time, even these can be destroyed and a patch of bulbs be completely wiped out.

The two methods of attack are the old, and one time only, method of contact poison which is directed against the adult fly when it lays its eggs; and the more modern method of stomach poison which is introduced into the plant's sap stream to poison the grub as soon as it bites.

The focal point in the pest's life cycle is the laying of the eggs, because they all have to be laid in the same position and within a relatively short period—in the neck of the bulb in the period between flowering and leaf die-back. As the flies jockey for position and climb on and around this part of the foliage, this is the position to lay on contact poison. It will have to be applied repeatedly throughout the period of egg laying, and beyond both ends of the period in order to catch the early risers and the late comers.

Dusting with Gamma BHC is the normal method. You can either use a puffer that squirts dust, or shake it down from a perforated can or a stocking bag. The former is best because this dusting is a two-handed job. If you are going to do it properly, you will need to use one hand to 'part' the foliage whilst you 'puff' with the other, getting the dust in between the leaves as they arise from the bulb necks as well as round the outside. This will have to be done weekly without fail from the latter half of April, normally until mid-July.

This will kill most of the flies, but you will not necessarily have got all the eggs, and as it is to be expected that some larvae will be able to bore down, it is a good idea to stop the dusting a little early, say, at beginning of June and to replace the end overlap of the egg laying period by literally poisoning the bulbs so that as the larvae begin to bite, they get a stomachful and die, hopefully before they harm the bud or devour the central cone. A full strength spraying over the foliage of a systemic insecticide every seven to ten days from the beginning of July until the foliage has yellowed and is well into die-back should ensure that the poison is carried down into the bulbs and thus render them toxic to any grubs that get that far. Add a few drips of liquid detergent to make sure the spray 'wets' the foliage, and don't waste the poison by letting it drip on the soil. Use a very fine spray so that it floats on and sticks.

334   Daffodils and ground cover

I want to plant 'King Alfred' daffodils in a border facing south-east. Can you recommend suitable ground cover I could grow with these daffodils?

The choice of ground cover plants in association with daffodils must be governed by the consideration that after flowering it is necessary to allow the bulb foliage to carry on growing, to die back naturally and completely. During this period, the border is bound to look somewhat bedraggled as the ground cover plants are submerged by the daffodils' top growth. For this reason, I would think that the best arrangement would be to set the daffs in well-spaced groups or clumps so that the ground cover is not over-powered by a more general spread of resulting top growth.

Suitable plants for your purpose—given in alphabetical order so that you can look them up easily in the catalogues—would be: *Ajuga reptans*, *Alchemilla mollis*, varieties of Anchusa, the beautiful Campanulas, *C. portenschlagiana*, *C. garganica* and *C. arvanica*, and the natural Geraniums, *G. sanguineum* and *G. endressii*. The shorter heathers could be used if your soil is acid. Heuchera is worth a place if only for the mass of fiery red hazy bloom that gets up high enough to smother the remnants of the daffs. The wonderful colour and form variation in the range of Hostas means that they cannot be left out, there are a great many to choose from and their 'lily' blooms are an added attraction.

The creeping forget-me-not *Omphalodes verna* would be useful at the front as it only gets up to about 6 inches. *Polygonum vaccinifolium* is worth looking into; it covers well and puts up pink bloom towards autumn, at a time when colour is getting a bit scarce.

The periwinkles, *Vinca major* and *V. minor*, often suffer the stigma of being regarded as 'common' which is a pity because the flowers are pretty and there are charming variegated leaf forms of both. There are several varieties of Viola that should do well; one of the best is the apricot-orange coloured variety 'Chantreyland'.

Finally, perhaps not quite what you had in mind but worth thinking about, is a massed planting of dwarf lavenders. There are several forms available now, giving blooms from deep blue to pale pink, and of course the grey-green of their foliage is a very effective background to the yellow of the daffodils.

335   Delaying bulbs starting into growth

We decided to have a lovely show of spring bulbs this year and a lot of bulbs we ordered have now been delivered. However, we have just learned that we have got to move house in a couple of months' time. As I shall want them for my new garden, can you suggest what I can do about my bulbs.

It depends upon just how later than normal the planting can be done. If by a few weeks or a month or maybe two, then by keeping small quantities in the bags in which they are packed (larger quantities should be opened so that air circulates around the bulbs) in the coolest driest place you can find, you should be able to delay their starting into growth, and then plant them very late. I would not recommend anything quite so drastic, but I have known of crocus, daffodils and tulips put in the vegetable drawer of a fridge, planted in late February and giving a marvellous show!

If it is to be close to the New Year before they are likely to be planted, it would be much safer to prepare boxes of peat. Tomato trays or something similar from the greengrocer are ideal for this. Examine your bulbs each week and if they show they cannot wait any longer and begin to sprout shoots and roots, you will have to plant them in the peat—otherwise they will be spoiled.

They can then go through the process of beginning their growth; keep the peat a little on the dry side to hold them back. Keep them in the same cool place and when you are able, transfer each growing bulb with a root ball of peat attached straight into a permanent position in the new garden.

Bulbs specially prepared to bloom quickly and early—hyacinths for Christmas, for instance—cannot be long delayed. These would normally be planted in bowls or pots, and perhaps you could take these with you. If this is not possible, it would be better to give them away to someone who would appreciate them.

336 Fritillaria : the Crown Imperials

Several years ago I was given several small bulbs of Crown Imperial, Fritillaria imperialis. *They came into weak bloom two to three years later, so last year after the second lot of indifferent bloom I dug some peat into the soil. This year they seem to be 'blind' and I haven't had a single bloom.*

Coming from Asia, this lily is very fussy, and there are a number of conditions it doesn't like and which can cause it to go blind.

Probably the most common cause of trouble is a soil that is too loose, and as they positively detest root disturbance, digging peat into the soil after they had settled and flowered was about the worst thing you could have done. If it should become necessary to remove weeds nearby, keep hoeing or forking to the very minimum and always firm the soil again by careful treading. The very best position for Imperials is in a grassed-down orchard where the soil is undisturbed and, in addition, they receive an annual mulch by virtue of the scything of the long grass prior to fruit picking plus the later leaf fall. You should have worked compost into the soil before planting and the peat you dug in would have been better laid as a mulch. This would also have been beneficial in conserving moisture, and this could be another clue to the loss of bloom because dryness at the root in spring will invariably cause the blooms to abort.

Finally, the bulbs should be deeply planted, with at least 5 inches of soil above the bulb. If your bulbs were not planted to these conditions, you should consider sacrificing bloom for another couple of years and do the job properly. Move these bulbs to a spot where they will be in dappled sunlight and undisturbed soil. Move them in October, planting 8–10 ins. apart and mulch well. Then leave them well alone to replenish themselves.

337 Gladiolus : will small corms flower?

I ordered a large number of '6–8 cms. gladioli bulbs', but when they arrived, I was astonished at how small they were. Will they flower this year? I have just finished planting them about 3 in. apart.

Small size corms can often be bought in bulk quite cheaply and this is an excellent way to build-up a stock, but you will have to be patient for a year or two further whilst they increase their size. The ideal size corms for good Gladiolus blooms are those described as 12–14 cms., that is, whose circumference measures between 12 and 14 cms. or if it helps you to visualise better another way, about $1\frac{1}{2}$ ins. diameter. See also *No. 342.*

The corms you have bought are small, but it is quite likely that some of the larger ones will put up a bloom in the first year, but don't expect anything very wonderful. Like the crocus, the Gladiolus corm withers and dies each year and is replaced by a new corm that forms immediately above the old. Given good growing conditions, all the new corms that will form in the first year should be considerably larger and should all flower next time.

338 Hemerocallis, the Day Lily

Could you tell me what is wrong with my day lilies? I have had three plants in the garden for at least two years and although they are very healthy, there have been no flowers yet.

Several plants, commonly and variously called lilies because their blooms are lily-like, are not true lilies. Hemerocallis are herbaceous perennials and have the name Day Lilies because each bloom looks like a lily and only lasts a day. However, despite the short life of each bloom, a fresh one is opened each day and the flowering is extended over a surprisingly long period. Their origins are widespread: most of the species come from southern Europe, and temperate regions of Asia from Siberia to China and Japan, and there are innumerable hybrids in cultivation.

Hemerocallis doesn't like root disturbance and takes time to settle down after replanting, usually a couple of years at least. The modern hybrid varieties, with a very much wider colour range of pinks, reds, maroons etc. usually take longer than the older yellow and orange varieties. The best way to shorten the settling-in period is to do all you can to make them feel at home. Leave them alone once they are planted and, because planting time is the very last opportunity for a long time to do anything about the soil underneath them, upon which they will be depending, it is essential to fork in plenty of well-rotted compost beforehand. This will help to ensure that they won't become thirsty in dry spells. Thirsty plants cannot be expected to flower, nor can hungry plants, and Hemerocallis are hungry feeders.

Supplementary feeding is essential, not only to bring new plantings into bloom but also, even in a rich soil, to avoid rapid decline into mediocrity. Cover new plantings with a mulch cover of compost or peat during mid-March, scratch into this a slow-acting balanced nutrient source like Growmore or Humber Eclipse at 2 oz. per sq. yd., and add to the mulch cover if necessary. Repeat with a second feed dressing at the same rate, scratched in four to six weeks later. If the foliage shoots are developing by this time, give them a quick flick over with the hosepipe after spreading down the fertiliser in order to avoid any possibility of scorch on the soft young growth.

Day lilies like plenty of light, so if they are not in a bright sunny position—and perhaps did not have plenty of compost dug in under them when planted—then you should consider an even further delay in blooming by re-planting during the autumn.

339 Hyacinths: correct treatment of bulbs after flowering

I've several pots of faded indoor hyacinths. Can I use the bulbs again next year?

Hyacinths are at their best in their first year, after that they decline year by year. This decline can be hastened, and usually is, by not allowing the foliage to grow on and thrive after blooming. This is the period when next year's embryo bud is being nurtured. All too often bulbs are grown in bulb fibre which, unless you make your own (see *No. 331*) does not contain much plant food. With nothing given other than plain water, the bulb is not given a chance to give even a second rate bloom next time.

When grown in bowls or pots the best way to deal with hyacinths is, immediately after blooming and with as little disturbance to the root ball as possible, plant the bulbs in an open but lightly-shaded position in the garden and allow them to grow on and build-up energy until the foliage dies back naturally. You can then lift them, dry them out and pot up again for next year. Or you can leave them in the ground. Naturalised like this, smaller but nonetheless attractive flowers will appear each spring for several years until the bulb finally declines through old age.

If the bulbs have been grown until blooming in bulb fibre and fed on little else than plain water, the bulb will be very very depleted, living mostly on the food reserve within the bulb. In this case, encourage them with a sprinkling of Growmore or Humber Eclipse and cover the bulb area with a light mulch of compost.

340 Iris: treatment for poor flowering

I have an ordinary purple border Iris which has been in the same position for three years. It is in full sun and the ground gets very dry in summer. The plant has now thirty or more sets of leaves, but had only two flowers this year. Can I do anything to get more flowers please?

Border Iris should be lifted, divided and replanted every fourth year, but as your Iris have done so poorly I wouldn't wait for the fourth year; lift them at the first opportunity, autumn or early spring.

If you are doing the job in autumn, each new division should consist of a young rhizome with a good fan of leaves attached. On the other hand, if you are dividing in early spring with little or no leaf growth yet showing after the winter, ensure that the divided rhizome(s) have a good growth bud. Choose the sunniest position you can and prepare the soil by forking in a little well-rotted compost and, most important, if you can get it, plenty of old mortar rubble, or you can make up a very good substitute. You generally buy sand from the garden shop by the bushel—a bushel contains 8 gallons dry measure—and a gallon of sand will be enough to dress a square yard so you can easily calculate how much you will need for the area you are going to plant up. Into each gallon of sand mix 2 ozs. lime and 2 ozs. gypsum; if you are on heavy clay make it 4 ozs. gypsum. Spread over each square yard of planting area and lightly fork or hoe it into the top 3 inches.

Plant the young rhizomes 15–18 ins. apart half-exposed on the surface and with the roots well anchored in the soil. It is a good idea to sit the rhizome on a little mound and let the roots fall down the slope on either side; then fill in and firm. In late March, or a little later if you have just recently planted, dust down a light dressing of balanced plant food, Growmore or Humber Eclipse, at 1½ ozs. per sq. yd. It will be risky to scratch it into the surface for fear of dragging up the roots, so water it in, and repeat the dressing once only, four weeks later. There is no reason now why you should not have lots of fine blooms.

Keep an eye open for snails, an arch enemy of Iris. You can clear them quite easily by setting slug traps as described in *No. 511*.

341 *Lilium regale : care and cultivation*

I have received ten Lilium regale *bulbs and I would like your advice regarding cultivation, i.e. distance apart, depth of planting, height, and if I should leave the bulb in the ground over winter? Also how often is it necessary for them to be lifted?*

As with all Liliums, the regal lily from western China flowers best in a soil containing plenty of humus. The white, gold and purple stained blooms on a single stem are beauty enough, but in a group the beauty is magnified. Depending upon the soil and conditions, the stems are going to grow from three to six feet tall so that with several large trumpet blooms they will be top heavy and subject to wind sway. It follows that each stem will need firm 'grasping' by soil round its base so that the heavy stem does not flop. Planting, therefore, must be deep, with the top of the bulb a clear 6 in. below the surface. They also derive protection and are better supported against wind sway, if planted in groups. If you can choose a gap or clearing in the border or between shrubs from which they derive protection from wind and above which they can hold their blooms, so much the better.

For planting in groups of three or four or more, take out a hole approximately 2 ft. sq. and a full spit deep; take out the crumb and then half a spit of the sub-soil and move this off-site or scatter it nearby. Fork in a full bucket of compost into the bottom of this hole, plus a couple of ozs. of Growmore or Humber Eclipse and lightly tread firm. To give fierce drainage under them, set the bulbs on little mounds of sand 9 ins. apart remembering to keep the tops a good 6 ins. below the surrounding soil. Fill in carefully around the bulbs firming as you go.

Mark the outer edges of the planting area by pushing in a few split canes so that you can at once identify where the bulbs lie, and finish off by laying down a 2–3 inch thick mulch of compost over the planting area. As the stem grows and flower buds form, extra roots appear at the base of the stem; this is the plant looking for even more nutrient to support the blooms and also to get better anchorage and stability for what will become a top-heavy stem. Keep these roots covered with more compost and this will encourage and help the stem roots to develop fully.

Prepare for this stem rooting beforehand, when the shoots are only about 6–9 inches tall, by carefully scratching into the compost—

around but not nearer than 3 in. to each stem—
a couple of dessertspoonfuls of Growmore or
Humber Eclipse. The purpose of the 3 in. gap
is to make the stem roots go and look for food,
and in doing so, lengthen and develop.

If the lilies should need extra support later
as they become tall, put several stakes in a
ring around, but well away from the group so
that roots are not damaged, and enclose them
within a tall 'cage' by stringing round.

Replenish the mulch cover as it becomes thin
and absorbed into the soil. In late February,
before the new shoots are near the surface,
scratch in a couple of ounces of the same
fertiliser as you used before (don't change to
another) and then once again, as before, when
the stems are at the 6–9 in. stage. With the
careful preparation outlined here, plus annual
feeding and mulching there is no reason why
the group of bulbs should not increase in
number and continue to bloom magnificently
for many years. If they become overcrowded,
choose a mild dry spell in October or as soon
after as you can, to carefully lift and replant
the young healthy bulbs in a fresh site as before
and rejuvenate the old place in the same way.

342   Measurement of bulb sizes

*Why do bulb suppliers advertise their bulb sizes
in centimetres instead of inches, and what does
the measurement exactly mean?*

Although now changing, Holland for a long
time has been the main centre of bulb production, and when we imported their bulbs we also
imported their system of measuring the sizes
which was expressed in the continental metric
system. The number of centimetres is intended
to indicate the circumference of the bulb or
corm, and although you can translate an inch as
approximately $2\frac{1}{2}$ centimetres, and a 10 cms.
bulb therefore as having a 4-in. circumference,
to do so could be a little misleading.

Bulbs are graded over a riddle—that is, a
grid with holes in it of the determinate size.
Thus a bulb described as 10–12 cms. is one
that would not pass through a 10 cm. circular
hole, but would fall through a 12 cm. hole. A
bulb that will not pass through a 12 cms. hole

must clearly be in a larger size range—i.e.
12–14 cms.—or above and, similarly, small
bulbs that drop through the 10 cms. hole but
are stopped by 8 cms. will be classified as 8–10
cms. et seq. Shape also plays an important
part: an awkwardly-shaped bulb but of relatively small bulk needs a larger hole than it
really qualifies for. But apart from this the
system works quite satisfactorily.

Now that we are adopting metrication in
this country, it should not be too long before we
learn to read and think in terms of centimetres, grammes and litres without the need to
make mental calculation to translate into the
familiar but out-dated impracticable inches,
ounces and pints.

343   Summer flowering bulbs

*After our spring Azaleas and Rhododendrons
have finished flowering they look very drab. We
now realise that we should also have planted
some summer and autumn-flowering shrubs, but
don't want to dig up our Azaleas and Rhododendrons which are well-established. Can you suggest any alternatives?*

A very interesting question, and here is a
suggestion that I am sure a lot of people will
want to try, with or without drab gardens!
Most people, when we speak of bulbs, tend to
think of spring with daffodils, tulips, hyacinths, crocuses and snowdrops. It is surprising how few people realise what an enormous
variety there is of bulbs that flower in summer,
even until late autumn. Many of these will get
up to 2, 3, 4 ft. or even higher and by planting
these under existing shrubs, so that they grow
up through the shrub foliage and hold their
flowers above the shrubs, you can bring colour,
beauty and interest to the garden for most
months of each year.

Outstanding for this purpose are the lilies
and probably the best place to see them used
in this way is at the R.H.S. Gardens at Wisley
in Surrey, where every year many, many
thousands of lilies grow through the Azaleas
and Rhododendrons to produce a sight that is
worth travelling a very long way to see. There

is a huge range of colour, height, season and cost among lilies. Write off for or collect a catalogue of summer bulbs from a good class supplier; and let your imagination run as far as your pocket will let it.

But, of course, you will not want to plant just lilies alone. For the edges of the shrubbery to grow through the dwarf Azaleas, try Nerines. They are often regarded as not quite hardy, which is not true, especially if you carpet the area where they are planted with a heavy protective layer of compost in the autumn. *N. bowdenii* is the best known, producing lovely rose pink blooms.

Getting up to 2–2½ ft. *Camassia cusickii*, bears in July, charming pale blue flowers with striking yellow stamens. Planted in groups of three or four, they will put a new lease of life and interest into the faded Azaleas and make your neighbours curious to find out what they are.

A little taller and later comes the 'summer hyacinth' *Galtonia candicans* with pure white wax-like bells. They multiply well and you shouldn't have to wait for single bulbs to form groups.

Not a bulb, but often classed with them, is *Crocosmia masonorum*, like a multi-headed, giant-sized orange scarlet Montbretia. It is inexpensive and should be grown more often.

In recent years the Gladioli have had a lot of attention from the hybridists, especially the Butterfly and Primulinus types. Many of these are hardy and can be left in the ground to multiply. They are well worth experimenting with and are surprisingly inexpensive.

These are some suggestions that can be relied on to put extra colour and interest into your garden. One thing is certain, summer and autumn-flowering bulbs growing through spring shrubs can put added interest into any garden.

Section VII

House and Indoor Plants

344 Achimenes: why the misnomer 'Hot Water Plant'

Could you tell me why my Achimenes will not flower? They were planted in late March, five to a 5 in. pot, in John Innes No. 2 compost. I keep the greenhouse at about 70°F. during the day and 55°F. at night.

Achimenes must have humid conditions and many gardeners fail with them by keeping them in a greenhouse which is also occupied by other plants and in deference to their opposing requirements, the Achimenes suffer. Unless you grow cucumbers in their own greenhouse or in a segregated part of one where they can be provided with the humid atmosphere they need, and you can move your Achimenes in with them, you will need to improvise and experiment.

Many enthusiasts faced with this kind of problem rig up a humidity case, like a miniature greenhouse within the greenhouse, in order to trap a mini-atmosphere which can easily be kept humid. However, in the absence of anything so elaborate, you can give the plants a weekly steam bath. Stand the plant in its pot on another upturned in a bowl, and pour very hot water in the bowl. The plants revel in the rising steam and this has led to their common name 'Hot Water Plants'. However, don't make the mistake that some people make, by watering the plants with hot water!

In order to keep the air humid around the plant, the best everyday cultivation procedure indoors is to stand the plants on a tray of sand or grit that is kept wet. In the greenhouse, water the floor several times a day and hang an old blanket in a bowl of water, like a large wick.

You must also change the growing medium; five tubers to a 5-inch pot is fair enough, but the compost needs to contain more organic matter. Use a mixture of half Levington compost or peat, and a half John Innes No. 1, compost. Plant 1½ inches deep into this compost, and loosely. Never firm the growing medium for this plant. Finally spread a ½ in. layer of coarse peat overall. 55°F. is an absolute minimum for Achimenes, but try to keep it a little higher, 60°F. if possible, and unless you are going to keep them in a humidity case, apply shading over head; they will not stand exposure to full sunshine.

345 Aechmea: watering is all-important

I bought an Aechmea plant about 3 in. tall about two years ago. It grew, but many leaves turned pink and died. I potted it on with, I think the correct soil, and carefully avoided getting water in the centre, as the florist advised. It is now 12 in. high with an off-shoot 6 in. high, but there has been no flower.

Aechmea is a sub-tropical plant from South America and, as you might expect, two primary conditions that should be avoided are temperatures less than 60°F. and draughts. This applies not only to the treatment that you give the plant, but also to what happens to it before you acquire it. It sounds likely in other words, that the plant was badly chilled before you acquired it. Aechmea needs a very moist atmosphere at all times with copious watering, with very weak liquid manure added during spring and summer, reduced only a little to moderate watering in autumn and winter—using rainwater at all times. The central cup should always be kept filled with rainwater; the advice given by the florist was wrong.

After it has flowered, the main rosette will naturally decline, but before it dies it should put out one or more new shoots, which can be left attached to the parent stump, or separated and potted in spring into the smallest pots that will contain their roots in a compost composed of equal parts, coarse moss peat, sphagnum moss and sharp sand. These should be mature enough to bloom in two to three years' time.

346 African Violets: care and cultivation

I admire African violets and would like to develop a good collection, but I don't seem to have much success. Can you please tell me about their cultivation likes and dislikes so that I can see if I am doing something wrong. And is there a better method of increasing them other than seed?

The cultivation of Saintpaulia is one of the most frequently raised problems because so many people want to grow this attractive small plant from Central Africa in their homes.

They need a growing medium that is not particularly rich but which contains plenty of organic matter—an ideal mix is three parts of the mild John Innes No. 1, plus 1 part moss peat that has been rubbed through a ½ inch sieve. Place drainage crock in the pot; they will not stand poor drainage. Healthy plants can be grown in 3½–4 inch pots but, as they grow bigger, they will resent root cramping and should either be potted into a larger pot or be propagated to produce fresh young plants. It is these that will give the best bloom.

Be careful not to overwater—little at a time and just enough to keep the soil moist. If you are growing cucumbers, perhaps, or other plants for which you are steeping manure in water, see *No. 412*, use this humus-laden manure water instead. Be careful, also, not to let the leaves become wet or allow water to splash into the plant centres especially in autumn and winter when the plants are naturally slowed down, because this is the surest way to cause rotting. Water just at the rim of the pot or, if there are too many leaves and you are not too sure, water from below by immersing the pot for a few minutes. Whilst they will not tolerate wetness at roots or on their leaves, they must have a moist atmosphere and this is probably the most serious fault affecting indoor culture. In the greenhouse it is a simple matter to stand the pots on a wet gravel bench, but on an indoors windowsill you can help them by standing them on a plate of sand that is kept wet so that moist air can rise round the leaves.

Standing Saintpaulias on windowsills can be another reason why they are unhappy; they need plenty of light—this is the most prevalent reason for poor flowering—but they must not be placed in full sunlight. Make sure they are not subjected to a temperature below 55°F. and they will continue to bloom for a surprisingly long time—even every month of the year is by no means uncommon. Incidentally, growing them on windowsills can be yet another reason for poor flowering because

pulling the curtains each evening isolates air behind from the warmth of the room, and in contact with an expanse of cold glass, the trapped air very soon cools down to below the critical 55°F.

Propagation can be by sowing seed in late spring into the same compost as they will later grow in, and in a minimum temperature 65°F. When the seedlings are large enough to handle, move them into 3½–4 inch pots. Seed is expensive, so if you want a variation of colours—violet, blue, through paler shades and pink to white—make sure you get a strain that includes all colours and is not a reselected strain to give mainly one colour. 'Fairy Tale' from Thompson and Morgan, Ipswich, contains a wide colour range.

When the plants are established you can reproduce your favourites true to colour—and of course pinch bits of your friends' plants —by propagating them by leaf cuttings. Select mature and healthy outer leaves. Cut them with a razor blade or very sharp knife as close as possible to the point of origin, and either place them in a small jar of rainwater where they will soon produce root and should at once be potted up with the rooted tip no more than a half inch below soil surface, or by dibbering the leaves around the edge of a large pot of sandy compost and moving the ensuing plantlets into individual pots. Plants propagated by cuttings will have exactly the same flowers—colour and single or double—as the parent, whereas you will not know what the flowers of seedlings will be until they flower.

347 *Anthurium, the flamingo plant*

I have a plant that I understand is called 'Flamingo'. It is in a 5 inch pot and the roots appear to be coming out of the top. What is the best way to look after this plant?

The flamingo plant, Anthurium, comes from South America and bears a yellow flower spike accompanied by a spathe, very like that of its close relation, the Arum Lily, except that the spathe is brilliant red and is flatter and shield-shaped instead of tubular.

As this plant is outgrowing its 5 inch pot,

repot it into a 7 to 8 in. pot during February, keeping the crown well up above the compost or, if possible, divide the root into pieces each with a growth shoot, and plant into separate 5 or 6 in. pots, using a compost mix made up of equal parts by bulk John Innes No. 1 and peat.

Stand the pots on rough peat or sphagnum moss in a position that is well shaded from direct sun, and heap more peat around the pot(s) so that each is standing in peat moss for about a third of its depth. From now on, this should be kept permanently wet so that a very humid atmosphere rises around the plants. Feed with liquid manure every fourteen to twenty-one days and allow the temperature to rise to 70–80°F.

The brilliant coloured spathes are carried for a long period during late spring and summer. From October, reduce the watering gradually so that by November it is just enough to prevent the evergreen leaves from shrivelling. During the winter rest, the temperature must not be allowed to drop below 55°F.

As February and March come round again gradually increase watering; liquid feeding and a rise in temperature will again bring the plants into active growth. Repotting should not normally be needed more often than at three-year intervals, when root divisions can be taken at the same time.

348 Aphelandra needs special conditions

Could you please give me some advice on how to look after a pot plant called Aphelandra? It appears to be tropical, has variegated leaves and yellow flowers.

Aphelandra is a native of tropical South America and although its attractively veined leaves and conspicuous yellow flower heads make it a popular plant, you will have to imitate its tropical environment in your home, if it is to be at all happy as a room plant. Its natural habitat is a humid atmosphere and a constant temperature—60°F. is ideal, 50°F. too low, and below that hopeless. In most homes, there is a temperature drop during the night and the air is often much too dry,

especially where there is central heating or electric fires.

The plant needs plenty of light, but not direct sunlight. This means light all round and even if stood in a well-lit window, there is always the dark side and the plant should be turned frequently so that all the leaves get a fair share of the available light. A greenhouse or conservatory therefore is the best proposition but if you must bring it into the house, bring it in for a few days only, returning it to the greenhouse or conservatory to recuperate.

During the growing period from May to August or September, the plant needs abundant watering with diluted liquid manure; any dryness at root level will lead to the first stages of leaf wilting—dull sheen, lifeless appearance —and if this is allowed to become wilt, with the leaves actually drooping, it can be too late. Aphelandra is one plant that soon reacts by shedding leaves.

During the winter months, watering can be reduced to just enough to keep the soil moist. An overwet soil and/or draughts at this time will also almost certainly cause leaf fall.

During the growing season, humid conditions must be maintained and you can go a long way towards creating the humidity it needs by mist spraying with clear rain water daily. Never use tap water because it contains lime. Position the pot on a peat or shingle tray that is kept wet at all times, so that this keeps moist air rising around the plant.

349 Aspidistra: the correct way to repot

When should I divide up and repot my Aspidistra and what kind of compost should I use? The last time I repotted it, I used ordinary garden soil and the plant did not seem to like it. Does it ever flower?

Aspidistra, the parlour palm, originates from China, and is one of the most tolerant plants of mismanagement; it will grow in quite poorly-lighted rooms, hence its popularity in Victorian times.

It does best away from direct sunlight, in soil that avoids stagnant waterlogging and in a soil structure that is more open than plain garden soil. A suitable compost would be equal parts of sieved garden soil (or even better, John Innes No. 1 compost) peat and sand, with a wad of rough peat over plenty of crock in the bottom of the pot. Repotting is best done in March, and at this time roots can be divided into pieces, each having a leaf or shoot.

Watering should be carried out by immersing the pot in rainwater at room temperature. An evergreen, it will need to slow down in winter, but not stop altogether. Watering, therefore, should be reduced but not withheld. Try to maintain a temperature of 50°F. — with a rock bottom minimum of 40–45°F.

An Aspidistra, growing well in the partially shaded conditions it likes, will sometimes produce a flower, a lurid pinkish affair at soil level. Its only interest is one of curiosity because in its native habitat, this bloom is pollinated by a snail!

350 Aspidistra: why the variegated kind turns green

About half the new leaves produced this year on my very large variegated Aspidistra are plain green. Is there anything I can do to keep them all variegated?

Loss of variegation in the leaves of ornamental plants is a problem that worries a lot of people but is quite easy to understand if you approach it in this way. In many plants—the variegated Aspidistra is one of these—the stripes, blotches or other variegation are not 'fixed' and the variegation is no more than a tendency that will occur and remain only if conditions are favourable. The variegation is caused by the absence —or very much diminished presence in the parts concerned—of the green colouring matter, chlorophyll. This is contained in small cells, called chloroplasts and is where the joining together of carbon dioxide gas and water takes place to form simple carbohydrate compounds, which are later elaborated into sugars, starches, cellulose, etc. The source of energy needed to do this is light and to produce all the carbohydrate a plant needs, sufficient light has to reach the plant and be absorbed. If there is more light than a plant needs it may— and only may because it is a tendency and there is no certainty that it will—be able to manage with a reduced amount of chlorophyll in its leaves. In some cases, this will take the form of areas of leaf left devoid of the green colouring, or where it is sufficiently reduced—i.e. lighter green—to produce the variegations that we find attractive.

This can only happen, however, where the light intensity is more than adequate. Place the plant in a position where the light intensity is reduced below critical level and it will have to produce more chlorophyll and increase its area of green, filling in the stripes and blotches and thus the variegation is lost. Some plants, variegated or not, are more tolerant of reduced light than others. This is one factor that makes them suitable as house plants, and the reduced light conditions that generally entails.

Other factors, like a pot-bound plant, for instance where the roots are working overtime in an overcrowded space trying to extract moisture and nutrient from a too small and worked-out volume of soil, can aggravate the position and trigger off a reversion, but the basic cause is a too low light intensity.

The 'tendency' factor, compared to a 'fixed variegation', also explains why some parts of a plant will vary in the 'tendency' to variegate and every gardener will know of examples where plants revert to type even in full light. Perhaps one of the most common examples is the Golden Privet hedge which reverts to green. The best way to maintain the tendency to variegation is to prune out or discard those parts that lose their variegation. In the case of Aspidistra this would take the form of repotting and dividing every three years or so, retaining only the best parts.

In the same way that reversion can be influenced by pot binding, nutrient availability will also aggravate the situation but you will now realise that although it will certainly help to follow the cultivation outlined in *No. 349*, the variegated Aspidistra is more intolerant of really poor light, and you should therefore move it into a much brighter position—but not direct sunlight.

351   Azalea : giving it a new lease of life

Where am I going wrong with an indoor Azalea that refuses to thrive?

The Azaleas grown and sold as potted plants for indoor culture are all bushy evergreen shrubs, and are less hardy than those that are planted in the garden. Their treatment is altogether different to the hardy kinds and there are all manner of things you could be doing wrong, probably the three most important likely causes of failure are lime in the soil or water, light intensity and incorrect watering.

Indoor Azaleas fall into three basic groups which flower at periods from November to April and in advising the time for repotting, one can only say immediately after flowering. Until you repot, water only with rainwater. Where an Azalea has been watered with tap water and there is the consequent possibility of lime having been introduced to the soil, you should use a method that is described in several other places in this book. Put tea leaves or tea bags from the tea pot into a bag and steep this in rainwater. Use this liquor to water your Azalea, renewing the tea leaves as they become worked out. The acidity of the tannin in the tea helps to overcome the lime already in the soil and which this plant detests.

At repotting time, turn the plant out and tease loose some of the roots from the root ball so that they bite into the new soil more easily. Scrape off any soil at the top of the ball that is free of root and replant in the same size pot, or if the soil ball is tight with root and a larger size pot is clearly needed, use only the next size pot. Use lime-free Bower's Ericaceous Mixture —most garden shops should be able to supply this—but if you have any difficulty and have to make up your own compost, try to collect some soil, perhaps from the countryside, from under a wild rhododendron or from a heather-covered common or moor where these grow wild, not where they are being cultivated because the soil may have had to be specially treated. Collect soil from where they grow wild, and you can rely upon the soil being lime-free. Use equal parts of this soil mixed with moss peat, and a little sand.

Not every gardener will be able to journey to an area where heather and rhododendrons grow wild, or for that matter live within reach of a garden shop or centre where lime-free compost can be obtained so here is a compost mix in which I have been able to grow excellent Azaleas: equal parts John Innes compost No. 1 and peat, and a half part each spent tea leaves and sand, and only water with 'tea-leaf rainwater' which will overcome the small amount of calcium in the J.I. compost.

The second important factor why potted Azaleas become unhappy and where they are often at a disadvantage compared with permanent outdoor plantings, is lack of light. After flowering, stand the pot in a position in the open where it can receive all possible light until it is autumn when it should be taken inside again.

It is this period of several months standing out in the open that inevitably pinpoints the third factor—i.e. the ease and speed with which the potted plant can dry out. Azaleas are particularly vulnerable because they have a very fibrous root system that completely permeates and fills the root ball with root. If this is allowed to dry out, watering from above is useless because it runs off and does not soak into the matted dried-out ball. Quite literally, many potted Azaleas which are allowed to get into this condition die of drought whilst being watered overhead twice a day!

If the plant foliage becomes dull and limp, it's a sure sign it is suffering from dryness at the roots. There is only one way to put this right; the pot must be immersed in water—rainwater—and kept there for at least half an hour after the bubbles cease. If, in the autumn you bring the plant into a centrally-heated house where the air is dry, stand the pot on a tray of shingle kept wet at all times so that humid air can rise. In addition, mist spray the foliage with tepid rainwater daily until the green buds begin to break colour, then stop as the continued spraying may damage the soft petals. See also *No. 352*.

352 Azalea: too much water will produce brown leaf tips

Can you tell me how to avoid the brown spots which appear on the tips of the leaves of our Azalea when it is brought back into the house, having been taken into the garden after flowering. Here it is placed in the ground and watered every day. Could the trouble be due to our central heating?

This is a symptom of overwatering. Azaleas must never be allowed to dry out, see *No. 351*, but your procedure is much too far in the other extreme. After the stress of blooming, the plant will need feeding and building-up whilst it gets on with the job of preparing next year's flower buds. Watering each day will soon wash out any plant nutrient in the soil within the pot. You would do better to put it into a moist peat bed where it can get plenty of light and feed it little and often with a long-lasting organic-based manure.

Rather than keep an Azalea in the centrally-heated house until it finally gives up, it is better to bring it into the adverse conditions inside the home for a day only, then out again to 'recuperate' and carry on growing more normally in the greenhouse or conservatory.

The fact that your plant rebels with brown spots so soon after coming back in the house, shows that it has not built-up vigour and health whilst outside and is not really healthy.

353 Barrels: suitable plants for

I have acquired a 45-gallon wooden barrel with 2 in. diameter holes drilled around the sides. I think it was used at one time for growing straw-berries but I would like to grow creeping perennial plants from the holes. Can you suggest some that would give a colourful display?

Growing colourful rock and trailing plants in barrels is a particularly good idea and especially suitable for those wishing to construct a highly decorative set piece for a patio or balcony. Several plants, perhaps usually associated with bedding, can be tried, particularly in the top of the barrel. Fibrous-rooted Begonia, Verbena and *Phlox drummodii* are ideal for the job and, topped off with an ivy leaf Geranium or a Fuchsia, with some blue and white edging of Alyssum and Lobelia, can provide a dazzling display.

However, you ask for creeping perennials—the point to bear in mind is that these must not be so rampant as to swamp everything else—and they will be required to hang down rather than ramble over. A number of 'rock' plants can be tried; Aubrietia, of course, in the many shades of lilac and mauve; the white blooms of Arabis and Iberis and the brilliant yellow of *Alyssum saxatile*. The unusual foliage of the yellow-flowered creeping Jenny, Lysimachia, will provide a nice contrast, but plant it high in the barrel so that the long stems can hang. *Campanula poscharskyana* is a must and, for providing colour later on into summer, try the yellows, oranges and reds of the many varieties of the rock rose Helianthemum.

Among the rock pinks, Dianthus, I have found the variety *D. temiscaming* very good for barrel work. Finally, try the *Fuchsia* 'Golden Marinka'. This is very much hardier than many give it credit for. Brilliant red flowers against yellow variegated foliage is attractive in itself, and trailing over the top of your barrel, it would make a very good colour foil to the other plants. Construct a drainage core and fill the barrel as described in *No. 246*.

354 Begonia: why blooms fail and fall

I have been trying to grow those tuberous Begonias with the very large flowers. Each year they start well, the buds form and then just as they begin to open, or even before, they suddenly stop in their stride and nearly always fall off. Can you suggest any reason why this happens?

The most likely reason for Begonias aborting bloom is that conditions do not suit them. However, the fact that you sucessfully cultivated it to the stage where it was about to bloom suggests that there was not a lot wrong during the approach to blooming and that the fatal condition came on fairly quickly. This would indicate dryness either at the roots or in the atmosphere around the plant, or both. The bloom of a double Begonia is very large and bulky and, as this is developing, the plant is demanding increasing moisture. Even a short period of dryness will put the plant in a state of shock; all it needs is a drop in temperature, a draught maybe, and the bloom aborts. This sensitivity is held by some growers to be more pronounced when the plant has been grown too lushly, and perhaps this is where you have gone a little astray. Therefore, here is a brief run-down on tuberous-rooted Begonia cultivation.

Begin by 'starting' the tubers in February or March by half-burying them in moist peat in a temperature of 60–65°F. When showing two or three leaves, pot up into 5 to 6 in. pots using a compost made up of one part by bulk John Innes No. 2, 1 part moss peat and a half-part sharp sand. Try to maintain the temperature between 63–68°F; a steady constant temperature throughout is essential, so is humidity, and as ventilation is important especially in hot weather in order to keep down the temperature, you will have to take special steps to keep the air moist.

Stand the plants on wet peat or wet shingle so that damp air can rise constantly over and around the plant. Keep them in a position where they have plenty of light but are protected from full sunlight. From May to October, water freely with very weak liquid manure. During the growth period the tuber and root ball must never, at any time, become dry. During October, however, the watering can be reduced to let the growth die down. This can then be cut off and the tubers stored dry and cool at a minimum of 40°F. If you can manage the extra 5°, 45°F. would be better, and in February or March you can start the tuber off again.

The big double blooms can become very heavy and are then quite liable to flop over, so take the precaution of tying the flower stalks individually to thin supporting canes to fit just below the blooms. Don't make the canes too obvious or you will spoil the appearance of your plant.

The spectacular large blooms are male and just below and to the side of them, two smaller comparatively insignificant flowers will appear.

These are females and because the plant will only use up energy in trying to set seed, which would be better reserved for the main bloom, remove them at the bud stage as soon as they are large enough to snap with the finger.

355 Beloperone : why the 'shrimps' fall off

A few weeks ago, I was presented with a lovely shrimp plant. Since then, the leaves and shrimps have been falling off (from the bottom) and I would like to know the cause and the remedy.

There are several species of shrimp plant but the one most commonly grown by far is *Beloperone guttata*. They are evergreens and come from the Grenada region of Brazil. The actual flowers are not very prominent, being almost entirely hidden and covered by the conspicuous pink sheath-like bracts which on good well-grown specimens are borne almost all year round.

To achieve this, the plant needs ideal conditions: plenty of light but not direct sun; no draughts and sudden variation in temperature; a minimum of 50°F. in winter, which means some heat in the greenhouse otherwise flowering and the pink 'shrimps' will cease.

They do not need a very rich growing medium—John Innes No. 1, compost is ample, but mix in a little coarse sand or grit to keep it open and prevent any suggestion of water-logging which harms the roots and hinders rather than helps uptake of moisture. This is the most common mistake made in growing Beloperone because keeping the soil reasonably moist is all that is needed. Too wet conditions can cause the root to rot and become unable to absorb moisture, causing the plant to flag. Many people react to this condition by thinking that the plant is dry and needs a drink and so give it even more water!

356 Beloperone: absence of shrimps after repotting

Why hasn't my two-year-old Beloperone flowered this year? I repotted it into a bigger pot and although it has made lots of new growth, there is no sign of a shrimp.

Repotting is the cause of the loss of your shrimps. Beloperone is one of those plants that need to have pressure put on them to make them flower more profusely (in this case the 'shrimps' are not the actual flowers but enlarged and coloured bracts that surround and almost hide them). The plant throws most flowers—shrimps—as a reaction to fierce overcrowded competition and you should therefore imitate this condition by confining the root system in a pot small enough to ensure that it is pot-bound.

For a plant to react by offering no shrimps at all suggests that the repotting was into a pot much larger than the original and probably also into a very rich compost. If there were a few shrimps perhaps and a not very large pot, one might suggest letting the plant grow and eventually create its own overcrowding, but in the circumstances described, there is really no alternative to reducing the pot size and getting the compost right.

During March, remove the plant from its pot and shake out the soil; remove long straggly shoots and use these if you want as cuttings to increase the stock. Select a pot into which the root system will comfortably go; then take the next size smaller! Pot up into this smaller pot using a compost mix of equal parts John Innes No. 1, peat and sand. Read *No. 355* about the conditions required for this plant. Because of the cramped root system, the plant will tend to become dependent on artificial feeding—which is as you want it— because it is this marginal fight for survival that produces the best shrimps.

Every fourteen days or so, apply a liquid feed made up by soaking old farmyard manure or mushroom compost in rain water to produce a golden brown liquor like cold brown tea. Add a few drops of proprietary liquid manure with a potash bias—like Sangral Tomato or Tomorite. These are normally intended to help ripening of fruit and putting colour into Chrysanthemums and Dahlias, and will have the same effect on your shrimps.

357 Bougainvillea: care and treatment

Please advise me on the care of Bougainvilleas. The one I purchased is in a pot and I was told that it had been hardened-off.

The spectacular Bouganvillea, so admired by those on holiday in warmer climates, must remain just a fond memory to all those who do not have a greenhouse because, coming from Brazil, it cannot be grown outside in Britain except in a very few favoured localities—the Scilly Isles and the Channel Isles for example. A greenhouse or conservatory is essential and it will have to be fairly large and tall because these are climbing plants and need plenty of headroom. They require a minimum temperature of 55°F. between February and May and 65–75°F. from May to September. During the winter right round to February, they need an absolute minimum of 50°F. Although no artificial heating is needed in summer, it is vital during the winter.

Actually it is not the flowers that produce the vivid colours of pink, magenta and orange, but adjacent large leafy bracts.

Set the plant in the greenhouse border, incorporating a little balanced plant food like Growmore or Humber Eclipse, plenty of peat or well-rotted compost and if you can get it, some builder's rubble containing old plaster. Every February at pruning time, spread 3–4 oz. of the same plant food on the soil surface up to 2–3 ft. away from the plant and cover with a 2 inch mulch of garden or mushroom compost. Hoe in half the previous amount of Humber during April. This heavy feeding is necessary in order to get the fullest colour into the bracts.

The plant needs full sunlight, and in summer full ventilation, which won't be difficult as you will need all the doors and windows open then to prevent the greenhouse becoming an oven. Water abundantly in March when growth is at its maximum, gradually reducing and drying from August so that by November watering has stopped altogether.

Prolific 'flowering' can be greatly enhanced in February, just before the heavy watering begins, by shortening back all shoots and growths of the previous year to a suitable bud within an inch or two of their base.

358   Cacti : making your own growing medium

I have a large collection of cacti and would like to know what form of lime is suitable for a potting compost. As the water in this area contains a lot of lime, is there any way in which it can be treated? Also, what fertilisers can I use which will not induce soft lush growth?

Cacti and other succulents are not so particular about their growing medium as many growers imagine. Having evolved on and become adapted to cope with dry arid conditions, they clearly do not need and will not relish a growing medium that is over-retentive of moisture. Use John Innes Potting compost No. 2, that has been made up from sterilised loam, so that you can be sure it is free of harmful organisms and weeds.

If you are making up your own—old stacked turves are fine for this—sieve the loam through a $\frac{3}{8}$-inch sieve to produce a quantity of friable crumbly soil. An old method of sterilising is to put about $\frac{1}{2}$–$\frac{3}{4}$ inch of water into an old saucepan, and bring it to the boil. Fill the saucepan with sieved soil, cover with a lid and allow to simmer for about a quarter of an hour. Since it is easy to burn the saucepan, use, if you've got one, an old porridge steamer and drill a few holes in the top part that usually holds the porridge. Or, a simple and safe method is to use a large tin can into which you have drilled several small holes. Fill this with loam. Stand it on a small tray or piece of wood in the bottom of the saucepan or a bucket so that the soil is clear of the boiling water. Subject the soil to fierce steaming for 20 minutes and it will be sterilised. Then it can be tipped out, and the can refilled for another batch.

The formulae given for most composts is normally quoted as so much fertiliser per bushel. But most amateurs will not be making up such large quantities so will need to calculate for lesser amounts.

When you have sterilised your loam and

allowed it to cool, use a small pot to measure out loam, sand and peat in the following proportions: 7 potfuls of loam, 3 of the same pot of sand and 2 pots of fine sieved peat. Mix thoroughly and into each gallon ($\frac{1}{8}$ bushel) of this, mix $\frac{1}{2}$ oz. of John Innes Base fertiliser (which you can buy in small quantities) plus a heaped teaspoonful of ground chalk. If you have difficulty in obtaining J.I. Base, use Humber Eclipse. Don't use lime; it is a little too fierce and chalk is milder.

This compost is normally quite rich enough for succulents, but for cacti you should add more sand in order to make it drain more fiercely. Most growers mix in an extra pot of sand to the original mix. If I can get it, instead of sand I prefer to use crushed plaster rubble (in which case the chalk should be omitted because the lime in the plaster will give you all you want), or crushed brick dust.

As your tap water is very alkaline, use rainwater. You will sometimes see the advice to add a little nitric acid to hard limy water, and my advice is don't. Nitric is a particularly dangerous and corrosive acid and not to be handled unless you know exactly what you are doing. It's far easier and safer to arrange for down pipes from the greenhouse roof to collect natural rain into water butts.

359   Cacti : are pencil-like shoots usual?

An Opuntia microdasys I grew from a cutting made normal oval-shaped leaf pads until recently. Then it started to produce round pencil-like leaves, and I wonder if this is unusual.

Opuntia—often called the prickly pear cactus —is not the only plant that has these thin pencil-like growths. They occur on many other cacti and succulents, notably on the so-called Easter Cactus, and are due to the plants being grown in insufficient light. These plants originate from regions of the world where the light intensity is much higher than in the U.K. It follows, therefore, that they need to be grown in positions where they can get all possible light. A greenhouse is the ideal, of course, or a conservatory, but failing such conditions, at

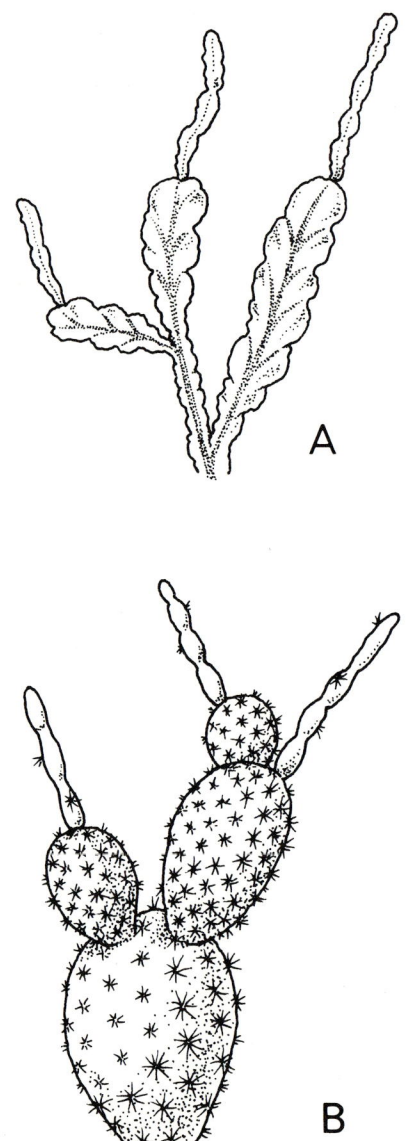

No. 359 *Echinocactus (A) and Opuntia (B) are two examples of cacti and succulents that put out thin uncharacteristic leaf growth in response to poor light.*

least position cacti and succulents on a sunny window sill.

The flowering cacti are very popular for the exotic, and sometimes extraordinary, blooms that they bear. Always bear in mind that the ability to build-up reserves and develop bloom depends directly upon enough light being absorbed.

360   Cacti: use of seashore sand in compost

I am making my own compost for growing cacti and succulents and I would be grateful if you could tell me if coarse sand from the seashore would be suitable for inclusion in the compost if the sand were first washed to remove the salt.

The use of seashore sand is naturally attractive because it is, to all intents and purposes, free to those who can collect it. Onions, asparagus and some brassicas relish a little sea sand because of the salt and other minerals that inevitably come with it, but there are many plants that are quite intolerant of it, and it is far too risky to use unless you are prepared to wash it very thoroughly. Furthermore, seashore sand is very likely to contain a proportion of shell, which in the soil will gradually breakdown to soluble lime, and for this reason should never be used in connection with lime-hating plants.

Spread out the sand or grit thinly on a board, trays, or some hard-standing for several weeks where rain or dousings from the sprinkler can wash it clean.

For use in a compost for cacti in particular, I would take a further precaution, after thorough washing, of mixing half an ounce of gypsum to every 1 lb. of sand before adding to your compost. The gypsum will help to remove salt that may still be hanging about.

361   Cacti: discoloured and flabby

What causes the stems of my Schlumbergera buckleyi *to turn red? The stems have become rather flabby, although the flower buds are retained. The plant is growing in a cool greenhouse.*

Formerly called Zygocactus, *Schlumbergera buckleyi* is commonly called the Christmas cactus and although belonging to the cactus family it can easily grow to the size of a succulent shrub. It is an epiphyte—i.e. a plant that receives most of its nutrient material from the air—and there are several cacti that grow in this way. Nearly all of them are remarkable for the size and beauty of their flowers. In nature, such plants frequently grow high up on the branches of trees or rock faces.

A flabby and discoloured plant indicates that any one of three main conditions are wrong, or perhaps all three—watering, soil medium and humidity. As epiphytes get most of their nutrients from the air, they will not need a rich compost, and indeed they only need to have a root system sufficient to anchor themselves in the little soil pockets and ledges on those rock faces, and that is what you have now to try to imitate. They will do quite well in the cacti compost described in *No. 358*, but it is worth making up the following variation for this particular plant.

Move your plant into a compost mix made up of equal parts of four ingredients: John Innes No. 1 compost; mushroom compost or peat that has been put through a $\frac{1}{2}$-inch sieve; crushed brick or plaster rubble—again put through a $\frac{1}{2}$-inch sieve—and silver sand. This, as you will realise, is a fierce draining compost.

Pot into this compost during April or May with one sixth of the pot occupied by drainage crock for large plants, and a quarter to a third for small plants. Plant very firmly with the compost pressed in hard and stand on a wet shingle base so that the rising air is always humid. In summer, most of these plants prefer some shade—dappled sunlight is best—and require as much humid air circulation as possible. It is a good idea to increase the humidity by lightly mist-spraying the plants every other day and if the plant looks a bit sickly, add a few drops of Murphy FF foliar feed. Remember they will take nutrient from dust particles in the air.

It is also a good plan to suspend the plants from the greenhouse roof, or to stand the pot on another upturned, or a pedestal, so that the flattened stems can trail and hang down below their own pot. Remember their natural habit is to grow from branches and rock faces.

With a fierce draining growing medium like this, it is hardly possible to overwater, but there is no need to overdo it. All that is needed is to keep the soil just moist and no more. As autumn and winter approach, ensure that a minimum temperature of 45–50°F. is maintained. The spectacular flowers will quickly deteriorate if they get very wet; therefore, as the largest of the buds reach half an inch in length and opening is imminent, stop the spraying in favour of watering with manure water.

362 Cacti for Christmas need darkness to flower well

Could you tell me why the buds of my Christmas cactus plant won't open? Last year there were no buds or flowers. This year there are many buds, but they don't open.

To flower really well Christmas cactus needs water, food and warmth during winter and darkness twelve hours a day from September to February. A shortage of any of these requirements will slow or stop the plant growing and, as always, it is the flower buds which will suffer first; they won't form or if they do, they will be reluctant to open and will probably abort.

Try to keep the plant in a minimum temperature of 50–55°F; avoid draughts and direct sunlight; in their natural habitat these plants grow in dappled light, see *No. 361*. It may be easy enough to ensure the length of darkness during mid-winter, but during September and October and again in early spring you may have to put on a little extra daytime shading to make up the twelve hours' twilight. When in growth and whilst still blooming, keep the soil just moist with rainwater to which has been added a few drops of liquid feed.

363 Campanula : care and cultivation

I have purchased two dwarf campanulas, one of which is supposed to be white and the other blue.

They are pot plants for keeping indoors and I would like to know their names and something more about them.

The Campanula usually sold for growing as a house plant is *C. isophylla* the so-called Italian bellflower. It has blue and white forms and has a natural trailing habit that makes it ideal for standing on a shelf or pedestal, or planting in a hanging basket. As they grow, pot on your plants into 5 in. pots containing a compost made up of equal parts by bulk John Innes No. 2 and peat (or if you have any, rubbed out and sieved mushroom compost and peat in equal proportions) plus a little gritty sand to keep it open and stop it becoming wet and soggy. Water moderately well, and every 10–14 days add a few drops of a general liquid feed to the water, Bio General Purpose or Sangral would do very well. Give plenty of light and air; they do not have to stay in the greenhouse.

After flowering, cut back the long shoots in order to encourage the production of new long flower bearing growth for next season. During winter move the plant under cover, preferably in a cool greenhouse or conservatory, reducing watering so that the plant is kept fairly dry. Repotting when necessary is best done in early spring, and as new growth appears, don't let too many new shoots develop because the largest trails and the best bloom comes when these are thinned out a little. You can use the prunings to strike cuttings; they root quite easily in sand.

364　Chlorophytum, the Spider Plant

My spider plant has fourteen blooms and I would like to know if these have to be trained to a support, or can be allowed to hang down; they are about 18 in. long. Can these blooms be planted to start another plant.

The spider plant—*Chlorophytum comosum variegatum*—is one of the easiest house plants to grow and takes its name rather fancifully from the shape of the small plantlets that form at the end of the arching stems arising from the centre of the cluster of long slender leaves. These form an attractive display and, inci-

dentally the plant is seen to best advantage when the pot is stood upon a pedestal or hung from a wall bracket or hanging basket, so that the 'spiders' droop and hang low.

These stems often carry both bloom and plantlets and can be pegged down with a bent wire stirrup—a paper clip or hairpin is ideal for this—into small pots of potting compost or into Jiffy 7s. Indeed, if the plants are growing well and these plantlets are not potted up, it is quite likely that they will show their impatience and zest for life by trying to form roots whilst still in mid air.

When rooted and growing away, sever from the stem and pot on into stronger John Innes No. 2 compost.

365　Chlorophytum: why the leaves turn brown

My Chlorophytum is giving me a great deal of trouble since the tips of the variegated leaves are turning brown. Can you suggest how to stop this?

This plant is among the most popular of house plants because it is so tolerant of low light intensity. The plant needs a copious moisture supply throughout the year and a moist atmosphere. The brown tips to the leaves can be ascribed to dryness either at the roots and/or in the atmosphere. The best procedure is to stand the plant on a tray of gritty shingle that is kept wet at all times, so that the evaporation area produces plenty of rising moist air.

Dryness at roots is often due to the way in which the thick fleshy rhizomatous roots overcrowd a pot with bursting pressure, so that the water from overhead often runs off rather than penetrating the compressed root ball. It is best to avoid this by splitting and dividing the root clump in March, every two or three years, or by layering the plantlets that form at the ends of the long arching stems so that you always have a succession of young plants growing (and swelling).

Use a compost therefore that is moisture retentive, yet porous so that it does not waterlog; and which also is sufficiently spongy to allow the root swelling to take place.

Equal parts by bulk John Innes No. 2, peat,

rubbed out and sieved mushroom compost, and sand is ideal. Copious watering will soon wash out soluble nutrients and if you want really good plants with lots of plantlets showering out of the central clump, give a liquid feed every 10–14 days—one with a slight, but only slight, nitrogen bias would be ideal. Bio General, or Sangral General would do very well.

Place in a position where the plant can get good light but away from sunlight, and try to ensure that the winter temperature does not drop below 45°F.

366 Chrysanthemum : 'Charm' varieties from seed

I would welcome advice on some 'Charm' Chrysanthemums which I grew from seed this year. They have turned out a failure; they are thin, spindly plants with no body in them. I potted them on in John Innes No. 2 into 6 in. pots. Where did I go wrong?

Maybe you went wrong even before you started because there are two strains of Charm Chrysanths—for greenhouse culture and for outdoors. Although the early stages of cultivation are identical, they diverge before flowering and to have had thin spindly plants suggests that you have been growing the outdoor type as greenhouse subjects.

Charms are better for a long growing period. So sow seed early, in January, no more than $\frac{1}{8}$-inch deep for both types in John Innes Seed Compost in trays and placed in a propagator set at 55–60°F. Germination is quite rapid; they should be through in 10–14 days. When germinated, move the seed trays outside the propagator; stand the tray on top of the propagator for a couple of days so that a little heat can be picked up. Then move them on to the staging—the weaning must be gradual. When the seedlings are large enough to handle, an inch or so high, they will be ready for potting. Don't leave it much longer or fighting each other to reach towards the light, they may well become drawn—the correct term is etiolated—and useless. Keep the greenhouse temperature steady at 55°F—not more or the

heat will also help to force them up and become spindly.

Prick out singly into $2\frac{1}{2}$ in. pots containing John Innes No. 1 compost. When a nice layer of root surrounds the soil ball, pot on to the next size pot $3\frac{1}{2}$–4 in. When tapping out the pot shows that the next layer of root is well-formed, move on to the 5–6 in. pot using the richer John Innes No. 2, and finally into an 8 in. pot in which the greenhouse type will bloom.

At this point the treatment of outdoor and greenhouse types diverge. During May, instead of potting on into the 8 in. pot, the outdoor types can be planted direct into the outside bed or border where they will bloom from September on. Plant them 21–24 ins. apart, and their blooms will merge into a solid mass of colour. They are hardy and can be treated as perennials for a few years until their vigour declines, but remember these are prone to slug damage so have the slug traps ready— see *No. 511.*

Referring again to the greenhouse types— you will not plant these out at the 8 in. pot stage. Stand the pots outside in a sheltered but bright spot making sure—now they are exposed —that they do not dry out. Keep them spaced well apart so that top growth can spread fully, and in September move them back into a greenhouse where a minimum temperature of 40°F. (frost free) can be maintained. Don't put on more heat than this or the plants will be drawn up and spoiled; keep them cool and hard. Don't overwater, give just enough to keep the soil nicely moist. These will begin to bloom from the end of September, and continue perhaps even into December.

The all important factors are successive potting on into pots only one size larger each time so that layers of assimilative root are built up; you cannot expect the plant to support a $2\frac{1}{2}$ ft. wide spray of bloom in an 8 in. pot unless there is a mass of root. Secondly, full light at all times is a must, otherwise the plant will be weak and drawn.

They should break freely and carry on sub-branching of their own accord, but if the plants are slow to break, pinch out the lead shoots.

367 Chrysanthemum: sterilisation against eelworm

I want to sterilise my Chrysanthemum stools against eelworm. What should the temperature of the water be and the period of immersion?

A very wise precaution, and anybody growing Chrysanthemums at all seriously should regard this as a vitally necessary part of the drill. It is not difficult to carry out, and the only piece of extra equipment needed is a special thermometer, to enable you to know exactly the temperature of the water that you are going to heat and to keep it at that temperature. You can obtain one suitable for this job from Brannan Thermometers, Cleator Moor, Cumbria.

Your first step is to assess what size vessel you will need, a bucket perhaps, to hold the stools and how many stools you are going to sterilise in each operation. This may seem obvious, but you have to think rather carefully about it because you are going to have to keep that vessel full of water heated to a steady temperature that is just a little over blood heat. In most households, this will mean standing a bucket on the gas stove which is easy enough to regulate; an electric stove on 'low' may be too much and you will have to switch on and off fairly often. In any case, make a trial run first, with water only. It's no good thinking that you don't need to practise and can make it up as you go along. First, try to determine from the catalogue or the grower whether a particular variety is 'soft' on eelworm sterilisation; that is to say, whether it can stand 115°F. or, being soft, you can only subject it to 110°F. That 5°F. difference is so little and yet it can wreck all your efforts. You can see therefore how important it is to have an efficient thermometer and also how important it is to always make sure that plants are correctly and permanently labelled. You will realise, also, why it is wise to obtain chrysanthemums only from a reputable and reliable grower who can provide such information about what he is selling; or to accept stools only from friends who know about these plants. It is the easiest thing in the world to gratefully accept a load of trouble.

First wash the stools clear of all soil in tepid water, laying them to one side until you have one loading cleaned and ready.

If the varieties are normal and 'hard', bring the water to 115°F. and immerse the stools; the temperature as shown by the thermometer, which should be kept immersed, will naturally drop a little as the stools are cooler and will quickly take some of the heat. Bring it back up to 115°F. and keep the stools completely immersed for five full minutes, but not any longer than is then required to lift them out. If you can use a chip frying wire basket, that solves that one.

'Soft' varieties are treated in exactly the same way except that the temperature is 110°F. only and the immersion period twenty minutes.

Wash the stools in clear tepid water—not cold water which would cause shock—and pot up into a compost that has been sterilised. This again may seem obvious, but it really is amazing how many enquiries are made by gardeners who have gone to all the trouble of heat-treating the stools to remove the risk of infection, and then pot up into soil which, because it has not been sterilised, is a very possible source of re-infection.

If you are unable to determine whether your varieties are soft or hard, regard them all as soft and test them for the 'hard' treatment by trying out a small stool that you can spare and afford to lose if it reacts badly and shows that the variety cannot take it. Finally, be very careful with your labels; it's all too easy to lose them during this job and it's no good swearing when you find a couple floating in the hot water.

368 Chrysanthemums: causes of petal fall

Why do the petals fall away from my Chrysanthemums once they are cut? I have been feeding them but I am wondering if I have been giving them too much, or using the wrong thing?

Petals, leaves, fruits and all parts that fall naturally from plants, become detached through a double layer of cells at the base of the petal, leaf or fruit stalk, called the abscission layer. These become more fragile and liable to fracture as a result of factors like ripening (of fruit), withering (of leaves), overloading (premature fruit drop), dryness, end of life span (autumn leaf fall) etc. and there are other sudden conditional factors like draughts and temperature drop.

In some plants and varieties, this layer is very fragile and it doesn't take much to cause the break. Consider a plant that carries a bloom with a large number of petals such as a Dahlia or a Chrysanthemum: as the bloom opens from the bud, it begins to transpire moisture from a surface area that increases rapidly until, fully open, the total area is very large and the evaporation rate correspondingly increased. The need to replace the lost moisture is therefore also great.

Any dryness at the roots therefore puts the bloom at risk, the petals become limp and may even wither at the tips. The Dahlia usually hangs on fairly well to its petals, but the Chrysanthemum's petal abscission layer is much more fragile and they are therefore much quicker to fall.

The moisture is drawn up from the root system where it is being taken in from the soil to the leaves, and blooms through long tubular cells in the stem. When you cut a bloom, it is inevitable that a little sap will be lost and that air will enter the tubes. Even though you may get the cut end into water very quickly, a bubble of air enters the tube and causes an airlock. In many plants this airlock effectively prevents the passage of liquid, now water instead of sap, and the flow stops all along the tube, right up to the bloom. The petals go on evaporating, however, and with no more liquid coming through, they fall limp. In the case of the Chrysanthemum, this is all that is needed to cause the abscission layer to fail, and the petals fall.

The precautions to be taken come before and after cutting. Never let the plants become dry at the roots so that you have a ready-made situation that predisposes the petals to fall as soon as you stop the sap flow by cutting. Keep the plants well-watered so that the liquid pressure is high; then, as soon as you can *after* cutting, remove the airlock.

This can be done in two ways. First, hold the cut stem end under the water in the vase and cut off an inch. Being under water, air cannot enter and the sap flow can continue without hindrance. Obviously this means that you must leave the cut stem in the vase; you cannot take it out to move it to another because air will get in and you are back to square one.

If the vase is narrow and you are putting in several stems, it can be impracticable to cut the ends in this manner. In this case, another method that works with Chrysanths is to spread the area and kind of damage done to the fluid-conducting tubes so that although airlocks occur, water may still be drawn into the tubes above the airlocks. Hold the stems so that the end couple of inches is on the table and hit this part with a piece of wood, so that the stem is split and bruised, then put it in water at once. Water then stands a much better chance of getting in and petal drop is averted, or at least minimised.

Don't try burning or dipping in hot water; the idea behind this is to seal off the tube ends so that more air cannot enter. The bloom then lives on the moisture within the tubes and which are soft enough to contract as the fluid is removed. Chrysanths are hard-stemmed and the contraction cannot occur so it is generally a waste of time to try that method.

369 Chrysanthemum : spray varieties

Could you tell me whether spray Chrysanthemums should be stopped? If so, when?

Generally, spray Chrysanthemums form a natural break bud without the need for any stopping or pinching back. However, sprays are grown because they bear bloom in sprays and not specimen single blooms, and the best results are obtained by forcing the plant to make many more flower-bearing tips than it would do if allowed to break naturally.

Removing the growing tip, and then waiting for the development of side shoots, can delay the formation of the flower buds and, therefore, you should make up for this by starting the plants into growth as early as you can. If you have a cool greenhouse, you should not have much trouble starting them in February and if you can introduce a little warmth, growth can even be induced during January. Soil warming cables are inexpensive and make a world of difference. I think that they are the most useful and important addition you can have in your greenhouse. They are cheap to buy and run. Write to Humex Ltd., Byfleet, Surrey for their catalogue.

Depending upon when you can start them, treat your sprays in much the same way as 'charms', see *No. 366*. Take out the main growing tip(s) when the shoot has 4–5 pairs of leaves and, if there is time, the tips of side shoots can be pinched out when these have 3 pairs of leaves. Try to get the second pinch completed before the turn of the year—the day of longest daylight hours.

Asking for intensive growth like this means that the plants should have adequate nutrient resources. Your plant will have to make a good root system to sustain and support the extra foliage and flower—that means phosphate. It will have to make a lot more leaf, which means nitrogen. This extra growth is going to put a strain on the vigour of the plant and you must not let it outgrow its own strength. There will also be a lot more bloom and this means potash.

You will realise, therefore, that a long sustained feeding action is needed, not short bursts, and that the feed must have an adequate content of all three—Nitrogen, Phosphorous, and Potash. Fertilisers are available, of course, in which the proportions are varied, ostensibly to improve blooming, fruiting or some other particular requirement, but I think that most amateurs would find it easier to concentrate on cultivating healthy balanced plants by using fertilisers in which the three main nutrients are balanced in equal proportion or nearly so. Use Growmore or the longer-lasting Humber Eclipse in the compost, and if you liquid feed later on when the buds are forming and want to add extra potash to put a little extra colour into the bloom, Sangral 'Tomato' or Tomorite would do very well.

370 Chrysanthemum : how to preserve and propagate a 'sport'

One of my Chrysanthemum plants (the variety is called 'Silver Rose') has sported a red bloom on one stem. I would like to propagate it and would be obliged for advice.

If you wait until the following spring to propagate in the usual way by rooting cuttings, it will be difficult to be sure that a cutting will be a re-emergence of the sported shoot or, for that matter, that the sport is still active. You will have to work much more quickly.

Bring the sported stem down carefully so that it lays in the soil. Position a deep tray alongside perhaps two if required. Fill with sandy peat and peg the stem into this with wire hoops. Cover each leaf joint with a handful of compost, a sand/peat mix will be ideal. It is not normally necessary to cut into the leaf joints and treat them with a rooting compound, as with aerial layering of many hard

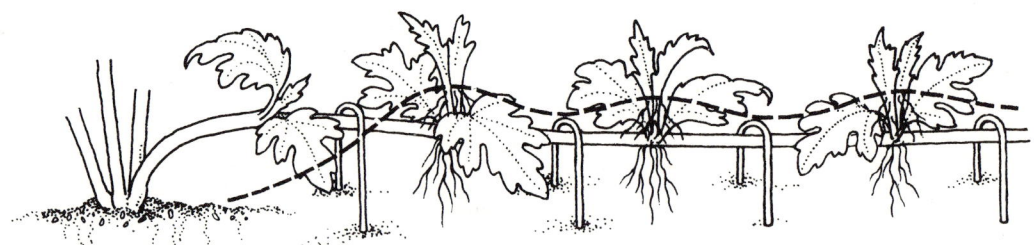

No. 370   *A quick method of producing cuttings from a Chrysanthemum 'sport' in order to preserve the different colour or other characteristics. The dotted line indicates how the soil can be heaped up as necessary.*

wood shrubs but of course if you do this your chances of success are much better.

With the change in the direction of gravity—the stem is now horizontal—the immediate effect is to encourage the production of shoots at each leaf joint and because they have emerged through their little mounds of soil, the base of each shoot will be pale green in colour—or even white and very similar to a cutting that would be taken in early spring from an old stool. It may even be rooting, as indeed may the main stem itself if it has been cut and treated with hormone.

Strike the cuttings or pot up the rooted stem sections and grow on in the normal manner. Vegetatively propagated, the cuttings should have exactly the same 'sport' colour blooms. However, do bear in mind that a 'sport' can just as easily and quickly revert to the original type, and it will not be for several generations of vegetative cuttings that you can rely upon the variation as having become fixed.

371 Chrysanthemum: treatment of a dwarf plant after flowering

How should I look after a dwarfed, potted Chrysanthemum when the flowers fade?

Dwarfed potted chrysanths have become popular house plants, but they are produced by very special treatment. If you look at the pot carefully, you will see that the 'plant' is in fact three, four or even five separate plants. These have been raised from cuttings and treated with chemicals—such as gibberelin—which causes the plant to grow dwarfed and thus become eminently saleable as a pot plant.

Cut back flowered stems to near the base and keep the plants in a cool, but frost-free place, because the varieties used for dwarfing tend not to be so hardy.

In spring—February or March—heap a couple of handfuls of peat or very light compost over each pot. Shoots will soon be emerging and like those described in *No. 370*; any that push through will quite likely be rooting into the compost cover. These can be detached and potted up but don't be disappointed if they grow taller and differ from the parent potted plants that were dwarfed with chemicals.

372 Cineraria: flopping and collapsing

Could you tell me what I have done wrong whilst growing Cineraria? Sown in August, pricked out into 3 in. pots and finally 5½ in. deep pots, they grew well until the flower buds developed. Then for some reason, all but two out of the twelve grown, flopped and did not recover. Compost was my own mixture of soil, sand and peat.

Although the symptoms described are fairly common it is difficult to say precisely what has caused this trouble because it is a combination probably of several adverse conditions. Cinerarias are peculiar in that they have a critical period at the bud stage when they become especially touchy about their pet hates—dampness at the roots, a stagnant atmosphere and overbright light. It is as though they are at that stage when the fine show of bloom and colour they are about to produce makes them like a nervous prima donna about to go on stage; the slightest little thing not quite right and they throw a tantrum.

Many amateur growers of Cinerarias make things worse by growing the plant too softly—in too high a temperature and in a too rich compost. If you are using John Innes formula composts, No. 1 is ample. They need little heat from sowing until flowering and then only in cold weather to maintain a minimum of 47–50°F.

The use of sterilised soil and compost at all times is important with Cinerarias, see *No. 374*, and after sowing from May to July in a sterilised John Innes seed compost, the main growing-on medium should consist of one part sterilised loam, two parts peat and one part sharp gritty sand—all by bulk. The grittiness of the sand is important because of the need to keep the compost open at all times. You will have to water freely in summer but at no time must there be any suggestion of waterlogging. Stand the pots on gravel or ash so that water does not hang around the base of the pot.

243

There are hardly any plant nutrients at all in this compost mix so far. So into each bushel mix 4 ozs. of Humber Eclipse semi-organic fertiliser, 1 oz. of Epsom salts and ½ oz. of lime. Water it moist and let it stand for a week, covered with moist sacks. When making your own growing medium, don't stray far away from these tried and proven proportions.

Grow on in a light unheated greenhouse. Ventilation at all times is imperative—a stuffy atmosphere is an almost certain guarantee of collapse; either the foliage will suddenly wilt or the whole plant will keel over at soil level.

As soon as the embryo buds can be discerned, give just a pinch of sulphate of potash to each plant and from now on gradually reduce the watering. You've got to harden and firm the plant ready for blooming, so water more sparingly and make sure that the plants are shaded from bright sunlight.

373 Cineraria: lace patterns on leaves

Some Cinerarias growing in pots in my greenhouse are being attacked by minute white grubs tunnelling through the leaves. They leave unpleasant white markings which spoil the appearance of the plants. Please tell me how to get rid of them.

Without a doubt, this is the Chrysanthemum leaf miner, so called because it tunnels or 'mines' inside the tissues of the leaves, commonly those of the Chrysanthemum, but from time to time of other plants too. Other leaf miners attack trees and shrubs, sometimes with very tough 'leathery' foliage—indeed the holly suffers badly, see *No. 85.*

As in the case of holly, the problem is that once inside the leaf and tunnelling, the pest is difficult to reach. The problem is a physical one—contact sprays do not touch, let alone reach him, and therefore cannot be relied upon to achieve a kill. However, you do have an easier problem to solve with Chrysanthemums, compared with the glossy leathery leaves of the holly, the foliage of Cinerarias and Chrysanthemums is softer, the 'skin' isn't so resistant. Therefore, systemic chemicals—whilst not entering quickly for an immediate

kill, at least are absorbed much more readily. Furthermore, the living rate of Chrysanthemums, Cinerarias and the like, is faster than the outdoor shrubs, the sap stream moves faster and systemic insecticides which enter the sap stream and render it toxic to biting and sucking insects spread throughout the plant much more quickly and thus give good control. They should however be applied as soon as the tell-tale tunnels are seen and before too many, indeed any, of the leaf veins have been 'crossed', stopping sap flow and the function of the leaf. A badly marked leaf cannot do its job and may well take more energy to prop it up than it is contributing to the well being of the plant.

The alternative advice is to pick off affected leaves and burn them. Whilst this may be acceptable in a Chrysanthemum, and even in a holly, which have a larger number of leaves and can perhaps stand the loss of several leaves, the loss of more than one leaf to a Cineraria is a serious matter and to be avoided—if at all possible.

Fumigation is another good control. Burn BHC smokes, three times at seven-day intervals. Overnight is the best time to do this: you will have to close down all ventilation to stop the gas escaping, and if you did this during the day, might risk the temperature soaring and that could easily wreck everything.

All in all, systemic insecticides offer the most practicable control, but spray at the very first signs of tunnelling.

374 Cineraria : wilting

Several times I have grown Cinerarias, but almost immediately after coming into flower they have wilted and died. Could you please advise what treatment I can give to avoid further disappointments?

In *No. 372,* you will read about sterilised soil and a sandy open compost. Fungus spore of one sort or another inevitably will be in unsterilised soil. Not all will be harmful but with a touchy subject like Cineraria it is best not to take chances, and the sterilisation has to be absolutely safe and sure.

However, you can't do much about spore

that arrives by other means—in the air, in the water from your water can, the pot, if you didn't clean it thoroughly before potting into it. Somehow or other, fungus will arrive. What you mustn't do is to create conditions that encourage fungus to develop and that is the reason for the rather large proportion of grit and sand.

Erratic watering and/or a compost that holds too much stagnant moisture do two things which are both fatal to the Cinerarias. The first is to encourage fungus diseases like collar rot and black neck each of which will cause the kind of trouble you describe and the second is to cause the plant to alternate between thirst and dropsy, and the plant suffering this will inevitably be less resistant to attack. Hence the advice in *No. 372.* to sterilise and make the growing medium quick draining.

An old tip was to heap up soil around the stem so that watering ran away to the pot edges. This is more theoretical than practical and shouldn't be necessary if the compost is open and the pots are watered without wetting the plant stems. The advice is also often advocated to water with Cheshunt Compound—this is all right as a depressant or precaution but no good at all if recourse to it in any degree lessens your diligence in creating the right growing conditions.

Cineraria, to many gardeners, is a very difficult plant. To grow it well is a challenge—but that is what gardening is all about.

375 Cobaea : grown as a trailer

Could you tell me how to grow a Cobaea as a trailer in a 6 in.-pot?

This was a very common technique in the days when gardeners in private service had a lot more time to work on decorative set pieces. When allowed to hang as a trailer, plants that climb by tendrils and twining tend to turn and climb up themselves, but most plants that trail and clamber—and normally have to be trained—can be set up high to hang down and cascade.

The 'cup and saucer' flowered Cobaea makes a spectacular specimen; it is a half-hardy perennial that can be raised quite easily from seed and will bloom in its first summer. Cobaea seed should be sown not flat but on edge, a half-inch deep in late February in a temperature 65–68°F. Germination is normally quite rapid and the first seedlings should be showing in fourteen days. Use John Innes seed compost and pot on the seedlings into 3½ in. pots, then 6 in. pots with John Innes No. 3 for climbing in the greenhouse. Alternatively you can pot into a wire basket for hanging. As the plant grows rapidly, so will its demands on moisture increase, so water freely, never let it become dry and as the flower buds begin to appear, give liquid manure once a week. This plant likes plenty of sunlight and can be moved outdoors in warm sunny weather. In autumn, shorten back the long stems so that new growth forms for the following year.

376 Dieffenbachia, the Dumb Cane : cutting it back

I have what I understand is called a Dumb Cane. It is getting unmanageable; it is now nearly 5 ft. tall and obviously very healthy and two pod-shaped flowers are now appearing. Should I prune my plant?

There are several varieties of Dieffenbachia, the Dumb Cane, and all come from South America where they can grow quite tall. The variety usually grown as a house plant is *Dieffenbachia picta*, the large green leaves carried around a central stem are blotched with cream-yellow.

They prefer a shaded subdued light, but the temperature and watering requirements they need are not in line with our normal living conditions and this means that they do best when brought indoors for short visits and are returned to the greenhouse for recuperation. From February to March, watering needs to be free, with frequent leaf spraying to maintain humidity and the temperature kept between 65–85°F. From September, watering should be reduced to just enough to keep the soil moist, and the temperature reduced a little—but not below 55°F.

To propagate the plant in this country, you will need a propagating case in which a bottom heat of 75–85°F. can be maintained. In spring, cuttings of shoot ends a couple of inches long can be taken and struck into sandy peat. This will cause side shoots to form lower down the stem and these also can eventually be taken as cuttings, followed by removal of the cane, which in turn will cause new shoots to be thrown up from the base.

Incidentally, and perhaps surprisingly to many, for a plant that is so popular, it is poisonous: the common name Dumb Cane derives from an unpleasant loss of speech that occurs for several days if the sap gets into the mouth. Don't take risks: always wash your hands thoroughly after cutting the plant.

377   Euphorbia : care and cultivation

I would be grateful for any information you can give about the plant Euphorbia fulgens. *Can I keep it from year to year and what temperature does it need? Should I repot or leave it alone?*

Euphorbia fulgens is a shrubby species of the same genus as the popular red-leaved Christmas poinsettia; both originate from Mexico.

With care *E. fulgens* can be kept for several years, provided that two pet dislikes are recognised and avoided: draughts and root disturbance. It differs in appearance and habit from the more familiar poinsettia (see *No. 411*) in having slender arching stems, narrower leaves with clusters of 'flowers' along its length. The 'flowers' are in fact orange-scarlet-coloured bracts, the true flowers being quite insignificant.

These arching stems are particularly useful for flower arranging and decoration; the cutting does no harm to the plant because it encourages the production of fresh new stems from the base. Indeed, pruning consists of heading back such stems as are left to encourage side shoots, or cutting them right back to within an inch of the base; this is best done during late spring.

The plant does not have a very vigorous root system, which is why root disturbance is best avoided until repotting becomes really

necessary—and then into a larger pot using John Innes No. 2 with peat and enough coarse sand to keep the compost open and free-draining. Repotting can be done at the same time as pruning.

Cultivation is similar to that for poinsettia except that winter temperatures should be a little higher. Position in a sunny dry part of the greenhouse. From May to September, water freely and exclusively with a very diluted liquid feed and try to maintain a uniform temperature of 65–75°F. Ventilation at this time is important, but there must be no draughts. From September when 'flowers' are forming, reduce watering by half and the temperature to 60°F. From January or the end of 'flowering', maintain a minimum temperature of 55°F. and keep the soil almost dry until pruning and 'wake up' again in spring.

378   Ferns : propagation not from seed

My indoor fern has recently produced fronds with brownish black blobs on their undersides. Is this a disease?

These are probably the quite natural development of the spore-bearing bodies called sori. Ferns do not set seed like other plants but reproduce by means of spores, which is the microscopically small 'dust' that falls as the spore cases open. If you would like to propagate your fern, make up some trays of a moist sandy/peat mix, surfaced with a thin layer of sand. Then, as the sori open, spray the sand surface moist and, holding the tray under the frond and tapping with the other hand, the 'dust' will be knocked out onto the sand. Place the 'seeded' tray in a moist propagator case and within a few weeks you will see a fine green mould appearing. This develops into little flat green growths called prothalli. This is the infantile stage, and you should keep it moist with a light mist spray as required. In a few weeks, small recognisable fern fronds should begin to appear. As soon as these are large enough to be handled between finger and thumb, pot up singly into small pots. The general 'terrestial fern' compost of equal parts John Innes No. 1 or 2, peat and silver sand should suffice.

379 Flies: minute pests that bother pot plants

There are often clouds of tiny black flies close to the soil of my pot plants, both indoors and in the greenhouse. Are these harmful?

Probably these are fungus gnats. The flying adults lay eggs in the soil, and the maggots normally feed on fungi that are living on decaying plant tissues. Fungus growth is part of the natural process of breakdown of organic matter and this indicates that your compost must contain organic material that is still at an early stage of decomposition.

They become dangerous to indoor and pot plants when the compost fungus dies out as decomposition proceeds and they turn their attention to the living roots of the plants. Fortunately, control is relatively easy. Drench the affected compost with Malathion—preferably all the pots in the greenhouse as there will undoubtedly be a few free flies to home in and lay more eggs. Have a mist sprayer on hand containing pyrethrum or the new insecticide Sprayday; this has a terrific 'knock down' effect. Eggs laid in Malathion-soaked compost won't get very far and the pyrethrum should stamp out the rest of the flying adults.

380 Frangipani: conditions required for flowering

We have a frangipani grown from a cutting and have repotted it once, using a mixture of garden soil and peat. It has several large leaves, but how de we encourage it to flower, and also, what is the minimum temperature it will withstand?

The Frangipani plant—*Plumiera rubra*, sometimes spelt Plumeria—is an evergreen flowering shrub that originates from tropical America, with brilliant flowers like a red jasmine. To get Frangipani into flower, however, you will have to maintain a minimum of 65°F. during winter; very high for most gardeners but if you want tropical flowers, you will have to provide nothing less than tropical conditions.

Your compost mix is not really satisfactory because it could consolidate and waterlog. You will have to wait until February when the plant has slowed and start again using equal parts by bulk of loam and silver sand and half a part coarse fibrous peat. You can prepare this by rubbing moss peat through a $\frac{1}{2}$-in. sieve, and using the roughage that remains. Stand the pot in full sunlight on a shingle sand or peat layer that can be kept wet so that humid air can rise and surround the plant.

In March increase the temperature to 75°F. and begin daily watering with very weak liquid manure and mist spraying until flowers appear in June or July on the terminal shoots. Immediately after flowering, prune back straggly shoots and from September or October reduce watering to moderation only—just enough to keep the soil moist. At no time must the temperature be allowed to fall below 65°F.

381 Freesia raised from seed; why no flowers?

Why do my Freesias carry so few flowers? They are raised from seeds sown in April, put into a cold frame in June and brought back into the greenhouse in September, where there is a minimum temperature of 50°F. They always make a tremendous leaf growth.

It could be due to poor seed, incorrect soil or unsuitable conditions; it is impossible from the evidence to say which, so I'll run through these points with comment so that you may recognise where you are going wrong.

It is no good if you don't start right. Good seed can be spoiled by poor cultivation, but you cannot expect to get good first-class flowers from third-class seed.

You are sowing too late and, in consequence, the plants are having to rush through their build-up period. Sow the seed very thinly indeed much earlier, in February. Sow them in 5 in. or 6 in. pots in a temperature of 60–65°F. in a compost of 2 parts John Innes No. 1 or 2, and one part of sand over a good layer of peat. Freesia seedlings do not like root disturbance, therefore they should not be transplanted in the first year. If you have sown too thickly and it is necessary to thin out you can, of course, try transplanting the thinnings, but you cannot rely upon them to give a good bloom. They may, however, provide corms and you can use these the next year. When seedlings have germinated, the tray can be moved into a well-ventilated position in the greenhouse until June, and then into an open position, where they will be exposed only at the most to dappled sunlight.

Under no circumstances should they receive a check at this time, particularly a check due to dryness, and as the pots or seed trays can very easily dry out in this exposed position, watering —or ascertaining the need for it—will have to be a daily routine.

By the latter half of September they will be ready to be taken back into the greenhouse but if the weather is warm, leave them a little longer. Keep the plants fully ventilated. The questioner's temperature of 50°F. at this stage is a little high and is probably responsible for the lush leaf growth: 45°F. is ample.

Don't take all the pots in at once. The more forward ones go first—it is not unusual to have some putting up a bud spike whilst still out in the frame—and move the others in gradually over a period of a few weeks. This is when you should be using a maximum/minimum thermometer alongside the Fressias. You must watch the night temperatures and the state of the moon and the weather: a clear night and a full moon can drop the night temperature considerably at this time of year. If your thermometer tells you that the temperatures have been getting near the 35–40°F. bracket, don't risk it any longer. Get the plants inside!

During all your care and attention to compost and conditions, keep a sharp look out for pests. Greenfly is the worst and far better than eradicating this pest is not to let it get a hold in the first place. A weekly spraying with Lindex will stop a build-up of the pest and during the spring and summer months, it is easy to give the Freesias a spray at the same time as you give the roses their routine spraying.

382   Fuchsia : sudden leaf shedding

I have two standard Fuchsias which bloomed beautifully last summer and are growing in separate 12 in. tubs filled with John Innes compost. Two weeks ago, one of them shed all its leaves and now looks dead. Can you tell me what went wrong as I don't want to lose the other one?

This sometimes happens with Fuchsias, Geraniums and other plants grown as standards by amateurs—and even on occasion by the professionals too!

The fundamental difference between a standard and a bush is that the head of a standard is separated from its root system by a long narrow roadway—the stem—upon which is running a lot of congested traffic, and it takes a much longer time to get a consignment from one end to the other than it does with a 'normal' bush type plant where the branches and root are much closer together. Inevitably, when there is an emergency up top, there must be a delay before supplies can be got through and, by the time they do, the emergency can have deteriorated to disaster. It only needs a shock, a cold draught perhaps, or a pest attack and you may soon have a burial job on your hands.

The basic remedy is, don't let a supply shortage happen in the first place. Reducing supplies from below is caused by reduced intake of moisture and nutrients and this can be caused by two factors—often together. First, too little water, and then too much! Dryness at the roots causes the minute root hairs, which constitute the assimilative part of the root system to wither and die. The internal sap pressure then reduces to the point where leaves become limp.

You now notice the limpness and conclude that your plant wants a drink. So you water it and if the soil ball is dry, most of the water runs off. The leaves will still look limp; for one thing the root hairs are largely non-existent, and the sap pressure takes a lot longer to be restored, so the leaves still being limp, you water it again, and again—or stand it in water for hours till the leaves do pick up. The root layer around the soil ball becomes waterlogged and the few remaining root hairs that have not dried out, now rot away. The assimilative power of the root system is thus almost nil, and it is no wonder that the plant looks dead.

Erratic and over-watering then is the basic cause, and the cardinal rule with all standards, because of their construction and inbuilt hazard, is to *never* let them dry out at the roots.

A crash programme for the seemingly dead plant must of necessity be drastic. Soak the entire plant stem and top part too for 24 hours in a bath of water and try to reverse the dehydration but then remove from soaking so that the soil ball can drain out the surplus water. Then follow with daily spraying of the foliage, to try to keep the leaves plump. At the very first signs of greenfly, add Lindex to the spray. The plant has had a bad enough time as it is without letting it suffer a pest attack. As soon as the new foliage shoots begin to appear add a few drops of foliage feed also to the daily spray in order to help the foliage develop fully without being completely dependent upon supplies being hauled all the way up the stem, which, in any case will not be very plentiful for some time.

383 Gardenia: care, cultivation and propagation

I have recently acquired a Gardenia pot plant. Would you tell me the best way of caring for it, and instructions on how and when to split up the plant?

Gardenias are sweetly scented, and the varieties most often used for pot work are *Gardenia jasminoides*, the so-called Cape Jasmine from China and Japan, *G. thunbergia* from South Africa, and several hybrids. In this country, it can only be grown really well in a greenhouse as it requires a winter minimum temperature of 50°F. and a humid atmosphere. They are evergreens and, in particularly favourable conditions, will bloom intermittently throughout the year. Of course not everyone has a greenhouse so if you are going to try to grow it in the dwelling house, you will have to try as best you can to simulate the moist atmosphere with one or two artful dodges. Stand the pot on a tray of permanently wet shingle or peat and frequently mist spray over and around the foliage. I have heard several times of Gardenias growing well in the windows of bathrooms—where they evidently find the steamy atmosphere to their liking.

Gardenia doesn't like full sun, so it will need shading. In the house, stand it if possible in a bright aspect, but away from direct sunlight.

Don't hasten to repot; Gardenia is one of those plants that does best with hard-packed roots. When you have to do so, use a pot just large enough to take the roots.

It doesn't need heavy watering like some tender subjects and we don't have to be so concerned about a fierce draining compost to avoid waterlogging—a common source of trouble with other plants. A compost of one part John Innes No. 2 compost and 1 part peat is ample, but as the plant is going to be allowed to become a little cramped in its pot, we can expect the nutrients to have become much reduced by the second year and then all the normal watering should be done with a well-diluted liquid manure—a quarter of the strength recommended on the bottle.

Gardenias are particularly prone to insect attack: in the greenhouse keep a special watch for aphis and bear in mind that this susceptible plant can easily 'host' the pest to other plants. Spray with Lindex contact killer at the first signs of attack or, better still, reckon that the plant will be attacked regardless and spray regularly as a matter of routine every 5–7 days from March on to prevent a build-up. In the house, where there is not the same risk perhaps of the pest being passed on, you can easily add Lindex to the daily damp-air spraying at the first signs of trouble.

Pruning merely consists of removing overgrown and old shoots, as necessary, to keep the plant to shape. This can be done in early February at the same time as repotting, if that is also necessary. In early March, you can begin to increase the frequency of watering and also raise the temperature gradually to 75°F. and try to maintain it there all through the summer. Keep the air moist by spraying the foliage; don't let this get on the blooms or you'll spoil them. During September bring the temperature down gradually to the winter minimum of 50°F., at the same time reducing the watering a little, but not too much or you may stop winter flowering altogether.

Propagation by splitting is generally impracticable. For one thing if you are not going to repot until it is necessary, the opportunity will not arise very often and old plants do not bloom very well either. The normal practice, and much to be preferred because the best bloom is carried on young plants, is to take cuttings of semi-soft shoots about 2–3 inches long. If you do this about late February or early March, there is every chance that you can take cuttings from the material that you may be pruning at this time to keep the shrub to a nice shape. Trim neatly, touch the cutting into hormone rooting powder and insert in a rooting compost of 2 parts peat and 1 part sand. These cuttings will need a temperature of 75–85°F., so a propagator (and a close humid atmosphere) of some sort is almost essential.

384 Geranium : cuttings turn black

I have a problem with Geranium cuttings going black on the stems. I take good cuttings in August and September, cut them through the joint and plant them in either John Innes or no-soil compost, having pre-soaked the box before planting.

Strictly speaking, the plants used for bedding and decorative pot plants, and commonly called Geraniums should be referred to by their correct name Pelargoniums. Bear this in mind if you look them up in reference books, because old names die hard and you may be somewhat confused if there is not a cross-reference to point out the common misnaming.

The trouble described here sounds like black leg, a disease that affects all members of this family and is at its worst when cuttings are soft and immature. There are also a number of other points discernible from the question that are at fault. The best time for taking cuttings is July or early August, whilst the length of daylight is still long; a month later, the hours of daylight are diminishing fast. Shoots for cutting should be semi-hard since soft lush growth is very prone to fungus attack of the kind you have experienced. Try to keep your plants well apart so that they get plenty of all-round light, and are not drawn and elongated by overcrowding. They should have short internodes (the distance between leaf joints).

Select shoots that are about 5–7 inches long and take them off with a sharp knife from just above a leaf joint bud from which a replacement shoot will grow. It is important that the cut stem on the living plant ends with this bud, not an inch or two of internode which cannot grow on and therefore rots back, providing a favourable starting point for fungus growth. Once established the fungus can spread back past the leaf joint where you should have cut, and then on down the entire stem. Trim this cut surface with a razor blade, perfectly clean so that it calluses and heals quickly.

Cut away the internode section on the cutting to just *below* the next leaf joint—not through it as you are doing. This is because the sugars and starches manufactured within the leaves of plants are stored in special cells at the base of the leaf stalks and in the stems at the point from which the leaf stalks grow. It is these storage cells that form the swelling of the stem at this point—called a node. Making a cutting just below a node therefore means that a food supply is adjacent to be utilised as the energy source for the production of the roots. Make the cutting away from the node and the energy source is not close by to form roots, the cutting stagnates and is more likely to rot. By cutting *through* the node as you have done means that you cut away half the energy store.

This cut surface must be a clean cut so that it forms callus tissue quickly—not a ragged torn surface that will be slow to heal and encourage infection. Also with a razor blade, remove the first two leaves and the leaf stipules left at the base of each leaf stalk. These add nothing to the food reserve, indeed, they may well have begun to wither and brown and are in fact one of the primary causes of stem rot as they soon become infected with Botrytis and may already be carrying airborne spores when the cutting is taken.

In addition, take off any flower buds. The cutting must not be allowed to expend precious energy on flowering; it will have quite enough to do to make root.

Lay the cutting aside on a clean sheet of newspaper for 20–30 minutes so that the cut surfaces can dry and a callus healing layer can

No. 384 *A typical Geranium cutting with the lower leaves and leaf stalk stipules removed. The cuttings should be positioned round the edge of the pot where the drainage is fiercest and the soil remains driest.*

form. This will be more resistant to infection by a possible soil borne infection than a fresh and moist open wound. Cuttings will normally make root without help, but hormone rooting powder encourages them to do it more quickly, so dip the cut end of the cutting into the powder after about 10–15 minutes drying time when it is still just moist enough for a light coating to adhere. Shake off the surplus, and continue the drying.

Don't use boxes for striking cuttings; wood is easily infected and very difficult to sterilise. Use 5 inch pots that have been washed and cleaned. Crocked with a wodge of peat in the bottom and fill with a mixture of 2 parts sharp sand 1 part fine peat. Soak the prepared pot by immersion 24 hours before inserting cuttings and allow to drain. Dibble in six cuttings firmly, equidistant around the edge of the pot. This is the fiercest draining part of a pot of soil, and cuttings are positioned in this way to avoid even the slightest suggestion of water-logging or wetness. Watering is not necessary; there is enough moisture left in the pot from the immersion and held in the peat content. Only if and when the soil shows a dry crust does the pot need watering and then by im-

mersion. Do not, at any time, allow the foliage to become wet.

Stand the pots up on a shingle or other well-drained surface, keep shaded from bright light and maintain a temperature of 60–70°F. A single sheet of newspaper laid over is ideal shading. Keep this on for a week. In fourteen days, the cuttings should be looking plump and firm and a further week after that could well be clearly 'growing away' indicating that they are forming a root system. Twenty-eight days after insertion, there should be no doubt that the cuttings have rooted. Slip your fingers between the cuttings and upturn the pot in the palm of your hand. Tap the pot on the bench if necessary, just enough to loosen the pot; don't take it off the upturned soil ball, in case, being very sandy, the whole lot collapses. Lay the pot on its side safely on the potting bench and slide the pot away. You should have six nicely rooted cuttings ready for potting up singly into 3½ in. pots, then when a nice layer of root has formed, into 5 in. pots. As winter approaches, prevent them from flowering by taking off any flower buds that form. The first flower heads that form next spring will then be large and full.

385 Geranium: when leaves turn yellow and plants fail

The leaves of my 'King of Denmark' geraniums turn yellow and the blooms lose their brilliant pink. What is the reason and the cure?

The answer is that your plants are not getting enough food, or what they are getting is unbalanced. This is more likely to happen when a plant is growing in a pot, than when in the open ground where its roots can go looking for nutrients far beyond the limitations of the pot.

The quick and short term solution is to push nutrients into the plants, rather like force-feeding an undernourished child. Give liquid manure which contains quickly assimilated nutrients, but make sure that the N.P.K. proportions are equal or very nearly so—i.e. Sangral, Bio, Maxicrop etc. There are so many liquid manures which you can buy, and not all are suitable for this purpose by any means. You can also push nutrient chemical into the plant via the leaves, by spraying on specially formulated chemicals that are absorbed into the leaf cells and so into the sap. The first effect of these foliar feeds is to step up the photosynthesis activity; this is the process by which plants join together carbon dioxide and water to form sugars, starches and cellulose and use the energy of light to do it. Therefore, if you use foliar feeds make sure that your plants get plenty of light.

Many plants have a dependency for a particular element in their make-up, although that element need only be present in the minutest amount. This presence of the element may be as low as 5 or even less parts per million and yet without it the dependent plants can become anaemic, weak and altogether sick. Because just the merest trace is needed such elements are called 'trace elements' to distinguish them from N.P.K. which are needed in much greater proportion. The geranium is one such plant, its particular necessity being magnesium and a shortage of this would indeed make the leaves pale, yellowish and even brown and scorched. As a precaution add half a dozen crystals of Epsom salts to each pint of the foliar feed and liquid manure.

Of course, these are all short-term remedies and in no sense are they a substitution for good cultivation in a soil medium containing adequate supplies of nutrients.

386 Ginger: how to care for it

After making chutney with some root ginger, I left a piece in a cupboard and it started to sprout. I potted it up and now have a plant with five shoots a foot or so long. How can I look after it?

Root ginger is the rhizome of a plant from the East Indies known as *Zingiber officinale*. It needs heated greenhouse conditions in order to thrive, 75–80°F. from March to October, a winter minimum temperature of 55°F., and a humid atmosphere. Considering how many gardeners maintain these conditions for other plants, it is surprising how little the ginger plant is grown, because it has bold foliage up to 3 ft. high with a spectacular spike of yellow-green, purple-streaked flowers each summer.

The plant should be in a compost mix of equal parts John Innes No. 2 or 3, peat and sharp sand to keep it open and well-drained. The foliage will die down during winter and you can re-pot in February, dividing the rhizomes if there is more than one—and they pot easily. From March to early October, watering must be quite copious with the pot standing on permanently wet shingle, in a shaded position away from full light. Through late autumn the soil should be watered only sufficiently to keep the soil moist; then from October or November until repotting in February, it should be kept almost dry.

If you haven't a heated greenhouse and can make sure that a minimum of 55°F. can be maintained you can try to grow it as a house plant. The relatively low light intensity indoors will be quite suitable, but without the humidity and the minimum temperature it may be reluctant to flower.

387 Gloriosa: its care and cultivation

I have some tubers of Gloriosa superba raised from seed sown six years ago. Each February I pot them up and they grow well in a cool green-

house until June, when they die down without flowering. The largest tubers are 3 or 4 in. long and I wonder if these should be cut up, and whether they are of flowering size?

Gloriosa—variously called the Malabar Glory Lily, the Mozambique Lily and the Glory Lily—are lovely climbing members of the true Lily family, with very spectacular reflexed flame-red and yellow flowers, produced continuously throughout summer. It is not difficult to grow, provided it is grown according to the rules—and you are breaking several—which is why you have not had bloom.

First, coming from tropical Africa you will need a winter minimum of 55°F., and during the growing season from February to September 70–85°F., and 70°F. should be regarded as the absolute minimum if you want flowers, so a greenhouse is essential.

Your tubers must not be cut: 4 ins. long is flowering size. Plant large single tubers 2 ins. deep in a 6–7 inch pot, or three smaller tubers in a 9-inch pot. Use a rich compost made up of equal parts of John Innes No. 2 or 3, peat and silver sand. Don't use sharp gritty sand; silver sand is much softer and if you can put a wad of well-decayed stable manure or mushroom compost in the bottom of the pot, so much the better.

The plants should be positioned on shingle, peat or sand that is kept permanently wet so that moist air can rise continuously. They will need full light but protection from direct sunlight so you will need to be able to provide partial shade when they need it later on into summer. Arrange wires, trellis, or large mesh netting from the pots up to and across the inside of the roof of the greenhouse, so that they can clamber on this and hang their flowers below; you should get all this done before positioning the plants.

Commence growth by watering once—and once only. Starting off must be done slowly; this is where many gardeners make a mistake. Two weeks later, give another light watering and, then as growth emerges, a little more. Increase the watering so that they are being watered freely in full growth and leaf. Every

ten days or so give a weak liquid manure feed. Ideally this process will have started in February, but if you cannot manage the rather high temperature demanded, delay until the second week in March.

Gradual to start, gradual to finish: after flowering slowly reduce the water supply so that by October they are dry, or nearly so. Remove the dead foliage and stems and keep quite dry until the next season. This rest period is vital, and so is dryness and maintenance of the winter temperature of 55°F. during it.

Finally, your last mistake; there are mixed opinions and mixed advice about Gloriosa. Many people repot every year and, in my opinion, this is ill-advised because this plant is resentful of root disturbance, and you are more likely to do better by keeping them in the same pot for three or four years, increasing the liquid feeding a little as time goes by to make up for the washing-out of nutrients from the original soil.

Rather demanding rules perhaps, but if you can stick to them you will get an astonishing show of bloom which makes it more than worthwhile.

388 Gloxinia grown from seed

What should I do with a box of Gloxinias raised from seed? They've made sturdy plants but they didn't bloom this year.

The plants with superbly coloured trumpet flowers and thick velvety leaves that are commonly called Gloxinias, are derived forms of a plant that originates from Brazil and which are correctly called *Sinningia speciosa*.

Ideally, seed will have been sown in gentle humid heat, 65–70°F. between January and March. Seed should not be covered, but merely pressed into the soil surface. As soon as leaves are ¾–1 inch across, very carefully ease them from the seed compost with as little damage to the roots as possible and pot singly into 2½–3 inch pots containing the same seed compost. They should not be given any soil change at this stage; transplanting is shock enough and they are not ready yet for rich living. Make the roots work, make them go and look for food and get established. If you make the compost too rich too quickly, you'll never get a well developed root system.

Arrange, either on the bench or in the greenhouse bed, a peat plunge bed into which the pots can be sunk to their rims. From this stage on, a regular unvarying temperature becomes important, and burying the pot helps achieve this. Connoisseurs and experts will have thermostats, heaters, automatic ventilators etc. but most amateurs will have to improvise and do their best. You must aim for a steady temperature of 60–65°F., regarding 55°F. as the absolute minimum; lower than that might wreck all of your previous work.

As the 2½–3 inch pot develops a full layer of root around the soil ball—and an occasional tap out will help you to keep a check—move them on into a 4 inch pot. Now you can step up the nutrient content in the compost—John Innes No. 1 Potting. Then, as that pot develops a thick layer of root, on to a 5 inch pot, and finally into a 6 inch pot using John Innes No. 2. By the time the 6 inch pot is reached, the soil ball will be full of root layers and that much root is needed to support a really large bloom head. Plant into a 6 inch pot first time, and you get only one root layer and not much root means not much bloom!

Keep the plants shaded from direct sunlight at all times, keep the atmosphere moist by damping down the floor, but try to keep the leaves dry. Botrytis and mould fungus can play havoc with young seedlings. Whenever outside temperature allows, open the ventilators to provide as much ventilation as you can. See also *No. 389.*

389   Gloxinias grown from corms

I have grown some Gloxinias from seed and wish to know how to save the small corms for next year's growing.

In autumn, early October, begin the process of reducing watering with the aim of having got the pot quite dry by about the middle or end of November. Opinions vary on whether the corm should be shaken out of the soil at this time, or whether it should remain in the pot and laid on its side to rest under the greenhouse staging. If you remove it early on, make sure that the pot has been quite dry for a couple of weeks so that the root activity has ceased completely. Carefully clean off the corms, remove old soil, and examine them—keeping a most careful watch for any signs of grubs around the corms and in the soil. Gloxinia corms are magnets to several pests to come and have a good feed. If the soil is clean, throw it on the compost heap. If there are any pests in it you will have to sterilise it before you can do anything else with it—there is no sense in spreading trouble. Place the corm right way up in dry peat and store in the dark where a fairly warm temperature of 50°F. can be maintained. If soil pests have been observed, dip the corm in a weak Malathion solution for two minutes, leave it to dry before placing it in the dry peat. Only store corms 'in pot' if you are very confident that the plant is healthy and you don't suspect soil pest damage.

In late February, examine all the corms and place them half buried in damp peat—ordinary seed trays will do for this. Raise the temperature to 65°F. You can do this by placing them in a propagator frame, on a propagating heat panel, on soil heating cables, on a tin box with an electric bulb inside—or even on the television! Mist spray overhead 2–3 times a day. Most gardeners 'start' corms and tubers in this way—Dahlias and potatoes are other examples. The already growing plants get away very much more quickly and, having half a lap start, have a longer growing period to run up to maturity. Shoots will soon emerge and the big danger is an early attack by greenfly. Put a little Lindex in the spraying water and this should control them and prevent a build-up.

When the leaves are about an inch long, you can carefully lift the corm complete with any peat held by any root action and pot into a 5–6 in. size. Pot in the normal way with the crown of the tuber just at soil surface level using a compost mix of equal parts by bulk, John Innes No. 2, peat and silver sand. Stand the pot on permanently wet sand, shingle or peat to create humidity. Keep shaded from bright light and especially direct sun, and don't get the leaves wet since they can easily be marked and spoiled.

390 Grevillea : ideal conditions

Can you advise me about a fern-like house plant known as Grevillea? When I had it four years ago, it was four leaves high and has now grown to a lanky 3 ft. Last year I re-potted it, but it still looks pretty poorly and the leaves are hanging down.

Grevillea comes from Australia, where it is called the Silk Bark Oak. Of the three or four species, the one grown in greenhouses for its handsome fern-like foliage is *G. robusta*. It is a tree-like plant which in its homeland can reach 100 ft. and soon becomes too large for the convenience of the average amateur greenhouse, and therefore is regarded as expendable, being replaced every few years by new plants grown quite easily from seed.

As the tree becomes older, grows taller, and more tree-like, there is a natural tendency for the lower leaves to be shed, and this tendency will be accentuated by disturbance or unsuitable conditions affecting the root system. Constraining into a pot a root system that likes to range in well-drained soil means that as it grows bigger you will find it increasingly difficult to keep it happy. In this questioner's case, the nutrients could have been exhausted from the soil and as the natural reaction to distress is more frequent watering to keep the plants alive, you are fighting a losing battle because this causes root rotting.

The biggest risk with all pot grown subjects is overwatering and this is most important with Grevillea. It does not like root disturbance—therefore when the young seedling is potted up for the first and last time, the pot in which it is to stay should be generously large—6 ins. is usually recommended but I prefer 9 ins. at least. The growing medium must be correct because you will not get another chance to get it right. A well-drained compost is vital; use a mix made up of equal parts John Innes No. 2; peat roughage—the tailings left in a half inch sieve, and silver sand. Water only

when the soil surface becomes dry and, when the plant has reached 18 ins. tall, introduce a weak liquid feeding once every 14–21 days at first, increasing in strength and frequency as it grows taller and bigger.

When the plant has become as tall as you want, prune out the growing tip and this will induce axillary side shoots to develop from the otherwise normally dormant buds at the leaf-joints of the leaves that have fallen.

Then, when the plant becomes too large, raise new plants from seed. You can obtain this from Sutton's of Reading, and Dobies of Chester. The seed is large and flat. Sow singly and on edge, not flat, in February or March, an inch deep in a Jiffy 7 or peat pot, so that they can be potted on without root disturbance. Germination will require a temperature of 75°F. so some form of heated seed raiser is therefore necessary. As soon as roots show through the mesh of the Jiffy 7, or sides of the peat pot, move into a 3 in. pot and when about 5 ins. tall set up in the big pot.

391 Heliotrope : its cultivation

I had a glorious show of heliotrope last summer. I have now boxed-up my plants which are resting in a warm greenhouse. How do I keep them through the winter and please tell me how to increase my stock for next year?

The sweet-scented *Heliotropium peruvianum*, sometimes called Cherry Pie, comes from Peru. There are several varieties, and although blooming is usually earlier with cuttings taken from old stools, many gardeners prefer to discard old plants and avoid overwintering costs, by sowing seed February–March in gentle heat. Geranium boxing is really intended not so much to keep plants for further use, but as a supply of fresh cuttings in spring.

Boxing-up the heliotrope stools in the same way is not really satisfactory for keeping specimen plants through the winter. Pot plants, and the best of your plants saved from the outside flower beds when cleared in the autumn, are best kept singly in good light in the greenhouse, with just enough watering to keep the soil moist, and the plant growing steadily through the winter months. If you want to take a chance and box them, follow the procedure as with Geraniums, see *No. 313*. They should keep reasonably well at a temperature not lower than 45°F. but do not overwater or you will lose the lot with black leg rot.

Maximum ventilation whenever temperature allows is vital. From the end of January to the beginning of February, a little extra heat to maintain a minimum of 50°F. will start the production of growth and new shoots very early in the year and give a little extra time to bring the new plants to flowering maturity during the summer.

No. 391 *Soft cuttings should be trimmed immediately below a leaf joint. A sharp knife or razor blade should be used.*

The ideal cutting is soft, going firm, about 2½–3 ins. long. Use a razor blade to cut very cleanly just below the leaf joint and also to slip off the two lowest leaves. Lay the cuttings aside for 5–10 mins. for the cut surface to 'dry'

slightly; this forms a layer of healing or callus tissue as precaution against too easy entry by black leg fungus spores should they be in the soil. Touch the tip of the cut into hormone rooting powder and insert firmly into sharp sand, four or five around the edge of a 4–5 inch pot. Don't set more than this number and certainly not in a seed tray because if black leg fungus does occur, it can spread very quickly through Heliotrope. This is the main difference to geranium culture; they are very susceptible to black leg and other fungus troubles. Keep them in small groups and you won't lose many, but several in a seed tray and you could lose the lot.

Place the cuttings in shade at a temperature of 65–70°F.—a propagator is ideal, of course—and rooted cuttings can be ready for weaning in 14–21 days. Pot them up a week later into a rapid draining compost mix, equal parts John Innes No. 2, peat and sharp sand. Move up pot size as growth requires until you end up in a 5 inch pot for flowering.

Of course, water a little more freely as growth increases, but beware of overwatering and ventilate as frequently as possible. This cannot be overemphasised. Cherry Pie is a charming plant with a wonderful scent but stagnant moisture and stagnant air will soon make a mess of it.

392 *Howea, the Kentia Palm : its care and cultivation*

We have recently acquired a Kentia Palm which is well established and some years of age. It stands in a good sized pot which is in a tub with a draining tap at the bottom. The plant is about 5 ft. high and has a similar spread. Could you please give me advice on its care? It will live in a humidified warm-air centrally heated house.

It sounds very much as though the previous owner of this palm has gone to some trouble— a tub with a draining tap which creates the best conditions for its welfare and not surprisingly has been rewarded with a plant that has grown well.

Commonly called Kentia Palm, it is correctly *Howea belmoreana*—its place of origin being

Lord Howe's Island in the Pacific Ocean between New Zealand and Australia.

Humidified warm air heating would seem to be a fair climate, but you will need to add to the humidity by mist spraying daily with rainwater, and sponging with tepid rainwater to keep their leaves quite clear of dust.

Repotting, recharging the growing medium, would be a fair-sized job for an amateur to tackle, especially as this is growing within an outer container, and yet, it is quite likely that a degree of root congestion has set in and nutrients are exhausted in the limited soil. Therefore, a plant this size will need a supplementary feed with a weak liquid manure, every 7–10 days from May to autumn.

Watering should be free enough to keep the growing medium well moist from March and all through the summer; reduce a little during the winter months. If peat or some other moisture-retentive material is contained in the outer tub, this is no doubt serving a useful purpose in keeping the growing medium moist. It may well also contain root that has found its way out through the drainage hole in the pot. The primary purpose of this outer tub however, should be to allow moist air to rise through the leaves. Therefore keeping this moist is just as necessary as the inner soil. A better and safer method, if you can accept this, is to have a shallow tray or two containing shingle and sand kept wet at all times placed near to or under the palm so that the greater wet surface area more effectively gives off vapour than the smaller surface area of the present outer tub.

The plant will need good light, but if you stand it near a window make sure direct sunlight does not reach the leaves or they will turn yellow; and avoid all draughts. Howea needs a winter temperature of 60–65°F. which should fit in well with your central heating, rising to 75–80°F. during the growing season.

393 Hoya: the importance of correct watering

Last year I bought a Hoya carnosa *wax flower plant. It had three blooms on, has grown very well, but the blooms dry and fall off before they grow and open.*

Hoya carnosa, the wax flower, an evergreen with clusters of pink white flowers, comes from both Australia and China where it is found growing on and climbing over the trunks and branches of trees, subsisting on debris, dust etc. collected in the bark of the host, and on moisture, taken from the air; rain, condensation, mist and humidity—referred to loosely as hygroscopic moisture. The origin of plants, is always far more important than of just academic interest because it is an indication to the temperature and conditions in which it has evolved, and therefore needs to be reproduced in order to grow well in this country.

Hoya will accept as a substitute for its tree trunk debris, a compost mix of equal parts soil with a low nutrient content, John Innes No. 1 will do, rough peat and sand (or a mix of sand and charcoal). The charcoal is advantageous if you can get it because the compost must be kept open and well-drained. The Hoya will accept this growing medium, but it will not accept water in any way other than the way it receives it in Nature.

Rain falls from above and the plant must therefore always be watered with rainwater from overhead. Stand the pot on wet shingle to encourage a moist atmosphere, but never allow waterlogging; this is why the growing medium is so fiercely draining.

Atmospheric conditions in a forest are more stable than those in an exposed position and this leads directly to some more likes and dislikes. Hoya doesn't like sudden changes or extremes. It likes plenty of light but not fierce sunshine; dappled sunlight, as in a woodland is best and is natural. The atmosphere must not be allowed to become too hot and too dry.

In dry hot weather when you may have to have greenhouse ventilators well open to keep the inside temperature down, rapid drying can then follow, so at least once daily it will be necessary to mist spray the foliage being careful to avoid the flowers. Always use tepid rainwater, never water from the tap.

The temperature range should be kept

fairly uniform–50°F. in winter, 60°F. during summer. By nature a rambling climbing plant, it is best displayed by providing trellis adjacent to the pot for it to clamber over.

Pruning should be limited to keeping the plant to shape and size, taking out stragglers and old wood. Finally, don't make the mistake that many gardeners do by removing the flower stalks after blooming, because these will often produce secondary flowers.

394 Hydrangea: moving a plant indoors

Can you tell me the proper time to dig up a small Hydrangea in my garden and transplant it into a large pot to grow indoors? It is very healthy and has borne a lot of beautiful flowers. Would it require any special attention?

Don't do it! A lot of people try this and are disappointed when the Hydrangea which has flowered so well in the garden doesn't do so well when it is moved into a pot. The spectacular mop heads that you see in the florist's shop are always young plants of specially bred varieties that have been grown and fed intensively. I think you would do better to leave your evidently quite happy plant where it is and to take cuttings for potting and growing indoors. They will not be as spectacular as the special indoor types but you will at least avoid the very likely probability of spoiling or even losing the parent plant.

Soft tip cuttings will root readily in sand in spring and can be potted up, taking out the growing tip when four full leaves are showing in order to produce four axillary shoots which should produce four 'flower' heads.

Bring the potted plant under cover if frost threatens and in March begin to gradually increase watering as foliage develops and increases moisture demand. There must be absolutely no check from dryness at root, and as soon as the 'flower' buds show, begin feeding either by scratching a dessertspoonful of Eclipse Garden compound into the soil or with liquid manure each week. Use one with an analysis as balanced as possible, Bio or Sangral 'General'.

If you are growing the plant indoors, you must realise that the light intensity will be much less than outside, and this disadvantage should be counteracted by standing the plant outdoors at every opportunity during the summer.

Incidentally, you will notice that the word 'flower' is in quote marks. This is because, strictly speaking, what we are referring to are not flowers at all. The spectacular 'flower' heads, whether pink, blue, white, or cream, are in fact modified leaves called bracts. The actual flowers are the insignificant little 'pips' in the centre of each 'flower'.

395 Impatiens: why it drips at the leaf tips

Can you explain why my busy lizzie exudes sugary crystals at its leaf tips?

Dripping is not at all unusual with Impatiens and is one way in which this plant is able to shed excess moisture. There are other plants that can do the same—notably the Swiss Cheese plant, *Monstera deliciosa*, which you may also have growing in your home. If the plant is taking up more moisture than it can transpire or link up with carbon dioxide to form sugars and starches, the excess sap oozes from the cells near the leaf tips, accumulates as a droplet, and may then crystallise.

It is more likely to happen to a plant kept in a very damp atmosphere, into which it is difficult for more water to evaporate; on the other hand it can be caused by overwatering—i.e. literally forcing water into the plant so that it has to come out somewhere! If you feel that you could have been providing it with too many drinks—a common mistake with many plants kept indoors—cut back a little on the kindness and the trouble should soon clear up.

396 Impatiens: the new short varieties

My busy lizzies grow tall and straggly with few flowers. Why?

This probably happens because they are etiolated—the technical term used to describe the condition when plants become drawn and spindly due to not getting enough light. You see the same thing happening with seeds which are sown too thickly in poor light so that they race each other to reach up to the light (mustard and cress are good examples). Move the plant to a brighter position and you should be able to overcome the difficulty. If the plant is already too tall, trim back the more straggly shoots using the tips as cuttings. These will root easily in damp sand.

Some forms of Impatiens have a natural tall habit and it could well be that you would like the compact dwarf growing forms better. Try the 'Zig-Zag' and 'Imp' strains—these are F1 Hybrids and become smothered in very brilliantly coloured flowers. You can obtain seeds from Sutton's, Reading, and when established, propagate more of your favourite colours by cuttings.

Your feeding could also be contributing to the problem. Check on the feed you are using and make sure that the proportions of N.P. and K. are equal; if they are not, switch to a feed where they are balanced. If the N.P.K. ratios of your feed already are equal, dissolve a very small pinch of permanganate of potash—Condy's fluid—and an equal amount of Epsom salts in a pint of water, and use this alternately with the general feed until blooming increases and foliage colour improves.

397   Impatiens : why do the buds fall off?

Could you please advise me about the care of a busy lizzie as a house plant? For many years I have grown them, but am frequently troubled by buds falling off. It cannot be caused by dryness because I have the plant standing in a saucer of water.

Although it will tolerate shade and a fairly dry atmosphere and will therefore grow quite well indoors, Impatiens needs a damp atmosphere if it is to thrive and bloom well. Watering should be fairly free, but this doesn't mean spending its life standing in water, neither does it mean waterlogging the soil. The compost therefore needs to contain plenty of sand or grit so that it is kept open and porous. Use a compost made-up of equal parts by bulk, John Innes No. 2, peat and coarse sand. Because the frequent watering will quickly dissolve out the soluble nutrients, every 10–14 days when in flower make one of the waterings a feed by adding a little liquid manure to the water. Use one with a bias towards the K or potash content, like Sangral 'Tomato' or Bio 'Tomato'. This will tone up your plants and put extra colour into the flowers in the same way as this feeding aids the ripening process of tomatoes and other fruit.

A far better method than standing the plant in water in a saucer—as so many people do—is to stand the pot on a shallow tray of gravel or shingle that is kept permanently wet. The surface area evaporating moisture is therefore much greater than the wet surface area of a saucer or pan of water. Furthermore, any tendency to over-watering and stagnation which is easily done if you haven't got your compost quite right—is reduced by the fierce drainage under the pot. Dry air, incorrect watering, these are two basic reasons why buds will drop.

A third could be light intensity if growing indoors in a subdued light so position the plant near the window where it can get more light. If you have a greenhouse or a conservatory you have no problems. Grow several plants, and, in turn, bring one plant into the living room for a day returning it to the greenhouse for a week to get over the dryness it has experienced in the home. That way you'll keep them all happy.

398   Ivy : why variegation is lost

A pot-grown ivy with nice leaves—cream in the centre and green outside—has been grown on a window ledge where it didn't get much light. It produces new leaves quickly but they are pale green. I have moved it to a sunnier position and would like to know if the leaves will change colour, or does it need more drastic treatment to bring back the variegation?

By the description 'cream in the centre and green outside' it seems likely that this could be the variety 'Gold Heart' or as it is sometimes called, 'Jubilee'.

It is vital with all variegated ivies to provide full light at all times because any reduction in light intensity means that the leaf must make more chlorophyll to keep up its production of carbohydrate. This means that the cream area will take on a greenish hue, reduce in area or be lost altogether.

Frequently, leaves do not develop variegation until approaching maturity, but if a shoot develops a succession of leaves that are all plain green, it is fairly certain that 'reversion' to type has occurred. This is a common fault with many variegated plants—particularly with ivies. Cut off any offending shoots as soon as it is clear that reversion has occurred.

You can best avoid this trouble happening by growing the ivy in good light, at a well-lit window, or by growing several outside and bringing them in separately for a day at a time.

At the first autumn opportunity, repot into a compost mix made up of equal parts by bulk John Innes No. 2, peat and sand with a sprinkling of Humber Eclipse. Always propagate from the best variegated shoots by cuttings or layering in spring and, if possible, from plants that have shown the least tendency to throw reverted shoots.

399 Jasmine: conditions required for its bloom

A few years ago my greenhouse paraffin oil heater failed and my jasmine was killed above ground. Now, although it has grown up to the roof again, no flowers are showing. What can I do to get flowers? It is growing beside a grape vine. Does jasmine need lime and if so would the lime be detrimental to the vine?

In addition to the Winter Jasmine *Jasminum nudiflorum*, and the Summer Jasmine *J. officinales* and its varieties, there are others that need the temperatures and conditions of a heated greenhouse. It is impossible from this brief description to say which of these tender greenhouse species you have, or for that matter, whether your plant is Stephanotis which is often called, most confusingly, the Madagascar

Jasmine. See *No. 418*. It all goes to show how important it is to know the full botanical name of your plants, and if you are not sure, get them identified properly.

However, assuming that your plant is a true jasmine, it will probably be one of the more popular kinds—one of a group that all originate from the warm climates of Borneo, Malaya and south China. A high winter temperature is therefore essential, 55–60°F., and you should have heating that is capable of maintaining this value.

Also, quite evident considering the place of origin, is the degree of light intensity needed and here is the most likely reason for lack of bloom. It could be that the grape vine is crowding out the jasmine and taking too much of the light. Jasmine can hardly get too much light in this country.

Another conflict of interests could be the humidity; these jungle plants like a damp humid atmosphere so when you have the greenhouse ventilation wide open, and not too much risk to the vines will ensue, spray the Jasmine foliage to get it well wet, but do this early in the day, so that the house doesn't remain damp overnight.

I don't think you should worry unduly about lime; the vine likes plenty of lime anyway and the Jasmine will soon tell you with yellowing 'chlorosis' of the foliage if it becomes too alkaline.

400 Kalanchoe attacked by fungus

Last year I bought a Kalanchoe and in February little red flowers appeared. In June I put the plant in the garden where it stayed until just before the frosts commenced. The plant has always had good light and has been watered sparingly, and it grew quite a lot during the summer and looked generally healthy. About a week ago I noticed that the bottom part of the plant was covered with white growths and these are spreading to the top of the plant. Please could you advise me if the plant is dying and whether there is anything that can be done?

This is a very attractive plant when in bloom and is increasingly popular as an indoor pot plant. Strange as it may seem, this is a clue to the most common problem with this plant: modern housing has a high degree of central or controlled heating. Under such conditions, drying-out of pot plants is fast and watering takes place more frequently.

Kalanchoe, however, has thick fleshy leaves in which it stores moisture so that it is able to avoid the effects of drying better than most other pot plants that are brought into the home. Watering on the same scale as most other plants is too much for Kalanchoe and can easily lead to soft pappy growth that is wide open to mildew and other fungal attack. The best remedy for this is to spray a fungicide and keep the plant much drier. Overwatering is something you must always be careful about. In this case, however, the description suggests something else—especially as it has been outside in the garden. It sounds very much like it has picked up a severe infestation of the pest known as mealy bug which looks like blobs of cotton wool around stems and leaves.

You can try the drastic method of dabbing with methylated spirits to arrest it, but if the trouble and damage has gone too far you will have to destroy the plants. But first, cut off the top of the plant plus any shoot ends, if it has made side growths, and after leaving these in the sunshine for 48 hours to dry, insert them into sand in the same way as you would cuttings. Destroy the old infected plant stool by burning.

When roots have formed on the new 'cuttings', pot up using a fresh compost mix, equal parts of John Innes No. 1 fine sieved mushroom compost or, if unavailable, peat, and fine sieved plaster rubble if possible or use sand. You will notice that this is not a particularly rich compost and we take this point one step further by always using a pot that you would normally consider rather small; this will restrict the roots. Kalanchoes flower best when they have to fight hard to survive, hence the barren soil and the small pot.

401 Mimosa : its care and cultivation

Could you advise me on the care of my Mimosa?

It is container grown and the garden centre tell me it is fully hardened-off.

The flowering Mimosa is really Acacia and it is likely that your plant is *Acacia decurrens* var. *dealbeata*. Unless you live in the warmest part of the country, it would be very unwise to regard your Mimosa as hardened off, whatever your assurances. Grown on a large scale in Spain and North Africa for British and European markets, it is actually native of Australia and, perhaps surprisingly, a close relation of the runner bean.

It needs a minimum temperature of 50°F. in winter and that means that it is really only suitable for a sheltered position against a south-facing wall, and needs protection from cold winds and from frost by sheets, straw mattresses, or specially cut evergreen foliage. Otherwise, it is best grown in a greenhouse or conservatory, and not a small one either because this is really a tree. In Australia, it grows to 50ft. and, at best, you would have to prune your plant pretty heavily to stop it from growing too big. The solution for most people is to grow it as a shrub in a large tub.

Although not a confirmed lime-hater like Azaleas and Rhododendrons, the plant will become chlorotic on chalky or limy soils, therefore when you plant or repot—February is the best time—do so into a compost of equal parts lime-free ericaceous compost, peat and sand. Pruning back to size and shape can also be done at this time. Watering is best kept to moderation at all times, otherwise growth will become lush and size a problem. If pots are not too large to be unmanageable, they can be moved outside during summer; otherwise provide plenty of ventilation during warm weather.

402 Mimosa will not keep over winter

I have two young 'sensitive plants' which were raised from seed last spring, but the leaves seem to have shrivelled and look poor. Will they revive in the spring? They are in the warm living-room and are watered about once a week.

Unlike the florists' flowering Mimosa which is actually *Acacia*, see *No. 401*, the 'sensitive plant' is so called because of its strange habit of folding its leaves when touched. It is *Mimosa pudica*, a true Mimosa, and often incorrectly but understandably confused because of its name with another and larger growing species, *M. sensitiva*. Both come from Brazil where they are perennial shrubs, but in this country, they are usually treated as greenhouse annuals. It is a waste of time to try to overwinter the 'sensitive plant' in this country because it resents low temperatures—65°F. or less—and subdued light. Seed is inexpensive and readily obtainable from Sutton's, Reading; Dobies, Chester; or Thompson and Morgan, Ipswich. Sow in 70°F. in February or March and set the seedlings into 3–4 ins. pots containing a loam/peat/sand compost or John Innes No. 1. Water freely with a weak liquid manure—quarter strength—and keep in a light airy place. With the onset of autumn and winter, the lower light intensity heralds the scrapping of the plants. You would need artificial light and a high winter temperature to get them to remain healthy and not drop all their leaves.

403 Monstera: what to do with the aerial roots

Is it normal for a Swiss cheese plant to throw out lots of thick roots from the main stem?

Despite its common name, *Monstera deliciosa* comes from Mexico, where the pineapple-flavoured fruits of the mature plants are highly regarded. The plants sold in this country as attractive cut-leaved house plants are small youngsters. In its natural habitat, it creeps and clambers up and over nearby trees, sending down aerial roots from several feet up like a bamboo curtain.

As a decorative feature, this plant is most often required to conform to a short standard form, as distinct from its natural tendency to flop and clamber around. Therefore, it is best to guide the first few aerial roots that form on a young plant so that they enter the soil and become supporting props. If too many form and get in the way, you can cut them off, but it helps your plant to take in more nutrient and remain vigorous if you can guide them all into

the soil, perhaps even into other pots alongside. Use a compost of equal parts John Innes No. 1 and peat, plus a half part sand.

Monsteras prefer a rather humid atmosphere, and as they are not likely to get that in the homes and offices where they are so often used for green decoration, they will appreciate the substitute of two or three daily mist sprayings to wet the foliage, using clear tepid water. The pet hates are draughts and bright sun. Dappled light or partial shade is best and a well-grown plant should produce enough lustre on its leaves not to need any artificial preparations for a glossy sheen. The plant is evergreen, so keep the soil reasonably moist at all times. In centrally-heated houses and offices, the moisture evaporation—called 'transpiration'—from the foliage can be quite rapid and this must be replaced because they must never be allowed to become dry at the roots. Indeed, this is one plant where it is better to overwater rather than the other way. Monsteras can sometimes be seen to be shedding excess water from their leaves in the form of droplets exuding from the points at the 'holes' in the leaves, see *No. 405*.

404 Monstera: how to reduce its size

I have a Swiss cheese plant which has grown to a height of 5ft. Can I cut it back to 3 ft. which is tall enough for me—and is there any way of stopping its growth?

Never let a Monstera become so tall that it needs such drastic treatment. You are contemplating cutting off a third or more of the main stem and as a plant growing vigorously would most likely bleed severely, prepare for the decapitation by slowing it down. You can do this by withholding water so that the pot becomes fairly dry and then watering only sparingly so that it remains dry for at least two to three weeks. Carry on daily spraying of the foliage by all means (see *No. 403*), but the sap flow *within* the plant must be slowed.

If you haven't been adding foliar feed to the daily spraying, do so now. Just a few drops to make a very dilute solution is all that is needed. As you should be spraying two or three times a day, the accumulation build-up of chemical feed has to be borne in mind.

Cut the main stem to a point just above a node (leaf joint) and have a little charcoal handy to sprinkle over the cut end, just in case bleeding does occur.

Three or four days after cutting, begin watering again slowly at first. Either give a balanced liquid feed every 10–14 days or scratch in a small teaspoonful of Humber Eclipse or Growmore to the soil surface at three-week intervals over a period of two to three months. All being well, you can expect this treatment to give you some side shoots and fine new leaves.

You can use the cut-off head to try your hand at making some cuttings. Use the same compost as for normal cultivation, see *No. 403*, using the cut-off portion to chop into pieces as though for vine cuttings, see *No. 203*. This can be done at any time of the year. You will need to have a propagator because a very humid atmosphere and a temperature of 70–80°F. will be required. Keep shaded from bright light and as soon as the roots are formed, move from the propagator gradually. Careful weaning is all important.

405 Monstera: drips around the leaf edges

I have a Monstera deliciosa *growing in the house. Every morning the edges of the leaves have water drops around them. Is this normal?*

Plants that live in a moisture-laden atmosphere naturally have some difficulty in evaporating—transpiring—excess water from their leaves. Sometimes conditions like saturated humidity and excessive moisture at root level will increase this difficulty and the moisture, unable to evaporate fast enough, simply collects at the edges of the leaves or, as in this case, at the ends of the segments. Coming from an area of high humidity, Monstera is one of the plants that has evolved the ability to cope with this condition. Plants that are not so evolved cannot cope and are likely to develop the bloated condition called oedema or 'dropsy'.

Probably the most frequently met condition causing dew drops is a warm day, causing the plant to work fast. Then with sap moving fast and the plant drawing hard on plentiful moisture at root level, the cooler night air is unable to absorb as much moisture as during the warm day, and since the plant does not slow down that fast, the water collects instead of evaporating and you find dew drops in the morning.

There is nothing much to worry about. You may have been overwatering a little; try reducing this and mist spray with rainwater every day. This is more important than moisture at the roots. You will find that the problem will abate when there is a more stable night/day temperature.

406 Neanthe, the dwarf palm: care and cultivation

Is it safe to split up a Neanthe bella *growing in a 9 in. pot, which has formed two distinct stems at soil level?*

There are very many different kinds of palms from many different places of origin, in all shapes and sizes and growing in a wide range of conditions. The smaller types, and younger specimens of the larger ones, are very striking in large rooms, halls, foyers, showrooms etc. and one of the best for cultivation indoors is the plant that you have, the so-called Dwarf Palm or Mexican Fiesta Palm, *Neanthe bella*. It is tolerant of shade and can be used indoors more permanently than many plants that really need to be brought in only for short visits and returned to the greenhouse again if they are to be kept in good order.

Neanthe is not only dwarf, it is also very slow growing, and it is unusual to have a twin-stemmed specimen—if it really is a twin stem, and not a pair of plants that have grown very closely together from a twin seed.

If it is definitely one plant, I think it would be extremely risky to try parting unless it could be done leaving one with a good root formation and the other with enough root to give it a reasonable chance of recovery and establishment. Both will require a recuperative period in a warm, humid, shady, draught-free position.

On the other hand, if it is in fact two plants, root separation will be a difficult job requiring much more care and patience. Either way it is a risk because the plant hates root disturbance. However, if you decide to take a chance the best time to do the job would be spring, using a compost mix of equal parts John Innes No. 2, peat and sand, and the warm weather hopefully following shortly will help recovery. Water freely and give it a liquid feed every month.

407 Orchids: correct potting for Cymbidiums

I have a Cymbidium orchid which I have had for two years. I have had it in the house and it still looks healthy, although it has not flowered. The size of the pot that it was bought in is 3 in. across the top. I have thought of moving it into our greenhouse, but the only heating we have is paraffin, and the temperature falls to freezing point as the glass is to ground level.

The first thing I would do is to get rid of the paraffin heater. Double glaze the greenhouse with polythene film to reduce both heat loss and heating costs. Use a clean fumeless electric fan heater that will still provide air movement when the inbuilt thermostat has automatically cut off the heating element as the required temperature is reached. Although Cymbidiums are regarded as one of the hardiest orchids, they should not be allowed to experience temperatures below 45°F if you want bloom: freezing point is hopeless. In time, a flowering-sized plant can be expected to require a 10–12 in. pot or even larger, so if this plant is still in a 3 in. pot after two years, little wonder it hasn't flowered!

The best time to re-pot is February to March but if you have read these notes during the growing season, rather than wait the better part of another year for February to come round again, repot at once causing as little root disturbance as possible. When repotting at the right time—February to March— prise out some of the old soil from the root system and repot using the next size larger only. If it is a new planting, use a pot that will just take the plant comfortably since a lot of spare room will discourage flowering.

Cymbidiums, although very popular, are one of the exotic orchids and if you are going to grow it well, you should be prepared to go to some trouble to get the rather specialised growing materials that many orchids need. Osmunda fibre is extremely difficult to obtain, but if you are lucky enough to get some, use this two parts by bulk to one part chopped sphagnum moss and one part ericaceous compost with a little crushed brick rubble to keep the compost open instead of settling into a wet mass. Failing the Osmunda fibre, the next best course is to obtain a compost suitable for Cymbidiums from a commercial orchid grower who, if he too cannot get Osmunda, will be making up his own compost. However, do be quite certain to stipulate Cymbidiums. Don't just ask for 'orchid compost' because different orchids flourish in different materials, proportions and ingredients.

If you prefer to make your own, try rubbing sphagnum moss peat through a half-inch sieve and use the roughage; also add a further part of ericaceus compost to the Osmunda formula given above. The shortage of Osmunda has forced many orchid growers to experiment. A large collection I know in Berkshire is grown in a compost made up of rough sphagnum, chopped bracken, leaf mould and crumbled polystyrene made by grating down a quantity of broken unsaleable ceiling tiles! I mention this to illustrate how in orchid growing, as in every other aspect of gardening, experimenting is important and of course can be the source of much satisfaction when you are successful.

Water freely with rainwater during the growing period—February to August—and try to maintain a steady temperature 65–75°F with shade from sunlight. Maintain a very humid atmosphere by watering the greenhouse floor twice a day and hanging up a wet blanket, see *Nos. 281* and *412*. If the weather becomes very hot with the temperature in the eighties, the plants will also need mist spraying with tepid water—but keep this away from the flowers.

The blooms of Cymbidiums are very large and generally fall into a flowering pattern of alternate years. The non-flowering year's rest contributes to the production of better blooms.

When this pattern has been established, it is the general practice to repot the February after flowering.

408 Orchids : care and cultivation of the hardy Pleione

I recently bought a Pleione formosana. *Could you tell me how to look after it? Also, is it possible for me to propagate it? I have a heated greenhouse.*

Pleiones are relatively hardy and are often grown by cool greenhouse and alpine enthusiasts. The growth cycle begins in February when watering and a temperature rise to 60°F. produce flowers very quickly and before much leaf growth has taken place.

The opportunity to repot comes as the flowers fade. Drainage must be fierce, and for this reason they are often grown in 'pans'—which are like 9 in. diameter flower pots but only 2½–3 ins. deep and the shallow soil depth therefore ensures that water drains through quickly. Pleiones can be grown just as well in a normal depth pot provided you place plenty of drainage crock in the bottom. Place a thin layer of sphagnum moss over the crock to prevent the compost falling through and top up with a compost of equal parts Osmunda fibre if you can get it (see *No. 407*), sphagnum moss, peat, roughage (the tailings left in a ½ in. sieve), ericaceous compost and silver sand. Into this compost plant the bulbs to about half their depth, 3–4 ins. apart and water them well. As the bulbs begin to grow, cover the pots with live green sphagnum; prodding this into the compost between the bulbs. Most bags of sphagnum that you buy will contain some pieces of light green living moss—or ask your florist (they use it for wreath making) to save some for you.

Shoots arise from the existing bulbs which are then replaced by new bulbs forming at the base of these shoots. The old bulbs fade and it is the new bulbs that will produce next spring's flowers. The live sphagnum covering creates the ideal conditions for the formation of the new bulbs.

Keep well-watered through the early sum-mer and then, about July or August, begin gradually to reduce and water sparingly so that from September the compost is kept barely moist. Maintain a minimum temperature of 45°F. until February when increased watering and warmth starts the process again. As the new pseudo bulbs form and increase, these can be divided at the repot stage and planted as separate bulbs.

409 Orchids : Lady's Slippers are easy to grow

I would like to grow some Lady's Slipper Orchids. Are they very demanding?

A native to the British countryside, the true lady's slipper orchid is *Cypripedium calceolus.* It is a pretty little yellow orchid that, as its name suggests, is found on limy chalky soils, but unhappily all too rarely. Its natural habitat is woodland settings where the soil is shaded, cool, sheltered from cold winds and with a high humus content, and it is these conditions that you should try to reproduce in your cool greenhouse.

Use a compost of equal parts John Innes No. 1, peat and a half part crushed plaster rubble and/or very coarse sand grit. If you can't get plaster rubble, try to obtain instead ground limestone chippings. Keep just moist, never allowing it to dry out. A good supplier of this orchid and many other Slipper Orchids is J. A. Mars of Haslemere, Surrey.

410 Phoenix, the date palm : will it grow outdoors?

For the past four years I have had a Phoenix Palm which has grown exceedingly well in a pot in the house. In the summer, it is placed outside until October. Now it is getting large and I am wondering if I could plant it outside permanently as it will soon be too large for the house?

Phoenix dactylifera *is the date palm and the species usually grown as an indoor plant is a dwarf form* P. roebelinii *which gets up to 4–6 ft. As a rule it is grown as a floor-standing specimen feature and thus requires plenty of* room to do it justice. Although it is becoming too large for your house, you cannot plant it in the garden because, unless you live in the relatively frost-free extreme south-west of the country, it is hardly likely to survive long. Palms hate draughts and sudden temperature variation—and outdoor conditions would be altogether too harsh for a Phoenix.

The conditions needed are very similar indeed to those indicated for the Howea, see *No. 392*.

If you have to part company with it, maybe a local hotel or restaurant would be interested in buying it.

411 Pineapple flower : why doesn't it grow fruit?

In April I bought a pineapple flower. This has now finished flowering but there is no sign of fruit. Will it flower again next year, and what treatment should I give it to make it fruit?

This is a case of confusion, and likely disappointment, due to the use of common names. The pineapple flower is not the fruit pineapple of commerce. So far as this country is concerned, pineapples can only grow in well-equipped greenhouses. The true pineapple is *Ananas satera*, a prickly fleshy-leaved plant from tropical America, see *No. 412*. The 'pineapple flower' is a common name given to a bulbous member of the lily family, *Eucomis punctata*, which comes from South Africa. It will grow outdoors in the mildest parts of the country, but needs protection from frost.

With pot culture, plant one single bulb to a 5-inch pot containing a compost mix of equal parts John Innes No. 1, sand, and peat or well-rotted mushroom compost. Pot up in March and from a moderate watering rate, increase with growth so that by May when foliage area is increasing fast, water is being given freely. As the flower spike appears, provide liquid manure every 10–14 days until the flower fades when watering should be reduced. By the end of September, the plant is virtually dry and has only an occasional very light watering.

Stand in a frost-free position, 45°F. minimum, and restart the growth again in March as

before, repotting with fresh compost at the third year, and dividing any offsets that come away easily. These can be potted up singly the same as the parent and will bear flowers in a year or two.

412 Pineapple : will the plant bear ripe fruits?

I'm growing pineapple tops in pots in my greenhouse. Some have produced some small fruits. Will these grow to maturity?

It gives intense satisfaction and not a little fascination to get pineapple tops to root, even more so to get them to produce embryo fruits (but you would be well advised to regard them as decorative plants and not be disappointed by expecting to get ripe fruit). To grow properly and to have any chance at all of developing its fruit, each plant will need to be in a large pot, at least 10–12 inches in diameter, and to ripen it will need a lot of bright sunlight, because coming from tropical America, it is at a disadvantage in this country. The recommended compost mix is equal parts John Innes No. 2 and peat, plus enough coarse sand to keep the compost open and well-drained. A moist atmosphere and free watering are important during spring and summer, but there must be no waterlogging, standing the pot in saucers containing water is definitely wrong, although often advised.

Although a moist atmosphere is important, it does not relish getting its leaves wet; indeed, the leaves of the variegated variety of pineapple can spot badly if water drops are allowed to remain. Therefore stand the pots on permanently wet shingle and nearby suspend a piece of old blanket in a bowl of water to act as a giant wick which will give off a lot of water vapour.

During spring and summer months, when fruits are forming, it is a good policy to irrigate with liquid manure water made up by putting some well-rotted stable manure or some of the denser less strawy parts of old mushroom compost, into a sack and steeping this in a water tub. Add a few drops of a liquid fertiliser with a potash bias—like Tomorite—and let one of the daily 'little and often' waterings per week be with this. The soil should be kept moist, no more. As soon as the fruit begins to ripen, discontinue all watering and remove the wet blanket so that the atmosphere becomes drier.

In order to give every encouragement, you will need to maintain a summertime temperature of around 80–85°F. which should not be too difficult in a sunny season but the minimum winter temperature 60–65°F. may be a bit demanding for most people. To minimise the effect should the temperature drop below this figure, keep the air dry and give only enough water to prevent the thick fleshy spiky leaves from flagging. If you can provide these cultural conditions you may expect to get a fruit on your pineapple plant in three to four years, but you will need a great deal of sunshine for it to ripen. In March, the cycle begins again with the return to increased humidity, watering and heat.

As well as growing from the tops of the fruits that you house successfully, pineapple plants may also be propagated by carefully parting shoots that begin to form as soon as the ripe or partly ripened fruit has been cut. You can pot these up like corms in small pots in a temperature of around 80°F., keeping them partially shaded until rooted and established.

413 Plumbago : re-potting and cultivation

Last year my Plumbago capensis *blossomed and climbed successfully. This year it produced no shoots at all, but after turning it out of its 5 in. pot, I found that it had enormous roots for what I thought was a dead plant. Can I repot it so that it has a chance to flower next year?*

A 5-inch pot is certainly much too small for a well-established and mature *Plumbago capensis*. The best time to repot is early spring, tease out what old soil you can without too much disturbance and then choose a pot that will comfortably take the roots—it may be 8–9 inches wide, possibly larger. Use a compost mix equal parts John Innes No. 3 and peat, plus a half part grit sand or a whole part if softish with not

many large grit particles in order to keep the compost open and free draining.

Watering will need to be fairly free from April through to end of September. Position the plant so that the foliage receives good light but not direct sun.

Plumbago is very susceptible to aphis and white fly; at the very first sign of greenfly, spray with Lindex, and for white fly, spray with Malathion or the new insecticide 'Sprayday', which should keep both pests under control.

The summer growth is sometimes so rampant as to constitute a problem in the confines of a small greenhouse, and the plant may be moved to a sheltered position outdoors and of course it is often used as tall contrasting 'dot' plant in summer bedding displays. See *No. 119*. Two precautions you must guard against when standing pot grown Plumbago outdoors are drying out and the tendency of the rampant foliage and flowers to catch the wind and topple over.

Bloom is carried on the current year's growth continuously throughout summer months. After flowering has ceased—this may be October, November or even December, although advisedly you shouldn't allow it to continue flowering for quite that long—all flowered shoots should be cut back severely to within 1 inch of the base of origin from the main lead stem, removing all weak and crossing growth.

Some people advise leaving all the pruning until March, but I don't advise this for amateurs, because ventilation and the passage of air through and around plants during winter is a vital factor in order to prevent stagnant air which encourages fungus.

Too much foliage on plants in a closed greenhouse will slow down, or even stop air movement, so, whenever you have the choice, and the chance, take out unnecessary growth and foliage early. The plant needs a rest during winter, so cut the watering down to just enough to keep the soil from drying out completely. Try to keep a minimum temperature of 45–50°F.—55° would be better—but never within 10°F. of frost. If your plant needs a further repotting, February to March is the time and then as warmer weather approaches, a gradually increasing rate of watering with liquid feed will restart the plant into vigorous growth.

414 Poinsettia : how to get colour into old stools

Once my poinsettia has bloomed it continues to grow beautifully, but only green leaves. I have had it three years now, but no sign of red flowers. What can I do? Is it worth keeping?

This is the frequent experience of many amateur gardeners who try to keep their Christmas poinsettias going. The Christmas poinsettia, so popular because of the brilliant scarlet bracts, is *Euphorbia pulcherrima*. The red flowers are not flowers at all but modified leaves, called bracts, that surround the true flowers which themselves are quite insignificant.

The plants that are sold at Christmas are usually the product of special growing conditions and, furthermore, these brilliantly coloured specimens are young plants from cuttings that always colour better than older plants. You will get better results from cuttings, but here is a procedure using the old stools which is worth trying.

After Christmas, the red bracts will decline and turn green. All shoots should be pruned back during April to the second bud or eye from the base. New shoots will then form and when these are an inch or so long, repot the plants. Turn them out of the old pots, remove as much old soil as you can, shake out the roots and cut away any long straggling ends. Choose a pot just large enough to take the root system. Use a compost mix of 2 parts John Innes No. 2., 1 part rubbed out and friable cowpat if you can get it—otherwise the more solid parts of mushroom compost, or failing that, peat will have to do—and finally a half part of silver sand.

Place the plant in a well-lit but not full sun position, with a temperature of not less than 65–75°F. Water freely and during June or July upturn and tap out the pots to examine the development of new roots. When a good layer of new root has been formed enclosing the soil ball, pot-on to the next size pot, using the same compost. Then water well and remove the plant outside to a sunny position, plunging the pot in a peat layer to help guard against drying out, the great danger at this time. Keep the pots moist and mist spray the foliage daily with clear water. It stays here until September, when it should be taken into the greenhouse with a minimum maintained temperature of 55–60°F.

In October, raise the temperature a little to 60–70°F. and, twice a week, give a liquid feed that has a slight potash bias—'Tomorite' diluted or Sangral 'Tomato' would do quite well. Keep this up until the new bracts are fully developed and coloured and then cease the liquid feed, replacing it with clear tepid water sufficient only to keep the soil moist. Your timing will probably be different to the Christmas period, for which they were originally prepared, but as soon as the coloured bracts fail, move to a greenhouse with a minimum temperature of 45°F. with pots laid on their side with the plants resting until April when the plants can be put back and the process repeated.

This may sound a rather elaborate procedure, but not everybody has the facilities for producing young cuttings. However, if you have a propagator you can take 2–3 in. long cuttings during the spring and root them in sand. Pot them up when rested then follow the above procedures. The mid-summer outside cool period is important to the later colouring of the bracts.

415 Polka Dot plant : care and cultivation

Recently I bought a Polka Dot plant. It is about 18 in. high, with light green leaves that look as if they have been splashed with pink paint. Can you tell me its proper name; is it suitable for the garden or greenhouse, and can you give me some more information about it?

The Polka Dot plant is *Hypoestes sanguinolenta*, a tender, shrubby foliage plant not suitable for planting in the garden but which can be grown in the house. Indeed it is very popular for this purpose as its pink dotted foliage makes it unusual and attractive. It will do very much better, however, and retain its spots in the better light of a warm moist greenhouse or conservatory. In the dry air of the home it is liable to drop its leaves, so daily spraying will be beneficial.

Repot in the early spring and at this time the rootstock can be divided, but only if it parts easily. As with so many of these sub-tropical foliage plants, the growing medium needs to be moisture-retentive, but at the same time well-drained, in order to avoid waterlogging. The Polka Dot will like a slightly rich nutrient supply as well, so make up a compost mix comprised of equal parts John Innes No. 2 or 3, peat and garden or mushroom compost teased out and sieved through a ½ in. sieve, and sharp sand.

416   Rubber plant: care and cultivation

Can you tell me how to look after a rubber plant?

The rubber plant, *Ficus elastica*, is the species frequently offered but *F. robusta* makes a more durable house plant with darker green glossy leaves and is one of the few plants which will grow in low light intensity, so it is little wonder that it is so popular as an indoor plant.

However, not everyone is able to grow rubber plants successfully and usually the problem is one or other of its pet hates—draughts, a too dry atmosphere and direct heat from a fire or radiator. It will stand temperatures as low as 40–45°F. but it is most important to try to maintain a constant temperature, with no great variation between day and night. Modern central heating systems often incorporate a measure of temperature control, but all too often this means that the air is dry.

Many people try to overcome this by standing the pot in a pool of water. This is not really satisfactory—Ficus is not a bog plant. It is more important to create atmospheric humidity,

and rather than a saucer or dish of water it is better to stand your plant on a tray of gritty shingle that is kept wet. The evaporation area is greater than that of the saucer and of course waterlogging is obviated by the fierce drainage under the pot.

Proprietary preparations can be purchased which give a sheen to the leaves, and it is a popular idea that sponging with milk is good for the plant. Using milk in this way could easily do more harm than good by encouraging mould and other fungi spores to develop on the milk traces on the leaves. If a plant is growing healthily, it will have a natural gloss and sponging every other day with clear water to keep the leaves dust free is all that is necessary. In a centrally-heated dry atmosphere, sponging may not create enough humidity you should then mist spray with clear water once, or even twice a day.

Keep the soil moist at all times and every 10–14 days add a few drops of liquid feed, with the NPK proportions in reasonable balance— Bio General or Sangral General will do very well.

When roots begin pushing through the drainage hole or appearing at the soil surface, you can take this as an indication that the plant is becoming pot-bound and needs a move into a larger pot. The best time to re-pot is spring, but if you are very careful not to disturb the root ball, you can repot into a larger pot at almost any time. Use a compost mix, 2 parts John Innes No. 1 or 2 and 1 part peat plus 1 part sand.

417   Rubber plant: white bugs and falling leaves

In the last few months, my rubber plant has shed seven leaves, leaving only four on top. I have repotted it in John Innes compost and while doing so found whitish bugs on the roots so I washed them in warm water. Would these bugs be responsible for the leaves falling off?

It is more than likely that the loss of the leaves is due to the shock of washing the roots, coming on top of the stress to the plant by the infestation of mealy bug. A compost mix containing more than John Innes would have been better. The important thing is not to disturb the roots any more than you have to. Read *No. 416* concerning care of the rubber plant, especially the points about humidity. As it now has only four leaves left, move the plant into good light—but not direct sunshine—so that the leaves can work at full speed.

You cannot rely absolutely upon having removed all the pests by washing the roots, so into the water which you give the plants add enough liquid Malathion to make a solution as recommended on the bottle. Water with this solution exclusively for a few weeks so that the whole root ball becomes permeated with the insecticide.

When your plant is thriving again and getting over its bad experience, you may consider aerial layering, see *No. 418*. The old stem may then produce side shoots or new growth from below.

418 Rubber plant : reducing an overgrown specimen

A rubber plant which almost touches our ceiling has recently grown side shoots and new shoots from the roots. How can I cut them away without harming the plant?

Side shoots are normal in healthy thriving plants and it would be sacrilege to cut them away. However, within the confines of a normal house, a rubber plant can become too high, too wide and altogether too handsome, and when this happens, the rational thing to do is not to slaughter the plant, but find it a larger home. You may well be very surprised at what a hotel or restaurant would pay you for it.

However, if you can live with the wider plant that it will become as the side shoots grow, you could reduce the height by aerial layering the too tall stem.

With a very sharp knife, cut up into the stem from a point which is an inch or so below a leaf joint, passing vertically through the leaf joint to an inch or so above. Get some-

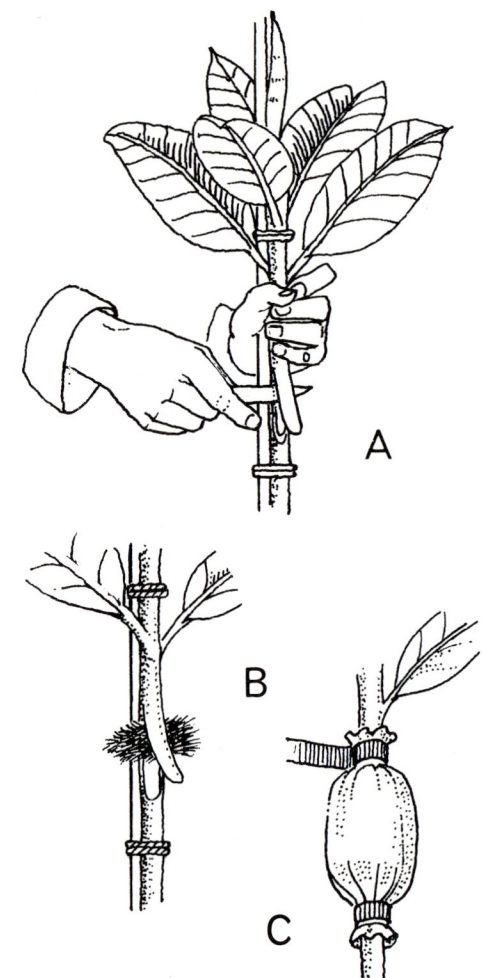

No. 418   Reducing the height of a rubber plant by aerial layering.
A.   Cut up into the main stem which has been tied to a supporting cane above and below the cut to avoid collapse.
B.   When the cut surface has been coated with hormone rooting powder, position moist sphagnum moss under the tongue prior to complete wrapping.
C.   After wrapping the moist sphagnum moss in polythene film, both ends are sealed with adhesive tape. Replace the supporting cane afterwards.

body to hold the topmost part whilst you do this; if you try it single-handed, you risk the top part bending over and falling away. If you *have* to work alone, at least fasten a supporting cane above and below before you start.

Wedge the cut open with a thin twist of sphagnum moss—this is when the greatest danger of toppling occurs—and with the blade of the knife, smear all the cut surfaces with Seradix hormone rooting powder. Remove the twist of moss and replace with damp sphagnum arranged so that as much of the cut and hormone coated surface is now in contact with the moss. Wrap a good handful of damp moss all round the wound area, and hold it in place by binding firmly with clear polythene film, sealed airtight above and below the operation with Sellotape.

With aerial layering, it is a good tip to foliar feed above the wound. Mist spray with Murphy FF foliar feed every 5–7 days, and when it can be seen that the polythene bag is well filled with root, you will be able to cut down the 'new plant' and pot it up in the compost mix given in *No. 416*.

419   Sanseviera : losing leaves

My Sanseviera plant is about eight years old and nearly 3 ft. tall. It has been no trouble until January when three leaves became wet and soft at the bottom, and then collapsed. Can you suggest why this should have happened. It is in a centrally-heated room, and in full sun and light.

There is not much doubt that the cause of the leaf rot was overwatering. The leaves of Sanseviera are very like succulents in their ability to resist transpiration and hold moisture. The leaves have a leathery texture, really a thick waxy surface for just this very purpose of conserving moisture. Even in a warm centrally-heated room, one watering a month is normally quite sufficient during the winter resting period. It is a very tolerant plant and will stand temperatures down to 45°F. but would do best in a room where the temperature variation between day and night is minimal.

Cutting off the soft parts and repotting was the best thing you could have done. As you will have realised from your experiences, any tendency to wetness in the soil has to be avoided and the growing medium must not only be well drained—equal parts John Innes No. 1 or 2, peat and sharp sand—but also given fierce drainage underneath by standing the pot on a shingle/grit surface. Whatever you do, don't follow the advice to stand the pot in a saucer of water. Keep the soil only just moist from spring to autumn, using a diluted liquid feed from May-June onwards and decreasing the watering from September to once a month until the spring.

Incidentally, don't discard any leaves that you may cut off. Trim them to clean healthy tissue with a razor blade, leave the wound for an hour to dry and then touch into rooting hormone powder. This can then be set as a cutting in a sand/peat mix. Placed in semi-shade and kept on the dry side of moist, rooting should take place, although rather slowly.

420   Shade : plants that will grow in poor light

Are there any house plants which will thrive in very shaded corners? My flat has a corridor entrance hall which no sunlight reaches. I like house plants rather than cut flowers, so your advice will be most welcome.

This is a cry from the heart that is received frequently, perhaps not surprisingly, from the many people who live in flats and whose gardening is therefore restricted to pots on window shelves and in hallways.

There are several plants that naturally grow in the shade of other plants and which are therefore likely to be able to adapt to the reduced light intensity within the home. The Aspidistra is a case in point; it is extraordinarily tolerant also of neglect and was very popular with the Victorians. See *Nos. 348* and *349*. It is gradually coming back into popularity after an 'anti-old-fashioned' period. Fashions change with plants in the same way as other things, and whilst the Aspidistra was being reviled as old-fashioned, it became 'trendy' to grow rubber plants, Ficus (see *Nos. 416-18*), and the Swiss Cheese plant *Monstera deliciosa* (see *Nos. 403-5*).

Philodendron scandens would be suitable for the low light intensity and you could also try *Fatsia japonica*, the False Castor Oil plant. Several ivies are suitable especially the hybrid between Fatsia and Hedera (Ivy) called *Fatshedera lizei*. Also try the Spider plant, Chlorophytum (see *Nos. 364* and *365*).

Ferns thrive in woodland and similar situations of subdued light, and most ferns offered by florists would be suitable.

Two points should be borne in mind: any variegated foliage subjects are quite likely to lose the variegation in low light intensity and secondly, the conditions of subdued light in which many of these 'house plants' have evolved in nature, are also very often conditions of high atmospheric humidity. This is the exact opposite of the conditions that are produced by modern centrally-heated and controlled environments. Counteract this and encourage your plants by standing them on trays of permanently wet sand or fine shingle. This wet surface creates a humid atmosphere around the foliage, and is a simple expedient that has often made all the difference between failure and success.

Another material that can be used for this purpose apart from sand and shingle, and which is quite acceptable aesthetically, is to crumble into very small pieces the kind of expanded polystyrene that is used for ceiling tiles and for packing around equipment in cartons.

Finally, as you are talking about an entrance hall, do try to do all you can to avoid—or at least deflect—cold draughts from the front door.

421 *Stephanotis : care and cultivation*

I have a nicely budded plant of Stephanotis on a small framework and I should appreciate any information about its treatment, such as suitable compost, feeding, propagation and winter care. Can I have it in the house rather than my greenhouse? It appears to be pot-bound, but I know this is an advantage with some plants.

Stephanotis floribunda, the Madagascar Jasmine, is a beautiful greenhouse climber with white flowers borne in clusters and is rather similar to its relative, the Hoya, but needs a higher temperature.

Although it needs shading from sunlight, it will need more light than it can get inside the home, and is far better left where it is in the greenhouse.

The best time to repot is February and until that time comes round, a pot-bound plant is best kept going on supplemental feeding with liquid manure. You can prepare this by steeping some well-rotted stable manure or mushroom compost in a sack suspended in rain water and using the tea coloured liquor as a base into which you can dissolve a little Bio or other liquid fertiliser. Never use tap water for watering or spraying Stephanotis because of the possibility of introducing lime which they dislike. A suitable growing medium often advised is John Innes No. 2 which contains a small amount of lime but not enough to hurt.

But if you want the plant to thrive and produce better flowers you will have to take a little more trouble. It is an old adage that the best results require just as much effort by yourself as the plant, and the ideal compost for Stephanotis takes a little trouble and effort. It is equal parts by bulk John Innes No. 2, peat, silver sand, and well-rotted stable or farmyard manure or mushroom compost that has been well rubbed through a half inch sieve.

At repotting time, prune out weak and straggling shoots and carefully tease out some of the old soil, and lift the bound-up roots clear. Try to do this without damage so that they can bite quickly into the new compost. Repot using a pot size that gives about $1\frac{1}{2}$ inches clear all round. Crock well—the pot must be well drained—and stand it on shingle so that the drainage is fierce from the bottom, in a position where shade from sunlight can be provided.

From now till autumn, spray daily with rainwater from a fine mist on all foliage, but keep the spray away from the bloom. About a month after repotting, raise the temperature to a minimum of 75°F. and scratch into the soil surface a level teaspoonful of balanced fertiliser or apply a dilute liquid feed every fortnight. Stop the fertiliser dry feeds at the end of July and the shorter-lasting liquid feeds by mid-August. Stephanotis, being an evergreen, does not stop completely but still needs a slow-down during the resting period. In October, reduce the watering to just enough to keep the soil moist, and reduce the temperature to an absolute minimum of 55°F. 60°F. would be better if you can maintain it.

422 Stocks : winter-flowering blooms

I have grown some winter-flowering stocks from seed. They are now in a cold greenhouse, about 1 ft. high, and I would like some advice about how to care for them. Can you also tell me the difference between Brompton and Lothian stocks?

The plants we know as Lothian, Brompton, ten-week, and night scented stocks have been developed from species of the genus *Matthiola* which originates from the mainland and islands around Greece. The type best suited for winter flowering is a strain called 'Beauty of Nice', sown in July, but Lothian, although usually used for late summer–autumn flowering and Brompton, usually spring flowering, can also be used for winter flowering by sowing from early July to August and planting out the seedlings into 3 inch pots.

When potting-up the seedlings, most people naturally select the biggest and best seedlings in the seed pan, and probably discard the rest. However, a good tip is that it seems to invariably be the weaker backward seedlings that ultimately provide the best double blooms. It is the strongest, most vigorous seedlings that contain the highest proportion of single blooms. Many of the seedlings will lift with a long tap root; cut this with a razor blade, and the plant will then develop a much more fibrous root system with a greater tendency to throw blooming side shoots, and not put all its energy into one main single spike. Of course if you want cut flowers on long stems for the house, then utilise the strongest plants with their roots intact.

Pot on at 6–9 ins. tall into 4½ in. pots and at 1 ft. tall, your plants should be in their finishing pots, about 6-inch size, and in a compost mix of equal parts John Innes No. 2 and peat. Allow them to stand out until October and then bring them into a cool greenhouse with pots standing apart so that air can circulate freely and each plant receiving full light.

Botrytis fungus is the problem at this stage and you can prepare the plants for this, and incidentally put a little extra colour into the bloom, by giving each a pinch of sulphate of potash two weeks before the move, and again as they are being moved. As you lift each pot, sprinkle a pinch and tease up the soil so that air can enter the compost. A stagnant soil surface encourages Botrytis. From now on, be very careful not to let the foliage become wet; water very carefully with the can spout, not through a rose. Water sparingly, only just enough to keep the soil moist.

423 Umbrella plant: conditions required

What is the name of a house plant with green, rather rushlike leaves shaped at the top like the blades of a helicopter? Mine is about 18 in. high and the ends of the leaves are continually dying and new leaves coming up.

Often known in florists shops as Umbrella Plants or Umbrella Grass, *Cyperus alterifolius* is a smaller-growing version of one of the most important plants ever utilised by man—the Egyptian papyrus reed *C. papyrus*. It is like the papyrus which grows in swampy marshy riverside areas since it likes to grow with its feet paddling in the water. It is one of the few plants that will enjoy the entirely mistaken and obnoxious habit that so many people have of standing house and indoor plants in saucers and trays filled with water.

The turnover of leaves can be fairly rapid with drying brown leaves being constantly replaced by fresh growth. However, I would suspect that in the case of this question, the trouble is due to not enough continous moisture at root. Repotting can be done at almost any time and, when large enough, the root crown may be divided to increase your plants. Upturn it and knock it out; if the root system appears congested and pot-bound, use a larger pot merely covering the drainage holes so that soil doesn't fall through. A layer of rough peat will do well because you are going to stand the pot in water. Use a compost mix, two parts John Innes No. 2, and one part each of sand, and—if you can go to the trouble of collecting it from the countryside—dried cowpat, crumbled and passed through a ½ in. sieve, or failing that, mushroom compost, similarly sieved—or failing that as well, peat will have to do!

During spring and summer imitate the Nile flood season by standing the pot in a saucer or tray of water and position it in full light but not direct sunlight. During the months of October to February, not so much water is needed; lift the pot out of standing water and merely keep the soil moist.

Natural leaching of plant nutrients will be rapid with this rate of watering so give a little balanced liquid feed like Bio or Sangral about once a week. This plant is fairly easy to manage in the greenhouse providing you don't let the temperature fall below 45°F. in winter but because of the light requirement you will have to position it in a well-lit window indoors. It might be best to bring it into the house only for short visits of a day or two at a time.

Section VIII

Greenhouse Practice and Principles

424 Cleansing a greenhouse

Please advise me on cleaning a newly acquired greenhouse. We have recently moved and for the first time find ourselves owner of a greenhouse, size 2 yds. × 4 yds. approx. with a wooden frame. We have tried growing some seed but the soil is so poor that they just haven't grown. Do I discard all the soil already in, and start again? If so, with what?

Very many people when moving house also acquire a greenhouse and have this problem. There is no knowing the past history of the greenhouse, what crops it has grown, what plants it has housed, so there is no knowing what pests and diseases may have been built up. Depending upon its age, the condition of the timber, paintwork and cleanliness, it could be harbouring all sorts of beasties. However, this is not to frighten you, merely to put the worst possible construction on things, and you will have to tailor the following advice to what is practicable in your own particular circumstances.

First, brush and scrape all the dust and loose paint from the inside, make sure all the glass is firm and clean, the timber in good condition and the whole structure sound and watertight.

Normally at this stage I would advise taking out as much of the soil as you can, and replacing with clean fresh soil and compost, but you may find this rather a big job, if so leave it since there is an easier alternative.

Clear out all dead leaves, and rubbish. Then wash out and fumigate the house using Jeyes Fluid as per instructions on the bottle. Whilst still wet and the smell is strong, close the door and windows and leave completely closed for a week whilst you attend to the outside, brushing off and re-painting, cleaning the glass. After a week when the Jeyes has done its job, paint the inside.

When this has been done, you will be ready to think about growing. If you want to grow plants like tomatoes you can completely avoid risk of any pest or disease remaining in the soil by using growing bags, see *No. 258*. It would be a good precaution to put down a layer of clinker, ash or gravel, to lay the bags on so that you get good drainage. Tomatoes do well grown like this and there are all sorts of other vegetable and salad crops that can be grown the same way. You can either take the bags out at the end of the season, or run them on a second time if you feel that they have remained clean and free of disease. If you do use them a second year, use liquid fertilisers to replenish what will have been washed out during the first year. When you finally get new bags, use the content of the old ones as mulching material in the garden.

425 Creosote is fatal

My plants are looking sickly after I painted my greenhouse staging with creosote. What can I do?

Get the staging outside as quickly as you can and everything else that has been painted or even splashed with creosote; the fumes are lethal and you won't be able to even think of using this timber for sometime. Expose it to the weather, and in time the timber will lose most of the smell.

You can then paint over the creosoted timber with a proprietary compound like Tarseal or a metallic aluminium paint. When this paint is perfectly dry and has weathered for two or three months, try to see if you can detect by smell the slightest suggestion of creosote odour. If you can, paint again until you are quite satisfied that even the slightest remaining trace has been sealed off. Then—and only then—can you take the staging inside again. You will have to keep it away from fierce sunlight, however, since this and hot air temperatures will have a strong 'drawing' influence on any viable creosote still left underneath. This is why you must let the aluminium paint or 'Tarseal' weather and become hard. Even after these precautions, it would be safest to cover the staging with gravel trays.

426 Fans and fan heaters, invaluable aids

In my greenhouse (which contains many flowering plants, including cyclamen) I have a small Humex air circulating fan which I used through-

out last summer. Can I use the fan on damp, muggy days? I feel I would like to use it without any vents open.

This is one of the big advantages that this type of heater has over all the others. Black leg, the common fungus problem that thwarts the efforts of many amateurs to keep their Geraniums, Pelargoniums, Fuchsias and other plants through the winter, thrives in still, stagnant, musty, humid air conditions. Getting air on the move at once makes conditions much more buoyant.

Of course, a fan heater with an inbuilt thermostat drastically reduces heating costs by cutting out the high wattage heating element when the air temperature reaches the pre-set minimum, the fan keeps going however using about the same current consumption as a small electric light bulb.

On a damp muggy day, there is no advantage to be gained by letting in the atmosphere. You can close the air vents to keep it out, and the fan then gives adequate air movement inside. Try to direct the air current diagonally across the greenhouse floor so that a circulatory air current is set up, distributing it throughout the house at all levels.

However, keep pots and especially cuttings and seedlings away from the direct line of draught because they can easily dry out too quickly. Put up a deflector shield if necessary. Be very careful, too, if you use a paraffin heater in a greenhouse in which a fan is running. A draught directed at a lamp could easily affect the flame so that it smokes and harms your plants.

427 Flowers all year without heating

My greenhouse is not heated and seems very dull during winter and early spring. What flowers can I grow to keep it bright and interesting in winter?

Even though your greenhouse is unheated there is no reason for it ever to be dull. Starting in September, you can pot-up Polyanthus, forget-me-nots, even wallflowers. Stand them in a protected position outside and bring them

in before the cold nights come. They will give plenty of colour in the New Year.

Several shrubs can be grown in pots, stood outside during summer and brought in during autumn and winter. The evergreen Japanese Azaleas, heathers, Daphne, Camellia, and even whilst these are in bloom the early spring bulbs will be starting, like the many varieties of *Iris reticulata*, Crocus species, hyacinths, tulips, Narcissii and then spring and early summer is on you again. With all the usual favourites like Geraniums, Fuchsias, heliotrope, etc.

You can always maintain a permanent interest by a collection of ferns, the effect of any of the above is enhanced tremendously by spreading them out against a background of greenery.

Then with the encouragement of a successful display, you can progress to the rather more difficult but beautiful plants *Primula chinensis* and *P. obconica*, Cinerarias, Salpiglossis and the Christmas cherry, *Solanum capsicastrum*.

428 Fumigation: does it affect polythene?

I have erected two polythene greenhouses and I now want to know the best method of fumigating them before the new season begins. Will a nicotine bomb or similar device have any chemical reaction on the polythene?

There should be no harm to the polythene. Most, if not all, of the fumigants available to the amateur are also used in commercial horticulture, where the use of polythene film is nowadays so widespread that any manufacturer would probably regard an adverse effect on polythene as a severe limitation to sales—and they would therefore not be made.

Just a couple of comments, though, on fumigating with nicotine. Effectiveness is dependent upon warm temperatures and you would probably get far better insecticidal and fungicidal control with the modern preparation Tecnalin. Secondly, do *not* as I saw demonstrated once on a T.V. 'how to do it' gardening programme, light your fumigation bomb and then step over it to get to the door! Leave the greenhouse door wide open and with your back to it and no obstruction on the floor light the bomb, low down near floor level, stand up, turn round, get out quick, shutting the door behind you, and keep the house closed according to instructions and stay out until the house has had a full day with the door wide open to disperse the fumes.

429 Leaky roof: the proper way to repair it

How can I stop the rain coming into my greenhouse? The roof is of reinforced glass which was puttied-in at first; then Sylglas was used, but all to no avail. Do you know of anything that would stop the trouble?

If putty has failed and Sylglas hasn't stopped it, then it is not the fault of the Sylglas because clearly water is getting in at the rebates in the sash bars and probably rotting the timber. Now, it probably hasn't occurred to you that every time you go into your greenhouse, you are walking and working under a hundredweight or more of glass and if that roof gives way whilst you're inside, you are not going to be very nice to look at. So safety first: take the glass right out, a bay at a time, clean out all old hard putty, scrape away paint, and prod the wood to see if it has rotted at all. You will have to use your own judgement as to whether replacement of the bars is required. If they are sagging or warped, you'll never make them watertight.

After scraping the paint away you may have to leave the bars for a day or two for the wood to dry out before painting them with red lead—it's no good painting damp wood—and then with white undercoat and white gloss.

In between coats, you can take the opportunity to get the glass thoroughly clean. A Brillo pad and Ajax scouring powder should shift even the worst of normal staining. If they can't make it quite clean, then don't bother since the stain will have eaten into the glass and light will be obstructed, so replace the panes and instead of using putty which sets hard in time and then cracks. Use Sylglas mastic, which is like putty but stays soft, and is watertight.

Many people dislike working with it because it can get your hands in an awful mess. The answer is to work with wet hands and only small quantities of mastic at a time. Keep a paraffin-soaked rag handy to wipe your fingers clean if you get gummed up, but keep dipping your hands in a bowl of water containing a little washing-up detergent, and you will handle the mastic without trouble.

You will have to reglaze, if only to be sure that the roof above your head is safe. However, before you do the job, a temporary—but only temporary—measure to prevent water dripping on the plants is to line the inside of the house with polythene, like double glazing. Don't make too good a job of this, otherwise you will be encouraged to put off the reglazing, and that you will have to do—better sooner than later.

Reinforced glass, mentioned in the question, usually refers to wire mesh reinforced and the thickness makes an appreciable loss of light. Plain clear horticultural grade would be very much better. If the reinforced glass was used as a precaution against snow avalanching from a roof—as is often done with a conservatory or lean to—clearly the greenhouse is in the wrong position and should be moved away from overhead danger.

430 Leaving polythene liners in position all summer

I have lined my greenhouse with polythene to prevent heat loss. Do you think I should remove it next summer or will it, as it tends to break the direct sunshine, keep it cooler as well?

The history of the use of polythene film in greenhouses goes back only a few years, to just after the war when cheap plastic film became widely available. A great deal of practical experience has been gained however, in that time about the many uses to which it is put.

When used as a 'double glaze lining', there is a further obstruction to light by clean polythene film—in addition to the glass—but this is very small. It is not enough to be of any consequence during spring and autumn, and it is no bad thing during high summer when most plants need a little shading. In addition to its primary purpose of retaining heat when the outside temperature drops, double glazing tends to slow down the sudden sharp increase in temperature that can occur when the sun comes out. This is especially useful for people at work or out shopping and who are not on hand to open up more ventilation. If this is a problem for you, however, fit an automatic ventilation control unit, like a Ventmaster. This is easy to fit, is entirely self-contained, requires no electricity or other power and is quite inexpensive. Get details from Humex Ltd., Byfleet, Surrey.

There is everything to be gained by leaving the lining in position, but note the above point about the small degree of light obstruction by clean film. A lining that gets wet by condensation collects dust and debris, even algae, and this causes light obstruction of a very different order. You may well have to take it down from time to time for cleaning, or replacing.

431 Making full use of the greenhouse

Which vegetables or flowers can I plant in a cold greenhouse when I clear my tomatoes?

One thing is for certain: food is not going to get any cheaper, and no food can be fresher than what you grow yourself. The space inside a greenhouse—heated or not—is far too valuable ever to remain empty.

Winter lettuce and endive are perhaps the obvious and best choice. The lettuce varieties Kordaat, Kwick and Kloek are especially suitable for just this purpose, and for those who haven't tried them the blanched shoots of chicory and sea kale will provide a pleasant and money-saving winter vegetable. Follow these with a crop of extra early peas and potatoes. There are several pea varieties to choose from—and a remarkably quick maturing potato for this purpose is Ulster Sceptre. A little later, sowing of dwarf French beans will give a good crop whilst the earliest arrivals in the shops are very expensive.

If you want to occupy the vacated space with flowers instead of food, you can bring in pots of late-flowering Chrysanthemums that will have been standing out during the summer, Gerani-ums and Fuchsias growing in pots can be brought in to lengthen their flowering period and over-winter.

Bulbs, especially hyacinths but also tulips, iris, daffodils and narcissi will all bloom much earlier if brought into better growing positions inside the cool greenhouse. See also *No. 427*.

432 *Plastic tunnel houses are very good indeed*

I would like a greenhouse to enable me to raise plants earlier and to grow them on much later than I can in the open garden. But I have been put off by what seems to me to be the very high cost of decent greenhouses. I have seen very long plastic dome-like greenhouses on nurseries and I wondered if I could get a smaller version, say 12 ft. × 9 ft; if so, how much would it cost?

It is an old adage, 'you only get what you pay for', and in most respects, this is true of greenhouses. There are expensive, not so expensive, and the other kind that are too cheap to be any good. However, the trade is sufficiently competitive to ensure that when you invest in a conventional rigid structure greenhouse—be it timber frame or metal—you will get good value and that with reasonable care and attention to maintenance, you will still have that same greenhouse in a good many years' time. Spread over those years, the initial cost is therefore not so great as it may at first seem to you. Indeed, when considered against the value of all the things that you would have been able to grow, you should be able to show a very clear profit.

However, costs have undoubtedly risen and the development of cheap plastic film has produced an initially cheaper structure which is the dome-like tunnels that you have seen. A plastic film stretched over a tubular metal frame is not so strong as a conventional greenhouse structure and is vulnerable to damage by strong winds, but in a relatively sheltered garden it would be perfectly safe. The plastic cover is reckoned to need replacing every three to four years but even with this periodical cost, it would take some time before the overall cost catches up with the higher initial cost of the traditional greenhouse. You will also avoid the heavy outlay in one go.

Small versions of the long commercial structures are now available for use in the private garden from 8 ft. × 6 ft., and also in larger sizes. Erection is extremely easy and another advantage over the rigid greenhouse is that you can move a plastic house to another part of the garden without too much trouble. I have found the plastic house so good for growing tomatoes, melons, cucumbers, salad crops and other plants that my one original has now become four. Economically, the plastic house is well worth the consideration of every gardener who has the space.

433 Reasons for scorch, and methods of shading

I recently bought a plastic tunnel greenhouse and am astonished at the difference it has made to the way the plants grow in it. My tomato plants are better than they've ever been. However, I am having a problem with seedlings, especially lettuce and some Geranium and Fuchsia cuttings that I am trying to propagate : they go brown at the edges. Can you suggest what I am doing wrong?

Greenhouses have a trapped and largely captive atmosphere which absorbs the sun's heat rays passing through the glass or, as in your case, the plastic film. This higher temperature is one of the ways in which better and faster growing conditions are created. Light also tends to be concentrated in much the same way and plastic film greenhouses are extremely efficient in this respect. In bright sunny weather it is quite possible for the combination of temperature and light to produce conditions that speed up the living processes within the plant to a remarkable degree.

The first effect, and the one that concerns us, is that the plants give off water vapour, transpire, at a very much faster rate than normal—water which they must replace that much faster by absorption through their root system. Even established plants with well-developed roots can have difficulty in keeping up when the pace really gets going. For a young seedling with an as yet infantile and undeveloped root system, it is much more difficult; for a cutting with no root system at all, it is well nigh impossible. The result is that the leaves dehydrate, the cell structure collapses beyond recovery usually beginning at the edges, this area then withers and you get the familiar scorched edge.

The precautions that you have to take are two-fold. Make sure that there is adequate ventilation so that the greenhouse does not get like an oven and also reduce the light intensity at the peak sunny periods by applying shading. In the past, this has either been something like whitewash, or blinds made of hessian or plastic, or even venetian blind-like shutters. All have their disadvantages. The whitewash washes off in rain or continues to cut out the light when it is not sunny. The blinds have to be rolled up or let out every time a cloud comes over, and a roll of wet hessian weighs a ton and is adept at cracking glass. The cost of shutters puts them beyond the reach of most amateurs.

However, a new product available in the U.K. effectively solves the problem of shading and scorching. Called 'Varishade', it can be sprayed, brushed or rolled on in liquid form. This material becomes opaque when dry but turns translucent when moist and wet—i.e. in mist, dew or rain—then opaque again when it dries out. It can be removed easily enough when required, but does not wash off in rain. Variation in shading is therefore in response not to sunlight but to humidity—not quite the perfect answer we are looking for, but there is enough correlation between sunlight and humidity to cover a large enough measure of our requirements. Effectively, it really is automatic on-off shading. I still take the extra precaution of laying a sheet of tissue paper over the soft cuttings like Fuchsias and Geraniums for the first ten days or so, taking it off at night when it is not needed. Cuttings apart, I have found that 'Varishade' meets all my needs.

The usual problem for amateur gardeners is what happens whilst you are at work, wondering if your plants are suffering from sudden changes in conditions in the absence of anyone on hand to vary the shading and ventilation. 'Varishade' and an automatic Ventmaster, see *No. 430*, will do the job for you and remove the worry.

434   Sour soil : sterilising is hard work

I wish to sterilise a 15 ft. × 6 ft. area in my lean-to greenhouse in which I have grown tomatoes for six years, and the soil is now sour. Will you please tell me the quantity of water necessary to mix with formaldehyde?

If by sour you mean that the soil is played out and devoid of nutrients or, conversely, that by heavy feeding with artificial fertilisers you have built up an over-supply—perhaps even an imbalance—then sterilisation won't help. And before growing anything else you should carry out a thorough soil test with a Sudbury soil testing kit to find out the relative strengths of N.P. and K. still remaining and whether the soil is acid or alkaline. This information is vital because without it you can have no idea what steps to take. Soil test kits are simple to use and cheap to buy.

On the other hand, six consecutive years committed to tomatoes could well have built up a disease and pest count that would make it practically impossible to grow the crop without an attack of some kind.

It therefore follows that if you need to sterilise the soil to eradicate pest and disease, you've got to do it properly and that is easier said than done. Sterilising by steam is a very tedious, laborious and costly performance, and for the amateur quite impracticable. Getting all the tackle on site to raise the steam is rather like getting a sledge hammer to crack a walnut.

Sterilising with formaldehyde gas is effective, but it needs to be done thoroughly. Use formalin—the liquid— at a diluted rate of one part in fifty parts water. This is applied at the rate of 25–30 gals. per cubic yard of soil. The procedure is to move all plants out of the house, turn the soil over on an area of a sq. yd., saturate with the solution, throwing up a 6-inch layer, soaking that, then another layer and so on. Build up the soil into saturated heaps

and cover each heap as completely as possible with polythene sheets. This is to trap and concentrate the fumes so that every particle of soil is permeated. Any gaps and the gas will escape and the effectiveness of the operation will be lessened; you cannot cover these heaps too thoroughly. Leave the heaps covered for at least two complete days, three would be better.

To disperse the toxic gas take off the covers. Put a wet handkerchief to your nose whilst you do this. Open the ventilators wide. Turn the soil every few days for five to six weeks to get rid of the gas, and to help the soil become dry and workable. Then make a test sowing of a fast-growing seed like mustard or cress. If it germinates and grows, try a few radishes. If they grow, the soil is safe; if not, keep turning the soil until the test crops grow unharmed by any gas residue.

This is how formaldehyde sterilisation is done: if it all sounds too much trouble, you have the easier alternative of growbags, see *No. 258.*

435   Sterilised soil: how long will it stay sterilised?

How long can I keep sterilised seed compost before using it?

Soil is sterilised, of course, to eradicate animal and plant life including viable weed seed, so that seedlings will not be attacked by pests and diseases or suffer from the competition of other germinating seeds. The sterilised soil may thus be clean, but experience generally has shown that, unless the sterilisation is 100% complete, or if the sterilised soil becomes contaminated, infection spreads more quickly.

The answer to your question, therefore, depends upon how thorough the sterilisation was and how thorough the measures have been to keep the soil isolated from possible infection. Fungal spores are always in the air ready to alight on a favourable growing medium. It would be wise to carry out a germination test with any soil over 3–4 weeks old from sterilising. Sow mustard and cress, or radish seed, before committing more valuable seed to it.

Steam-sterilised soil should be bagged airtight in perfectly clean plastic bags as soon as it has cooled and then, if sterilisation has been thorough, you can reckon on it remaining so for anything up to twelve weeks. It is generally reckoned however that it is best to use sterilised soil as soon as possible after the sterilisation process—i.e., as soon as it is cool after steaming. Sterilising by formaldehyde presents a number of problems and is generally considered impracticable for small quantities. See *No. 434.*

436   Thermometers placed correctly

Where should I place a maximum-minimum thermometer for true readings?

This type of thermometer not only tells you what the temperature is when you look at it, but what the hottest and coldest temperatures have been since you last looked at it, and reset the indicators. If you are at all concerned with knowing what maximum and minimum temperatures have been—which is the whole function and purpose of this kind of thermometer—you need two. One should be placed outside, so that you know just how cold or warm the general outdoor conditions have been, and the other inside the greenhouse so that you know how well or not so well your heating arrangements have been able to cope with those outside temperatures. One might feel satisfied on seeing a light frost to note that the thermometer records that the temperature inside did not drop lower than, say, 45°F. when outside it fell to 35–40°F. but then the heater has not had a lot of work to do. A harder frost one night bringing the inside temperature down below a set minimum of 45°F. would indicate that the heating capacity is not enough to deal with a really heavy frost and, if that happens, the only thing that a single thermometer can tell you, is that you didn't have enough information to avoid being caught out, and perhaps suffer damage. It's the difference that matters. If you can see a recorded ten degrees of frost with the inside temperature still remaining at 45°F., you can sleep soundly at nights.

Place an outside thermometer about 4 ft. from ground level in a position where it is shielded from direct sunlight and where air can circulate freely, so that it can fairly record air temperature and not radiant heat from sun or greenhouse. Therefore, hanging it outside the greenhouse door is not the best position. The inside thermometer should be positioned as far away from any heating appliances as possible—i.e. in the coldest part of the greenhouse. Rising warm air from any heating appliances can give a false reading.

Propagators, of course, are for creating specialised conditions and should have their own separate thermometer.

437   Tomatoes, cucumbers and strawberries : do they mix?

Would tomatoes, cucumbers and strawberries be compatible in the same greenhouse? Can you suggest other fruits or vegetables for greenhouse cultivation?

This question is asked as often as any other and the usual answer is No, they are not compatible. Then letters are received from gardeners who protest that they grow them together and have done so for years, which only goes to show that there is nothing definite and dogmatic about gardening; what does well in one place, doesn't do well in another. There is always the exception to prove the rule.

However, the nub of the controversy probably is what is regarded as a worthwhile crop in these mixed conditions and it is virtually certain that the respective yields of tomatoes, cucumbers, strawberries and other greenhouse crops would be much better if they were each accorded their own specialised conditions. Cucumbers require warm and very humid conditions; on the other hand tomatoes and strawberries need plenty of direct sunlight and full ventilation at all times.

If the house is large enough, you can erect a partition so that you can have a dry end and a moist end. As the tomatoes finish, you can follow on with winter lettuce and endive, see *No. 431,* and grow very early crops of peas, potatoes, beans, chicory and spinach. Of course, the moist end can be brought into use too, simply by discontinuing the creation of moisture procedures like spraying and keeping the floor wet, hanging up wet sacks or blankets.

Comments about growing strawberries will be found in *No. 245*.

Other fruits are more permanent and you must decide whether it is more economical for you to take up space and wait for a few years for fruiting maturity to get a crop of grapes, peaches or figs, or make more profitable use of the greenhouse by growing more essential crops to mature at times when they are fetching high prices in the shops.

Section IX

Seeds and Sowing

438 Slow and erratic germination of cacti and succulents

I sowed a packet of mixed cacti seeds two months ago, but so far nothing's happened. Are they so difficult to grow?

As you might expect, most cacti come from desert-like areas where the soil is generally barren, and temperatures are a good deal warmer than here. These are the most important factors when it comes to raising them from seed. Germination of cacti seed is sporadic at the best of times, but if you follow this procedure you won't go far wrong—and you might try it also for the seed of succulents and other cacti-like subjects.

For all cacti you will have to provide a steady temperature, within a degree or two either side of 72°F. This really means a propagator or a heat pad or soil cables preferably controlled by a thermostat to control a steady temperature plus, of course, a maximum/minimum recording thermometer so that you can check that the heating apparatus is working efficiently. This makes you independent of the weather conditions outside and although cacti grow away best from a spring-time sowing, they can, in fact, be sown at any time.

Prepare a normal seed tray by placing a layer of crock over the drainage holes. Cover this with a ½ in. layer of charcoal or, failing this, with peat mixed with an equal quantity of fine rubble or smashed brick passed through a ½ in. sieve.

This gives you a fierce drainage. Complete filling of the tray with a mixture of equal parts John Innes No. 1 and sand, plus a half part crushed brick rubble passed through a ¼ in. sieve. Your seed tray is now very near the cacti's preferred desert-like conditions. Press the surface level with a piece of flat wood and you are ready for sowing.

Don't water overhead; it would probably run off the dusty surface anyway and the soil wouldn't be properly soaked and the flat surface would be broken up. Soak the tray by very carefully, and slowly, lowering the tray into water. Don't do it quickly or the lot will float out.

Prepare about a teaspoonful of powdered brick dust and drop this *into* the seed packet. Shake so that the small quantity of seed is mixed up thoroughly with the dust. This will give you enough material to take several 'pinches' between finger and thumb to spread evenly over the wet surface of the tray seed bed. The seed will be spaced out more evenly this way than if you try to do it with seed alone. Cover the seed with as thin a layer of fine brick dust as you can manage—a finger and thumb job again. Old bricks are invaluable to the cactus grower, especially plaster rubble.

There is no need to water the freshly sown seed since enough moisture will soak up from the wet soil below and subsequent watering should only be done by lowering into water or by spraying with a fine mist sprayer. Cover the tray with a pane of glass to create a moist mini-atmosphere and place in the 72°F. heat away from sun and reflected bright light.

Mixed cacti seed will germinate at different times and can be lifted from the seed bed as soon as large enough to handle. Do this by making a tiny fork from a wooden plant label or something similar; cut a V-shaped notch directly into the point so as to make two prongs. Then, with a pointed label in one hand to carefully dip under the infantile root and the fork in the other hand to lift the seedling, prick off the seedlings as they appear into pots containing the same compost as described above but with a wadge of moisture-holding peat in the bottom. As you lift the seedlings, don't disturb the soil in the tray any more than you can help. Other seed nearby may be in process of germinating, and too much disturbance at this crucial time could easily kill them.

439 Saving and sowing seed of Camellias and other shrubs

Last autumn I picked a fat, fleshy pod from one of our Camellias, but this has now shrivelled and dried up. Can you tell me how to treat the seeds and when to sow them?

Many of the trees, shrubs and plants that grow in our gardens derive from other climes where the light is more intense, the summers are longer, and the temperatures warmer. Therefore, for the seed to ripen and become viable in our climate, it often has to be left on the parent plant as long as possible, literally until it drops of its own accord or only taken off to avoid being frosted.

The mistake in this questioner's case was in picking the seed much too early. The seed of some plants—Camellia is one—does not remain at its most viable for more than a few days, and you have to get it just right. Provided they are not sterile forms, the following procedure will give a good chance of obtaining viable seed not only from Camellia but from most other plants too.

As a seed capsule or pod forms, leave it on the plant and when it is nice and plump, slip a small transparent polythene bag over it and fasten with a piece of thin wire or an elastic band. Puncture a few small pin holes in the bag so that the seed head can breathe. Keep a close watch for the seed casing to begin to crack open. The seed inside is then ripe and you can detach it, leaving it in the bag. Bring the bag into a warm room where the seed casing will then open completely. If the seed doesn't spill out naturally, shake it out, but don't pull or scrape it; the seed should detach naturally.

In the case of short-life Camellia seed, sowing must take place within fourteen days; after that the viability begins to fall. Leave it beyond twenty-eight days and you'll be lucky to get one to germinate. Prepare a seed tray with an inch deep layer of sand over a full $\frac{1}{2}$ in. layer of peat. Soak the prepared tray by lowering it into water and after bubbles have stopped rising, allow to drain for ten minutes. Then sow thinly on the surface, covering $\frac{1}{4}$ in. deep with dry sand. Don't water—moisture will rise from below.

Cover with a pane of glass and place in a warm temperature, 60–70°F. It is important to keep the temperature within this range. Germination can take anything from twelve to thirty six days. Lift out carefully as soon as seedlings are large enough to handle. As Camellias do best in lime-free soil, either pot into a compost mix 2 parts Bowers ericaceous compost and 1 part washed sand, or dibber them into special Jiffy 7 acid peat balls.

Dibber a hole in the peat ball and set the seedling with sand. Never water with tap water, always rainwater, and when the seedlings are 2–3 ins. high, pot on into a $3\frac{1}{2}$ in. pot. Don't try to remove the net mesh of the Jiffy 7; plant the lot intact using the same compost as above. Pot up later into a larger pot or plant out in a permanent position in an acid peat bed.

440 Chipping seed: essential for hard seeds

I have tried without success to grow Cannas from seed for two years. I soak the seeds thoroughly before planting in February but even by early May there is no sign of life. Can you give me any advice?

The common name for Canna is Indian Shot and this is a clue to your trouble; the seed is very hard, almost like a shot pellet! In addition to being hard, the seed coat also is extremely impervious to water and you will wait a long time for moisture from the soil to soak through it to stimulate germination. There are many seeds which germinate more readily after being soaked for half an hour or so; beans and peas are good examples, and there are some which if not so hard as Canna, nevertheless benefit by some assistance—lupins and sweet peas for example, see *Nos. 319, 328* and *329*.

Such seed has to be chipped—that is, an opening created in the seed coat for water to get in. Old time gardeners with their hard-skinned fingers used to do this with a knife cutting a chip in the hard covering. However, I would advise you not to chip it with a knife. Hold each seed very carefully in a pair of pliers and file carefully through the seed coat with a nail file. During February, and after soaking the seed for a couple of days, sow $\frac{1}{2}$ inch deep, singly, into 3 inch pots of John Innes Seed Compost and place in a temperature of 60–70°F.—unless you have a heated greenhouse you will need a propagator or soil heating cables. The warm temperature is vital and germination will take from three to ten weeks; it is very erratic indeed.

Later on, the young plants can be planted out when all fear of frost has gone. If they try to flower during the first year, don't let them; take the flower head out and make them concentrate on forming a good rootstock to sustain a first-class bloom head next year. Lift them before frost and dry them for storage during winter; be sure to keep them away from frosts and mice. See also *No. 307.*

441 Special technique for germinating conifers

I brought back some cedar tree seeds from Corfu. Would you tell me the best way to get these to germinate?

It is only likely that seed will be viable if you collected it fallen, but not if you pulled cones while they were still 'green'. Cedars are generally hardy enough in this country but with seed originating from Corfu, you may have some difficulty with our colder climate, however there is no reason why you should not try to germinate them. Here is a method I have seen on forestry nurseries in Wester Ross, Scotland, that gives good germination of most conifers.

Sow seed $\frac{1}{8}$–$\frac{1}{4}$ in. deep and $1\frac{1}{2}$–2 ins. apart in April in John Innes Seed Compost with one half part by bulk silver sand. Use a 3–4 in. deep pan or box and soak the compost by immersion. Allow to drain and slide the seed box into a large black polythene bag. Position two wire hoops diagonally, corner to corner, to hold the bag up like a small tent and screw the neck of the bag by slipping on an elastic band. In this dark forest-floor-like atmosphere, germination is usually good—if the seed is viable. After seven days, take a peep every day and as soon as the first seedlings show, remove to a clear plastic bag, partially covered with a sheet of newspaper to keep the light subdued. In three days the newspaper can come off and in another three days, prop the bag open to the air; then in another week remove the bag altogether. After germination, the weaning process must be gradual. If you rush this introduction to the outside world, the shock may well prove fatal.

Keep the boxes in a sheltered position, away from fierce sun—dappled light is best—and

never allow drying-out to check the growth of the seedlings. Protect from fierce frost and lying snow and at twelve months old, the seedlings will be ready for planting out or potting into 4–5 inch pots using John Innes No. 1 compost, with a half part sand added.

442 F1 Hybrids: what are they?

Reading seed catalogues, I see references to F1 Hybrids and warnings not to save the seed. Why not, and what are F1 Hybrids anyway?

In concentrating breeding programmes on qualities like weight of yield, colour, rate of growth etc., it is not uncommon for other factors like vigour and resistance to be lost or impaired and, when this happens, it is a logical step to cross back with hardier, wild and native varieties in an attempt to inherit some of their vigour. In recent years 'crossing back' has been done more perhaps with roses than with any other plant, and many of our modern varieties have a 'wild' species at no great distance back in their pedigree.

The idea behind what is called F1 hybridisation goes even further. It is to have two specific breeding programmes, neither especially intended to produce a final commercial end product in themselves but which, when crossed, throw up a hybrid with exceptional growing vigour, or other qualities—just for this one generation. Plants raised from seed saved from F1 Hybrids are invariably quite useless because you only get the desired characteristics in this *one* generation and seed does not come true.

Of course, there is in this a big advantage for the seed firm that puts a lot of money and effort into the research and business of breeding new and better varieties. They alone know the secret of the family tree in each ancestry for their particular hybrids, and they are therefore able to put them on the market and recoup their investment without rivals cashing in and exploiting the new introduction before the raisers have had a chance to recoup their outlay.

However, all that apart, modern gardeners are very fortunate compared with their forbears because this F1 hybridisation technique has produced many really outstanding flower and vegetable improvements over the old varieties. In addition to vigorous growth, the improvements for the private gardener include better colours, bigger yields and quicker growth to maturity. F1 Hybrids cost a little more but this is negligible compared with the improvements.

Every year, new hybrids are introduced and this is important because in our present precarious economic position and diminishing area of land available for food production, anything that increases and improves yield is vital.

443 'Stratification': special technique needed

Which is the best way to raise hawthorn bushes from seed, in order to make a long hedge?

Hawthorn seeds and many others, holly for example, are hard-coated and need special treatment called stratification, after which they usually germinate quite well.

The stratification procedure may well seem rather involved, and you may wonder if it is worth going to all the trouble. Certainly you will not save much money by raising a thorn hedge from seed because quickthorn plants for hedging are quite cheap. However, the nurseryman has to take the trouble to stratify his seed, and if you want to germinate hawthorn berries this is how you will have to do it.

Collect the seed in late autumn when fully ripe. Prepare a large clay pot by crocking the drainage holes closely, then add a 1 inch layer of sand. Spread a layer of seeds, one seed deep and preferably thinly enough to be not touching. Then add another one-inch layer of sand, more seed and so on in alternate layers until full. Wrap the entire pot in small mesh wire netting to keep out mice, water the pot well and bury it in the garden where the soil is fully exposed. Here it remains for more than twelve months.

Weather and time breaks down the tough seed coat and prepares the embryo for germination; it is most unlikely and unusual for germination to occur without this preliminary weathering.

In early spring when the pot has been in position for about 15 months, lift, sieve out the seed and sow thinly in a shallow drill. Seedlings should quickly appear, and 12 months later, these should be lifted. Cut off the end of the tap root to encourage fibrous root, and as you want these plants for hedging, also prune off the growing tip to encourage side shooting. Plant out into the nursery 9–12 ins. apart in rows 18 ins. apart for 12 months and then lift and plant into the final hedge position.

The lifting of the twelve-month-old seedling procedure is essential in order to cause fibrous root activity. If you leave it any longer than this in the seed bed a heavy tap root can develop, making later removal more difficult. Such plants will be poor with a minimum of side shooting and a minimum of fibrous root. This means that re-establishment after transplanting is delayed with a consequent increased risk of the plant not taking at all. This is why good nurserymen will often lift shrubs in the nursery rows, and replant almost in the same holes! Also see *No. 444*.

444 Berries: a longer alternative to stratification

Can you tell me how to grow holly trees from berries? I covered some berries with sand in December in a small plastic bowl. In May I planted the berries but there is no sign of the berries coming through the soil.

You can use two similar methods to raise holly and other berry seed, but both will require at least a year—most likely several months longer—to achieve germination.

Holly seed needs special conditions to make the embryo viable and ready for germination. This includes the simulation of a natural process of being buried in the soil and weathered for a year. Young self-sown seedlings that you may find growing under a tree have come from seed that has been there for a long, long, time.

The controlled method is called stratification because it consists basically of arranging seed in layers—strata—in some sort of container and exposing this to weather, after which the seed is sown in the normal way. The process is described in *No. 443*.

The second method is by sowing thinly in shallow dishes or scratching the seed into a patch in an exposed position. Rain and frost will get at the soil and you should then cover the area with a one-inch layer of coarse grit or gravel. Then leave them alone except for the removal of any weeds that have the strength to push through the cover; this should be done as soon as they show and before they can develop a root that will cause a lot of disturbance as you pull them out. Sow seed in early spring, as with stratification, but don't expect to see anything till the summer after next at least; more than likely for a year or two after that.

445 Last year's seed : how long will it stay viable?

Every year I seem to have a few packets or part packets of seed left over. Is there any general rule as to how long they will keep? Is there any difference in this respect between flowers and vegetables?

There is no general rule concerning the length of time that seeds retain viability—some lose it very quickly and have to be sown within a very short time of ripening, others will germinate well even after a period of several years, particularly those we call weeds which is why they are so successful in resisting our efforts to clean them out of cultivated soil.

Seeds sold in the UK are subject to stringent acts and laws which control minimum percentage germination. These percentages often fall drastically in seed kept over from one season to the next which is why the date is always stamped on seed packets. Viability is affected by conditions—too much warmth can shorten viability and, of course, dampness and moisture can also spoil seed.

The seed coat and remains of husk and pulp are ideal material for the growth of mildews and other fungi. This is why the cleaning of seed is so important and more likely to be carried out thoroughly by a reputable seed company with equipment and know-how than by the amateur. At least one commercial producer now offers seeds in hermetically-sealed foil packets from which all moisture has been extracted. Seed stored in this manner will retain its viability much longer, provided the packet remains unopened and the miniscule atmospheric conditions inside remain unspoiled.

Bearing in mind the relatively inexpensive cost, it is hardly worth keeping used seed beyond the season for which it was intended and, particularly it is most unwise to rely upon old seed for an early sowing because by the time you find out it is not going to germinate properly and have to make another sowing with fresh seed, it is no longer an early sowing!

446 Why seedlings 'hang' and do not grow away

I can germinate seed, but the plants do not grow away. This is particularly the case with marrows. I use soil-less compost which should be disease free.

This can happen with any seedling, but is a fairly common problem with marrows, cucumbers, courgettes and melons—all members of the Cucurbit family. As the seedlings do not grow away, it is fairly evident that your compost is not suitable. The young seedlings are exhausting the food supply within their own seed and are not assimilating nutrient through the root systems and becoming established due to nutrient deficiency, wrong conditions, or both. The early stages of germination and growth of any seed are dependent entirely on the food material stored within the seed until the seed leaves emerging into light turn green—i.e. make chlorophyll—and begin to photosynthesize carbohydrate and until the infertile root develops sufficiently to begin absorbing nutrient chemicals from the soil. Further more, the 'soil' that greets the emerging infantile root has to be favourable not only as regards its nutrient content, but also with regard to its physical structure.

For the marrow family, try changing your

seed compost to one consisting of equal parts of John Innes No. 1, peat and sand; soak the seeds for an hour in tepid water and sow the seed on their edges—not flat—two to a $3\frac{1}{2}$ in. pot. This should be done at the end of April and the pots placed in a temperature of 60°F., later selecting the strongest seedling and removing the other. Keep moist but not wet—waterlogging causes root rot and then nutrients cannot be absorbed.

When two or three true leaves have formed, stand the pots in seed trays and move outdoors during the day, taking them in at night. Do this for a week when, with all danger of frost gone—it should be the end of May by this time—you can plant outdoors. Gradual hardening-off is vital; marrows are soft, and sudden chilling can be fatal. Always plant out on a little mound because the main stems of young marrows are prone to rotting when the soil remains wet. Planting on a mound helps to keep the stem drier and safer.

447 Pelleted seeds : are they any better?

Should I get better results from sowing pelleted seeds?

Putting a coating—usually of clay-like material—around a small seed makes it much bigger and easier to handle. Seeds can then be spaced out evenly in the drills and you don't waste so much. This method is much better than sprinkling unpelleted seeds along a drill which, however carefully spread, always need to be thinned out as seedlings.

You get better seedlings too, not only because being spaced apart they don't have to compete with near neighbours as soon as they germinate, but because the pellets can contain a little insecticide and fungicide to protect them through the early vulnerable stages.

However, there is one important point to bear in mind: the pellet has to break down before moisture can penetrate and the seed emerge. Always sprinkle a little moist peat along the drill, water thoroughly and then sow the seed. This helps to ensure a rapid breakdown of the pellet and a rapid start to growth.

448 Polyanthus seed germinates poorly : a reliable method

I experience great difficulty in germinating Polyanthus seeds, even when purchased in tin-foil packets. What are the best conditions for them?

The seed of the Primula family does not enjoy a very long viability and Polyanthus seed should always be fresh. See *No. 445*. In this particular case, the seed has the advantage of being in foil packets, which usually prolongs the viability, so it is more likely that there is something wrong with your sowing technique—sowing too deep or allowing a period of dryness, perhaps. I have raised very many thousands of first class plants using the following method, and there is no reason why you should not be equally successful.

Prepare seed boxes in late January–February with a compost consisting of equal parts John Innes seed compost, fine sieved peat, and soft or silver sand. Press level with a flat piece of wood—gently, not too hard—and soak thoroughly by immersion. Mix the seed with three times its own volume of silver sand—this will not only enable you to sow the seed thinly, but the light-coloured sand will also show you where it has fallen, and you can then get an even spread. Polyanthus must have fierce surface drainage, so don't cover the seed with soil, but a very thin layer of sharp sand, just enough to cover the seed and no more. Stand the tray in a mild steady temperature (55–60°F.) and cover the tray with a pane of glass. Lift this and wipe off condensation every day. With this moisture-retaining compost, you will probably get germination in about three weeks without the need to water. However, if the sand shows dry, give just the merest flick with the finest rose you have, or even spray clear water with a single-handed sprayer. The very fragile seed will be germinating and it must not be knocked down.

As soon as germination occurs, place a wooden label across each corner of the tray and place the glass on these; the gap will give just a little surface ventilation. Then, as germination proceeds, take off the glass. The hardening off must be done gradually. Prepare seed trays with the same compost as above and as soon as you have thirty-five seedlings large enough to handle between finger and thumb, prise them out carefully without disturbing the others into 3 in. deep trays as follows.

With a small dibber, scratch seven marks into the soil surface evenly along the long edge and five down the sides. This will enable you to position 5 rows of 7 neat and in straight rows equidistant apart. Carefully dig under the seedlings with a wooden label, lifting with soil particles adhering to the infantile root system; of course, try not to disturb the smaller ones more than you can help. Dibber them in very carefully, water, and stand out in a shady position taking care that they do not dry out or you will lose them for sure. As soon as they are established, they can be moved into a more open position but still away from direct sun. When the plants are 2–2½ inches across the leaves, they can be transplanted into prepared open ground, 10 ins. apart in rows 12–14 inches apart. Here they should grow into nice plants ready for planting around September–October into the positions where they will flower the following spring.

Like their near relations primroses, Polyanthus like plenty of organic matter in the soil, so dust some peat or crumbled compost along the rows as a mulch, but keep a wary eye open for slugs and snails. Be ready to place traps as described in No. 511.

If you don't have heat in the greenhouse, sowing will have to be delayed until April–May and the entire process follow on later, although the end products will not be so large and well-developed. Sometimes, with the greenhouse-sown early starters, some plants may try to throw a bloom in that first summer. Don't let this happen, the plants are not mature enough yet to support a bloom and will only exhaust and ruin themselves. Take out the bloom so that strength is conserved and you'll get far better blooms in the spring.

449 Poor germination after liming: use a soil test kit

For several years I have been successful in growing lettuce and carrots. This year germination was poor, and the seedlings ceased growing beyond 1 inch high. I had an attack of club root on my cabbages last year and I limed the soil heavily; could this have anything to do with it?

Carbonate of lime or hydrated lime which is the usual method of applying lime to the soil is known to inhibit germination when applied fresh, and for sometime after.

I don't think that this is the cause in this case, however, for two reasons. Firstly, the lime was applied long enough ago to have weathered and been dispersed before the seed came into contact with it; keeping liming and sowing apart is, of course, correct practice. Secondly, germination has been achieved although the seedlings failed at 1 inch.

Therefore I would suspect that the soil is still acid and in fact needs much more lime. However, before you begin adding more, you should find out exactly what the alkalinity/acidity balance is (called the pH factor) and then you will know whether you need to put down more lime, and if so, how much.

You can resolve this quite easily with a Sudbury soil test kit obtainable from Boots or your local gardening centre.

It could be that this problem has crept up on you because of a persistent use of artificial fertilisers, many of which are sulphur-based compounds and which leave sulphur end-products in the soil causing acidity. If you have been using straight chemicals and feel that your N. P. and K. ratios could have been unbalanced, you can check this too with a little more elaborate but still quite simple soil test kit. Take a careful look at your soil structure, especially the organic content, make as much use as you can of mulching so that organic material is always being added to the soil and use slow-acting long-lasting organic-based manures instead of short-lived quick-acting tonics and pep pills.

450 Poor germination after early sowing: why?

Wanting to get an early crop, I sowed vegetable seeds early and, although there was no frost, very little came up, whereas seed from the same packets sown only 3–4 weeks later in exactly the same way, germinated well. Why should this be so?

This happened basically because the soil had not warmed up after winter's cold, and your seed simply rotted. Invest in some cloches— either glass or corrugated polythene sheets— and 2–3 weeks in advance, place over the soil where you are going to sow seed so the soil becomes warmer. Don't make the mistake that a lot of people do in keeping the ends open; close them in with a pane of glass so that the inside warms up, like a miniature greenhouse.

Now you can sow earlier than normal with a much better chance of success; excessive rain will have been shed aside by the cloche and the seed will not so easily rot in wet soil.

Before you sow seed, tip a little 'combined seed dressing' into the packet and shake it up so that seeds are coated and given protection against fungi which cause root rot and damping off, and against soil pests like wireworms and leather-jackets.

Before sowing into the drill, first dust fine peat along the row; this not only improves soil texture, but also makes all the difference to moisture retention around the seedlings. Water with the fine rose on the can, cover again with the cloches, and you should have no more trouble in stealing a march of a few weeks on the normal season.

451   Seeds collected in old stockings

This year I am saving seed from a leek for the first time. Some people have told me I should cover the seed head with muslin and others say I shouldn't. Can you tell me the right method please?

In a warm dry summer, ripening can be considerably advanced and the seed be shed very early—sometimes unexpectedly. The sole purpose of the old practice of enclosing in muslin the seed head of onions, leeks, and other plants with similar-shaped seed heads, is to trap the seed inside and prevent it from being lost by falling to the ground. A better material is a synthetic fibre stocking, such as a piece cut from women's tights, since this material dries after rain much more quickly than muslin.

After pollination is completed, the flowers gone and the seed head seen to be swelling, entirely but loosely enclose the head with a single layer of the material so that air and light are hindered no more than necessary. Tie it closely around the stems because this is where the seed will collect if it falls. Don't let fallen seed accumulate in the bag because if it gets wet with rain, it will take longer to dry, could spoil, or even begin to germinate.

As soon as the seed is seen to be capable of being shaken loose, cut the stem towards the end of a dry sunny day so that the bag and its contents are dry. Cut it well below the bag and hang it upside down in a dry airy place for a few weeks. When all the seed has fallen or can be shaken out, collect it in a large envelope, add a little 'combined seed dressing', shake and mix thoroughly so that the seed becomes coated, and seal the envelope. Write the name on it and store in a dry place until it is required for sowing.

452   Seedlings which are long and leggy

Although I can get seeds to germinate, the young plants tend to become leggy and drawn. How can I overcome this?

This condition is called etiolation and although it can be caused by too much heat underneath, literally driving the seedlings out of the soil, the more usual and basic cause is insufficient all-round light.

It may be that the natural light in your greenhouse is being obscured by dirty glass or too many shelves or too many other plants. It could be that the sides of a propagating case are too high, or it could be the most common cause of all—seed sown much too thickly so that as the seedlings germinate, they have to fight each other to reach up to the light. The only time you want this to happen is when you sow mustard and cress, or when you put a bucket over your rhubarb to draw out long stalks.

If you have difficulty sowing seed thinly, mix only a little with silver sand so that you have a greater quantity of material to spread but, of course, only a small part is viable seed and inevitably it is more thinly dispersed.

Section X

Lawns

453 After every mowing, the lawn turns brown

Every time I mow my lawn it turns brown next day. Sometimes this lasts for a few days, sometimes for longer. Can you say what is happening?

This is typical of a blunt mower. Instead of cutting cleanly, the grass leaves are being squeezed between, or bashed and bruised by blunt blades. What should have been clean-cut mowings in the grass box were not cleanly detached and badly bruised sections have remained on the lawn, died and turned brown the next day.

The debilitating effect on the individual grass plants is tremendous. Very soon your grasses will be so weakened that many of the individual plants will die, the sward will become thin and moss and weeds will take over.

You should get the blades sharpened at once, and if you value your lawn, have the mower serviced before the beginning of each mowing season.

454 Only one way to make a bumpy lawn level

What is the best way to level a lumpy lawn? I have rolled it many times but it doesn't make much difference and a heavier roller is very expensive. I am not sure that I could pull it about either.

No lawn was ever levelled with a roller so get rid of it. More damage is caused by rollers than any other garden tool. A lawn is a living community of plants and when you subject the high spots to rolling pressure, all you do is compress and compact the soil in that spot. The only way to get the lawn surface level is to get the underlying soil level, either by taking some away from the lumps or adding some to the hollows. To what length you will need to go, depends upon how bad the inequalities are to begin with and how true you eventually want it to be.

If the humps are pronounced and readily identifiable, variation between high and low will, in consequence, be considerable. This can be reduced by flaying back the turf and removing a little soil from under the humps. Using the corner of the spade (or a half moon knife), cut a letter H with the middle bar across the hump, pull back the two tongues of turf, remove enough soil and relay the turf. This will at least reduce the bad inequalities. Further levelling must now take the form of raising the low spots and this is done by top dressing with fine crumbly soil, at no faster rate than the grasses can grow through and colonise.

The vigour and speed of growth of the grasses is therefore of some importance; a soil cover that is too thick on slow growing grasses can effectively mask out and kill the plants. The best time to begin the top dressing is therefore from spring onwards when growth is naturally at its most vigorous. The soil material to use for this job is dry fine sieved soil taken from the surrounding garden. This is because it will at least be in keeping with the soil type of which the lawn consists.

To fill the hollows to the point where the surface is quite level will probably cause considerable thickness and this, if made up with brought-in and therefore 'foreign' soil, will produce patches of uneven growth and colour. This is not idle theory; I have seen it happen many times when the warning has not been heeded. Therefore, rob the surrounding garden and if soil has to be brought in, use it on the garden to replace what has been taken for the lawn; the plants in the garden border or beds will not show such disfigurement to soil fertility variation as the lawn certainly will do.

Where hollows are apparent, or can be felt when walking across the lawn, sprinkle a small handful of the soil, sieved fine and kept dry for the purpose, rubbing it into the turf, putting no more down until all signs of the previous soil have gone. This part of the procedure will take several soil droppings and may take some time. However, it is a task not to be hurried, and it will considerably level the surface without disfigurement. In time, of course it will be more difficult to discern hollows as they fill and you may well feel satisfied that this is as far as you wish to go.

If you are looking for a billiard table level, further levelling will take the form of spreading down a fair quantity of soil. This can be brought in since the entire lawn is going to receive a fairly uniform coating. Pull it level with a straight edge, as in cement levelling. The longer this straight edge can be, the more level your lawn will be, but for the amateur, 3 ft. is probably about the comfortable maximum. Buy a piece of perfectly straight timber 3 in. × $\frac{5}{8}$ in. × 3 ft. long, hardwood and for preference beech or oak. It must be absolutely straight because any curvature or bend will be transmitted to the lawn surface—and you'll never get it level. Fasten this by screwing or bolting to the inside face on the prongs of your garden rake. Choose a dry day, mow the lawn closely and at once put down along one side of the lawn enough soil to form a ridge. Drag the soil ridge with the straight edge no more than a foot at a time towards the other side. Add to the soil as required to maintain the ridge as soil is left behind in the hollows, and little or nothing on the hilltops. You must keep a surplus ridge going all the time. If you let it run out, there will be no soil to drop into the hollows under the straight edge.

After a few weeks, when the grass has grown through the soil layer and the soil has been absorbed and become the new surface, repeat the mowing, top dressing and levelling procedure, but at right angles to the first; if the first was north and south, carry out the second east and west. The lawn surface will now be very much more level than before and a year's weathering will bring the hollows back a little as the soil settles and the procedure can be repeated if you want the level to be absolutely precise.

The above procedure is basically how the professional groundsman produces a true level surface. By doing the same, you too can produce a level lawn—with a roller you never will.

455 Worms on the lawn

Since worms are supposed to be so good for the soil, must they be killed on the lawn?

In a mild muggy autumn and again in spring, the worms come to the surface in great numbers to breed, and as they re-enter the soil they leave many casts behind them. Worm casts smother and blanket the finer grasses of the sward, and when they are exceptionally numerous they smother the main grasses as well. Leave these casts undisturbed and you decimate the grass population. You must seize every opportunity—if and when they dry and become crumbly—to brush and disperse them. They also make first-class seed beds and thus you have the old and proven axiom of the two Ws in the lawn—'weeds and worms go together'.

The good that worms do for a lawn is far outweighed by the harm. In the old days, physical contact with the worm by using paralysing toxins like Mowrah meal and derris was necessary. As worms often burrow to considerable depths, it was a skilful job to persuade them to the surface layers where the poison could be brought into contact with them and so achieve a high percentage kill.

Nowadays, 100% eradication is simple and fool-proof. Simply mix and water down Chlordane—the dilution rate will be on the can or bottle. This material gradually weathers down into the soil where it creates a soil atmosphere which is toxic, not only to worms but to all soil creatures like wireworms and leather jackets that breathe by a system called diffusion. In these creatures the toxin accumulates and reaches a fatal level but birds and animals are unaffected because they have ventilated lungs like humans. The toxicity remains effective for about a year until the concentration disperses: then you simply apply a further solution.

456 How can a good lawn be made on clods of clay?

I have been putting down sand for three or four years on my clay-ridden lawn, but it has made no difference. The soil is as sticky as ever.

Clay can be improved and made more easy to work with, but it is not a quick or simple matter. It's one of the most frustrating problems that beset gardeners and is worst in a clay-based lawn, where disturbance and working of the soil would ruin the lawn. Many people have spent a lot of time and money trying various remedies, with no other reward than frustration due to not understanding what clay is and why it behaves the way it does. It is no good trying to overcome its sticky heavy nature with sand, grit, ash or even compost. That is only treating the symptoms and doing nothing about the cause. Understand the cause, and you can then do something about remedying it.

With the naked eye you can see individual grains of sand, but the size of particle that constitutes clay is microscopically small and the remarkable fact is that these clay size particles only need to constitute approximately 30% of a soil sample for that soil to have the characteristics of a clay—heavy, wet, sticky, poorly draining and difficult to work. Thirty per cent of clay is enough to cover the larger particles and fill the spaces of sands, grits and gravels—and so they behave like clay.

If you begin with a soil that is almost 100% clay, consider how much sand, grit, ash or whatever else, will be needed to reduce the clay proportion to below 30% of the whole. It doesn't take much to realise that a 'physical and brute force' method of altering the clay character—which is what sand and grit is— is completely impracticable. To alter merely the top 3 ins. of your clay soil, you would need to put down and mix with it at least 7 inches of sand and grit and there would still be the original impermeable waterlogging clay subsoil under that.

Clay stays wet and sticky, i.e. water does not pass through it because water will not pass through a very small aperture, and the spaces between the microscopically small clay particles are correspondingly small, and as described above, 30% clay-sized spaces is enough to make the passage of water difficult.

Clearly the problem is to make these spaces larger and there have been some ingenious ideas that have sought to do this, and which have been put on the market.

In addition to such man-made solutions—

none of which have lasted very long—there is a natural solution that has stood the test of time. It is not expensive and that is probably the best reason why it is not more commercially promoted and well known.

Where in geological history clay has become overlaid and become permeated with rock gypsum, the clay does not resist the passage of water, and to explain simply why this is so, we need an analogy. Most people will know the old party trick of rubbing a comb or pen or a stick of sealing wax with silk or flannel, and then making small pieces of paper attach themselves. This is caused by static electricity. Each clay particle has a static electrical charge upon it; gypsum particles have a very strong opposite charge and, according to the principle 'like charges repel—opposite charges attract', the clay particles are attracted, cling to and group around the gypsum particles in the same way that the pieces of paper cling to the comb.

The spaces between the groups of clay particles are much larger than when the clay is not grouped—the correct word is 'flocculated' —and water can thus pass more easily through these larger gaps. Really a very involved scientific subject, this simplified explanation will no doubt still be heavy weather for some. However it is necessary to have a basic comprehension of the principles involved (a) in order not to waste time and money on remedies that do not treat causes and (b) to give yourself confidence to carry on applying gypsum over a possible lengthy initial period when no improvement may readily be apparent.

8 ozs per sq. yd. per annum is the maximum rate that a clay can assimilate gypsum and it is best applied as 2 ozs. per sq. yd. dressings, 3 months apart. Persist with this rate of application to the lawn, and as the grouping of the particles develops gradually, it will become less wet and sticky and in consequence the grass will grow much better.

The process may take two or three years to achieve significant improvement. You will have to be patient, but at least it will be patience with an awareness and understanding of what you are doing and that will ultimately change the nature of your clay. See also *No. 2*.

457 Control of coarse wide-leaved grass

A very coarse, wide-leaved bright green grass has started to spread rapidly in patches over our lawn. Can you identify this from my description and tell me how to get rid of it and prevent its return?

This grass sounds like Yorkshire fog, *Holcus lanatus*. It is a difficult 'weed' grass to control by chemical means because there is no easy and simple way for the chemical to distinguish between the leaves of grasses as there is between broad-leaved weeds like daisies and dandelions and grasses. However, if you read *No. 459*, you will find the clue to its control.

Yorkshire fog does not like frequent close cutting and because it can lay flat to escape the mower blades, it should be raked so that it stands up, before mowing. Using a garden or a springbok rake for this job can be time-consuming and guaranteed to produce the most excruciating backache. Most domestic lawns are not too large to come within the scope of a wheeled hand-pushed, scarifying rake. A very good type called the 'Aerake' is made by Sisis Ltd. of Macclesfield, and turns a tedious chore into an easy pleasant task. This is very important because the key factor is frequency of combing up the fog grass and cutting it with the mower so that it bleeds.

Do not ignore, however, the warning that the spread of this fog grass indicates. Your fertility is dropping and the weed is only advancing because it is not getting enough competition from the finer grasses. Read the adjacent items on lawn care and realise why you must get the finer grasses growing vigorously so that they crowd out invaders. The Aerake will also enable you to carry out slit aeration and this, with correct feeding and frequent mowing, are the keys to a good lawn and the prevention of fog grass.

458 How to control the daddy-long-leg invasion

Daddy-long-legs have invaded my lawn. Am I too late or can I yet save the grass?

You cannot stop daddy-long-legs (crane flies) from alighting on the lawn, and good lawns are just as liable to be attacked as are those in poor condition. The long-legged flying insects are familiar in August and September. The female is the one with the long pointed 'tail'—not a tail at all, in fact, but an ovipositor—a long egg laying tube—and each time she alights for a split second on her flitting hopping flight across the lawn, she lays an egg through the turf, near the soil surface.

This soon hatches into a grub—known as the leather-jacket—which then burrows down to feed on the grass roots for up to three years before pupation, and emergence as an adult. All the care you take with your lawn will go for nought if there is an army of these pests chewing away.

You can rid the lawn of them, together with the cast-making worms, by watering down a solution of Chlordane worm-killer. This renders the soil atmosphere toxic to all creatures that breathe by diffusion, see *No. 455*. This is best applied when you see the crane flies on their egg-laying flights so that the hatching grubs burrow into toxic soil; however, it can be applied at any time you become aware of the trouble.

Bare patches may appear if too much of the root activity has been destroyed. Feeding and aeration should soon encourage recovery, but if you sow seed into these patches, don't use selective weed-killers for at least six months because the selectivity doesn't become effective until the grass is maturing. This also applies to a combined feed and weed-killer like Humber Eclipsall, so use Humber Eclipse Garden Compound instead.

459 Why a Cumberland turf lawn disappoints

I laid Cumberland turf because I wanted a good lawn. It was very expensive but is proving unsatisfactory. It is difficult to keep green and also it is being spoiled by a lot of large-leaf grasses appearing that were not there to start with. What do you suggest?

A mown lawn is unnatural and 'in the wild' short sward turf only occurs where it is grazed frequently by animals, where the depth of fertility is so shallow as to make it difficult for other rooting plants to become established, as on chalk downland, or when other local or special conditions prevail that favour or even can only be tolerated by dwarf-growing grasses.

One such special condition is periodic immersion by sea water, as on the flat marsh areas of the coast where sea-washed turf is cut. One of the largest of such turf areas was around Silloth in Cumbria, hence the description Cumberland turf. Because that county's turf areas were not inexhaustible, the term has increasingly become applied to similar turf cut from similar places.

With diminishing areas and escalating transport costs, true Cumberland turf is very, very expensive to start with and so much more expensive to maintain in its original condition as to be, for all practical domestic lawn purposes, a waste of time and money. This is because the very moment the turf leaves the sea-washed conditions in which it evolved naturally, it is also subject to invasion by the grasses that are native and indigenous to the new area where it is expected to grow. In other words, it ceases to be Cumberland sea-washed turf, and begins the transition to Acacia Avenue turf, Surbiton, or wherever.

Some of the grass species comprising the mixture in the Cumberland turf may be able to accept the transition, but the vast majority, the dwarf-growing species for the most part, that give Cumberland type turf its character, cannot accept the change in conditions and begin to die out. Worm casts hasten the process—see *No. 460*—and the thinning sward readily admits invading large leaf grasses which are native to your area and conditions.

You can hardly give the turf periodic washing with sea tides and the heavy rainfall—not hosepipe—of the Lake District. What you can do, however, is to try to emulate one of the conditions which are much more widespread throughout the U.K. and which produces the short sward turf found on downland and meadows that are heavily grazed by sheep. The resulting turf on the shallow fertile downland hilltops is different from the turf in the lower and more fertile meadows, but frequent regular close cropping produces a short sward in each case.

The common factor in both cases is sheep and your mower has to become a flock of sheep, with the emphasis not on 'close' mowing but on frequency.

Probably the finest and shortest turf outside the Cumberland sea-washed marshes is to be found on (some) bowling greens, to where the turf has been transported and laid. A close examination soon reveals that, although they are often called Cumberland greens, the turf contains hardly any of the original sea-washed species. The sward has, however, been kept short, thick and free of broad-leaved invaders by receiving downland treatment, i.e., frequent close cropping. A good bowling green is mown every day with a sharp mower and, other factors apart like incorrect feeding which, in any case, are consistent with bad cultivation, bowling greens that are in poor or declining condition are invariably not mown every day or are mown with blunt blades.

It is this daily mowing that is impracticable for most amateur gardeners who have jobs to go to, and a once-a-week slaughter when the sward is cut as close as the mower will go so that it lasts until the following weekend has the very opposite effect to what is required. The added effect of mowing with unsharp blades is dealt with in *No. 453*.

Whilst a stretch of fine green lawn may be every gardeners dream, it is not buying the best or the most expensive turf to begin with that is the governing factor. A lovely lawn will remain a dream unless you understand, and can go a long way towards providing the right conditions. All the fertilisers in the world will do little to preserve a Cumberland lawn unless you mow it frequently. If you cannot mow daily, forget Cumberland, lift the mower cutting height to $\frac{1}{2}$–$\frac{5}{8}$ ins., mow twice weekly and settle for cutting respectable grass, instead of mowing a fine lawn.

460 Dog's brown patches : how to stop them

How can I stop my dog from bringing my lawn out in brown patches?

This is a frequent problem with bitches squatting on the lawn and, of course, the ideal way is to keep the dog off the grass, either by not letting it loose in the garden, or by taking it out on the lead. Repellent substances would be effective but you would need to ring round the lawn, and that is hardly practical.

The only method that I know to be really effective is always to have a can of water standing ready, go out with the dog and as she finishes squatting, water the area at once.

Two further procedures will also help. Mix a dessertspoonful of hydrated lime and a cupful of gypsum. Tip this into an old stocking and, after watering with the can of water, dust the area at once by shaking the dust bag over and around the damp patch.

Secondly, the acid and other chemicals causing the scorch are organic and contain nitrogen. Decomposition and utilisation of this nitrogen can be encouraged by making sure that the soil bacteria population is as numerous as possible. You will do this by regular slit tine aeration.

If you do not aerate regularly (you should, of course), at least aerate each spot as it occurs with an Aerdrain fork fitted with root action slitting blades. This useful tool is very simple to use, and is manufactured by Sisis Equipment Ltd., of Macclesfield.

461 How to grow a chamomile lawn

Can you give me any information about chamomile lawns?

There are a number of dwarf-growing plants other than grasses that can be used to make a lawn, the basic difference being that they cannot stand close and repeated mowing like grasses. This was not so important in the days long ago when lawns could only be mown by hand swing-knives like sickles, or by scissor-like shears normally used for clipping sheep, when the many pairs of hands needed to 'mow' an area of any consequence were cheap to hire.

Of course, the plants used for these early primitive lawns in addition to being dwarf-growing would have needed to be spreading in habit so that they merged, covered the soil surface and thus crowded out rogue plants— weeds. An added attraction would be an aroma created whenever the lawn was walked on, crushing and bruising the leaves. In this way many aromatic plants and herbs were used of which perhaps the most suitable and certainly most widely used was chamomile.

The invention of the lawn mower altered everything enabling one man to do the work of many and the cutting was so much closer. The aromatics and herbs could not stand such close mowing and therefore declined in favour of the grass that could.

Aromatic chamomile lawns still have a curiosity value and if you wish to try cultivating one, you should first face up to what you are letting yourself in for. In the same way that a grass lawn is constantly under invasion threat by weeds, an exclusive chamomile community will also be invaded and, in this case, grass itself becomes a weed. However, there is no selective weedkiller to help you, and weeding the chamomile lawn is a tedious hands and knees job.

If you are prepared for this, plant young divisions 4–6 ins. apart into a level prepared site, from March onwards. Because of the subsequent weed problem, it is best to prepare the soil by spending a little time over it. Rather than let the weeds germinate after the chamomile has been planted, encourage germination before planting, then kill the weeds; germinate again, kill again—possibly several times until the soil has been cleaned of weed seed for at least an inch or two in depth. This will be done by repeated soil disturbance—raking and watering. You should eradicate each germinated weed crop by hoeing, *don't* use a selective weedkiller because of the danger of toxic residue affecting the chamomile. If you wish to use a chemical eradicator, use one of the Paraquat-based ones which break down within

THE COMMONSENSE OF GARDENING

seconds of touching the soil, but will effectively kill all green leaf. Use a fine mist from a hand-sprayer kept solely for total weedkilling and no other purpose. You cannot afford the risk of spraying anything else with a contaminated sprayer, and of course keep both it and the concentrated chemical in a perfectly safe place beyond the reach of others, especially children.

When raking and watering fails to show any weed germination, you can fairly assume that the soil is clear of weed. Then go ahead with the chamomile planting. You can obtain plants from Treneague Chamomile, Trevorder, Wadebridge, Cornwall—who have a dwarf non-flowering strain—Moorhavens, Adlams Lane, Sway, Lymington, Hampshire and Dorset Herb Growers, Shipton Gorge, Bridport, Dorset; all are excellent suppliers.

462 Effect of repeated sulphate dressings on the lawn

Many years ago I read somewhere how sulphate of ammonia and sulphate of iron could be used to feed a lawn and keep it bright and green. Is this really correct?

Sulphate of ammonia is a quick-acting boost to the nitrogen supply and contributes nothing beneficial to the soil structure. See *Nos. 456, 465* and *475*. Feed is the wrong word. Grass is a plant the same as any other so far as basic nutrient requirements are concerned. Phosphorus, potash and nitrogen are needed, in approximately balanced proportions. Nitrogen is required for leaf development and you might think all that is needed is plenty of it to encourage plenty of leaf—but not so. A lawn will not remain healthy on a diet of nitrogen alone, any more than you would remain healthy on a diet of all greens at every meal without meat, potatoes, puddings or bread.

The use of quick-acting nitrogen fertilisers like sulphate of ammonia and nitrate of soda should be regarded essentially as a booster. It is all very well asking a correctly fed lawn for an extra effort but if you keep on forcing leaf growth with highly nitrogenous fertilisers, the other two main nutrient sources will quickly become out of proportion and you get

what is called an induced deficiency. The ratios of the lawn feed you use should never be much in excess of $1\frac{1}{2}$ nitrogen to 1 of potash to 1 of phosphorus.

As you will appreciate when reading *No. 465*, it is in the interests of long term fertility if the nutrient source is organic-based and there are a number of materials available. Because it has never failed me I always advise the use of Humber Eclipse Garden Compound Manure with N.P.K. ratios of 1–1–1 and Humber Eclipsall Turf Compound (which has an inbuilt selective weedkiller) with ratios of $1\frac{1}{2}$–1–1.

Iron sulphate does not supply nitrogen but it is often advocated for putting colour into a lawn. What does this mean? Let's turn to man for an illustration. An undernourished man looks pale because the red cell count in his blood is low. This is because red cells die every fifteen days or so and the iron needed to make new ones is usually obtained from our food intake. Therefore anyone who doesn't get enough food looks anaemic. So you give him the usual cure for anaemia which is an independent source of iron, usually iron tablets and pills. His body makes more red cells, his colour returns and he looks much fitter, but is he really? His blood count is fine, his body processes work well again, but his stomach is still empty and what little food resources he has get used up quicker than ever. Soon he is a very sick man because you haven't got to the real cause of the trouble—starvation.

Plants don't make red corpuscles as man does; they make green chloroplasts and they too contain iron. A poorly fed lawn doesn't look very green because its chloroplast count is low —and thus the advice is given that iron sulphate will improve the colour. It does—the grasses make more chloroplasts, they look greener, and you think your lawn is better. So did the undernourished man look better with the improved blood count. All you are doing in each case is rushing faster towards exhaustion and at this stage, moss, weeds and fungi invasions meet no resistance whatever from the struggling grasses. See *Nos. 465* and *471*.

Indeed, many sulphate fertilisers, including the two in question, are acidifying in their effect. Repeated use must therefore also be seen as increasing the acidity of the soil, with the risk that it can eventually become so acid that grasses have difficulty in tolerating it, leaving the way open for moss which thrives in acid conditions.

463 Fairy ring : not easy to control

There are four fairy rings on my lawn which I have been trying to get rid of with Epsom salts and sulphate of iron. Then I decided to dig one out and found the soil all streaked with white. I would like your advice about getting rid of the rings which have not responded to the usual recommended treatment.

The streaky white appearance of the soil from under a fairy ring is due to the fine threads called mycelium by which the fungus travels through the soil. This mycelium is waxy and has the effect of waterproofing the soil so that water can no longer penetrate. As a result, the grasses are deprived of moisture and often die before the fungus moves outwards to the next 'ring' of soil. As the old mycelium dies, water begins to penetrate again and sometimes rescues the grass, or adjacent grasses spread into the vacated band of soil. Because of the decaying mycelium and dead grass root, the humus content is higher, and nitrogen content is therefore a little higher and the grass often responds and appears a darker green.

There are several chemical remedies including proprietary preparations, but a fairy ring is notoriously difficult to eradicate. Sterilising with formaldehyde is not to be recommended because the lawn can be severely disfigured and digging out the affected ring is a rather drastic remedy. A successful remedy is described in *No. 473*.

Any toadstool-like growths that appear should be removed at once, before they have time to mature, drop spores and spread the trouble. Although Fusarium fairy rings will attack turf in good condition, there is little doubt that it will be more readily attacked if the turf is under nourished. Therefore, read the items on fertility, *Nos. 456, 462, 465* and *475*.

464 Weeds on the lawn sown from good grass seed

In my new garden, I sowed good quality grass for my new lawn, and a forest of weeds has appeared. Do you think that they came with the grass seed and what can I do?

You have nothing to worry about. The seeds of many weeds can remain viable in the soil for very many years, waiting for the soil to be disturbed so that they are brought to germinating level. This is what happened when you prepared your lawn seed bed. You could have used preparations that would have killed these weeds as they emerged a few days before the grass seedlings but it is too late now to use weedkillers.

Make sure that your mower is very, very sharp. Bashing and bruising with a blunt mower is very weakening to even well-established grass and to do it to young infantile seedlings is simply asking for trouble—see *No. 453*. Set the mower to cut very high—at least an inch but higher still if possible, and only lower it very slowly indeed, taking the whole of the first cutting season to come down, one notch at a time to no lower than $\frac{3}{8}-\frac{1}{2}$ in. This gives the young plants a chance to make plenty of leaf and to thicken up and become established before you make the heavy demands of close mowing. Indeed, if you can accept a 'long' lawn, leave the mower at the $\frac{5}{8}-\frac{3}{4}$ in. setting. Mowing too closely is the most frequent single cause of all lawn troubles.

As soon as you commence mowing, most of the weeds you see now will die out because they cannot stand the knife repeatedly. In fact, the finest lawn weedkiller of all is your mower, and the only 'weed' plants that can live in a lawn are those that already have or can adapt (like a buttercup) to a prostrate growth habit that keeps below the mower blade.

Under no circumstances, use a selective hormone weedkiller within six months of sowing, because the young seedlings do not develop the immunity to the hormone, do not get 'selected out' and will die with the weeds. Naturally this applies also to any seeding of thin patches that you may do from time to time.

465 *The way to eradicate moss*

*Can you tell me how to get rid of moss on a lawn?
Last year I raked it over, got rid of barrow loads,
and dressed it with fertiliser. This year, it is
worse than ever.*

Leave it alone for the moment. Moss is a
highly complex subject, and first of all you
need to understand it. In the same way that
man regards himself as the highest of animals,
plants also can be placed on the rungs of an
evolutionary ladder. Algae are very simple and
come at the bottom, then lichens and mosses up
through the ferns to the higher plants with
grasses, especially wheat and corn, very near
the top. Now it is reasonably and generally
true—and for our purposes, certainly so—
that the higher a plant is placed on this scale,
the higher is the degree of fertility required to
sustain it, i.e. the higher plants have only been
able to evolve on this planet as fertility has
evolved and become more elaborate.

The botanical family of grasses is exceptionally large and the degree of fertility requirement by various species is extremely variable.
Likewise, many grasses are very tolerant of
variation in fertility levels and will continue to
grow, if not thrive, when conditions become
adverse and fertility much reduced. The
grasses that comprise our lawns come into
this category and it is because they are so
tolerant, that declining fertility is thereby
masked and passes unnoticed for some time
before warning signs appear, and when moss
occurs the decline is already well advanced. At
this point read *No. 467.*

When moss invades a lawn, the fertility has
become so low that the higher forms of life
find it difficult to live, much less offer resistance, and so those life forms that only need a
very low and primitive fertility are able not only
to grow, but grow without competition. Moss
in a lawn indicates the inescapable fact that the
soil is very, very low in fertility, and it is
important to appreciate in this context that
fertility has not so much to do with fertilisers as
it has to do with soil structure because, in
addition to moisture and nutrients, a fertile
soil must contain humus, bacteria and air and

it is the last that is in many ways the key factor.
See *Nos. 2, 456, 462, 465* and *475.*

You cannot dig or hoe a lawn like a vegetable
garden and therefore the soil will not contain as
much air—hence the need for lawn aeration.
Every box full of grass cuttings removed from
the lawn represents a box full of humus being
removed from the soil of the lawn. Add up the
number of boxes per mowing, per week, per
season and you will see how large a bulk of
humus material is being removed. You may be
able to replace the plant nutrient chemicals with
packets of fertiliser, but these do nothing to
replace the cumulative loss of humus, and its
effect upon the soil structure of the lawn leads
inevitably to degeneration into a dense, solid
mass, devoid of humus, air, bacteria, and consequently, devoid of fertility.

The cardinal fact is that it is a waste of time,
money and effort killing moss, or raking it and
scarifying it, if you do nothing about the mismanagement that caused it in the first place.
The natural source of plant nutrients is as the
end product of the decomposition of organic
matter by bacteria. Without air in your lawn
bacteria cannot live and, anyway, there is
precious little humus in your lawn soil for
them to live on. Begin to improve fertility and
vigour in the grass by getting air into the soil.
This is best done with an aerator of the type
that slits not spikes, because the soil surface
area thus exposed is a great deal larger. Sisis
Ltd. of Macclesfield, Cheshire, make aerators
with slitting root action blades in sizes to suit
all lawn areas and pockets. Slitters do not harm
the lawn surface and you can hardly aerate too
often. To begin with, the blades will not penetrate very far; you cannot expect them to
since the soil is solid and compacted. Depth is
something that will come with time and repeated use as the compaction is relieved and,
in any case, all you need worry about at the
start is the top inch. To begin with, slit as
often as you can manage it, in all directions.
That will at least help the ingress of air—you
are 'digging' your lawn without destroying the
surface.

Next, manuring: a good top dressing of
peat or organic matter each autumn and spring

will begin to put humus back into the soil—regular slitting will also help this. With the return of air and humus, bacteria will soon proliferate. Eventually, try to settle down to regular slittings every week throughout the year, stopping only when it is frosty or too wet for you to be on the lawn. You will now begin to get the best return from the use of organic plant food dressings (see *No. 462*) and you have a huge backlog to make up on.

With good cultivation, fertility will improve, the grasses will respond, begin to thrive, and you can start exerting pressure on the mosses—they won't like the more fertile conditions anyway. When you can see your improved management resulting in more vigorous grass pushing out the moss, showing that you are now moving in the right direction, then is the time to help the grass by using a moss killer.

As I suggested at the beginning, the way to get rid of moss is to leave it alone until you understand why it is there, and why it will come back unless you improve your management. Moss is Nature's indicator about which way your fertility is going. Leave it there until you know where you are going.

466 New lawn failure : get rid of the roller

Although we dug, raked and rolled the ground very carefully, the lawn we sowed in mid-March is very disappointing. The grass is still not long enough to cut and there are bare patches everywhere. The soil is very heavy ; can we do anything to rectify matters?

First of all, read *Nos. 2, 456,* and *465*—and then you will realise that you should next get rid of the roller. It is the most damaging thing in the garden. No lawn was ever levelled with a roller, nor can be; all it can do is compress the lumps, squeezing the air and life out of the soil, which is why your lawn develops bare patches.

Sowing in mid-March would be much too early. Unless winter has been exceptionally mild and quite frost-free the soil will still be very cold and much of your seed is bound to shiver and rot. The end of April is quite early

enough and then only if the temperatures have been mild ; otherwise leave it for another couple of weeks. The grass will always catch up from a faster start.

With young seedlings growing, it is now much too late to attempt to level the surface and you must wait until what grass there is has become established.

Follow the feeding pattern outlined in *No. 471*, but because you must not let selective weedkillers get near young grass, substitute Humber Eclipse Garden instead of Eclipsall Turf Compound, picking up the programme as indicated according to the time of year you start. That will make sure that the grass is not deprived of nutrient.

Next, and as soon as you can, something has to be done about the heavy soil. This must be made more porous so that surface water can get through. Put down agricultural gypsum at the rate of 2 ozs. per sq. yd. every three months, no heavier and no more frequently as this is the fastest rate that the soil can assimilate it. Keep the mower blades set high to give the grass a chance and when the grass is responding and becoming established, any patches remaining can be resown, using the same seed mixture, and during late summer levelling can begin, see *No. 454*. Additionally, and most important in a heavy soil which tends to become dense and airless, you can help your grass a good deal by helping air to get into the soil. Use a slit tine aerator as often as you can afford the time.

467 Plantains, daisies and dandelions : how to get lasting control

How can I get rid of hundreds of plantain weeds on a large lawn that has been down for two years? There seems to be almost more weed than grass.

The way to keep plantains out of your lawn is *not* to kill them; an explanation of this statement is needed.

Plantains, like daisies and dandelions, have big wide leaves that lie flat and are therefore ideal for being thoroughly wetted by a selective weedkiller spray. They are probably the easiest weed of all to kill off and one spraying of any of the selective weedkillers knocks them over like ninepins—but it's almost the worst thing you could do. Ask yourself how they got there in the first place, and secondly why they are still there, thirdly what will you have when they are gone?

If you read the adjacent *Nos. 465* and *471*, you will appreciate that weeds don't get into a healthy vigorous lawn because they are pushed out. The plantains are remaining in this lawn because they are *not* being crowded by the grasses.

Wipe out the weeds and you will be left with an immense area of bare soil, constituting an ideal seed bed for another weed invasion. Therefore, it is no good whipping out the weed until and unless you do something to ensure that the bare area vacated by killed weeds will be quickly colonised by grasses spreading in.

Any time before July—after which, delay until the following spring—begin by putting down 2 ozs. per. sq. yd.—not more—of Humber Eclipse Garden Compound which is a powdery dressing. You will need a decent distributor capable of putting it down at the required rate. There is no weedkiller in Garden Eclipse but I suggest you use it for two basic reasons. First, it is a balanced feed that in 2–3 weeks after application will have grass, and weed, beginning to respond vigorously. This action will continue for another three months. The weeds will love this and grow like cabbages —never mind them, it's the grass we are concerned with. Keep the mower blades very high and let the weeds and the grass make plenty of leaf.

The second reason for using Garden Eclipse is that the kinds of bacteria that will be concerned with the decomposition of the Eclipse organic material will proliferate and the bacteria count will increase, so that when you put down another dressing later of the same organic base, there will be a much greater number of the right kinds of bacteria waiting to deal with it.

Four weeks after the first dressing of Eclipse Garden, put down a light 1 oz. to the sq. yd. of the Turf Compound counterpart of Eclipse Garden called Humber Eclipsall. This contains a weedkiller and must be used only on the lawn, not on the garden.

You should not be aiming to knock over the weeds yet although in response to the earlier dressing they will be growing so well that they will take in the first 1 oz. weedkiller dressing so fast, that they are going to be mighty sick.

Probably the first effect of the hormone you will notice is that the weeds grow much more quickly. The short stubby leaf stalks begin to stretch and the leaves lift clear above the grass. This will happen slowly enough for the grass to get under and start filling in the bare areas under the leaves. Keep the mower set high since you don't want to take off too much of the plantain leaf; you will want enough left to go on working for a little while longer yet.

In two weeks' time, maybe three depending on the weather, the grasses should have so responded to the Eclipsall dressing as to be already crowding under the plantain leaves. If you are not satisfied that this is so, repeat the 1 oz. Eclipsall dressing and come back in two weeks for the kill. For this, put down a 2 oz. per sq. yd. dressing of Eclipsall and you will soon have the greenest lawn you could wish for—with not a weed in sight.

Your mower will still be set high; don't make the mistake that so many make in trying to carve the lawn down low in one go. Be patient; take the mower down one notch, $\frac{1}{4}$ inch, every other week, mowing as often as you can, so that the cuttings coming off are very small and the grass is not weakened by taking off too much leaf at one cutting.

Of course, if you are able to include aeration with a slit tine aerator into your lawn cultivation, so much the better.

468 What does rush grass indicate?

Patches of an extremely coarse, tough, round-leaved grass are now appearing in my lawn, which was made from turf about three years ago. Until now it has been of quite good quality and I would like to get rid of this tough grass which the lawnmower won't cut. An expert who visited our garden society said it was a rush or reed of some kind, but our soil is very dry indeed.

The 'weed' grass undoubtedly is a rush, quite likely field woodrush which is native to poor, low fertility soils, generally acid and heath-like, and to dry grazing meadow.

This is consistent so far with your description of your soil. For the three years that your lawn has been laid, it has probably been living for the most part on the fertility imported in the soil of the turf, and this is now becoming used up. Three years of weathering, leaching of nutrients into the poor soil underneath and mowing have taken their toll, and it sounds as though you have not done much to improve fertility. Your lawn is becoming more similar to the natural soil below it and, not surprisingly, as the fertility reduces, plants requiring less fertility are gaining a hold. See *Nos. 2, 456* and *465*.

Short of digging it out as it appears, wood-rush is difficult to eradicate, and the best method of control is a combination of cultivation and worrying persistence.

First, feed the grasses with an organic-based long-lasting nutrient as outlined in *No. 471* in order to get the grasses moving and responding. Secondly, the indications are that the subsoil is low in humus and you will have to regard a spring and autumn top dressing with peat or a fine sieved crumbly organic material as part of your routine for a couple of years at least. Compost could be used provided that you rub it through a ½ inch sieve so that the small crumbly material can easily work down through the grass sward. However, you will have to be prepared to risk the introduction of weed seed, although this is not likely to be serious if you feed with Humber Eclipsall which contains a hormone weedkiller. Thirdly, as you will realise from the other items on lawn care, aeration and assimilation of the organic matter are important. In the face of regular wounding by the slitting blades of the aerator, the wood-rush will undoubtedly begin to face increasing pressure from the increasingly vigorous grasses.

Selective weedkillers applied in the usual manner do not have much effect; this is another of the advantages of Eclipsall since the hormone is presented in a persistent manner. Whenever you have a few minutes to spare you can help it to get into the rush by using an old kitchen knife to lacerate the tufts of rushes right through the roots.

As the woodrush is indicative of acid conditions, its appearance in three years suggests that acidity may be quite pronounced. Carry out a soil test with a Sudbury test kit which you can obtain quite cheaply from a garden shop. Follow the instructions and, if acidity is indicated, put down ground chalk at the rate of 2–3 ozs. per sq. yd. every two months until the acidity is reduced. You may have to do this several times before you get it right and then bear in mind, because of the nature of the soil underneath, you will probably have to put down a little chalk from time to time to prevent it becoming too acid again.

469 Sand and peat for a lawn top dressing?

The grass on my lawn is very sparse, but otherwise weed free and of good colour. I have been advised to top dress with sharp sand and garden peat. Is this correct?

Subject to certain safeguards, sand and peat are satisfactory for top dressing but first read *Nos. 2, 456* and *465*. You must understand how this peat and top dressing is going to affect the soil structure.

Be careful about putting down any bulk top dressing material that could affect the surface level by introducing inequalities that do not already exist. On the other hand, if the purpose of this exercise is also to level the lawn, then I would not use peat and sand because the peat can dry and shrink considerably. It would be better to use a solid non-shrinking top dressing like the natural garden soil, and level the lawn properly with a 3 ft. lute, see *No. 454*.

If the purpose is to introduce humus-forming material into a level which is low in fertility, a peat only dressing should also be pulled level with a 3 ft. lute, because every operation involving the addition of a substantial amount of material to the lawn surface is a further opportunity to at least maintain, if not improve, the level.

The almost invariable advice given is to brush top dressings into the surface; in theory, this is right because it helps to work the material through, avoid overcoating and masking the finer grasses. In practice, and without the correct equipment which an amateur is very unlikely to have, it is very risky because, with a narrow stiff broom, it is virtually impossible to avoid brushing the top dressing material into ridges and inequalities. It is far better practice to get your grasses growing quickly by feeding and aeration so that they will quickly grow through a luted level dressing.

However, peat or any other bulk organic material should not be left lying on the soil surface where it can oxidise and be largely wasted, or if it gets and remains wet as on a heavy soil, can putrify and quickly contribute to a build-up of thatch, see *No. 475.*

Slit tine aeration to expose the maximum soil area to the free atmosphere not only encourages the proliferation of beneficial soil bacteria but also facilitates the descent and incorporation of the humus-forming material into the soil, where it is needed. There is no point in putting down fertilisers and lawn feed materials if they are going to be washed out before any benefit can be gained. Furthermore, slit tine aeration does not mark and disfigure the lawn surface, as spiking does, and is the most important single process of cultivation you can use on your lawn.

The sand ingredient in the top dressing proposed is subject to much misgivings. If the sand is intended to improve a wet clay, you are wasting time, effort and money; see *No. 456.* If you want to level the lawn, use something more natural to the rest of the lawn. Sand will produce an unsightly, blotchy mess due to the unequal response to uneven fertility; there is no food material whatever in sand.

Provided that you have considered the above, and understand what you are doing, go ahead and top dress your lawn with fine peat. Feed with an organic-based plant food and don't be afraid to augment the humus intake by flying cuttings from the mower, but always remember to aerate with the slit tines.

470 Soak the lawn, or leave it alone: why?

I read recently that it was inadvisable to water a lawn with a hose; that one should either use a sprinkler or leave it alone. I assumed that the advice was correct, and so this year I have not watered my lawn at all. It is now pale yellow. I am confused, and with so many lawn conditioners and tonics available, I am afraid I may make matters worse. Can you please advise a good tonic to get the lawn back into condition?

The advice about not watering a domestic lawn with a hose is sound, but is much better expressed as 'either flood the place or don't water at all'. The reason for this is that root growth is attracted in the direction of moisture and when a lawn is allowed to become very dry those roots will be searching rather desperately for any moisture they can find.

Most people when watering the lawn with a hose do not keep at it long enough for sufficient water to soak right through the soil to root level and below. Dry soil can absorb so much water that even a heavy downpour may soak in no more than an inch or two. The roots will be actually encouraged to come up to the moisture rather than go deeper for it.

The danger now becomes apparent—if your watering during a dry period is not enough to get right down, and merely wets the top inch or two, it doesn't take too long for most of the root activity to become concentrated near the surface. If you then go away on holiday or miss out the watering and a further dry spell ensues, the entire root system dries out like a biscuit.

If you are going to hose the lawn, put a sprinkler on the end, and leave it running whilst you go away and do something else. This way the lawn gets a long and thorough soaking—and is not so dependent upon the time you can spare for the job.

As for a good tonic, this is not what the lawn needs. The number of lawn products currently available is confusing but after what it has been through, your grass will need a balanced diet of food and drink—and plenty of kind treatment. First let the floods commence so that the water goes down deep—an oscillating wave sprinkler is better than a revolving one because the water is spread evenly over an area instead of being concentrated in a puddle in the centre and nothing in the corners.

Next, feed with a balanced nutrient, preferably organic or semi-organic, in which the nitrogen, phosphate and potash proportions are fairly even, you can tell this by looking at the analysis on its sack or bag. Phosphate is usually indicated as soluble and insoluble phosphoric; add the percentages together and compare this total with the figures for nitrogen and potash—they should be fairly equal. National Growmore or Humber Garden Eclipse semi-organic are as good as you'll get. Two dressings of 2 oz. per sq. yd. four to five weeks apart, preferably in early spring, but any time up to the end of July, and you'll soon be getting new growth.

In order to rescue a very dry lawn, give the grass a chance to grow, to make leaf and build up its reserves. Stop all mowing until the grass is at least an inch long and then mow as frequently as you can with the blades set high —and leave the box off. Never cut lower than an inch until the whole area is evenly grown over again. Then gradually you can reduce the cutting height, but I would suggest that you do not go below ⅝ in. for at least a year.

471 Special lawn sand used as a weed-killer

I have a low growing round-leaved weed in my lawn and have read that it can be controlled by lawn sand. How does it work?

Lawn sand kills weeds in exactly the same way that over-strong applications of fertiliser chemicals can cause scorch damage and even kill.

Plants absorb nutrient chemicals by a process called Osmosis. Put simply this means that when two chemical solutions of unequal strength are separated by a membrane through which liquids can pass; the weaker solution passes through to the stronger, diluting it until the solution strengths are equal.

The very fine hair-like feeding roots of plants have a fine skin covering—the membrane—that separates cell sap within the plant root from the moisture in the soil outside. The soil moisture has dissolved plant nutrients in it —which is why we speak of 'soil solutions'— and all the time the strength of the soil solution is weaker than the cell sap within the plant, it will flow through the membrane of the root hair into the plant.

If you put down too much fertiliser so that the soil solution becomes stronger than the cell sap within the plant, the moisture flows out of the plant instead of into it. It is like osmosis in reverse, and the correct word is 'plasmolysis'. This explains why plants can be killed by over-strong fertiliser applications.

Lawn sand kills weeds in the same way. Iron sulphate has very strong powers of absorption, and when mixed into sand and sprinkled over the lawn, use is made of leaf shape to determine which plants are killed and which are not. Wide flat leaves like daisies, dandelions, buttercup and many others, are the right shape to catch the sand as it is sprinkled, and the chemical sucks the life sap out of them, whereas it bounces off and does not remain on the narrow vertical leaves of grasses so they remain unharmed.

If you spread lawn sand when the grass is wet, some of it may stick and scorch the grass leaves; therefore apply it only when the grass is dry. Also, of course, if you put down too much lawn sand so that some of the sand cannot fall through and remains in contact with the grass leaves or renders the soil solution too strong, the grasses also will be killed.

There are several lawn weeds that answer to the general description 'low growing, round leaved' and it is not possible therefore to positively identify which one is the subject of this question, and consequently know whether you have to deal with a special peculiarity or difficulty.

Modern hormone selective weedkillers should give good control, and are to be preferred, but if you really want to use the old-fashioned lawn sand method, heed the above warnings and don't exceed the rate advised in the instructions printed on the bag for general spreading or confine the use of the sand to spot treatment, i.e., sprinkling just a small quantity on to the weeds only.

472 What do starlings on the lawn indicate?

After I have mown my lawn, starlings descend and make a real mess of it. Is there no way of stopping them? The trouble has gone on for three years now and I can never understand why they do not seem to damage other lawns in the district. The grass is fed with lawn fertiliser in the summer and autumn.

The diet of starlings includes leather jackets, wireworms, grubs, worms, insects, and large numbers of birds picking and scratching into a lawn indicates fairly conclusively that they are finding what they are looking for. In fact, you might consider what would be happening to your lawn if the starlings were not taking such a heavy toll.

The obvious control is to eradicate the grubs and insects so that the birds go away to feed elsewhere. You can do this by watering down Chlordane which, although used in the main as a wormkiller, will also control the other soil creatures that breathe by diffusion. See *No. 461*. Use it exactly as the instructions indicate on the can and you will have no lawn pests or birds feeding on the lawn for a year. After this period, the poison dissipates and you will have to repeat the treatment. There is no risk to bird life or animals, all of which have ventilated lungs breathing free atmosphere.

473 Controlling toadstools

During the last two autumns, a lot of toadstools appeared on my lawn. Last year I dug them out, but they appeared again. How can I get rid of them permanently?

The first thing is to find out what is causing the toadstools. If they occur in large numbers it could be due to rotting timber, root or other woody matter buried in the soil in which case the best course is naturally to get it out. Various methods of chemical control can be tried. A mercury-based fungicide would be easy and straightforward to apply and is probably all that is required to knock it out if it is not deep seated. But it could be rather expensive if there is a lot to do.

In this case, try permanganate of potash, sometimes called 'Condy's fluid', obtainable quite easily from chemists. Dissolve the crystals at the rate of 1 oz. in a gallon of water. Let the liquid stand for half an hour or so, but stir frequently. It is a very strong fluid so keep it well away from your clothes and skin. Then with a fine sprinkler rose on the watering can, apply the gallon of solution evenly over an area of 3 sq. yds.

Another method, I have seen used with success several times—including on fairy rings—is to use sulphate of iron dissolved at 1 oz. per gallon. At this concentration, it will certainly scorch the grass, so it must not be sprinkled. Instead use a crowbar or iron bar to make holes about 6 inches deep into the heart of a toadstool patch or about 7–8 inches apart if the area affected is large like a fairy ring. See *No. 463*. Holes should therefore be made for a foot or more outside the ring. To help overcome and penetrate the mycelium wax, mix in half a teaspoonful of liquid washing-up detergent to a gallon of solution and, using a funnel to avoid spilling, fill the holes to about $1\frac{1}{2}$–$2\frac{1}{2}$ inches of the top. Refill when soaked away.

When drained for the second time nearly fill the holes with crushed plaster, rubble, or crushed brick, or failing either of these sand will have to do, and top off with a little soil. Scorching around each hole is almost certain to result as the root systems are affected by the strong solution but the grass usually recovers quickly if care has been taken not to overfill the holes so that the top layer of soil is also saturated. The idea of this method is to create a scorching permeation and soaking from 2 to 10 inches deep, but not to the surface 2 inches where the grass would be harmed.

The porous tube of plaster or sand backfill ensures that even if the mycelium is not killed, water will be able to penetrate more easily and of course, in the other extreme, surplus surface water will be able to drain away.

474 Laying turves

What is the right time and method to lay turves?

I have successfully laid turves in every week of the year and there is no hard and fast rule on the time to do the job. It is really a question of avoiding adverse weather conditions, and using plain common sense. Rooting will be more successful on warm soil than on cold, and so spring, summer and autumn are most favourable.

Don't make the mistake that many gardeners do of deep-digging the lawn area beforehand. Nothing will settle soil like time and weather and despite all your firming and levelling, deeply-dug soil will go on settling long after the turves are growing away and all your most painstaking efforts to produce a billiard table level surface will have been wasted.

Disturb only sufficient soil to produce enough tilth to rake into the hollows and get the surface reasonably level. Firm the soil by treading; never under any circumstances use a roller. See *No. 466*. It causes more damage and trouble than any other tool in the garden.

Rake and tread, rake and tread several times; stones must come out in case they work through the turf and chew a piece out of the mower blade. A good watering will help to settle the soil and show up unsuspected low spots; allow to dry and rake again, and again. If you are on heavy clay soil, it will help considerably to mix in gypsum at up to 8 ozs. per sq. yd. whilst you are raking. When you are finally satisfied with the level, forty-eight hours before laying is due to begin give the entire area a thorough soaking, flood it so that when you come to lay the turves they go down on soil that is well-moist in depth. Then, as you are ready to lay, sprinkle down Humber Eclipse Garden Compound or Growmore at an ounce or two per sq. yd. Give a final light raking to work in this nutrient dressing and to raise a very slight tilth from the sodden surface. This will help the roots work in more easily.

Now you are ready to actually lay. The turves should go down in the familiar staggered pattern like bricks in a wall but don't just lay them like doormats. Normally, turves are cut 3 ft. × 1 ft. and are folded or rolled, unless you stipulate 18 inch × 1 ft. unrolled flats, which I think are best. In any case, they always begin to shrink as they begin to dry. Drying and shrinking can continue after laying, and once a laid turf has shrunk, you'll have an awful job stretching it. Nothing looks worse than the all too common sight of a newly laid lawn, covered with dried and shrunk turves, curling up at the edges with inch-wide gaps between them.

To avoid this, kick the turves tight against each other, make a turve 3 ft. × 1 ft. go into 2 ft. 9 ins. × 10–11 inches. This, plus making-up faults and breakages, can easily amount to at least 10% of the area and the calculated number of turves you need. Therefore, you should always allow an extra 10% on the straight calculation of the turves required for a specific area. For example, an area of 300 sq. ft. would need not 100 3 ft. × 1 ft. turves, but 110. Or if you are laying 18 in. × 1 ft. 'flats', you will need 220, not 200. The most expensive turves are the odd number that have to be delivered afterwards to finish the job.

Lay them, tread them with your feet, don't beat them since that's worse than rolling. If your feet feel a high spot, take out a little soil from underneath. Try to get the job done in one day, or if the uncovered area is showing a dry crust, water it again, ready for next day.

If your soaking prior to laying was heavy enough, there should be no need for overhead watering and this should be avoided for at least a week unless the weather is very warm and drying. This is because the roots must be made to reach down to where the moisture is. They must be made to work and become established. If you water from above, there won't be the urge to get digging. See *No. 470*.

If you follow the above procedure properly, in seven days' time you will have a job to lift up the turves, in a fortnight it will be impossible, indicating that rooting has been well established. Begin mowing with the blades set high, mow frequently and lower the blades only very slowly, no more than one notch each two weeks and not below $\frac{5}{8}$ in. for the first year. After the first four weeks, slitter blade aeration can begin in order to cause root pruning and promote maximum root activity.

475 *Thatch eradication*

We need some help with our lawn on which there is a thick layer of old grass below the green leaves and on top of the soil, so that the lawn always seems a yellowish green, particularly after cutting. One reason may be that the soil here is very sandy. We always water it in dry weather.

Thatch in a lawn needs a lot of understanding and is the subject of a lot of quite illogical advice! Instead of raking it out, I suggest you leave it there till you understand why it is there in the first place. The best thing to use on thatch is commonsense.

A sandy fast-draining soil is always very quick to suffer from lack of moisture and then when rain comes, it rapidly leaches out the plant nutrients. It is a waste of time and money using quick-acting chemical fertilisers in these circumstances; it's rather like gardening in a sieve—a splash of water and it's all gone. Read the adjacent items on lawn care and then, relating all this to your case, you will realise that you will have to work hard to get as much moisture-retaining organic matter into your sandy soil as possible.

Everything you do must be in the direction of adding humus. Peat and mushroom compost will need rubbing through a ½ inch sieve in order to extract the small sized crumb particles that will work down easily into the turf. However, such materials cost money. You can go a long way towards providing all the organic matter you need, not only for the lawn, but for the rest of the garden as well by shunning the dustbin and consigning all household waste to the compost heap. See *No. 480*. Now this really is important, because on a hungry sandy soil, fertility will be entirely dependent upon soil structure, how much humus you work into it, and therefore how much you make or buy. With your sandy soil, making compost is vital to every aspect of your gardening, and everything of organic origin should go on the compost heaps, from cabbage trimmings to flower stalks, eggshells to newspaper.

In this context you should also consider how you mow the grass. With so little moisture-retentive power in the soil, you cannot expect the grasses to live at a fast rate—which is what they will try to do in order to replace the leaf if you mow too closely. Therefore, the first thing to do is to set the blades high to leave as long a sward as you find acceptable but certainly no lower than ¾ in. Secondly, and this is going to sound revolutionary to the general advice that you will read and hear, on your sandy soil always fly the cuttings, take the box off your mower and put it away. At this point I would suggest, if you haven't already done so, you read *Nos. 456* and *465* which are relevant. Why take humus away from the lawn when you are trying to increase humus in the soil underneath? The objection is usually three fold: the cut grass treads indoors, the cut swarfage left on the lawn makes it look untidy, and the accumulation of cuttings eventually produces a stifling springy coconut mat layer of 'thatch'. All very true but easily avoided.

The first two objections are met by mowing more frequently so that the size of the cuttings coming off is very much smaller, they don't lie around making a mess, but dry out to dust very much more quickly and return more easily into the soil. The last objection is worth considering at some length because understanding why 'thatch' builds up—and you already have 'thatch'—helps to understand how it is bound up with fertility. Organic matter is decomposed by bacteria, and grass cuttings decompose very quickly. See *Nos. 476* and *489* on composting which are relevant. When they accumulate into thatch, instead of being decomposed into humus, it is clearly due to the simple fact that cuttings are being deposited more quickly than can be decomposed. This can be due to two or three reasons: insufficient air which decomposition bacteria must have in order to live (not likely in your open sandy soil), insufficient humus in the soil (not on top) to support a high bacteria population, and extreme acidity at the soil surface. Thus you have the anomalous situation of thatch on the surface being caused in very great part by a lack of organic matter not much more than a couple of inches below the surface.

The logical remedy for thatch, therefore, is not to rake it off and take it away, but to put it where it is needed—down under. You can do this quite easily and effectively by frequent and regular aeration with a slitting blade aerator, not a spiker. If you scarify and rake out the thatch especially with the low fertility of your soil and poor vigour of the grass, your next problem will probably be moss because you are creating the ideal conditions for it to get in and gain a hold. Read *No. 465* and you will see how repeated mowing with the box on the mower removes a large bulk of organic matter from the soil, how the humus content of the soil declines and with it the bacterial population. This condition requires top dressings of humus-forming materials like peat and compost. Thatch is caused by the same lack of humus in the soil, and the logical solution is to turn it into a top dressing by aerating and encouraging bacterial decomposition.

Section XI

Soils, Composts and Fertilisers

476 *Compost heaps*

Try as I may, every compost heap that I make becomes a wet, horrid, evil-smelling mess, instead of the crumbly friable stuff that it is supposed to make and that I have seen on television programmes. They never explain where I go wrong. One says cover it to keep off the rain; another says there is no need and that it does more good than harm.

The decomposition of once-living animal and vegetable matter is a living process carried out by living micro-organisms—in the main, soil bacteria—which fall into two basic groups. Aerobic bacteria require nitrogen and oxygen for their own body processes and prefer it to be in a gaseous form—hence the need for the presence of air in the soil. Decomposition occurs step by step, involving several—and sometimes a great many—different strains of bacteria until the complicated chemical compounds that comprise all vegetable and animal matter—wood, leaf, stem, flower, bone, hoof, horn, feather, blood, etc.—are reduced to very simple chemical compounds that can dissolve in water and be assimilated by living plants.

The second group, anaerobic bacteria, does not need air, and indeed, proliferate only when it is absent. They are responsible for the process called putrefaction, the end products of which are not the simple compounds of decomposition but compounds which have disagreeable odours.

What happens in your compost heap can be illustrated by explaining something else that occurs rather more quickly and is familiar to most gardeners. Let us suppose that you mow your lawn and tip all the cuttings in a heap. When you collect them up a little later, you will know that they have become very warm. This is familiar to all gardeners—but what is happening?

Although the grass is dry when you cut it and you think the cuttings are quite dry as well, in fact the grass leaf structure consists of approximately 85% liquid cell sap and only 15% dry matter—cellulose, sugars and starches, mostly carbohydrates. Mown off the surface of the soil, perhaps with some worm cast as well, it is inevitable that the cuttings box will also contain a lot of soil bacteria. As you tip the cuttings on the compost heap, a lot of air goes in too and you have all the ingredients for decomposition to begin.

Bacteria would like to have an optimum temperature of 130–160°F. and they set about creating it. A lot of the energy that goes into the lawn in the form of light and is tied in the elaborated compounds, is now released as they begin to be decomposed—in the form of heat—and only a couple of hours after mowing, you can feel it.

Go back to the heap in a few weeks' time, and it will be much smaller, usually a soggy mess. The green grass is browny yellow—and most noticeable, there is a horrid smell. Grass leaves are comprised of cells which, as you might expect with an 85% liquid content, are very thin-walled and as the bacteria break these down, the cell sap is released. As the leaf matter breaks down, the strength of each particle weakens, the heap settles and the air spaces become smaller—liquid is being released into them and the air is being used by the bacteria at a terrific rate. As the heap settles, it becomes increasingly impossible for more air to enter. The aerobic bacteria stop dead in their tracks, decomposition is arrested and anaerobic bacteria take over. Their process is putrefaction—bad smelling compounds, and in a fortnight you can smell them!

To ensure uninterrupted decomposition, an uninterrupted air supply is necessary. So you should simply shake up the heap, break it open, turn it, fluff it loose so that air can get in. Relate all this to your compost heap, where exactly the same thing happens and you will see that you will have to turn it repeatedly in order to re-charge it with air—and whilst you are doing that, incorporate some roughage like old bean haulm, Brussels' stems, old tomato stems, stuff from the border, even twisted newspaper, etc. so that the heap does not settle again into a dense air-less mass. Roughage preserves little air channels to the interior and as the bacteria continue to get air, they continue their work.

A compost heap decomposing properly generates heat for a considerable period and it is usually reckoned that this is enough to drive off any surplus moisture; therefore, except in very wet conditions, there should be no need to cover the heap. But, of course, a so-called compost heap with insufficient roughage to keep it open, is destined to become a soggy mess anyway which can only be made worse by not being covered. See also *Nos. 483* and *489*.

477 Dealing with a garden prone to waterlogging

When dry my soil is very good and easy to handle, but most of the time it is very wet as there is a small stream at the bottom of the garden. Can you suggest the best way to avoid it.

With your water level, I believe it would be worth your while to try an experiment. You cannot drain away the water because it won't go lower than the stream, so you'll have to climb up out of it by raising the soil level.

Before embarking on anything too ambitious, see if the idea works by starting with the 'Lazy Bed' system. The Scottish crofters used to use this method quite widely—and some still do— to grow vegetables in their sodden peat bogs. Dig ditches 3 ft. wide and 9 ft. apart, and throw the top two spits on the ground in between. You now have a raised bed and a wide drainage channel which may or may not soon contain standing water, depending on how high the water table is. Tidy up and smooth the sides of the raised beds so they don't dry and crumble, and grow your vegetables on this drier higher level.

If this shows improvement in your vegetable crop, you can consider making the arrangement more permanent by building retaining walls of stone and brick. Perhaps a local builder would welcome the opportunity of a site close at hand to get rid of a load of hard-core instead of hauling it off to a distant tip. Don't be over-anxious and tell people that you want old bricks, or they will ask you to pay for them. Just let them know they can tip a load at any time in your drive or in the road outside, and you should get all the material you need.

478 Counteracting lime soils

The soil in my new garden was tested and found to be exceptionally alkaline. I have used an iron chelate solution, but there has been no very marked improvement. Could you suggest what else can be done, as even ordinary plants are very yellow.

Whilst acidity can be corrected fairly quickly by dressings of lime, the opposite course is a very different matter and can take some years of treatment before marked improvement is obtained. Even then, it is quite likely to require continuing treatment to maintain a more neutral balance because the underlying lime and chalk quickly affect the top soil. This is why, unless you put in a physical barrier like a plastic sheet, see *No. 117*, it is a waste of time digging out holes and filling them with acid soil for planting lime-hating plants, like Rhododendrons.

Yellowing of the foliage in excessively chalky conditions is a condition called chlorosis, see *No. 38*.

Deal with a chalky limy soil, first by incorporating into the soil as much organic matter as it is possible to lay your hands on. Read the items in this book on composting, especially *Nos. 476* and *480* and utilise everything you can. Bracken peat is particularly useful as it has an acid reaction.

Secondly, if you use fertilisers, use sulphate forms like sulphate of ammonia, sulphate of potash or sulphate of iron which have acid reactions. Conversely, do not use materials like bone meal, hoof, and horn, or superphosphate which have alkaline reactions, and will only make matters worse than ever. Let everything you do in the short term be a move in the direction of acidity. In the longer term, carry out regular testing so that you know exactly what is happening to the acid/alkaline balance, see *No. 488*.

Finally, it will help the worst affected plants to put down very finely ground powdered sulphur which you should be able to obtain from the chemist's without much trouble. Be careful how you use this however. It is very acidifying and should only be used a little at a time. The following is a safe method that I have used myself and seen used many times, but don't expect miracles overnight. Nature doesn't work that fast. Calculate the number of square yards to be treated and mix the same number of ounces of the powdered sulphur into a fair quantity of peat or finely crumbled compost. Throw this out evenly over the area so that the sulphur has been carried and stretched to the relatively light rate of only 1 oz. per sq. yd. Three months after the 1 oz. sulphur dressing, do it again, except that this time use half the amount of sulphur. Hoe this into the soil/mulch. After another three months give another ½ oz. dressing, and then before the next three-monthly dressing is due, carry out acid/alkalinity tests with a simple testing kit, see *No. 488*. By observing the gradual rise of the acid ratio, you will know when to ease up with the sulphur, but in a limy, chalky soil the reasons already given must lead you to expect to have to carry out this treatment on and off indefinitely.

479 Should lime be put on the compost heap?

Should I add lime to a well-rotted leaf heap before I dig it into my vegetable garden?

This is not necessary unless your soil is known to be acid, and then it would be better in autumn to spread lime on the surface to be weathered in, and this only as indicated as required by soil testing. Too many amateurs seem to regard lime as a panacea, the more profligate use of which is to entail that much more fertility. On gardens and allotments, tons of the stuff are put down every year with no more understanding than 'it's the thing to do every year, isn't it?' Simple acid/alkaline kits are very easy to use and very inexpensive considering the mistakes they help to avoid. See *No. 488*.

Digging in compost is best done at that stage of a crop rotation programme, just before the soil is to be occupied by gross feeders—potatoes certainly, but not other root crops like carrots, parsnips, and beet, and trenched under beans and peas. Some potato varieties resent fresh lime and go scabby, so for this crop —no freshly applied lime.

When you spread lime on top of a compost mulch, hoe it in. The lime can be concerned with chemical reactions which cause the release of ammonia. This gas has nitrogen as one of its constituents—the very nitrogen that our plants need and which you may have spent good money on putting down as a fertiliser.

Fresh lime or compost will be at or near the surface, and any ammonia resulting will be easily and quickly lost to the atmosphere. If it is hoed in, there is a much better chance that before the ammonia is lost, soil bacteria will have converted it to nitrite and prevented its loss. One more bacterial conversion to nitrate and plants can absorb it and utilise the nitrogen.

480 Making more compost by shunning the dustbin

All our garden waste and kitchen waste, such as potato peelings and outer leaves of greens, are put on the compost heap but I seldom have enough to go round. What can I add or use to make more? I don't want to buy more peat.

Anything that was once living, whether of animal or vegetable origin, is part of the cycle of life, sometimes referred to as 'ashes to ashes and dust to dust'. Living plants work up simple chemical compounds absorbed from the soil into the more complicated chemicals that comprise plant structure—stem, leaf, fruits, roots, branches and trunks of trees, etc.—and the animal life that devours them further elaborates these chemical compounds into flesh, bone, blood, hoof, horn, hair and feather.

Read *Nos. 476, 487* and *492* and related subjects, and you will be able to take a long hard look at the contents of your dustbin. Far too much potential fertility is thrown away in this nation's dustbins.

Although straw is now a very much more valuable commodity than it was, you might find a farmer willing to let you have some broken or rotting straw bales which you could carry off in a sack, or on a roof rack.

If your neighbours are not compost conscious, offer to take their kitchen waste, lawn mowings, leaf sweepings, and other organic matter. Even old cottons and woollens will break down—these are best put under peas and beans to form a spongy moisture reservoir. Newspaper can be used; treat it rather like wood shavings. See *No. 492*.

Always remember the importance of the air content of a compost heap. Screw up all newspaper and material in twists so that it physically forms 'roughage' to keep the air passages open. See *No. 480*.

481   *Nitro-chalk as a top dressing needs care*

Could you tell me the correct uses of nitro-chalk as I assume it is all lime?

Certainly nitro-chalk has an alkaline reaction, and for this reason is particularly useful on sour acid soils. Its primary purpose, however, is as a supplier of nitrogen since it contains up to about 15%, compared with perhaps the most commonly used nitrogen fertiliser, sulphate of ammonia, which has 18%. Not a lot of difference, but sulphate of ammonia has a definite acid effect, and as soils tend to become acid with the repeated use of artificial fertilisers, the alkaline reacting nitro-chalk therefore helps to restore the balance. It is much to be preferred on all soils other than those that are chalky, limy or known to be already alkaline.

It is useful for leafy crops, particularly cabbages, brussels, broccoli and other brassicas which can be attacked by the fungus disease club-root, which is at its worst when the soil is acid and is discouraged by alkalinity.

Since nitro-chalk is a stimulant fertiliser, not a slow-acting manure, use it sparingly— 1 oz. per sq. yd. is quite enough; more than that, and you are liable to cause scorch.

482   *Mould growth on soil*

In my greenhouse and garden there are areas about six yards square that get a heavy mould growth on them. This is green and of a tiny fern-like type. Can you tell me what I can do to get rid of it?

'Fern-like type' means that it is something more than just algae, which is quite common. Most likely this is liverwort, a primitive plant form that requires only a very low degree of fertility and thrives in wet conditions. Calomel —which you can get at the garden shop or centre and is normally used for controlling club-root—is reckoned to control liverwort as well.

As you will read elsewhere in this book the sensible and successful gardener prevents causes. You should recognise that the presence of liverwort is an indication that your soil structure needs improving.

The surface of soil that is dug fairly frequently, as in a vegetable plot, or hoed perhaps as in a rose bed or flower garden, should not remain stagnant long enough for liverwort to get a hold. When the affected area is under cultivation, as in a greenhouse, then the soil must be in a horrid state. If the soil can be dug over, do so, incorporating a three- or four-inch layer of compost, or as much as you can spare, plus agricultural gypsum at the rate of 4 ozs. per sq. yd. The compost will help to open up the soil and let air into it, to overcome the stagnation that is directly encouraging the liverwort and, more important, reducing the fertility of the soil.

The gypsum will cause the clay particles in the soil to adhere together in groups, called flocculation, making the soil more porous, allowing surplus water to drain through quicker, and air to get in. I would guess that this soil is a heavy clay type, or inclined that way. If so, top dress the soil with gypsum at the rate of 2 ozs. per sq. yd. every three months. Either hoe it into the soil surface, or just spread it over the surface for watering or weather to take it in gradually. Slowly, this heavy sticky clay will be made much more friable and easier to work.

If the area is permanently planted, i.e. with roses or shrubs, these plants will benefit by maintaining a permanent mulch cover of peat, mushroom or garden compost. This will make weed and liverwort control by hoeing much easier. Liverwort itself is not serious, but the infertile and probably increasingly infertile condition it indicates is serious enough to demand your attention.

483   Different kinds of peat

What is the difference between moss peat and sedge peat?

Moss peat comes from marsh and bog areas in which sphagnum moss thrives or, being now drained, has thrived in the past. As you buy it in bags or compressed into packs and bales, decomposition is usually well advanced and beyond the denitrifying stage. See also *No. 489.*

Irish peat is an example of moss peat, invariably a uniformly dark brown colour, in a well advanced stage of decomposition and safe to dig in. There are other moss peats available however that are much lighter in colour and often contain moss that is scarcely more decomposed than merely collected and dried, and have been known to contain still living green moss. If you find fresh or green moss in any peat you buy, either put it on the compost heap or use it as mulch, but don't dig it in.

Prepared for transport and storage, moss peat is dried and compressed and in this condition has tremendous powers of water absorption. Dug into soil or mixed into composts in this condition, it can literally suck all the moisture out and leave plants gasping. Never, ever mix moss peat into soil or compost unless it is well soaked. Peat should give moisture, not take it.

Sedge peat also derives from marsh and bog areas where layers of decomposing bog plants have built up, mainly sedges as the name implies but also containing some other plants like cotton grass. This peat breaks into a much finer and more powdery texture than moss peat, and is therefore much more easily assimilated into turf. Usually it is less acid than moss peat but there's very little difference. Use moss peat for preference for digging in, mulching and putting moisture-retentive power into light sandy dry soils. For lawn care, the fine textured sedge peat is much the more useful.

484   Removing weedkiller applied by mistake

Having treated my garden with sodium chlorate, what is the procedure before cultivation?

With all the modern specific weedkillers available, it was very unwise to use sodium chlorate. The weedkiller paraquat kills off all green leaf and growth with which it comes into contact, but breaks down within seconds of touching soil and leaves no toxic residues. Although quite safe when used properly, paraquat is dangerous if it gets inside the body and following all the publicity about it, you should need no further warning to keep the liquid well away from the reach of children.

There are several proprietary weedkillers in both liquid spray and dry pellet form which control the soft growth of weeds but which leave the established plants and more woody roses and shrubs unscathed. Eradication of weeds and grass is now quite sophisticated and soil can be cleared so that cultivation can begin very soon after, even during treatment.

By contrast, the old-fashioned chlorate is very crude and puts the soil out of action for a long time. Left to the natural process of rainfall and weather, it will take several months for the chlorate to drain out of the surface layers, and much longer still for it to leach out of root depth of very many vegetables, herbaceous plants, and even longer before deep-rooted shrubs and trees are safe. You can speed up the natural drainage process considerably by treating the soil with agricultural gypsum. See *Nos. 2* and *456.* How much you apply and how you use it depends entirely upon the practicabilities of the situation, what area is involved, whether you can dig it in deep, whether you have a cultivator, and so on.

If you have a cultivator, it's a very different matter. A Wolseley Merry Tiller will dig 1 ft. deep and 2 ft. wide and churn the soil thoroughly so you can put down 8 ozs. per sq. yd., followed by 2 ozs. per sq. yd. and another churning at three-monthly intervals. Hand digging is much slower and the churning less thorough. Start with 4 ozs. and at each three-monthly digging over, another 2 ozs.

There is not much point starting the above process within two months of putting down chlorate since it will be far too strong. After that, start any time of the year, using whichever procedure is appropriate. Four weeks after the first three-monthly treatment, try a germination test; sow mustard or cress in small patches. If germination follows successfully, try something a little deeper rooted, radish for example and grass seed for a lawn area; then lettuce, then globe beets and carrots, feeling your way down as the gypsum dressings drive out the poison. If you plant anything deep-rooted too quickly, like roses, potatoes or shrubs, before you have checked it out with something expendable, you stand to make another expensive mistake.

485   Re-use of soil-less composts

Could you tell me about Levington's soil-less compost. Last year I bought six large bags for my tomatoes and I would like to know if it can be used again for anything, or treated again.

Many gardeners rejuvenate both John Innes and Levington composts for reuse, but the wisdom of doing so is often to be questioned.

With a crop so prone to diseases as the tomato, it is definitely very bad practice, because growing the same crop a second time in the same soil or compost is the quickest way to make sure that any disease is carried over and fresh new plants put into it are quickly infected. Of course, infection doesn't always occur; but the risk is not worth taking. This is why commercial growers, who have taken in a big way to growing tomatoes in peat-based compost in plastic bags as a less expensive alternative to annual sterilisation of the soil, carry all out these bags at the end of the season and carry in new. They cannot afford to take the risk, and I advise you not to try it.

Furthermore, you cannot tell how much nutrient depletion has occurred, taken out by the crop and leached out by watering, and it is virtually impossible for the amateur to determine what and how much should be put into the used compost to restore the balance of N. P. and K. and the essential minor elements.

In my opinion, the best and most profitable use that you can make of Levington is to regard it as organic matter like compost and put it down as mulch. By all means, mix in a fertiliser that contains N. P. and K. in balance, and you will have a first-rate mulch for the vegetable garden. Some imbalance will still remain from the original partly-used content, but used as a mulch, this is not all that important as it is unlikely to upset the total nutrient supply in the soil.

486   Risks of adding straight chemical fertilisers to compost

I have acquired a large quantity of leaf mould compost made from bracken. It is well-rotted and has a texture similar to peat. Would this be suitable for mulching fruit trees and should I add some potash or other fertiliser to this and other garden compost?

The main function of bracken peat is its wholly beneficial physical effect upon soil structure. Rotted bracken has an acid reaction and is a very useful material for mulching, particularly for lime-hating plants and when an over alkaline condition needs to be combated.

The nutrient content however depends upon how the bracken was originally cut before the composting process began. If the fronds were already brown and dead when cut, there won't be much plant nutrient, and what there is will be mainly potash. Read *No. 487* for the best place for potash. Its usefulness, however, would be increased tremendously by spreading and hoeing in beforehand a balanced compound nutrient like Growmore or Humber Eclipse at a couple of ounces per sq. yd., so that the moisture-retaining mulch layer covers it.

If the bracken has been cut when green, however, the resulting compost contains considerably more plant nutrients and, used in the same way, only half the extra quantity of balanced fertiliser needs to be used.

I would never advocate the use of potash or nitrogenous 'straight' fertilisers to restore 'balance' to a compost. It is virtually impossible for an amateur with limited technical resources to determine what is needed. If you want balance, add slow-acting, long-lasting balance, which is why throughout this book I suggest the use of Humber Eclipse or Growmore. Of course the original imbalance may still have an effect to slightly upset the equal response to the Eclipse or Growmore, but this will be nothing compared to the trouble that you will bring on yourself if you start guessing. Single element fertilisers should only ever be used as additionals for specific purposes, on plants that are already thriving on balanced diets.

487   Seaweed makes good compost

I have access to a good supply of seaweed and, during autumn, plenty of leaves. How can I speed up decomposition and what, if anything, should I add to make them more balanced?

First read *Nos. 476, 480* and *492*: seaweed can also pack into a wet soggy mess. Treat as for grass cuttings. By incorporating plenty of roughage in the form of your leaves, you will let in the air. Decomposition is normally very rapid. Potentially seaweed compost is rich in potash and trace elements, and can be ready for spreading as a mulch in three months and digging in after four to five months.

Because of the high potash content, it is particularly useful as a mulch before fruit ripening time. The soft fruits benefit, especially gooseberries, currants, strawberries and all the raspberry family. So do tomatoes and all flowering plants with bulky flowers like roses, Dahlias and Chrysanthemums.

Unless you are going to chop it up finely for use as a mulch on onions and asparagus, both of which are partial to the sea salt, it would be wise to wash the salt off the seaweed before adding it to the compost heap or using it as a mulch.

488   A simple method of soil testing for acidity

Is there a simple way that I can test whether my soil is acid or alkaline.

A very simple acid-alkalinity test can be done quite easily. Take a small handful of the soil you wish to test and put this into a jam jar full of fresh rainwater. Tap water should not be used because in many areas domestic water supplies have a marked lime content and, in any case, the hard and soft characteristics of tap water vary from area to area.

Even rainwater is not neutral; in falling through the air, rain can dissolve carbon dioxide gas, forming a weak solution of carbonic acid and other airborne impurities. You will have to bear this in mind when making a judgement, but a known slight bias is much better than the unknown quality coming through the tap.

Dip into the soil water a strip of litmus paper which you can buy from any decent chemist. If it turns a pale pink, your soil is acid, definitely pink, very acid, and if it turns red, it's a wonder anything is still alive! Pale blue means that the soil is slightly alkaline, and definitely blue, that it is very much so.

You can illustrate the effects by dissolving some lime in the water and comparing the reaction of litmus when dipped into it, with the effect when dipped in vinegar.

Some litmus papers take on a greenish hue when the reaction is balanced, others remain white but, allowing for the fact that the fresh rainwater is very slightly acid and the fact that most plants like a soil just the slightest degree on the acid side of neutral, you should be looking for the palest shade of pink, and you can add or withhold lime as appropriate.

If the soil is already too alkaline, utilise acid-reacting fertilisers such as sulphate of ammonia or sulphate of potash to gradually increase the acidity ratio. Never add lime or any alkaline reacting fertilisers like superphosphates. Of course, this is a very simple method of determining the acid/alkaline balance of your soil. A more elaborate Sudbury soil-testing kit indicates the content of the major plant nutrients—nitrogen, phosphorous and potash.

489   The correct way to stack and compost a load of manure

I recently got a load of horse manure. This is unfortunately nearly all straw with just a little fresh horse manure. Could you tell me the best and quickest way to compost this?

First read *Nos. 476, 483* and other items on composting in order to understand why this load of manure should be rotted down before being applied to the soil.

A load of fresh stable manure (or mushroom compost for that matter) upended by a tip lorry is a pretty formidable prospect for many amateurs, especially if it is in the road outside and has to be cleared quickly. Don't rush at the job of carting it with a wheelbarrow, without first thinking about the job. And even if it can be off-loaded nearer, don't simply tip it and leave it; the heap must be set up correctly. Look at the heap and try to imagine it as a cube —just a little smaller at the top than the area it will stand on, but as roughly as tall as it is wide.

Mark out with four sticks the floor area where the heap will eventually stand, and cover this area to a depth of about 9 inches, breaking up lumps and tossing it open with your fork to get plenty of air into it; try also to keep a fair mix of straw and fresh manure. A load with lots of straw in it is no bad thing because it is less liable to settle into a solid airless mass. Over this sprinkle just a little soil from the garden; this is to ensure that soil bacteria will be present and can begin the job of decomposition. Add another 9-inch layer of manure, another sprinkling of soil and so on in layers until the whole heap has been carted and stacked. By this time, you should have something like a cube with near vertical, only slightly sloping sides. As you build the stack, throwing the manure on with a fork, a lot of air will be trapped. Bacteria will need air so don't firm the heap by treading or patting with a spade, since this will only squeeze out the air.

When the stack is complete, take your fork and lightly 'comb' down the side walls so that the straw ends all lie in the same downwards direction rather like a thatched roof. This not only helps to shed rainfall, and prevents the heap becoming overwet and soggy and therefore airless but also looks more professional. Combing down will pull some material loose, of course; throw this up on top.

Within a couple of days the stack will have heated up nicely, and on a cool morning it should be steaming. This heat has to be kept in which is why it is stacked like a cube. If it is made in any other shape, like a long low bank, much more of the inside is near enough to the outside for the heat to be lost.

Three weeks after stacking, re-build the heap alongside, turning the outside to the centre, and centre to the outside. Shake up the material as you re-stack, getting air into it again. Soil is not needed this time, the bacteria are already there, but if the first stack has become wet and settled, you may have to lay sticks or other roughage in layers in order to keep open the air channels. See *Nos. 476, 480* and *483*.

The stack will need turning every three weeks or so and by the fourth turning, rotting down should be sufficiently far advanced for you to have difficulty in recognising any of the original straw. If this hasn't happened at the fourth turning, carry on with a fifth or sixth, building the cube shape each time and fluffing the material so that you recharge the heap with air. Continue until the entire heap has been reduced to a crumbly structure. If you have done the job properly, it will be nicely moist, quite friable, and smell sweetly—almost like moist peat.

At this stage it can be used, but will benefit from just one more turning, in 4–5 inch layers this time, with a sprinkling of Humber Eclipse or Growmore at the rate of 2 ozs. each sq. yd. surface area.

After fourteen days, you will have a load of compost ready for use, as mulch or for digging in, it will be full of plant nutrients, and be worth its weight in gold.

You will often read that you should only use well-rotted compost or manure: if you use only compost in which you can no longer recognise any of the original matter, then it is safe to dig in. If you can recognise any of it, then it is still in early enough stages of decomposition for strains of bacteria to be involved that require nitrogen. If this unrotted or 'short' compost or manure is dug in, the bacteria will most likely take the nitrogen they need from the soil, so that plants are robbed. Compost or manure in this 'de-nitrifying' stage should be used as mulch where atmospheric nitrogen is close at hand for the bacteria or, if it is very short and fresh, build it into the compost heap.

490 Growing vegetables on chalk soils

I am a novice vegetable grower and would like to know what, if any, vegetables will grow on a chalky soil. I have just taken over an allotment recently made from a long-established grass field.

The first task is to appreciate how crop rotation varies the demands made upon the soil by various crops, how in a systematic sequence each crop makes use of residues and soil conditions left over from the previous one. If you are going to make the best use of your plot, time and effort, you must plan ahead and get the sequence for the next two or three years written down on paper.

You will have to modify the ideal rotation to suit your chalky soil, obviously avoiding the crops that do not like chalky and limy conditions. For a few years at least, leave potatoes, carrots and parsnips out of your plan. These staple root crops don't like a lot of lime.

The next most important task is to build compost heaps and to activate an intensive household campaign to conserve every morsel of organic manure that you can. See *Nos. 476, 480* and *492*.

By its very nature your soil is potentially very fertile but it will also be very deficient in organic content. Humus, therefore, is the vital key to the successful production of crops on your plot. Feed generously with slow-acting organic-based manures—Humber Eclipse is ideal. Quick-acting boost chemicals will be so short lived in these conditions as to be largely wasteful. Given time, as the humus content increases, you will be able to grow a wider range of crops. For the time being however, you would be wise to concentrate on brassicas, cabbage, broccoli, kale and light root crops like kohl rabi and beetroot, or peas and beans and, of course, upon quick-maturing radishes and lettuce.

491 Don't put weedkiller-treated lawn cuttings on the heap

Why shouldn't I add grass mowings from a lawn treated with selective weedkiller to the compost heap?

Because there is quite a risk that some of the weedkiller may persist and find its way to vegetables and flowers. But if you can guarantee that your compost heap heats up properly, if by turning frequently and stacking long enough you achieve even and thorough decomposition so that the weedkiller is decomposed, grass cuttings from selective weedkiller-treated turf can be put on the compost heap for general use.

On the other hand, if you are in doubt, make another compost heap and use the produce exclusively on the lawn where the weedkiller will do no harm.

However, there is another point this question raises. Why is it that so many gardeners use selective weedkillers on lawns and then take away the cuttings , with the hormone in them? This weedkilling hormone is still active and capable of killing weeds. The most effective use of the grass cuttings would be to return them and the weedkiller to the lawn at once, by leaving the box off the mower, and flying the cuttings. You may not like cuttings on the lawn, but put up with this for a little while and give the hormone a chance to do its job. It is a waste of money to put weed-killer down, and then mow it off. Just one precaution however, if you fly the cuttings at the edge of the lawn, there is the danger that weedkiller can be thrown onto the flower beds. Therefore, leave the box on for the first two or three mower widths alongside the flower beds and borders, throw these cuttings to the centre of the lawn, and fly the rest.

In the case of a rotary mower, cuttings can be thrown considerable distances, so when the collector box is off always have the ejector vent or direction of throw towards the lawn centre, and away from plants that can be harmed by hormone-carrying cuttings being thrown onto them.

492   Why wood shavings are slow to rot

Why does it take three or four years for wood shavings used for horse bedding to turn to manure and how can I speed up the process?

First read *Nos. 476, 489* and the other items on composting in order to understand how the natural living process of decomposition works. Many trees reach a size and weight which exert a constricting force upon the heartwood at the centre of the trunk so great as to prevent the cells functioning properly. Because in Nature, non-function is the prelude to decay, a great many trees have evolved the ability to elaborate their own antiseptic with which the non-functioning heartwood becomes inpregnated and so resistant to decay. This antiseptic often colours the wood, renders it attractive and gives it commercial value—examples are oak, mahogany, ebony, and walnut—and in addition to this conifers also contain resins. You can frequently see this 'staining' when you cut through a log.

The chemical compound structure of wood is considerably more complex than, for example, grass cuttings, and in addition of course there is the protective effect of the antiseptics and resins to resist decomposition. Consequently, wood shavings will be a lot slower to start decomposing and have a much longer process of breakdown to go through. You have to do all you can therefore, to encourage and help the bacteria and this can be done in several ways. *No. 476* illustrates the other extreme where a lot of soft material settles into a soggy mass and the initial decomposition sets in very quickly. It is sensible therefore to mix in with the wood shavings plenty of quick-rotting, heat-producing grass cuttings, and to add all the spoiled and urine-soaked hay and stable straw you can; the nitrogen gas coming off in the urine ammonia will be a great help to the bacteria. However, even shavings can settle, and become soggy and airless, so have an iron rod handy which can be plunged into the bed frequently to help air penetrate to the interior of the heap. If the shavings are dry, moisten the heap a little as it is made up. This will help heat transference. A heap that is too dry can be a perfect insulator and the heap may not heat up evenly.

Nicely moist and made-up properly, there should be no difficulty in heating up from the first stacking. Watch it carefully and as the heat begins to subside—but don't let it cool—turn the heap by re-stacking it alongside, inside out. See *No. 489*. At this stage, moisten any over dry material by watering with a solution of a dessertspoonful of sulphate of ammonia and a small pinch of permanganate of potash—Condy's fluid—in a gallon of water. These will help to supply nitrogen and oxygen respectively. Heating-up should build up again without trouble.

You may need another couple of turnings and moistenings with the solution, the entire process taking at least twelve months, even two years for very hard wood shavings, in order to get breakdown to the point where the material is crumbly and quite unrecognisable as having been shavings.

Don't be tempted to rush things and do the job more quickly. Decomposition must be thorough, and because of the technical difficulty in decomposing all the shavings completely, it is wisest not to risk digging shavings compost into the soil. Use it instead as mulch for which it is ideal.

Fourteen days before intended use, mix into the compost material 1½ ozs. Humber Eclipse Garden manure per bushel, in the same way as outlined in *No. 489*, and you will have a first-rate organic mulch, and because the bacteria will have had a fortnight's work on the Humber, it will be rich in quickly available plant nutrients.

Section *XII*

Pests and Fungus

493   Ants: how to entirely eliminate them

My garden is overrun by ants and now they are coming into the house. Under the back step there is a nest which I cannot reach with boiling water, and although I put some recommended ant killer right in front of the entrance to the nest, the ants haven't taken the slightest notice of it. Please can you suggest what to do.

It is likely that you put the bait too near the entrance to the nest! Ants live in highly organised communities with special foraging workers whose job it is to wander far and wide searching for food. Let them do their job in future—placing the bait not so obviously near the entrance but a foot away, so the foragers will take delight in finding it.

Synchemicals 'Nippon' has for a long time been a good and reliable killer and another recently introduced remedy, cleared under the Pesticides Safety Precautions Scheme and which may well rival Nippon, is Rentokil Ant Killer which is based upon the insecticide chlordecone. Packed as a jelly in small tubes, it is available from most chemists and garden shops.

To make a bait, place a blob of either product in a foil milk bottle top and position two or three of these, near where you can observe a run but not nearer than a foot to the nest entrance. Cover these baits with an upturned flower pot —a clay one if possible so that it doesn't blow away in the wind—and prop it up slightly to give access. The message soon gets around that a new food source has been found, and worker ants take the jelly back to feed the colony where it acts like a virulent plague. Numbers are reduced after a few days and in a week, the colony should be entirely eliminated.

The process can be used throughout the garden wherever they are a nuisance, but you should also consider why your garden is being overrun. A nest will only build up if there is sufficient food supply, and for a garden to be overrun by ants—there must be plenty of food about.

A tree perhaps, or shrub, infested with aphis and excreting sugary honeydew is capable of supporting an enormous number of ants. In this case, clearly, the first step in eradicating the ants would be to remove the honeydew food supply, and that means eradicating the aphides. See *No. 1*.

494   Aphis inside lettuce hearts: how to control

My cloched lettuces, which are almost ready to eat, are being spoiled by greenfly. What can I do?

Lettuce are easy to protect against pests like aphides and caterpillars because the sap is moving fast enough to quickly spread a systemic insecticide throughout the entire plant and render it toxic to any insect that bites it or sucks its sap.

There are several proprietary systemic insecticides that will do this, sprayed on every 14–21 days from the seedling stage until near maturity. The plant is then protected by the toxic chemical it absorbs through the leaves into its sap stream. Although the chemicals used are reckoned to be lethal only to insects, it is not impossible for you to have a tummy ache if you take it into your own system. Therefore, with all food crops upon which you are using systemic insecticides, stop application 3–4 weeks before harvesting in order to allow sufficient time for natural processes within the plant to decompose the chemical and render it quite harmless. This breakdown, of course, is why, in order to maintain protection during the growth period, you have to spray every 2–3 weeks.

As the crop referred to in the question is near harvesting, you will have to use a *contact* insecticide which is quite safe, such as derris or Lindex, but of course this cannot be expected to control the fly that is already under cover and beyond reach in the lettuce heart.

495   Butt infested with wriggling creatures

Every time I go near my water butt great numbers of little wriggling creatures dive below from the surface and if I stand still they gradually come up again. What are they, do they do any harm and if so how do I eradicate them?

These creatures are the larval stage of mosquitoes and they cling to the water surface in order to breathe, diving down when disturbed and climbing again when they think danger no longer threatens.

If you draw water from a tap at the bottom of the butt, the most simple way to eradicate them is to add a teaspoonful of a very light oil like paraffin, turpentine or even fuel oil from the central heating tank, to the water. This light oil will quickly produce a film over the water surface.

This prevents the larvae—not from breathing through the oil as is commonly supposed—but from clinging to the water surface tension in order to breathe, and, unable to do so, they must die.

Of course, the precaution you must be sure to take with this method is that you must not let the water become so low in the butt that oil is drawn out through the tap, to possibly harm plants that you are going to water.

An alternative method is to spray the water surface with Lindex or Malathion whenever you see larvae rising. You are perhaps less likely actually to destroy all the larvae this way because of the immense dilution rate, but if you move slowly and spray when the larvae are at the surface you should get good control. I find it also helps when using Malathion to spray the inside walls of the butt so that there is plenty to evaporate, and set up a toxic atmosphere for the larvae to breathe—but of course you must cover in the top of the butt to entrap the toxic air.

Covering the butt is the best permanent answer, excluding both egg-laying mosquitoes and also light which can lead to a build-up of algae.

496   Control of leaf-cutter bees

Several of my rose bushes have had the foliage damaged by the leaf-cutter bee. Can you tell me if there is anything that will deter them from attacking the leaves, and something about their habits?

Most people associate bees with swarming colonies that live in hives and make honey.

But not all bees behave in this way, and the leaf-cutter bee is quite different from the honey bee. There are many species that don't swarm, and which are known as 'solitary' bees. Some dig little holes in the soil in which they lay their eggs, and this kind is not uncommon on the lawn. The one that is attacking your roses is carving off lumps of rose leaf to carry off as building material for its little nest which it likes to build in a dry place, well-protected from wet weather and where the young queens can hibernate through winter, and start new broods in spring.

Apart from being unsightly, a bad attack can materially reduce the effective leaf area and therefore must be checked before becoming serious. A deterrent is not a lot of good in this case because the bee will simply find other unprotected plants, and as it is not so beneficial as the honey bee, you have to use a toxic material to stop the damage. An insecticide like Abol X will give good control but in order to build-up a good thick layer of the poison on all the leaf surfaces, spray three or four times with a day or two between each spraying so that each coating can thoroughly dry before the next coating comes on. Use a finemist spray so that the minute drops 'stick' and don't run off as wasted drips.

497   Birds which strip buds from fruit bushes

I have trouble every year with birds stripping the buds from gooseberries and red currants. I have been told to spray with alum. Can you tell me the strength to use and how often to spray?

Dissolve alum—which can be obtained from the chemist or garden shop—at the rate of 2 ozs. per gallon. There is no need to drench the bushes till they drip; use a hand-held mist sprayer, and spray daily for three days. The second and third sprays should dry on top of the first so a good covering of alum is deposited. Then spray every seven to ten days. The birds will soon learn to leave the fruit alone.

Wash the fruit well before using them yourself.

This method can be used with Crocuses and

Polyanthus, both of which often are the objects of attack by sparrows. The difficulty is that frequent wetting of the blooms can spoil them; however it is worth trying.

498 Bullfinches, beautiful marauders

How can I persuade bullfinches to stay away from my plum trees?

Bullfinches are notorious for attacking the buds, and as they can wreck a fruit crop, you must do something about it. Indeed, in some parts of the country, the damage to commercial crops is so great that growers go to considerable lengths to stop them. They regard the birds as enemy No. 1—which is a pity because the bullfinch is a pretty and highly coloured bird.

The methods of control are open to questions of practicability in the particular circumstances of each case: i.e., what is economical and possible in an orchard is not necessarily so on a single tree in the garden. Spraying an entire tree with a bird repellent like Morkit can be terribly wasteful and therefore expensive, but to paint or selectively spray each vulnerable bud unless the tree is still quite small, would take more time than the average amateur gardener has available. Furthermore, the material lasts only for about a fortnight and has to be done again, maybe three or even four times before the vulnerable bud stage grows out.

Netting has been tried, but it is quite a job putting the net over a tree, and practically impossible to get off once the shoots begin to grow through it. However, netting does positively stop the birds getting at the buds, and this led to the idea of Scaraweb, a fine mesh net which is left on the tree and which gradually disintegrates and disappears over ensuing months. It can sometimes look a bit of a mess when the tattered remains flap in the wind, but it all goes eventually.

An alternative and possibly more humane alternative that I have known several times to be quite effective is to provide other food for the birds to attract their attention away from your trees and to leave you with enough buds to provide a worthwhile crop. You may finish up feeding most of the birds of the district but the overall cost of providing fat and seed may well be a lot less than the value of the lost crop.

499 Cauliflowers spoiled by aphides

My cabbages and cauliflowers have been spoilt by tiny black insects which seem to be impossible to wash off when preparing the vegetables for cooking. They don't cause a lot of damage to the plants but are very unpleasant when they appear in the cooking water.

There are so many different kinds of aphides, besides the more familiar greenfly and blackfly, and they are all horrible. Apart from a few exceptions, aphides are easy to kill—they are soft bodied—when you can get at them.

The problem with this particular type—the description fits the mealy cabbage aphis—is that the first insects get to the heart of the seedling or young plant and increase in number within the heart as it is forming, thus avoiding all contact killers.

Modern insecticides should enable you to stop this pest before it builds up. As soon as the young plants are established, begin a programme of spraying every twenty one days with a systemic insecticide. This will make the entire plant poisonous to biting and sucking insects. Make the spray solution as directed but add a little washing-up detergent to make sure that the foliage is thoroughly wetted and the spray doesn't run off the 'waxy' surface of the leaves. This run-off is the problem with all brassicas, and detergents solve the problem.

Gradually, the toxicity of the insecticide breaks down within the plant and you will have to judge when you can safely apply the last spraying to allow enough time for the poison to be degraded before you harvest for your own eating. This is usually about four weeks but keep strictly to the manufacturers' instructions on the bottle in this respect. Give it a little longer if you want to feel really safe, but don't use the crop before the minimum time has elapsed. The systemic insecticide will not kill you, but might give you the collywobbles.

500   How to keep cats away

What can I do to keep cats from my garden?

Much as we may at times be annoyed by the ginger tom from next door, the object should be to drive him away but not do him physical harm, and there is something sick and callous about people who resort to broken glass and barbed wire on the top of walls and fences. A little whiff of something unpleasant is usually enough to make a cat go away, so by stretching the unpleasantness along a fence or wall, you stand a good chance of stopping the cat from crossing over it.

You can do this by fixing a cord impregnated with a dog and cat repellent—the initial letters DCR providing the name under which you can buy it at most garden shops. This has an effective life of several months. Another very good repellent made by Synchemicals is sold under the name 'Scent off'.

A method that I have found to be effective many times, when all else fails, is ammonia. Collect some small glass bottles, pill bottles will do well, and fill these with ordinary household ammonia and position them at strategic points. Where the cat habitually comes through the fence or jumps down, bury a bottle up to its neck. It is no good just standing the bottle up as it will fall or be knocked over and the repellent ammonia be lost. Where the cat jumps up, fasten a bottle with wire or string.

Position several around any area that a cat has made its habitual toilet. One good whiff of ammonia and pussy will move quicker than he has for a long time.

Bottles will need routine inspection and refilling in order to hammer the idea into the cat's mind that your place is some sort of smelling salts factory and it should keep well away.

501   Control of chafer grubs

As soon as I plant any type of cabbage their roots and the bottoms of the stems are eaten by large fat cream coloured grubs, with brown heads. Now they have taken over the rose beds too. Can you please advise me as I am fighting a losing battle. I believe that during the last war, whizzed naphthalene was used on allotments to control soil pests. What is this?

These are chafer grubs and the difficulty is that they operate below the soil surface where contact killing is difficult to effect. If the soil can carry a long-standing crop and remain undisturbed for several months, apply Chlordane as suggested for clearing worms—see *No. 455*—which is as effective as anything, and it would be ideal in the rose beds. If the soil is to be dug or worked for short term, use Gamma BHC or PBI Bromophos.

Whizzed naphthalene which comes in small flakes was used widely at one time for digging in, and this strong smelling material highlights the difficulty with all soil fumigants: root crops so easily become tainted. The best course when eradicating soil pests is not to grow the same crop repeatedly in the same position so that a heavy infestation is built up. Adopt a rotational plan and follow on with different crops, see *No. 516*.

502   Cockroach control

What is the best way to deal with cockroaches?

Cockroaches, although not normally regarded as a widespread or serious problem in gardening, do occur, especially where there are animals and their bedding nearby, e.g., stables, biers and sties.

A widely used cockroach killer in the catering industry is Zaldicide M. You should be able to get it from larger chemists, or they can get it for you. If you have any difficulty, contact the manufacturer: Newton Chambers and Co. Ltd., Thorncliffe, Sheffield, Yorkshire. Use it as directed around crevices and such places where the creatures hide up during daylight so that they remain in contact with the material long enough for it to knock them over permanently.

503   Control of cutworm soil caterpillars

What can I do about freshly planted lettuce seedlings being eaten off at soil level?

Almost certainly this is the work of surface caterpillars: fat, slow-moving, green-brown creatures which tend to curl up when disturbed. There are several that answer this description and called, collectively, cut worms because they cut off the seedlings at ground level.

Control is quite easy. In future, put out a few test seedlings to see if the cut worm is about and if they get eaten, put down an overall dressing of Sevin dust or Gamma B.H.C. on the area that you intend to plant up. Three days later you can plant, taking the further precaution of a little dusting over each seedling as you plant it. You can do this by putting the dust in a piece of stocking and giving this a shake. Then very lightly scratch the dust into the soil surface round the seedlings.

504   Trespassing dogs

I've pleaded with my neighbour to keep her dog off my garden. I'm sick of the mess it makes. What can I do about it?

What a pity that some people are so selfish as to let their animals spoil other people's gardens. Of course, it is easy to suggest that you make the boundary fence or hedge dog-proof, but you shouldn't have to go to a lot of trouble and expense to keep somebody else's dog out of your garden.

However, it may be the only solution. You could plant a row of the pleasantly flowered but very long-thorned *Berberis sargentiana*. This will form a thicket through which no dog will venture. Not so positive, but effective whilst it is fresh (you will have to renew it from time to time) is cord impregnated with a repellant such as Curb, Renardine or Animoil.

If you feel the dog constitutes a health risk, have a word with your local Sanitary Inspector; if he feels that the risk is justified he will be able to take action. The only other alternative, if it has to go this far, is to consult a solicitor about taking legal action to prevent the dog being a nuisance.

505   How to control the Turnip Flea Beetle

Each year my cabbage seedlings are attacked by tiny hopping beetles that bite the leaves to pieces. What can I do about this?

Variously called Flea beetle, Turnip beetle and Turnip Fleabeetle, this is one of the worst garden pests. Although the holes they make are individually quite small, there are soon so many of them that they merge and cause whole areas of leaf to collapse and be lost. As the beetles rarely go for anything other than seedlings, the resulting damage is often devastating. As well as root crops, turnips, radish, kohl rabi etc., all varieties of the brassica family are attacked, and several flowers too. Rarely seen, they are small, dark and hop off at the first signs of danger.

The first precaution to take is to treat all seed with a protective before sowing. Tip into the seed packet a little Murphy Compound Seed Dressing, and give the packet a good shake up so that all the seed gets a thorough coating. This gives a good measure of protection at germination time not only against Flea beetle, but also against many other pests and diseases. Rain and watering will dissipate the protection, however, and as the seed leaves and first true leaves appear, the beetle will soon reappear.

As the young and susceptible leaves appear, you will have to spray with Malathion or dust them with Gamma B.H.C. powder immediately. You can easily make a spreader by putting some of the powder in an old stocking and shaking this along the row so that the seedlings and adjacent soil area receive a coating of insecticidal dust.

Normally, brassicas become too large and tough and the beetle leaves them alone. Radishes and turnips, however, are particularly susceptible and are at risk all the time they are in the soil, from germination to maturity.

506   Leatherjackets in the vegetable plot

How can I get rid of leatherjackets? Is there a method of getting rid of them by spraying some kind of insecticide on to the soil but which will not damage my plants?

This is a serious pest in lawns where it devours the roots of the grasses. See *No. 458*. Leatherjacket grubs will also attack a wide variety of plants and can be serious in the vegetable plot.

Insecticides will not harm your plants if used as directed, but root crops are very apt to pick up taints by being in very close contact with toxic chemicals in the soil. Best results depend on what you are going to do over the next couple of months or so. If the soil can remain comparatively undisturbed, long-standing brassicas following peas and beans for instance, you can eradicate this and other diffusion-breathing creatures by rendering the soil atmosphere toxic with Chlordane, used primarily as a lawn wormkiller. If the soil is to be dug and ventilated, Chlordane should not be used because the toxic soil atmosphere will then quickly dissipate. Instead, drench the soil with Gamma B.H.C. solution. See also *No. 455.*

507   Mealy bugs in the greenhouse

Mealy bugs have spread at an alarming rate in my greenhouse, appearing on the growing points of cacti and succulents, and on the undersides of the leaves of Cinerarias. Someone has suggested the use of methylated spirits. Would this be safe to use on such plants?

Mealy bug, very often looking like little spots of cotton wool, is a difficult pest to control because it has a waxy covering that very effectively sheds water-based insecticidal solutions. It is because methylated spirit dissolves the wax that it is often used. Normally, meths is dabbed onto the pest with a paint brush so that the dabbing action assists the meths to cut through the wax. Effective, but the degree of control can be improved by following up quickly with a Malathion spray, to which you should add a little washing-up detergent.

The thicker skinned cacti will probably tolerate the meths without trouble, but the Cinerarias are much softer and may well resent it. When in doubt, try it out sparingly on a mediocre plant that you won't be too distressed to lose. Systemic insecticides, making the whole plant toxic, would be more effective on the Cinerarias, since the sap stream moves fairly fast.

However, whichever method is used, you will have to attack the pest repeatedly. Mealy bug is a persistent problem, and once under

control must never be allowed to build up again. Having now had it, you know what it looks like so keep a sharp look out for it.

508   How to control mice devastating crocus corms

What could be eating my crocus bulbs? The soil's pushed away and only the shoots and skins are left.

This question is a common one. There is no doubt that your corms are being dug up and eaten by mice or other rodents. You can put a stop to their antics by putting down bait containing Warfarin but, like most other baits, effectiveness is increased by noting the pests' habits and turning these to your advantage.

Mice are not so suspicious of something new as are rats, but even so control is better for a little expertise. They will take bait fairly readily but there can be a far better kill with a little preparation.

Each evening put down baits of clean food— bread, cheese parings, fat scraps—under the cover of tiles and upturned pots out of reach of birds, other animals and pets. Clean up all baits in the morning, noting those that are being taken, and trying a different place for those that are untouched. It is important to clear up all food every morning, touched or untouched, because the idea is to get vermin used to taking food that is put down fresh each evening. After several nights of this, and with bait being taken regularly, adulterate the nightly feast with Warfarin. This way you will not just kill a few mice, but get a good clearance.

509   Moles : how to persuade them to go away

I am plagued by moles. Their escape tunnels are ruining my lawn. How can I stop them? What's the plant called that's supposed to drive them away?

Moles are easy to deal with if you go about it the right way. It is not so much a case of knowing what to do, or how, or when—but why.

They construct tunnels not for escaping, but for trapping their food.

If you examine a mole's fur, you will find that the 'pile' can be brushed all ways and is an incredibly efficient polisher. As the mole runs through his tunnel, the soil walls are polished smoothly, so that worms and other soil creatures breaking into the tunnel are unable to get a hold on the smooth surface to bore their way out. There they remain until Moley comes shuffling along.

A mole has to consume at least his own weight in worms and earthly creatures every day, and relies entirely upon acute sense of smell and hearing to lead him to any prey that falls into his tunnel trap. So—remove his food and he will go away. You should not have worms in your lawn anyway, so use a worm killer like Chlordane (See *No. 455*). An old trick is to drive him to distraction by putting an overpowering smell into his runs. Camphor balls will do this; or more quickly and effective is half a teaspoon of PDB (Paradichlorbenzine) crystals which you can get at the chemist. Close the hole afterwards so that the gas stays in the runs and you will not be bothered again.

Moles are said to detest and avoid the plant Caper Spurge. This may be so, but it can so easily seed itself that you'll then have an awful job keeping it in check. It's rather like solving one problem by creating another.

510 Hollow potatoes are caused by keel slugs

For the last two years my potatoes have been attacked by small black slugs which have eaten two-thirds of my crop. How can I get rid of these pests, and should I miss out potatoes for a time?

Underground or keel slugs tend to build up where food is highly nutritional for their needs, and is readily and repeatedly available. This is no more than you might expect, and the way to stop them building-up is to stop putting the food there. For slugs to take two-thirds of a crop, you must have a bad attack and it will be necessary to deal not only with the potato patch, but for some distance around. This may be a sizeable area, involving large quantities of control chemicals, so the overall cost could well be a very important factor.

The new slug killer, Draza, is very effective as a surface bait killer, but physical contact has to be achieved. It is impractical to put it in the soil because it will dissipate and decompose before all the slugs make contact with it.

Sports groundsmen have to remove worms from the fine turf of cricket squares, tennis courts, golfing greens and bowls' greens etc. They cannot disturb the playing surface, and for years the basic problem was bringing toxic material into physical contact with worms that could be as much as four feet underground.

The modern method is to set up a toxic atmosphere in the soil—worms and slugs have to breathe. One of the chlorinated hydro-carbon poisons is therefore spread to work down slowly into the soil atmosphere. The diffusion breathing creatures that inhabit the soil, worms, slugs, grubs, wireworms etc., absorb it into their bodies and accumulate it until it reaches toxic proportions and they die. The material is marketed as Chlordane: use it exactly as instructed as for turf, and repeat in twelve months' time. There is no danger to birds or animals who have ventilated lungs and cannot take in the stuff by breathing soil atmosphere.

You should not undo the good work by putting slug food straight back into the soil, so for two years whilst two successive doses of Chlordane are working (it is effective for twelve months) plant no root crops in this soil. Grow them some where else. Whilst the Chlordane is active, try not to disturb the soil any more than you can help since this will only allow the Chlordane to dissipate into the free atmosphere. Therefore, if you sow peas and beans, you will have to dispense with trenching compost under them and feed from above instead with liquid manure and foliar feed. Then follow these with brassicas to utilise the nitrogen residues.

After two years, you can try potatoes again, but only plant earlies for the first year, and don't rely on the ground for your main crop until you have proved that the ground has been cleared.

An alternative method is to drench the ground with a formalin solution. This is impracticable for anything other than a small area because the soil must be thoroughly soaked; a lot of water and a lot of formalin has to be used to prepare a lot of solution, it is not a cheap way of doing the job but it is thorough. The area has to be covered with a plastic sheet dug in at the edges at least a spit deep to hold it down in wind and to trap the formaldehyde gas. After two to three weeks, the cover should be removed and the toxic gas dispersed by digging over the soil two or three times, a week apart.

This, of course, is soil sterilisation on a large outdoor scale. Plant life will be inhibited until the gas has gone, and you will have to test for this by sowing a quick germinator like radish or mustard and cress. If they germinate and grow, you are safe to plant but, as with Chlordane, keep root crops away for two years at least so that any slugs that manage to survive are not encouraged to build up their numbers again.

511 Slugs : how to make an effective killer trap

Could you please tell me what to buy from the chemist to mix with bran as a good slug bait?

The active ingredient in slug and snail bait is metaldehyde. Proprietary slug and snail bait contains about 1 oz. of metaldehyde mixed with 1 lb. of bran then slightly moistened so that it can be compressed into pellets which are sprinkled around susceptible plants or those you wish to protect. The disadvantage with these pellets is that they absorb moisture and disintegrate quite quickly. A longer lasting, and very effective slug killer is the proprietary preparation Draza.

Here is a method of using it that is very effective indeed and remarkably economical because sprinkling pellets on the surface is so wasteful. Slugs and snails usually work during darkness, and move away to hide up with the coming of the dawn, so you should provide them with a convenient hiding place—with the bait inside.

Save your cracked plastic pots, cut them into two halves, and with a quick drying glue, make three or four dabs about the size of a ½p piece

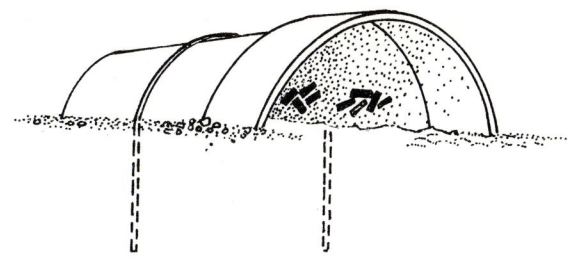

No. 511   *A good use for broken flower pots. Slug pellets are glued inside the half pot which is held down by a long nail or wire hoop.*

near the edges around the inside of the half pot. Whilst still tacky, press some pellets into each dab of glue and leave to dry. In the evening, set these traps by simply resting on the soil, the bait covered, protected from rain, and waiting for any slugs and snails that come in for shelter. There is no need to clear up the corpses: they will soon decompose.

Wind can turn over these traps so either weight them down with a stone or drill a hole in them and push a 6 in. nail or piece of wire through into the soil. As the bait is taken by successive slugs, it can be renewed and the trap used indefinitely.

512 Squirrels : arch pests

Although we used to be amused by the grey squirrels in our garden, they have multiplied and have ruined several young fruit trees by stripping the bark. They have invaded the fruit cage and the vegetable garden, dug up crocus and other bulbs, and robbed the bird table so that we don't get tits and other garden birds anymore. Is there any way to control them?

The biggest problem with the grey squirrel is to get gardeners and others to see the creature realistically for what it is, and to stop letting judgement be clouded by sentiment. In listing the several crimes of the pest, this question nearly says it all and is so typical of the many people who learn the hard way that the delightful creature springing around the garden is the devil in disguise.

The loss of birds in the garden is probably due not to them robbing the birds' feeding table but to robbing the nests, for they will take both eggs and young birds. They themselves breed twice a year, producing an average of five to six young. Contrary to popular belief, they seldom really hibernate through the colder weather and can often be seen foraging for food on a mild winter's day. It belongs to the rodent family and is really a tree rat with a bushy tail. You may have a soft spot for the squirrel, but it is a very serious and damaging pest.

Whether you wish to eradicate the grey squirrel or only deter it, both courses are beset with difficulties. I find they soon learn to avoid and leap over deterrents based upon smell. Poisoning is more positive, but dangerous to other garden life and for you to handle. It is no good for you to be taking such steps in your garden without similar wholehearted support from those around you. The creature is entrenched in the neighbourhood and as fast as you destroy those in your garden, fresh invaders will take their place. There are too many of them for you to destroy entirely, and they can leap over your deterrents, barbed wire fence, or other defences as easily as they can leap from tree to tree.

The only really feasible way to deal with the problem is to enlist the help of the one authority that has the power to approach the job on a large enough scale to be effective—contact your local council and let their professional operatives do the job.

513 Roots and stems eaten hollow by weevils

On investigating some failing Begonia semperflorens, *kept in pots in a greenhouse, I found that the bases of several plants had been eaten hollow by whitish grubs about ½ in. long with red heads. They appear to lodge at soil level, and the damage only occurs at the base of the stems as they attack neither the roots nor the leaves. Could you identify this pest and suggest an appropriate control measure?*

This sounds like the grub of the vine weevil. Normally rather grey-white in colour, it feeds at the base of a wide variety of plants, especially bulbs, corms and tubers.

Control method depends largely upon the stage of growth of the infected plant; if it is in full growth, you cannot shake out and handpick the grubs. BHC solution will give control and the most efficient way to use it would be to make a sufficient quantity in which to immerse the entire pot for twenty minutes, as though watering by immersion, and so thoroughly soak the soil. Spray the foliage with BHC in case there are adult weevils about: these are about ¼ inch long, black with a long snout. If you see damage to the edges of leaves of Begonias, Cyclamen, Saxifrages and, of course, vines, it's as certain as can be they are about.

Immersion may be needed several times, but during the dormant period, break out the corm or tuber examining it for grubs, and make sure the soil in the pot is sterilised by burning before you do anything else with it.

514 White fly, like clouds of ash

My conservatory plants are looking yellow and have stopped growing. When I approach them, a cloud of tiny white flies burst into the air. How can I stop these pests?

You have a severe infestation of white fly and you must stamp it out quickly, not only because of the inconvenience of having them flying in your face every time you pass near but because of the very serious debilitating effect on the plants. A weakened plant is more liable to attack by other pests and diseases.

There are several ways to deal with this pest. Liquid Malathion, made up as directed to white fly strength, will give good control but you will have to be careful how you use it. Use a hand-held mist sprayer to thoroughly coat all surfaces, especially the soft undersides of leaves and soft shoot tips. Direct the spray away from yourself and try not to inhale the spray or vapour.

In practical terms, depending upon how many plants you have, carry them all outside and spray over the inside surfaces of the conservatory, making sure all cracks and crevices get a thorough soaking. Drench-spray the plants one by one, outside so that the vapour is dissipated in the open air and you don't fill your lungs with it. Carry the plants inside again whilst still wet so that the liquid evaporates into the air, inside the greenhouse. Spray the greenhouse air to saturate the place with vapour, shut all ventilators and doors to keep in the vapour and keep out of the place for at least twenty-four hours.

That will knock out the flying adults; now you have to catch the larval stage which will have resisted your onslaught and will soon begin to emerge as mature flying adults.

There is only one way now to keep the pest under control and prevent it getting on top of you again, and that way is persistence. Keep the sprayer always filled and ready to hand from now on. Because you are going to rely on contact killing, add a few drips of liquid detergent to the spray in order to thoroughly wet the fly. Every time you pass by, look for the pests. Give them a squirt and make sure the spray hits them. Be persistent about this and gradually you will wear them down.

Never assume that you have completely cleared white fly; there will always be a larval stage around somewhere hatching out. You may bring it in on a new plant, or it can literally come through the windows from next door. In future, as soon as you see one, kill it with the spray, or you'll soon have a cloud. A recently introduced insecticide containing a synthesised form of the organic insecticide pyrethrum called Mezrethrin has the same rapid knock down effect. Manufactured by Pan Brittanica Industries (PBI), the preparation is called Sprayday, and you should have no difficulty in obtaining it from your garden shop. Observe the instructions meticulously.

515 White fly, its natural predator

Can you tell me where I can obtain supplies of Encarsia formosa, *the predator of white fly?*

Instead of the more usual method of controlling a pest by one or more means of poisoning with toxic materials, a natural predator is employed —*Encarsia formosa*. At one time white fly was a considerable problem because it was so resistant to the then known insecticides, and introducing a live natural predator was an unusual way of dealing with a pest when all else wasn't much good.

Encarsia was used—and still is in commercial horticulture—for controlling white fly in greenhouses where it could be 'caged' to do its work and not escape into the open air. You will have to arrange fine gauze at the ventilators and curtains at the door to keep them inside on the job.

Modern insecticides are a great improvement over those available even only ten years ago, and normally I would recommend that Malathion spray and fumigation, or the new Mezrethrine-based insecticide 'Sprayday' should provide adequate control.

However, exploring new ideas and discovering new methods is part of the satisfaction of gardening and there is no reason at all why you should not try this novel and interesting way of combating a pernicious pest, providing you take steps to prevent the predator from straying.

Contact the following suppliers, describing your greenhouse, size, plants, etc.

Botanical Developments Ltd., Challock, Ashford, Kent.

Organic Farmers & Growers, Longridge, Creeting Road, Stowmarket, Suffolk, IP14 5BT.

Springfield Nursery, Peckhill, Waltham Abbey, Essex.

The last named have also produced a predator for greenhouse Red Spider called *Phytoseiulus*.

516 Control of the wireworm

I found thousands of small, leathery, yellow worms when I dug my soil over. Are they harmful?

These are wireworms, one of the most damaging of all pests; they will eat into every root crop in the vegetable garden and a lot else besides.

You can control them by applying Chlordane wormkiller, see *No. 455*, or by working Gamma BHC dust into the soil, but root crops can pick up a taint so, in areas where you are going to grow root vegetables, use Bromophos granules. An equally effective method of ridding the soil of these pests—and incidentally it is much better husbandry—would be to run a four-year rotational plan instead of just three —root crops, legumes, brassicas and, in the fourth year, let the ground lie fallow under some hens.

You can easily arrange wire netting each year to confine them to their quarter of the plot. Roughly dig the ground over three or four times a year, and the birds will not only manure the ground for you and scratch it to a fine tilth, but also eradicate all the grubs and pests in it. See *No. 539*.

517 *Woodlice need persistent control*

Can you tell me of a way to get rid of woodlice in my greenhouse? They are eating the roots of my cucumbers and killing off the plants.

Woodlice are controlled by Malathion and, as this is also a certain control of that arch greenhouse pest, greenfly, it is a good idea to have a small single-handed sprayer, like the ASL Spraymist or a Spraygen, always ready loaded and ready to grab quickly so that you can give them a good squirt as soon as seen.

Greenfly are easy enough, they don't run away and control is relatively simple, see *No. 1*. The difficulty with woodlice is that they move around and hide away in cracks and crevices under staging, pots, trays, and even under loose mulch where it is nigh impossible for spray to reach them and achieve physical contact. If the numbers are tolerable, you can prevent a build-up by dusting around the places where they are seen or lurk with the dust form of BHC.

On the other hand, if you know that they have penetrated into a friable compost, say, and are eating the roots of your plants, dust will not get down there any more than spray would and you will have to make up Malathion solution at about half the spray strength and water the soil with this for a few days so that the poison is carried right down and permeates the soil.

However, this still doesn't control any of the pests tucked up under the staging and ready to send out their offspring to re-infest. In the last resort, you will only get them by fumigating with BHC smoke cones, shutting the place for forty-eight hours so that it works into every hiding place, and you may still have to repeat the job about fourteen days later.

Having cleared the greenhouse, you could easily suffer invasion from the garden the following day. You can't blame them for wanting to come in where it is drier and warmer, and the only way to stop them getting on top of you is to be more persistent than they are. Don't allow rubbish to accumulate, especially stacks of pots and trays that provide ideal cover for the pest.

518 *Precautions against Antirrhinum Rust*

How can I prevent my Antirrhinums *suffering from rust next year?*

Appearing on the leaves, first as small brown pin head spots, which increase in number to form discolouring 'rusty' patches, this disease is the scourge of the Antirrhinum. You cannot positively prevent this crippling fungus disease from attacking your Antirrhinums but you can go a long way towards preventing it crippling your plants by only growing varieties that have been bred with a high degree of resistance in their make up.

Most seedsmen offer these rust-resistant varieties, but you should bear in mind that soft flabby growth makes all plants more susceptible to fungus attack. Therefore at all times—from germination, through pricking out, and when planted into beds or the border —avoid quick-acting boost fertilisers, and go for the more natural slower acting manures that provide a balance of N.P. & K. Don't let the plants become dry either: dry plants mean soft flaccid foliage, and that makes it much easier for fungus to gain entry and undo much of the resistance that the plant breeder has bred into the variety.

If you have a bonfire, collect the ash as soon as it cools and before it can be affected by rain. Dust this around the plants. In addition to enhancing flower colour, the potash will harden the leaf tissue and make it more resistant to fungal attack.

Raise your seedlings in sterilised compost and as you have had a serious attack it would be a wise precaution to insert and dip your young bedding-out plants into a fungicidal solution— Zineb, Maneb or Benlate—before planting-out. This should protect them in the early stages and you can prolong the protection by subsequent spraying every ten to fourteen days until blooming commences.

519 Recognising and dealing with Honey Fungus

How can I recognise honey fungus? How can I treat the ground close to where a tree killed by the fungus has been felled?

Apart from the sudden death of infected trees, the main visible indication of *Armellaria mellea* is the emergence of mushroom-like fruiting bodies in clusters around the base of the infected tree stump. These are rounded and parasol-shaped, 4–6 inches in height and yellowish-brown, honey-coloured, thick stems, white to cream gills, and white acrid flesh.

Any premature falling of leaves or die-back of shoots calls for an examination of any area of dead bark; any presence of whitish thread-like growth—mycelium—with a smell suggestive of mushrooms, must be interpreted as being highly suspicious. Confirm by carefully digging into the top soil to look for the highly infectious brown-black leathery strands that give the fungus its other name, the boot lace fungus. These radiate in all directions for incredible distances and attack all manner of trees and shrubs. Death is invariable and quick.

Once found, digging out of these 'boot laces' is vital, however tedious. They must be burned at once as should any honey mushrooms before they have a chance to spread spores. A killed tree or shrub, of course has to be removed, either off the site for disposal or to the fire heap.

Untreated dead stumps, even if not killed by Armellaria, are an open invitation to the disease and are then a haven and starting point for Heaven knows what death and destruction round about. Stumps should be burned out by drilling out holes and repeatedly filling them with saltpetre (potassium nitrate) solution so that the whole stump becomes permeated. Then, when ignited, the whole stump smoulders away, gradually but completely. See *No. 541*.

The ground round about should then be treated by drenching with Armillatox solution 1 part phensic emulsion to 12 parts of water. This is obtainable from Armillatox Ltd., Fernhurst, Sussex, and use it strictly as directed.

Honey fungus is a vicious disease, difficult and expensive to eradicate. Don't encourage it by allowing dead stumps to remain.

520 Cause and eradication of puff balls on a new lawn

Three years ago we moved into a new house which was built on the site of an old orchard. We cultivated the garden and laid turf in June, which I think must have been infested because, in July, a large white fungus started to grow which we were told was puffball. We carefully removed it, and applied sodium chlorate, but others have now appeared. How can we get rid of them?

It is most likely that the puffballs have nothing to do with your turf, but are due to woody or other vegetable matter under the surface, rotting and supporting fungal growth. Most new lawn preparation involves soil levelling and when this is done with land that previously carried scrub or even trees, as is often the case, it is very easy to bury woody material, ranging from pieces of root to chunks of timber. Your lawn having been laid on the site of an old orchard, is almost certainly suffering from this.

Short of digging up your lawn and removing the decaying wood, the best solution is to hasten decomposition beyond the point where it can support fungus growth. In order to thrive, soil bacteria need plenty of air in the soil, and regular systemic aeration of the lawn by root action slit tines must therefore be an important first step. The woody material may be much deeper than this surface aeration can reach. Therefore pierce more deeply the area around any puffballs by driving in a digging fork several times. Drive the fork in to half the depth of the tines and prise up the soil a little so that the surface lifts and 'heaves' slightly. Drive the fork in another quarter in the same holes, heave again; then full depth and heave yet again lifting out the fork so that the holes remain clean with air access unhindered and as little actual damage as possible to the lawn surface. Do this several times around the trouble spots.

Any tendency towards lessening the air content of the soil can only slow up this decomposition process, therefore guard against anything that can cause compaction however slight. Don't walk on the lawn when the soil is wet and soft. *Never* use a roller. If the soil is at all inclined to be heavy, you can reduce this by spreading gypsum on the surface and letting the weather take it in. Give 2 oz. per sq. yd. every three months, but no heavier dressings than this or more frequent. See *Nos. 456, 465* and *475*.

Treating the puffballs with a total growth inhibitor like sodium chlorate is not only damaging to the lawn, but a waste of time because you are treating a symptom and not getting at the cause. Depending upon the size and extent of the buried woody matter, this problem may be with you for several years, but other than digging out every piece that causes trouble, the above methods are the most practical course for you to follow.

521 Stinkhorn is often difficult to eradicate

Can you tell me what the horrid-looking fungus is that keeps growing out of my rockery? I have removed it several times but it keeps coming back. It starts like a white ball, then turns into a red cap which grows bigger and bigger and attracts lots of flies.

This sounds like the stinkhorn fungus, often difficult to eradicate. The fungus thrives where there is a high level of organic matter in the soil. This one seems well-established, and will have white wool-like strands—which are the vegetative part of the fungus—permeating the soil where the surface part has been observed. Despite disturbing the rockery and digging out the white mycelium wherever it is found, all infected soil must be directly sterilised by burning.

Short of dismantling the rockery, two other procedures will together give you a fair chance of eradicating the fungus: starvation and chemical attack.

First, objectionable as it may be to remove the evil smelling thing, remove it you must. All further growth should be removed at the white ball stage, and certainly before the evil smelling stage is reached to prevent the development and spread of the spores which in turn lead to renewed spread.

By repeatedly trying to send up growth, which you will just as repeatedly remove, the fungus will eventually exhaust the food supply in the organic matter upon which it is living. You can further help this policy of containment by soaking the area with a weak solution of Jeyes Fluid. If you can clear the immediate area of plants you may be able to hit the fungus very much harder by soaking instead with a formalin solution—1 part formalin to 20 parts water—covering the soaked area for seven to ten days with plastic sheeting in order to keep in the sterilising formaldehyde gas.

Afterwards, turn over the soil to open it up and free the soil of all fumes. Before planting up with new plants sow some mustard, cress, radish or other quick germinating seed to see if the sterilising effect has passed.

Section *XIII*

Paths, Patios and Rockeries

522   Crazy paving : the easiest way to lay it

Which is the easiest way to lay a crazy paving path?

If you don't lay crazy paving properly, you will have lots of trouble later, let alone danger, with moving and tilting stones. The easiest way to lay crazy paving is to get it right first time. Set up boards to mark the edges of the path and fix the boards with stakes or by placing heavy weights on them. Within these edge boards or a little wider than the confines of the path or area you intend to lay put down a base of crushed brick and rubble. Ram it hard with a punner, or heavy wood block and water it well with the hose pipe to help settle it further. A couple of days later, ram it again, add more water and ram it a third time. If it is going to move and settle, it is better it should do so at this stage. Over this lay a 2 inch thick layer of coarse gravelly sand.

Firm the sand by watering and punning as with the hard core. Onto this lay the side stones first, dry for the time being and with about a half-inch gap between the stones, straight edges to the boards. It is advisable to arrange all the side stones completely before filling in the centre so that the supply of suitably shaped pieces does not run out half way. With the edge pieces arranged satisfactorily, lift them one by one and wet them by dipping in a bucket of water. Then put down a good dab of concrete—3 parts sand and 1 part cement—at each corner, replace the wet stone on the concrete dabs and tamp down, level with the stones either side of it. Obviously, don't walk on them yet.

When the edge stones are set complete, fill in the centre, a couple of feet at a time. In the same way as the edges tamp down the stones onto concrete pads, so that they exactly fit under a straight edge laid across the already fixed edge stones, from side to side. This will keep the finished surface level.

Fill in between the stones to about half an inch below the top surface using the same concrete mix but make it very wet so that it flows easily into the gaps, and especially if you are laying natural stone, wash off any that remains on the surface of the stones before it dries and disfigures them. Leaving the fill-in 'grout' half an inch lower than the stones, provides little gullies which will carry off surface water when it rains. Leave small gaps in this concrete grouting every few inches, filling them instead with coarse sand. This is to allow water to drain through instead of collecting on the surface. If you wish you can leave holes in the stone pattern for rock plants to grow in.

The Cement and Concrete Association have produced a very useful booklet on path laying. It is free and you can obtain a copy by writing to them at 52 Grosvenor Gardens, London, SW1. See *No. 529.*

523   Crazy paving : the safest way to kill weeds on it

What is the best and safest weedkiller for crazy paving?

It depends upon the type of crazy paving, whether there are plants growing in the crevices or alongside, and whether you want a total plant killer to completely sterilise the area or one that will kill weeds but not prevent later planting desirable plants into holes and gaps between the stones.

If you want a total killer to completely sterilise the area, you should not use sodium chlorate because this crude plant killer creeps horizontally through the soil, putting at risk plants several feet away from where it is put down, a risk that could be even more serious with the rain-shedding nature of the paving, i.e. rain water running off to the edge carrying chlorate with it. There is also an element of fire risk. In its expanded form—i.e., when it has been dissolved, spread and dries again—it can ignite to a carelessly dropped cigarette.

A Simazine based total plant killer would be preferable in this respect and also does not 'creep' like chlorate. However, heavy rain can cause small areas of wash off and drainage flooding, picking up weedkiller and possibly putting nearby plants at risk. Therefore, to be on the safe side, any wanted paving plants should come out before the weedkiller is applied.

Total weedkillers are now available in pellet and granular forms and whilst there are several advantages in this method on a paved area you may find the pellets can be moved by wind and rain. Those are the pros and cons of total plant killers. If it is total sterilisation you want, a killer based upon Simazine is probably the best bet, provided you heed the above and apply it with care.

On the other hand if you want to preserve or later plant rock and crevice plants, total killers are out, and you will have to use a plant killer that does not sterilise for a long time. In this case wet the foliage of weeds and unwanted plants with paraquat solution—Weedol or Gramoxone W. Paraquat kills by destroying the greenleaf, breaks down within seconds of touching the soil or path and there is therefore not the risk to other plants as with the other total weedkillers.

Provided it is not grass that you are trying to destroy and against which it will not be very effective, you can try a 'Touchweeder'. This is a small stick of wax (it is in a container and you can carry it in your pocket) that has been impregnated with a hormone weedkiller. To use it, you need only 'touch the weed' for a little of the wax to rub off, and being impervious to rain and wind the hormone is held in contact with the weed long enough for the hormone to kill.

524 Hypertufa—man-made ornamental rock

Can you please tell me about the rockery stone one can make oneself. What is it made of and how does one make it? Would it be suitable to put around a pool?

Tufa is a natural stone, traditionally used for shallow pans and troughs in which to grow alpines and rock plants. However, being alkaline, it is not suitable for many plants. It is also fairly expensive.

Hypertufa is a comparatively inexpensive substitute in which most plants thrive and which has the great advantage that it can be shaped as you will—not only like pots and pans but also to simulate weathered rock shapes incorporating, if you wish, smaller pieces of natural stone.

The ingredients by volume are one part cement, one part sharp sand, and two parts Sorbex peat. If you cannot get Sorbex, use moss peat. Sedge peats are not suitable because they break down too finely. Don't use the peat dry: soak it well and then squeeze out as much excess water as you can. Mix the ingredients thoroughly and then add just enough water, very little at a time, to produce a stiff porridge-like consistency. Mixing this 'porridge' can get a lot of air into it which will make it set 'fluffy' and 'fragile'. Therefore you must knead it as you would dough, with your knuckles, back of a trowel or with a piece of wood like a palette knife in order to remove any air pockets and to make sure that the peat is thoroughly permeated with the cement 'bind'.

This mixture can be used to cover flower pots and pans or you can use them as moulds to make rough cast pots. Old glazed sinks can be made to look like natural stone, and then used to house miniature rock gardens. You may need to chip or apply a thin layer of binding compound or glue to glazed surfaces in order to give the mixture a chance to obtain a grip. See *No. 528.* If you like the idea of incorporating pieces of natural stone, push them into the mixture whilst still soft. When you have made your sculpture, cover it with a wet sack so that drying and curing takes place slowly; this usually takes at least a week.

Very attractive rockeries can be made with this material—pumelled into random shapes, with hollows and pockets where small plants can be set to grow. It looks rather like a mellow weather-worn rock and, if the fancy takes you that way, you can colour your handiwork, with cement dyes. Don't make your rocks solid; make them hollow so that the same amount of mixture will make more rocks.

Hypertufa is suitable also for retaining walls, such as the peat beds, described in *No. 116*, and for banks, provided that you remember that it is a porous rock and cannot be expected to bear or restrain much weight or stress.

Due to the porosity imparted by the peat, plants seem to thrive on Hypertufa, driving their roots right into it.

I have seen it flaked and crumbling where frost has got in and 'lifted', but this is not so likely to happen if during the making you make sure you get out all the air and fluffiness. If you are in an exposed area and doubtful about extreme cold, reduce the peat proportion from 2 parts to $1\frac{1}{2}$.

I have not seen Hypertufa used in *direct* contact with water and feel that the porosity would make it unsuitable, but it can, of course, be used to form a rock and boulder surround.

525 How to remove iron stains from concrete

Old beer barrels used for growing plants in have left rusty rings on my concrete patio. Is there any way of removing them?

The usual way of removing iron rust stains from stone is with oxalic acid which you should be able to obtain from the chemist or they will get it for you. Make up a solution of $\frac{1}{2}$ fluid oz. in a pint of water, taking care not to wash or splash this solution onto nearby plants—or on yourself.

Always follow the basic rule when making up a solution containing strong acid or alkali. Always add or pour the strong liquid to water so that if a splash does occur, it will be of water or weak solution. If you do it the other way round, you will be splashing dangerous solution.

Deeply ingrained stains may need repeated treatment but don't make the solution any stronger than the above and let the stone dry from one treatment before applying another. Oxalic acid is poisonous, so keep it labelled properly and make sure it is safely locked away from children and pets.

Stop the iron bands of the barrels from making further marks by killing oxidation with a phosphoric acid preparation. First clean them with a wire brush and then paint the bands with Foscote or Jenolite—which you can obtain at the hardware shop. Make the bands very wet at the edges so that the acid soaks well in behind

the bands. Then stand them in a sheltered position away from rain where the iron can slowly dry and pickle. When completely dry, paint the bands with black bituminous paint paying particular attention to the outside edge where it will come into contact with the ground, and then paint the woodwork with clear varnish or colour paint.

It will help to prevent further staining and, incidentally, improve drainage from the pot if you lift it clear on to spacing blocks; these need only be an inch or so thick and should be of soft wood. If you use brick or stone, they can wear and break the paint seal and thus expose the iron to weather and rusting again.

526 How to remove oil stains from tarmac

Is there any method of removing oil stains from a red tarmacadam drive?

Oil drip from motor vehicles is a common trouble with driveways of virtually any colour other than black or dark grey, and even then it makes an unsightly mess. The staining and discolouring of hoggin, gravel, and concrete are bad enough, but when you have gone to the expense of red or other coloured tarmac, it is annoying to have it spoiled in this way.

You will have to be very careful about using oil solvents because these can weaken the bitumen bond. I have used two methods quite successfully. One is to use an old worn short stubble paint brush to stir into the oil with a strong and hot solution of caustic soda. Wear rubber gloves for this method, and don't get it on your clothes. Confine the soda to the area of the oil stain only. Wash off forcefully with a hose jet. Alternatively, and much safer, use an emulsifier like Gunk which you can buy at motor accessory shops. Use a directed, stirring the paste into the oil with a short bristled brush and washing off with the hose jet.

In both treatments, success largely depends upon getting at the oil very quickly before it has time to react with the bitumen bond and create a permanent and irremovable colour change.

527 Constructing and planting sink gardens

I would like to make a garden for small rock plants in an old sandstone sink, but though it measures 42 in. by 18 in., it is only 4 in. deep. Are there any rock plants that I could grow in such shallow soil conditions? The sink could be sited in sun or shade.

This is a very shallow pan but being made of sandstone, it is going to look very natural and is therefore worth a try.

Clearly the most important factor is the rapidity with which the pan will be liable to dry out. Conservation of moisture will be vital. Therefore the first thing to do is to cover the plug hole, so that excess water seeps out rather than gushes: a flat disc, piece of metal or a jar top would do. Lay in a full inch of peat or compost, piled up gradually to a mound of two inches at the centre. Over this, work in a nice firm filling of John Innes seed compost to $\frac{1}{2}$–$\frac{3}{4}$ in. of the rim at the edges and still mounded at the centre. At this stage, test place the stones or rocks that you will use to decorate the top and choose one at the far end from the hole under which to bury a small funnel. You can make one quite simply by cutting off the slop-ing top of a detergent plastic bottle. Scoop away the soil so that the neck rests on the bottom, with the top of the funnel an inch above the soil. From the remainder of the bottle, cut a piece of flat plastic to wrap around your finger to make a tube, which is then similarly inserted at the other end of the sink. Again, this tube should be an inch clear of the soil. Place your plants. You will do best with plants which can tolerate dryness such as Sempervivums, Sedums, Crassulas and you can try also one or two Saxifrages and perhaps a small conifer. Place stones over the funnel and the tube, and finally cover the entire surface with a half inch of fine shingle. This is to keep the soil surface insulated from wind, air and sun so that evaporation loss is reduced, and explains why the soil stopped short of the top, and why the funnel and tube protruded an inch.

Watering will then consist of lifting the stones under which the funnel and tube are concealed and pouring water into the funnel from a spouted can until you can see water rising in the 'spy tube' at the other end, indicating that water has percolated through the compost bottom layer and that it is nicely sodden.

Make this a regular weekly operation and you should have no trouble.

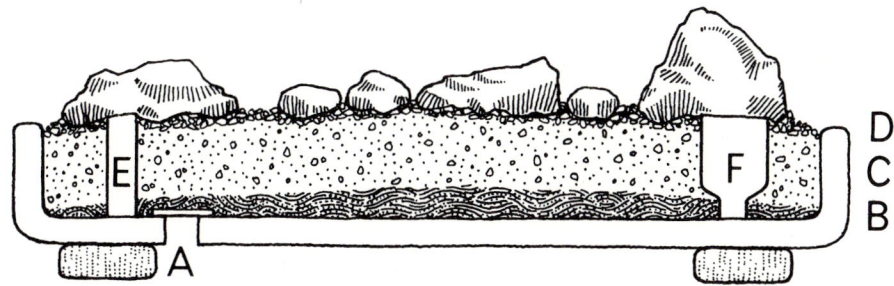

No. 527   Construction of a shallow sink garden.
A.   Covered drainage hole.
B.   Moisture-retaining layer of peat.
C.   Soil layer.
D.   Shingle or grit layer to retard evaporation.
E.   Observation tube.
F.   Irrigation funnel.
Position the sink so that there is a slight fall towards the drainage hole.

528 Sink gardens : sticking concrete to glass

Which is the best way to get concrete to stick to an old glazed sink that I'm trying to make into a miniature garden?

A shiny glazed surface is too smooth and does not give concrete anything upon which to grip and bond, and it is therefore necessary to roughen the surface, or to cover it with something to which concrete will stick. I have seen an adhesive like Bostick used very successfully but it has to be very liberally plastered on and can be a messy job.

By far the most simple method, although dusty, is to fit a coarse carborundum disc to an electric drill, and not only remove the glaze but bite into the sink in a series of deep scoring marks to give the cement a good grip.

For the first concrete layer, use a strong mix, 2 parts fine sand, 1 part cement, plus a little waterproofing powder additive like 'Puddlo' to make a really strong bonding layer. This need not be thick and you will not need very much. Before it is dry, slap on a thicker coating, made up of 3 parts sand and 1 part cement mix, scoring the finished surface and leaving it as rough or as natural as you wish. If you want an artificial finish, brush on Silexine or Sandtex or, alternatively if you want a mature and weathered look, make up a paste of a little clay with some cowpat, stable manure or as a last resort, mushroom compost. Brush this on and leave it to dry. Green algae and yellow lichen will very soon take a hold and look as though they have been there for ages.

529 Ideas for walls, paths, patios

I am planning to build a patio surrounded by screen block walls. Where can I get some ideas?

For gardeners who would like some design ideas before starting with their own patios and walls and who need guidance in construction methods the Cement and Concrete Association, 52 Grosvenor Gardens, London, SW1, have produced a 32-page booklet which explains all you need to know. It consists mainly of illustrations of patios, paths, steps, raised beds, water gardens, etc., and step-by-step construction principles all accompanied by explanatory text. Write to them and they will send you a free copy, especially if you mention this book.

Several manufacturers offer moulds with which you can make your own screen blocks. These save a lot of the cost as against buying them. Their advertisements appear in the gardening and national press, and the information leaflets they offer contain more illustrations and sketches showing how the various blocks can be used.

Section *XIV*

Eradication and Removal

530 Bamboo spreading : treatment for removal

How can I eradicate bamboos which, having grown under the garden wall, are spreading through the garden.

Bamboos can get out of hand and become a nuisance. They spread by means of runners just below the surface, which so multiply that it is virtually impossible to remove them completely by digging. However, you can control effectively with Dalapon grass herbicide which is obtainable from a good garden centre or shop.

During spring make up a solution strictly according to directions. You should spray this to wet the bamboo growth and foliage where it is growing thickly. Where it grows among other plants, you will have to be careful to confine the solution to the bamboo. This will be difficult with spray, so there is an easier way. Wear a long rubber glove and over this, a glove of cloth or some absorbent material. Make the palm and fingers wet with the solution, and then transfer the solution to the bamboo by grabbing the shoots low down and gently pulling the foliage so it slips through your fingers and becomes wet with the killing chemical. Do this two or three times at two to three days intervals when rain is not expected. In a month or so, the bamboo should be ailing and in another couple of weeks, you should be able to pull out dead canes. New shoots can be expected to show for some time so spray or repeat the glove method of applying the herbicide.

531 Bindweed 'bellbine' : its control

Please can you tell me how do I get rid of convolvulus or 'bell-bine' which is growing up fences, up and over roses and smothering everything it can climb over? Weedkillers sprayed on kill the leaves but do not prevent new growth.

Other than questions about lawns, this is probably the most frequently asked question of all. Spraying with a hormone weedkiller is often risky because the spray can so easily kill plants like roses which you don't want to lose. The leaf growth of convolvulus is generally very susceptible to hormone killers, and dies before the hormone has been translocated—i.e., before it has passed in the sap stream to stem and root system. The root system is the food storehouse and, as you know if you try digging it out, every little broken off piece can throw up new shoots. Therefore, killing off the leaves is not getting to the heart of the problem.

The root has to be attacked hence the absurd-sounding advice is that to kill the plant, you must make sure that you do *not* kill the leaves! They must stay alive, at least for a while, so that they can have time to transmit the hormone to the root.

Collect some large fruit tins—as used for canned peaches—narrow ones are not so good because they knock over too easily and the spilled liquid you are going to put in the can will be dangerous to other plants. Carefully unwind the bellbine, taking care not to damage the leaves and stems. Gather these stems together, roll them up carefully and stuff them into a tin. Do this with as many tins as you can and stand them where they can't be knocked over. Fill each with a weak solution of hormone weedkiller, such as S.B.K., using three to four times as much water as recommended. The living stems continue to absorb the weak hormone which then travels throughout the plant, reaching the roots before the whole plant begins to collapse. Repeat the procedure with all new growth that appears, and you should eradicate it completely. But remember, it is a persistent weed and there is only one way to beat persistence, and that is to be more persistent yourself.

532 Bramble in a rockery

Having just moved house I am faced with a well laid-out but neglected rock garden which has a lot of brambles growing out from beneath the rocks. Since some of these rocks weigh well over 1 cwt., it is impracticable to dig out the offending plants. Should I cut them off close to the ground and then inject concentrated sodium chlorate solution into the stems? Any advice will be appreciated.

Whatever you do, don't ever use sodium chlorate anywhere near where you have plants growing or will want them to grow. It is a crude killer, will poison the soil for several months, and has the vile tendency to creep horizontally through the soil and kill plants well away from where it was put down. With natural drainage on a rockery being broken up and diverted by the stones, heaven only knows where it will get to.

The most effective way to deal with brambles is to paint the stems with a solution of a shrub and brushwood hormone weedkiller in paraffin as described in *No. 533*. You will probably have to paint the bramble stems several times, and keep a careful watch for any signs of resurgence from roots not completely killed off.

The hormone is quite effective when used in a water solution but bramble is a tough resistant beast, and the paraffin is used therefore to punch a way into woody stems which carry the life stream of the plant.

In paraffin solution, the hormone is lethal so be very careful that it doesn't reach any other plants on the rockery which is why you should paint it, not spray it. Keep the tin in your hands at all times. If you put it down, you can be sure it will slide, fall, or be knocked over, with results that are not at all funny to contemplate.

Cut away the killed stems and chop them in pieces so that they can be put on the fire. Don't put them on the compost heap. Quite apart from putting hormone and paraffin residue in the compost, there is the added danger of running a thorn into your hands at a later stage. Hard and woody bramble thorns become extremely resistant to rotting down.

533 Clearing rogue growth from a holly hedge

I have neglected a holly hedge, and now elder, thorn, dogberry and brambles are growing through it. What is the remedy?

'Weed' growth of other plants—especially wild hops and bramble—in a hedge is a common problem because once such plants become established with a well-developed root system, physical removal is difficult and, in the case of holly, a very uncomfortable job.

A more simple method than digging out is therefore to be welcomed, and you can achieve this in the following manner, which can be adapted for any type of hedge.

Make up a solution of one tenth of a pint of SBK or similar brushwood killer (which you should be able to obtain quite easily from your garden shop) in one gallon of paraffin. Holly is reckoned to be rather resistant to this killer, but at the strength recommended here and which I have found necessary to get a good response—after all you will not want to go poking in a holly hedge very often—you would be safer not to take any chances. Therefore, you must be very careful and make quite certain that you don't get this on the holly. You can apply the killer at any time, but the most effective time is during late summer/autumn as the sap is beginning to recede and the hormone is thus more quickly carried back to the root systems.

Paint the solution on the main stems of the intruding 'weed' growth you wish to kill. If this is difficult to reach, pull the holly aside, tie it back to leave a 'hole' and fasten a paint brush to a stick to reach in.

If the main stems are very thick, $1\frac{1}{2}$ inches or more, they will likely be very resistant against mere 'painting', and you will have to be more drastic. You really will have to pull the holly aside so that you can get right into the target. With a carpenter's swing brace, bore a $\frac{1}{2}$ in. hole into the main stem(s) at a point 3 inches above soil level in a downwards direction, some 2 inches or more deep. Don't come out the other side since you want the hole to fill with liquid—the same hormone/paraffin solution which you can pour in through a small funnel. Thus impregnated, it will soon succumb.

Removing killed wood from the hedge may present difficulties. You will find it easier to pull it out if you first cut the material into short lengths. This you can do simply enough from outside the hedge with a long-arm pruner, using the hook of the open blade to reach in and pull the stuff out.

Anything too thick for the pruner will have to be sawn, and this too is quite easy if you use the light-alloy long-arm pruner made by Standard Engineering Ltd, Rowditch Park, Derby. They also supply a long curved pruning saw that fastens to the end of the pruner, and means you can do all the removal work from a position where you will not be scratched by the holly.

Don't leave dead material in your holly hedge; in time, it could harbour coral spot fungus.

534   Clearing tangled overgrown mass

I have taken over a large garden that was originally planted with shrubs, but which is now overgrown and a tangled mess of bramble, wild hops, bell-bine, nettles, and sycamore and ash saplings. I realise that a weedkiller will be impracticable but it will take ages to get it all under control with secateurs. I suppose I shall have to get stuck into it with a bagging hook unless you can suggest a better way.

Clearly you will have to slash a way through the rubbish but you will have to be careful not to damage any of the choice subjects. The brambles and saplings will need attention with a cutting tool or tools that can be aimed with a fair degree of precision and safety—and that is not the kind of work for a bagging hook or a sickle.

The most effective tool I have used in conditions like this is the kind of long-bladed slashing knife that the British 14th Army used to cut through the Burma jungle—and called a machete. There are two basic types: the outsweep with the cutting edge on the outside curve like an oversized carving knife, which would be ideal against brambles and nettles, sweeping the work away from you. The other type, the insweep with the cutting edge on the inward curve, is good for slashing hedge growth and trimming down saplings.

Between them, these machetes should handle all the material within reach with you standing up. Then, as you make room for yourself to take a swing, you can clear the rubbish down to ground level—without a back-aching stoop— be using a double-edged long-handled jungle knife shaped something like a hockey stick. This will deal with overgrown grass, soft weeds, and with a little practice, you can cut it all down as clean as with a scythe. These military-type jungle machetes are still being made and considering the way they slaughter this kind of job are surprisingly inexpensive. They are obtainable from Gardenwork, Catherine de Barnes, Solihull.

Most people not used to this kind of work may find it a little hard on the hands at first, and possibly raise a crop of blisters. This can happen with any hand tools like secateurs, shears, even a spade or fork during a long session of use. Blisters are painful, and here's how to prevent them. Have some French chalk or talc powder handy, either in a small tray or you can make a small plastic-lined satchel-like pouch or a pocket to hold some. Slip your hands in frequently so that they always have a good covering of chalk. This acts as a lubricant and your hands will slide easily around the tools without any skin friction. At the first sign of soreness, pack up work for the day to allow the fluid under the skin to disperse.

535   Couch grass, twitch or wick

Our allotment contains a lot of wick grass. I am endeavouring to remove all this and wonder if there is any other way—i.e. chemically—to get rid of this other than burning, which seems to be the accepted method. I am having to dig up a lot of good topsoil whilst getting rid of this grass.

When a plant, desirable or objectionable, is widespread all over the country, it is inevitable that it will pick up many local names. Therefore, what it is called in one place, may not be recognised in another. A case in point is the grass that sends up wide coarse leaves and long wiry roots through the soil with astonishing rapidity and headlong vigour. The most common name is couch grass, less widely known as 'twitch', sometimes 'wick', and there are very many other local names.

If you want to cultivate an infested area fairly quickly, the safest method is to dig over the area using a fork, and remove every piece you can find. A spade will slice through roots, cut them into pieces and make extraction more difficult. A fork will enable you to ease the roots out more effectively in longer lengths, but do be very thorough and remove every single piece because, like bindweed (see *No. 531*) even the smallest piece of root left in the soil can grow again.

This is why scorching off the foliage with a green leaf killer like Paraquat and then burning the dried and withered 'straw' is a complete waste of time and money. Not enough heat is generated to bake the roots underground, and they simply send up more leaf, thriving on the ashes of the old.

Forking out can be done at any time that the plot is vacant, and as it is almost impossible to get 100% removal, some re-emergence is to be expected, probably when crops or other plants are in position with not much room for forking out. This is where a broken fork can come in useful—many gardeners unfortunately break a tine or bend one (spring it) at some time. (Incidentally, if you bend a tine, don't straighten it yourself; it will only bend again more easily than ever and become useless because the steel hardening temper will have gone. Take it to a blacksmith.) Useless fork or broken, don't throw it away. Remove the tine on the other side (it is invariably an outer tine that goes) using a hacksaw. This will produce a narrow two-tined fork that will be useful for forking out couch in confined places, between rows etc.

Synchemicals' Dalapon is the chemical to use to avoid the tedious chore of digging out couch. It is most effective sprayed on the foliage when it is at its maximum growth period in spring and early summer. However, you will not be able to crop the area for at least four months, and your programme will have to be planned accordingly with the area out of action whilst the chemical remains toxic. Dalapon is remarkably inexpensive, and is available in packs as small as 4 ozs., which will control 80 sq. yds.

As with all chemical herbicides used in areas where food is to be grown, adhere very strictly to the manufacturers' directions for use.

536 Elm suckers and an easy removal method

Left with 3 ft. diameter stumps after having some infected elm trees cut down, I am plagued with sucker growths. What can I do?

The elm has a propensity for putting up suckers at the best of times but the frequency with which this question has been recently asked seems to suggest that the Dutch Elm Disease doesn't always kill the root at once. Deprived of its natural trunk and branches when felled, the root continues to send up suckers.

Eradication is quite simple: make up an oil solution of $\frac{3}{4}$ fl. oz. of SBK brushwood killer to half a gallon of paraffin and paint this on to shoots and stumps. If the sucker shoots arise from stumps, bore a hole into them and destroy them by smouldering as described in *No. 541*.

537 Ground elder: how to control a persistent nuisance

What is the best way of killing ground elder?

Once ground elder makes an appearance, it is a most difficult weed to eradicate. It has an extensive root system and this is what gives it the ability to keep coming back when the foliage is destroyed.

The best way to defeat persistence is to meet it with even greater persistence and fortunately this does not involve you in any great effort.

The modern green leaf killer Paraquat will take out the foliage. The usual way to apply this is by using a special sprinkle bar fitted to a water can. But I consider these to be pretty useless because Paraquat is effective only against green leaf; all that falls on the soil is wasted and the droplets from sprinkle bars, whilst easy enough to place where you want them without wetting and harming other plants, all too easily bounce off.

Use a Paraquat solution, made up strictly as directed but add a few drops of liquid washing-up detergent to make sure the liquid spreads and wet with a minimum of run-off and drip. I prefer to use a sprayer with the jet set slightly more coarsely than a fine mist which can easily drift and do damage. But don't make this so coarse that it is no better than a dribble bar or rose. You will need to repeat the procedure as new foliage emerges. This new foliage will be weaker on each appearance, and you must attack it before the green leaf can begin to send back sugars and starches to the root to replace the used food store. Finally the plant will collapse. Repeated use of SBK hormone weed-killer plus the washing-up detergent trick will cripple ground elder, but you must be very, very careful indeed to restrict it to the ground elder. Don't let it run off and get near other plants.

Another possibility—on an otherwise quite vacant plot—is to apply Amcide. This is a short-term herbicide based on sulphamate of ammonia and because it decomposes in about six weeks, it is best used in spring and early summer when the weeds are growing vigorously, and will therefore absorb the poison quickly. The area should be safe for planting two to three months after application. Make some test sowings first with cheap seed like mustard, cress, or radish, to check the poison has gone.

538 Ivy: clearing the ground prior to cultivation

How can I eradicate ivy from a neglected patch of ground which I now want to cultivate.

If a neglected patch of ground really means there is nothing of value growing there, the technique can be a little more drastic than if there are plants or shrubs that you wish to preserve.

Ivy is very largely surface rooting, and it is easier to get the hormone into the root system than with bindweed for example—see *No. 531*. The foliage of ivy has a leathery texture and the basic problem is to get the hormone past the resistant leaf surface.

If you are having a clean sweep of the area, use SBK or a similar brushwood killer at half the recommended strength—according to which one you use—but in paraffin, not water. The oil will penetrate quickly into the leaf carrying the hormone with it. Don't overdo the spraying: just enough to wet the foliage is all that is needed. If you make the soil underneath wet with paraffin, you may have trouble with oil residues when you come to plant up. One spraying should do the job; if not, repeat in three weeks' time which should finish it off. In

four to six weeks, depending on the speed of the kill and withering of the growth, you can burn it off if it is laying thick enough or you may have to rake it into a heap before it will burn.

However, if there are plants you wish to keep, you will have to use a less lethal water solution of SBK. Make it up to the same strength as above, plus half a teaspoonful of liquid washing-up detergent. Choose a windless day, and make quite certain the spray doesn't drift on to the plants you do not want to kill. With a water solution, you may have to repeat the spray in about four weeks, because despite the wetting effect of the detergent the leaf surface is very resistant to water. When the ivy is dead and dry, burn it off as with the paraffin method.

Shallow dig over, 3–4 ins. deep to break open the soil, get air into it and assist the bacterial breakdown of any toxic hormone and oil residues. Any residues that have penetrated to the soil will not have reached below this and deeper digging to begin with might put them well down where they may not decompose so well and cause later problems to deep rooting plants you wish to grow. Then, about six to eight weeks after the first spraying, you will be able to make a test sowing of a fast germinating seed like mustard or cress. If these remain healthy a week after germination, the soil should be safe for deep digging and/or planting.

Paraquat will scorch off the foliage with no residual effect on the soil, but you will have to spray two or three times with a few weeks in between to allow fresh foliage to arise from the still living root system. The third spraying will probably exhaust it, but by this time it will have taken as long as the more positive SBK method.

539 Nettles: control of, and what they indicate

Our chicken run is becoming covered with nettles. What can I kill these with, without harming the soil?

Eradication of nettles is very simple; spray them in the morning of a warm sunny day with a water solution of SBK, plus a few drips of washing-up detergent, and they will be in a sorry state by evening.

However, the following may be of interest to you. Poultry not only supply eggs, they manure the soil with their droppings, scratch and peck out a great many grubs and other pests. A healthy crop of nettles in a poultry run indicates that, potentially, the soil is very, very fertile, full of plant nutrients and would give very good crops.

The way to utilise poultry to the full is to split their run or your vegetable plot into four sections; the normal three sections of the three-year rotational cycle plus one when the fourth area is dug over several times but allowed to fallow with the poultry free ranging over it. This is quite easily achieved by putting up a light fence of 3-inch mesh to confine them to the fallow area. If you can position the hen house in the centre of the whole plot, so much the better; if not, simply use more wire mesh to give them an access lane. See also *Nos. 501* and *516*.

540   Persistent weed with pale green shamrock leaves

I am besieged by a weed which is like a pale green shamrock leaf and each stem has a small bulbous root. I can't find anything that will satisfactorily destroy it. I have tried pulling them up, one by one, but they soon grow again.

This is Oxalis, one of the most persistent and difficult weeds to eradicate because it is very largely resistant to hormone weedkillers. The bulbous roots give it an immense and long-lasting ability to come back when the foliage is removed by mowing or scorching. It is sometimes a nuisance among cultivated plants where the use of total weedkillers is precluded, not only because of the risk to nearby plants, but also because the soil would be made toxic to all plant life for a long time.

Fortunately, however, the range of total weedkillers contains an exception: Amcide, the common or brand name for ammonium sulphamate. This is a total plant killer, but short-lived. In about five to six weeks it decomposes, mainly into sulphate of ammonia and therefore has a secondary nitrogenous fertilising effect. You will have to be very careful how you use it; make up the solution exactly according to the instructions on the tin and add detergent to break down the water surface tension so that it wets the leaves thoroughly,—and paint the oxalis leaves, being careful not to let it splash and drip through to the soil underneath.

More effective—and you will have to decide in your own case if the extent of the weed is too great for you to adopt this method—is to use it dry. Part the foliage with one hand to reveal the main root clumps and shake on dry Amcide from an old salt shaker.

If you have any difficulty in obtaining Amcide at your garden shop, write to Herbon Ltd., Downton, Salisbury, Wiltshire.

541   Tree stumps: complete removal without digging

How can I get rid of an old tree stump without digging it out?

The best and least troublesome way is to burn it out but judging by the number of letters received on the subject, a lot of gardeners seem to have difficulties in burning out completely. The secret, and reason for the lack of complete success, is haste and incomplete preparation.

With a carpenter's swing brace, bore $\frac{1}{2}$–$\frac{3}{4}$ in. holes 6–8 ins. deep and 5–6 inches apart. If made in every part of the stump, from the sides, make these in a downwards direction because they will be required to hold liquid. You will find that the best bit to use in the brace is the long fluted type called an Irwin bit; this pulls out all the chippings and leaves a clean hole. Of course if you have an extension lead and can reach the job with an electric drill, there is no reason why you should not use it.

Make a saturated solution by stirring saltpetre—potassium nitrate—which you can obtain quite easily from the chemist, into warm/hot water, adding more, stirring, adding more and more until the liquid will take no more. You will now have a saturated solution. Fill the holes, using a small funnel. In a week, the liquid will have partly soaked into the wood—perhaps completely, depending upon the dryness and absorbent texture of the stump. Top up or refill the holes with more solution, leave the stumps uncovered and exposed to the weather—rain will help the saltpetre to diffuse.

If the stump is old and the wood well dead and rotten, keep up the hole filling at weekly intervals for four to six weeks and then leave the stump for a further two weeks for the salt-petre to soak in.

Should the stump be recent, with wood still green or sappy keep hole filling for eight weeks. Then, leave for another two, and, in both cases after the two-week soak period, cover the stump with a polythene sheet, securely enough to keep the weather and rain off, but loosely so that air can get at the stump and help dry it completely. This may take several more weeks.

When a spell of fine dry weather with no rainfall can be expected for a few days, fill the holes with paraffin, and begin a small fire with small dry sticks in the centre of the stump. As the flames from the sticks and the paraffin die down, you should see the stump beginning to glow and smoulder, like a big cigarette. There should be little smoke and no inconvenience to neighbours. The smouldering will continue perhaps for days, even a couple of weeks, and eventually the stump will disintegrate into a pile of ash.

If you have done your preparatory work thoroughly and with patience, the smouldering should extend right down to the roots. Most of the failures that occur are due to hasty and incomplete preparation.

542 Weedkiller with unwanted long-lasting after-effects

When our house was being constructed, a product called Atlavar was used on the ground which was very weed infested. We have since sown grass seed, first last autumn and again this spring, but both times the young grass turned yellow and died. Can you explain this?

Atlavar is a mixture of the hormone weedkiller 2-4D, the total plant killer sodium chlorate and Monuron. Sodium chlorate alone can persist in the soil for many months—up to a year in some soil types. But the effect of Monuron makes the chlorate very much more persistent and it can take four and quite likely more *years* from the time of application before the soil becomes free

of the chemicals and be safe for planting.

You could try to speed up its removal by using the flocculating agent, gypsum. This will also have the added advantage that when the weedkiller has gone, your soil, especially if it is a heavy clay type, will have become a good deal more crumbly and easy to work see *Nos. 2, 456, 465* and *475*. How much gypsum you can put down as a first application will depend upon what methods you can apply.

If you can dig over the site by spade, spread gypsum on the surface at 4 ozs. per sq. yd. Dig it in, breaking up the soil as much as you can and spreading the gypsum through the soil. If you can use a cultivator which will churn up and aerate the soil much more effectively than a spade, put it down at 6 ozs. per sq. yd.—or if you can use a super cultivator, like the Wolseley Merry Tiller, down to its full operating depth of almost a foot, you can make it 8 ozs. per sq. yd. Whichever method you use, follow up every three months with 2 ozs. per sq. yd. dressings, and dig or rotate with the machine each time to get air into the soil, which will encourage decomposing bacteria.

Whilst all this is going on, collect all the household waste and other material you can to build compost heaps, see *Nos. 476* and *480*, since you are going to need all you can get.

Two and a half years after the application of the weedkiller, begin spreading the compost and working this into the soil. This will help to boost the soil bacteria population and speed up the final decomposition and removal of weed-killer residues. By the time they have gone, the compost itself will be decomposing into humus and you should finish up with a very fertile soil.

After three years, especially if you are speeding things up with gypsum, deep aeration and composting, you can take a chance with a test sowing of a cheap expendable seed like mustard or cress. If this doesn't fail, you will have made some progress, and can move onto something that roots a little deeper. Try radish, and then slowly feel your way down from shallower rooting plants to deeper rooting, at all times using inexpensive expendable seed before committing and possibly failing with plants you would not want to lose.

Section XV

Aquatics

543 Fish forever blowing bubbles

My goldfish are constantly coming to the surface of my garden pool and gulping for air. Is this normal? I have plenty of oxygenating plants.

This is a sure sign of oxygen starvation. The fish not only come to the surface water where it is in contact with the air, but also try to increase the oxygen content by bubbling the water as they gulp it in.

Oxygenating plants only give off oxygen in daylight; when it is dark they actually use it up, and aggravate the problem.

A spell of dull, close, thundery weather hinders oxygenation of the water and can put the fish under severe stress. Even if the thunder brings rain, which has air dissolved in it, an awful lot will be necessary to put enough oxygen into a depleted pool to make it safe.

The solution is quite simple. Get the water on the move. Install a small pump that circulates the water over a waterfall or cascade so that the splash oxygenates the water. This need not be expensive if you use the submersible type of pump. No plumbing is required. The pump goes into the water, with its electrical lead connected via a weatherproof connector hidden under a convenient rockery stone to a lead from the domestic electricity supply. Hose from the pump water outlet conveys water to a high point above the waterfall, cascade—or a special spout will give you an attractive fountain. Apart from helping the fish to breathe, it will also add interest to your pool.

544 Repairing a cracked pool

Which is the best way to repair a hairline crack in my concrete garden pool? I have tried cementing it several times, but the crack keeps re-appearing.

Repairing a crack is easy enough if you can find it through the algae on the pool sides and bottom. The usual procedure is to scrub the crack area clean and apply Aquaseal 40. However, the more important question to ask yourself is, why did the crack occur in the first place?

When full of water, a pool represents a considerable dead weight of water, all resting on what may be a relatively thin shell of concrete, resting in turn on soil which, like sand, may be incapable of bearing weight without moving.

Judging by the number of questions that are received concerning pool cracks that reopen further every time they are repaired, there must be very many concrete pools consisting of shells that are too thin or have insufficient foundations. Clearly, it is then pointless to repair a crack. In a construction that keeps moving under the weight, you will have to cure the problem in a way that makes quite sure it won't happen again.

Clean out the pool and lay in a plastic or butyl liner. Then if the concrete shell moves again there is enough 'give' in the liner to move or stretch with the movement underneath, and the leak does not occur.

Cleaning out the pool is an opportunity to check over the plant life in it, making sure that there are sufficient oxygenating plants—and if necessary arranging for the addition of a cascade or fall powered by a small pump. See *No. 543.*

545 Effect of lawn fertiliser in the pool

Can I safely use a lawn fertiliser close to a plastic-lined garden pool without endangering the fish?

If a little fertiliser gets into the pool, either by seepage or perhaps by falling into the water when being put down on the lawn, the only likely effect will generally be to encourage plant life to grow, perhaps quite vigorously, especially blanket weed. This could have the effect of taking a lot of the oxygen from the water and the fish may suffer. However, this is the only likely danger to them and even oxygen shortage is unlikely if you have a pump circulating the water through a fountain or waterfall. See *No. 543.*

If the fertiliser contains a weedkiller, however, it could very well be a different matter and you would be wise to take great care to stop spreading the fertiliser well short of the pool side, and make quite sure that seepage does not occur.

If you have any doubts about this, cut a gully three or four inches deep around the pool so that there can be no run-off during heavy rain.

Beware, especially, if you have occasion to use worm-killer or other toxic materials anywhere near the pool or a greenfly killer and other insecticides on plants that overhang the water. Fish are very susceptible to some of the modern potent chemicals.

546 Herons taking goldfish

Recently a dozen of my goldfish were eaten by a heron. A friend tells me these birds are very territorially minded and will not visit a pool if another heron is there, so an imitation heron might deter the real herons. Is this likely? I have suspended a net just below the surface of one pool, but it is not easy to do this in irregular shaped pools.

Because herons are generally seen fishing alone, it doesn't follow that they always do, nor does it follow that they would be put off from alighting near to another heron, especially an imitation one which they would soon get to know. The heron is not a stupid bird and there are many instances reported where the imitation heron idea has failed.

It is generally observed that herons like to alight on dry land and from there wade into shallow water up to about 9–10 ins. deep, but very seldom in water any deeper. Therefore, a pool constructed with sheer or very steeply-angled sides to a depth of 18 ins. or more, is probably fairly safe from visits, and this is a point to be borne in mind when constructing a pool but not much help to an already existing one. However they don't always wade in. Where they learn that water is shallow and they can alight safely, they will do so. If they have become familiar with your pool and know they can drop straight into the water, it won't be much good putting up strings round the pool edges to frighten them.

In your case, I think you will have to resort to netting, but not as you have it suspended below the water surface as is often advised, because this can catch fish by the gills. It is much better

to suspend dark coloured Ulstron or Nylon netting—the kind used for fruit cages—above shallow water so that the bird is definitely kept off. Suspending single strands is often advised, to break the bird's alighting flight path. It is not reliably effective however because, although flying or wandering into an unseen wire may startle the bird and send it off, it doesn't prevent it from returning and trying again.

547 Leeches will attack fish

What can be eating the snails in my well-stocked garden pool? All I can find are empty shells.

It is extremely likely that at sometime you have introduced a water plant carrying the egg capsules of leeches. Fish will sometimes take the odd snail, but leeches have an insane passion for them, and the empty shells are a sure sign.

You will have to make absolutely certain, and if they are found to be present, you will have to eradicate them or they will next turn their attentions to your fish.

Tie a piece of raw liver to a stone or heavy object and place this in the middle of a shallow tin or tray some 9–10 inches diameter or square to which you have fixed a wire handle. This is a baited trap which you can lower into the pool on a cord so that it rests on the bottom. The leeches will soon be attracted to the liver and by pulling up the bait and inspecting several times a day, you can soon take them out. Draw up the bait carefully and slowly because when leeches are fully fed, they drop away from their victim; bloated leeches will therefore be lying on the tray. A quick upward movement through the water can easily wash them clear.

Once you have proven their presence, you will have to decide whether to press on with this baiting until you gradually exterminate them, or clean the pool out thoroughly. Whichever method you adopt, 100% clearance cannot be guaranteed because egg capsules may be on the plants, and a later hatching will re-infest the pool. Therefore, even if you clean out the pool, you should bait for a while afterwards in case a new generation emerges.

In future, any new plants or fish should be kept separately for a while, like a quarantine period, before being introduced to the pool. This is the only way to be sure they are not carrying pest or disease to infect the rest.

548 Keeping pool water clean

Can you tell me how to clear the water in a concrete garden pond which was cracked by frost? I bought a good liner and it has now been lined for 18 months. The water is green and the sides of the pond are slimy. I've been told that I should not have put in water plants (they are in containers) but I thought that plants were supposed to keep the water fresh.

Without doubt, this pool is receiving too much light. Very simple algae—minute plant organisms which colour the water green, or more elaborate forms with masses of very thin filament-like threads which strangle everything with a cotton wool-like growth (the common name blanket weed is therefore apt) proliferate where the water is still, where the water contains plenty of plant nutrients and where plenty of light penetrates. You can add chemicals which will suppress the algae, but I question the wisdom of this because it is an artificial cure and doesn't correct the mismanagement.

The leaves of waterlilies floating on the surface would reduce the light intensity of course, but even so you will probably need to do more than this.

In order to reduce the amount of light entering the pool, and at the same time improve the aesthetic appearance, you could arrange rocks and stone to overhang the edge and so cast shadow. Shrubs like Astilbe and small conifers planted on the sun side will also help reduce direct sunlight reaching the water, as would a small weeping birch or cherry.

Remove the excessive weed to begin with by twirling a forked stick around between the palms of your hands. You can make a fork stick by splitting a cane for 5–6 ins. and forcing the two prongs apart to form a fork, or bend a 12 in. long piece of wire like a hairpin, force the folded end into a bamboo cane, open out the two loose ends and there you are.

Be careful not to touch fish with the fork, especially the wire one whilst you are removing the weed in case you damage them. This could cause fungus infection and then you'll have more trouble than ever.

Introduce a submersible pump, and circulate the water over a little waterfall or cascade. Frequent examination and clearance of the pump filter will help to trap a lot of the free floating weed, and aeration of the water will both help the fish and the release of harmful chemicals which are retained in still and stagnant water.

Section XVI

Poisonous Plants

549 Is Laburnum poisonous to other plants?

Are the poisonous seed pods of a laburnum tree harmful to my vegetable garden which grows beneath it and to fish in a pool nearby?

After the Yew, the Laburnum is the most poisonous tree grown in Britain. All parts are poisonous—wood, bark and roots. The flowers are too but these soon wither and fall. Young leaves are poisonous, but this tends to diminish a little as the pods form. As the seeds ripen, the poison concentration builds up in both seed and pod and these are then very dangerous. Cases are on record of death in humans, and in horses and ponies that have consumed foliage, see also *No. 551*.

As there is no specific antidote to the poison concerned, Cystine, treatment of the very painful and distressing symptoms—stomach pain, vomiting, lack of coordination, convulsion and asphyxia—involves enemas, emitics and stomach pumping. That should be enough to cause you to take a different view of a beautiful but very dangerous tree.

There have been circumstantial reports from time to time of poisoning of other plants in the vicinity of Laburnum but there does not appear to have been any published reportage of controlled scientific investigation. If you detect any distress or difference in the appearance of vegetables or other plants nearby, regard that as fairly conclusive and take the tree out, move the affected plants, or grow your vegetables further away. Seeds and pods dropping into pools will definitely harm fish.

In the soil, bacterial decomposition will gradually destroy the toxicity of fallen foliage and pods but they would be better cleared up and consigned to the compost heap. Fallen seeds will be quick to germinate in the loose fertile soil of the kitchen garden. Remove all seedlings as soon as seen; you can easily spot their characteristic leaves. Laburnum seedlings soon make a long tap root and if you don't get them out whilst still very young, they will be beyond pulling and you will have to dig them up.

550 Old Man's Beard, the wild clematis

I try to discourage Old Man's Beard growing in a hedge by cutting off the tendrils close to the ground, and then pulling them down. This gives me a stinging itch which lasts from four to five days. Is there a cure? Also is there a better way of dealing with this plant?

Old Man's Beard, or Traveller's Joy as it is also called, is *Clematis vitalba*, the only climbing clematis incidentally which grows wild in the U.K. All parts of the plant are poisonous. The toxin involved is a severe irritant, and therefore it is not so much a question of being allergic as your having skin that may be a little soft, or at least not hard enough to resist light contact with the sap. Applied wet to any skin, however hard and corny, the sap can cause severe blistering and irritation which, as you have found, can last for days. You are not likely to ingest it because it is very bitter, but if you inadvertently get it into your mouth, off the back of your hand or your fingers perhaps, or if animals bite the leaves, severe irritation inevitably follows.

In future, wear gloves and long sleeves before touching it, and with all plants that you know to be poisonous, see *No. 551*, don't take chances by putting the haulm on the compost heap—burn it.

Your safest course would be to eradicate the plant once and for all. You will find advice on how to do this in *No. 531* which deals with removing bindweed from shrubs and other plants and in *No. 533* dealing with rogues in a holly hedge.

551 Poisonous plants in the garden

I've heard that Daphne odora *is poisonous. Is this true? Also, which other plants should I avoid growing while my children are small and liable to 'sample' leaves and berries?*

There doesn't seem to be any record of anyone being poisoned by this particular Daphne, but that is nothing to go by because the collation of information and evidence about poisonous plants is woefully lacking in this country, and whenever I have made enquiries about poisonous plants either to hospital or botanical garden authorities, it becomes apparent just how much we lack and need a centralised and therefore authoritative information centre on this very important subject. For instance, there is no authority controlling advertising on this subject, and it is quite easy for a poisonous plant to be advertised—albeit unwittingly. It has happened.

The one thing that can be said with certainty about *Daphne odora* is that it belongs to a genus that contains two species, *D. mezereum* and *D. laureola* that are well authenticated as having been fatal in both humans and animals —*D. mezereum*, in fact as recently as 1973 when a young child died in Britain after eating its seeds. Where children are concerned—like unrestricted and out of sight access to swimming and garden pools—there is only one rule for any sensible parent: safety first and take no chances. I should put this Daphne out of reach, either by fencing or by moving it to another position—or even removal from the garden. Better to sacrifice a beautiful flowering shrub than have a tragedy.

The following is a list of plants likely to be found in gardens which are recorded as having been poisonous either to humans—in some cases fatally—or to animals.

Trees, shrubs and hedges

Arbutus unedo	Strawberry Tree
Azalea – various	Azalea
Berberis – various	Barberry
Buxus – various	Box
Cytisus scoparius	Common Broom
Daphne mezereum and *D. laureola*	Daphne
Euonymus—various	Spindle Tree
Frangella alnus	Alder Buckthorn
Fraxinus—various	Ash
Hedera—various	Ivy
Hypericum—various	St. John's Wort
Kalmia	Calico Bush
Laburnum	Laburnum
Leycesteria formosa	Flowering Nutmeg
Ligustrum—various	Privet
Prunus laurocerasus	Cherry Laurel
Quercus—various	Oak
Rhamnus cathartica	Common Buckthorn
Rhododendron—various	Rhododendron
Skimmia—various	Skimmia
Spartium junceum	Spanish Broom
Symphoricarpus	Snowberry
Taxus – various	Yew

Flowering and other plants and bulbs

Aconitum	Monkshood
Aquilegia	Columbine
Arisaema (Arum)	Cuckoo Pint, Lords and Ladies
Colchicum	Autumn Crocus
Convallaria	Lily of the Valley
Delphinium	Larkspur
Dieffenbachia	Dumb Cane
Digitalis	Foxglove
Endymion	Bluebell
Fritillaria	Snakes Head
Galanthus	Snowdrop
Helleborus	Hellebore, Christmas Rose
Hyacinthus	Hyacinth
Iris	Flag, Iris
Lupinus	Lupin
Narcissus	Narcissus, Daffodil, Jonquil
Papaver	Poppy
Ranunculus	Buttercup
Ricinus	True Castor Oil Plant
Scilla	Scilla, Squill, Bluebell
Trollius	Globe Flower
Viscum	Mistletoe

Vegetables

Cochlearia	Horseradish
Lycopersicum	★Tomato
Rheum	★Rhubarb
Solanum	★Potato

Particular attention is drawn to the vegetables marked★—the foliage and green parts of all three have caused death in humans. Others are on record as having caused no more than distress to varying degree—age, personal susceptibilities and allergies also influence the effects—and others have a record with animals only. However, as little children have a remarkable propensity to put all manner of things in their mouths with the speed of lightning, I believe it is wise and safety conscious to direct a warning, to name those plants with known records—whatever the degree of severity and advise the need for your awareness and care. After all, you will not want your children to achieve fame as victims.

552 Strawberry Tree is not for dessert

Can we eat the fruits of a strawberry tree? After having planted one, I have heard that it is poisonous.

There are a great many plants that have fruits or leaves that are border-line cases. See *No. 551*. Sometimes it is a question of the amount consumed. Many herbs and the prussic acid in almonds are good examples. A few or a little perhaps for flavouring are all right but too many or too much can prove harmful.

It is very very difficult to be dogmatic about what constitutes 'poisonous' and even more difficult to be fair to a nurseryman, for instance, who would like to advertise and sell a plant, and to unsuspecting readers who may respond to an advertisement and let themselves in for trouble.

How does one answer a question about the strawberry tree? It is edible and in Portugal one berry dropped in gin makes a well-known national drink. Very true, but it is also a fact that the botanical name, *Arbutus unedo*, means something – *un* – one, and *edo* – edible; 'one edible' or, in other words, eat only one. That could mean that, because it is so bitter, you are unlikely to eat two. If that is the case, why grow it for the fruit? Or it could mean eat only one because two will make you ill and, in that case, it could be foolish to find out!

I have to deal with this subject at length because in recent years it seems to have become a growing practice with some nurserymen to think that gardeners are always on the look out for unusual plants and shrubs and that there is a ready sale for the exotic and strange. My advice is don't fall for such ideas: your time and garden space are much too valuable to grow anything other than established and proven successful plants. Concentrate on growing these well and you will get all the flavours you want without the need to take risks with questionable and risky gimmicks. When the Royal Horticultural Society have tested a new fruit in their fruit trials and pronounced it good for amateur growing, by all means try to grow it yourself, but until the R.H.S. or a similar reputable authority give the all clear, my advice is don't risk it.

553 The Thorn Apple

I'd like information about a plant which has grown among my runner beans. I understand that it is grown in India and its name is Datura stramonium. *Where it has arrived from I do not know. I always save my own beans every year so it could not have been in them.*

The Thorn Apple—*Datura stramonium*—is a member of the botanical family Solanaceae. All the native and most of the introduced and cultivated members are wholly, or in part, poisonous, some extremely so. The family includes this species the Thorn Apple, which is normally confined to the southern half of the country; the wild plants of henbane, woody, garden and deadly nightshades, and the cultivated plants of potato, tomato and tobacco. See also *No. 551*.

Now, before you panic and sign the pledge never again to eat potatoes and tomatoes, it is the foliage and green parts that are poisonous and which can remain so even when dried. So don't let the haulm of either get into hay or fodder or bedding for animals. (See also *No. 293*).

The Thorn Apple can turn up at any time especially in ground that is freshly opened up so that dormant seeds are brought to germinating level. In fact there are well authenticated records of seed germinating after being buried for eighty years. The entire plant is poisonous, the seeds particularly so, both to humans and

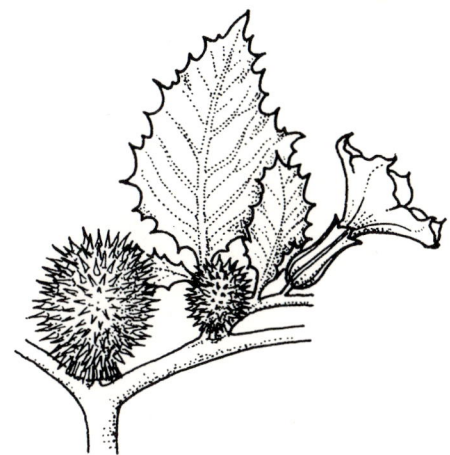

No. 553 Datura stramonium, *the Thorn Apple: the white, sometimes purple-stained trumpet bloom with its thorned fruit is one of the most poisonous plants found in the garden.*

animals. It is an annual, and will grow to perhaps 2 ft. tall with many branches bearing large coarse leaves that are irregularly lobed and pointed. During July and August large single white—sometimes stained violet purple —flowers are borne from the axils of the leaves on short stalks. These flowers have a sickly scent, and are followed by a large prickly seed capsule hence the name Thorn Apple, and not all that unlike the husk of the common conker. This capsule contains a number of wrinkled black seeds in which the alkaloid poisons are even more concentrated than in the rest of the plant.

To let the capsules burst is to ensure that you get a whole crop next and succeeding years. The precautions therefore are to treat with care and with gloved hands and covered arms; pull up and burn every leaf and piece of each plant. Do not spray with weedkiller. Apart from the obvious danger of damage to other plants, there is the added risk that because the poisons do not disintegrate in the dead plant, the dried withered leaves will still be a potential danger.

There is only one safe method of dealing with it; whilst it is still young and before those seeds are scattered, burn it.

Incidentally—since you mention it—it is not a wise policy to save your own beans year after year. It is inevitable that vigour will decline no matter how well you grow them, and quite unwittingly you may be contentedly growing plants that are sub-normal and producing a crop far less than you could be getting. Use fresh seed each year and you will get much better cropping—especially if you use F.1. Hybrids.

554 Do fallen yew needles poison the soil?

We are worried about some shrubs growing close to a yew tree in the garden. Although they were chosen as being shade-lovers and seem to be doing well, I wonder if the falling yew needles will eventually kill them. Will the needles release poisonous substances into the soil when they decay?

The yew tree, Taxus, is well known as a distinguished evergreen tree which can live to a great age. It will tolerate clipping and being slow growing is much used as a hedge that does not need a great deal of attention to keep it in shape. However, it is poisonous in all parts, especially the berries and in particular the seed within the berry, to all warm-blooded animals and also to fish. Birds eat the berries, but presumably not enough at any one time to prove fatal, and furthermore they do not digest the lethal seeds voiding them before being affected.

The yew is a conifer, and the leaves—like most conifer trees such as pine and firs etc.— are leathery, spiny, and as they dry, become very hard and woody. Being evergreen, they do not drop in one big autumnal fall, but gradually over a long period and being woody take a long time to even begin the process of rotting down, so that a thick layer can eventually develop.

It is not any poison in these leaves that can harm other plants and, in any case, being organic in origin the poison will be completely broken down by bacteria like everything else that is organic. The trouble can come, first to shallower rooting plants like ground cover in and around the tree and occasionally to the tree itself, from this thick, undecomposing mat soaking up rainfall, holding it so that it doesn't penetrate through to the soil and roots. On a sloping site, this effect is intensified by the increased tendency of rain to run-off this thatch-like mat. Left undisturbed so that it gets thicker and thicker, this mat can eventually develop a permanently wet, putrient layer, that is an effective barrier to the passage of air into the soil. This causes fertility to be reduced, see *Nos. 456, 465* and *475*, and other shallower rooting plants naturally suffer.

The best policy is to help the decomposition process and break up the mat by lightly forking with a small border fork. This admits air and encourages bacteria to decompose the woody yew leaves. If you already have a heavy build-up, there is no reason why you should not treat them like wood shavings and mix them with other material on a special compost heap, but you will have to make the heap properly so that heat is generated and the resistant yew leaves are thoroughly decomposed. See also *Nos. 476* and *492* which are relevant.

555 *Bowls and dishes made of yew wood*

Would food vessels of yew be dangerous to use because of the tree's poisonous capacity?

The yew is the most poisonous of all trees, containing hydrocyanic acid, the alkaloid ephedrine, and an irritant volatile oil. Drying and storage—seasoning the wood—does not lessen the toxicity.

It would be difficult for you to ingest toxic amounts from bowls and plates, but small though the risk may be, it is enough to deter yew turnery being offered for sale for domestic purposes. Hot moist food may well become tainted, though it is not likely that you would suffer anything more serious than a tummy upset.

If you are contemplating wood turning or wood carving, seal the wood with two coats of clear polyurethane varnish and restrict use to holding fruits with peel, cakes in paper or metallic cups, or use a paper liner for the bowl. See also *No. 554.*

Section *XVII*

Miscellaneous

556 How to avoid blisters when pruning

I have over four hundred roses and many shrubs in a lovely garden but I get terrible blisters every time I have to do the pruning. I have tried the french chalk method on my pair of secateurs, but it hasn't really helped. Do you have any other ideas?

The best way to avoid blisters is to analyse how they are caused, and then try to avoid that cause. Hand blisters on the pads of the fingers and the ball of the thumb are due not so much to the repeated *direct* pressure but to rolling pressure which tends to 'slide' the layers of skin under each other.

This occurs also, but to lesser extent, when digging, where most of the trouble is caused because the spade is being handled too tightly. A looser grip allows the handle and shaft to move with far less skin friction and resulting blistering. A polished lubricated surface further helps to prevent the top layer of the skin from sticking and sliding against the layers underneath. French chalk to make the handle slippery (see *No. 534*) and a lighter grip can make a lot of difference to digging blisters, but the use of secateurs is somewhat different.

If you look carefully at the position of the finger pads as the hand curls around the handles, you will see how ideally placed the pads are to be rolled each time the secateurs are squeezed and of course you cannot handle them lightly because their very use and action involves squeezing pressure. Various easy-action secateurs have been evolved from time to time intended among other things, to reduce this pressure. Although they are a tremendous improvement, they do not stop the likelihood of blisters when a lot of work has to be done because the same basic skin sliding and rolling is still there.

Allowing the top layer of skin to slide more easily against the handles and so less against the skin layers beneath, is much better and this is why shiny plastic handles are fitted to most makes, certainly the better ones. However, you still have the basic cause of trouble, skin rolling or sliding, and it is clear that the only way to avoid blistering altogether is to make the rolling and sliding take place somewhere other than between the layers of skin. This is achieved by turning the finger handle into a roller so that with each squeeze, the handle rolls and slides instead of the skin.

Each year professional rose growers have to prune many, many thousands of plants in a concentrated non-stop pruning session—a job lasting for many days on end, and even allowing for hardened hands, you can trust the trade to have found out by sheer experience which secateurs best permit the work to go on unhindered by blisters.

By far the most frequently used secateurs in the trade, and you can therefore draw your own conclusions, have a revolving handle. They are made in Switzerland by Felco and are distributed in the U.K. by Burton McCall Ltd. of Leicester.

Incidentally it is wrong to speak of a 'pair of secateurs'—you use secateurs, not a pair of them—unless you have secateurs in each hand!

557 Building a peat retaining wall

How can I construct a peat wall and what sort of plants can be put into it?

By its very nature, a peat wall cannot have the structural strength of brick and stone and, indeed, if a peat wall were to stand exposed on both sides, it would not be long before drying and oxidation reduced the wall to a heap. Therefore, a peat wall is for its appearance and support of plant life, and essentially a facing to a bank or raised bed of soil. It is used, for instance, when constructing an acid soil bank in an area of alkalinity, see *No. 116*, or walling to a 'lazy bed' in an area subject to a high water level and flooding, see *No. 478*. The surface blocks never dry out completely and absorb moisture from the soil at their backs. In the former case, the entire 'acid' bed will be built upon an insulating sheet of plastic.

Peat blocks suitable for making a peat wall are obtainable from Alexpeat, Burnham-on-Sea, Somerset, and as they are cut in various sizes, write for details. You should be able to

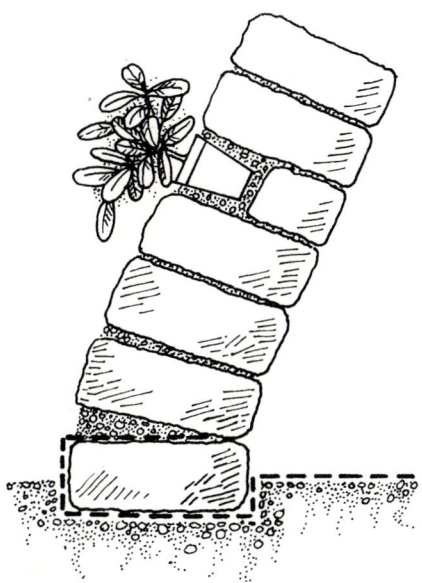

No. 557 *A peat block wall construction showing method of 'laying back' to avoid the later possibility of the wall collapsing outwards as the bank settles. When laying on a plastic sheet on chalk soil, tuck in the edge protruding from the trench between the first and second layers of blocks, as indicated by the dotted line.*

calculate roughly how many you will want; always calculate as though the blocks are going to be laid touching. This will produce a surplus that will cover any loss due to breakages, settling and replacement.

Begin by taking out a shallow trench about 1–1½ ins. deep and as wide as a peat block. This is to lock the base of the intended wall. If you are making an acid bed, lay the plastic sheet across the trench and place the first row of peat blocks touching. If you have any broken roughage, use this – otherwise use some of the soil/compost/leaf mould/peat with which you are going to back fill—to form a wedge an inch thick at the outside edge, sloping down to nil at the inside edge, so that the second row of blocks tilt slightly. Set this second row and every succeeding row slightly back towards the centre of bed so that the row below juts out

about ½ in. As the wall is built, it will therefore lean inwards and so reduce any later tendency to settle, move and fall outwards.

The second and succeeding rows of blocks should be laid midway over those in the row underneath—like a brick wall—with about a ½–¾ in. gap between. These gaps should be filled with back fill soil tamped in firmly. Lay another wedge of soil or roughage not quite so thick this time and lay the third row, again with each block directly above the gaps below. Back filling the bed with soil should now begin, firming by treading. The fourth row will not need a wedge, this and succeeding rows will be sloping enough so that heavy rain is led down the sloping peat blocks into the bank rather than being shed. Continue laying and back filling to the desired height.

If you intend putting plants into the wall face, use a half block or a broken one and fill the space with a flower pot. This can then be taken out later and a suitable plant tamped into the hole. Of course, the kind of plants that you will grow will depend upon the purpose of the raised bed, and the type of back fill used. As the usual reason is to enable lime-hating plants to be grown in limy chalk areas, one would expect to plant the dwarfer (unless the bed is very large and deep) kinds of Rhododendrons, Azaleas, Camellia, Pieris, Enkianthus, Eucryphia, Kalmia etc. enhanced by patches of heather. The flowering season can be extended by underplanting with spring- and summer-flowering bulbs, especially lilies which can rise through the shrubs and hang their lovely blooms above.

Do bear in mind, though, that a raised bed is an exposed bed, and subject to drying out faster than the soil at ground level. Never allow plants to dry out, and of course try to use only rainwater.

558 *Cleaning white marble garden statues*

How can I clean stains, algae and lichen from a white Italian marble garden statue?

How successful you will be will depend upon the scale and nature of any damage to the surface of the marble. Using a brush to work into cracks and crevices, wash with a solution of a proprietary algacide like Dinamin. Swab down with clean water to remove all killed algae and remove surface dirt. Alternatively, use domestic bleach at about 2 tablespoonfuls per gallon of warm water. As your hands will be in contact with this liquid for some time whilst you are doing the job, rubber gloves would be advisable. Swab down with clear water as before.

If this doesn't clean the statue sufficiently, you will have to be a little more drastic. Professional stone cleaners may use oxalic acid at this stage, but it is poisonous and you would need to be very careful and I would not recommend it for amateur use. Use instead a very mild abrasive with a soft plastic brush—I have seen very effective cleaning done with a soft nylon brush and Ajax bleach powder. If the surface has become roughened, even coarser abrasive may be called for and you will then have to use marble dust. You should be able to get this from a monumental mason; they use it for cleaning head stones.

When you have it clean and dry, paint the entire statue with a water repelling silicone solution so that water is shed at once and the effect of weather is minimised. The stone mason would probably advise you and perhaps supply a suitable repellent, or you can use Nubex which you can obtain from a builder's merchant.

559 Recipe for making Gardener's Ale

Our local horticultural society is planning a social evening, and all the refreshments are to be made from garden produce. Someone remembers having a drink called Gardener's Ale, which he believes is home-made. Could you please provide us with a recipe for this?

This is an alcoholic drink of the home-made variety, except that it does not use produce from the garden, despite its name.

The following is a recipe given to me by a friend who learned the recipe and art of making it from the shepherds and farming folk of Romney Marsh, and the story is that it has been handed down from the times when the area was notorious for smuggling and hard drinking. It is very potent—you have been warned!

You will need a handful of hops—all right for those who live amongst the hop fields of Kent. Everyone else will have to translate this as 2 oz. of the dried variety from the wine-making section of a supermarket or chemist. These should be steeped in 2 gallons of cold water overnight in a large enamel preserving pan; at no time use a galvanised vessel. In the morning, bring to the boil and keep boiling fairly rapidly for about half to three quarters of an hour. Whilst still very hot, pour off the liquor through butter muslin or a strainer into an earthenware or non-metallic vessel. Knowing what is coming, I suggest you use a large plastic bucket or bin, but one which you can stand in a bowl. Stir in 2 lbs. of malt extract—you'll probably get this from the same wine and beer making department, and 2 lbs. of brown demerara sugar.

If you like a really 'gutsy' brew with lessened bitterness but increased potency, also stir in up to 1 lb. of golden syrup. Give it a frequent stir whilst cooling. Towards evening, when cool, take a little of the liquor, now called 'wort', and use this with 1 oz. of brewer's yeast—or failing that use baker's yeast—to whip up a frothy paste. It is important to whip plenty of air into it so that it gets a good froth. Some people used to tip this straight into the 'wort', presumably they were in a hurry, because the fermentation starts at a terrific pace, very often overflowing the vessel—hence the bowl or tray in which it is stood. A more gentle fermentation is obtained by smearing the frothy paste on a thick slice of toast, wholemeal bread is best, like a thick layer of butter and floating this on the surface.

When the initial burst of violent fermentation steadies down, skim off the scum that forms. In about ten days, the fermentation will be almost complete with only a few bubbles still rising. If it is still working fast, leave it for another day or so until it has quietened down further, then syphon off the brew with a clear polythene tube into screw top beer bottles.

Corking is not really advisable unless you can secure them because you are going to build-up pressure in the bottles and the corks can easily pop.

Into each 1 pint bottle, add half a level teaspoonful of white granulated sugar; if you are using quart-sized bottles, a level teaspoonful of course, or if you like a real fizzer with a good 'head' on it, double this last sugar addition but don't blame me or write to me if the bottle bursts! The addition of this little extra sugar prior to stoppering and just before fermentation finally ceases, is just enough to revive the yeast bacteria and cause a slight secondary fermentation. The carbon dioxide gas cannot escape as it did when the wort was exposed and, instead, builds-up pressure within the bottle and has to dissolve in the ale. Don't shake to dissolve the sugar or you'll risk exploding the bottle; leave it to the bacteria to convert it.

Screw the stoppers tight and handle the bottles gently from now on. In about eighteen to twenty-one days, the ale will be ready for drinking. When pouring, handle the bottle steadily, being careful not to stir up and pour out any sediment at the bottom of the bottle. Don't overdo it and drink too much especially if you are only a casual drinker; it is very potent.

Remember that you need a licence to *sell* alcoholic drink, so no money must pass hands.

560 Hedgehogs in the garden

How can I deter hedgehogs from digging my lawn?

You can deter the hedgehogs from digging in the lawn but, whatever you do, don't harm them. They are the most efficient exterminators of slugs, snails, woodlice and other pests that damage your plants. It is a pity that they are scratching into your lawn, but evidently they are interested in grubs, worms and insects which probably are present in large numbers to have attracted their attention. You can deter them by removing the food source from under the lawn and diverting their attentions elsewhere.

Chlordane will clear worms and grubs from the lawn (see *No. 455*) so that any further digging and scratching will be a waste of time, and the hedgehogs will have to seek food somewhere else. Don't let them stray too far, however. Hedgehogs are entirely beneficial to the garden, so it is better to encourage them to stay around by putting out a saucer of bread and milk each evening. They adore this and will come regularly for it, taking a good toll of garden pests as well.

561 How are plants classified?

How are plants classified? Is it by the similarity of the flowers? I always wondered why Lobelia cardinalis *is so different from the little blue lobelia, but the other day I realised that the flowers of the two plants were identical except for the colour. Also, why do plants have to have such tongue-twisting names; surely there is an easier way?*

The classification of plants is based upon first, the basic characteristics, then major distinction and finally of minor variation. In the case of flowering plants, the classification will be based upon the floral parts. Plants belonging to the same family have the same kind of flower, although the leaves, stems and habit of growth may be entirely different. Thus flowers with four petals arranged in the form of a cross belong to the family or botanical order Cruciferae—crucifer—a cross.

Apples and pears belong to the order Rosaceae which may be surprising since, on the face of it, the bloom bears little resemblance to a rose. The basic connection is explained by the fact that the natural species of rose, perhaps typified in most minds by the single type, has five petals—the same as apples and pears. Although the bloom that most of us associate with the rose has many more petals, these are always in multiples of five.

Each family or order is divided into genera. Thus we have Rosa, the generic name for the rose, and Pyrus, the generic name for apples and pears. The genus Pyrus is often subdivided into species—*Pyrus malus*—the apple,

Pyrus communis—the pear, and these are further subdivided into varieties.

The Lobelia is a genus which is part of the family Campanulaceae. *L. cardinalis*, with scarlet flowers, grows to 3 ft. and originates from North America, whereas the small blue edging plant, *L. erinus*, comes from South Africa. Poles apart in origin, height and colour, but they have enough fundamental construction in common to place them in the same genus. As you say, it is remarkable how members of the same family can differ, but one sees variation no less in other walks of life.

Latin and Greek are the internationally accepted languages of learning and the long names you have difficulty in pronouncing are anglicised forms of those ancient languages and are used throughout the world. If you were to converse with a gardener from another country and you called a daisy 'a daisy', he most likely would not understand, but call it by its proper name *Bellis perennis*, he will immediately know exactly what you are talking about.

The reason why common names are not used is simple: what is common? That which people in the south of England call bluebells, a Scotsman calls harebells. Write to an Indian nurseryman and ask for Arisaema, he will know at once what you want; but ask him for the same thing and call it by our common hedgerow name of Cuckoo pint or Lords and Ladies and he would be totally lost.

Each locality and every country has its own common names, but there is only one botanical name. Your tongue may be a little confused getting round these, but that is nothing to the confusion we would all be in if we began using our own localised names.

You will note that the Index to this book has been compiled under the Latin names, with cross-references to the English common names. This is so because of the very reasons given above.

562 *Invasive roots from the next garden*

Roots from my neighbour's boundary hedge are invading my garden, and I've a strip 3 ft. wide where nothing will grow because of them. What can I do?

There is only one solution in a case like this: physical obstruction. Visit a builders' scrap yard, or watch out for a local demolition job, and try to get sheets of corrugated iron. This way, you should get them cheaper than buying new. The most common size sheet is 6 ft. × 2 ft. 3 ins. and you will need to cut these into two 3 ft. halves. This is not an easy job and probably the best way, without the specialist tools, is to saw through the tops of the ridges with an Eclipse Junior hacksaw, (this is quite inexpensive and is a very useful tool to have around for other jobs); then turn the sheet over, and saw again opposite the first cuts.

Paint the sheets with bitumastic paint so that they resist deterioration in the soil. Take out a 3 ft. deep trench as close up to your boundary as you can get—you will have to sever any roots you come to. Position the sheets with a good tight overlap fit each time, and back-fill the excavated soil.

If you can get asbestos sheets, corrugated or flat, so much the better. They will not rot and will not need painting.

563 *Mistletoe without berries*

A bunch of mistletoe grows on an apple tree and increases in size every year, but it has no berries. Why?

The mistletoe, *Viscum album*, is unisexual—plants are either male or female. Only the female plant can bear berries and, in order to do so, its flowers have to receive pollen from a nearby male plant.

Even if you are able to determine the sex of your plant, you would not be able to positively determine the suitability of the seed before implanting it into the tree—whether it will produce a plant of the required sex—and in any case it is most unlikely that good berries would be borne by the female of a solitary pair.

Your best course is to take the seed from several berries and implant them about eighteen inches apart around your existing plant. You can save berries at Christmas time, allow them to dry and in late March, implant them by cutting notches through the bark of the apple or a hawthorn, and pressing a seed into each cut so that it makes contact with the green cambium layer beneath the bark. Do this with several plants and it is virtually certain that some will be berry bearing females.

564   Re-starting the mower after the winter lay-up

I need advice on starting motor mowers after winter storage. Can you please help?

There are two basic causes of difficulty of starting after a long lay-up: mechanical and fuel degradation. The more important mechanical causes are dampness resulting in a poor or even no spark, worn sooty plugs, and lowered compression due to the engine cylinder having become dry during the long period of inactivity and therefore being unlubricated. During the winter, rising damp, which can affect the electrics—those parts of the engine concerned with generating the spark—can be largely eliminated by storing the mower off the ground so that there is plenty of ventilation around it to prevent condensation.

However, that's what happens to a great many machines despite all the warnings and admonitions in magazines and journals to take better care. So here are a few steps to take with a reluctant engine.

In the case of a four-stroke engine (you do not mix oil and petrol in this type) if the cord pulls easily with little or no resistance from the engine compression, you can suspect that a valve has stuck open. Take out the spark plug, and shine a torch in the hole. It is usually possible to make out at least part of the circular tops of the two valves, inlet and exhaust. One of them—usually the exhaust—may be open, raised, and when the starter cord is pulled to turn the engine, it doesn't move. When the engine last stopped, this valve was in the open position and it has remained so all winter and is now stuck.

Squirt in a little diesel oil, penetrating oil, or a little Redex oil (which is sold on the garage forecourt as an oil shot when you buy petrol), mixed with a few drops of paraffin and then go and have a cup of tea. By the time you come back, the oil should have worked in and freed the valve. If it still doesn't move when you pull the cord, take a piece of hardwood, not metal under any circumstances. Try to reach the valve top with it and give it a sharp tap. If that fails, do no more as you will need professional help.

With a freely moving valve and oil under the valve seats, you should now have good compression but before trying to start the engine, clean the plug with a wire brush and reset the spark gap, or fit a new plug, making sure it is the right type or you can do very serious damage. Do this also with two-stroke engines; and from now on the advice applies to both two- and four-stroke types.

Take off and clean the carburettor in clean fresh petrol. This is necessary to remove any gum or sediment. Completely drain off the petrol tank of any old fuel, flush it out with fresh petrol and drain off again, throwing it all away since it will have deteriorated. Reassemble, tank up with fresh petrol and you should get life. If not, suspect the electrics.

If the engine has a stopping switch, make sure it is on! Every mower mechanic in the country has at some time been called out to a mower that refuses to start despite everything —and has found the switch—'off'! Check for a spark by removing the plug, reconnect the lead and lay the plug on the cylinder or other bare metal. Turn the engine over quickly to see if it sparks. If it doesn't, you need professional help.

This advice may seem elementary to those gardeners who own motor cycles or cars, but to others it will seem a great deal of trouble. Here is a tip that will avoid much of it, will help easy starting at all times, and drastically reduce wear within your engine.

Get a can of a very special oil called UP4 Silicone oil if your engine is a four-stroke and runs on neat petrol, and get UP2 if it is a two-stroke engine and have to mix oil with petrol. Never buy ready-mixed petrol mixture from a garage. Mix your own so that it is always fresh and follow the mix instructions from the mower handbook.

You will *not* get this oil at a garage, and unfortunately not many mower service depots stock it yet either. So write to Messrs J. Gibbs, of Bedfont, Middlesex for details. Dissolve one teaspoonful of the oil in every gallon of petrol you use in your mower at all times including the two-stroke oil-petrol mixture. A special additive causes this silicone oil to put an extremely hard silicone lining on all interior surfaces of the engine. The lubricating oil bonds firmly onto this rendering the engine permanently lubricated right through the winter so that the engine can be re-started each spring with a lubricated cylinder and piston.

Normally it is wise to run an engine out to exhaust the petrol tank after the last cut, because petrol can degrade to a poor turpentine-like quality when left to stand for long periods, and no petrol engine will start on that. With this 'doctored' petrol, degradation is inhibited but it is still wise to run the tank out, when laying up for the winter.

Ideally, all cylinder mowers should be sharpened and overhauled properly during the close season, but with escalating costs more gardeners are bound to be tempted to dispense with overhauls. Rotary mowers at least have the advantage that they do not need regrinding— sharpening the blades is very much a DIY job. Always keep the cutting edges sharp, mowing with blunt blades is a life shortening overload on the engine of a rotary mower and murder for the grass. With the cutter bar type, always check the bar after sharpening by balancing on a knife edge across the centre of the attachment hole. Not a precise way to balance a blade, but better than putting it back regardless. Running an engine with an unbalanced blade can cause vibration bad enough to damage the engine. Simply file more metal away from the heavier end until you achieve a good balance.

565 Recipe for making nettle beer

I have heard that nettle beer is very good, and since I am besieged by them, I'd like to try but cannot find a recipe. Can you tell me something about it please?

This is a very old country drink and a favourite in parts of Lancashire and the north-west where it is quite a cottage industry, catering for tourists.

The recipes naturally vary a little from place to place and maker to maker, but here is a good general one that allows for quite a bit of variation and experiment to suit your own particular taste.

Collect a two-gallon bucketful of soft nettle tops and after giving them a good wash, put them in a preserving pan with 2 gallons of water, 2 ozs. of hops (you can get these from a herbalists, some large chemists or a shop specialising in wine and beer-making materials), 2–3 lbs. of malt and about a level teaspoonful of ground ginger. Bring to the boil, stir and simmer for 15 mins. Strain at once, and stir to completely dissolve up to 1 lb. of sugar which should be added slowly. This will vary according to how strong you want the resulting beer, but don't add much over the 1lb. since fermentation can be fierce and too much sugar has been known to explode a bottle. Allow to cool naturally, and whilst it is doing this, whisk up ½ oz. of yeast in just a little of the liquor. Again this is where there can be some variation; different yeasts can be tried. One used for lager beer would probably be the best to begin with and you can experiment with other yeasts at a later date. Whisk to a froth, get as much air into it as you can, and by the time the main liquor, now called 'wort', has cooled to 65°F. the yeast should already be working. Add the yeast froth to the liquor, stir it well to get it thoroughly mixed, and using a funnel, bottle it into screw-top beer bottles. You can begin sampling your brew after 12 hours, but it is better after standing for a couple of days.

If you do vary the above recipe, make only a slight variation at a time so that you do not get a brew you cannot control. I have known the above recipe to be very potent, so take it very steady until you know the strength of your brew. By all means swap drinks or give your friends a bottle, but always remember, that no money must change hands or you will be in trouble with the law.

566 Plants delivered in poor condition

I received an order of shrubs in poor condition,

*and the nursery blame this on the carriers and dis-
claim responsibility. Can I claim replacements?*

Whether you can acutally claim replacements
depends upon the terms of the sale and whether
you have complied with them. No nurseryman
who has produced and nurtured a young plant
likes to be told by his customer that it has failed
to grow—and nobody likes to have to complain.

Good nurserymen are good nurserymen
because, apart from other things, they appreciate the hazards of dispatching by post, BRS and
rail. They therefore take care to protect the
plants from damage, cold and the worst problem of all, drying out.

However, problems can and do arise even in
the best of nurseries. When you receive your
plants, if some are drying out or even dead, contact the supplier at once, by telephone if
possible, backed up by a confirming lettei, then
return the plants to the nursery.

In their terms of business, nurseries stipulate the terms upon which they offer replacements or refund, and provided that you have
complied with those terms—which you will
have done by returning the plants immediately
—the supplier is bound to honour your claim
in full, including all postal and carriage charges.
If, despite such compliance you do not receive
satisfaction, and your order was placed in response to an advertisement in a national newspaper or a journal, complain to the paper
concerned, giving full details—dates, cheque
numbers, correspondence etc., and ask them to
intercede. All advertisers have to give under-
takings to uphold standards in accordance with
a code of advertising and mail order practice
and a good paper will pursue a breach of the
undertaking.

Of course, undue delay in transit is not the
fault of the sender, but is a matter for both the
sender and yourself, the receiver, to take up
with the carrier. The best advice I can give in
this respect is to hammer them hard because
they are transporting live and perishable goods
that will spoil if delayed too long.

If you decide to accept the plants, follow the
advice in *No. 94* about heeling in and treatment of dry plants, but bear in mind that you
definitely do not have grounds for complaint
when you plant trees, shrubs or plants knowing
they have arrived in dry or poor condition, and
do not notify the nursery until several months
after, when they haven't grown.

You may be very disappointed and annoyed
but there is nothing to be gained in taking it out
on the nurseryman or complaining to the newspaper about the advertisements they carry. The
sender has no control over plants the moment
they leave his premises and an irate unreason-
able approach by you will not help.

Good nurserymen are concerned about their
goodwill, and are always ready to respond to a
reasonable approach.

567 Removing bitumen paint from teak furniture

*I have a teak garden bench which has been
painted with black bituminous paint. How can I
remove this?*

Teak is an extraordinarily durable wood and is
a favourite material, therefore, for garden
seats and tables that stand out in all weathers.
Even so, not only can this longevity be improved
by treating with suitable preservatives, but the
natural beauty of the wood is heightened.

Painting teak garden furniture with bituminous paint is sacrilege. Soften the bitumen
paint with bitumen solvent, and leave it for a
while. From a DIY shop or ironmongers you
can get a Skarsten scraper to which can be fitted serrated and plain interchangeable blades.
Begin with the serrated blade to cut into the
paint but don't scrape so hard that the serrations dig into the surface of the wood. As the
wood is bared, switch to the plain blade and
work to a smooth paint-free finish.

Rub down with wire wool and paint with a
proprietary teak oil like Cuprinol Teak, or
make your own: equal parts linseed oil and
turpentine well shaken and mixed. Apply
several coats and let it soak well into joints so
that the water repellent nature of the oil can
build up and do its job of preserving. Let it dry
thoroughly before sitting on the seat. Alternatively, give the seat a few coats of clear
polyurethane varnish and it will last for years.

568   Weedkiller sprayed over the fence

Can I lawfully spray weedkiller over my neighbour's fence to prevent his weeds from growing in my garden?

Certainly not! Unless you get permission to do so, you could land yourself in all kinds of trouble, trespass for a start, and if the neighbour chooses to be awkward, the weeds could suddenly become 'valuable plants' that you have destroyed.

If your neighbour will not respond to rational discussion, and recognise the mutual advantages of bringing the weeds under control, perhaps even letting you do the job for him, you may have to think in terms of putting in a barrier. You are entitled to remove all overhanging and intrusive plant growth, including roots, to the fence line, but not beyond. See *No. 562.*

You could resort to legal action, and in that case you will have to be able to demonstrate or prove nuisance.

569   When a tree obstructs light

How do I stand with my neighbour who has ordered me to cut down my chestnut tree which he claims is blocking his light?

Some people will act big and officious in the hope that others are gullible enough to be frightened into letting them have their way. Legally, your neighbour has no right to order you to cut down a tree growing on your own land. To make you do so, he would have to get a court order, and to get this he would have to prove that the tree constitutes danger or nuisance and that it trespasses on his land—i.e. that it takes light and that the roots draw excessive nourishment and hinder cultivation. See also *No. 568.*

If you are quite certain that the tree does not contribute nuisance in any way, and that such a claim could not be substantiated, you have nothing to fear. Indeed, if the tree is well-established you may well be able to turn the tables by getting your local council to make a protection order on the tree.

What your neighbour can do, is to request you to remove growth that overhangs his land and if you do not comply, he is then entitled to remove such growth himself and this applies to roots also. But he can only go as far as the boundary line, not beyond, into and above your ground.

There is another point, however, about this question of which you, and your neighbour, do not seem to be aware. If a chestnut is near enough to a building to be arguably obstructing light, it may well be near enough to constitute a greater danger to drains and even foundations because of soil shrinkage. See *Nos. 122* and *138.*

570   The Venus fly trap: how to gain optimum growth

Having tried to grow two Venus fly trap plants and failed I am writing to ask your advice. I watered the last one I purchased with distilled water according to the instructions that came with it, but it still failed to break into leaf.

The insect-eating Venus fly trap *Dionaea muscipula* comes from the bogs and marshes of Carolina, U.S.A. and, as always with plants from other climes imported into Britain, basic cultivation must consist of trying to create conditions as similar as possible to the home habitat.

Dry living conditions, possibly standing on a sunny window sill, or near the apparently optimum place, by an open window where the flies come in, are quite wrong, and if the plant is to be really happy you may have to go to some lengths, depending upon your particular circumstances, to create a mini 'bog and marsh' atmosphere.

The plant really needs to be grown in association with living sphagnum moss. It is not at all uncommon to see the plant being sold in kit form—pot, cover and growing medium consisting of peat and sphagnum that is completely dry and dead, and I have seen them in peat only with no sphagnum at all. Such plants are doomed from the start.

Living green sphagnum can usually be obtained from a good florist. Mix enough of this with an equal proportion of peat to fill the pot and set the plant in this, the best time being March–April. If you use a clay pot, which is porous and preferable to plastic but not absolutely necessary, pull a little peat through the central drainage hole. This is going to act as a wick to carry moisture to the plant.

Now you have to create a little surrounding marsh area. Position this pot in another, larger, pot giving 1–1½ inches clearance all round. Place enough coarse peat in the bottom so that the central pot containing the plant is lifted level with the top of the outer pot, and note how thick this layer is, an inch, an inch and a half or whatever. Pack the space around the sides with sphagnum and if possible with live moss at the top. The double pot should now be stood in a bowl, pot, saucer or tray containing rain water nearly as deep as the layer of peat that you noted. In this way, you will know that the pot with the plant in it is almost level with, but very slightly clear of water which will, of course, enter the drainage holes of the outer container and soak into the peat and up into the moss. Then via the 'wick', it will be passed through the inner drainage hole to reach the plant itself. This arrangement ensures that the plant will not be in standing water, but it will be marshy!

Many Venus trap outfits are sold with a clear plastic cover. This is intended to maintain a small humid mini atmosphere around the leaves. You will do very much better to arrange two wire hoops stuck in the outer container and then put the entire arrangement—water saucer as well—into a large plastic bag which, supported by the wires, becomes a canopy. Leave the bag propped wide open so that you can easily replenish the water in the tray as it evaporates; so that flies and insects can get in and so that you can see them being gobbled up as the jaws close.

Finally, you must keep the plant cool. It positively hates temperatures much above 55–60°F., and although the water tray and outer 'marsh' pot of sphagnum will take care of the humidity, if you stand the plant in sunlight it is going to get like an oven inside. A dappled light, even partial shade, is best. Keep the tray topped up to the required depth, not with distilled water which is sterile and quite unnatural, but with rainwater. If you live in a flat and cannot collect rainwater easily, thaw out some frost from the refrigerator or freezer but don't use ice cubes since they may contain lime from the tap water. Use the frozen condensation—frost—which will be lime free but which contains dissolved air and other gases in the atmosphere. After natural rain this is the next best. See also *No. 571*.

571 The Venus fly trap : dying leaves

Why do the tips of each leaf of my Venus fly trap plant die back after having trapped a fly, which seems to disintegrate and rot on the leaf. The plant is small but it catches plenty of flies.

First read *No. 570* concerning the cultivation of the plant and get that right, because the symptoms you describe so often are due to a plant that is only just about living, not thriving, and therefore cannot cope with the flies it catches.

A growing plant will be risky to disturb by replanting but there is no reason why you cannot get the pot into an outer container and water tray, and into a humidity canopy. You can then expect your plant to begin to thrive in the better conditions and when healthy and vigorous, you can expect it to develop a new trap about every 9–10 days and at any one time to bear as many as sixteen traps. Each should last from 6 to 10 weeks, at the end of which they gradually turn black. You can then snip them away with scissors, to be replaced by other traps which rise from the bulbous root.

As autumn approaches and your plant exhausts the local supply of flies, keep the plants just ticking over by removing the water from the tray, but of course keep the tray in place to collect any seepage. A plant that has done poorly will appreciate an artificial feed once a fortnight with a very weak balanced liquid feed —Bio Sangral or Maxicrop—before it dies back for its winter rest.

If it has grown well and successfully digested plenty of flies, it will have built up its reserves and be looking for a rest until it resumes its wholly admirable fly gobbling next spring. You will frequently see the advice that you should drop pieces of minced meat into the jaws—well, if you think that this is what happens in its natural habitat, do that. Some of the apologies that one hears about, no doubt need this supplementary feeding of artificial flies but the plant would do a lot better if given conditions more closely resembling its natural habitat and being allowed to catch its own menu.

If flies are scarce and unwilling to sacrifice themselves a very effective lure that I have never known to fail is to put two tablespoonfuls of beer in a saucer placed alongside the plant—at the entrance to the canopy bag is ideal. In a few days as the beer becomes stale the flies will come flocking.

572 Domestic geese for keeping down the grass

Which is the best breed of domestic goose for keeping down grass?

Without doubt, Chinese geese. They are not very large, 10 to 12 lbs. only—which is something to consider because geese are a little frightening to some people. They are good layers of large eggs and will graze on grass when it is actively growing, but in winter and early spring they will need the supplement of mash, corn, cooked potato and/or pellets.

A good nucleus would consist of a gander and four or five geese and as they are hardy they will not need elaborate housing, just a shelter from the worst weather, cold winds and for sleeping. Where foxes are about, however, it is advisable to shut them in at night.

It is a nice idea to keep grass down easily and cheaply, plus eggs, but there are a couple of points to bear in mind, however. They do not like long grass, and if forced by hunger to take in long strands, will impact themselves disastrously. The fresh young growth or sward they have grazed and have themselves manured seems to suit them best. A fairly large ranging area is required as they foul their habitat very quickly if it is too small, and it is therefore natural for them to walk continuously in the search for fresh clean grass.

Chinese geese are excellent guards; nobody will ever approach your house without your knowledge but, like other birds, they have their drawbacks. They tend to be noisy and rather troublesome if they don't have water for swimming. A child's paddling pool, about a foot deep, is the answer to that.

573 Kale for poultry

How can I ensure having kale for my hens throughout the year?

Kale is particularly good for poultry, not only for its nutritional value, but also for giving them much needed exercise, avoiding boredom and keeping their minds off such vices as feather picking. Kale should not be thrown on the floor where it can be fouled, but hung up just above head height so that the birds have to reach up, but not jump up for it. See also *No. 574*. Hang it fresh every morning, remove what is left at mid-day and use the remainder chopped and boiled in the mash. Using the cooking water to mix the mash—it is too full of goodness to tip down the drain.

Old, dry or withered kale or other brassicas —cabbage, sprouts, etc.—are a short cut to diarrhoea.

The following method should provide you with a steady supply and you can enter the cycle at the appropriate time when reading these notes. During February to late March, sow Dwarf Extra Curled under cloches for planting out in early May (always puddle them: see *Nos. 269, 270* and *271*) and cropping in early winter. In April sow Cottager's or Scotch Kale to puddle out in late May for cropping in late January to March or April.

Sow either of these varieties again in May, puddling out in July and cropping in March or April through to early June even to July. Between then and the first autumn early winter kale becoming available, you should have ample surplus lettuce and cabbage to keep up the green food supply. Don't forget, however, that what is good for poultry will be very attractive to the pigeon. Give it just half a chance to settle and it will strip you of kale, peas, strawberries and anything else you care to give it. This pest has an ability to consume food in huge quantities and its crop seems like a bottomless pit.

Various bird and pigeon scarers are available but all the pigeons I have ever known soon get used to them and their effectiveness depends largely on ringing the changes and introducing a different scarer as they learn to ignore another. The one really effective scarer is quite impracticable unless you live a long way from anyone else. This is a machine that produces a very loud bang every few minutes that is so violent that the birds don't seem to be able to get used to it.

574 Feather-pecking amongst poultry

What can I do to stop my hens feather pecking?

The causes of feather pecking are incorrect diet and overheating food, insufficient fresh greens (stale, wilted greenstuff is not only useless but can be dangerous, see *No. 573*), overcrowding and a too strict confinement, too long spent on the same ground which has become hen tired and sour, insufficient exercise, and probably the most important of all—boredom.

Hang fresh greenstuff every morning so that the birds have to reach for it without jumping and snatching. Anytime you have unwanted fatty food—dripping perhaps, stale fat, rancid butter, margarine, or meat scraps—mix this into their mash so that their fat and oil protein intake is improved.

If you can lay your hands on a bale or two of wheat or barley straw, as used for animal bedding, the birds will show a lot of interest in pulling it to bits and then scratching among the litter. All the time they have something to do their minds will be directed from trying to peck each other bald.

Some poultry keepers resort to debeaking and fitting 'bits' to the beak so that they cannot grip feathers. This tackles the symptom whilst ignoring the causes.

Try to run your birds over a different area of ground each year. See *No. 539*.

Glossary

Abscision Layer—A double layer of cells at the base of each leaf and fruit stalk which become corky, brittle and easily broken as the leaf nears the end of its useful life or the fruit ripens.

Acid Soils—Although not necessarily accurate in a strictly scientific sense, for most practical purposes acid soils may be regarded as those that are deficient or devoid of lime.

Adventitious Roots—are those that develop not from the main root but from other parts of the plant, i.e. the roots that form from cuttings and from layered stems are adventitious as are the above ground growth shoots that arise from damaged roots—one of the causes of suckers.

Annual—The descriptive term given to a plant that grows from a seed, flowers (to set seed for next year) and dies—all in the same year.

Artificial Fertilisers—are chemicals and nutrients prepared from sources that were not 'once living' and are therefore artificial. The opposite to 'organic'.

Axil—The axil is the angle between a leaf and the stem from which it arises. Similarly, an axilliary shoot is one that arises from the axil between leaf and stem. The side shoots removed from tomato plants are a familiar example.

Bass, Bast—A cream-coloured vegetable fibre, straw-like, thin, soft and supple. Split into thin strips, soaked and used wet to make it even more supple so that the knots do not slip loose, it is very useful for tying in and supporting shoots and stems.

Bastard Trenching—A form of double digging, with which term it is often confused. As in double digging, the soil is trenched two spits deep. In double digging, the spits are reversed so that what was the bottom spit comes to the top and the most fertile top layer finishes two spits down. In bastard trenching, the spits remain in their original positions, the bottom spit being merely dug and turned by fork, with the opportunity taken, perhaps, to work in compost. Especially when soils are mulched, fertility tends to increase in the top spit layer, and whether a patch is double or bastard trenched depends upon what is to be grown. For deeper-rooting subjects—shrubs, trees, roses— that would better utilise fertility at the deeper root level, the soil should be double dug with the spits reversed. For most garden plants and vegetables that are not so deeply rooted, the more fertile top spit should be at the top and the soil bastard trenched.

Biennials—are those plants the seed of which is sown one year, usually spring or summer, to produce plants that flower in the following year.

Bleeding—A plant is said to bleed when it exudes and loses sap after cutting or wounding.

Bolt, Bolting—Applied, in the main, to vegetable crops. This term describes the reaction of many leaf and root, annual and biennial plants—crops—to growth check, particularly dryness at root, in hastening to produce flower and thus seed, in an attempt to perpetuate their own species before anticipated death. Familiar examples are lettuce, all members of the cabbage family, beets, turnips, radishes and onions.

Bottom heat—is warmth applied from below seedlings and cuttings by equipment like a paraffin lamp, soil warming electric cable, or more naturally by fresh manure at the early heating-up stage of decomposition. It is the rising warmth that hastens germination, and encourages the development of root action which strives to work towards the warmth.

Bract—Botanically, a modified leaf on the flower stalk, usually quite near the flower when it may be highly coloured and mistaken for part of the flower itself. A familiar example is Poinsettia: the attractive scarlet parts are leaves, i.e. bracts, whilst the true flower is the small insignificant yellow centre of each cluster of bracts. Another example is the Hydrangea whose large mop head 'blooms' are composed entirely of bracts. The actual flowers are the tiny 'pips' in the centre of each floret.

Brassica—is the generic name for all members of the cabbage family, i.e. cabbages, broccoli, Brussels sprouts, cauliflower, Kohl Rabi.

Breaks—Shoots that are goaded into increased growth, and dormant buds that 'break' out, after a main growth shoot has been pinched, stopped or pruned. When a break occurs which has not been so prompted, it is called a 'natural break'.

Budding—is the term used to describe the method of propagation that involves a dormant bud or eye being taken from a special variety of rose, ornamental shrub or tree, fruit etc., and implanted under the bark in contact with the cambium layer of another type, usually, but not always, of more vigorous habit.

Calcifuge—A plant that has evolved in and become so adapted to living in acid lime-free soils that it does not thrive or indeed may find it impossible to live in soils where lime is present.

Callus Tissue—This is a layer or layers of special cells that form around a wound in both plant and animal tissue. Callus tissue is sometimes called healing or scar tissue and its speedy formation after wounding is important as a barrier against the ingress of disease.

Calomel—A compound of mercury and chlorine, effective as an inhibitor of many kinds of fungal growth.

Cambium Layer—A layer of cells, just one cell thick, through which most of the sap and nutrient flow is concentrated and may therefore be regarded for all practical purposes as the very lifestream of a plant. Its presence may be detected in woody tissue by lifting a tiny part of the bark tissue. The cambium is seen as the green layer beneath and this is a simple test to tell whether dormant wood is alive or dead.

Carbohydrates—are a range of complex compounds including starches and sugars formed of the three elements—carbon, hydrogen and oxygen. They are formed mainly in leaves in the presence of the green colouring matter, chlorophyll, during the process called photosynthesis in which light is the energy source. To enable the carbohydrate union to be formed, the energy is trapped within this union and when the compound is broken down, the energy is released as both light and heat (i.e. burning) or as the energy utilised by the plant for its own living and growth processes.

Catch Crop—A crop, usually a vegetable but it can as easily be flowers, always of rapid growth and coming to usable size or maturity —and grown between rows of slower-growing main crops—in order to 'catch' or 'snatch' an extra crop before the ground is wanted for another crop or before an already planted main crop grows to a size where it needs all the available space. Perhaps the most familiar examples are crops of lettuce, radishes, spring onions— even early peas when grown under cloches— taken whilst waiting for a crop of potatoes to sprout through the soil surface.

Chlorosis—is usually taken to mean the visible evidence in discoloured, deformed, even damaged leaves caused by a shortage in the soil of one or more essential plant nutrients. Nitrogen is needed by all plants in the elaboration of chlorophyll which colours leaves green and which is vitally concerned with photosynthesis (c.f.). Any shortage of nitrogen means less green colouring, chlorophyll, and leaves look pale and sickly. This condition of nitrogen shortage is called chlorosis—or more strictly nitrogen chlorosis—and as may be imagined can be a problem with plants that make a lot of leaf. Another main cause of chlorosis is caused either by an actual shortage of iron, or when this element is present in the soil but is locked into a chemical combination by the calcium in chalky and limy soils, and in a form that the plants cannot absorb. Other, not uncommon, causes of chlorosis may be shortage of magnesium, boron and other trace elements (c.f.).

Cloche—Devised in France, the earliest cloches were bell-shaped glass domes, hence the French name for a bell—cloche. The name has stuck ever since and is still applied to the very long tunnel-like glass, and in recent years plastic, coverings put over short-growing crops. The objective, like a miniature greenhouse, is to trap the sun's warmth, to raise the temperature of the soil, to protect from wind and cold, and to create congenial conditions sufficiently better than the open ground to induce quicker germination (and consequently a little longer growing season), and/or ripening, i.e. strawberries.

Cotyledon—This is the name given to the first leaf, still in embryo form in the seed, that appears when the seed germinates.

Crumb—This is the loose broken soil that remains and lies in the bottom when a trench is dug out by spade. 'Taking out the crumb' therefore means working back along the trench, shovelling out the loose crumb so that the trench bottom is left clean and firm.

Cuttings—Shoot tips or pieces of stem or root which, when severed from the parent plant, are encouraged to form adventitious roots and thus form new plants.

Damping Off—The term used when seedlings suddenly wilt, 'go down' and die. Caused by fungal attack which is encouraged by insufficient ventilation and the use of infected soil—hence the need for sterilised seed composts.

Deciduous—The opposite to evergreen. Trees and shrubs whose leaves die and are shed each autumn and winter are called deciduous.

Dibber, Dibble—A dibber is simply a pointed wooden, metal or metal-tipped tool for making a planting hole in the soil when pricking-out seedlings or planting out—which are then said to have been 'dibbled' or 'dibbered'.

Dot Plant—Usually a taller growing subject, sometimes specially trained to a cane like a standard, and invariably with contrasting coloured leaves or flowers, and planted among a bed of smaller or dwarfer growing plants, i.e. dotted here and there to provide form and colour contrast.

Double Digging—A term generally used to describe digging two spits deep. The top and bottom spits are reversed in double digging. *See also* Bastard Trenching.

Drawn—The word can have two meanings. A shallow trench or drill made in the seed bed for sowing seed is said to be drawn, and sowing instructions often refer to 'drawing' or 'taking out' a drill. The second meaning is when plants are grown in poor light, too congested conditions—as with seed sown too thickly—and when in reaching for the source of light, growth becomes stretched, long, lanky and 'drawn'. The correct word for this condition is etiolated (c.f.).

Dress—The term given to an application of fertiliser, mulch, insecticide or other substance to the soil surface. The material itself being referred to as a 'dressing'—the amount of which may be described as so many ozs. per sq. yd.

Drill—A shallow trench made in a seed bed when seed sowing.

Etiolated—The correct word to describe the stretched or drawn (c.f.) condition when plants are congested and grown in poor light.

Evergreen—The opposite to deciduous (c.f.). This term describes plants that retain their leaves instead of shedding them each autumn and winter.

Fallow—Soil is said to lie fallow when it is left for a period without a crop of any kind.

Fastigiate—The correct word to describe narrow upright growth. Familiar examples are the Lombardy poplar, Irish yew, and several conifers.

Forcing—By growing in a warmer than normal temperature, or darkness, or both, plants can be hastened—i.e. 'forced'—into earlier flowering or maturity out of their normal season.

Grafting—differs from budding (c.f.) in that instead of one dormant bud from a select variety being implanted under the bark of a wild natural or more vigorous variety, a short piece of young stemwood, perhaps containing several buds, and called a 'scion', is joined on to the root stock.

Guano—Although sometimes applied to animal droppings, is correctly confined to bird droppings and, to be precise, to the vast accumulated sea bird deposits at one time imported from the Pacific islands off the coast of Peru.

Half-Hardy—The term applicable to annuals, biennials, perennials and also to bulbs which will not withstand the winter outdoors in Britain and therefore require the protection of a frame or greenhouse from which frost can be excluded.

Hardening Off—In order to avoid shock and severe growth check, early seedlings and plants raised in very favourable conditions, as in a propagating frame or greenhouse, need to be gradually introduced and 'hardened' to normal outdoor conditions.

Heel—When a side shoot is pulled away from a main stem, with a small part of the main stem attached, it is said to have a heel.

Heeling-in—This means the temporary 'planting' or covering with soil in a trench in order to protect plants, especially trees and shrubs, from drying-out whilst waiting for permanent planting.

Herbaceous—Perennial plants where, although the root-stock remains in the ground throughout the winter, the above-ground parts —stems, leaves, etc.—die down to grow again in the spring.

Hormone—In very simple terms, hormones are substances elaborated and secreted within both plants and animals that control factors like growth and response to temperature, light intensity and day length, season, and other conditions.

Humus—The word has by common usage come to be applied to all forms of organic matter—farmyard manure, compost, peat, leaf mould, straw, grass cuttings, etc. Strictly speaking, as beneficial as such organic matter is or becomes to the soil, humus is more exactly a dark brown material with a gelatinous consistency that all organic matter becomes only in the final stages of decomposition.

Internode—The name describes the area or length of stem between two nodes.

Jiffy 7—These are discs about $1\frac{1}{2}$ ins. in diameter and $\frac{3}{8}$ ins. thick, made of dried, compressed peat and enclosed within a fine plastic mesh. When soaked in water they quickly swell to become a peat ball which does not break up, being held by the enclosing mesh. They are immensely useful for striking cuttings, particularly of plants that resent root disturbance.

Layering—The same basic principles apply to layering as to cuttings (c.f.). The main difference is that as many plants do not so readily produce adventitious roots from a severed cutting, the cutting is left attached to the parent from which it continues to draw sustenance whilst the roots form.

Leaching—Fertilisers and plant foods which dissolve in soil moisture and then drain away or are washed out of the soil before they can be of benefit to plants, are said to leach away. Thus quick-draining sandy soils are said to suffer from rapid leaching.

Lead—The main central growing stem or shoot, to distinguish it from secondary and side shoots, is referred to as the lead shoot.

Legume—The botanical order of plants that bear their seeds in pods like peas, beans, lupins, clover, laburnum, etc.

Metabolic Rate, Metabolism—Refers to the rate or speed at which a plant lives. A young healthy thriving plant responding to adequate supplies of moisture, nutrients and congenial conditions has a faster metabolic rate than an old struggling plant.

Mulch—A layer of organic matter—compost, peat, lawn mowings, etc.—spread on the soil surface is called a mulch.

Nitrification—Plant roots are not able to absorb the free nitrogen of the atmosphere until it has been converted into soluble nitrate, or reduced to simple nitrate from other more complicated compounds especially organic matter by bacterial action. The entire process of nitrate elaboration is called nitrification.

Nitrogen Fix—A specific part of the entire process of nitrification (c.f.), this is the term used to describe the action of the specialised types of bacteria that live in colonies within and in association with the roots of legumes.

Node—This is the swollen area in a stem at the base of a leaf and is caused by special cells that store the carbohydrate, starches and sugars elaborated in the green leaf during photosynthesis (c.f.).

Organic—Material which was 'once living'. This includes materials in which plant nutrients may be highly concentrated like dried blood, bone meal, guano and fish manure; materials where nutrients are far less concentrated but more bulky, like farmyard and stable manures, garden and mushroom compost, hop manures, etc., or bulky material like peat which although advantageous to soil structure may contain very little plant nutrient.

Osmosis—When a strong solution is separated from a weak solution by a permeable membrane, the weaker solution flows through the membrane, diluting the strong solution and will so continue until the strengths are balanced. This is called osmosis, and is the principle by which plants absorb nutrients from the soil, the sap solutions within the plant being stronger than the nutrient solutions in the soil and from which they are separated by the thin membraneous 'skin' of the very fine 'hair' roots. See the opposite effect—plasmolysis.

Ovary—The seed-carrying part of a flower.

Ovule—The unripened seed whilst still carried within the ovary.

Perennial—Usually applied to herbaceous plants, the root stock of which lasts for several years, fresh growth arising each year.

Photosynthesis—is the process by which plants join together carbon dioxide gas and water, and then further elaborate this into starches, sugars, celluloses and other carbohydrates. This is done in the presence of chlorophyll, the green colouring matter of all plants utilising light as the energy source.

Pinching out—Describes the operation when shoots, especially main lead shoots, are removed in order to divert growth energy into side shoots, buds, etc.

Plasmolysis—Plants absorb nutrients from the soil into their root systems by the process

called osmosis (c.f.). When the direction of the process is reversed, as for example when too strong applications of fertiliser render the soil solution strength stronger than the cell sap within the plant, the process is called plasmolysis and leads to dehydration and possibly death of the plant. This is the weed killing principle utilised in lawn sand.

Pot on—This is when a plant is removed from a pot and replanted in a larger pot.

Pot up—This is when a plant, a seedling perhaps, or one growing in open ground is removed and replanted in a pot.

Pricking out—This is the technique of removing young seedlings from a congested seed bed, or tray where they have germinated, and replanting them at a distance from each other so that they have space to develop properly.

Puddle, Puddling—Puddle is simply mud—soil and water—to which has been added a fungicide—usually calomel (c.f.) but others are equally effective—when planting out. Puddled roots derive a degree of protection against soil borne fungus attack. Puddling is very important with all members of the brassica family and others subject to Club Root disease.

Ringing—refers to a deliberate wounding of shrubs and trees by making cuts in the main stem or trunk. These ring the trunk but do not go entirely round as this would stop sap flow altogether and cause the tree or shrub to die. Nevertheless, obstruction is caused to the sap flow by the partial cutting off and the natural reaction to the shock is to try to ensure perpetuation of its own species before its anticipated death. This it will do by setting seed which has to be preceded of course by flower and fruit. Ringing is practised therefore to bring shrubs and trees into flower and fruit, when for some reason they show reluctance and need encouragement.

Root Pruning—is practised on established shrubs and trees for the same purpose as ringing. Root pruning is also done with many plants as they are planted, to cause the quick production of new side or lateral roots, called adventitious roots (c.f.) and which therefore materially assist the plant to become established following the disturbance of transplanting.

Rotational Cropping—Varying the crops grown varies the demands on the soil's N P & K resources, and interrupts the build up of pest and disease. Rotational cropping is a logical utilisation of the residues and effect upon the soil of one crop to the benefit of the crop that follows it. Thus peas and beans fix nitrogen in the soil which can be utilised by leaf crops—cabbage, lettuce, etc.—which therefore follow on, to be in turn succeeded by root crops and/or potatoes, which need heavy manuring which, in turn, is beneficial to peas and beans, et seq.

Scion—This is the 'top part'—the choice variety—that is grafted on to a stock—see Grafting. Sometimes also used to refer to the growth that emanates from a bud—see Budding.

Selective—A term normally used in connection with hormone weedkillers. A very great many man-made synthetic substances have been developed that have effects upon the growth and characteristics of plants in a similar way to natural hormones (c.f.). Some of these hormones have a particular and remarkable property. At certain rates of dilution, they cease to affect some plants—mainly monocotyledonous—but continue to have a fatally disruptive effect on dicotyledons. At further dilution even the dicots may not die although suffering distortion. Thus within a specific maximum/minimum rate of application the hormone chemical may be said to be selective in that it has a fatally disruptive effect on dicots whilst leaving monocots unharmed, i.e. it selects and kills the weeds in lawns and corn crops.

Sour—A soil that is excessively acid for the crop growing in it is said to be sour.

Spit—This is the term used to describe the depth of soil dug by a spade, i.e. digging a trench—the full depth of the spade blade is one spit deep—and digging into the bottom of that trench is two spits deep.

Sport—Many plants will—sometimes for no explicable reason—produce blooms or foliage of unusual colour or form. This is called a sport, and can often be preserved by vegetative propagation. Very many of our choice varieties have risen in this way.

Stipule—This is the name given to modified leaves—usually very much smaller than the main or basic leaf shape and quite different in appearance—that some plants bear adjacent to the main leaves or leaf stalks. Probably the most familiar example for gardeners is the small frill like appendages at the base of the leaf stalks of the common pelargonium (geranium).

Stock—This term describes the 'lower' or 'root' plant onto which is implanted or grafted a choice or select variety—itself called the 'scion' in the conjoining operations called budding and grafting. The word is also used to describe plants sometimes quite large and old which, because they are very true to type are particularly good examples and always highly prized, are repeatedly used as a source of cuttings for the propagation of young specimens. Such parent plants are then called stock plants or 'stock stools'.

Stopping—Rather like the action of pinching (c.f.) stopping is the removal of leading shoots, side shoots, buds, etc. for the purpose of diversifying growth, as in the removal of the main shoot, concentrating growth when the main shoot is retained but side shoots are removed, developing a main bud when secondary buds are removed, or as in the case of chrysanthemums, preventing bud production, and delaying blooming so that bigger and better blooms result.

Suckers—Adventitious shoots arising from the root system sometimes at some distance from the main trunk, stem or growth. Some plants are more prone to suckers than others, but the tendency is often magnified by grafting where a vigorous rootstock unable to push all its energy into a weaker growing scion finds an alternative outlet for its excess vigour in sucker growths—this is very common for example with plum and other stone fruits.

Take out—This phrase has two basic meanings in gardening. Removal of main and side shoots is often referred to as 'take out' or 'taking out' side shoots, etc., and perhaps not quite so obviously 'take out a spit' or 'take out a drill' simply means 'dig the soil out a spit deep' and 'make a drill preparatory to sowing seed'.

Tap Root—In the same way that some plants will make a main leaf shoot with very little or no side shoots, roots may also be of a similar configuration, one main central root with little or no lateral and secondary rooting. This main root is called the tap root, and it is in order to encourage the production of adventitious side roots that the tap is cut when seedlings are being transplanted.

Thinning—Some seed is so small, that no matter how careful with a pinch twixt finger and thumb, seed is sown thickly and seedlings grow too close for them to be able to develop properly. Thinning out is then simply the removal of the small, weak, backward surplus to leave the better seedlings to remain more spaced apart with enough room to grow.

Tilth—The term used to describe a layer of loose, fine soil particles on the soil surface. A tilth may be created by raking so that seed can drop between the particles and be covered, or it may be raked or hoed to create a moisture conserving barrier between the firmer soil layers underneath and through which moisture can move by capillary action, and drying air above.

Total—This word is used in gardening to distinguish the action of plant growth inhibitors—those substances that will kill all plant life.

Trace—The three familiar elements, nitrogen, phosphorus and potassium—N, P & K—are needed in the soil in a fair amount in order to support plant life. There are many others like Cobalt Zinc, Copper, Magnesium, Boron, etc., that need only be available in very small amounts, as low as two or three only parts per million, and yet without that mere trace the plants would suffer and die. Because only a trace is required they are called 'trace elements'.

Translocation—quite literally means the movement of location. The movement of carbohydrate sugars, starches, etc., as elaborated in the leaves to the storage cells at the nodes, and later to root storage cells as in tubers and swollen roots like carrots, turnips and beets, is called translocation.

True Leaves—The first 'leaves' to appear when a seed germinates are the 'seed leaves' or to give them their correct name cotyledons. Normally they are quite simple leaves, and unlike the leaves that follow and which are more characteristic of the foliage you associate with the plant and expect to see. These later leaves are called the 'true leaves'.

Wadge, Wodge—Localised colloquial expressions to describe a substantial wad of peat or compost roughage, inserted in the bottom of a pot when potting, to act as a sponge and retain plenty of moisture.

Weaning—Seeds that have been germinated and cuttings that have been rooted in warm humid conditions will sustain shock if suddenly removed to normal—but cooler—conditions. The move has to be done gradually and slowly —hardening off (c.f.). Weaning, although aptly describing this process, is also and more literally applicable to the gradual severing of a rooted layer from the parent plant.

Appendices

John Innes Compost

Frequent reference is made in this book to 'John Innes Compost'—'J.I.' for short. There are a number of J.I. Composts, varying in texture, i.e. soil structure and nutrient content, and intended for different uses and plants. The basic purpose is to provide a uniform scale of standardised composts in order to produce consistent growth characteristics in a wide variety of plants.

Apart from ensuring nutrient availability, another purpose of these composts is to ensure freedom from soil borne pests and diseases—at least to begin with, there being no guarantee that these may not invade or be introduced later. Therefore all loam used in these composts must be sterilised (and in what follows, it should be understood that all loam and soil referred to, will have been sterilised). This is best achieved by subjecting the loam to steam heat so that its temperature is raised to 180°F—use of a soil sterilising thermometer is essential—and held at that temperature for 10 minutes, not longer.

Various proprietary sterilisers can be purchased which are satisfactory in performance, and which deal quite adequately with the relatively small quantities that most amateur gardeners will need. However several of these appliances are graduated to indicate weight of contents. This is very misleading when it comes to making up the various composts and my advice is always to calculate in terms of bulk, i.e. gallons and bushels of loam—8 gallons = 1 bushel—and not in terms of weight by the lb.

Most garden centres and garden shops sell proprietary prepared J.I. composts, and many garden shops prepare and sell their own—made up loose.

Having regard to the foregoing, you will appreciate why it is advisable to ensure that all 'bought in' J.I. composts have been made up with loam that has been sterilised.

For those wishing to make up their own, and also in order to indicate the relative nutrient strengths, the formulae are as follows.

Note: Where dried and/or compressed moss peat is being used, which is normally very dry, this first should be broken loose, sieved and moistened—not saturated—before measuring and mixing.

J.I. Seed compost

2 parts by bulk medium loam — both should be passed through a $\frac{3}{8}''$ sieve to remove roughage.

1 part granulated peat

and 1 part coarse sand

Mix the above ingredients thoroughly, and to every bushel add and mix in $1\frac{1}{2}$ ozs. Superphosphate, and $\frac{3}{4}$ oz. ground limestone, ground chalk, or ground whiting.

J.I. Potting composts

7 parts by bulk medium loam (sterilised and sieved as seed compost), 3 parts by bulk granulated peat (teased, sieved and moistened), 2 parts coarse sand.

Note: Gardeners relying upon their own resources may have to vary these proportions slightly in order to ensure that the final product has a good texture. For example: using a soil in a light sandy district the proportion could be 8 parts to $2\frac{1}{2}$ parts of peat perhaps, with the sand proportion reduced to $1\frac{1}{2}$ parts or even less. However a heavy 'fatty' loam could well have the peat and sand proportions increased in order to keep the compost open and not let it settle into a badly draining stagnant mass.

Variation from the basic formula is a matter

for experience and there is no substitute for that. Perhaps the best idea is to buy a little proprietary compiled compost, and get the 'feel' of the correct mixture, and then vary the proportions of your own soil accordingly.

Into each bushel of the above, mix in $\frac{3}{4}$ oz. of ground limestone, ground chalk or whiting.

You will now need what is called John Innes Base fertiliser and this is made up of:

Parts by weight
- 2 Hoof and horn meal passed through a $\frac{1}{8}$ inch sieve
- 2 Superphosphate
- 1 Sulphate of Potash

The sole purpose of J.I. Base fertiliser is to ensure that the proportions of plant nutrient contained in the ingredients is calculated exactly; therefore they are measured by weight not by bulk as are the loam/peat/sand. Mixed thoroughly, the three ingredients of J.I. Base will give approximately 5% nitrogen, 7% phosphoric and 9–10% potash. 4 ozs. of J.I. Base fertiliser is regarded as one dose and the various J.I. potting composts are made up as follows. To each bushel of the basic loam/peat/sand/chalk mix add accordingly:

J.I. No. 1 Potting compost one dose (4 ozs.) of J.I. Base fertiliser.

J.I. No. 2 Potting compost two doses (8 ozs.) of J.I. Base fertiliser.

J.I. No. 3 Potting compost three doses (12 ozs.) of J.I. Base fertiliser

J.I. No. 4 Potting compost four doses (16 ozs.) of J.I. Base fertiliser.

The mild chalk or limestone is an essential ingredient in the composts except where the plants to be grown are known to be lime haters in which case it is best to omit the chalk/lime.

Seed and potting composts are clearly very different in nutrient content and have a markedly different effect on plants growing in them—indeed to attempt to germinate seed in a rich potting compost could be disastrous.

However, the composts look very alike and many gardeners have difficulty in telling them apart. In order to avoid making costly mistakes, it is a good idea to add smashed red brick rubble and dust to the potting compost. Pass this through a $\frac{1}{8}$ inch sieve and add the fine dust at a rate of about 2–2$\frac{1}{2}$ cupfuls per bushel. This should be enough to just colour it and make distinction.

If brick dust is not available try a couple of ounces of red ochre which you can obtain from an oil shop or hardware stores.

Plant Health

Here is a quick reference guide to pests and diseases, the plants and crops affected, and the chemical controls available to counteract them.

Pest or disease	Plant or crop attacked	Control chemical
Ants	various	BHC Dust
		Insecticides containing mezrethrin
		Nippon
		Rentokil ant destroyer
Aphides (including greenfly and blackfly)	various	Abol X
		Fentro
		Lindex
		Liquid Derris
		Malathion
		Super-Kil
		XL-ALL
Bacterial canker	cherries, plums and other stone fruits. Also apples, pears, Forsythia and other shrubs	Cheshunt compound
		Copper fungicide
Bees—leaf cutter	roses and other plants	Malathion
		XL-ALL
Bees—solitary	lawns	BHC Dust
		Chlordane
		Derris
Beetles	various	Fentro
		Sevin Dust
		Zaldicide M.
Big bud mite	blackcurrants	Lime sulphur
Blackfly	various	see Aphides

Pest or disease	Plant or crop attacked	Control chemical
Black spot	roses	Benlate
		Captan
		Elvaron
		Maneb
		Orthocide
		Systemic fungicides
Blight	potatoes and tomatoes	Bordeaux mixture
		Cheshunt compound
		Dithane
Cabbage root fly	brassicas	Bromophos
		Calomel dust (and puddling at planting time)
		Chlordane
Capsid bug	various, but especially apples and similar fruits	Fentro
		Lindex
		Systemic insecticides
Carrot fly	carrots	Bromophos
		Dipterex
		Kilsect
		Soot
		Sybol
Caterpillars	various	Derris Dust
		Kilsect
		Malathion
		Sevin Dust
Celery fly	celery	Bromophos
		Dipterex
		Kilsect
		Soot
		Sybol
Chafer grub	roses	BHC Liquid
		Bromophos
		Chlordane
		Sevin Dust
Club root	brassicas and wall-flowers	Calomel Dust (especially puddling at planting time)
		Cyclosan
Cockroaches	various	Zaldicide M.
Cutworms	various, especially seedlings	BHC Dust
		Bromophos
		Sevin Dust

Pest or disease	Plant or crop attacked	Control chemical
Damping-off fungus	various seedlings	Captan Dust
		Cheshunt compound
		Liquid copper
		Orthocide
		Use of 'protected seed'
Downy mildew	various	Cheshunt compound
		Dithane
		Mildew specific fungicide
		Zineb
Earthworms	lawns	Chlordane
Earwigs	various	Dipterex
		Lindex
		Sevin Dust traps
		Zaldicide M. traps
Fire blight	tulips	Benlate
		Systemic fungicides
		Zineb
Flea beetle	brassicas, radishes and turnips	BHC Dust
		Malathion
		Sybol
		XL-ALL
Foot rot	seedlings	Captan
		Dithane
		Liquid copper
		Orthocide
Greenfly	various	*see* Aphides
Grey mould	various	Benlate
		Elvaron
		Fumigation with TCNB smoke
Leaf curl	almonds and peaches	Dithane
		Lime sulphur
		Liquid copper
Leaf hoppers	various	BHC Dust
		Fentro
		Sevin Dust
		Systemic insecticides
Leaf miners	Chrysanthemums, Cinerarias and holly	Kilsect
		Malathion
		Sybol
		Systemic insecticides

Pest or disease	Plant or crop attacked	Control chemical
Leaf mould	potatoes and tomatoes	Benlate
		Liquid copper
Leaf spot	various	Benlate
		Cheshunt compound
		Dithane
		Systemic insecticides
		Zineb
Leatherjackets	lawn grasses and many other plants including vegetables	BHC Liquid and Dust
		Chlordane
		Sevin Dust
Mealy bug	greenhouse and indoor plants	Malathion
		Super-Kil
		Systemic insecticides
Midges	blackcurrants, Chrysanthemums and others	BHC Sprays and Dust
		Lindex
		Malathion
Mildew	various, especially roses	Benlate
		Captan
		Karathane
Millepedes	various	BHC Dust
		Chlordane
		Sybol
Narcissus fly	daffodil and narcissi bulbs	BHC Dust
		Lindex
		Sybol
Onion fly	onions	Calomel Dust
		Dipterex
		Kilsect
		Lindex
		Soot
Powdery mildew	various	Benlate
		Dinocap
		Mildan
		Mildew specific fungicide
		Systemic fungicides
Red spider	various	Azobenzene smoke fumigation
		Malation
		Super-Kil
Root aphis	greenhouse and indoor plants	BHC Liquid
		Malathion

Pest or disease	Plant or crop attacked	Control chemical
Rust	various	Cheshunt compound
		Dithane
		Zineb
Sawfly	various	Dipterex
		Derris
		Fentro
		Super-Kil
		Sybol
Scab	apples and pears	Benlate
		Lime sulphur
		Systemic fungicides
Scale insect	greenhouse and indoor plants	Malathion
		Systemic insecticides
Slugs and snails	various	Draza pellets set in traps
		Metaldehyde in liquid and pellet form
Snails	various	*see* Slugs
Springtails	greenhouse and indoor plants	BHC Liquid and Dust
		Sybol
Thrip	various	Liquid Derris
		Malathion
		Super-Kil
Wasps	various	Derris Dust
		Sevin Dust
		Sybol
Weevils	various	BHC Liquid
		Fentro
		Malathion
		Sevin Dust
White fly	various	Fumigation in greenhouses and enclosed atmospheres
		Malathion
		Super-Kil
Wireworm	various, especially root	BHC Liquid
		Bromophos
		Chlordane
		Sevin Dust

Metric Conversion

CONVERSION OF IMPERIAL MEASURES TO THE METRIC SYSTEM

Gardeners are concerned with five basic forms of Imperial measurements that are currently being changed, or soon will be, to the Metric system. These are linear measurement, weight, capacity and volume, area, and temperature.

Experience has shown that for some time after conversion to metrication, many people reconvert to the old and familiar Imperial values in their calculations as happened, for example, with money decimalisation. The following explanations and comparative scales should be useful.

Some measurements peculiar to horticulture, like pot sizes, seed box sizes, hosepipe fittings, etc., will for the time being continue as before.

1. **Linear measurement**

In the metric system, length is based upon the metre which is approximately 39 inches, i.e. just over one yard. Lengths less than one metre are expressed in hundredths of a metre—centimetres—and thousandths of a metre—millimetres. One thousand metres are expressed as one kilometre.

Metric symbols in common use

km. kilometre
m.   metre
cm. centimetre
mm. millimetre

Equivalents

Imperial measurement	*Approx. Metric equivalent*
1 in.	2·5 cm.
1 ft.	30·5 cm.
1 yd.	91·5 cm.
3 ft. 3 in.	1 m.
5/8th mile	1 km.

2.   Weight measurement (also called Avoirdupois)

In the metric system, the basic unit is called the gramme. It is a relatively small unit—approximately 28 equal the Imperial ounce. Gardeners are not likely to be concerned with weights less than one/twenty-eighth of an ounce, so there is no need to worry about fractions of a gramme. More important is the commonly used multiple of the gramme—the kilogramme.

Metric symbols in common use
kg.   kilogramme
g.   gramme

Equivalents

Imperial measurement	*Approx. Metric equivalent*
1 oz.	28 g.
4 oz.	112 g.
1 lb.	448 g.
1 lb. 1½ oz.	½ kg.
2 lb. 3 oz.	1 kg.
11 lb.	5 kg.
22 lb.	10 kg.
½ cwt.	25 kg.
1 cwt.	51 kg.

3.   Capacity and Volume

In the metric system, the basic unit for measuring liquids is called the litre which is approximately 1¾ Imperial pints. Quantities of less than a litre are usually measured in thousandths of a litre—millilitres. Larger quantities of dry materials may be measured as in Imperial measure by cubic quantity, i.e. cubic yards will be measured as cubic metres.★

Metric symbols in common use
l.   litre
ml.   millilitre
cu. m. cubic metre

Equivalents

Imperial measurement	*Approx. Metric equivalent*
1 gill	140 ml.
½ pt.	280 ml.
1 pt.	570 ml.

★As metrication is being implemented, increasing use is being made of the mathematical methods of expressing square units of area and cubic units of volume.

Thus, square metres may be abbreviated and expressed as sq. m. or as m^2. Similarly, cubic metres may be abbreviated and expressed as cu. m. or as m^3.

1 qt.	$1\frac{1}{8}$ l.
1 gall.	$4\frac{1}{2}$ l.
$1\frac{3}{4}$ pt.	1 l.
$1\frac{1}{8}$ gall.	5 l.
1 bushel	36 l.
1 cu. ft.—$6\frac{1}{4}$ galls—$\frac{5}{8}$ bushel	22·5 l.
1 cu. yd.	·8 cu. m.
$1\frac{1}{4}$ cu. yd.	1 cu. m.

4. Area

Areas that have concerned the gardener are square inches, square feet, square yards and acres. Area will be expressed now as square centimetres, square metres and hectares.* See footnote, p. 391.

Metric symbols in common use
ha.   hectares
sq. m.   square metres
sq. cm.   square centimetres
Equivalents

Imperial measurement	*Approx. Metric equivalent*
1 sq. in.	6·5 sq. cm.
1 sq. ft.	930 sq. cm.
$10\frac{1}{2}$ sq. ft.—$1\frac{1}{4}$ sq. yd.	1 sq. m.
$30\frac{1}{4}$ sq. yd.	25 sq. m.
1 acre	4000 sq. m.
$2\frac{1}{2}$ acres	1 ha.—10,000 sq. m.

5. Temperature

Although both scales have been in use for some time, there is still plenty of confusion concerning the comparisons between Fahrenheit and Centigrade. The following explanation should make it quite simple to understand.

The freezing and boiling temperatures of water are defined as 0°C. and 100°C. respectively on the metric Centigrade scale, whereas on the Fahrenheit scale the freezing and boiling points are 32°F. and 212°F. respectively. Thus the ranges between freezing and boiling points are 100° on the Centigrade scale and 180° on the Fahrenheit scale.

Therefore, 1°C. is equal to 1·8°F. and it will be seen that, commencing at freezing point, the Fahrenheit scale advances $5 \times 1·8°$ for every 5° on the Centigrade scale.

	Fahrenheit		Centigrade
Freezing	32°	Freezing	0°
	41°		5°
	50°		10°
	59°		15°
	68°		20°
	77°		25°
	86°		30°
	95°		35°
	104°		40°

Rates of Application

The two most common rates of use concerning gardeners are ounces per square yards—oz. per sq. yd.—for dressings and ounces per gallon—oz. per gall.—for solutions.

Two useful scales are listed below.

Dressings—ounces and pounds per square yard become grammes and kilogrammes per square metre.★ See footnote, p. 391.

Imperial measurements	Approx. Metric equivalents
$\frac{1}{8}$ oz. per sq. yd.	4 g. per sq. m.
$\frac{1}{4}$ oz. per sq. yd.	9 g. per sq. m.
$\frac{1}{2}$ oz. per sq. yd.	18 g. per sq. m.
1 oz. per sq. yd.	35 g. per sq. m.
2 oz. per sq. yd.	70 g. per sq. m.
4 oz. per sq. yd.	140 g. per sq. m.
8 oz. per sq. yd.	280 g.—$\frac{1}{4}$ kg.—per sq. m.
16 oz.—1 lb.—per sq. yd.	560 g.—$\frac{1}{2}$ kg.—per sq. m.
2 lb. per sq. yd.	1 kg. per sq. m.

Solutions—ounces per gallon become grammes per litre

Imperial measurements	Approx. Metric equivalents
$\frac{1}{8}$ oz. per gall.	1 g. per l.
$\frac{1}{4}$ oz. per gall.	1·5 g. per l.
$\frac{1}{2}$ oz. per gall.	3 g. per l.
1 oz. per gall.	6 g. per l.
2 oz. per gall.	12 g. per l.
3 oz. per gall.	18 g. per l.
4 oz. per gall.	25 g. per l.
8 oz. per gall.	50 g. per l.

Index

The folio references given are Question numbers, not page numbers

The folio references given are Question numbers, not page numbers

The folio references given are Question numbers, not page numbers

The folio references given are Question numbers, not page numbers

The folio references given are Question numbers, not page numbers

The folio references given are Question numbers, not page numbers

The folio references given are Question numbers, not page numbers

The folio references given are Question numbers, not page numbers

The folio references given are Question numbers, not page numbers

The folio references given are Question numbers, not page numbers

The folio references given are Question numbers, not page numbers

The folio references given are Question numbers, not page numbers

The folio references given are Question numbers, not page numbers

The folio references given are Question numbers, not page numbers

The folio references given are Question numbers, not page numbers

The folio references given are Question numbers, not page numbers

The folio references given are Question numbers, not page numbers